MW01134582

MAOISM AT THE GRASSROOTS

Maoism at the Grassroots

Everyday Life in China's Era of High Socialism

edited by JEREMY BROWN

and MATTHEW D. JOHNSON

 Harvard University Press

Cambridge, Massachusetts

London, England

2015

First printing

Library of Congress Cataloging-in-Publication Data

Maoism at the grassroots : everyday life in China's era of high socialism / edited by Jeremy Brown and Matthew D. Johnson.
      pages cm
    Includes bibliographical references and index.
    ISBN 978-0-674-28720-4 (hardcover)
    1. China—Social life and customs—1949– 2. China—Social conditions—1949–
3. Communism—Social aspects—China—History—20th century. 4. Politics and culture—China—History—20th century. 5. China—Politics and government—1949–
6. Crime—China—History—20th century. 7. Political participation—China—History—20th century. 8. Communication—Social aspects—China—History—20th century. 9. Discontent—Social aspects—China—History—20th century. 10. Power (Social sciences)—China—History—20th century. I. Brown, Jeremy, 1976– II. Johnson, Matthew D.
   DS777.6.M36 2015
   951.05—dc23   2015002580

Contents

Part III. CULTURE AND COMMUNICATION

Part IV. DISCONTENT

MAOISM AT THE GRASSROOTS

Introduction

JEREMY BROWN AND MATTHEW D. JOHNSON

When analyzed as history, the Mao Zedong era (1949–1978) looks different than it did when scrutinized by social scientists. Ever since the founding of the People's Republic, contemporary observers have identified an underlying reality at odds with the goals and policies pursued by top leaders in Beijing. That underlying reality, scholars found, was characterized by conflict, tension, and variation.[1] Factionalism divided bureaucratic institutions; mass campaigns failed to achieve their aims; local officials subverted policies; groups pursued their own interests. In other words, state control was not always total or centralized but at times appeared limited and tenuous.

As historians, we embrace this picture of the Mao era, but our approach differs in two main ways: where we look and what we are trying to explain. Social scientists have analyzed China's political and social system by looking at policy implementation, group behavior, and the origins and outcomes of such events as the Great Leap Forward and the Cultural Revolution. Their concerns have been mainly top-down and state-focused. In contrast, the historians whose research is collected in this volume look at individual people in villages, factories, neighborhoods, counties, and ethnic minority regions from the bottom up, and in everyday contexts that make the familiar analytic categories of "state" and "society" impossible to clearly distinguish from each other. And while we do not shy away from putting together our local case studies (like a jigsaw puzzle, in Elizabeth J. Perry's apt coinage)[2] to form broader conclusions about China, our main task is to explain processes of change and continuity over time from the perspective of relatively unknown historical actors. We call this approach "grassroots history." In writing China's history from the perspective of the grassroots, we are also making a statement—that the story of change in post-1949 China is more than a story of policy implementation via relentless group mobilization, or of chaos and terror unleashed by factional infighting in Beijing.

What does our grassroots historical approach add to an understanding of the Mao years? How does it differ from what social scientists discovered decades ago? First, we have found even more diversity and variety in behavior, outlook, and viewpoints. Men had gay relationships in factory dormitories; teens penned searing complaints in diaries; mentally ill individuals in the Beijing suburbs cursed Mao; and farmers formed secret societies, founded new "dynasties," and worshipped forbidden spirits. These diverse undercurrents—barely hinted at in openly published sources but plentiful in archival and grassroots documents—were at least as "mainstream" in people's everyday lives as the ideas found in Mao's Little Red Book or *People's Daily* editorials. Second, we agree with Joseph Esherick, Paul Pickowicz, and Andrew Walder that earlier generations of social scientists underestimated the extent of routine violence, resistance, and repression during the Mao period.[3] These traumas took different forms, from armed rebellion to harsh prison terms for saying the wrong thing or being gay, and they were not limited to such major campaigns as the Great Leap Forward or the Cultural Revolution but were present throughout the Mao years. Third, by departing from what historian Gail Hershatter calls "campaign time" and looking at particular moments of change and at the Mao years as a whole, we have discovered multiple turning points as well as shared experiences that together defined the period we have termed "high socialism." Before discussing turning points and high socialism, we begin with the concepts of grassroots and everyday life.

Everyday Life

Focusing on everyday life means taking what people actually did as a starting point rather than starting with what top officials wanted people to do or to think. The chapters in this volume examine what Michel de Certeau calls "ways of operating," meaning the tactics individuals used as they engaged with the people, ideas, and spaces around them.[4] This concept encompasses private life, family dynamics, entertainment choices, workplace relationships, religion and cosmology, and anxieties about clothing and money. It examines how people watched films, how they seduced their coworkers, how and why they cursed and complained, and what they wrote in their diaries.

Looking at everyday life does not mean ignoring the role of the state, which was undeniably intrusive and influential during the Mao era. We approach politics, however, through the eyes of villagers and urbanites, not through elite policy-makers and propagandists. We also depart from imprecise paradigms. Two decades ago, Elizabeth J. Perry critiqued the state-society relations model that then dominated studies of contemporary China, writing that "terms such as 'state' and 'society' are simply too gross to capture the enormous variation that differentiates one Chinese region—or level of government—from another."[5] There was no monolithic Chinese society during the 1950s, 1960s, and 1970s, nor was there a single Chinese state. The chapters in this volume validate Perry's point and take up her call to disaggregate the "unwieldy concepts of 'state' and 'society.'"[6] It is impossible to understand the Mao years without shining a bright light on the diverse ethnic, regional, religious, family, and urban or rural identities that gave meaning to people's lives.

Aside from its imprecision, the other problem with the state-society relations paradigm is that it sets up state and society as separate, oppositional entities. As Joseph Esherick has shown in his research on rural Shaanxi during the late 1940s, representatives of the Party-state at the county level and below were themselves "members of society" who were "deeply enmeshed in a variety of local networks from which they could never be completely separated."[7] Following Esherick, we find that throughout the Mao years, the Party-state and society were intertwined. In factories, an immediate supervisor or a comrade in the workshop represented the Party-state. In villages, the face of the Party-state was a neighbor, a family member, a member of a minority ethnic group, or a fellow clandestine worshipper. As Gail Hershatter has shown in her study of rural labor models, becoming an embodiment of the Party-state did not sever a person's relationships with family members or neighbors, but it did alter them. People knew who was a labor model or a cadre; they treated local representatives of the Party-state differently because such representatives were genuinely different. Local leaders were responsible for nothing short of "rearranging space, establishing hierarchies, organizing surveillance, recalibrating time," as Hershatter writes.[8] They also had special powers: they bestowed rewards and punishments, and assigned labels. The chapters that follow refrain from referring to an amorphous state set apart from society and instead show clearly the significant roles that local officials played as representatives of the Party-state, as community and family members, and as mediators between national policies and particularistic interests.

The Grassroots

We use the term *grassroots* to encompass this complex interplay between provincial, county, commune, and village officials, and among people who had no official titles whatsoever. Grassroots history has as its antecedents the village and urban studies, ethnographies, and micro-level social analyses of previous generations of scholarship on China.[9] Our notion of the grassroots is first and foremost meant to distinguish our subject from previous studies of Mao Zedong and other central officials and bureaucrats in Beijing.[10] It used to be that studies of elite politics were overrepresented in scholarship about the Mao years because sources from and about life at Party Center were more readily available than grassroots sources. Times have changed. Although the Central Archives remain closed to academic researchers, forcing even the best of recent works about elite politics to rely on anonymous testimony from "well-placed oral sources,"[11] an explosion of grassroots sources over the past two decades has fueled a new wave of scholarship on the history of the Mao years.[12]

Grassroots sources include archival documents, internal circulation (*neibu*) collections, oral history, and unpublished diaries and manuscripts. They allow us to describe the lives of people at the grassroots—officials and nonofficials; farmers and technicians; Han, Miao, or Uyghur—with unprecedented accuracy and detail. While many of the chapters here draw from material held in official provincial, municipal, and local archives, even more of them use documents collected from flea markets, peddlers, and other underground channels. The school of "Sinological garbology" (the collection and study of "rubbish materials," or *laji cailiao*) has gained momentum among an international cohort of scholars in China, Europe, and North America who use diaries, personnel dossiers, public security and legal files, Red Guard leaflets, and other ephemera to shed light on phenomena—family life, petitioning, and sexual behavior, for example—that official archives redact, withhold, or simply do not contain.[13]

Examining everyday life from a grassroots perspective, we find a complex, particularistic web of interests in every social context. Previous scholarship by Vivienne Shue and other social scientists has located particularism—often defined as interests that competed with those of the Party-state—in villages where state "reach" appeared more constrained, or in factional networks that divided the political elite.[14] Expanding on this perspective, the chapters in this volume show that particularism also existed in and through structures of governance, or was manifested in such difficult-to-document forms of behavior as sexuality, abuses of the legal system, illicit commercial activity, conspiracy, and covert acts of religious worship. Our findings thus connect the history of China after 1949 to histories of the late Qing and Republican eras, when particularism was more readily observed as a basic feature of social life, whether described as corruption, networks, *guanxi,* localism, or the private sphere.

As a result, the "grassroots" can be understood as both a methodological starting point and an objective structure of society. Methodologically, it is aligned with subaltern studies and other approaches to "history from below" in the sense that it privileges sources and readings that cut against the grain of established narratives and state-centered readings of historical sources, including those that, like archives, are themselves produced by institutions of state power. (Some might note that the term *grassroots* itself connotes the lowest level in Party-state hierarchies, but our term—derived from both Anglophone scholarship on grassroots political history and the Chinese sense of grassroots (*caogen*) as connoting nongovernmental forms of organization or counterhegemonic social forces—is not restricted to this narrower Party-state usage.)[15] As a category of social description, the grassroots might best be thought of as a localized "contact zone" where nonelite individuals interact with more powerful social structures. The presence of diverse individual and collective responses to centralizing, hegemonic forms of state power is significant. Although we do not deny that social control was created through some combination of propaganda and political terror—and much in between—we would also argue that the notion of a comprehensive post-1949 consolidation of power by the Mao-led Communist Party cannot account for the diversity of behavior described in the chapters that follow.

High Socialism

In our reevaluation of the history previously subsumed by monolithic constructions of the Mao years, periodization is also important. While some chapters in this volume look back to the early 1950s for precedents and others see Maoist legacies in the reform era, each case study centers on events during the period from the mid-1950s until 1980. We refer to this period as "high socialism," meaning the time between agricultural collectivization and nationalization of industry in the mid-1950s through the end of the 1970s. High socialism was characterized by state ownership of property, Party-state fusion, the politicization of everyday life, and a planned economy that privileged heavy urban industry by extracting grain from the countryside and restricting internal migration. These broad aspects of high socialism came to life at the grassroots in the form of class status labels, grain rationing booklets, propaganda written on neighborhood blackboards, loudspeaker broadcasts, mandatory evening meetings, and anxious interactions with local officials who wielded arbitrary authority.

One advantage of focusing on these shared elements of high socialism is that it sheds new light on understudied moments. An abundance of studies about the Great Leap Forward and the Cultural Revolution means that we know far more about what happened in China in 1958 and 1966 than we do about events in 1955, 1965, or 1975. As it turns out, 1955, 1965, and 1975 were just as significant at the grassroots as were the starting points of the Leap and the Cultural Revolution. Many of the chapters in this volume fill in these chronological gaps in our knowledge about the Mao years. Inspired by Gail Hershatter's point that "campaign time" did not necessarily match lived experience, we find that the labels "Great Leap Forward" and "Cultural Revolution" were not especially meaningful starting points or finish lines at the grassroots.[16] As Michael Schoenhals has argued, the term "Cultural Revolution" loses its explanatory value when scholars inaccurately use such labels as "manic" or "bizarre" to depict what happened between 1966 and 1969 as an abnormal exception to PRC politics.[17] The violence, abuses of power, and resistance associated with the Leap and the Cultural Revolution were far from abnormal. They were present at every point along the historical timeline between the 1950s and the 1970s. Even though both events exacerbated the preexisting conditions to tragic degrees, they did not introduce them de novo from 1958 onward. And in some places the most significant turning points began not with the Leap or the Cultural Revolution but with collectivization (in Miao areas of Guizhou in 1955–1956, for example), state control over the cotton market (in rural Shaanxi gradually throughout the 1950s), or reassessing villagers' class labels (in 1965). And, as we shall see in Chapter 1, the year 1970 proved to be a painfully important turning point in the life of a factory worker named Zang Qiren.

*   *   *

Our exploration of everyday life at the grassroots begins with a group of four chapters that zoom in on the effects of repression, surveillance, and political labeling at the individual level. As crushing as such repression could be, people insisted on asserting their personal beliefs and identities, even though they knew that by doing so they risked being sent to jail or labeled as a class enemy. We open with Yang Kuisong's microhistory of a "bad element" named Zang Qiren, who worked in a factory in Henan. Leaders at Zang's factory expended huge amounts of time and resources investigating Zang's pre-1949 history for evidence of counterrevolutionary behavior. Zang indeed concealed the truth about his past in the many self-confessions he wrote during the Mao period. In 1968 he was so afraid of getting in trouble that he ran away from his factory and hid in a neighboring county. But in the end it was Zang's unwillingness to stop what he knew was risky behavior in the factory, rather than his political history, that prompted public security officials to incarcerate him as a bad element.

Although only a small percentage of people living in China between the 1950s and 1970s were labeled as bad elements, everyone had a class status label. As Jeremy Brown shows, the class status system that divided China's population into such categories as poor peasant, middle peasant, rich peasant, and landlord was more dynamic and unstable than previous scholarship has assumed. This instability peaked during the early and mid-1960s. In Henan in the aftermath of the Great Leap famine and in other provinces a few years later during the Four Cleanups, work teams reinvestigated and reassigned the class labels of millions of rural Chinese people. Even though central policy had already changed direction and no longer required the reinvestigation of class labels, officials in many villages continued the practice in 1965 and 1966. This is but one example of local cadres being more influential than

Mao himself at the grassroots. Many rural families, terrified at the prospect of a negative change (for example, from lower-middle peasant to rich peasant), petitioned for the restoration of their original labels. In arguing their cases, they appropriated official language and policy, accepting the class status framework while protesting its capricious and arbitrary implementation.

Perhaps no political campaign of the Mao period was as capricious and arbitrary as the Anti-Rightist Movement of 1957–1958. Cao Shuji demonstrates that in rural China, the Hundred Flowers Movement and anti-rightist rectification were wrapped together in a single package. County cadres and village teachers were aware of what had befallen urban elites who spoke out during the Hundred Flowers and knew that the entire point of soliciting criticism was to identify rightists. Many rural people were afraid of being labeled as rightists, but some could not restrain themselves from opening their mouths. Why? Some people's personalities made them inveterate critics—they could not help themselves. Others were naïve and gave in to pressure from local officials, who played a crucial role in pushing people to speak out one day and punishing them the next. In addition, a significant number of rural educators and bureaucrats willingly sacrificed themselves as rightists in order to expose food shortages caused by collectivization and the state grain monopoly.

After the Anti-Rightist Movement, the cost of saying the wrong thing remained high, but even during the extreme political repression of the Cultural Revolution, people expressed critical and independent views. Daniel Leese draws on legal case files from suburban Beijing to explore how hundreds of people were imprisoned as counterrevolutionaries during the Cultural Revolution and then rehabilitated after Mao Zedong's death. Leese finds that the Party's "transitional justice" in the aftermath of the Cultural Revolution was limited. Aggrieved suburbanites who had been jailed for criticizing Mao, praising Lin Biao, or questioning the leadership ability of Hua Guofeng were eventually exonerated, but the broader systemic nature of their critiques remained unaddressed. Taken together, the first four chapters show the intensely personal human toll of anxiety-inducing political movements, labels, and persecution during the Mao years. Rather than backing down in the face of such traumas, however, many people maintained "strong political views and individual standards of evaluation," as Leese concludes.

The second group of chapters, titled "Mobilization," examines how people reacted when local authorities resorted to less punitive measures to convince them to make personal sacrifices for socialist construction. During the era of high socialism, mobilization proved just as influential as persecution in changing how and where individuals lived and worked. The changes, however, turned out differently from what authorities had originally intended. Rural women in Shaanxi, as Jacob Eyferth describes, understood success in terms of textile work. A family's social status depended on weaving an adequate amount of cotton to wear and to offer at such culturally meaningful rituals as weddings and funerals. It was shameful to wear shoddily stitched clothing or to fall short on wedding gifts. Yet when agricultural collectivization pushed women into farmwork, they came under great pressure to meet their obligations to the state (which at the grassroots was represented by village cadres who also happened to be friends and neighbors) as well as their obligation to produce textiles for family use. The result was that women worked double shifts: in the fields during the day and hunched over the loom at night. In addition to working longer hours than their male counterparts, some village women resorted to pilfering cotton from fields and exchanging finished cloth for cotton on the black market in order to maintain minimum standards of social success during the Mao years.

The next two chapters explore how young people grappled with their role in a Maoist revolutionary project that pushed their lives on a trajectory they had not chosen for themselves: the sent-down youth movement. Sigrid Schmalzer finds that rural scientific experiment mattered deeply to propagandists, policy-makers, and sent-down youth during the 1960s and 1970s. Propagandists depicted science as an opportunity for educated youth to contribute to the revolution, and many young people embraced this vision. Propaganda about science, however, was not all rosy. In fact, propaganda celebrated the usefulness of failed experiments. Youth in the countryside knew that failure was a common—and healthy—part of scientific experimentation, but when their efforts did fall short, they were extremely hard on themselves. Recognizing how sent-down youth and propagandists alike conceived of scientific experiment during the 1960s and 1970s helps to explain why people willingly participated in official projects and found them personally meaningful.

This is not to deny, however, that many teens dreaded the prospect of going to a village. By the mid-1970s, ambivalence or opposition to revolutionary projects was becoming more and more common, as Sha Qingqing and Jeremy Brown show in an essay that draws on a diary kept by a young man in Tianjin during the summer and fall of 1976. The diarist, named Tongshan, recorded the devastation of his Tianjin neighborhood during the Tangshan earthquake of July 1976. His descriptions of aftershocks, anxiety, and rumors about how top Communist leaders were responding to the crisis were quickly subsumed by his own worries about how the quake might affect his assignment to a village as a sent-down youth. Tongshan's writing reveals that he appropriated and internalized propaganda while simultaneously doubting key Maoist policies. The street fights, petty thefts, and visits from the police he experienced while waiting to go to a village added to his stress and exacerbated his doubts. Enthusiastically repeating revolutionary bromides on one page of a diary and then bitterly complaining about them the next day might seem contradictory or hypocritical, but the coexistence of official ideology and critical ideas was a central part of everyday life during the Mao years.

The mix of the personal and the political in Tongshan's diaries reflects his exposure to a realm of official culture that had become well established but not all-powerful during the Mao period. Our third group of chapters focuses on culture and information at the grassroots, specifically in the areas of film, Red Guard periodicals, and local religious practice. Matthew Johnson examines the urban core and the immediate rural environs of Shanghai and concludes that, although the propaganda system became a central feature of China's state structure after 1950, the creation of a single, nationalized mass culture was considerably less successful than other historians have imagined. Treating institutions of mass culture as local and social phenomena rather than mere manifestations of state ideological dominance reveals that cultural transmission was far from an assured process, whether viewed in terms of dissemination or reception. Shanghai was essentially a multicultural space in which local, national, and international culture all coexisted. In addition, uneven and heterogeneous patterns of cultural distribution within the city and between Shanghai and its rural hinterland reflected broader imbalances in the Mao-era cultural landscape. Shanghai's cultural scene became even messier in the aftermath of the Great Leap Forward, when state and nonstate actors co-opted cultural resources and institutions, or simply introduced their own apolitical or oppositional alternatives, all of which were viewed by the Shanghai cultural bureaucracy as troubling indicators of systemic failure. Even when the Cultural Revolution came, Shanghai propagandists could not totally overcome the economic and organizational constraints that prevented state culture from becoming a unified, national phenomenon. Moreover, censors were hardly the sole arbiters of taste. Profit-mindedness—a hallmark of official and unofficial culture alike from the 1950s onward—has proven to be a powerful, and easily ignored, force in shaping China's cultural landscape.

Grassroots communication during the Cultural Revolution was, as argued by Michael Schoenhals, one of the era's most striking features. The flourishing of publications produced by "revolutionary mass organizations" in 1966 and 1967 revealed a plurality of values and opinions in Chinese society— a picture at odds with conventional stereotypes about Red Guard chaos and violence. Red Guard groups printed and distributed newsletters that mimicked official internal reference publications, reporting on how the Cultural Revolution was unfolding throughout China and reprinting top leaders' speeches. Before 1966, such independent reporting would have been considered counterrevolutionary networking. Given the mass organizations' quasi-official status at the outset of the Cultural Revolution, however, their information-gathering and dissemination activities were tolerated until September 1967, when the Central Cultural Revolution Group decided that translocal and multipurpose groups gathering intelligence throughout China constituted a threat. Information networks had become unofficial cultural spaces. Their sudden emergence during the Cultural Revolution's early years suggests, at the very least, that the potential for such unofficial space to exist was present throughout the Mao years generally. The restraint of unofficial culture went hand in hand with its creation. In other words, what defined the "unofficial" was a process of criminalizing and squeezing out nonstate alternatives to official cultural and information flows.

Themes of cultural pluralism, unofficial networks, and official co-optation all appear in an essay by Xiaoxuan Wang, who shows how the Communist Party continued earlier state efforts to brand local, communal religions as superstitious organizations, and to close and confiscate their temples, monasteries, and schools. Official policies, however, did not necessarily achieve full or successful implementation at the village level. Wang brings fieldwork and archival research to bear on the issue of religious control, focusing on Ruian County in Zhejiang Province to demonstrate that local customs such as rainmaking and dragon boat rowing were never driven underground by increasingly harsh state measures against religion. In fact, Wang finds that during the Cultural Revolution, the Christian population in Ruian increased significantly. Even as previously protected leaders and institutions were displaced, the "revolutionary masses" themselves exhibited a striking tenacity in their devotion to both legal and illicit practices. Often the line was blurred. The chief cause of this dilemma in religious policy implementation—the question of how to classify and transform (or simply eliminate) surviving religious organizations—was local cadres themselves. As Wang shows, overburdened rural cadres were members of communities in which religious practice remained a vital part of the fabric of social life. In a manner reminiscent of Andrew Walder's description of "neo-traditional" patronage in post-1949 Chinese factories, such cadres represented a new local elite and potential patrons for religious rituals and other activities. Many grassroots officials saw rituals as legitimate practices; others simply ignored them. From this perspective, the religious revivals of the 1980s and 1990s were largely extensions of a status quo that had existed since the 1950s. Local cadres themselves facilitated the survival of unofficial and illicit practices.

Our finding that heterogeneity, limited pluralism, and tensions between official and unofficial cultures were persistent features of grassroots society during the Mao years builds on existing scholarship that has pointed out the limited reach of the state in rural China.[18] Indeed, some of the earliest insights into conflict in Mao-era society have come from the rural sector.[19] Struggles over peasant surplus and property during the formation of the state grain procurement system and collectivization in the 1950s revealed the high levels of discontent that could be incurred by an aggressively modernizing socialist regime. The Cultural Revolution also exposed the political system's capacity for group conflict and violence. Since then, new sources have allowed researchers to identify instances of violence dating back to the earliest years of the PRC. Many of these accounts, however, have focused on state-directed excess.[20] The story of grassroots discontent and resistance against everyday forms of control is the topic of our final group of chapters.

Conflict, violence, and discontent at the grassroots had a strong ethnic dimension in non-Han areas. Many scholars would readily agree with the assertion that "liberation" remained far from complete in Tibet, Xinjiang, and southwest China after 1949. What has received considerably less attention is the degree to which interethnic tensions smoldered following the military takeover, only to erupt in the course of rural collectivization or campaigns to identify and punish enemies.[21] Wang Haiguang connects Guizhou province's mid-1950s transition to socialism and the experience of forced collectivization to the explosion of anti-Han, antigovernment grievances among minority villagers in the Mashan region. This case study provides insight into the broader dynamics of ethnic antigovernment resistance throughout Guizhou, Yunnan, Sichuan, Gansu, and Qinghai during the same period. By 1956, ethnic tensions in China's interior had reached such a pitch that Liu Shaoqi and Mao Zedong personally addressed the issue. By advocating nonviolence and an end to "Han chauvinism," central leaders sought to calm the uprisings and bring peace to geopolitically sensitive frontier regions. In Mashan, soldiers in pre-1949 guerrilla bands reemerged as charismatic local leaders and catalysts of opposition to socialist policies. Myths, rumors, and polytheistic religious beliefs also provided templates for rejecting regional authorities. Failure to completely curb Mashan's rebellious inhabitants through violent coercion led provincial leaders, some of whom had experience as ethnic guerrilla resisters themselves, to consider a more peaceful path. Nevertheless, these softer policies were not implemented until formulated and authorized by central leaders. Left to their own devices, officials in regions riven by interethnic tensions were often inclined to choose harsher methods, just as resisters resorted to violence as a way of standing up to state extraction and persistent discrimination.

In Xinjiang, grassroots attempts to directly counter Han chauvinism and state expansion were denounced as "local nationalism." Zhe Wu presents a complex case of tension between Han and non-Han cadres in the former East Turkestan Republic territory of the Xinjiang Uyghur Autonomous Region—directly on the border with the Soviet Union. Here, anti-Han or "local" ethnic nationalism remained a potent force within the Communist Party itself, as onetime East Turkestan Republic ("Ghulja regime") leaders joined Han Communists to form a ruling coalition. Faced with unfavorable policies at all levels of society, Xinjiang's non-Han cadres and ordinary inhabitants alike viewed Communist pro-unity policies as a ruse. Pastoral lands were seized, acculturation forced, and the interests of the largely non-Han population neglected in key areas such as health and education. By 1956—a critical year in the history of China's interethnic relations—Muslim identity seemed under attack. Non-Han cadres such as Saifudin Azizi appear to have initially worked to downplay the severity of the brewing backlash but could not conceal the frequent appearance of "counterrevolutionary" anti-Han organizations in society, or even within the Party. As patterns of unrest and political conspiracy mounted, the crisis began to further erode popular faith in the benefits of Party-led government. The sudden onset of the centrally directed Anti-Rightist Movement led to criminal investigations, finger-pointing within the ranks of non-Han cadres (who, despite allegations, did not represent an ethnic "bloc within"), and ultimately an effort to bring Xinjiang under firmer Communist control through communization and de-Sovietization. This chapter thus highlights the mix of local, transregional, and international forces that shaped and unsettled social relations throughout the 1950s. By the early 1960s, the Ili-Tacheng (I-Ta) zone of Sino-Soviet competition was rocked by uprisings, insurrection, and the migration of political refugees from China to the Soviet Union. As Wu argues, the causes of the turbulence were not simply Sino-Soviet competition writ local. Rather, persistent patterns of interethnic tension in Xinjiang kept majority non-Han regions tense throughout the Mao years.

Conflict was consistent and localized during the era of high socialism. S. A. Smith uses a macrohistorical and multisited perspective to shed light on the extent to which violence across multiple locales constituted—or was even intended as—a threat to central authorities. Drawing on public security materials to produce a bird's-eye view of the phenomenon of redemptive religious societies, Smith documents an astonishing pattern of uprisings ostensibly carried out in the name of universal salvation that also included a diverse range of participants and motivations beneath their shared religious veneer. Violent crackdowns could not fully eliminate the sects, some of which were networks of thousands of people following newly declared "emperors." Just because redemptive societies did not provide a sustained challenge to the existing political and normative order does not mean that their members did not envision alternatives to that order. As Smith notes, the image of imperial restoration proved particularly attractive to sect members who sought to create their own "statelets" within the larger geobody of the People's Republic. Discontent was thus expressed in archaic, opaque, and traditionalist terms that, though labeled as superstition, reflected millions of villagers' direct engagement with the experience of living in a country whose politics proved baffling, injurious, and even deadly.

The chapters that follow provide an account of post-1949 social change from the perspective of everyday life and using the methodological and analytic lenses of the grassroots. In exploring themes and categories viewed by past scholars as integral to the centrally directed state-building project, we have found particularistic interests in the context of each, as well as within the very structures of the Party itself. This shows that studying the history of the People's Republic solely from the perspective of state-society relations, mass movements, and official categories and discourse overlooks many aspects of everyday experience, including networks that linked state and nonstate actors and made room for a wide range of bottom-up agendas. By going to the grassroots, however, we have encountered a familiar historian's dilemma: as voices proliferate, the credibility of a unified national narrative recedes. There is no single grassroots narrative to replace the voice of the center. Instead, we are left to ponder whether "Mao's China" ever existed at all.

Part I

CRIMES, LABELS, AND PUNISHMENT

1

How a "Bad Element" Was Made

The Discovery, Accusation, and Punishment of Zang Qiren

YANG KUISONG

The term "bad element" (*huaifenzi*) has a history of use by both the Nationalist and Communist Parties. Initially, it was a general reference to all corrupt, degenerate, and opportunistic "elements." Later, it became a specific term in Communist Party documents, referring to all people whose actions were vile and thoughts impure, and who had a damaging effect on the Party's work.

Party Center issued an official document defining the differences between "counterrevolutionary elements" and "other bad elements" on March 10, 1956. The document noted, however, that "all counterrevolutionary elements are bad elements." Based on this definition, the "other bad elements" referred to those outside the group of people who had been investigated and proven to be "counterrevolutionaries"—"political imposters," "traitorous elements," "hooligan elements," and "degenerate elements of extremely vile character."[1]

In 1957 Mao Zedong categorized *huaifenzi* as criminals. In Mao's words, dictatorship was to be imposed on all "thieves, swindlers, murderers and arsonists, hooligans' organizations, and elements that cause serious harm to socialism."[2] But because most *huaifenzi* "harmed socialism" indirectly, they were different from "counterrevolutionaries," who stood in direct opposition to the Party. Therefore, the conviction and sentencing rates of *huaifenzi* were usually lighter than the punishments meted out to counterrevolutionaries. But because *huaifenzi* still "cause[d] serious harm to socialism" from a class struggle standpoint, the regime treated these people and class enemies as birds of a feather. As a result, policies toward *huaifenzi* were similar to those governing counterrevolutionaries. The authorities usually deprived these people of their political rights and personal freedoms, handing them over to local governments through which they would undergo reform through labor or supervised reeducation.

Even by the standards of the time, however, the definition of *huaifenzi* was broad, and the factors leading to conviction were numerous and complex. Many criminals did not necessarily oppose socialism, and many of them fell afoul of the political system and its policies without necessarily committing "bad" acts. It is therefore worthwhile for historians to question just how bad convicted "bad elements" actually were and to what extent they may have opposed socialism. This chapter tells the story of a "bad element" whose badness was ambiguous and contested.

A Bright Future

Zang Qiren was born on August 26, 1925, in Lishui County, Jiangsu Province. His family belonged to the class of urban poor, and his father, Zang Nansheng, was a low-ranking clerk in charge of grain receipts in the county government's land tax office. After the junior Zang's mother died in the wartime chaos of 1937, the senior Zang remarried, after which time the entire Zang family, which included younger brothers and sisters, subsisted on Zang Nansheng's tiny income. With his schooling cut short by financial difficulties, Zang Qiren worked for a living from age fifteen onward—as an apprentice in a cigarette factory and a sock factory, an intermittent hawker, an intern at the Kunshan Public Roads Bureau, and finally as a bus conductor. When Nanjing was occupied by Communist Party forces in 1949, Zang had already lived a difficult life. Recruited on the day of his twenty-fourth birthday into the Lishui County Grain Bureau as a tax collector, Zang soon became an enthusiastic supporter of the new society and its politics and applied on his own volition to join the New Democracy Youth Corps.[3]

Zang's fortunes changed again in April 1951, when arrangements were made for him to be transferred to a factory in Nanjing as a temporary worker. He was soon promoted to a permanent position. Zang's new job coincided with the Campaign to Suppress Counterrevolutionaries. Responding to the campaign's emphasis on placing loyalty to the Party above all, Zang reported to the authorities that the landlord relatives of the very person who had secured him a new job in Nanjing were then hiding in Nanjing. Zang also reported his mother's cousin for possessing firearms.[4] While the campaign raged on, Zang devoted his own spare time to studying and to improving his coworkers' literacy. The factory named Zang "Excellent Anti-Illiteracy Teacher" for three consecutive years from 1954 to 1956, and he was elected to the organizing committee of the factory Youth Corps.

In 1956 Zang's factory was relocated from Nanjing to Xuchang in Henan Province. By this time Zang had married, but his new wife, who worked at the looms in a wool factory, was unable to make the trip with her husband because of her own family circumstances. Zang, now a Youth Corps cadre and confidante of the factory's Communist Party secretary, responded enthusiastically to this impending assignment. Although his wife had given birth to their first child only a few months before, Zang did not exercise his right to request that he remain in Nanjing and instead worked hard with little outward complaint. Regularly exceeding both quotas and expectations, Zang's good fortune continued after the factory finally moved to Xuchang. He was elected vice-chairman of the factory workers' union and was a representative at Xuchang's fourth union congress. In 1957 he received the Union Activist Award, Second Level.[5]

Zang had reached the apex of his political career. At the same time, however, a change in factory leadership and worker dissatisfaction brought about by the move to Xuchang had transformed the factory's political atmosphere. When a new rectification campaign unfolded alongside the Hundred Flowers and Anti-Rightist Movements, mobilizing ordinary people to criticize bureaucratism within the upper ranks, Zang Qiren began to make his first series of mistakes—mistakes that, given Zang's personality and experience, seem surprising.

A Guilty Conscience

Zang Qiren was short, with small, elongated eyes and a natural smile. His easygoing appearance allowed him to mix comfortably with his coworkers, even if Zang himself spoke infrequently. Although Zang had a strong sense of self-esteem, he was sensitive and became hesitant when he encountered problems. Documents that Zang wrote over the years confirm that he viewed this particular trait as his most significant shortcoming, noting that "I do not take setbacks well" and "I have the weakly cowardice of the petty bourgeoisie." Zang's superiors agreed. In their eyes, although Zang "sought to improve himself" and "had a positive work attitude" most of the time, he had a "weak capacity for struggle," "could not take criticism," and "possessed certain petty bourgeois thinking."[6]

Zang's personality had a lot to do with his past. When asked to write up his personal history during each of the political campaigns of the 1950s, Zang's résumé always looked the same:

September 1938–June 1940: Stopped schooling because of the Japanese invasion.

September 1940–June 1942: Studied and completed education at Lishui Model Elementary School.

September 1942–June 1944: Studied at Lishui Normal Junior High School; schooling interrupted because of family difficulties.

October 1944–June 1945: Apprentice at XX Socks Factory in Nanjing; left because of bullying.

September 1945–August 1946: Medic trainee at Shaoxing Zhangzhen Civilians' Hospital; dismissed.

January 1947–June 1948: Trainee at Kunshan bus station of the Public Roads Bureau; dismissed.

July 1948–March 1949: Unemployed; became a hawker.

August 1949–April 1951: Lishui Grain Bureau, municipal and district governments; drew up books and accounts; helped with tax collection during summer and fall harvests.

April 1951–present: Washer, Decorations Department [*penhua bu, xiban*] XX Factory, Nanjing.[7]

This matter-of-fact narrative concealed several details that Zang held back even when called on to confess and reconfess his personal history. Zang's 1953 election to the factory's Youth Corps Organization Committee had brought him good political standing and a sense of satisfaction. But it also made his superiors pay more attention to him, contributing to his unease. He was especially nervous about speaking to his superiors. The situation went on for several months before Zang submitted a resignation letter in May 1953:

Lacking sufficient knowledge of political theory and work experience, I cannot progress in my work and lack confidence. . . . I have little time to connect deeply with the masses, with the serious outcome that I have cut myself off from them. For this reason, I have had many criticisms directed at me from the Youth Corps. Some people say I am selfish because I am only concerned about my own education. In addition, after getting married last year I have had many family problems, and these have taken up part of my time. The above reasons have made me depressed, and my attitude toward work has become worse. For the sake of my other responsibilities, I wish to resign from my posts in the Youth Corps and to be replaced by another Organization Committee member chosen by the branch who will play a leading role in educating young workers, striving ahead with them and improving links with the masses.[8]

The letter's fluency and cohesion (most workers in Zang's factory were illiterate or had received only an elementary school education) drew the attention of factory Communist Party secretary Wan Shihong, who took time to counsel and encourage his distraught young subordinate. During his spare time, Secretary Wan would seek out Zang for conversation and a game of table tennis. With Wan as a mentor, Zang's work in the Youth Corps once again began to progress, and he was promoted to the position of acting branch secretary. Zang's resignation was postponed for less than a year, however, before his anxiety returned, and he abruptly quit the Youth Corps with the excuse that he had become too old to continue.

What Zang did not realize was that his experience and position as branch secretary would make it impossible for him to ever reclaim normal worker status. In January 1955 he was asked to complete a cadre résumé form, implying that the factory bureaucracy still considered him a political functionary. In the context of the ensuing Campaign to Eliminate Counterrevolutionaries—in full swing by summer that year—this meant that Zang was subject to investigation as a potential "bully, spy, and counterrevolutionary" and was a candidate for expulsion from the cadre ranks. For personnel in leading positions, every blemish in one's personal history had to be checked. As an ordinary worker, Zang might have remained untouched by the movement. Yet coupled with his guilty conscience, the compulsory review soon forced him into a surprising confession. As more people from the factory, including some he knew well, became targets of the purge, Zang's resolve broke down. In September 1956 he confessed to the Party branch that before 1949 he had been "forced by life's circumstances to work on the other side" and that he had thereafter concealed this fact from the organization.[9]

Historical Problems

What specifically had Zang done wrong? According to his written confession he had (1) underreported his age by two years during the time of the Japanese occupation for fear of being conscripted and had never corrected the deception; (2) during the Anti-Japanese War, he had been forced by the Nationalist Army to become a medic, deserted, then returned when he was unable to survive without his military connections, and also worked as a tax collector; (3) also during this period, he had joined a secret organization called "Ten Sworn Brothers" and pledged loyalty to a leader called the "Old Man." Zang's revised personal history also reflected the new revelations:

August 1932–June 1937: Fifth Grade, Lishui Normal Affiliated Elementary School.

August 1937–June 1938: Took refuge from the war in Maoshixiang.

August 1938–June 1940: Completed elementary education at Lishui Model Elementary School; enrolled at Lishui Normal Junior High School.

June 1940–September 1940: Left school, remained at home.

September 1940–November 1940: Apprentice, XX Cigarette Factory, Nanjing.

November 1940–August 1941: Unemployed, at home.

August 1941–June 1942: Apprentice, XX Socks Factory, XX Road, Nanjing.

June 1942–April 1943: Medic, 89th Regiment Civilians' Hospital, Zhangzhen, Shaoxing County.

May 1943–September 1943: Unemployed, at home.

September 1943–June 1944: Medic, 88th Regiment Rear Hospital, Tianjiashan, Shangyu County.

June 1944–August 1944: Unemployed, at home.

August 1944–January 1945: Revenue Department, 88th Regiment,
    Jinjishan, Xiaoshan County.
January 1945–May 1945: Unemployed, left home.
May 1945–April 1946: Unemployed, at home.
May 1946–January 1947: Hawker, Suzhou.
January 1947–June 1948: Trainee, Kunshan Public Roads Bureau.
July 1948–March 1949: Bus conductor, Kuntai Bus Station.
April 1949–August 1949: Cigarette stallholder, Lishui.
August 1949–April 1951: Assisted with tax collection, Lishui Grain
    Bureau.
April 1951–present: Joined factory.[10]

In his written confession, Zang Qiren reiterated several times that the
Nationalist troops he had joined were engaged in combat with the Japanese
behind enemy lines. His first encounter with the army was after he had left
the XX Socks Factory in Nanjing and was traveling to Zhejiang in search of
his relatives. While on a boat from Xiaoshan to Zhangzhen, Zang was captured by scouts of the 89th Regiment of the Nationalist Army's 30th Brigade
and was forcibly impressed into the regiment's medical unit, where he
became a medic. After a few months, Zang escaped home but could not get
along with his stepmother or stand the scorn of his neighbors, so he left.
Unable to find a new job, he then worked as a medic for a new unit, the 88th
Regiment, for several months. Finding life in the military too arduous, Zang
managed to secure a new job as a tax collector through his network of personal acquaintances and lasted for three months at the new post before the
sudden arrival of Wang Jingwei's collaborationist "Peace Army." Fearing for
his life, Zang again deserted his post.

Zang's fear of confessing this period in his personal history was partly
because of the stigma that would accompany his brief service with the
Nationalist forces. In the context of the Campaign to Suppress Counterrevolutionaries and Democratic Reform Campaign, however, the more
serious of Zang's omissions were his involvement with Ten Sworn Brothers
and pledged loyalty to the Old Man—later revealed to be Nationalist army
officer Yu Jipeng. Not only would Zang be investigated for past criminal
transgressions, but the very fact of his membership in this "reactionary
underworld organization" would be seen as a grave political offense. This is

presumably why Zang tried to play up his youthful ignorance and naïveté in his written confession, in which he explained:

> My motivation for joining a sworn brotherhood was that I was influenced by old-style novels and thought joining was an act performed by heroic outlaws. My motivation for pledging loyalty to Yu as the "Old Man" was that I thought he was a hero for not cowering before the enemy. I was also curious about the celebrated Green Gang and Red Gang and wanted to find out what they were really like.

When he confessed, Zang was still on good terms with the factory leadership and friendly with the Communist Party branch secretary. He still harbored illusions of evading punishment, writing, "I request that the organization be lenient toward me and hope that it will give me additional education and assistance." He added, "If this matter can be kept secret, please keep it a secret, so that I will suffer less emotional distress."[11]

Looking for Trouble

Zang Qiren's confession came just as his factory was preparing to relocate from Nanjing to Xuchang. This massive undertaking left little time for factory authorities to continue investigating Zang's case; the leaders also hoped that Zang would mobilize other workers to help the factory resume production. Rather than being denounced and investigated for his confessions, Zang was instead promoted in the union. A year passed, and still no inquiries were made into Zang's past. With new responsibilities and accolades to his credit, Zang again began to speak up and incur the unwanted scrutiny of superiors.

In relocating from Nanjing to Xuchang, the factory had moved from a bustling metropolis to a remote town. Many workers resented the move. Factory head Niu Keyong had promised that the future would be bright, praising Xuchang for its low prices and convenience. Yet after their arrival, the workers found that goods in Xuchang were often more expensive than those in Nanjing and that the factory itself was located in the countryside, nearly four miles from Xuchang proper. Transport was inconvenient and living conditions spartan. Medical care proved difficult to obtain, and single workers—by far the majority—were dissatisfied with the lack of entertainment. They clamored to return to Nanjing.

As vice-chairman of the union, Zang was obliged to help the factory pacify the workers, but at the same time he opted to serve as their advocate. During this crisis, Zang's mentor, Secretary Wan, was transferred away from the factory. The new secretary, Deng Rongxian, was almost immediately at odds with the union cadres, criticizing them during a rare visit to the factory floor for neglecting their educational and disciplinary responsibilities. Deng was short and frail, and Zang thought little of this new superior. The fact that Deng had been transferred from a recently closed kiln factory only made Zang more willing to challenge the secretary's criticism.

Zang quickly earned Deng's ire through a series of ill-timed attacks. When the Hundred Flowers Movement encouraged workers to criticize cadres and oppose bureaucratism, Zang's coworkers posted big-character posters targeting factory leadership. Zang, who himself had borne the brunt of worker insults for his role in suppressing their demands following the move to Xuchang, had frustrations as well. Lacking Party membership, he sought to rebuild his self-esteem by acting as a scribe for the less educated workers, collecting their criticism during small group meetings. Zang also urged the more talented artists among the workers to adorn the posters with cartoons lampooning factory head Niu Keyong and made his own big-character poster attacking Secretary Deng. Among Zang's accusations were that Deng spent time in his office rather than on the factory floor and that his mismanagement of the kiln factory boded ill for their factory, which was now doomed to fail as well.

In grassroots units such as Zang's factory—much like the conditions of the rural counties Cao Shuji describes in Chapter 3—the Hundred Flowers Movement was quickly followed by the Anti-Rightist Movement. Factory Party branches repeatedly encouraged workers to speak out, rectify the Party, and oppose bureaucratism. With discontented members of the factory thus exposed, the branches were then instructed by superiors to label as "rightists" those who had been most active and critical during rectification. A smaller number of participants, mostly those with a track record of poor performance on the job, were labeled bad elements. As vice-chairman of the workers' union, Zang Qiren was not labeled a rightist but was nonetheless investigated. Just as the Great Leap Forward was ramping up in the summer of 1958, Zang was compelled to write an account of his words and actions during the rectification movement.

The resulting document gave a detailed account of the big-character poster attacking Secretary Deng. Zang stressed that his writing of the big-character poster was "not an attack against the Party. . . . The main idea was to get Secretary Deng to go down to the factory floor and mix with the masses. This was because at the time Secretary Deng had already been in the factory for a few weeks, but all he did was go with X to the decoration room for a brief look." Zang admitted that his "political awareness was very limited, had serious rightist tendencies, and could not distinguish right from wrong." He emphasized, however, that he was "always loyal to the Party" and had "never conspired with the rightists and bad elements on how to attack the Party and the leadership." Zang said he was willing to submit to a thorough investigation.[12]

Alarmed but Unharmed

Before the Anti-Rightist Movement had ended at the factory, the Great Leap Forward was launched. Once again, everyone in the factory was mobilized and busied themselves with big meetings and small meetings, pledge-making ceremonies, overtime hours, "putting up red flags and pulling out white ones," and making revolution. Zang Qiren found himself transferred from the factory floor and into the union offices, where he turned out daily news-sheets and bulletins that featured production reports and news of techno-logical innovations. When the Leap collapsed in 1959 and 1960, Zang returned to the factory floor as a clerk and auditor. Once again, his past was seemingly behind him.

Were it not for a report filed on August 24, 1959, by Ji Zhengqi, himself labeled a "bad element" in the Anti-Rightist Movement, Zang might have escaped the notice of the factory's Party branch in its hunt for ideological deviance. Ji alleged that during the Hundred Flowers Zang had abused his position and power as vice-chairman of the union to slander the leadership, writing big-character posters and producing many cartoons (which Zang would later blame on other small-group members). Ji claimed:

Zang once told me in his own words that Secretary Deng's work style was bad. During the first factory committee meeting convened by Deng, the factory union committee members were all criticized. A Party branch secretary such as Deng must really change his style, Zang said, because otherwise our factory will collapse like the kiln factory. At the same time, Zang also called Secretary Deng . . . an opium addict. All in all, he was very dissatisfied with Secretary Deng. He was always conspiring with Tang Jinhu and Wan Liang, but I do not know what they talked about.[13]

In late 1960, the factory Party branch began an external investigation of Zang Qiren's political history.[14]

Based on the investigation plans drawn up by the Party branch, we know that Zang's 1956 confession was to be verified by traveling out of Xuchang to interview the people named in Zang's account. The investigators' questions included:

1. When Zang was working at Zhuji and Xiaoshan, what reactionary organizations did he join? What positions did he hold? Did he commit any crimes?
2. Under what circumstances did the Ten Sworn Brothers become sworn brothers? What was the aim of the sworn brotherhood? After pledging loyalty to Yu Jipeng as their "Old Man," did they act as his agents?[15]

Zhu Hongzhong, chairman of the factory workers' union, was the first person dispatched to investigate Zang's personal history. Yet even after two months of searching, few of the individuals named in Zang's history could be found. Zhu did locate Hong Zhenglong, a former coworker of Zang's in the Nationalist Army medical unit, who confirmed that Zang's statements concerning his two tours as a medic and brief stint as a tax collector were all basically true.[16]

Zhu remained skeptical. He reported:

Most of Zang's associates in the past committed various crimes and were reactionaries, which was why some of them were suppressed and some of them were sent for reeducation through labor. Some later returned to their former haunts, some died in labor camps, and some escaped to Taiwan or areas around Jiangxi. There are individuals whose whereabouts are still unknown, and I have not been able to locate them. But according to what various local Party organizations tell me, people such as these often joined reactionary organizations and activities during the time of the reactionary government and were in cahoots with bandits, repressive landlords, and the like. . . . Zang was quite young when he became a reactionary organization member, and his period of membership in the brotherhood was short. It is likely that he was no more than an ordinary minion. According to Zang's coworker Hong Zhenglong, Zang did not commit any crimes, and he was not a member of any other reactionary groups. But how is it that Zang came to know these reactionary types and repressive landlords, let alone become their sworn brother?[17]

Zhu Hongzhong's investigation discovered little, but this fact was not enough to exonerate Zang.

Unable to get to the bottom of Zang's preliberation activities, the factory Party branch dispatched four additional investigators to locate Zang's past associates. This time, they were able to locate the son of one, although they could only prove that Zang had sought employment with the Youth Battlefield Service Corps, not that he had joined.[18] The investigation team turned up another promising lead when they located Chen Liang'en, mentioned in Zang's confession, who could verify whether Zang had indeed been unemployed, as he claimed, in early 1946. But Chen was no longer in Jiangxi, and the investigators waited several months before learning that he had been sent to Xinjiang as a criminal sentenced to reeducation through labor. In subsequent correspondence, Chen insisted, "I have never heard of a person called Zang Qiren."[19] The factory Party branch, incredulous, sent another request for information through the Xuchang Party Committee's Industrial Investigation Office to the cooperating Xinjiang unit where Chen was housed; Chen's answer—and attitude—remained unchanged. In the end, another letter sent through the Industrial Investigation Office elicited a response directly from the local procuratorate in Xinjiang: "Chen escaped while checked into a hospital. If recaptured, we will inform you."[20]

Falling In with the Wrong Lot

Unexpectedly, the investigation ground to a halt. Zang Qiren, apparently unaware of his predicament, was transferred to his factory's decoration workshop as a production group leader in late 1962. With the arrival of a new supervisor from Zang's hometown, Zang's fortunes again improved. He was transferred off frontline production duty and given the position of workshop technician, formulating workshop operations and job descriptions, as well as overseeing scheduling, quality control, and processing. In this way Zang enjoyed the relatively comfortable life of a workshop worker-cadre until the outbreak of the Cultural Revolution.

Behind the scenes, however, Zang's tangled history had a profound effect on his career and promotion prospects. By the end of the 1950s, it was clear to factory leaders that Zang was not politically reliable. During the earlier part of the decade, Zang's steady rise from acting branch secretary of the Youth Corps to vice-chairman of the factory union and his selection for the position of union representative indicated that he was a rising star, despite the scrutiny briefly elicited by his 1956 confession. Following the big-character poster incident of 1957, however, political suspicion dogged Zang's career. Although well educated and technically experienced, during the early 1960s Zang was a second-tier leader in the factory and workshop, passed over for further promotions, excluded from Party branch-organized meetings, and no longer invited to participate in political and propaganda work.[21]

This uneasy state of affairs collapsed during the Cultural Revolution. At the moment of the new movement's inception, two major factions quickly emerged in Xuchang: the "royalist" faction, represented by the Third Red Guard Headquarters, and the "antiroyalist" faction, represented by the 8-24 [August Twenty-Fourth] Rebel Headquarters. Zang threw in his lot with the royalists, believing that the more insurrectionist 8-24 organization was full of junior workers who were "mischievous," "full of complaints," and "impolite to leaders"—and thus doomed to fail. Instead, he stood on the side of the senior workers and active members of the Party and youth organizations.[22] The strategy worked at first—the 8-24s were suppressed by locally stationed military forces. But support for the 8-24 group from central authorities suddenly gave the rebels the upper hand; factory head Niu Keyong and his immediate subordinates were the first to fall, while second-tier leaders, such as Zang, who had stood with the royalists found themselves targets of further attacks.

Zang's first alleged crime was his ties to the workshop supervisor, Chen Wenlong, who shared Zang's birthplace and had favored him as a technician. Chen was labeled a "capitalist roader" by the rebels and continuously denounced. In the course of mass meetings, Zang's name emerged as Chen's "trusted aide." To avoid falling into the political abyss along with Chen, Zang immediately began to write big-character posters exposing and criticizing his boss. He was not brave enough, however, to engage in face-to-face "struggle" with Chen during the struggle meetings. Targeted in big-character posters and exposed by the 8-24 rebels, Zang was also compelled to write one self-criticism after another explaining his relationship to Chen Wenlong. In these documents Zang Qiren revealed that he and Chen had been neighbors as children, living on the same street and attending the same primary school as classmates until the second grade. After that, their contact had broken off, only to be restored again when Zang joined the factory in 1951 and discovered that Chen was already an employee. Chen did not disclose Party matters to Zang but did assist his former childhood classmate in carrying out the more complex requirements of his job.[23]

Zang could not guess that the rebels might learn about the investigation into his suspicious history, and so in his self-criticism he repeated the now-familiar narrative:

> I too came from a poor family. I dropped out of school and became an apprentice in a shop in Nanjing, where I suffered physical and verbal abuse. I suffered all kinds of inhumane treatment in Old China. I finally found a proper job after liberation, and my life became stable. I was a slave in Old China, but my true master is New China. . . . But I studied Chairman Mao's writings poorly, and my worldview was not thoroughly reformed.[24]

Confessing His Problems

On the night of May 31, 1968, Zang Qiren was summoned to an office by rebel faction workers to "confess his problems." An unprepared Zang hemmed and hawed and was reported by the interrogators to have "performed badly." He was not allowed to return to his dormitory and instead spent the night in the factory's air-raid shelter, now used by the revolutionary committee as a makeshift jail.

Xuchang was one of the first cities in China where the armed battles of the Cultural Revolution took place. Beatings and deaths were common. A guilty and nervous Zang, fearing for his safety, escaped the factory at 3 A.M. following his incarceration, ran on foot to the neighboring town of Hanzhuang, and boarded a train. On June 1, 1968, Zang got off the train in Zhongmu County. It was noon, and Zang had nowhere to go and little money with him; he was, however, able to telephone his younger brother, who urged Zang Qiren not to run away. Zang followed his brother's advice and returned to the factory. He wrote a public confession in which he attributed his earlier flight to "distrust of the masses" and repented having "provided an opening for class enemies and people with hidden agendas to achieve their aim of attacking the revolutionary committee and revolutionary rebels."[25]

On June 3, the terrified Zang supplemented this document with an additional written confession to the workshop group charged with guarding him, in which he wrote that he "was scared and afraid of being beaten up" and in severe discomfort owing to the "hordes of mosquitoes" that visited the air-raid shelter. Being incarcerated made him "feel like a criminal" and "miserable." Since the attacks on Chen Wenlong had begun, Zang wrote, he had been engaged in a constant process of self-evaluation, realizing that his "political awareness was low, [he] had always stood with the wrong people, and [his] break with Chen Wenlong remained incomplete." "Only by making a clean break with Chen could I return to Chairman Mao's revolutionary line," Zang continued. "If I chose not to speak because of my ineloquence during denunciation meetings, others would have said that I have not made a clean break, but had I decided to speak, my nervousness meant that I would have spoken poorly." Trapped by these circumstances, Zang concluded, he had decided to prevent them from escalating by "running away once and for all."[26]

Zang was desperate to disassociate himself from Chen, end the investigation, and secure his release from the mosquito-infested shelter. As a result, he began to produce an amazing amount of detail concerning the history of their relationship: during the two-day period from June 9 to June 10, he produced eighteen pages of material written in tiny characters, in which he revealed that Chen Wenlong had been involved in a plot to "restore capitalism." Zang further documented multiple instances of Chen's dispensing favors to those around him, his promotion of cronies, formation of various cliques, aid to trusted subordinates, complaints about the factory, and "corruption of the workers' revolutionary resolve." The most damning line uttered by Chen, Zang alleged, was delivered at a leaders' meeting in 1965: "People need education, just like cabbages need manure." According to Zang, Chen's comparison of the Party's wholesome nourishment to manure was "reactionary in the extreme."[27]

The rebels, however, were not placated. In their eyes, Zang was a criminal, to be caught and punished. For two hours on June 11, rebel interrogators "sounded out" Zang with a barrage of questions and oblique references to his past, none of which implicated Chen Wenlong. The matter, they insisted, was serious and one of "fundamental principles." Zang was to hold nothing back. Finally realizing that he was in grave political danger, Zang agonized over the motives of his questioners throughout the following night, racking his brains to guess what information they already possessed and what crimes he would be expected to confess. The solution, he decided, would be to divulge that he had made a "political mistake," which was a common-enough offense in the context of the Cultural Revolution and thus unlikely to incur grave punishment. The following day he wrote in his self-criticism:

> In the first half of 1967, I listened to a revisionist Soviet radio program three times. The first time I accidentally discovered the program, and I listened out of curiosity. But then I listened two more times. At the time I thought it was all right if I listened to the program with a critical mindset. I did not realize that it was a serious mistake and that, if I were to listen to it over a long period of time, I would slide toward Soviet revisionism and onto the road of anti–Party, antisocialism, and anti–Mao Zedong Thought, becoming close to the enemy and turning revisionist.[28]

The rebels were not interested in Zang's radio listening. Though still unaware of his shady preliberation history, they were bent on confronting him about his royalist stand at the outset of the Cultural Revolution. Zang responded by divulging additional details of how he had joined the Red Guards and opposed the 8-24 rebels. Because Zang had never become a conservative leader and had merely followed Chen Wenlong, these confessions amounted to little, even when couched in terms of fundamental conflicts between "revisionism" and "Mao Zedong Thought."[29] Zang was briefly off the hook.

Confronting His Past

In the ensuing days, it appears that the rebels finally became aware of the suspended investigation into Zang's incomplete autobiography. During the second half of June 1968, they organized a struggle session in which Zang was confronted and required to give a full account of his historical problems. In early July, Zang gave a public account of his history, addressed to the factory's "revolutionary masses" in the form of a big-character poster. These accounts were basically unchanged from what Zang had written more than ten years earlier. The rebels remained unsatisfied. Still lacking sufficient evidence to push the investigation further, however, the rebels allowed Zang to return to the workshop and ordered a new round of field trips to investigate Zang's personal history.

What the rebels had already learned about Zang's dubious history was not terribly damning. At most he had served as a medic in the Nationalist Army and had assisted the preliberation government as a tax collector; Zang had never even properly enlisted as a soldier. Although once a member of Ten Sworn Brothers and a follower of the Old Man, he had engaged in no criminal activities. Like the earlier Party branch members who had rallied around Secretary Deng, however, the rebels were convinced that there was more to this story. By moving the investigation away from the issue of Ten Sworn Brothers, they found their suspicions confirmed.

All at once, evidence for Zang Qiren's status as a political criminal began to accumulate at a rapid rate. The breakthrough came from Jiang Tao, a cousin of Zang's mother who admitted to the investigation team:

> In 1948 the chief of the Jiangsu Public Roads Bureau, Zhang Jingcheng, distributed forms in various offices to encourage people to join the Nationalist Party. At the station where I worked, Zang and Mao Benqing asked me, "Are you going to join the Party?" I replied, "Deputy Chief Yang does not belong to any political party. I am not interested in such

things. Since Yang is not the one who wants us to join, we can ignore it."
I seem to recall that Zang then said, "Whether one joins or not doesn't
mean anything. I once joined the Three People's Principles Youth Corps
and it was pointless." At the time we were just chatting casually about
the applications and I did not press him further to find out where he
had joined.[30]

Ironically, investigators already knew about Jiang's involvement because
Zang himself had mentioned it to an external investigation team from Jiang
Tao's work unit, saying that when both men had been employed by the Public
Roads Bureau, they had encountered mailed registration forms for membership in the Nationalist Party. Zang then remembered Jiang saying that if he
had wanted to join, he would have done so a long time before but that he did
not believe in political parties. Therefore, Zang recalled, "Jiang Tao did not
encourage us to join."[31] Questioned by the investigation team charged with
Zang's own case, Jiang could not avoid confirming that the conversation had
taken place.
    For Zang Qiren, the investigation was now reaching a crisis point. To
verify Jiang Tao's revelations, the rebel team sent another emissary to
Nanjing to requestion Jiang, who suddenly became evasive and claimed that
he could not recall Zang's original words, adding that "as I understood it
Zang did join the corps, but I did not press him further and can't be sure."[32]
Proving Zang's connection to a reactionary political party was difficult, but
now the main issue was class struggle rather than "political mistakes." In the
second half of November 1968, rebel organizations in the factory held
another mass struggle session, demanding that Zang Qiren confess to his
reactionary past.
    On November 25, December 4, December 25, and December 30 Zang
delivered a series of written statements that, though embellished with new
details, repeated the basic pattern of his previous accounts and asserted that
he had voluntarily participated in all investigations against him.[33] Zang
swore that apart from joining Ten Sworn Brothers, he had not been a member
of any reactionary groups and that he had only met the Old Man in order to
acknowledge him as a patron.[34] Finally confronted with the issue of his
alleged membership in the Nationalist-affiliated youth corps—which he did
not voluntarily confess—Zang delivered two accounts of the events described

by Jiang Tao. The result was a complete denial: "If I had been a Nationalist Party member, I would not have been furloughed from work in August 1948 and would not have remained an apprentice for more than a year and a half." Zang also gave a complete list of his former Public Roads Bureau coworkers and requested that factory investigators contact all of them. In conclusion, he reiterated:

> I swear before the Party and the revered Chairman Mao that I never joined any reactionary party, religious organization, secret service, or front organization. In the past I was never politically active nor was I engaged in other clandestine activities. I never took up arms. After meeting the Old Man, I never sought him out for aid, and as for my sworn brothers, apart from coworkers such as Jin Jishan, I only met the other five twice—first at the oath-taking ritual and then at the ceremony making the Old Man our leader. There were no other meetings, and we did not commit crimes. I have not concealed any aspect of my past employment.

Zang's only admissions of wrongdoing were that he should not have worked as a medic for the army or as a tax collector but had been compelled to do both because the Nationalists were everywhere.[35] The gambit worked. Although struggle against him was now in full swing, Zang had guessed correctly the limits of what his investigators knew and the extent of their investigation's progress. Mao Benqing could not be located to supplement Jiang Tao's testimony; none of Zang's other former coworkers had ever heard him mention the Three People's Principles Youth Corps. Even former members of the Youth Battlefield Service Corps, of which it had once been suspected that Zang was a former member, denied that he had Nationalist Party connections.[36] Once again, Zang's political opponents found themselves at an impasse.

A Failed Suicide Attempt

In the absence of any proof that his history contained evidence of heinous crimes, Zang was instead made a target for regular harassment and monitoring. In early 1970, the national "One Strike, Three Anti Campaign," which focused on countering sabotage and economic malfeasance, resulted in Zang's subjection to a series of political education classes and struggle sessions. Zang had become a permanent suspect in the hunt for sabotage.

The campaign's primarily economic focus meant that Zang's past history and political errors could not be used effectively against him. Instead, the revolutionary committee opened a new series of investigations into his behavior as a factory employee, and soon acquired several leads from Zang's former friends and coworkers. Zang was alleged to have exchanged his food ration tickets for millet in 1962; later he used his authority to arrange hardship subsidies for a friend, then used that same friend's name to borrow money with which he ultimately purchased a radio for personal use. Armed with this new information, interrogators were able to pry out of Zang the additional confession that during the Great Leap Forward and its aftermath he had "eaten and taken a lot, harming others for his own benefit, and engaged in graft and embezzlement to line his own pockets." Zang further admitted to using his status in the union and workshop to obtain additional cigarette rations and nutrition coupons, the latter valued at 2 jiao; he had also given factory-produced washbasins as gifts in exchange for food, failed to return dozens of coupons for steamed buns, and had taken cooking oil from the canteen without paying.[37] In keeping with earlier confessions, Zang also revealed that, as early as 1960, he had listened to "enemy radio programs"—including Voice of America, Voice of Free China, and broadcasts from the Soviet Union—with a coworker. When Zang bought the coworker's radio in September 1962, he was able to listen to broadcasts from both Taiwan (with difficulty) and the United States (clearly). In January 1967 Zang began once more to listen regularly to Soviet programming, which, as he recalled, praised Soviet economic development while criticizing the treatment received by Soviet delegations abroad in China. He swore that he had never encouraged others to listen, nor had he discussed the programs with coworkers.[38]

No longer compelled to discuss politics, Zang Qiren then proceeded to detail a long list of shameful "hooligan crimes." This admission pushed the investigation of his behavior in new and unexpected directions. What most pained Zang about his past, he recounted, was that, as a Nationalist Army medic in 1942, he had been forcibly sodomized by a Nationalist stretcher platoon commander. Zang claimed that following that incident he was unable to repress his own homosexual tendencies. From his teens to his forties, Zang pursued these urges; although he also married and fathered a child, Zang sought out sexual relations with men during prolonged absences from home.

In China during the Mao years, homosexuality was considered a form of "hooligan" behavior. Zang's repeated encounters with investigation and interrogation had given him ample time to reflect on the possibility that his sexual behavior might get him in trouble. Thus, while the basic facts about Zang's preliberation associations had been established in 1956, every new campaign brought with it new waves of fear and anxiety that his closeted sexual identity would be exposed. While accusations against him mounted during the Cultural Revolution, Zang had written thirty-four letters to twelve different men who were his previous sexual partners, and he had met with these individuals on thirty-two different occasions—all to conceal the evidence of his homosexuality by creating convincing pretexts for these otherwise-illicit relationships.[39]

The confessions were not completely without precedent. In early December 1968, Zang had buckled under repeated questioning by interrogators, revealing that though he had "no other problems," he had previously touched the genitals of male comrades, "an extremely low and vile act, and a serious error—I will turn over a new leaf."[40] Such incidents were not unheard of in factory dormitories but were rarely acknowledged or were in some instances treated as subjects of gossip and rumor circulated among the workers themselves. Zang's December 1968 questioning is a rare instance in which such rumors were used to hound a suspected political criminal, but because Zang's history as a former reactionary was the real target of such investigations, the issue of sex was dropped. In the context of the One Strike, Three Anti Campaign, Zang's political problems were no longer subject to scrutiny. As a suspected hooligan, however, Zang appeared to the revolutionary committee as an undesirable of a different, though equally dangerous, kind.

Interviews and interrogations of workers who were Zang's former roommates and friends revealed that several men had maintained sexual relationships with Zang over the years. On the morning of May 25, 1970, Zang was summoned by the workshop Party branch for a meeting, during which he was informed of the serious nature of his crimes and the breach in regulations they represented. He was ordered to give a full confession. Threatened with humiliation and the exposure of his numerous sexual liaisons, Zang Qiren could no longer withstand the mental strain of further interrogation. After a day of excruciating deliberation, he chose to end his life by swallowing a toxic substance. In a suicide note addressed to his family and children, Zang wrote that he had committed crimes and let down the Party and Chairman Mao. He hoped that his downfall would serve as an important lesson to others: to assiduously read the works of Chairman Mao, obey the Party, and make revolution with Chairman Mao forever.[41] Despite his preparations, the suicide attempt failed. Zang, given away by his own cries of pain, was carried away for emergency treatment and restored to health.

Pouring Out Beans from a Bamboo Tube

On June 21, 1970, Zang Qiren, recently discharged from the hospital, was taken along with several other "elements" whose reeducation had been arranged by the revolutionary committee to a meeting in Xuchang, where he was made to again confess his crimes and receive political instruction. Once again, Zang sought to think ahead of his captors and reveal only what was already known. Addressing his failure to disclose his homosexuality, he wrote of his fear that a full confession would have harmed others as well as himself and that he would have disappointed those who knew him: "These two thoughts stayed with me and churned around in my head. With no full confession, my days were miserable. The burden got heavier and heavier. I lost my appetite and couldn't sleep. The pressure was so great that I couldn't even breathe. I was a wreck."[42] The answer, as Zang knew well, was to play down the extent of his mistakes, if not their nature. He admitted to having had only a few sexual encounters with people outside of the factory.

This time the gambit was unsuccessful. The revolutionary committee widened its search for Zang's sexual partners. On July 21 and July 27, Zang was taken to educational sessions intended for counterrevolutionaries, at which a military representative, Secretary Wu, attempted to elicit confessions. Trapped and "squeezed" by Secretary Wu's authoritative presence, Zang was like a bamboo tube filled with beans—opened, then poured out for the committee to examine. By the end of July 1970, Zang had confessed to having had relationships with more than ten men. In early August he added another three names to the list. Some verified the details of Zang's confessions. Others were angry, denied the claims, and accused Zang of "framing" them. Zang's depression returned, and he once again contemplated suicide. On August 26, Zang managed to sneak out of the factory and briefly thought about throwing himself into a nearby lake. Halfway there, he recalled a discussion that had taken place in one of the small-group reeducation sessions about how the family members of a recent suicide victim had been forced into confessions themselves. Zang returned to the factory.

In early September 1970, Zang Qiren was once again subjected to public struggle sessions. These highly charged events frequently elicited unfounded and speculative accusations from members of the audience, and Zang realized that if he did not give a full confession about the extent of his homosexuality—if he did not allow the beans to be completely poured out—innocent people might be implicated. What followed was a systematic confession of what Zang called the "crimes of my private life." In this document, Zang confessed that since the late 1940s, he had engaged in sexual acts with more than twenty men, giving the year, month, location, and specifics of each liaison.[43] Zang also described his life as a young man in the "old society":

> Although I did not stay long in the old [Nationalist] army, its corrupting influence on my private life was severe. Nie XX, commander of a medical corps stretcher platoon, sodomized me by force while I was sleeping. He took advantage of my youth and timidity to sodomize and masturbate me many times. He harmed me, but being young and ignorant, I did not consider the relationship to be homosexual. Instead, I thought it was all quite silly and nothing more. Because of my ignorance and my desire for sexual release, I began to masturbate. From that point onward, I was poisoned and trapped by unhealthy influences and began to read pornographic books, such as *Secrets of the Manchu Court, Weird and Wonderful Tales of Past and Present Ages, Sexual Knowledge,* and so on. All of these described sexual acts between men and women, as well as sexual acts between men. The descriptions gave me knowledge of these immoral behaviors, and the poisonous wares of imperialism, revisionism, and feudalism gradually seeped into my brain. Step by step, they took over my thoughts, searing me with the mark of capitalist degeneracy. In 1948 I was a bus conductor at Kunshan Station and

became very friendly with a driver's assistant, Xu XX. We became very close. I was twenty-two; both of us were of the same age, unmarried, and had sexual urges. As I had been ideologically poisoned by unhealthy ideas, I seduced Xu into a relationship. That was my first criminal act, but it occurred before liberation. In Old China I was surrounded by bad influences (having been raped, led astray by pornographic books, and so on), and I did not know that I had committed a crime. Perhaps I could have been forgiven, because the old society was to blame for my wrongdoing. Then liberation came, and Chairman Mao and the Party rescued me from my hard life. My livelihood was assured, and I had good political status. By rights I should have then fortified my mind with Mao Zedong Thought and swept away the filth and dregs left by the old society. . . . But a change in worldview cannot be created by will alone, and there are some people in our society who still refuse to walk the bright and broad way of socialism. Zhang XX was one such person. In 1950, when I was still an assistant tax collector in Lishui, Zhang not only sodomized me but also forced me to engage in oral sex with him on numerous occasions. This further poisoned me to the core, and it played a considerable role in turning me toward crime in the future.

Following Mao Zedong's instructions on determining causality, Zang's self-examination traced his crimes back to their ideological roots. Believing that his primary flaw was "selfishness," from which stemmed an inability to follow the path of revolution, Zang attributed his mistakes to his pursuit of self-interest at the expense of socialism:

I attended several years of high school at night, not for the sake of the revolution but to increase my own likelihood of promotion and to receive a higher wage and higher social status. I carried out research on production methods, not to improve the work of the union but to make use of my position and connections, open doors, eat and take more than I should have, and engage in corruption and theft. I was chipping away at the foundations of socialism and sabotaging socialist development. . . . For a long time, I engaged in abnormal homosexual activities, to the extent that these began to replace my normal marital relations; I became a criminal. All of these behaviors were manifestations of my bourgeois worldview, which shaped my entire life and my yearnings.

Zang proceeded to detail additional manifestations of his corruption and debasement. For example, he thought nothing of using his radio to listen to enemy jazz broadcasts and committing the counterrevolutionary act of tuning in to proscribed radio stations, thus becoming a "commando" of imperialism, revisionism, and counterrevolution. He concluded: "I have degenerated into an ideologically backward, morally depraved, and politically muddled representative of the bourgeoisie."[44]

Reeducating a Nonpolitical "Bad Element" through Labor

The confession was accepted. Evidence of Zang's "other bad element" crimes, including those of "hooligan element" (*liumang fenzi*), put him on the same level as people labeled anti-Party counterrevolutionaries, even though his alleged political crimes remained unproven. In winter 1970, the factory authorities closed their investigation of Zang and forwarded the case to the Public Security Bureau, where military control authorities would review the evidence and decide on a punishment. The preliminary decision was swift: Zang was to be temporarily placed under public surveillance and then confined and made to perform penal labor.

In August 1971, the Xuchang Public Security Bureau (PSB) began carrying out the terms of Zang Qiren's incarceration. Zang was once again compelled to write a series of confessions. The entire process took several weeks. After that, Zang was subjected to "supervised labor." He was also required to submit a monthly ideological report to the factory authorities while awaiting the results of the PSB's ongoing investigation. In the reports, Zang sought an end to the uncertainty that had dogged him for decades:

I have committed heinous crimes, which result from a contradiction between the people and the enemy. I have become an enemy of the people and will lose my rights as a citizen. I hope that the government will be lenient with my case. If so, even if I am subjected to the most severe punishment (such as losing my factory membership, remaining under surveillance in the factory, losing my position and my wages, or being sent to the borderlands for wasteland reclamation or to the rural areas for reeducation among the poor and lower-middle peasants), I will be willing and grateful. Even if the government gives me another sentence and I am made to wear a criminal "hat," I will have deserved it and will not protest.[45]

The Xuchang PSB recommended no further sentencing. Instead, his case was sent back to the Municipal Light Industries Bureau Special Investigation Group, with the recommendation that Zang's verdict and punishment be reconsidered.

In January 1972, the Special Investigation Group confirmed the veracity of the case as submitted by Zang's factory and sent the materials compiled by the factory to Zang for his approval. Zang's only objection was to the accusation that he had used the rectification movement to maliciously attack Secretary Deng and assault the Party, which was attributed—erroneously, according to Zang—to his dissatisfaction with the factory's relocation and feelings that his career had "no future."[46] On April 14, 1972, the factory Party branch, in consultation with the Special Investigation Group, reached its conclusion:

Zang Qiren was a medic, corporal, and tax collector with the 88th and 89th regiments of the 30th Brigade of the Nationalist Army from June 1942 until 1945. He also became one of the Ten Sworn Brothers, a group that included Xiang Weiming (enemy army lieutenant), Tong Binhui (suppressed after liberation), Zhu Chuanzhang (presently in Taiwan), and others. Their acknowledged leader, aka the "Old Man," was Yu Jipeng, commander of the Shaoxing County militia. During this period, Zang forcibly collected so-called "taxes" and engaged in sodomy with Nie XX, a medical corps platoon commander. In 1947, as a conductor for the Kun(shan)-Tai(cang)-Liu(he) Bus Company, Zang engaged in mutual masturbation and other perversions on numerous occasions with Xu XX. In 1950, following liberation, Zang was working in the Lishui County Grain Bureau where he fondled and masturbated Zhang XX, plying Zhang with liquor and forcing him to engage in oral sex acts. In 1951, Zang joined Factory XX and his hooligan crimes increased in severity; by the end of April 1970, more than twenty workers, peasants, and students had been fondled, masturbated, and sodomized by Zang and had been made to perform oral sex acts on him and engage in other perversions. All told, seven individuals were sodomized by Zang, five made to perform oral sex acts, and three to engage in other perversions; Zang also molested a female worker. When worker Fan XX was transferred to the countryside, Zang urged Fan to return the money that he [Fan] had borrowed from the union; Zang then asked Fan to come to his room and made Fan spend the night there. In the middle of the night, Zang fondled Fan and made him perform other perverted acts, applied lubricant to Fan's anus, and sodomized him. After being sodomized, Fan could no longer control his bowels, inadvertently defecating in his trousers. Using games of "horse" and other pretexts, Zang also fondled and masturbated a young worker who lived in the same dormitory, causing the worker to ejaculate. In addition, between 1960 and 1961, Zang listened to radio programs broadcast by the U.S. imperialists, the Chiang Kai-shek gang, and the Soviet revisionists on multiple occasions, either in the house of Lu XX or in his own dormitory. Of the behaviors listed above, Zang has only confessed voluntarily to his political problems (in 1956) and to secretly listening to enemy radio broadcasts (after he was exposed [during the Cultural Revolution]). As for his hooligan crimes of perversion and sodomy, Zang deliberately concealed them. During the Cleansing the Class Ranks and One Strike, Three Anti campaigns, Zang colluded with others to form a united alliance. When accused by the authorities, he resisted by attempting suicide and fleeing the factory. Only later, after being criticized and educated by his leaders, struggled against many times by the people, and made to accept Party policy did Zang finally make his confession.

As for how to punish Zang, the factory Party Committee wrote:

Zang Qiren is an experienced worker. He bears some guilt for his criminal association with the Ten Sworn Brothers and for his reactionary employment record. After liberation Zang continued his transgressions by listening to enemy radio broadcasts; he also engaged in hooligan activities such as perversion, sodomy, and oral sex for nearly twenty years. The nature of these crimes is serious and their details vile; they are punishable offenses. But Zang did confess. After further discussion with the workers and examination of the case by the factory Party Committee, our decision is to identify Zang as a bad element. He is to wear a "hat" and to undergo reform through labor while under public surveillance.[47]

The Xuchang Public Security Bureau disagreed. Zang had committed no political crimes. He had no reactionary motives for listening to enemy radio broadcasts. As for his sexual relationships with other individuals of the same sex, such behavior was not uncommon among workers, and the Supreme People's Court had in 1957 ruled that it was "best not to punish" voluntary homosexual activity.[48] With no evidence that Zang had used force to assault others sexually, the Public Security Bureau instead recommended a punishment focused on reeducation; there was no need to officially label Zang as a bad element.

The Party branch at Zang's factory was dissatisfied with this recommendation. Finally, both sides agreed on a compromise—the PSB would call Zang a bad element, but he would not carry an official label as a bad element (in the parlance of the time, he would not "wear a bad element cap") and he would be allowed to remain in the factory for reform through labor. The PSB identified Zang as a bad element on August 2, 1972; as an additional sign of leniency, his case was treated as a contradiction among the people rather than a counterrevolutionary crime.[49]

The Road to Prison

While still awaiting a decision on his case, Zang was placed under surveillance and assigned to push heavy carts of bricks at the factory. After the more lenient sentence was issued, the factory assigned him to be a mixer in the decoration workshop. Since 1968, Zang had been denied family visitation rights. His return to factory life was a lonely one; Zang immediately sought out male companionship. Though former friends were wary of him, Zang developed a close relationship with Sun Furong, who like Zang had been identified as a bad element within the factory. Sun had served in both the Nationalist Army and People's Liberation Army, had been transferred to the same factory as Zang, and had also been found guilty of engaging in sexual acts with other male workers. Between August 1973 to July 1976, Zang and Sun had sex more than ten times, arranging their trysts in factory locations including the communications room, air-raid shelter, pantry, and milling room. In 1976, Zang also struck up a relationship with a young male coworker named Xiao, who soon became the primary object of Zang's affections. Zang frequently visited Xiao's rural residence in Xuchang County, where the two would have sex; before long, Zang's unexplained disappearances resulted in the discovery of his liaison. This time he faced conviction and real imprisonment.

Brought before factory authorities in July 1976, Zang admitted to his sexual relationships with Sun and Xiao. The leaders were incensed. They saw homosexual relationships as a persistent problem that had been caused by the factory's move inland and the presence of "bad elements" who, like Zang Qiren and Sun Furong, had been polluted by their experiences before liberation. Factory leaders demanded that the two be arrested and brought to justice. A report on Zang stated that despite the lenient terms of his previous punishment, he "naturally takes to evil ways and has deeply harmed the physical and psychological well-being of youths. . . . He is a bad fellow who will not repent despite repeated reeducation; he must be severely punished. After discussion with the workers and examination of the case by the factory Party branch and revolutionary committee, we propose that the judicial department arrest Zang and sentence him to prison. This will appease the people's anger."[50] On December 8, 1976, the municipal police held a preliminary trial for Zang Qiren, but based on the judiciary's decision to avoid treating private issues as criminal offenses, the trial concluded with the judge's decision to assign Zang a course of "policy education" and return him to the factory.

Zang descended into a state of fear, heightened emotion, and anxiety. The unexpectedly light punishment came as a release of sorts. In a report to the factory, Zang wrote, "I feel that although I have committed a serious crime, rather than beating me to death with a pole, the Party's leaders are still patiently educating me and pointing me in the right direction."[51] This understanding of the situation was overly optimistic. Though let off by the municipal police, Zang had become an enemy to the factory leadership. Following repeated appeals to the PSB, the factory's recommendation to arrest Zang was finally accepted.

The events that followed made Zang a convict and criminal as well as a bad element, thus sealing his fate within the factory. On December 27, 1976, Sun Furong was arrested and tried publicly, paraded onto a stage by the workers' militia, and his head forced down while other coworkers read the charges against him. Sun was then handcuffed by police and driven away, to the applause and cheers of several hundred factory employees. Zang, still technically a free man, was filled with dread. On January 20, 1977, he was informed that the factory was preparing to deal with several criminal cases and that his current position as mixer was to be filled by a new transfer. Sensing that his time had come, on January 22 Zang contacted his younger sister to tell her than he was likely to be arrested and imprisoned and told his younger brother to look after their parents in Lishui. Whereas a less experienced Zang might have contemplated suicide in such a situation, years of enduring the threat of exposure and punishment enabled him to calm himself. Zang even harbored some hope that he might return to the factory after serving his prison term.[52]

Arrested a month after Sun, Zang was treated to the same public humiliation, criticism, and trial, followed by a posted notice that read:

> Despite repeated efforts to reeducate him, Zang Qiren did not repent of his heinous crimes, reactionary thoughts, and corrupt character. He is in fact a Nationalist dreg and remnant who has infiltrated our working class organization. To carry out the Party's basic line and fortify the dictatorship of the proletariat and to strike a severe blow against sabotage carried out by the Gang of Four and other class enemies, the factory's revolutionary committee has examined the issue and decided to revoke Zang Qiren's factory and union memberships and to petition the public security organs to have him arrested and brought to justice.[53]

Following three months of preliminary trials and sentencing, on April 21, 1977, the Intermediate People's Court of Xuchang issued a criminal verdict against Zang:

The criminal Zang acquired the evil habit of sodomy from the old society. He did not repent after liberation. Even after being identified as a bad element, he was not given an official label, and his case was dealt with as a contradiction among the people. Yet he continued to commit offenses, owing to his evil and depraved nature. In order to safeguard social order and strike out against hooligan criminal elements, the court sentences the criminal Zang Qiren to seven years of imprisonment.[54]

This time, the sentence came as an unpleasant surprise—Zang had not expected that his period of incarceration would exceed that of Sun Furong. In April 1977, the month of his sentencing, Zang was already fifty-two years old. The length of the prison term ensured that he would never work at the factory again.

* * *

Judged by the moral and political standards of the time, Zang Qiren was sometimes "good" and sometimes "bad." By 1973 most other workers, including his former friends, had distanced themselves from Zang. This did not, however, prevent Zang from starting a sexual relationship with the much younger Xiao. Viewed from the perspective of the factory community, Zang's inability to control his sexual urges was not "good." But at the same time, Zang had a long and established history of being "good." According to the standards of the Chinese Communist Party, Zang's impoverished background made him a reliable and grateful beneficiary of "liberation," which had allowed him to find a stable job and advance his career. In the 1950s, responding to the Party's exhortations, Zang had placed duty before family. He did not complain about the factory's relocation from Nanjing to Xuchang and did not seek to use his son's birth as a pretext to avoid the move. In the factory he became an educator of other workers and received many personal honors and commendations. In other words, people around him had reasons to call him a good person.

Others' perceptions of Zang began to change from "good" to "bad" because he had been caught concealing his past. But Zang's murky political history, in spite of repeated, lengthy, and costly investigations, was never enough to warrant an official verdict, let alone give him a label of bad element or counterrevolutionary. It was Zang's sex life, not his pre-1949 political background, that pushed him into the category of "bad" by the standard of the time. After Zang confessed to his relationships, factory and public security officials paid no further attention to his alleged ties to reactionary organizations before 1949. It was all about sex.

Although Zang certainly transgressed certain moral and political standards of factory life during the Mao period, in other ways he was a victim. First, if we take his word about how he had been raped in the late 1940s and in 1950, he was a victim of sexual abuse. Second, like many others during the Mao years, the socialist planned economy forced him to live apart from his family for years at a time. After the factory moved from Nanjing to Xuchang, workers faced long-term separation from their spouses. In 1962, the State Council ruled that workers who were unable to spend their regular weekly day off with their spouses were to be given an annual two-week family visitation holiday. Even this concession was difficult for many workplaces to implement, and many workers endured long-term separation from their loved ones. Under these circumstances, extramarital relationships were bound to occur. To understand Zang Qiren's path to becoming a "bad element," we must take into account the political-economic system that produced this outcome.

Translated by Wee Kek Koon

2

Moving Targets

Changing Class Labels in Rural Hebei and Henan, 1960–1979

JEREMY BROWN

Gao Yongcheng watched bemusedly as his dog took off in pursuit of a car that was passing through his village in Lankao County, Henan. Motor vehicles rarely drove through Henanese villages in 1964, so the car's appearance was a novelty for the dog and for Gao himself, a young man in his mid-twenties who led his production team's militia. As the dog caught up to the car and tried to bite it, Gao's smile turned into a look of shock, quickly followed by rage. His dog, unfamiliar with the dangers of cars, had gotten tripped up and crushed by a tire. The animal was still alive, but one of its legs was mangled.

Gao shifted his attention from his dog to the occupants of the car. He and several friends flagged it down and began shouting at the driver. Gao yelled, "Stop! You have to compensate me for my dog!" The driver of the car, which belonged to the Lankao County Paper Factory, stepped out and tried to assuage Gao, who responded with curses, saying, "You guys should be driving on the main road. What the hell are you doing coming through our village?!" The driver then got back in the car and shut the door, but Gao grabbed him. At this point, another occupant of the car, factory director Yu, tried to intervene. When Yu's words failed to calm Gao, the factory director took a 5-yuan bill out of his pocket and gave it to Gao. Gao responded angrily, saying, "No, 5 yuan isn't good enough—it's got to be 10." Yu, a Red Army veteran, opened up his empty wallet, showed it to Gao, and said, "I don't have any more money today, Comrade. I'm sorry." As Gao continued to argue, an official from the village arrived and criticized Gao; then the car left.

We know about Gao Yongcheng's bad temper because this story was included as evidence in his production team's May 30, 1966, petition requesting that Gao's father's class status be changed from poor peasant to sublandlord (*er dizhu*).[1] As part of the Four Cleanups movement's reinvestigation of every village household's official class status (*jieji chengfen*), Gao Qiwang's changed label was approved in July 1966 by his village's Poor and Lower-Middle Peasant Association, by the Four Cleanups work team in the village, and by higher-level work team leaders at Zhuaying Commune Headquarters.[2] Gao Qiwang's new class status referred to his having rented land from a landlord and then subleased it to others before "liberation," and he would be treated as a "landlord element" (*dizhu fenzi*) until his death in 1977. Gao Qiwang's 1966 identity change was posthumously revised in November 1979 to a "family status" (*jiating chengfen*) of "tenant middle farmer" (*dian zhongnong*).[3] He was one of 393 "four bad-type elements" in Lankao whose "erroneous" class label changes were corrected in 1979; that same year, county authorities also removed negative labels from 5,035 people without admitting that their original classification had been wrong.[4]

Gao Yongcheng's bad behavior (he had also punched a soldier's wife in the mouth) was not the sole reason for his father's new class label in 1966. Gao Qiwang himself had indeed hired laborers to help with planting and harvesting in the late 1940s and had been less than a model citizen during the 1950s and 1960s. Many factors contributed to Gao's status change. Millions of people in China faced the prospect of a new class label in 1965 and 1966. Like Gao Qiwang's family, villagers' economic situations and behavior before and after "liberation" came under intense scrutiny from outsiders on Four Cleanups work teams, who asked rural people to testify about their neighbors.

In China during the Mao period, each individual's official class status was a marker of identity as significant as race, gender, and national citizenship are in North America today. People who had "good," politically reliable class labels such as those of worker and poor peasant could participate in politics and enjoyed privileged access to education and jobs. Those who had "bad" class status, including landlords and capitalists, suffered discrimination and were often passed over for work or school opportunities. Each rural family's class status was first assigned during land reform on the basis of the household's economic situation during the three years before "liberation," whenever that moment came in a particular area.[5] Children and others without independent incomes were assigned a "family status" (*jiating chengfen*), which was based on their family's main source of income—a rule that essentially made class status hereditary.[6]

We have a fairly good understanding of how class status labels shaped life chances and granted or denied rights and privileges during the Mao period. Scholars have noted the irony that a classification scheme aimed at eradicating exploitation and promoting equality created new forms of inequality and harsh discrimination. But previous studies have underestimated the class status system's dynamism, instability, extreme variation, and sheer confusion.[7] Class status labels in Mao-era China were part of a complex modern categorization scheme that merged "formal" restrictions and "informal" workarounds.[8] Because of source limitations, however, scholars of Chinese politics and history have mostly focused on the formal aspects of class status (regulations emanating from Beijing) and have neglected the informal dynamism of how the system worked at the grassroots. As Geoffrey Bowker and Susan Leigh Star write, classification rules "often come to be considered as natural, and no one is able completely to disregard or escape them. People constantly fiddle with them, however, and work around the formal restrictions."[9] Newly available sources from Chinese villages show that rules about class status labels affected reality, but did not dictate it.

In 1960s China, with the stroke of a pen and the stamp of an official seal, poor peasants became landlords or middle peasants became lower-middle peasants. A renewed emphasis on class struggle, fueled by Mao's concerns about the death of the revolution in the wake of the disastrous Great Leap Forward and famine, made such changes possible. But while central policy permitted reclassification and created a political atmosphere that encouraged work teams to identify hidden enemies, local dynamics determined who was affected. What justified a change from a good or neutral label (poor peasant or middle peasant) to a bad one (rich peasant or landlord)? Sometimes historical problems that had been covered up or ignored during land reform came to light during reinvestigation. More often, bad behavior in the 1950s or early 1960s—including violence or breaches of community norms during the Leap, sexual misconduct, or intravillage feuds—led to new class labels. Even bullying, like Gao Yongcheng's violent demands for compensation when his dog's leg was crushed in 1964, contributed to status changes.

Significant changes to class labels occurred in Henan Province in 1960 and 1961 during the "remedial course in democratic revolution" (*minzhu geming buke*) movement. The "remedial course" targeted local officials who had made mistakes during the Great Leap Forward, and in its methods and results it presaged a massive effort four years later to reinvestigate and classify the background of every rural household in China. The reclassification project of 1965–1966 was part of the Four Cleanups movement. While most villagers maintained their original, land reform–era class status during the Four Cleanups, the millions whose labels were reassigned had to live with the consequences until 1979, when Party Center's repudiation of class struggle led to a final round of investigations and changes.[10]

This chapter draws on the class status files of individuals and families from Hebei and Henan. At a used book market in Tianjin in 2006, I bought a full five-folder set of files about Mochagang Village, west of Tianjin in Hebei Province. In summer 2009, I purchased five folders from Henan (one from Nanyang County, four from Kaifeng County) from vendors and read class status reinvestigation files from Henan's Lankao County, held at Shanghai Jiaotong University's History Department. I also viewed a full run of class archives from Houjiaying in Hebei Province, held at Nankai University's Chinese Social History Center. The forms from Henan were completed in December 1965, January 1966, and July 1966, while a full year separates the Hebei class archives (Houjiaying's were completed in August 1965; Mochagang finished its forms in July 1966).

The files offer a glimpse into how rural people dealt with the messiness of changes to class status labels. They also challenge the 1966 and 1976 "divides." While the 1949 divide has been dismantled by scholars exploring continuities between the Nationalist and Communist regimes, the 1966–1976 period, almost always referred to as the Cultural Revolution, is remembered as a "ten-year disaster" that stands starkly apart from what came before and after. The ten-year straightjacket and the label "Cultural Revolution" obscure long-term trends that spanned the 1960s and 1970s, and also paper over important changes that took place between 1966 and 1976.[11] The most meaningful dates for shifts in the class label system were 1960–1961, 1964–1966, and 1979. The Great Leap Famine and the Four Cleanups movement—more so than the Cultural Revolution—were the impetus for class label changes in villages. The Four Cleanups movement has not garnered the same scholarly attention as the Cultural Revolution. This is because the Four Cleanups preceded and then merged into the Cultural Revolution, and also because the Four Cleanups was a primarily rural event that was not covered in newspapers at the time. For many people in China, Four Cleanups policies issued in 1964 and then carried out in 1965 and 1966 were at least as important as the events of the Cultural Revolution.

Remedial Democracy

In 1960, Guo Zhaotai's identity in the official class status system changed from middle peasant to landlord. Specifically, Guo became a "landlord who had slipped through the net" during land reform (*louwang dizhu*). At the time of the change, Guo was the thirty-six-year-old vice-head of Xiaolizhuang Village in Lankao County. Guo and others in Henan had their labels changed by work teams carrying out a "remedial course in democracy," an effort to punish local officials in the aftermath of the Great Leap disaster. Peasants and local officials in Henan also called the movement "reforming the third type of brigade" (*gaizao sanleidui*), which referred to "backward" villages that needed special attention during the rectification campaign of 1960–1961.

The phrase "remedial course in democracy" invoked China's "democratic revolution," meaning the Communist Party's attempt to overthrow feudal forces and eliminate rural exploitation through land reform. The Party's transition toward socialism in the 1950s was based on the assumption that the democratic revolution had been a success. But when the Great Leap Forward ended in tragedy, Mao blamed the failure on feudal forces that had managed to survive the revolution's first stage. On November 15, 1960, responding to reports of widespread famine and political terror, Mao Zedong said that in many districts "bad people are in charge, beating and killing people. Grain production has dropped and people do not have enough to eat. The democratic revolution is still incomplete and feudal forces are causing great trouble."[12]

Because the democratic revolution had not been sufficiently thorough, a remedial course was necessary, especially in the "third type of brigade," in which class enemies had wormed their way into positions of power. According to Mao, as many as one-third of all villages belonged to this category.[13] Many such brigades were in Henan Province, where massive numbers of famine deaths were accompanied by murder and torture carried out by local officials, who punished people for refusing to hand over grain or for attempting to flee the region. The center of this disaster was Henan's Xinyang region.[14] Xinyang Prefecture's report of November 22, 1960, called for "doing a rectification movement in a big way, just like land reform. This is a remedial course in democratic revolution, and also the continuation of the socialist revolution."[15] The movement to correct land reform's shortcomings spread beyond Xinyang to other parts of Henan, including Lankao County, where it changed the class labels of Guo Zhaotai and at least thirty-nine others.[16]

Land reform first came to Lankao in 1950 and 1951. At the time, today's Lankao County was made up of two separate counties—Kaocheng and Lanfeng. More than 50 percent of households in the two counties were classified as "poor peasants and farm laborers" (pin-gunong), almost 40 percent as middle peasants, and around 6 percent as landlords. Three separate reinvestigations in 1951 and 1952 fixed errors in land distribution and class label assignments.[17]

During land reform, Guo Zhaotai was classified as a middle peasant; later reinvestigations confirmed this label. According to the Government Administration Council's guidelines on how to "differentiate rural class status," those in the middle peasant category usually worked the land themselves and did not exploit others and also generally did not sell their labor to others.[18] Guo was lucky that land reform work team members assigned class status only on the basis of the three years before the Communist takeover of Lanfeng and Kaocheng in late October 1948. When Guo was born in 1924, his grandfather was a landlord and the family was prosperous, but his father's heavy opium habit put the Guos on a downward spiral. In 1943, in the midst of a terrible famine in Henan, Guo Zhaotai's father sold the last of the family's land. From 1946 through 1948, Guo Zhaotai supported himself by grinding and selling soybean oil. He also tilled seven or eight *mu* that his sister's husband's family had given him when she got married. Between liberation and land reform, Guo purchased an additional four to five *mu*, giving him a total of twelve.[19]

These details seemed to place Guo firmly in the middle peasant camp. Between 1946 and 1948, he had not rented out land, had not hired laborers, and had no income derived from exploiting others. What made him a land-lord in 1960? None of the documents accompanying the Lankao County order restoring Guo's middle peasant status in 1979 date from the remedial course in democracy, but his file does contain transcripts of interviews with villagers who recalled why Guo's status changed. When asked in October 1979, "Why was Guo classified as a landlord who slipped through the net in 1960?" one of Guo's fellow villagers replied:

> It should be said that before the thirty-second year of the Republic [1943], Guo Zhaotai's family was prosperous and owned many things. Guo Enxiang [Guo Zhaotai's father] had also served in bandit leader Zhang Laowu's army. On top of that, during the Great Leap Forward, Guo Zhaotai severely beat people, grabbed more than his share, and so on. He was classified as a landlord who slipped through the net. He was also given a sentence of fifteen years.[20]

In other words, it came down to distant history and recent misdeeds. As seen in Yang Kuisong's chapter in this volume (Chapter 1), this is the exact same combination that sealed Zang Qiren's fate as a "bad element."

Other testimonies consistently repeat these two main reasons for Guo's status change: first, Guo came from a landlord family and his father had done bad things in the years before the founding of the People's Republic; second, Guo had "violated discipline" during the Great Leap Forward. Details vary: the brigade leader of Xiaolizhuang in 1960 said of Guo that "If there was an argument, he beat people, but not severely,"[21] and only one person recalled that Guo had been sentenced to serve time. In his own testi-mony, Guo said nothing about beating. He claimed that he was framed: "Because I had always worked for the Party and had the guts to speak out and butt heads, I offended quite a few people. Certain people hoodwinked commune members who did not know the truth and had them create false materials."[22] Guo's behavior during the Leap clearly contributed to his reclassification in 1960. According to central policy governing class status, Guo's family history before 1946 should have been out of bounds, but instead it was used to justify a change in status that punished Guo's more recent transgressions.

Local cadres in Henan were blamed for the province's disastrous Leap. One way to punish them was to give them an unfavorable class label. While this contravened land reform policies, it bolstered Mao's claim that the catastrophe in Henan had been caused not by central policies, but by class enemies at the local level.[23] The reassignment of class labels in Henan in 1960 shared several aspects with the more widespread class status changes that would follow in 1965 and 1966. First, Mao created an atmosphere conducive to identifying people who had "slipped through" land reform's net, by accusing hidden class enemies of trying to kill the revolution. This atmosphere was limited to a few provinces such as Henan in 1960 and 1961, but would encompass all of China by the mid-1960s. Second, recent bad behavior and personality disputes determined who was targeted, with evidence about preliberation exploitation "uncovered" only after work teams identified potential enemies. Preliberation history could easily be adjusted to deal with postliberation problems. Finally, genuine confusion about class status policies and definitions led to considerable variation at the local level.

For example, in Guo Zhaotai's 1979 file, there are at least four competing terms for Guo's official class designation. The official county order restoring Guo's land reform label corrected his "family status" (*jiating chengfen*) to middle peasant, while the commune's written report claimed to be reinvestigating his "class status" (*jieji chengfen*), which was first middle peasant and then landlord. A standardized form for Guo's biography noted that his "family background" (*jiating chushen*) was middle peasant, and Guo began his own testimony with "I am Guo Zhaotai, male, age 53 *sui*, peasant status" (*nongmin chengfen*). The words for class, status, family, background—and sometimes also "identity" (*shenfen*), "element" (*fenzi*), and "label" (*maozi*)[24]— were often mixed up throughout the 1960s and 1970s. In practice, the class status system was hardly systematic.

Four Cleanups Policy and Revising Class Labels

It makes sense to view the Four Cleanups movement as the continuation of remedial democracy on a much broader scale.[25] Scholarly accounts of the Four Cleanups tend to focus on elite politics, particularly on Mao's growing unhappiness with Liu Shaoqi. Mao kept changing his mind about the campaign between 1963 and 1965, but he eventually made it clear that he wanted an attack on "capitalist roaders in positions of authority," rather than a cleanup of petty cadre corruption. Mao wanted this attack to be led by the masses, including newly established poor and lower-middle peasant associations, rather than by large outside work teams.[26] The problem with a Mao-centric history of the Four Cleanups is that localities did not follow central policies in lockstep.

Another problem with describing the Four Cleanups from Party Center's perspective is that to do so totally overlooks one of the most important parts of the movement: the reexamination and classification of rural class labels. Class label investigations and reassignments continued in villages nationwide well after the policy document that authorized them (the Revised Latter Ten Points of September 10, 1964) was superseded by one that Mao preferred (the Twenty-Three Articles of January 14, 1965).

The Revised Latter Ten Points introduced significant changes to the draft Latter Ten Points of September 1963. While the earlier document called on "all comrades engaged in rural work" to study documents about how to determine rural class status, it explicitly stated that this did "not mean that a new division of classes is going to take place in rural areas."[27] Party Center reversed course on this question in September 1964, when "cleansing class status and establishing class files" became one of the main parts of Four Cleanups work.[28] Specifically, "Because in villages there is currently a rather widespread situation of confusion in class status, it is very necessary to undertake a serious, one-time cleansing of class status as part of the work of the Socialist Education Movement." The next sentence of the Revised Latter Ten Points targeted everyone in rural China: "In other words, *every family's status* should be investigated and assessed through thorough mass discussion, and class files should be established."[29]

It is unclear who ordered a reinvestigation of every rural Chinese family's class status. According to central economic official Bo Yibo, politburo member Tan Zhenlin was initially charged with supervising the revision of the Latter Ten Points in June 1964, but Liu Shaoqi took over the job in August.[30] Bo Yibo does not specify how the mandate for reassigning class labels made it into the document, but he is clear about the order's effects. Some of the masses (meaning noncadres) were given new class status labels that were worse than their land reform designations, and because Party Center had not given a clear standard for how to reclassify people, many localities were overly punitive in assigning class labels. Leaders in Guizhou, Bo Yibo wrote, determined that the democratic revolution had been incomplete in more than half of the province's districts. Newly discovered landlords and rich peasants in Guizhou were treated even more harshly in the Four Cleanups than the exploiting classes had been handled during land reform in the early 1950s.[31]

During the last quarter of 1964, the Revised Latter Ten Points—along with nationally circulated investigation reports about model brigades in which work teams had seized power from village leaders who had hidden their true class identities—radicalized the Four Cleanups.[32] The publication in January 1965 of the Twenty-Three Articles, a new guiding document for the Four Cleanups movement, should have been a moderating influence. The Twenty-Three Articles were supposed to take precedence over previous Four Cleanups policy documents.[33] The new articles did not mention investigating and assessing class labels or creating class files. The sentences in the Revised Latter Ten Points about examining "every family's status" had disappeared.[34] This absence makes it easy to assume that the reassignments called for in the Revised Latter Ten Points would stop in 1965. But they were just getting started.

Registration Forms and Class Files

The Twenty-Three Articles were silent about class labels but did not explicitly instruct Four Cleanups work teams to quit assessing class status. In the absence of clear instructions, many teams forged ahead in 1965 and 1966, creating dossiers for rural families and confirming or changing the labels people had been given during land reform. In order to figure out how to assign class status, work team members consulted compilations of convoluted and sometimes contradictory land reform policy documents.[35] The process and timing varied widely. In Houjiaying, a village between Tangshan and Beidaihe in Hebei, the Four Cleanups work team posted updated lists of class labels for all village families at least three times in 1965.[36] Gao Qiwang, the father of the young tough whose dog was crushed in rural Henan, did not learn about his change from poor peasant to landlord until a dramatic village meeting in late September 1966, although the Four Clean-ups work team had arrived in February and paperwork for the change began in May.[37]

In many counties, work teams followed the Revised Latter Ten Points and created "class archives" for each household, using fill-in-the-blank forms. The class archive forms confused and disconcerted Yang Shangkun, director of the Central Committee General Office. Yang, who took on an assumed name and joined a Four Cleanups work team in Shaanxi's Chang'an County, called his deputy Gong Zirong and asked him to query Party Center: "Should we do 'class archives' or not? Some places in Shaanxi have already printed and distributed 'class archive forms.' This type of form is loaded with trivial details, very difficult to complete correctly, and could be impossible to rely on in the future."[38] Central Secretariat member and Beijing mayor Peng Zhen eventually offered a vague response to Yang's questions, writing, "It is best to synthesize all of these questions and look at them together. Wait for the Northwest Bureau to discuss them, and listen to the Bureau's opinions." We do not know if Yang ever got a clear answer.[39]

The files in my collection confirm Yang Shangkun's complaints. Bound together in folders and titled "class registration forms" (*jieji chengfen dengjibiao*), paperwork for each family ranges in length from two to three pages. Forms from Hebei and Henan differ considerably. The Hebei forms include three separate spaces for the household's economic situation during land reform, at the time of collectivization, and "the present" (*xianzai*); there is also a larger space for "family history." The Henan files are brief, with a small box for "family economic situation before liberation," nine lines for information about family members, and a half-page space for miscellaneous notes (*beikao*). But they include a crucial element missing from many of the Hebei forms: a clear indication of what happened to each family's class status during the Four Cleanups.

Whereas the Hebei forms only provide space for the household head's family background and class status, the Henan forms are more specific and give a sense of change over time with three separate blanks under the heading "family's class status": "designated at land reform," "designated at land reform reinvestigation," and "examined and approved in the Four Cleanups movement." The last category shows which families had their class status reassigned. This is great to know, but the Henan forms do not explain why the change occurred. Fortunately for researchers, scribes in Hebei's Houjiaying made up for shortcomings in their class registration forms. Whenever necessary, they appended an extra handwritten page titled "Reason for class status change."

Going Down

Of the 141 households in Houjiaying during the class status investigations of 1965, the status of 17 "went down" (*xiajiang*), meaning a favorable change to lower-middle peasant or poor peasant, and 8 suffered a "rise" (*shangsheng*) to a worse class status such as rich peasant or landlord. Even though only one-fifth of the families in the village experienced changes in status, because the Four Cleanups work team investigated every family and announced results publicly, the underlying instability in the class status system affected everyone. If a villager's class status remained unchanged during the Four Cleanups, seeing neighbors' and relatives' labels change based on flimsy or confusing evidence sent the message that nobody's class status was a sure thing.

In some production teams, only favorable changes occurred. Of the 208 Henanese families for which I have files, 40 had their class status improve in late 1965 and early 1966, usually from middle peasant to lower-middle peasant or poor peasant. What did an improved class status label mean? It is likely that while outside work teams fueled punitive revisions because they felt pressure to expose hidden class enemies, some villagers themselves pushed for downward changes because better labels translated into practical political benefits. Edward Friedman, Paul Pickowicz, and Mark Selden write that during the Four Cleanups, the leaders of Wugong Village in Hebei reassigned "politically favored middle peasants" as lower-middle peasants in order to "solidify the position of friends" and grant them political clout.[40] Lower-middle peasant status became more politically valuable in 1964 with the formation of Poor and Lower-Middle Peasants' Associations (*Pin xia-zhongnong xiehui*, hereafter referred to as *pinxie*). The associations were meant to encourage mass involvement in exposing cadre corruption during the Four Cleanups; membership was limited to those with poor and lower-middle peasant labels.[41] In both Hebei and Henan, downward changes in class status made villagers eligible to join the newly formed associations. That was the whole point of a favorable revision.

The connection between a downward change and membership in *pinxie* is evident on class registration forms from Henan. On each form's list of family members—next to name, sex, and date of birth—there is a box for "Member of *pinxie* or not." All of the families whose status was changed from middle to lower-middle peasant or poor peasant had at least one *pinxie* member. Families who retained middle peasant status were ineligible to join, and their corresponding box on the form is either empty or reads "nonmember" unless they found a way to get special "treatment" (*daiyu*). Some villages constructed multitier class status labels, with the official status accompanied by separate tag that indicated how a family or individual was to be "treated" in practice.

In the number 6 production team of Liutie Village in Kaifeng County, thirteen of the thirty households changed from middle to lower-middle peasant. The class status of six other families in the production team remained unchanged, but remarks in the "miscellaneous notes" section explained that certain members of those families were to be "treated as lower-middle peasants." Huang Fa remained a middle peasant but received lower-middle peasant treatment and joined the *pinxie*. The form filler justified this special treatment by noting that Huang Fa was a member of the Communist Party. Huang Ji was also a middle peasant who received lower-middle peasant treatment and joined the *pinxie,* probably because he was Huang Fa's younger brother (the form does not say). Huang Ji's wife, Zhou Guiying, got to join the *pinxie* too because her father was a poor peasant, so she followed his class status.[42] The Revised Latter Ten Points had authorized changes in class status but did not sanction Liutie Village's unorthodox practice of "treating" a middle peasant as a lower-middle peasant. Nor did *pinxie* policy guidelines permit middle peasants to join the organization. Villagers in Liutie cleverly realized that because central guidelines did not expressly prohibit special treatment, they could probably get away with the practice.

When pressed to justify downward changes in class status during the Four Cleanups, how did village cadres do so? Weakly. Party branch and *pinxie* leaders in Hebei's Houjiaying provided vague rationales for revised class labels. Houjiaying's "reasons for class status changes" were two-to-three sentence explanations, generally approved and stamped by six individuals: the village's Party secretary, the vice-secretary, the *pinxie* chair and two vice-chairs, plus one Four Cleanups work team member. Sometimes the papers were stamped by a five-member class reconsideration committee (*jieji fuyi weiyuanhui*).

Fifty-seven-year-old Hou Daxiang was a member of the class reconsideration committee and also a beneficiary of recategorization; he stamped a form approving his own change from middle peasant to lower-middle peasant. During land reform, Hou Daxiang's family's status had been assessed solely on the basis of their economic situation, Hou argued. In the years before land reform reached Houjiaying, the Northeast had already been liberated, improving peasants' standard of living even as far away as Houjiaying, he reasoned. This joyous development made Hou Daxiang's family more prosperous immediately before land reform, which led to a middle peasant label. "But under current class status classification policy, we should look at questions historically," the explanation continued. Because Hou Daxiang and his father had worked for landlords for more than twenty years, "the poor and lower-middle peasants have discussed this. [Hou Daxiang] should be lower-middle peasant, and his status is hereby changed."[43]

Land reform classifications were ostensibly based on a family's economic circumstances during the three years before liberation. Land reform–era policies had been distributed to Four Cleanups work teams, and nothing in "current class status classification policy" changed the three-year window. But in order to give Hou Daxiang lower-middle peasant status, his fellow villagers thought "historically" and invoked a more distant past.

In other cases, vague statements or extraneous family details justified improved class status labels. Forty-one-year-old Hou Dazhi and his father "had been exploited a small bit, so they do not meet the standard for middle peasant." Concrete evidence of Hou Dazhi's family's suffering was absent from his class archive: he had worked in Shenyang between 1941 and 1949; his father was a carpenter. But because of a "small bit" of exploitation he had once suffered, he became a lower-middle peasant in 1965. Another member of the Hou clan, Hou Yongju, had peddled and done odd jobs in the Northeast for at least twenty years. In 1947 his eldest son, a soldier in the People's Liberation Army (PLA), had been killed in the civil war against the Nationalists; Hou's third son had joined the PLA in 1964. A year later, his sons' military service was cited in support of Hou Yongju's status change from middle to lower-middle peasant.[44]

Going Up

People such as Hou Yongju and Hou Daxiang must have quietly accepted their favorable class status changes. The affirmation of political reliability was useful, and nothing good would come from pointing out that the status revisions had not been handled in accordance with central policies. When people in villages "went up" in status during the Four Cleanups, however, the reasons were just as arbitrary but their responses much noisier. Becoming a lower-middle peasant and joining the *pinxie* might have been a nice change, but it was not as earth shattering as the shock of being reclassified as a class enemy.

Class status revisions during the Four Cleanups went beyond rural cadres and could touch any villager. Gao Qiwang was not an official, and while his dog-owning son was on the production team's militia, he did not hold a village-wide post. But the elder Gao had served in the Nationalist Army in the 1930s, and he and his sons had a penchant for angering fellow villagers. A May 30, 1966, report from Gao's production team requesting his change from poor peasant to sublandlord detailed Gao's problems and dwelled more on recent history than on the preliberation past. "After liberation," the report noted, "Gao should have sincerely participated in production and followed government laws, but he disguised himself as a poor peasant and did evil, spread rumors, destroyed the collective, and rode roughshod over the poor and lower-middle peasants."[45]

Gao's "evil" included helping a woman sell trees that had been felled at the gravesite of her late husband in 1953. The husband was a landlord who had been executed during land reform. In 1963, Gao sang a "reactionary" song from his army days, with lyrics cursing the Red Army: "Their ideas come from Lenin, who isn't even Chinese; they make wives kill their husbands; liberated women kill people too!" In the early 1960s, Gao had also overfed livestock (two horses died), kept money he earned transporting goods for the village instead of giving the proceeds to the collective, and he and his family members had "beaten the poor and lower-middle peasants seven times and cursed them too many times to count."[46]

In a self-criticism dated June 10, 1966, Gao admitted selling two cypress trees from the landlord's grave, keeping transport income for himself, and singing a reactionary song. He also said, "I have a bad temper. . . . I don't know how many people I have cursed in Lizhuang, and I have also beat up many people."[47] The ostensible reason for changing Gao Qiwang's class status was that he had subleased land in the late 1940s. But the bulk of the materials supporting his class status revision emphasized his recent nastiness.

Other class status revisions during the Four Cleanups focused more on disputed details from the three years before land reform. At issue in Qin Xinde's rise from middle peasant to landlord in 1966 was the precise timing of when his family had hired a farm laborer. Qin was a thirty-year-old production team leader in Lankao County. In a 1966 letter to the Kaifeng Prefecture Four Cleanups work team office appealing his class status change, he claimed that his family had done a mutual labor swap with a man named Qin Xiang that had only lasted six months in 1943, before the three-year preliberation window.[48] Work team members in the village wrote back to their superiors, arguing that many villagers had claimed that Qin's family had exploited others immediately preceding liberation. But Qin was refusing to accept the new label, and his mother lay down in front of the village office in protest and would not leave.[49]

The work team's word trumped Qin's, and his landlord label stuck until November 1979. During a 1979 reinvestigation, Qin recalled that his illiterate mother had been "tricked" into affixing her fingerprint on a document confirming their family's landlord status. After Qin sent his appeal letter in April 1966, Four Cleanups work team leader Wang Jinhai called him in for a late-night talk, put a pistol to Qin's head, and mused about what it would be like to blow Qin's brains out. After that, Qin and his mother were subjected to several public struggle sessions and his mother was nearly beaten to death.[50] An investigation report by commune officials in 1979 stated that the family's original middle peasant label had been correct: the Qin family hired a laborer in 1946 to help after Qin Xinde's father died, but the arrangement had not lasted long. Qin Xinde had argued with the Four Cleanups team about this many times, the report continued, and had appealed to higher levels, "but because the Cultural Revolution started, the problem remained unresolved."[51]

The Cultural Revolution began in Beijing in May 1966; the last Four Cleanups work teams were ordered to leave villages in February 1967.[52] The overlap between the Four Cleanups and the Cultural Revolution added to confusion in villages, but in terms of class status changes, this much is clear: for some people, the Cultural Revolution froze what the Four Cleanups had set in motion. On January 25, 1967, Party Center issued a directive about "protecting the achievements of the Four Cleanups movement," noting that the Ten Points and Twenty-Three Articles had been "personally directed and formulated by Chairman Mao."[53] Which Ten Points? The directive was unclear. A follow-up article in *Red Flag* in March 1967 cited the full name of the document known as the Latter Ten Points, without the word "revised." Extremely careful readers would have assumed that the Revised Latter Ten Points and its endorsement of class status investigations had been repudiated. But the article was vague and gave no guidance on what to do about class status changes that had already occurred.[54] Party Center's terse declaration of victory in the Four Cleanups meant that families who contested their changed class labels would be opposing the movement's "great achievements."

Fighting an Unfavorable Change in Class Status

The Cultural Revolution set in stone some of the Four Cleanups movement's class status changes, but that did not mean that affected families remained quiet after work teams departed. Some pursued appeals for years. The Liu family of Houjiaying expended a huge amount of energy battling a new rich peasant status, but the more the Lius fought, the worse things got. In 1965, the Liu household included patriarch Liu Wanchen, age sixty-one; his wife Liu Zhao Shi; a thirty-eight-year-old son who was mute and played no role in the drama except as proof of preliberation bitterness; the eldest son's wife, who was also mute; third son Liu Binxiang, who at twenty-six was a production team leader; Binxiang's wife; and fourth son Liu Binqing, a twenty-five-year-old university graduate and cadre at the Hebei Provincial Water Department who was far away from home as a member of a Four Cleanups work team in Hebei's Xuanhua County.[55]

In 1965, the Four Cleanups work team changed the Liu family's status from middle peasant to upper-middle peasant. As soon as the family's status changed, fourth son Liu Binqing took the lead in advocating for the restoration of a middle peasant label. Binqing appeared to be in a good position to help his family: he was a well-educated member of the Communist Youth

League, worked in the provincial capital (Tianjin before April 1966, Baoding until January 1968, Shijiazhuang after that), had firsthand experience as a Four Cleanups work team member, and was familiar with class status policy documents. Between 1965 and 1969, Binqing wrote many letters. Some went to his parents and to Binxiang, advising them on how to handle the class status change; others appealed to officials at every level of the bureaucracy, from village cadres all the way up to Chairman Mao. The result? Binqing was punished by his work unit, his brother was labeled a bad element, and the family's status went up even higher, to rich peasant, a label that stuck until 1978.

As a production team leader, third son Liu Binxiang was already a likely target during the Four Cleanups. Two issues put the Liu family on even shakier ground. In 1958, Binxiang had been kicked out of the Communist Youth League because he had an affair with a landlord's daughter. That same year, father Liu Wanchen had been labeled a rightist. This label had been officially removed in 1960.[56] Binqing wrote that the initial status change from middle to upper-middle peasant occurred when village *pinxie* members met to discuss what the family's status should have been at land reform. Villagers' fifteen-year-old memories were fuzzy, but most said the status was upper-middle peasant, so the matter was settled.[57] One problem: there was no upper-middle peasant category during land reform— lower-middle and upper-middle peasant gradations were only introduced in 1955 (before that time there were middle peasants and "prosperous middle peasants," *fuyu zhongnong*).[58] Another problem: the *pinxie* members' recollection was wrong.

Fourth son Liu Binqing left his Four Cleanups work team and rushed home after his family's upper-middle peasant status was announced. Binqing confronted Wen Binghe, political instructor of the Houjiaying Four Cleanups work team, who told him that "before 1945 your family was poor peasant, but after that your life got better." Binqing and his mother searched their home and found a household registration booklet from 1950. The old document listed the family's class status as middle peasant. Binqing handed the proof to Wen Binghe, who promptly "lost" or "burned" it. Angry, Binqing wrote to the commune Four Cleanups work team in early September 1965. Receiving no response, he sent a complaint to the county work team headquarters three weeks later. He waited a month and then fired off a letter to

Mao, telling the Chairman, "I am writing to you because I have nowhere left to appeal."[59]

In his letters, Binqing singled out Wen Binghe as a bad work team member, detailed the family's suffering before liberation (so bitter that his eldest brother had become mute), complained that certain other families in the villages had unfairly "gone down" in status to lower-middle peasant, and presented several possibilities for his family's actual status. His father had been a blacksmith, so if labels were based on a household's main source of income, should the family's status not be "handicraftsman?" But the Lius were also truly poor farmers, Binqing wrote, with a lower standard of living than the average middle peasant. He took a conciliatory tone in his letter to Changli County officials: "I do not necessarily want the leaders to change my family's status. But I do want a correct understanding: Does the work team have an unclear grasp of policy, or did we change from poor peasant to upper-middle peasant in just two or three years?"[60]

Liu Binqing got no response, but every time he sent a letter, the Four Cleanups work team in Houjiaying received a copy and a query from superiors at the commune or county level (the letter to Mao seems to have been intercepted by the Hebei General Office and forwarded to Changli County). Four Cleanups official Wen Binghe knew exactly what Binqing was writing about him, and the more Binqing appealed, the angrier Wen got. Wen had already been criticized by his superiors for his failure to compel Liu Binxiang to admit to corrupt behavior.[61] Now that his name was appearing on letters addressed to Chairman Mao, he was convinced that the Lius were the enemy. Somebody in the village once heard Wen say, "None of the Lius in Houjiaying are any good."[62]

Liu Binqing also coached his family members on how to behave. In a letter to his parents and middle brother, dated February 23, 1966, Binqing expressed happiness that the village—perhaps pressured by his appeals to higher levels—was conducting a Four Cleanups reinvestigation. Binqing instructed his parents that they should emphasize how poor the family was before liberation by citing their eating habits, housing, and elder brother's muteness. Binqing sensed that his parents might be embarrassed to play up their poverty. "Don't be afraid that people will laugh at you," he wrote. "Our poverty was caused by the old society, so explain the true depths of our bitterness." Binqing then gave his brother Binxiang four points of advice:

1. No matter who you talk to, earnestly speak from your heart about how your past mistakes were wrong. There's really nothing to your problems.

2. Work hard in the fields, whether or not you're still a cadre. The Four Cleanups movement is good.

3. Have a kind attitude no matter who you're talking to; don't say anything bad about anyone. We are speaking the truth.

4. You can talk about the bitterness we suffered in the past and compare it with today's happy life.[63]

Liu Binqing thought that a conciliatory attitude combined with an emphasis on preliberation poverty would convince investigators of his family's true class status. But he undermined his own advice by continuing to send inflammatory letters in 1966.

Binqing sent off eleven more missives between May and July 1966. Instead of restoring his family's middle peasant status, the Four Cleanups reinvestigation changed it for the worse in the summer of 1966, from upper-middle to rich peasant.[64] Binqing accused Wen Binghe of changing the family to rich peasant status because Wen was so enraged about all the new appeal letters. Addressing Wen directly, Binqing wrote, "You instigated people who did not understand the truth at a mass meeting in May 1966, saying with great hype, 'These eleven letters are poisonous. Because of these eleven letters, your family will be categorized as rich peasants.'" Binqing insisted that there was no poison in his letters. The real poison, Binqing claimed, could be found in Wen's decision to change his family's status to upper-middle and then to rich peasant.[65]

At the end of July 1966, a week after the Liu family's rich peasant label was finalized, third son Liu Binxiang sought out his elder sister, Liu Shuyan, for advice. She lived in Nijing, where the commune was headquartered, and because she had married into another family, she was not listed as a member of the Liu household in Houjiaying. Binxiang said he wanted to contest the new class status; his sister told him not to bother with Changli County officials. The two set off right away on a trip to the next highest level of the bureaucracy, Tangshan Prefecture. When the siblings arrived at the gate of the prefectural headquarters compound in Tangshan, they were disappointed—they had not realized that the office would be closed on Sunday.

Binxiang and Shuyan spent the night at a bus station and returned to the prefectural headquarters at 7:30 on Monday morning, August 1, 1966. Forty-five minutes later, an amiable "comrade" at the prefecture's reception office listened to Liu Binxiang's story. After Binxiang finished, the cadre responded that the family's class status could be middle peasant, upper-middle peasant, or rich peasant. All were possible, all sounded fine to him. Binxiang could request another reinvestigation if he wanted to, the cadre told him, but nothing good would come of it, because the Party did not make decisions based on class status. The Party considered your ideology and whether you were revolutionary, he said. The prefectural cadre urged the Lius to go home, draw near to the Party, work hard, and refrain from petitioning to any higher levels—further appeals might add to the severity of the Liu family's "sins," he warned.[66]

Back in Houjiaying the next day, Liu Binxiang wrote a self-criticism describing his trip to Tangshan. The prefectural comrade's words had eased his worries. He pledged to stop petitioning, to obey the Party, and to work hard. Binxiang's promises failed to satisfy the Four Cleanups work team and its village allies, who promptly named Binxiang a "bad element" as punishment for "willfully stirring up trouble" by petitioning in Tangshan.[67] The bad element label, combined with his new class status, may have broken Binxiang. On a document in 1970, he signed his name "Liu Binxiang, rich peasant status, bad element." Both stigmas stuck until December 1978, when Changli County restored the family's middle peasant status and formally stated that it had been incorrect to label Liu Binxiang as a bad element.[68]

Liu Binqing fared little better than his older brother. He was heartened by the events of January 1967, when power seizures in work places and villages gave hope to people who felt they had been wronged in 1965 and 1966. Binqing sent an "urgent summons" to Houjiaying villagers on January 31, 1967, attacking Wen Binghe and complaining about the injustice of his family's class status change.[69] A few months later, the brothers were still strategizing about how to restore their family's middle peasant status. Binxiang wanted Binqing's work unit, the provincial water department, to affix stamps of approval on Binqing's letters about the family's class status. Binqing wrote that it would be impossible to get approval from his workplace.[70] Liu Binqing was unable to get help from his office because his appeals about his family's class status revision had led his work unit to discipline him with a "double expulsion," meaning that he had been expelled from the youth league and removed from his job.[71]

Naturally, Binqing responded to this punishment by writing more letters of appeal. Letters he wrote in 1968 and 1969 included detailed mathematical calculations about the percentage of his family's income before liberation that was derived from hiring laborers. Binqing knew that central documents about land reform mandated that a family that earned more than 25 percent of its income from exploitation could be in the rich peasant category. When Binqing did the math in early 1968, he arrived at an exploitation income of 18.1 percent (next to this number he wrote, "under 25 percent, not enough to be a rich peasant").[72] A year later, when Binqing revisited the issue, his ratios for exploitation income were even more in his family's favor.[73]

Liu Binqing's number crunching seemed to bolster his case, but because his conclusions questioned the results of the Four Cleanups movement, he was wasting his time. His calculations may have shown that his family did not deserve to be categorized as rich peasants, but instead of garnering agreement and sympathy from higher officials, Binqing only brought himself more punishment. Binqing's last appeal about his class status in the Houjiaying files is dated January 13, 1969. We do not know whether Liu's "double expulsion" was resolved after 1969 or whether his appeals caused even more severe punishment during the 1970s. We do know, however, that his letters did not improve his family's class status. Local dynamics had been the key to whose labels were changed during the Four Cleanups, but after that, only a shift in central policy would help families such as the Lius. That shift only came at the end of 1978, when an order from Changli County finally canceled Liu's father's rich peasant label and restored him to middle peasant status.[74]

Removing Labels, Correcting Errors

A *People's Daily* article from January 1979 notes that between land reform and 1979, farmers in one Henan village had their class status assessed on seven occasions.[75] The article does not specify when each separate class status designation occurred, but we can guess that the seven instances included land reform in 1950, two land reform reinvestigations in 1951 and 1952, the remedial class in democracy in 1960 and 1961, the Four Cleanups in

1965 or 1966, probably a Four Cleanups reinvestigation later in 1966, and the Cleansing the Class Ranks campaign of 1968 and 1969.[76] In 1979, a final eighth class status assessment would follow.

The class status changes of Gao Qiwang (poor peasant to sub-landlord), Guo Zhaotai (middle peasant to landlord), and the Lius of Houjiaying (middle to upper-middle to rich peasant) stuck with them past the end of the Cultural Revolution. Mao's funeral and the arrest of the "Gang of Four" in late 1976 came and went with no immediate effect on class status. Major changes came quickly, however, at the end of 1978. In a speech at the Central Propaganda Department on January 3, 1979, Hu Qiaomu proposed a new way of thinking about class struggle, blaming the Gang of Four, Lin Biao, and Kang Sheng for distorting Mao's statements about the continued existence of classes in China. Hu also claimed that Kang Sheng had written "continuous revolution" into the ninth Party constitution in 1969, proclaiming that class struggle would exist "from beginning to end" in Chinese socialism. Hu Qiaomu derided this change as illogical: "Lenin said that socialism is the eradication of classes. If that's true, then if class struggle exists from beginning to end in a socialist society, how can classes be eradicated and how can we enter communism?"[77]

Hu Qiaomu argued that it would cause "chaos in ideology and practical work" to continue to emphasize class struggle in the form of the masses exercising dictatorship over and depriving rights from former exploiters. A new approach to class struggle and class status was codified on January 11, 1979, when Party Center issued a decision about removing labels from "landlord and rich peasant elements" and about handling the status of sons and daughters of landlords and rich peasants. The policy change mandated that villagers from landlord or rich peasant "family backgrounds" (*jiating chushen*) would without exception be given a status (*chengfen*) of "commune member" (*gongshe sheyuan*). Children of these villagers would have their "family background" revised to "commune member."[78] In an interview with *People's Daily*, Minister of Public Security Zhao Cangbi clarified that rural counties nationwide would see two types of changes: first, landlord and rich peasant labels would be removed from all but a tiny number of people, even if such individuals had originally been correctly identified as landlords or rich peasants. Second, people mistakenly classified as landlords and rich peasants would have their status corrected, posthumously if necessary.[79]

This second category mostly affected people who had experienced class status changes during the 1960s—such as Gao Qiwang, Guo Zhaotai, and the Lius of Houjiaying.

Party Center's decision that almost all villagers' status would be "commune member" and that landlord and rich peasant "family background" labels would not be transferred to a second generation seemed to imply that the class status system would wither away naturally. Nonetheless, in 1979, families that had been adversely reclassified during the 1960s assumed that the stakes were high and once again actively appealed. They were not interested in a bland "commune member" label. They wanted their old class status back.

"Mistaken classification" (cuohua) correction files from Henan in 1979 include reports from villages, communes, and counties and often append testimony from the family involved. They also usually contain records of conversations with other villagers about the family's economic situation before land reform and about why the family's status changed in the 1960s. The 1979 class status investigations share many common elements with the status revisions of the 1960s. Applicants once again emphasized their families' preliberation poverty. They attacked bad Four Cleanups work team members by name, much as Liu Binqing pilloried Wen Binghe, and complained about "certain individuals" who had been manipulated by work teams. And just like in the 1960s, appeals addressed to central leaders were intercepted and dealt with locally.[80]

As it turned out, people petitioning for corrections need not have worked so hard. All they had to do was ask or simply wait for commune investigators to come to them. Preliberation history was as easily changed or ignored in 1979 as it had been in the 1960s. Commune-level reports often made perfunctory and vague statements such as this one about Gao Qiwang: "at the time of liberation, even though he did exploit others, the amount was small, not enough to be classified as 'sublandlord' status." Therefore, Gao's poor peasant status should be restored, the report concluded.[81] But if Gao had committed any exploitation at all during the three years before liberation, according to land reform regulations he could not be given a poor peasant label. A clerk at the county level noticed this mistake and changed Gao's status one last time, to tenant middle farmer.

In other cases, commune and county investigators confirmed that Four Cleanups work team members had uncovered genuine deception about families' economic histories. In 1966, Ren Zishi's family went from middle to rich peasant status, mostly because the family had failed to disclose ownership of 37.5 *mu* of sandy land during land reform. Rural cadres interviewed old villagers who knew the Rens. They learned that "It was true that the 37.5 *mu* of land was hidden during land reform, but this land was bad quality and not very productive." It did not really matter that Ren had hidden land in 1950, denied it in 1966, and lied again in 1979, commune officials wrote to the county revolutionary committee in justifying his return to middle peasant status:

> It needs to be pointed out that this serious problem of Ren Zishi's hiding land and exploitation during land reform was extremely mistaken. In this current effort to confirm written materials, Ren was even more mistaken to have taken an improper attitude and to have simply copied down the original amount of land that he admitted to [during land reform].

In 1979, still worried that his total landownership and rental to tenant farmers made him a rich peasant, Ren Zishi had once again underreported his acreage. "He should be criticized and educated by the masses," the commune revolutionary committee concluded, "but these problems should not affect the correction of his status."[82]

In 1965 and 1966, Four Cleanups work teams had reshaped or ignored history in order to meet their goal of discovering and punishing hidden class enemies. Rural officials in 1979 had a different objective—to correct erroneous changes to class labels—but they were almost as blasé about what had actually happened before land reform. Facts could not be allowed to get in the way of successfully following a new central policy, especially when the historical details had become irrelevant: the landlord and rich peasant classes had been eliminated, and former exploiters had almost all been reformed through labor. It was time to move on.

The changes of 1979 came as a relief to the families that had suffered the stigma of bad class labels for more than a decade, but they should be forgiven for feeling bitterness about the ordeal. Central leaders ordered widespread class status reassessments in September 1964 but gave no clear instructions about how to carry out the task. Four months later, they dropped the idea without telling anyone to wrap things up, so work team officials and village cadres kept going, granting good labels to allies and friends, punishing foes with bad labels, and leaving others alone. Relationships, personalities, and grudges at the grassroots determined the extent to which central policies would be implemented, tweaked, or simply ignored.

3

An Overt Conspiracy

Creating Rightists in Rural Henan, 1957–1958

CAO SHUJI

Many scholars studying the Anti-Rightist Movement of 1957 tend to focus on the initiators of the movement, meaning Mao Zedong and other central leaders, and on the question of whether the movement was an "overt conspiracy" (*yangmou*) or a "covert conspiracy" (*yinmou*).[1] Scholars have paid most attention to the Anti-Rightist Movement in Beijing, Shanghai, Guangzhou, and other provincial capitals. There has been little research on middle-tier cities, let alone county towns and villages. This chapter explores county-level rectification (*zhengfeng*) and anti-rightist movements from a grassroots perspective. But even when examining the issue from a new grassroots angle, there is no escaping the classic theme of overt versus covert conspiracy. Based on recently obtained county-level files and memoirs, this chapter argues that the Anti-Rightist Movement at the grassroots was in fact an overt conspiracy from beginning to end.

By "overt conspiracy," I do not mean that Mao set a premeditated trap for critics in the countryside. In rural China, county leaders were the ones who set traps. The Party's attack against rightists at the grassroots was a ruse meticulously planned by the local leaders who carried it out. Amazingly, the campaign's targets knew full well what consequences their unrestrained airing of views would bring. Because both sides of the "struggle" knew what the movement's outcome would be, it makes sense to call it an overt conspiracy.

This bizarre situation arose because the Anti-Rightist Movement unfolded on distinct timelines at different administrative levels in 1957 and 1958. Party Center had originally ordered that the first phase of rectification would occur only in the central bureaucracy, in provincial- and municipal-level agencies and in universities. This is the event familiar to most scholars as the "Anti-Rightist Movement." The second phase extended the movement to county- and subcounty-level agencies and to secondary and elementary schools. This chapter focuses on the relatively understudied second phase, for which it makes most sense to refer to multiple "anti-rightist movements."

At the provincial and municipal levels and in universities, the rectification and anti-rightist movements also occurred in two distinct stages. The first stage involved the unrestrained airing of views (*mingfang*) and criticisms of the Party, commonly known as the Hundred Flowers Movement. The second stage was attacking rightists. It is generally accepted that the Anti-Rightist Movement started on June 8, 1957, with the publication of the famous editorial "Why Is This So?" (*Zhe shi weishenme?*) in *People's Daily*.[2] From that day on, the Hundred Flowers turned into the Anti-Rightist Movement. On October 15, 1957, Party Center issued "Criteria for Classifying Rightist Elements" (*Huafen youpai fenzi de biaozhun*).[3] These criteria came too late to help people who had already been labeled as rightists, because the Anti-Rightist Movement had already ended in many provincial- and municipal-level agencies and universities. At the local level, however, where rectification and anti-rightist movements had not yet begun, it was a guiding document.

In Henan's Nanyang Prefecture, about 130 miles south of Luoyang, the rectification movement at the county level was not put on the agenda until September 1957. Because of the fall harvest, rural rectification did not begin in earnest until December 1957. Grassroots rectification was scheduled to shift to anti-rightist attacks in early January 1958.

Why would people in rural counties repeat the same mistakes that urban rightists had made months earlier by giving their honest criticisms of the Party in the hope of rectifying its shortcomings? Widespread media reports at the time made it clear to everyone that criticizing the Party as part of the rectification movement and the rightists' attacks on the Party were two sides of the same coin. Why would people, fully aware that the purpose of rectification was to identify rightists, place themselves in a dangerous situation?

In Tongbai County, on Henan's southern border with Hubei Province, rectification got off to an abortive start in autumn 1957 before finally starting with a conference for county-level cadres between December 16, 1957 and January 19, 1958. From December 27, 1957, through early February 1958, the county committee held a separate rectification conference for the county's educational and business sectors. After that, rectification and anti-rightist movements were carried out among village cadres at the grassroots. Precisely when schoolteachers or village cadres were starting to air criticisms of the Party, anti-rightist movements in other parts of the county's bureaucracy were in progress or had already ended. Given the palpable evidence of other people's mistakes, which had been made literally the day before, why would local cadres and village teachers plunge themselves eagerly into the movement like moths to a flame? Remarkably, critics simply could not keep their mouths shut, well into 1958.

When Nanyang Prefecture organized a new "Open Your Heart to the Party" (*Xiang dang jiaoxin*) campaign for schoolteachers in May 1958, many teachers continued to voice "anti-Party thoughts." Some people also exposed and informed on others. As a result, 1,914 teachers were labeled rightists.[4] On August 18, 1958, an "Anti-Rightist Tendency" (*Fan youqing*) campaign, focusing on criticizing Henan Party Committee secretary Pan Fusheng, was launched throughout the whole province. A large group of grassroots cadres and village teachers once again articulated their spoken and written criticisms to the Party, were labeled as having "rightist tendencies" or "severe rightist tendencies," and were demoted, had their wages reduced, or were sent for reeducation.[5] I have to ask the question again: Knowing full well what had happened during the rural anti-rightist movements of late 1957 and early 1958, why did those who "opened their hearts" and voiced "rightist tendencies" keep coming forward to criticize the Party and tell the Party the "truth"?

A Failed First Attempt to Air Views in Tongbai County, Autumn 1957

The *Chronology of the History of the Chinese Communist Party in Nanyang Prefecture* reveals that 8,693 people were "erroneously" branded rightists in the entire region.[6] Of these, 157 were from Nanyang City; they suffered their fates in 1957.[7] Because they were rightists of the first stage, I will allow them to drop out of the narrative at this point.

In May 1957, Henan Province and Nanyang Prefecture began to prepare for a rectification movement that would encourage people in rural counties to air critical views. The goal was to start the movement in September and end it by December. Tongbai County Party leaders quickly responded with their own plan, which did not contain even a hint of belligerence.[8] This is not surprising, because they had no clue that the Hundred Flowers would turn into the Anti-Rightist Movement on June 8, 1957.

On September 17, 1957, Tongbai leaders drew up a more specific draft plan for the rectification movement. After listing a number of "reactionary" statements uttered by urban elites during the Hundred Flowers, the document states that "at the same time the rectification movement is implemented, all county cadres must organize to carry out the anti-rightist struggle to isolate the rightists and counter their furious attacks. This will facilitate the successful completion of the rectification movement."[9] By September 1957, Tongbai County leaders knew that rectification and the anti-rightist movement had to be part of the same package.

Rectification had to come first, of course. Without the unrestrained *mingfang* of rectification, rightists could not be properly identified. Tongbai County authorities therefore listed debate topics for the airing of views: state grain purchases and farmers' livelihoods, the Campaign to Eliminate Counterrevolutionaries (*sufan*), cadres' work and cadre policy, and democracy and freedom. Apart from these basic issues, individual sectors also had to debate their own particular problems. For example, teachers had to discuss Party leadership in schools, the reeducation of intellectuals, and teaching policies.

It was possible from the beginning that the airing of views might lead nowhere because people were afraid to speak out. Tongbai leaders were aware of this. They therefore proposed that debates in all sectors "focus on food supplies and agricultural cooperativization, because wrong thinking and muddled understanding about these issues are more prevalent." In Tongbai County, the state grain monopoly had set annual rations for individuals at only 180 kilograms of unprocessed grains, whereas the daily processed grain ration was a mere 375 grams per person. People were hungry throughout the county.[10] By choosing to focus on grain, county leaders were guessing that people would have plenty to say.

In the second half of September 1957, 3,749 county cadres, teachers, shop-keepers, doctors, and craftspeople took part in rectification meetings organized by the Tongbai Party Committee. The committee's report about the meetings reveals the doubts and resistance of many participants:

> [They] had reservations about this study session. They did not say much, or said nothing. There was a feeling of fear. Even those who spoke said mostly good things. Some individuals were frightened, behaved with a guilty conscience, and pretended to be enthusiastic. These people, who accounted for some 10 to 15 percent, are normally troublemakers. They are backward, dissatisfied, and are the ones who would be expected to say a lot. But during this study session they always spoke cautiously.[11]

The climate of fear created by the urban Anti-Rightist Movement in summer 1957 had clearly spread to the countryside. People in Tongbai were trying hard to avoid becoming rightists.

Wang Ziting, a reporter, approached his boss and told him, "In the past I said there was not enough to eat. I was just joking." Li Yongchun, a deputy section head at the county grain bureau, had once said that he would "definitely have some criticisms" about the Campaign to Eliminate Counterrevolutionaries. But when this remark came up at the rectification meeting, he denied having said such a thing. "It doesn't sound like something I would have said," Li explained anxiously. "Wouldn't that make me a rightist if I had said it?"[12]

Despite the general cautiousness in September 1957, some people actually expressed dissatisfaction. For example, Du Jialin of the commerce bureau said: "In reality, the rightists are insignificant, but they have been stirred up under a magnifying glass." Lin Zhongzheng, a staff member in the production office, thought that the rightists were not counterrevolutionaries, but had been antagonized into an "us versus them" situation. But people who actually opened their mouths, such as Du and Lin, were a tiny minority. For the rest, their strategy was to say nothing, say little, or say only positive things. For this reason, Tongbai County "leaders and activists felt frustrated because they are worried about not being able to obtain any material."[13] If participants remained silent, the plans of the county committee would come to naught.

Before Party Center issued its "Criteria for Classifying Rightist Elements" on October 15, 1957, no one knew that sympathy for the rightists would also be grounds for being labeled a rightist. Du Jialin and Lin Zhongzheng's seemingly sympathetic statements about other unnamed rightists were recorded and later used as evidence against them. Beyond this, however, there were no genuinely "rightist" opinions aired during the study sessions in Tongbai that fall. The boring meetings failed to meet the organizers' expectations.

Speaking Out in Tongbai, Winter 1957

In December 1957, the Tongbai County committee tried again, convening a meeting for county, district, and village cadres. Participants were exhorted to help overcome bureaucratism by enthusiastically making speeches and big-character posters. A total of 1,329 cadres attended the meeting.[14] On December 16, Sun Lijun, the county committee secretary, summarized central and provincial policy. The next day, county head Ge Jinglu said that the rectification movement would focus on great debates and an airing of views about the Party's problems.[15] Not once did he mention the term "anti-rightist."

On December 18, the criticism session began. The county committee exhorted participants to "air your views boldly, firmly, and thoroughly." The county's *Rectification Bulletin,* published the next day, listed a number of criticisms, including a request to dismiss two cadres who had not done any work for long periods of time. The most crucial critique was a suggestion to ban people from attending the meeting who had lost their political rights because of criminal sentences. County leaders accepted this suggestion, but it was not what they were looking for.[16] As the meeting went on, however, people did raise more criticisms, and "large quantities of poisonous weeds appeared."[17]

The county committee achieved this by mobilizing activists to "fire up and lead the masses in airing their views." County leaders also allayed people's fears by issuing rules prohibiting anyone from influencing or interfering with the airing of views. No one was to engage in persecution or revenge attacks. Six cases of interference were dealt with swiftly, the most serious of which involved Cao Qisheng, deputy secretary of the Pingshi District Party Committee. Under cover of darkness, Cao had torn down big-character posters that criticized him. Tongbai County leaders ordered a swift inspection and then stripped him of his position in the rectification leadership group. Apparently the "masses responded positively" to Cao's dismissal after the news was reported in the county's *Rectification Bulletin*.[18] Seeing Cao punished gave others the courage to speak out.

On January 17, 1958, the Tongbai County committee submitted a concluding report to its superiors in the Nanyang Prefecture Party Committee. Tellingly, the report linked *mingfang* with exposing rightists:

> At first the rightists were hunkering down and did not stick their necks out. They put up a few big-character posters to watch which way the wind blew and followed what others were doing. Then they became more active. Some people exposed their tails; some exposed their whole bodies. Next, they were completely naked before everyone. Finally, comrades with high political and ideological consciousness started to refute them.[19]

Everything went according to the plans of the Tongbai Party Committee. These plans had been in place as early as September 17, 1957, when the county committee had instructed cadres to "stay cool-headed, not responding immediately to reactionary critiques," and to "vigorously muster your strength to strike back after the rectification and anti-rightist movements begin."[20]

If these events had taken place in the spring and summer of 1957, there might have been some doubts about the real purpose of launching unrestrained *mingfang*. It is still reasonable for scholars to debate whether certain people took advantage of the Hundred Flowers to attack the Party and the socialist system, angering certain leaders in the process and thereby triggering the Anti-Rightist Movement. But the events in Tongbai took place in the last twenty days of 1957, and the entire process was controlled by county leaders. It was an unequivocal "overt conspiracy."

Luring the Snakes out of Their Lair: How Rural People Became Rightists

By April 1958, 129 people in Tongbai County had been labeled rightists. Of these, 52 were elementary schoolteachers and 8 were secondary teachers.[21] How exactly did these people become rightists?

The Indecisive Wang Jianxin

Wang Jianxin, a young man in his late twenties at the time of the Anti-Rightist Movement, joined the Party in October 1950. He first worked as a clerk in the county's finance and trade bureau but was later sent down to the Maoji district office, where he became Party branch secretary. Born into a poor peasant family, Wang's personal class status was that of a student. Before the Communists came to power, he had served as a soldier in the Nationalist Army.

Given Wang Jianxin's downward transfer to a subcounty district office, we can deduce that his career as an official was not very promising. We also know that when Wang was transferred to Tongbai from Nanyang City in 1954, his wife had not been allowed to accompany him to his new post. He had had disagreements with his leaders about this. Interpersonal relationships, especially those between superiors and subordinates, often determined whether someone would be labeled a rightist.

At the county rectification meeting on December 22, 1957, Wang Jianxin made eight criticisms.[22] His first remark was that the county Party Committee did not take finance work seriously. His second criticism was that county Party secretary Sun Lijun did not listen to his reasonable suggestions and was too harsh in his criticisms of his staff. Third, Wang had requested that his wife be transferred to work in Tongbai, but Secretary Sun's response was "stern in voice and mien . . . criticizing more than educating him, and showing not a bit of warmth." Fourth, there was bureaucratism in the county committee, which had labeled Wang a "backward element" (*luohou fenzi*). Wang Jianxin's fifth, sixth, and seventh criticisms had to do with unclear personnel matters and will not be discussed here. The eighth criticism was that political life in the county committee was abnormal.

Examining the specific content and wording of Wang Jianxin's remarks helps to explain his classification as a rightist. In his first criticism, Wang said there were seven people in the finance and trade bureau, but "only two people did operational work, and political work was not good. The department head should get involved in operations." By saying that the department head should do operational instead of political work, Wang might have provided others with an angle from which to criticize him. In his second criticism, Wang should have stopped after making his point about Secretary

Sun, but he had to add that "because the leaders of the county committee support unhealthy trends and evil doings, the political atmosphere is bad." This could have been seen as a broad attack on the Party leadership. In his fourth criticism, Wang believed that the authorities "demanded too much food" from the farmers. This could have been construed as opposition to the sacrosanct state grain monopoly. Wang's sixth criticism reveals that he had actually written to the *Henan Daily* about a personnel matter, which was finally resolved when the prefecture intervened. Clearly, Wang Jianxin often rocked the boat and liked speaking out. He had offended top county leaders on numerous occasions.

Wang Jianxin spoke again on December 25, 1957. He criticized the county committee for being unfair in 1956 when it assigned the ranks of cadres. Such criticisms were common at the time and could be heard in all departments. But toward the end of his speech, Wang made a broader point: "During this round of *mingfang*, I think that even if I don't say anything positive, I will not be condemned as a rightist. People who exercise freedom of thought are considered backward, and people like us who are always loyal to the Party are seen as disloyal. People who perform well at work are called backward, but those who suck up to their superiors are considered good people by the county committee." During the Hundred Flowers of 1957, "exercising freedom of thought" (*fahui ziyou sixiang*) was quite a trendy phrase. But why would Wang Jianxin persist in self-identifying as someone who "exercised freedom of thought" shortly after the urban Anti-Rightist Movement, and when he himself was already so deeply embroiled in the rectification madness? Did he actually believe that his superiors wanted him to "exercise freedom of thought?"

It is unclear why Wang insisted that he would "not be condemned as a rightist." Given Wang's penchant for making suggestions and contradicting leaders, his criticism of the county committee and the state grain monopoly on crops, and his self-identification as a person who exercised freedom of thought, he was already on the verge of being labeled a rightist. Wang Jianxin certainly viewed the rectification and anti-rightist movements with some degree of fear. But all his fears could not stop his desire to air his views—his heart could not control his mouth—and he finally said what he wanted to say. His personality made it difficult for him to toe the official line or speak untruths. So he was classified as a rightist.

Lu Jinfu Denounced at a Mass Meeting

Relatively speaking, Wang Jianxin was not a major rightist. The most extreme rightist in Tongbai was Lu Jinfu, the twenty-nine-year-old editor of the county newspaper. At meetings on December 22 and 23, 1957, Lu Jinfu spoke up twice. He began by complaining that the county "government is less important than the county Party Committee, and its orders are ignored. This situation should be reversed." Lu's remark that the government was subordinate to the Party could have been seen as an attack on China's political system. Lu continued by criticizing the county's management of villages and its handling of the market in the county town. He then complained that the children in the county theater troupe sang badly at a welcoming ceremony for dignitaries, which was a major "loss of face."

Lu saved his harshest criticisms for the end of his speech:

> Development plans for mountainous areas began with a great bang, only to peter out to a mere whimper. The measures did not suit local conditions. Whatever the leaders say goes. . . . It's all a mess. Can irrigation work be completed this year? Of course, the Party does not make empty boasts. Could it be that I have rightist tendencies? As for irrigation, the leaders must study the issue and not just say big words that cannot be put into practice.

Others had also spoken out against the county committee's planning of mountainous areas, but Lu Jinfu went beyond previous criticisms by denouncing leaders' hyperbolic statements. At the end of his tirade, he could not hold his tongue and began to question whether he had "rightist tendencies." In the process of airing his views, Lu seems to have gotten carried away. He then dug himself into an even deeper hole by naming names.

"County head Tian should be more involved in governing," Lu continued. "His political and ideological leadership is lacking." Lu next turned his attention to his immediate superior at the newspaper, Tu Xianglin. "He can reel off points on doctrine and Marxism-Leninism, but he does not apply them," Lu complained. "He yells at people in the newsroom . . . but county head Tian did not educate or help him." Lu realized that he might be labeled a rightist, but he could not stop himself.

On January 11, 1958, the county committee held a mass meeting attended by 1,000 people to condemn Lu Jinfu as a rightist.[23] The following specific charges were lodged against Lu:

1. Someone filed a story saying, "The cooperatives are so good." Why did you edit it to "It is so good in the cooperatives?" Was this not an attempt to diminish the superiority of socialism?
2. When vice-editor Tu Xianglin was away at provincial-level meetings and in the countryside, Lu Jinfu said, "Even when vice-editor Tu is not around, we can still put out a newspaper." Was this not subversion and an attempt to negate the Party's leadership?
3. In upholding his bourgeois style of journalism, he went around uncovering the dark side of society and publishing it in the newspaper.
4. Lu Jinfu opposed the Party's leadership by saying, "the cadres' policy is that officials look out for one another," and "we ask you now: Who did you wine and dine to get your promotion?"
5. Lu Jinfu said that farmers' lives had gotten worse. He said his father did not have enough to eat when he came to the county seat and had lost weight.

The first and second criticisms against Lu seemed to be grasping at straws. There was no proof for the third one, and even if there had been, Lu Jinfu could not be held solely responsible for what the newspaper published. The fourth charge was the only one directly connected with Lu Jinfu's airing of views in December 1957, and it was the most crucial. Lu's denunciation of higher-ups brought about his downfall.

Like Wang Jianxin, Lu Jinfu could not hold his tongue. He knew very well that he might be going down the rightist path, but he still forged ahead. Lu's personality sealed his fate. He had a penchant for making overly broad points about the people and issues he criticized. This gave his foes ammunition to depict him as opposing the entire socialist system.

Snakes Remember How They Were Forced Out of Their Lairs

The archival files from Tongbai do not shed much light on what people might have been thinking as they aired their views. Memoirs, however, allow people who had been labeled as rightists to explain why they spoke out. Among the many books and shorter pieces by rightists, three articles written by rural elementary schoolteachers and administrators are particularly valuable in depicting how the movement unfolded at the grassroots. Two of the educators, Li Shugang and Feng Xianzhi, were from Xinyang County in Henan; the other, Ye Fangying, worked at an elementary school in a village in Guangdong.[24] Of the three, Ye's account is the most detailed. These three memoir articles can be read in tandem with files from the Tongbai County Archives for a more comprehensive understanding of the rectification and anti-rightist movements in rural China.

Ye Fangying was born in 1927. In 1950 he was an elementary school principal in a village in Guangdong. He was forced to relinquish his position because of ill health, and he found himself in dire straits. Later, he petitioned the South China Bureau and had himself reinstated to his former post. This entire ordeal made him "grateful for the Party's kindness" and "determined to work hard to produce results."[25]

Ye Fangying had read newspaper reports about anti-rightist movements in cities all over China. He agreed with and was partial to the political standpoints of elites such as Zhang Bojun, Luo Longji, and Chu Anping, all of whom had been excoriated as rightists in the national press.[26] At the end of 1957, the schools in Ye's county moved the winter holidays forward so that 2,000 teachers could assemble in the county seat for rectification meetings. The same thing happened in Henan's Xinyang County, where the winter holidays were moved forward and around 1,600 teachers headed to the county seat for a conference. Back in Guangdong, before the teachers in Ye Fangying's county assembled, the county organization department had sent people to the schools to investigate the situation on the ground. For this reason, Ye recalled, "all the teachers in the county were aware that the final goal of this rectification study session was an attack on rightists." Ye wrote: "Because many teachers had read about the rectification movements in the center, provinces, and cities, they had learned from others' past mistakes. All those who came for the rectification meeting were nervous and wary about *mingfang*."[27]

Li Shugang and Feng Xianzhi in Xinyang County expressed the same worry in their memoirs. Feng wrote:

Although the teachers had heard the mobilization speeches and reports made by the cadres of the county leadership, they were still full of worries when the rectification movement began and were "as silent as cicadas in winter." The *mingfang* could not get started. The few pathetic big-character posters posted on the teaching wall featured the usual hagiographic praises of the county and school leadership or teachers' suggestions about trifling everyday matters or criticisms about the private lives of school leaders and female teachers that barely scratched the surface.[28]

Like Feng Xianzhi and his colleagues, Ye Fangying was determined to keep his mouth shut.

On the day after Ye and other teachers arrived in their county seat in rural Guangdong, the county committee held a mobilization meeting. The head of the county propaganda department, surnamed Zhang, who was also a vice-secretary on the county Party Committee, delivered a speech at the meeting. Zhang began with an exposition on international and domestic affairs. According to Ye's recollection, Zhang implied that teachers' unwillingness to speak out was tantamount to disloyalty:

> I sincerely plead with you on behalf of the Communist Party and the People's Government. Based on your immeasurable loyalty to the Party, say everything you know and say it without reservations. Be bold in making various criticisms and suggestions to the Party and government. The more pointed, blatant, and malicious the criticisms, the better. Because "bitter medicine cures illnesses and loyal words that are tough to hear help those who govern," your sharp criticisms will help cadres at various levels of the Party and government. Our great leader Chairman Mao once said that even if only 1 percent of all the criticisms made were true, we the Party would not only accept them in humility and make swift improvements, but we would be deeply grateful for your loyalty toward the Party and would commend and reward you.[29]

The official's encouraging words were insufficient to allay the teachers' worries that they would be labeled as rightists. Zhang understood this fully, so he went a step further. He continued: "You are all very worried that by saying too much you will be classified as rightists. So, privately you decided to keep your mouths shut, say as little as possible, and make no criticisms." Zhang then openly admitted that the movement would have three phases. The first would be the "airing of views," the second an "anti-rightist movement," and the third "rectification and reform." "To be perfectly honest," Zhang explained, "some rightists will be ferreted out" in the process. "But do not be afraid—rightist elements are an objective reality. Even if a bona fide rightist does not utter a single word, he will still be a rightist. Even if nonrightists air their views without restraint and spew forth a whole litany of nonsense, they are still not rightists. . . . If there are no demons in your heart, what is there to be afraid of?"[30]

In Tongbai County, some people were indeed denounced as rightists despite their not uttering a single word during the airing of views. Also in Tongbai, the contents of people's speeches were not the only criteria for determining whether they were rightists. From this perspective, Zhang was telling the truth. If there was a conspiracy to entrap rightists, it was out in the open.

Zhang was still worried that the teachers would not speak, so he dragged out Chairman Mao as a guarantee. He said: "Our great leader Chairman Mao and the Chinese Communist Party are aboveboard, conducting only 'overt conspiracies,' not covert conspiracies. We are upright gentlemen who keep our word and are resolute in our actions, not mean, despicable men who go back on our word and who delight in intrigue and ruses."

After Zhang's mobilization and encouragement, the airing of views began. It was rather quiet in the beginning, and the few who spoke heaped praise on the leadership. County leaders then announced threateningly: "We did not ask you here to sing praises and say only good things. If anyone insists on saying only good things, he will be mercilessly criticized or even punished for not trusting the Party and for harboring disloyal thoughts against the Party." The county then specified the punishment for not speaking out: starting the next day, to remove everyone's reticence about making suggestions, every person had to air more than fifty views. The views could be spoken or in the form of big-character posters. Those who aired fewer than fifty views a day would not only be criticized, but they would have to attend extra lessons after the meeting ended to accomplish their mission even if it meant that they could not go out, rest, or sleep. Given such pressures, coupled with the encouragement of activists, Ye Fangying and his colleagues finally began to criticize the Party.[31]

Each issue of Tongbai County's *Rectification Bulletin* from late 1957 and early 1958 contains a substantial amount of statistical data, which record in great detail the number of big-character posters posted in every small group, the number of suggestions, and the targets of criticism. Tables quantified and divided the statements into different categories: correct, incorrect, and reactionary. Before I read Ye Fangying's article, I questioned the veracity of these figures. Now I believe that these data are reliable. To meet the quota of fifty views, Ye Fangying tried to come up with all sorts of trifling issues to talk about. Something similar must have occurred in Tongbai County.

The situation in Xinyang County was comparable. Even as late as February 1958, there were still very few views aired at the teachers' meetings. To break the impasse, the rectification leading group took school principals and some teachers to nearby Huangchuan County to see how it was done. They saw that *mingfang* had reached a feverish pitch; it seemed as if the whole county was covered with big-character posters. Li Shugang recalled that the posters were "petitions to the leadership or criticisms of food supply, personnel, the relationship between the Party and the masses, education policies, and so on. We were bedazzled by the sheer variety." Following the tour, it was time to force the snakes out of their lair. Li wrote:

> Everyone was given twenty sheets of white glossy paper, and we were to imitate Huangchuan in writing our criticisms. Those who did not meet their quota were not allowed to sleep. Then the second and third groups of visitors to Huangchuan returned. Twenty big-character posters a day became a fixed quota, and they were submitted to the group leader for vetting before they were put up. Those who "picked only sesame and not watermelon seeds" were seen as wanting in quality and ordered to go back to work.[32]

This was how *mingfang* reached its peak in Xinyang County.

Let us return to the story that was unfolding in rural Guangdong. After a meeting one day, Ye Fangying's younger brother—a small-group leader of the rectification movement and an activist—came to see him under the leadership's orders. They wanted Ye to "unleash a surge in the group's *ming-fang*." Ye's brother urged him to start speaking out. He said: "You don't have to worry. It would be a bad idea to make the Party pay special attention to you" by failing to meet the quota of criticisms or by only making superficial suggestions. What came next was incomprehensible to Ye Fangying.

County leaders praised those "who had been the most enthusiastic in speaking out, aired the most views, whose criticisms were the most pointed and blatant, and whose tirades against the Party were the most vicious." Supercritical posters, poems, and drawings were displayed as models for all to see. "Those who vilified the Party were commended, while those who sang its praises were investigated," Ye recalled. "I was like a person riding a blind horse into a *bagua* maze—bedazzled, dizzy, losing all sense of direction." So he began airing his views. He criticized cooperativization as "making saplings grow by pulling on them" and the agricultural tax as "killing the hen for eggs."[33] In his remarks, Ye made the same mistake that Wang Jianxin and Lu Jinfu had made in Tongbai: they tended to make broad conclusions instead of sticking to specific issues. Ye's fate was as good as sealed.

Not long after, attacks on rightists began, just as Vice-Secretary Zhang had promised. Merciless in his vilification of the rightists, Zhang said, "Over the past twenty days or so, we have deliberately created false appearances to inveigle the rightists, enticing them to 'dance their demon dances.' Today their exciting performance must come to an end. Their true natures as bourgeois rightists have been completely exposed. Let us now drag them out one by one and uncover their true natures in broad daylight. Let them be debated and criticized by the masses." Zhang then read out the names of rightists. Without exception, all those activists who had previously been commended for their views were labeled as rightists.[34] Those who had been most vicious in attacking the Party were deemed to have broken criminal laws and were sent to labor camps for reeducation. Both Ye Fangying and his brother were classified as rightists and spent the next twenty years under a cloud of shame.

Ye Fangying, Li Shugang, and Feng Xianzhi were indeed like snakes that were forced out of their lairs. They had been tricked by an overt conspiracy. Even though they knew what was coming, they were still duped by local Party leaders.

Willingly Coming Out of the Lair: Those Who Sacrificed Themselves to Air Their Views

According to Ye Fangying, when news of the results of the rectification and anti-rightist movements trickled back home, people were surprised and shocked. Ye recalled:

> These teachers were all intellectuals who were refined and educated. They often read the newspapers and knew very early on about the anti-rightist situations in Beijing, Guangzhou, and other places. They also knew very well the adage that "talking too much causes strife, and putting yourself forward creates trouble." So why were they so stupid as to entrap themselves by being so enthusiastic in airing their views? These teachers were too sincere and naïve; they placed too much trust in what the Party leadership said. They were really pitiable.

When Ye Fangying asks why people were "so stupid as to entrap themselves by being so enthusiastic in airing their views," he is essentially rephrasing the research question I posed at the beginning of this chapter. His answer is that the "rightists" were too trusting. This does not seem to be an adequate explanation, because in a crisis, naïveté is no match for the instinct of survival.

Let us go back to Tongbai County. In late December 1957, county cadres were meeting to air their views and the anti-rightist movement had not yet begun. Cadres finished airing views on January 1, 1958, and the next day, the anti-rightist movement for county officials began. Meanwhile, Tongbai teachers were on a different timetable. During the first phase of *mingfang* for schoolteachers, between December 29, 1957, and January 6, 1958, most views aired were "superficial" or focused on personal disputes or issues within the schools.[35] There were only a few critiques of Party policy. Under the personal leadership of the county committee secretary, teachers reached a second peak of *mingfang* between January 7 and January 9, 1958. The teachers mentioned fewer trivial matters, "with a corresponding increase in the number of issues pertaining to the Party leadership and important policies." The third peak came after January 9. I believe that teachers' "rightist" views were aired during the second and third peaks. But precisely when the schoolteachers were moving into these high points, the county three-level cadres' conference had already turned into an anti-rightist meeting, and more than one hundred rightists were labeled and attacked. In such a small county seat, it was impossible for information not to circulate between the two meetings. What was going on in the heads of the schoolteachers who were airing their views?

The situation in Tongbai was even more incredible than Ye Fangying's decision to speak out in Guangdong. If Ye could be considered honest and naïve, then what can we say about the teachers attending the rectification meeting in southern Henan? Just next door, criticisms and attacks were already raining down on newly labeled rightists, but the teachers were still raring to go, seemingly desperate to squeeze themselves into the ranks of rightists. Why?

A report prepared by the Tongbai County rectification office, completed on January 14, 1958, provides many examples of views aired by the schoolteachers. These views were more emotional than those given by county cadres and make for more vivid reading. First, teachers vented about the food supply. Li Xicheng said, "Do you know how watered down the rice is these days? You can plunge your head into the pot and not even a grain of rice will stick to you." Along the same lines, Liu Yaohua said, "Now we have the 'three verys': the rice is very watered down, one gets very bloated after eating, and one gets very hungry after taking a few pisses." Li Yunsheng made a more systemic critique and excoriated collectivization:

> A landlord-class household in my village did not join the cooperative. That household has food to eat and is are better off than cooperative members. Those who go it alone are so much freer, but the cadres ostracize them. We do not wish to become socialist, but they force us to. . . . Cooperativization is undemocratic. We have nowhere to go to voice our grievances.

In addition to complaining about farming and food, teachers offered broader criticisms of the county Party Committee's work. Niu Xingnan wrote a damning summary of how the bureaucracy functioned. Work, Nie wrote, was nothing more than "writing reports, asking for materials, and researching policies." According to Ye, one could only "connect with the masses" at huge conferences and meetings, not at the grassroots. Grain policy was so bad that food was being wasted while peasants went hungry, and rural cadres were "on a rampage."

Finally, there were views on the Campaign to Eliminate Counter-revolutionaries. Tang Yuying said, "What good was there in the elimination of counterrevolutionaries? All it did was persecute people to death. My older sister only taught a few days of school in the Old China, but cadres running the *sufan* campaign kept calling her in. Each time they speak with her, she dies another death. Since the beginning of the campaign, she has died five times." Lu Mingxuan said, "The Campaign to Eliminate Counter-revolutionaries was bungled. There are more negative side effects than positive results."[36]

Teachers continued speaking out in the following days. A report prepared by the Tongbai County committee rectification office, completed on January 16, 1958, stated that between January 13 and January 15, Ma Guoyuan had said: "These days the Party is not going down the proletarian road, but a capitalist one. The lives of the people after cooperativization have not improved, but it insists otherwise." Wang Xinshan said: "The lives of farmers are even worse than those of prisoners in the cities. The agricultural economy has definitely stalled. There is a shortage of lamp oil and cooking oil." Li Yunsheng said: "The Party does not practice what it preaches. It keeps saying that the farmer's lot has improved, but how has it improved? The Party is only concerned about the lives of the workers; it is not concerned about farmers' lives. Workers and farmers ought to switch places for a while."[37] Other teachers made many similar comments, the intensity of which far surpassed those uttered by Tongbai bureaucrats such as Wang Jianxin and Lu Jinfu at the separate county cadres' rectification meeting.

According to the Tongbai "Statistical Table of Registered Rightist Elements," all the abovementioned people who aired their views were classified as rightists. The teachers' criticisms had more literary flair and were more sophisticated than those made by county cadres. Some of their theories and formulations were almost at the same level as those articulated by the major national-level rightists in the first half of 1957. Perhaps they had been inspired by the statements of elites in Beijing. But as teachers in rural areas, they had a palpable understanding of the farmers' plight. They were the sons and daughters of farmers. Their most vivid and candid criticisms were about rural life. But as heartfelt as their critiques were, the village teachers possessed one thing that the rightists in Beijing lacked: hindsight. Why, then, did they still plunge headlong into the trap and sacrifice themselves?

I believe that apart from the "snakes" that were lured and forced out of their lairs, such as Ye Fangying in Guangdong, some emerged by their own volition. When we speak of intellectuals in late 1950s China who were willing to sacrifice themselves and serve the country, we must include this group of ordinary and inconspicuous rural intellectuals. Their strength came partly from book learning and partly from the land. Because they had witnessed the farmers' hardship during collectivization, they could not stop themselves from speaking up. Even though they were fully aware of the dangers of speaking, they felt obligated to do so. They were enticed, not forced, to say what they did. They spoke their minds bravely, honestly, based on what they had seen and heard, and because they simply wanted to. As a result, they were condemned as rightists. They were not deceived, nor were they gullible. Without understanding why they sacrificed themselves, we cannot understand the many changes in Chinese politics in the following decades.

Opening One's Heart to the Party

For both China's farmers and rural intellectuals, 1958 was a year of unease. In the past, scholars only knew that the Great Leap Forward was ruinous for China's rural economy. Now we know that politics in 1958 had a cause-and-effect relationship with the Leap catastrophe. In Tongbai County, the whole year was taken up by political movements, including continued attacks on rightists.

The rectification and anti-rightist movements among Tongbai teachers finally ended by early February 1958. In villages, the movements might have concluded even later. Then, in May 1958, rural teachers faced another political movement: the "Open Your Heart to the Party" campaign, which I will refer to as *jiaoxin*. Only two files on this campaign are held in the Tongbai County Archives, so many details remain unknown. We can still ask one crucial question, though: When the schoolteachers' superiors asked them to "open their hearts," would the rural intellectuals who had somehow escaped being labeled as rightists just a few months earlier be a little smarter? In other words, would they keep their mouths shut and protect themselves?

People said all kinds of things during *jiaoxin*. According to a bulletin about the campaign, "there were conflicts and dissatisfaction with previous political campaigns and different views on the Party's various policies, decrees, and measures; nostalgia for landlord families and thoughts of vengeance for relatives who had been persecuted; bourgeois pedagogy and actions; and deep-seated and mutual criticism between leaders and leaders, comrades and leaders, comrades and comrades."[38] A few examples are worth examining.

During *jiaoxin*, cases of colleagues informing on one another or students informing on teachers began to surface. When he was teaching a natural science lesson on magnetic force, Li Jiaxun had illustrated how like poles repel and unlike poles attract by telling an anecdote about relationships between male and female students. After someone snitched, Li's lesson was criticized as an example of vile bourgeois pedagogy. That was not the end of his problems. Li could hardly have predicted that encouraging his students with the following truism would get him in trouble: "You must study hard. If you do not study hard, you will let your parents down. Your parents are farmers whose faces are bent toward the yellow earth and whose backs face the sky. They spend so much time in the hot sun that oil flows from their bodies." This statement was circulated as a prime example of bourgeois teaching.

It came to light that teachers had been spreading even more serious rightist opinions in their classrooms. Zhao Kewen was conducting a lesson on "The Communist Party Is Our Life" when he said that "rightists opposing the Party and the Party struggling against rightists" could be considered "mutual attacks" conducted on equal footing. He said: "Rightists opposing the Party is determined by their nature. We do not oppose the Party because we don't dare to."[39] This might have been the final nail in his coffin. For reasons unknown, it was only on September 28, 1958, that the Tongbai County committee labeled him a rightist. He was finally rehabilitated on May 30, 1962.[40]

When a teacher named Gao Wansheng was opening his heart to the Party, he had this to say about the rectification movement: "The Communist Party's treatment of intellectuals is like a weasel with evil intentions paying a visit to the chicken. A round of political campaigns will sweep away a batch. That is why I was very careful not to say anything when I aired my views. But after so many rightists started making comments, I could not keep quiet." These were the genuine political views of teachers in the rural schools of Tongbai County. They had many reasons to keep quiet, but some still felt the need to speak. Gao Wansheng and Zhao Kewen were not lured or forced to say anything. They spoke because they wanted to.

Of course, more threatening methods were used to force people to open their hearts to the Party. Meng Fanxin, a teacher, did not wish to say anything. He told his principal: "Isn't [asking me to *jiaoxin*] no better than making me go to the Public Security Bureau?" Then the leadership "made use of Hu Ming, his closest comrade, to have a private chat with him." Hu said: "Even if you wanted to go to the Public Security Bureau now, you would not be allowed to. Next time, you may have to go even if you don't want to." Apparently Hu's "sincere and pragmatic words" moved Meng to "confess his problems." This was the same method used during the rectification movement in rural Guangdong, when the Party sent Ye Fangying's younger brother to urge Ye to air his views.

A total of 1,914 secondary and elementary schoolteachers in Nanyang District were newly labeled rightists after the *jiaoxin* campaign, according to a recent publication by Nanyang education authorities.[41] This number cannot be verified in the archives. Nonetheless, by looking at files from a reinvestigation of rightists in 1962, we can draw conclusions about why those who "opened their hearts" in 1958 were classified as rightists.

A document from 1962 titled "Conclusions upon Reinvestigating Rightists and People with Rightist-Tendency Mistakes" records the verdicts reached after the Tongbai County committee reexamined thirty-one "rightists" plus forty-one people who had "serious rightist tendencies" (*yanzhong youqing*) or who were "rightist-tendency elements" (*youqing fenzi*). The biggest difference between this document and other similar documents is that fifty-eight of the reports provide examples of the original evidence for the labeling of "rightists" or people with "rightist tendencies," as well as the reasons for their rehabilitation. An example of this is the decision by the Tongbai County committee to rehabilitate Gao Hongde on May 31, 1962. Gao, an elementary school teacher, was classified as a rightist on December 9, 1958. As punishment, he was demoted and had his wages reduced.

More than three years later, authorities revisited the justification for labeling Gao a rightist. His original classification had been based on four statements he made in 1958. Upon reinvestigation, none of them seemed quite so severe:

1. One morning in March 1958, he was preparing a meal in the school kitchen and, while casually chatting with his comrades, said: "For the sake of joining the Party, Wang Xinshan spoke up during the meeting and was labeled a rightist. I will never again apply to join the Party." This problem came from Gao's personal understanding.

2. One evening in September 1958, Gao said: "Meng Guanglie made mistakes because his school is far away from a grassroots Party branch and the Party did not educate him sufficiently. That was why he was labeled a rightist. This has everything to do with the Party." Gao had a confused understanding of the facts, so he cannot be judged on the basis of this statement.

3. Gao cannot be punished based on what he said about low grain rations during the *jiaoxin* movement in September 1958.

4. During the small-group meeting to oppose Pan, Yang, and Wang on August 9, 1958, what Gao said about feeding the farm animals separately was correct, not mistaken. The county committee has examined the above factors and decided to revoke Comrade Gao Hongde's rightist label and punishments. He is to be reinstated to his job at his previous salary level.

Conclusion 3 is especially significant. What Gao had said about food shortages in September 1958 at a *jiaoxin* meeting actually became part of the evidence for his classification as a rightist. It was but one short step from *jiaoxin* to repercussions. In rural China, attacks on rightists extended all the way to the end of 1958, overlapping with the Great Leap Forward.

It is also significant that in the fifty-eight reinvestigation reports, almost all the rightists and people with "serious rightist tendencies" and "rightist tendencies" committed the crime of complaining on the farmers' behalf that their food rations were too low, that the average annual allotment of 180 kilograms of grain per person was not enough, that farmers' lives were hard and their status low, and that rural education was substandard. Among those who were reexamined, all admitted to this in the "personal views" (*benren yijian*) column of the paperwork. If it were not for the Great Famine of 1959–1961 and the postfamine remedial measures, the Henan grassroots organizations would not have reinvestigated and rehabilitated these rightists. Although history has confirmed that these rightists' statements about food shortages and hunger were accurate, the price to pay for presenting the facts was heavy.

*   *   *

The rectification and anti-rightist movements, as well as the movement to open one's heart to the Party, all unfolded chronologically and followed the Party's top-down hierarchy, beginning at the center and gradually progressing down through the provincial, municipal, and county levels. Throughout the process, the airing of views at different levels had sufficient precedents so that participants could decide for themselves whether to speak and what to speak about. Despite substantial enticements and heavy pressures, most people chose silence or evasion. Nonetheless, a group of "rightists" still stood up to air their critical views and offer suggestions to the Party. Even when they had a certain inkling of the tragic consequences that would result from their actions, they chose to speak, whether hesitantly or resolutely. Seen from this perspective, China in the late 1950s did indeed have "rightists" who opposed the Party and opposed socialism.

The reason for this state of affairs was that in the 1950s, China's political evolution and the turbulent changes in its social and economic structures had given rise to genuine grievances and hardships. The actions of the rightists demonstrated that not everyone could calmly and silently accept the direction China had taken in the 1950s. From this perspective, the commonly held view that China had only 5 actual rightists is incorrect. The Party rehabilitated 550,000 rightists in the 1980s and left only 5 prominent rightists unrehabilitated because it had changed course and members of the former opposition were no longer considered enemies of the Party.[42] But analyzed from a historical perspective, a large number of "rightists" actually were so opposed to Maoist policies that they willingly sacrificed themselves in order to speak their minds.

From the standpoint of the Party, the rectification and anti-rightist struggles were justified and necessary to maintain its socialist course and safeguard its authority. From the perspective of most of the people in rural counties such as Tongbai who were labeled "rightists," speaking out against injustice and unfairness was second nature. At the time, most of them were young people in their late twenties and early thirties who had promising futures. Rural China's most brilliant lights had been extinguished by an anti-rightist "conspiracy" that unfolded openly and in the light, not secretly or under cover of darkness.

Translated by Wee Kek Koon

4

Revising Political Verdicts in Post-Mao China

The Case of Beijing's Fengtai District

DANIEL LEESE

To ensure people's democracy, we must strengthen our legal system. Democracy has to be institutionalized and written into law, so as to make sure that institutions and laws do not change whenever the leadership changes, or whenever the leaders change their views or shift the focus of their attention.

—DENG XIAOPING, DECEMBER 1978

The lawlessness of the Cultural Revolution is a well-known fact. Many memoirs and scholarly works have dealt with the arbitrary detention and brutal confinement of the movement's victims.[1] Similarly, the crucial importance of the Third Plenary Session of the Eleventh Central Committee in December 1978, and especially the role of Hu Yaobang in rehabilitating Communist cadres, has been pointed out.[2] Yet our knowledge about the fate of ordinary citizens who came into conflict with local authorities, as well as the actual procedure of rehabilitations (*pingfan*) or at least corrections (*jiuzheng/gaizheng*) of former verdicts at the grassroots is highly limited. Studies have usually been confined to the macro level of the legal system or to Party-internal revisions of verdicts concerning high-ranking officials.[3] Based on original court files, this chapter provides insights into the cases of some forty citizens revised by the Beijing Fengtai District Court. The court documents cover the period from immediately after the Third Plenum until August 1979, when the bulk of counterrevolutionary cases had been settled in Fengtai. This material not only sheds light on how legal norms and procedures were reinstated after 1978, but also allows insights into how counterrevolutionary crime was defined and dealt with before then. The revision of verdicts, as well as the accompanying rhetoric of socialist legality and modernization, played a crucial role in strengthening Party rule and thus provides an important link between the eras of revolution and reform.

A Plethora of Problems

On December 13, 1978, five days before the advent of the Third Plenum, the Beijing Fengtai District Court delivered a first batch of counterrevolutionary cases to the local Party Committee with suggestions about how to revise verdicts that had been handed down by the court itself or by military author- ities during the Cultural Revolution. The spectrum of crimes deemed "counterrevolutionary" was considerable. Many cases dealt with acts of "slandering" or symbolic transgressions. Among the files was the case of a fifty-seven-year-old woman of poor peasant background surnamed Wang who on August 7, 1976, had been arrested for an act of active counter- revolution. During an assembly of her production team to discuss the efforts of Party Center in ameliorating the fate of the Tangshan earthquake victims, she had approached production team member Hao, sitting beside her, with the words: "Did you know? Chairman Mao has already died."[4] Hao had duti- fully reported these words, and Wang, now branded a counterrevolutionary, was held in custody for half a year until investigations carried out by the court itself revealed that Wang had been confused by the death of Marshal Zhu De in July 1976. The court traced the reason for this confusion to Wang's lack of education and cleared her of counterrevolutionary charges. She had already been released in early 1977 with an oral notification, but this proce- dure was considered insufficiently formal, and therefore a written court document was issued. Around the same time, upon Mao's actual death on September 9, 1976, a sixty-year-old production team member from a nearby commune was reported as having told his children: "This is really good. A main pillar of the Communists has crumbled."[5] The man, named Li, had forbidden them to wear a black ribbon as a symbol of their grief because they had failed to do the same when their own mother had died. The district court, in a verdict delivered on July 23, 1977, sentenced the man to seven years' incarceration due to a reactionary class standpoint and his act of out- rageous "malicious slandering" (*edu gongji*). By December 1978, the court declared that these utterances stemmed from incorrect thinking but did not constitute a criminal offence.

Besides acts of slandering, the files included much more complicated cases, such as that of a fifty-two-year-old peasant who during the Four Cleanups and under Red Guard torture had confessed to having been an accomplice to the murder of two Communist Party cadres back in 1946 but who had later recanted his confessions and been held under mass supervision ever since. After renewed investigation, the court advised dropping all counterrevolutionary charges because of a lack of evidence.[6] Many cases also included discontent about living conditions under socialism, such as the court files of a forty-two-year-old temporary worker named Liu, who had been convicted to fifteen years in prison for "counterrevolutionary theft" by the military authorities in charge of adjudication in Fengtai in 1972. Liu had allegedly stolen and attempted to sell over 130 meters of electric cable from the Beijing Zhoukoudian highway construction site—an act which delayed this national project for two days.[7] At home, he had frequently complained about his job status, sarcastically saying: "This is the great advantage of Mao Zedong and the liberation through the Communist Party. . . . In America there exists unemployment, in the Soviet Union too. What do China's temporary workers count for? Before the Cultural Revolution I blamed Liu Shaoqi. Now that the Cultural Revolution is over, there is still temporary work. What is that supposed to mean? Temporary work does not guarantee a living. . . . The poor are still poor. The poor have nothing to eat. All of this has taken place under the leadership of the Chinese Communist Party."[8] The court recommended reducing the former sentence from "counterrevolutionary theft" to "ordinary theft" and the corresponding prison sentence from fifteen to nine years because Liu's complaints had not incited others to act. The verdict was considered basically correct, with the exception of the charge of counterrevolution, and the revision amounted to a "correction" (jiuzheng) of the former verdict, not a complete rehabilitation of the defendant.

Similar incidents were reported from all over the country and required central-level instructions about how to resolve the millions of cases adjudicated during the Cultural Revolution. On December 29, 1978, a mere week after the end of the Third Plenum, Party Center circulated a report that had been submitted by the Supreme People's Court's Party Group a month earlier. The document targeted the reexamination and revision of what came to be termed "unjust, false, and wrong cases" (*yuan jia cuo an*) that had been adjudicated under the influence of the so-called "pseudo-Left but genuinely Right counterrevolutionary revisionist line" of Lin Biao and the "Gang of Four."[9] In order to ease future case revisions through local people's courts, the document listed five categories under which the vast majority of cases should be subsumed and handled in the future. First were the victims of the "three types of cases" (*san lei anjian*), hinting at previous criticism against Lin Biao, the Gang of Four, or complaints about the treatment of Deng Xiaoping after the Tiananmen incident of April 1976. Most of the defendants had been accused of "maliciously attacking" the policies of the Cultural Revolution and been sentenced according to the "Six Regulations on Public Security Work" starting on January 13, 1967.[10] The second category dealt with criticism of Party cadres or policies aside from the aforementioned "three types." The accused had commonly vented their anger about personal misfortune endured during the Cultural Revolution by way of writing slogans or poetry critical of the central or local leadership. Besides these cases of intended criticism, the third category comprised symbolic transgressions, such as the unintended misspelling or writing of certain characters. Among the convicts were a fair number of juvenile delinquents who had shouted slogans in praise of recently purged leaders, as well as people who had unintentionally defiled or destroyed Mao icons. "Class vengeance" (*jieji baofu*) constituted the fourth category. The term basically referred to deeds and utterances committed by persons with a "bad" class background, the spectrum of action ranging from derogatory comments to petty theft and violent brawls. In many cases the crimes had already been tried and the sentence served before or during the Cultural Revolution, yet the victims had often been charged again, retroactively, on grounds of their class background. The fifth and last category referred to cases of so-called "political lunacy" (*zhengzhi fengzi*), which included utterances or deeds of mentally handicapped persons. Despite a long-standing tradition in China of exempting cases of madness from normal procedures of criminal justice—acknowledged by the Supreme People's Court in June 1956[11]—many had been held fully accountable for their actions.[12]

The Supreme People's Court did not supply numbers to estimate the national scope of "unjust, false, and wrong" verdicts. One year later, it finally offered more specific information. Between 1967 and 1976, approximately 287,000 sentences of counterrevolutionary crime had been issued, of which some 241,000 verdicts had been revised by late 1979. Among these, some 131,000 cases had been considered "unjust" and the victims therefore rehabilitated.[13] The overall number of sentences delivered by judicial and public security organs during the Cultural Revolution was much higher, and given at over 2 million in 1983, of which some 670,000 cases implicating more than 725,000 persons had been reversed and the defendants rehabilitated.[14] Another 33,000 counterrevolutionary cases had been tried in 1977 and 1978, and 21,000 of these were later revised.[15] The scope of judicial revision was thus enormous and yet dealt with only a fraction of the grievances inflicted by Cultural Revolutionary violence, many of which were not addressed by courts but rather, if at all, through local *danwei* authorities or petition bureaus.

The early reform-era rehabilitations did not mark the first time the Party had revised previous verdicts to reshuffle the balance of power after a Maoist mass campaign. Quite to the contrary, the constant reexamination of its Party personnel under changed discursive parameters had been a crucial feature of Party politics.[16] During the Cultural Revolution, efforts to revoke erroneous verdicts within the Communist Party had first taken place in the wake of the Lin Biao incident as experienced administrators were needed to staff the reemerging state and Party institutions. The civilian cadres were to wrest power from the hands of the PLA Military Control Committees that had assumed de facto power in many units after the anarchic period of 1967–1968.[17] The early 1970s further witnessed the initial rebuilding of judicial institutions such as local people's courts that had by and large been rendered defunct, since "lawlessness" had explicitly been decried as a hallmark of Cultural Revolutionary policies.[18]

The end of military rule in China's public security apparatus also eased the situation of many prisoners wasting away in jails and detention centers. Mao Zedong in December 1972 had criticized the predominating "fascist examination methods"[19] when commenting on the fate of former railway vice-minister Liu Jianzhang, who had been detained without trial for more than five years. While Liu's fate was by no means extraordinary, Mao's short comment and a follow-up instruction of Premier Zhou Enlai demanding a reexamination of Liu's case and prison conditions in general, as well as inter-dicting the use of force against prisoners, had a notable impact.[20] A critical revision of past work routines by the Beijing Chongwen District Public Security Sub-Bureau revealed that during 1972 about 36 percent of the working staff had violated Zhou's directive and that "open or disguised vio-lence" against prisoners had been "fairly common."[21] About 2,000 prisoners had temporarily been confined in "small, black chambers," where some of them had been tied up or handcuffed, received all types of corporal punish-ments, or had been "taken out at [the warden's] pleasure."[22] As a conse-quence, the chambers were closed, work routines changed, and prisoner provisions ameliorated. Yet the fate of most political victims remained uncertain.

In December 1977 it was the recently rehabilitated Deng Xiaoping who twice commented on unresolved cases of former high-ranking officials and advised the CCP Organization Department to thoroughly deal with the issue.[23] Of crucial importance for instigating the revisions was the appoint-ment of Hu Yaobang as head of the CCP Organization Department on December 10, 1977, putting him in charge of cadre job assignments and han-dling Party members' files. During the following year, the Party-internal case reexaminations commenced. At the Eighth National Judicial Conference in April 1978, local courts were called upon to revise unjust verdicts among non–Party members as well, the degree of reversal depending on the nature of the respective case. Yet the local response remained slow owing to polit-ical uncertainty and the fact that the institutions envisioned to fulfill the task had not yet been effectively reorganized. Only as the Third Plenum shifted full weight behind the revision of verdicts as part of advocating socialist legality and "seeking truth from facts" did local implementation gain momentum.

At the Fifth Session of the National People's Congress on July 1, 1979, a first set of seven groundbreaking laws was finally promulgated after a twenty-year period during which, with the exception of the 1975 and 1978 constitu-tions, not a single national law had been passed.[24] The seven laws included the Organic Laws on the People's Courts and the People's Procuratorates, as well as a Criminal Law and a Criminal Procedure Law, and became effective on January 1, 1980.[25] The laws offered, for the first time, clear guidelines about the responsibilities of state institutions, the length of sentences, and court procedures. They provided groundwork for the rebuilding of legal institutions that continues until the present day.

Case Revisions in Fengtai District

Compared to national statistics, the number of cases dealt with by the Fengtai court seems marginal. During the Cultural Revolution, a total of 1,117 cases had been handled by local authorities, including some 260 cases of counterrevolutionary crime.[26] The sample discussed here contains 39 of these verdicts. Fengtai District, covering the southwestern section of suburban Beijing, had a population of roughly half a million by the mid-1960s. Despite its proximity to the nation's political center, Fengtai in the late 1960s and 1970s bore little resemblance to its present-day counterpart. Although all major southbound railway lines crossed through the district, little industry seems to have developed in Fengtai before 1978. The local annals mention some 167 state-owned enterprises at the outset of the Cultural Revolution that had "outdated equipment and simple technology."[27] Instead, they emphasize Fengtai's traditional role, dating back to imperial times, of supplying the capital with vegetables, fresh flowers, and livestock.[28] More than half of the defendants in the sample were of peasant-class background, and agriculture features prominently in several cases. Livestock are occasionally mentioned, for example, in a case of "counterrevolutionary theft" when the convict had not only stolen food coupons, bicycles, garments, and cash, but also "more than 100 rabbits."[29] The cultivation of flowers had been terminated because it was deemed to be a capitalist venture. In the early stages of the Cultural Revolution, even a plantation of apple trees was cut down on the pretension of "removing revisionist roots."[30] Fengtai was thus neither fully urban nor truly rural in 1978, reflecting in many ways the nature of the crimes detailed below.

Judicial work until 1966 had been handled by the district court in close cooperation with the local people's procuratorate and the public security organs. Crime rates had steadily been decreasing since the Great Leap Forward, with around 100 criminal cases being handled per year in the mid-1960s. At the outset of the Cultural Revolution, the judicial system came under heavy criticism. By February 1967, the court, the public security sub-bureau, and the procuratorate had all been placed under military control. The procuratorate was abolished in April 1967, and all judicial personnel, with the exception of five court employees, were sent to the countryside for ideological reeducation. The so-called "Beijing Municipal Fengtai District Public [Security], Procuratorate, [People's] Court Military Control Committee," assumed complete judicial powers.

After the Fengtai court was reestablished in early 1973, the Military Control Committee was disbanded as part of the nationwide attempt to curb the influence of the military in the wake of Lin Biao's fall.[31] The local people's procuratorate was formally reestablished in January 1979 but did not immediately take up its tasks. None of the case materials mention its involvement or a defense counsel. Investigation work was commonly conducted by the public security organs and the indictment filed by the court itself. The local court, and in rare cases the Fengtai District Public Security Sub-Bureau, thus took on the responsibilities of the procuratorate.[32] The case revisions were compiled by the court, which submitted the results of its investigations by way of reports to the local district Party Committee or political-legal committee and the presiding local Party secretary, who enjoyed the right of final decision. Hence, the system was also referred to as "approving cases by secretary" (*shuji pi'an*).[33]

Owing to the prominent role played by the local Party Committee, the court verdicts are called "requests for instructions" (*qingshi*). They usually start out with a short characterization of the defendant, mentioning name, present age, sex, class background (*chushen*), and class status (*chengfen*), as well as current address and *danwei*. This introduction is followed by a brief account of the crime, the date of detention and incarceration, and finally the sentence with administrative number and the type of crime. Occasionally, remarks about ethnicity or education level are included. At least eleven convicts were of bad class background (on the arbitrary nature of defining class background, see Chapter 2 by Jeremy Brown). Their current class status labels, however, included only one "active" landlord. The biographical information in the first section is commonly followed by a paragraph summarizing the main arguments of the original verdict. It also mentions possible revisions prior to the district court's case review. Among the thirty-nine cases analyzed here, ten had been subject to revisions through the local unit, the Public Security Bureau, or the district court itself. Three cases state the date of the revisions. All of these deal with the spreading of rumors in the immediate wake of critical events, such as the Tangshan earthquake or Mao's death. The remaining seven case revisions without exception appear in the latest available batch, filed in August 1979. Although they do not provide information about the precise date of the earlier revisions, they mostly involved two layers of review, first through the local *danwei* or people's commune and then through the local public security organs. All criminal offences were committed between late 1969 and mid-1971 and, unlike the case revisions cited above, did not stem from hastily taken judgments in the immediate wake of sensitive political events. Instead, the seven revisions are all based on administratively registered and documented verdicts issued by the Military Control Committee. Most revisions ascertained the basic correctness of the former judgments but dropped the political charges. In these cases, only a partial rehabilitation was granted, in order to show that the original verdict had been basically correct, albeit excessive.

Besides providing details about earlier revisions, the verdicts' second paragraph also offers information about unusual legal incidents. While it is commonly assumed that criminal procedures had been in complete shambles since the outset of the Cultural Revolution, at least four convicts had formally appealed their sentences. The most astounding example is the case of a forty-three-year-old temporary worker of "unclear" class background, surnamed Xi, from Bin County in Shandong. Xi had been sentenced to ten years' imprisonment for active counterrevolutionary crime by the Fengtai Military Control Committee in November 1972.[34] He had been accused of harboring a reactionary standpoint and of being hostile to the socialist system, as exemplified by various malicious speech acts and jottings. The accused had further sent a letter to Mao Zedong complaining about the injustice of not being able to attain a permanent job. Evidence in his case had been provided by family members, including his ex-wife and brother-in-law, who had testified that Xi had referred to the CCP Chairman as "Old Mao" (*Mao laotou*) in private. Xi had further compared the rustication of the Red Guards with the "reform through labor" system and had frequently instructed his son not to forget the death of his grandmother, who had been beaten to death by Red Guards.[35] Xi did not accept the verdict and appealed to the local court after it was reestablished in 1973. Upon being rejected, he filed an appeal at the Beijing City Intermediate People's Court in 1974 and again in

1976 at the Beijing City Higher People's Court, both of which dismissed his case. Xi's verdict was finally revoked by the Fengtai court on February 9, 1979. The report stated that although Xi had committed erroneous deeds and harbored capitalist thoughts, these did not constitute counterrevolutionary crimes. The local Party Committee approved this revision on March 2, 1979.[36] Xi's case is highly interesting because it reveals that the possibility of filing appeals actually existed, at least after the demise of the Military Control Committee. It was even possible to circumvent the two-tiered court system by simply continuing to file appeals to higher levels.

The third and longest section of the court reports is made up of the reasons for the revisions. It discusses the crimes and the veracity of the evidence in considerable detail and thus allows for interesting glimpses into both the nature of political crime during the Cultural Revolution and the standards of adjudication. This section often includes several quotations, the accuracy of which cannot be verified. Labels for criminal offenses were by no means standardized, as shown by the changing labels mentioned in Chapter 1 by Yang Kuisong. Yet all included a strong political element and thus can be subsumed below the headings provided by the Supreme People's Court's categorization. The dividing lines between the different categories cannot always be strictly drawn, because the crimes often overlapped and included several charges. The reports end with a request for instructions addressed to the local Party Committee and the date. Half of the sample files also include the original handwritten comments of a Party Committee member. Of the comments, 80 percent simply state "Agreed" and the respective date. Three cases were referred back for further information. One comment mentions dissenting opinions within the district committee, which had been resolved by "relying on the masses," without giving further indication about the consequences.

The results of the revisions were either declared at the defendant's work unit by representatives of the judicial organs or, in the case of major crimes, publicly during so-called "pronouncing judgment assemblies" (*xuanpan dahui*). These assemblies, which had been held regularly after the reestablishment of the Fengtai District Court in 1973, aimed to "frighten the convict" and "educate the masses."[37] Between 1974 and 1990, 211 of these assemblies were organized in Fengtai and attracted some 734,800 spectators. In the adjacent but more urban Chongwen District, such assemblies had, with varying designations, been conducted throughout the Cultural Revolution by the revolutionary committee and later by the district court. The *Chongwen District Public Security Annals* mention several of these assemblies, each with 1,500 to 15,000 spectators. During the assemblies, sentences were not only proclaimed or revoked but, in case of death penalties, also executed on the spot.[38]

Several case reports not only changed the political verdict but also recommended offering financial compensation, restitution of outstanding wages, or reemployment in the person's former *danwei*. The amount of financial remuneration is never given in detail but was to be decided upon by the former responsible *danwei* or the relevant local financial institution, as the Supreme People's Court had ordered in December 1978. Most cases handled from mid-1979 onward at least define the limits of financial restitution. The financial aspects of rehabilitation were much more complicated to solve than the change of political verdicts, which in many cases were fast-tracked. In its report the following year, the Supreme People's Court mentioned several unresolved problems about financial compensation. Recently released convicts tried to return to the labor camps that had once confined them, to receive daily food rations, saying, "Criminals have food to eat, the innocent remain hungry."[39] In eight suburban districts of Hunan Province, 133 recently rehabilitated persons even committed new crimes to solve this problem and gain readmission to labor camps. The Supreme People's Court declared that the judicial system alone was unable to cope with this problem and urged local organization departments, personnel bureaus, and labor departments to assist in making the revision of verdicts a success.

Another difficult issue to solve was the question of restoring urban residency to students and others sent down to the countryside during various campaigns. Although by the late 1970s many students had long since returned to the city by way of instrumentalizing personal relationships, the official line was harsh. Unless they managed to pass the university entrance exams or could prove official employment, there was to be no change of *hukou* registration.[40] Despite these regulations, many victims of the Cultural Revolution flocked to big cities in the late 1970s and petitioned for a reversal of their verdicts. Within the suburban Fengtai setting, however, the question of *hukou* registration plays only a marginal role. In spite of the attempt at procedural standardization, the case files reveal that local courts were faced with unforeseen difficulties or unaccounted-for loopholes that needed to be solved pragmatically. This becomes quite clear when we turn to the specific content of the case files. While in theory every case revision had to be rooted in overturning the evil acts of the Gang of Four, these linkages turned out to be fairly haphazard in local court statements dealing with ordinary citizens. Some of these cases are detailed below, arranged according to the categories provided by the Supreme People's Court, which directly shaped judicial practice in Fengtai.

The "Three Types" of Cases

There are no examples of the first category—criticism of Lin Biao and the Gang of Four or criticism associated with the first Tiananmen incident in 1976—in the files I collected. The official *Fengtai District Annals,* however, mention the case of a middle school teacher surnamed Li who in March 1970 was sentenced to seven years in jail for his unspecified criticism against Lin Biao.[41] Li's sentence was revoked during a public "rehabilitation assembly" (*pingfan dahui*) on August 30, 1978. Most cases in this category were dealt with before the Third Plenum and therefore do not appear in the present sample. In contrast, there is one case of a forty-eight-year-old worker surnamed Tan who in July 1976 was sentenced to fifteen years' imprisonment as an active counterrevolutionary for continuing to praise the military genius of Lin Biao. Even after Lin's death, Tan held steadfastly to the view that without Lin Biao the Communist revolution would never have been successful. He accordingly had been reprimanded by the production team leadership, which he berated as a "fascist dictatorship worse than Hitler's Nazis."[42] After suffering a leg injury in 1972, his work points had been reduced, and his new tasks included guarding sorghum fields against sparrows. Tan disapproved of this demotion but still fulfilled his duties, armed with a bamboo stick to which he had fastened a white plastic bag. Upon being asked by passing children about his job, he told them he was swinging the flag of Lin Biao. These utterances led to further punishment, and tensions came to a head in December 1973, when Tan, upon arriving late at a group study session, mocked the attendants: "Are you studying Lin Biao's instructions?"[43] The ensuing debate sparked a violent brawl, which led to Tan's arrest and later sentence. The verdict at the time charged Tan on grounds of "reactionary thoughts," for "singing the praises of Lin Biao in a big way," and for "attacking local cadres." The revised sentence tried to trace the personal frustration of the accused and characterized the relevant remarks as "wrong but not counterrevolutionary."[44] The report therefore advised rehabilitating and releasing Tan, and offering him a basic living allowance. This is the only case in which the Party secretary did not comment with an affirmative or critical remark but simply left a question mark, waiting for further instructions by higher authorities. Tan's fate remains unknown.

Malicious Attacks

The main bulk of the cases can be subsumed under the second category and deal with criticism directed against high-level Party leaders or against the impact of Cultural Revolutionary policies. The labels "counterrevolutionary" (*fangeming*) and "active counterrevolutionary" (*xianxing fangeming*) appear to be attached at random.[45] Among the cases in the present sample, two-thirds contain "malicious attacks" against the former CCP Chairman by way of crude curses, symbolic transgressions, or hidden allusions. The reasons for attacks against Mao, who assailants often considered a personification of the entire Chinese socialist system, were manifold but usually related to feelings of injustice. Thus, a sixty-one-year-old peasant surnamed Liu who had been leader of the local production team until the outset of the Cultural Revolution, when he was purged and struggled against, held Mao responsible for his fate and attacked him as a "bastard, not conceived by human beings."[46] He was sentenced as an active counterrevolutionary to ten years in jail on grounds of reactionary thoughts and malicious attacks against the "proletarian headquarters" (i.e., Mao Zedong). The revision argued that Liu had been unable to understand the course of the movement and therefore failed to comprehend the negative impact of the Lin Biao and Jiang Qing cliques. The court explicitly recognized the discontent arising from Cultural Revolutionary policies but did not criticize the movement as a whole. Instead, the utterances were redefined as wrong and reactionary but certainly not aimed at a subversion of the system, a criterion that basically defined the meaning of "counterrevolution."

Transgressions during periods of political uncertainty involved drastically higher sentences. This is illustrated by the fate of a thirty-one-year-old worker surnamed Li and a sixty-five-year-old poor peasant named Song, who received the highest punishments in the present sample on grounds of "malicious attacks": a death sentence with a two-year suspension in the first case and lifelong incarceration in the second. The crucial event in question was Mao's death. Upon hearing the news of the Chairman's passing, Li suggested drinking some alcohol and Song rejoiced: "Today we are very happy, so let's drink something."[47] They made themselves comfortable in Song's apartment, enjoyed the beverage, and offered a toast to the deceased. Their celebration was noticed by neighbors, who notified the public security organs. Both men were arrested on the spot and held in custody until mid-February 1978, when their sentences were determined by the Fengtai court. The original sentence describes their acts as "mad attacks, hurling abuses, slandering and vilifying Chairman Mao and other central leaders."[48] The case revisions made by the very same institution just one year later conceded "highly backward and reactionary" thinking but questioned the existence of subversive thoughts. Continuing ideological education, rather than punitive justice, was regarded as the fitting measure to cope with the convicts' problems. In case of the younger worker, the court specifically demanded that he be reinstated in his former job and retroactively receive outstanding wages. The district committee agreed with this rationale, and the accused were released and rehabilitated by early 1979.

Besides the timing of certain speech acts, the class background and status of the convict played an important role in Cultural Revolutionary adjudication. This fact is exemplified by the fate of the only "active" landlord within the sample, who was detained on the grounds of vilifying Mao through symbolic allusions. When watching the growth of vegetables with other members of his production team, he commented: "This cabbage is rotten, and this old stinking piece of flesh has also died."[49] His fellow workers had asked him to behave himself when speaking of his kin. Only later did it dawn on them that he had alluded to Mao Zedong. Landlord Wang was sentenced to twelve years in prison. Wang's case, which is among the first batch of case revisions at a time when the Third Plenum had not yet ended, is the only document that continues to use the language of class justice in the revision section. This is all the more conspicuous because other reports passed the same day, but dealing with "former" landlords, explicitly criticize class terminology as unsuitable for legal reasoning. The report states that the landlord's enmity toward the socialist system and his malicious attacks constituted severe offenses that had correctly been pointed out. Yet it was recommended to solve the problem by commuting the sentence to three years of mass supervision.[50] Despite a similar evaluation of the case, the revised verdict—which was approved by the local Party Committee on December 14—still resulted in a massive reduction of the former penalty. Nonetheless, Wang's case underscores the importance of the Supreme People's Court intervention, circulated two weeks later, ending the consideration of class background when revising cases.

Among the most detailed case reports is the file of forty-three-year-old Ms. Shen, a woman from Daxing County of poor peasant stock. Daxing had achieved tragic prominence during the early Cultural Revolution through the slaughter of 325 people with bad class backgrounds in late August 1966.[51] Shen's troubles commenced in the summer of 1969 with the leveling of her tiny private vegetable patch by the neighborhood Mao Zedong Thought Study Group, apparently for "hygienic" reasons. In March 1970, the situation escalated further when Shen misinterpreted the chanting of slogans during the "daily read ritual" (*tiantian du*) in her neighbor's home as a continuation of the criticism against herself. She splashed water against her neighbor's window, inciting the study group to recite Mao directives on class struggle. On April 14, a local police officer asked her to participate in the study class. According to the court report, this request resulted in the following dialogue:

> SHEN: Well of course, you guys have things to eat and things to wear. You go to study classes all day. I do not get enough to eat; therefore I won't participate in study classes.
>
> POLICE OFFICER: Chairman Mao said: If we have made mistakes, we have to correct them.
>
> SHEN: I have never seen Chairman Mao.
>
> LOCAL CADRE: You have never seen the Chairman, but did you never see the Chairman's portrait?
>
> SHEN: When I see the Chairman's portrait, I simply get angry. If Chairman Mao were not there, would I still be suffering from hunger? Liu Shaoqi is bad, Soviet revisionism is bad, American imperialism is bad, but I simply don't know what exactly is bad [about these].

LOCAL CADRE (SHOUTING): We will smash the dog heads of all those who oppose Chairman Mao!

SHEN: That's exactly what I do—I oppose Chairman Mao! So what are you going to do with me now?[52]

Shen was immediately seized by the local public security organs and sentenced the same day to five years in prison. The original verdict stated that the accused harbored "reactionary thoughts," took a hostile standpoint toward socialism, had continuously slandered the Party and the proletarian headquarters, shamelessly flattered "thief Liu" (*Liu zei*), and disturbed the masses in studying Chairman Mao's important works. Shen served her full term and was released in late 1975. She continued to be labeled a counterrevolutionary until the local Party Committee finally rehabilitated her on August 27, 1979. The revised verdict described her case as based on a "lack of understanding"[53] of contemporary politics. The charge of counterrevolution was therefore dropped in lieu of continuing ideological persuasion.

Although criticism of Mao entailed the harshest consequences, the slandering of other leading cadres also bore drastic results. In the wake of Mao's death, this held especially true for Mao's short-term successor, Hua Guofeng. Three cases in the sample are based solely on skepticism about Hua's leadership skills. The Chinese public had not been thoroughly prepared for Hua's accession, but utterances such as "Hua Guofeng has just been working for a few months; he does not have experience. It would have been good if he had spent a few more years at the Chairman's side"[54] were sufficient to merit a five-year prison sentence. Similar indictments continued at least until late 1977. In December 1977, the Fengtai District Court sentenced a sixty-seven-year-old worker to six years' imprisonment as an active counterrevolutionary for maliciously attacking the "wise leadership of Chairman Hua" during a marital row.[55] Criticism of Hua Guofeng also sealed the fate of a thirty-one-year-old female student surnamed Wei from Hubei's Mianyang County. In February 1976, when Hua Guofeng had taken over the duties of acting premier after Zhou Enlai's death, Wei, upon seeing a newspaper photo of Hua receiving foreign dignitaries, had told a colleague: "Hua Guofeng looks ugly and ferocious; his appearance is repulsive. This is not ideal for a premier—it won't do. Premier Zhou looked superb; he had authority. What kind of authority does Hua Guofeng command?"[56] Wei had furthermore continued to praise the looks and likeness of Chiang Kai-shek and Liu Shaoqi. She was arrested in April 1977 and sentenced to ten years' imprisonment as an active counterrevolutionary. After spending one-and-a-half years in prison, the court advised dropping the sentence because Wei's mistakes had been caused by her capitalist education and thus did not constitute a major offense. She was fully rehabilitated soon thereafter.

With the exception of the "active" landlord case, all political verdicts based on verbal criticism of Party leaders were completely overturned and the victims rehabilitated. The local courts had been advised by the Supreme People's Court that single utterances should not be taken as primary evidence of a crime, but, instead, the person's general conduct.[57] The case revisions therefore aimed at reducing the overuse of criminal justice and favored administrative penalties or an instant release. The Supreme People's Court furthermore stressed the importance of ideological work and of winning over the populace by channeling hatred toward Lin Biao and the Gang of Four.[58] By providing common scapegoats, the Party aimed to distance itself from the dark sides of the Cultural Revolution and to regain public legitimacy through political and financial rehabilitation.

Class Vengeance

Cases associated with category 3 of the Supreme Court report—the unintended vilification or destruction of Mao symbols—are not included in the present sample. Similar to the crimes of attacking Lin Biao or the Gang of Four, they ranged among the more bizarre verdicts and thus probably were among the first to be revoked. Several cases, however, prominently include the intentional defilement of Mao icons. All of these cases are to be found in association with categories 4 and 5: class vengeance and political madness. While "class vengeance" explicitly was the driving force in only two verdicts, it is used as additional evidence in five other cases. All of these deal with individuals of bad class background and in the original sentence contain a strong element of class justice.

The example given by the Supreme Court for using past crimes to justify a renewed sentence appears in only one case of the sample that links the destruction of Mao effigies with supposed class vengeance. A thirty-three-year-old peasant surnamed Zhang with landlord class background had in

July 1967 not been able to attain medical care for his sick son. In anger, he cut sixteen holes in a Mao portrait on the wall and proceeded to shred it and urinate on the scraps.[59] Zhang further criticized Mao for being unable to resolve his misery: "Everyone says Chairman Mao is great. I have nothing to eat and still he doesn't care." Zhang was detained for nine months and released after intense "education" in April 1968. After serving his sentence, he remained under mass supervision. In January 1970, however, the Military Control Committee sentenced him to seven years in prison for the same offences. Zhang served the full term. The Fengtai court in August 1979 declared the first sentence of nine months to have been correct. The renewed sentence in 1970 was nullified for reasons of procedural errors. Zhang had after all served twice for an identical charge. He was to receive future living allowances but no compensation for the nine years spent in prison. Again, this verdict did not constitute a full-scale rehabilitation but rather a correction.

The two verdicts immediately designated as class vengeance crimes deal with violence against Cultural Revolutionary authorities. In one case, a forty-seven-year-old former rich peasant had attacked a people's militia member during a struggle session against the convict's father on August 24, 1966. Upon witnessing the pain inflicted on his elderly father, the accused jumped on the podium and smacked the militia member in the face. For this "outburst of fierce and ugly class hatred"[60] committed at the very outset of the Cultural Revolution, he had been sentenced one day later to six months' detention by the still-existing district court. The other case involved a forty-one-year-old former landlord whose parents had been humiliated in similar fashion by a leader of the local poor peasant association. Furthermore, their home had been ransacked and their only bicycle confiscated. The accused continued to harbor resentment and later, unsuccessfully, tried to reclaim the bicycle. He was prevented from attacking the peasant leader; finally, on July 29, 1969, he destroyed the furniture of the local production team office. He served a five-year sentence for "counterrevolutionary class vengeance" on grounds of "being born to a landlord family," "harboring reactionary thoughts," and for violent behavior. The court report argued that the original sentence had to be revised, because a bad class background did not constitute a criminal offense. No trace of reactionary thinking had been detected with the exception of anger about the fate of his family during the Cultural

Revolution. Thus, he was to be released and entitled to basic living allowances.[61]

These two cases reveal both the lingering impact of class justice and the differences between sentences issued by the pre–Cultural Revolution judicial organs, even in their last moments of existence, and those by the makeshift military authorities. In two comparable cases of committing a violent act in the heat of the moment without resulting in lasting injury, the two accused had been sentenced to six months of detention and five years in prison, respectively. The first verdict, handed out in mid-1966, still followed former judicial conventions. By 1969, a harsh line against political slandering and "counterrevolutionary acts" was obviously deemed to be an expression of political loyalty by the local Military Control Committee as it carried out court functions, irrespective of previous legal norms.

The last case involving class vengeance to be discussed here is slightly more complex and involves several individuals. Fortunately, all case materials are included in the sample. The case centers on two brothers of landlord class background surnamed Wu who by the time of the revision were thirty-seven and thirty-three years of age. For the sake of convenience, I will refer to the elder brother as Lao Wu and the younger as Xiao Wu. Red Guards had ransacked their home and struggled against their mother, who poisoned herself as a consequence of repeated criticism sessions in July 1967. Xiao Wu had furthermore been expelled from his job as primary school sports instructor on grounds of upholding a reactionary standpoint, criticizing the banning of the Qing novel *Dream of the Red Chamber,* sexually molesting two of his students, and, finally, for "conducting an 800-meter track race during a seventh-degree storm."[62] While Xiao Wu soon set out to "exchange experiences" (*chuanlian*) across the country, Lao Wu and his friend Xie, according to the reports, had made a habit of listening to Soviet radio broadcasts and frequently criticized Cultural Revolution policies. They voiced their bewilderment about the purge of state leaders such as Liu Shaoqi and expressed disgust over former actress Jiang Qing ("all film directors who used to perform with her in the past have been purged") as well as Minister of Defense Lin Biao, whom they described as a "toady" and "treacherous court official."[63] They had furthermore vilified Mao icons—for example, by intentionally destroying statues or by symbolically burying Mao buttons near Xie's father's grave—and mocked official propaganda by reciting, "Let them in the grave give eternal prominence to Mao Zedong Thought."[64]

Xiao Wu had in the meantime fallen in love with a young woman named Zhou, whom he met at the Red Guard Liaison Station in Chengdu. Zhou was of landlord class background, and her family had been expelled from Chongqing and sent to a rural tea farm during the Four Cleanups.[65] The loss of her city residence permit had darkened her life prospects considerably, and thus Zhou took advantage of revolutionary upheaval to try to regain her former residence status. Her hopes turned out to be in vain, and marriage plans with Xiao Wu seemed to be illusory.

When he learned of his mother's suicide in July 1967, Xiao Wu wrote a letter to his brother expressing his anger and fury:

> There is no love greater than a mother's love, and there is no hatred more profound than hate toward one's father's murderers. Today, thief Mao [*Mao zei*] has slain my mother; in future years I will kill all Communist bandits. I will use my twenty-two years of age to kill the people who killed my mother. I will use your blood to clean my knife. If these wrongs remain unavenged, I won't be able to close my eyes in death. . . . The Chinese people cannot be duped. China's sons and daughters cannot be humiliated. Today, how many sons and daughters have been killed by thief Mao? How many mothers and fathers have been killed, how many persons have experienced either the destruction of their family or have been killed themselves, how many sons and daughters have killed their parents with tears in their eyes? Just you rise, thief Mao's felons. Take our heads, take our blood, but return our country to us.[66]

Wu and Zhou decided to turn their back on China and seek their fortune abroad. They met a returned overseas Chinese, who told them that they could "easily make a living abroad by circulating reactionary propaganda."[67] They set out to Kunming to cross the Yunnan border to Vietnam and start a life as traders in Burma or Indonesia.[68] After burning their remaining Mao buttons and their little red books, they attempted to cross into Vietnam in September 1967. Because they lacked the necessary documents, they were

detained by the border guards and released again only after "intense education." In the following weeks, they discussed alternative options and decided
on crossing the border in less strictly controlled minority areas, but they
lacked the money for further travel. Therefore, in January 1968, Zhou
returned to Beijing to obtain further funds. She met with Lao Wu, Xie, and
others to discuss the possible border crossing. Lao Wu cautioned against
hasty moves. He accompanied Zhou back to Kunming in order to persuade
his brother to give his motherland one last chance. They would try to reverse
the school verdict so that Xiao Wu would be able to take up his old profession. Should this plan fail, they would leave the country together.[69]

Lao Wu managed to convince his brother, and they returned to Beijing.
Upon their arrival at the Beijing railway station on March 1, 1968, the Wu
brothers and Zhou were arrested by public security organs, who had been
alerted by unspecified informants. The three students were detained without
trial for more than six years. Xie and others implicated during the interrogations were arrested in June 1968, only to face the same fate. In November
1974, their cases were finally tried before the reinstated district court. All
four were accused of counterrevolutionary crimes, class vengeance, and
treason. Zhou was sentenced to seven years' incarceration; Lao Wu received
ten years; Xiao Wu and Xie, who in jail apparently carved numerous counterrevolutionary slogans such as "Mao Zedong is the second Qin Shi Huang"
and "Long live the Communist Party, long live Liu Shaoqi"[70] into the wall of
the prison cell, received the longest terms (fifteen years).

The reevaluation of the Wu brothers' case led to controversies in the district Party Committee because the case not only dealt with word crimes, but
with attempted treason as well. Xie and Lao Wu had filed appeals in late 1978
and restated their positions. The court reports of February 1979 suggested a
complete reversal of verdicts in all four cases. The hatred voiced against Mao
and the Cultural Revolution accordingly was to be perceived as misguided
criticism of Lin Biao and the Gang of Four, in line with the ideological work
suggested by the Supreme People's Court. All four of the defendants had suffered during the Cultural Revolution, owing to their bad class background,
and had tried to distinguish between true communists and the culprits
responsible for the chaotic situation. While their criticism had been misguided, their crimes should not be perceived as counterrevolutionary
actions. Instead, the court recommended reinstating them to their former

positions and fully reimbursing them for the financial losses and medical costs incurred during the period of detention. The court also instructed the local education department to consider rehiring Xiao Wu as a school teacher.

The Party secretary had great difficulties in determining the correct handling of this case. In a long handwritten comment, he cited opposition to the court's suggestions on the side of the Party Committee and the local political-legal committee. The decision was therefore delayed until more detailed instructions about similar cases could be supplied. This finally happened in December 1979, when a Supreme People's Court report explicitly discussed cases of treason and committed to a differentiation between political, economic, and personal reasons for trying to cross the borders.[71] Only in a fraction of these cases had counterrevolutionary activities been planned. The report therefore advised not to indiscriminately apply political labels and encouraged the revision of treason verdicts as well.

The Wu brothers' case is a highly interesting example of many phenomena that governed Chinese society and adjudication during the Cultural Revolution. It sheds light on the stark restrictions experienced by children born into families with bad class background and simultaneously portrays the temporary freedom of movement and speech enabled by the nationwide anarchy. The case offers examples of youthful heroism and patriotism, as well as criticism against misguided policy guidelines. It further highlights the long periods of unofficial detention that came to be the norm rather than the exception during these years. This holds especially true for cases first dealt with in 1967 and 1968, when Military Control Committees carried out few if any legal proceedings. No other institution reviewed the status of former verdicts until the reestablishment of local courts in the early 1970s.

"Political Madness"

The fifth and final category deals with cases of "political lunacy"—supposedly counterrevolutionary acts committed by mentally ill persons who nevertheless were punished according to the same standards as other political offenders. Four cases in the present sample can be subsumed under this label, three of which shall be discussed in detail. In the first, a thirty-one-year-old student with poor peasant background surnamed Wang was charged for counterrevolutionary murder. Wang, about whose pre–Cultural Revolution history the report mentions basically nothing, had in May 1969 been sent to Beijing Anding Psychiatric Hospital in order to receive medication to treat his schizophrenia. While at the hospital, he had voiced erratic criticism and destroyed Mao portraits, but was soon released. On October 14, Wang entered the house of a poor peasant and killed the inhabitant with a stove poker for no apparent reason.[72] After being detained, he was sent twice for medical examination in Anding in December 1969, where doctors confirmed that he suffered from schizophrenia. He nevertheless continued to languish, first in a detention center and then for seven years without trial in an unknown prison. On July 13, 1976, his case was tried before the Fengtai court. Wang was held fully accountable for the murder and sentenced to death, with a two-year suspension. Since he had killed a poor peasant, the crime was not simply defined as murder, but instead as "counterrevolutionary murder." By August 1978, the Supreme People's Court reissued its 1956 decision regarding the exemption of convicts with a proven record of mental illness from the usual court procedures.[73] Therefore, the Fengtai court revised its verdict in December 1978. It advised releasing the accused based on his proven record of medical illness, dropping the former charges without commenting on financial compensation.

The second case deals with a fifty-seven-year-old worker named Qiang from Anci County (Hebei), of bad class background. Qiang was sentenced in March 1970 by the Military Control Committee to ten years' imprisonment on grounds of counterrevolutionary crimes. The original verdict cited four reasons for his imprisonment: he had delivered military information to the Japanese in the 1940s and in 1954 caused a traffic accident; Qiang had also criticized the Cultural Revolution and, finally, written two counterrevolutionary letters to Mao Zedong in July 1968 that constituted the main evidence for his crimes. The letters contained two "poems," one of which read as follows.

> Mao Zedong:
> It is still the same that I can't sleep
> Who is it? It is your Communist
> Party members it is your military army
> I think by myself that it is maybe the military

that disturbs me. If it disturbed me to death you still would not care. Well, then I simply die!

The court on August 1, 1979, argued that the first two crimes had either come under the statute of limitations or had been dealt with already. As for the remaining evidence, the court cited medical sources stating that the accused had been treated at Anding Hospital five times between 1957 and 1968 to cure his "severe unknown mental illness." The court report advised releasing and rehabilitating the convict without further inquiries about his psychological well-being, permitting him to work, and reissuing his wages. The Party Committee agreed on August 27, 1979.

The last case to be dealt with in this chapter is that of thirty-seven-year-old former landlord Yang, who in August 1971 was sentenced by the Military Control Committee to seven years' incarceration on grounds of "counter-revolutionary theft." Unlike the other cases of "political lunacy" mentioned above, Yang had no history of mental illness. The military committee had based its argument first of all on Yang's class background—"born as landlord, reactionary thinking"—and had further argued that between 1967 and 1969 he had committed theft more than 140 times, including the robbery of one hundred rabbits.[74] He had also criticized the Party and Mao Zedong, for example by praising the North Korean standard of living. Problems with Yang's mental health first appeared during the "One Strike, Three Anti Campaign" in late 1970, when his thefts were finally discovered. During the interrogations, he suddenly collapsed and cried:

I hate Chairman Mao. I have been buried under the Lei Feng pagoda[75] for thirty years. Today, after the pagoda collapsed, I only started to truly live among mankind. I am Yang Kaihui. I am the reincarnation of Mao Zedong's first wife. I lived for Mao Zedong and I died for Mao Zedong. . . . I am Mao Anlong.[76] I am deaf, my brain wrecked after being fractured. I want to see Chairman Mao, so that he can cure my illness. . . . Mao Zedong, this old chief hooligan, drinks the people's blood and betrays the people. The people do not have enough to eat and wear. They have to work all day; illnesses are frequent. Mao Zedong should be burnt until nothing but ashes is left of him; let him ascend to the Guanghan palace[77] on the moon to meet the ghosts. . . . Long live

the people! Long live the great, glorious, and correct Chinese Communist Party![78]

During the following day's interrogations, Yang tore off his clothes and
started eating animal feed, and he announced a few days later that Mao
Zedong had already died. What was Yang's motivation for these seemingly
lunatic utterances? Had he tried to fake madness to receive favorable treatment, or had he cracked under the pressure of interrogation and been driven
into insanity like many other prisoners during the Cultural Revolution?
Faking madness was definitely no viable path for bypassing harsh verdicts
during these years, especially since the highly prominent case of the
"Madman of the new era," Chen Lining, had strengthened public perception
that madness was a social construct rather than an illness.[79]

The court report does not provide further clues about Yang's motives. The
original verdict interpreted the utterances as malicious attacks. The revision
simply skipped this section and focused instead on criticizing the arguments
related to class background. Furthermore, the report discussed the personal
situation of the accused as a major reason for committing theft. Because Red
Guards had destroyed his home and belongings, Yang had relied on theft to
survive. Once his situation changed for the better, the crimes stopped. The
court thus advised dropping the criminal charges. The Party Committee, on
August 27, remained unsure about the verdict and extended its delibera-
tions, so again we remain uncertain about the fate of the accused.

*   *   *

Individual case histories show the difficulties of coming to terms with the
Cultural Revolution's legacy. By late 1978, no official evaluation of the tumultuous period had been issued, and the judicial organs had to toe a thin line
between righting individual wrongs and not making themselves vulnerable
in case of a new change in political direction. Especially in such peripheral
regions as Tibet, Fujian, and Ningxia, local courts until mid-1979 did not
dare to revise the Cultural Revolutionary verdicts for fear of committing
errors.[80] Distinct from the experiences of other post-communist societies
that tried to cope with the horrors of the past by way of a complete renunciation of the former dictatorship, the CCP did not fall from power despite
having endured a most severe crisis. The Party thus had to regain public

legitimacy without discrediting its own claim to rule China. Redressing the Mao-era verdicts served to appease the exhausted population and reclaim public legitimacy through formal procedural justice.

The Fengtai court closely followed the directions of the Supreme People's Court, and critical verdicts, such as in cases of treason, were delayed until higher authorities had passed a clear directive about how to deal with these issues. The main difference between the cases tried or revised during the Cultural Revolution and the ones analyzed in the present sample may be observed with regard to the role of class background and the importance of judicial procedure. While class background had clearly influenced previous decision-making, its influence on adjudication receded in the late 1970s. And although the Fengtai court by late 1978 still displayed caution in handling the case of the remaining "active" landlord and the revised verdict even reproduced certain stereotypes of Cultural Revolutionary class justice, the court simultaneously reduced the former sentence through the backdoor. Concomitantly, previous procedural errors were pointed out and corrected. Especially in times of high political sensitivity—for example, after the death of a political leader or after major catastrophes such as the Tangshan earthquake—similar crimes had been sentenced more harshly. In basically all cases that did not involve physical assaults or state subversion, the court pleaded for immediate release, and the Party Committee usually followed the court arguments. The same held true for criticism of Mao Zedong or Cultural Revolutionary politics. These "malicious attacks" in most cases were declared to stem from either incorrect thinking or as having originally targeted the policies of the Lin Biao and Jiang Qing cliques.

By solving these cases on an individual basis without addressing larger questions about who was responsible for previous injustices, the Party relied on selected measures associated with the concept of "transitional justice"[81] in a post-conflict society, yet without destabilizing its claim to rule. Public debates about the reasons for Cultural Revolutionary excesses were only tolerated as long as they served current political interests, and soon enough the limits of criticism were sharply defined in trials against new "counter-revolutionaries" such as Democracy Wall activist Wei Jingsheng. Although official attempts at administering transitional justice culminated in the trial of the Gang of Four and the remainder of the Lin Biao clique in late 1980, society-driven forms of coping with the Cultural Revolution and its continuing legacy assumed other shapes, including literary expressions such as Liu Binyan's famous reportage stories, or "scar literature." Official attempts at transitional justice thus remained partial.

Nevertheless, the mechanics of local case revisions present us with a detailed example of how the CCP managed to distance itself from the Cultural Revolution while simultaneously retaining its monopoly of power. And, even more important, the cases reveal the machinations of state control and the practices of informing on family members but also the resilience—not necessarily resistance—of ordinary citizens in the face of political persecution. Quite unlike common and sometimes self-exculpatory stereotypes about brainwashed and indoctrinated masses unable to assess the political situation, the cases reveal strong and informed political views and individual standards of evaluation that often conflicted with official guidelines. While many individuals were detained, perished, or were driven to madness as a consequence of state-sponsored violence, it was ultimately insufficient to crush these independent assessments. The study of China at the grassroots during this period of political transition presents us with the unique opportunity for reflecting on the extent of state control during the turbulent Cultural Revolution, and also on the extent of local discontent in the Mao and post-Mao eras.

Part II

MOBILIZATION

5

Liberation from the Loom?

Rural Women, Textile Work, and Revolution in North China

JACOB EYFERTH

The socialist revolution promised to transform the material life of China's rural inhabitants, to bring new objects and technologies—"two-story brick houses, electric light, and telephones" (*loushang louxia, diandeng dianhua*)—to the countryside, and in doing so to radically alter existing divisions of labor and patterns of everyday life. How people experienced socialism at the grassroots levels depended as much on the halting and uneven changes in material life as on the sequence of struggles and political campaigns through which we usually analyze socialist China. Few changes in the countryside were more momentous than those related to how rural people clothed themselves. By this I do not mean sartorial change, which was relatively slow, but the way cloth and clothing was produced.

As late as 1936, more than two-thirds of China's cloth output was produced manually, in small urban workshops and rural households.[1] While the old adage that "men farm and women weave" was never strictly accurate (most women participated in farmwork at least seasonally, and some men spun and wove), it is true that *all* women in late imperial China, from commoners to the elite, were expected to perform textile work. Textile work shaped women's lives at many levels: it kept them cloistered at home but also linked them to faraway markets; it was associated, in elite poetry and ritual laments, with loneliness and physical isolation but also gave rise to all-female forms of sociability and networks of technical exchange.[2] Textiles were the public face of women who were expected to spend much of their lives indoors and make themselves as invisible as possible if they ventured outside. In the form of betrothal gifts, dowries, and graveclothes, the fruit of women's labor created and reinforced human relationships: women weavers re-created the social fabric with their hands. Textile work even shaped women's bodies: women who spent much of their life squatting in front of the spinning wheel or sitting at the loom developed a set of bodily postures and sensory habits that set them visibly apart from women who did not spin or weave.

Numerous studies have shown that rural hand spinning and hand weaving held out remarkably well in the face of mechanized competition.[3] Imports of foreign yarn in the late nineteenth and the rise of mechanized spinning mills in the early twentieth century led to a sharp reduction of laborious, inefficient hand spinning, so that by the turn of the twentieth century, about one half of all yarn used in China was machine-made. Thereafter, however, the advance of machine yarn slowed down, in part because weavers took to combining machine-spun warp threads with homespun weft.[4] Hand spinning survived in cotton-growing areas, where households continued to use household labor to spin yarn for their own consumption and, in some cases, for commercial weaving.[5] The picture is more complex in the case of weaving. Imported and domestic factory cloth competed with Chinese handloom cloth; at the same time, the increased availability of cheap factory yarn stimulated the growth of new handloom weaving centers near Shanghai and Tianjin.[6] As late as 1935, 24 percent of Chinese rural households spun or wove; in cotton-growing provinces such as Henan, close to 60 percent did.[7]

When the Chinese Communist Party came to power, the vast majority of rural people wore homespun *tubu* cloth, and millions of rural women spent much of their working life producing cloth and clothes. Within less than ten years, the socialist revolution replaced the horizontal division of labor between men and women in the farming household with a vertical division between countryside and city. *All* rural people, men and women, were mobilized to work in agriculture—and increasingly *only* in agriculture, as local handicrafts and sidelines were phased out. Textile production, for centuries as integral and necessary a part of rural life as grain cultivation, was taken out of the countryside and redefined as part of urban industry. In the Communist Party's view, hand spinning and hand weaving were wasteful of raw materials and labor; their very existence in the twentieth century was proof of the distortions that semifeudalism and semicolonialism had imposed on China. Once the revolution had put the economy back on a healthy track, demand for such technically outmoded industries would evaporate and they would quickly disappear.[8]

Disappear they did—but neither quickly nor naturally. In the Guanzhong area of Shaanxi Province, most rural people continued to wear homespun cloth until the end of the collective period, and anecdotal evidence from other parts of China suggests that this was no exception.[9] This situation is perplexing because cotton farmers were obligated to sell their entire harvest to the state, with the exception of small amounts of "self-retained" cotton (*ziliumian*) intended for padding. Moreover, under the system of "unified purchase and marketing" (*tonggou tongxiao*) introduced in 1954, rural people received ration coupons that gave them the right to buy factory cloth, albeit at levels that were substantially lower than those for urban people. Finally, from 1960 on, central and provincial governments issued increasingly strident calls for the suppression of hand spinning and hand weaving, in order to ensure that all of China's cotton harvest was processed in state factories. The reasons for the survival of *tubu* in the face of state pressure are complex: some farmers may have preferred sturdy handmade cloth to factory cloth, which was initially of poor quality, and many rural people—men as well as women—may have associated handmade textiles with "proper" gender roles and respectability. The main factor, however, was that state-owned cotton mills failed dismally in supplying rural people with the cloth they needed. Average rural rations remained below replacement levels for much of the 1960s and were only marginally above these levels in the 1970s. Rations differed widely from place to place, and in many parts of China, people relying solely on state supplies would have found themselves with fewer clothes on their bodies year after year for about twenty years. Scarce as the rations were, large numbers of rural people never claimed them but instead sold their coupons on the black market, to earn cash for more urgent demands. Rural women, in short, often had no choice but to produce cloth at home with whatever scraps of cotton they could pilfer from the fields or buy on the black market.

Textile work is enormously time consuming: it took about sixty labor days to provide a family of five with the absolute minimum of clothes—one summer suit (to be replaced every three years), one winter suit (replaced every five years), and half a quilt and mattress (replaced every ten years) per person. Making shoes took an additional thirty days at least. If the family was to be clothed decently according to modest standards (a good suit for the household head to wear on market days, new clothes for children every second year), a woman might have to spend one-third to one-half of her waking hours working with spinning wheel, needle, and loom.[10] Yet the Chinese state did not acknowledge the existence of a rural textile crisis, nor did agricultural production teams make special provisions for women who clothed their families. Like men, women were expected to work full time in agriculture, though their attendance was less strictly enforced. Women dealt with this situation by working "overtime" (*jiaban*), spinning by lamplight for hours after men and children had gone to bed.

In the following pages, I look at everyday Maoism through the lens of cotton cultivation and textile work. My focus is on the choices of rural women under conditions of great scarcity. How did women find the time and the materials to clothe their families? How did they cope with conflicting demands from families, relatives, and the state? What were the moral valences of different choices? Did a young woman who embroidered a tobacco pouch for her father-in-law fulfill a customary duty, or did she waste time and materials that would have been better spent in collective work? Answers to these questions, I hope, will help us understand how socialism was experienced locally and how this state of affairs changed over time. Most of my material comes from fieldwork in Zhouzhi and Xingping Counties in central Shaanxi and from research in county and provincial archives.[11]

Textiles and Women's Work in Guanzhong

The Wei River valley—also known as Guanzhong, the area "within the passes"—contains most of the flat and fertile land in Shaanxi Province, with Xi'an at its center. Cotton production in Guanzhong dates back to the early Ming dynasty and underwent a major revival in the 1930s, thanks to the linking of Shaanxi to the national railroad network and energetic measures by the provincial government to promote cotton cultivation.[12] Cotton exports to coastal China increased amid high hopes that Guanzhong would become a main supplier for the textile mills of Shanghai and Tianjin, until the outbreak of war in 1937 cut short the expansion. Despite the opening of new irrigated cotton districts along the Wei and Jing Rivers, export-oriented cotton cultivation did not replace an older pattern of cotton cultivation for home use. In Xingping County, it was said that "all families spin, but no one sells cotton; all villages weave, but no one sells yarn" (*jiajia fangxian bu mai hua, cuncun zhibu bu mai sha*).[13] This was not entirely true: cotton cultivation could be very lucrative, especially at the height of the 1930s cotton boom, and many farmers sold part of their harvest. However, farmers rarely put more than one-third of their land under cotton; a common plot size was one to two *mu*. Cotton was a risky crop: one week of heavy rains in the fall could destroy the entire harvest.[14] It also required a high investment in seeds, fertilizer, pesticides, and irrigation, as well as three times more labor input than wheat, maize, or sorghum.[15] The percentage of land under cotton, therefore, tended to increase with wealth: only farmers with surplus cash and labor could plant much of their land in cotton and benefit from high prices during the 1930s boom.

While not a road to riches, weaving for the market was not as badly underpaid as is often assumed.[16] A standard piece of cloth sold for the equivalent of 50 to 70 *jin* of wheat in normal years, although it might only buy 30 *jin* in crisis years. If we subtract the cost of cotton, we are left with a net income of 23 to 43 *jin* of wheat for the twelve days it took to complete a standard piece— 1.9 to 3.6 *jin* for each day of work.[17] In other words, a textile worker earned enough to sustain herself and one to three other household members. Old people in Xingping, where commercial weaving was particularly widespread, maintained that women's contribution to household incomes outweighed that of men: as much as three-quarters of a household's grain income could come from women's textile work.[18]

Each stage in the life course of rural women in Guanzhong was marked by the exchange of textiles or the acquisition of new textile skills. Most girls learned to spin at age seven and to weave at age ten to fourteen. Families that did not need their daughters' labor in the fields groomed them for marriage by cloistering them soon after they had learned to spin. One woman I interviewed was told to stop visiting friends when she was nine. With the exception of trips to nearby temple fairs, during which she and her sisters watched village operas from behind the closed curtains of an oxcart, she did not leave her parents' home until her wedding day.[19] Cloistering was not always that strict, and recent research by Gail Hershatter suggests that the centrality of cloistering in rural women's memories may in fact be the result of systematic misremembering.[20] In my experience, as in hers, women often recalled episodes of seclusion that fitted easily with the official narrative of feudal oppression before liberation. Continued conversation brought out memories of farming and other outdoor work, which was often remembered as more painful, emotionally and physically, than domestic work. At the same time, most of the women I interviewed insisted that their farmwork was seasonal, and that much of their childhood was spent at the wheel and the loom.[21] This regime of intensive textile work was relaxed around the seventh day of the seventh month, when girls and young women came together to pray to the "Seventh Sister" (*qi jie,* also known as *qi xian,* the Seventh Immortal) for needle skills as well as the skillful mouths, eyes, hands, and hearts that would win them the love of their future husbands and the respect of their marital families. This was an all-female festival in which girls and unmarried women met to sing, dance, and pray; married women were only allowed to watch from behind a screen.[22]

The training of daughters was often very strict, since mothers felt that their chances on the marriage market depended in large measure on their textile skills.[23] Folksongs from Zhouzhi County reflect the hopes and fears of future brides:

> The poplar tree is split in two, two neighbors to the left and right
> This household's sons can read and write; that household's girls do
>   needlework
> First daughter embroiders peonies, second daughter pomegranate
>   flowers
> Third daughter, alas, can't embroider; she's told to sit in the dirt and
>   spin cotton
> The drive band snaps, the spindle bends; she hasn't spun a
>   single skein
> Tears in her eyes, her back is sore; poor thing who can't embroider!
> Look at you, what will you do? Who will ever marry you?[24]

The first years after marriage were often the hardest in women's lives. Folksongs describe the fate of young women who were treated by their inlaws as a source of cheap labor:

I had finished my embroidery when mother-in-law told me to spin
Not daring to reply I carded cotton and turned the spinning wheel
Midnight came and the cotton was still piled high
I spun until daybreak. With the first morning light I returned to
    sewing.
My hands were lumps of ice, blood oozing from their backs
My ears like wooden bowls; too numb to hear the cock crow
My feet like icy bricks; when I tried to rise I could not stand.[25]

Once she had children of her own, a woman would spend much of her time producing cloth and clothes for her own small family rather than working for the extended household under the supervision of her mother-in-law. Over time, a woman's needlework became her public face—more public, in some cases, than her own person, since married women spent much time inside the family courtyard. Neighbors and relatives judged a woman on the basis of her family's clothing: neat stitches were the sign of a well-ordered household and an industrious wife and mother.[26]

Almost all important interactions in rural Guanzhong involved the exchange of textiles. Births, cyclical festivals, and visits to the natal family were occasions for giving textile gifts, and no marriage could be concluded without gifts of cloth and cotton. The customary standard for a bride price in Zhouzhi was "two bundles of cotton and four bolts of cloth" (*liang kun mianhua, sige bu*)—enough for two padded winter suits and two thickly padded quilts.[27] These gifts were in fact a form of reverse dowry; most of it was transformed by the bride's family into clothing and bedding for the bride, so that she could enter her new home in style. During the first few years of her married life, a woman was expected to produce gifts for her relatives: embroidered pillowcases for her mother-in-law, tobacco pouches for the father-in-law. If her marital family allowed it, she would also take textile gifts home to her natal family. Gifts of cloth or clothes were also mandatory when children were born. Even the dead had to be clothed, and since they wore their clothes for the entire length of the afterlife, these had to be of the highest quality.[28] Three sets of graveclothes—one unlined set for summer, a lined one for spring and autumn, and a padded one for winter—were the norm. Preparing graveclothes for oneself and one's relatives was seen as an appropriate and dignified end of a woman's working life.

Women's social status was intimately bound up with textile work. Elite and nonelite families alike pursued what Kenneth Pomeranz termed the "economics of respectability": the gain in social standing and earning power that resulted from keeping women at home.[29] Complete, year-round cloistering was most common in elite families: only these families grew or bought enough cotton to keep women constantly employed, and only they subscribed to the strictest notions of propriety. In most families, women participated in farmwork during the busy planting and harvest seasons. Only women of very poor families worked in the field day in and day out, a situation that they and their male relatives experienced as degrading. For a woman, skill in planting crops or handling animals did not bring recognition: her proper work was indoors, and she could earn praise for herself and her family only through domestic work.

Despite the stereotypical image of the lonely woman at her loom, textile work was intensely social. Girls and young women spun in groups, and their work was often accompanied by songs and storytelling. Weaving was solitary work, but before a woman sat down at the loom, she had to size and reel the yarn and warp the loom. These tasks required close coordination between several workers, and since women learned these skills in their natal families, they often asked their mothers, aunts, or sisters to help with this task. In China's exogamous kinship system, which isolated women from their closest kin, cooperation around the loom allowed women to reactivate their kinship networks and connect with close relatives from their natal home.

Textile work created specific bodily postures and sensory skills. In winter, spinning women sat cross-legged on the *kang,* in a way that allowed them to absorb warmth from the heated surface; in spring and summer, they squatted in front of the hand-operated spinning wheel with feet flat on the ground and body slanted forward. Women who have spent much of their life spinning and weaving assume these postures with great ease, while women born since the 1970s tend to find them uncomfortable and prefer to sit on chairs. Ways of sitting are associated with specific types of sociability; the way one sits and moves about the *kang,* in particular, is both intimate (people sit close to one another, legs covered by a shared quilt to preserve the heat) and regulated by a set of tacit rules.[30] Another example of bodily conditioning through textile work is the way women learned to spin an even thread in the dark. Wu Xiujie reports that this led to frequent conflicts between mothers-in-law, who had learned over time to "see" the thread with their fingers, and daughters-in-law who still relied on their eyes and therefore "wasted" lamp oil.[31] Ways of sitting, standing, walking, etc., do not directly produce subjectivities, but there is a striking difference between the low and "earthbound" posture of a woman who has spent much of her life squatting in front of the spinning wheel or hunched over her needlework and the more erect and expansive posture of a younger woman who has never done such work.

Cotton and the Socialist State

Textile work, in short, shaped all aspects of rural women's lives, in ways that could be both oppressive and empowering. This complex social world disappeared in the course of the socialist revolution. During the Yan'an years, CCP leaders encouraged women to spin and weave, because local cloth production strengthened the economy of the CCP-controlled border regions and drew women into public life. This changed in 1949: as an article in the *People's Daily* explained, the liberation of Beijing and Tianjin put the new government in possession of 400,000 power spindles and more than 10,000 power looms, whose voracious appetites had to be fed. Manual spinning in the countryside was therefore to be phased out, and the women whose labor was made redundant were to be mobilized to grow cotton for urban industry.[32] CCP leaders objected to household-based spinning and weaving because it tied up two resources that were crucial to socialist modernization: cotton—China's most important crop after grain—and women's labor power. Cotton and cotton textiles were central for capital accumulation: cotton mills were the single largest source of state income in Maoist China, accounting for 10 percent of revenue,[33] and the export of cotton cloth and garments paid for much-needed technology imports from the Soviet Union and other friendly nations.[34] Women's work was central to China's development strategy because industrial expansion depended on a more productive agricultural base, and in the absence of capital inputs (which were reserved for industry), productivity gains in agriculture could be achieved only through increased labor input. Rural women were China's largest untapped labor source, and CCP leaders hoped that their full participation in farmwork would free men to work in rural industry and capital construction.[35] Obviously, women could work full time in agriculture only if they were first liberated from time-consuming textile work.

Cotton acreage in Guanzhong expanded rapidly in the first two years of the PRC but reached a ceiling in 1952, when almost all usable land was either under grain or cotton. Area yields did not reliably increase until synthetic fertilizer became widely available in the 1970s.[36] At the same time, demand from newly built or repaired cotton mills outstripped cotton supplies. After a series of good harvests in the late 1940s and early 1950s, Guanzhong had been designated a "cotton base" for northwestern China, with the task to supply the clothing needs of Gansu, Ningxia, and Qinghai, and a large number of cotton mills had been built in Xi'an and Xianyang.[37] The state-owned Cotton, Yarn, and Textile Company (huashabu gongsi) was hard-pressed to satisfy demands, and since harvests could not easily be increased, much of its effort focused on suppressing private competition and, above all, reducing the amount of cotton that remained in peasant hands.[38] Somewhat paradoxically for a socialist state, local officials were ordered to increase the commodity rate (shangpinlü) of cotton—that is, to break open the unity of production and consumption in the rural household and turn self-sufficient peasants into market-oriented farmers.

In order to achieve this aim, the state trade companies used bait-and-switch tactics that were as ruthless as those of any private trader. Even before the formal ban on private cotton trade in 1954, the state aimed to procure 80 percent of the cotton harvest, leaving only 20 percent in the hands of cotton farmers.[39] Actual procurement fell far short: in 1952, the state cotton company obtained only 36 percent of Shaanxi's estimated harvest, less than in all other major cotton-producing provinces.[40] To increase its harvest share, the cotton company introduced a system of advance purchases (yugou) under which farmers were asked in early spring to pledge their future harvest in exchange for an advance payment of 20 percent of the expected harvest value, to be paid in cash or raw materials. Survey reports conducted by the cotton company and the supply and marketing cooperatives show that many farmers were reluctant to accept these loans, for fear that a poor harvest would leave them in debt. They were particularly skeptical about accepting goods (grain, seedcake fertilizer, or factory cloth) instead of cash, partly because of the poor quality of the goods offered, partly because they feared "that later on, we [would] find ourselves without cash and thus lose our freedom" (*jianglai meiyou lingqian yong, bude ziyou le*).[41] Anxious farmers pleaded: "Can we perhaps order less, or perhaps not order any goods at all?" The answer, it seems, was no—the cotton company, and above all the supply and marketing co-ops, were so eager to tap into the "great latent purchasing power" of rural households that they pushed for high sales pledges and high ratios of payment in kind, depicting the purchase of factory goods as a "patriotic and collectivist" duty and as cotton farmers' contribution to "strengthening the worker-peasant alliance."[42] Unsurprisingly, many farmers overcommitted, leading to sharp recriminations the following year.

In 1951 and 1952, state traders pushed aggressively for early sales; in 1953, the situation was reversed. The summer wheat harvest in North China was so poor that state planners expected serious problems in supplying the urban population with food grain. Cotton farmers were among the largest non-urban grain consumers, and state officials feared that putting cash in their hands would drive up grain prices in a market that was not yet under complete state control. Since higher purchase prices could not be passed on to urban consumers, increased rural demand would cause massive losses to the state. Therefore, the central government lowered cotton procurement prices from a level of 9 kilograms of wheat for every kilogram of cotton to a ratio of 1:6.25.[43] In addition, local cotton procurement stations were ordered to delay purchase as long as possible without provoking open protests—ideally until the spring wheat harvest.[44] Since cotton deteriorates quickly if not properly dried and stored, farmers had no choice but to stand in line at the procurement stations, often for several days on end. Once their cotton was weighed, company personnel often arbitrarily downgraded it. Worst of all, farmers were not paid in cash but in IOUs, to be cashed in only after the spring harvest. In late 1953 and early 1954, angry cotton farmers took to torching cotton warehouses, and the situation became so tense that the police handed out firearms to procurement station personnel.[45]

Cotton farmers reacted to the 1953 crisis by reducing the area under cotton cultivation, in some cases destroying unripe cotton crops and replacing them with winter wheat.[46] With the introduction of "unified purchase and marketing" in 1954, cotton became a formal state monopoly. Only a minority of farmers had joined mutual aid groups or cooperatives by that time, and in theory, independent farmers were free to grow as much or as little cotton as they chose. In practice, however, township and village governments were given production quotas, and almost all cotton farmers had signed mandatory contracts that were enforced even after floods and droughts. Farmers who had pledged more than they could sell—often under pressure from above—were criticized in public and had to repay their cash advances; those who had cotton left after fulfilling their pledge were "to be mobilized and persuaded" to sell it to the local procurement station, at a slightly higher "negotiated" price (*yijia*).[47] Cotton farmers were allowed to retain only enough cotton to pad winter clothes and quilts, in most localities 1 kilogram per person. This "self-retained cotton" (*ziliumian*) became the main source of textile fibers for rural people's clothes in the collective period.

Women's Work under Socialism

Early PRC gender politics were more concerned with reforming the feudal family than with changing the patterns of women's work. Freedom of marriage and divorce and the right to resist cruel and unfair treatment in the family: these were the slogans that attracted many women to the CCP. Yet from early on, equal participation in productive work—always understood as work *outside* the household—was portrayed as the final aim of women's liberation. Songs and plays at that time depicted women's liberation as a process of stepping out of the darkness and loneliness of the feudal family and into the sunshine of public life and public work.[48] There is no reason to doubt that many women, especially young women, experienced the revolution this way. Strict cloistering came to an end, and women were encouraged to participate in politics, although this often meant no more than the passive attendance of village meetings. Women I interviewed in Gedatou Village, Zhouzhi County, remembered little change in their daily life and work routines during the first years of the PRC. Most of them worked primarily indoors until collectivization in 1956–1957, when participation in farmwork became the norm. After collectivization, women worked in all-female teams (*funü dui*) under female leaders, sometimes alongside men but usually on separate tasks. Like men, they worked three daily shifts (morning, forenoon, and afternoon), though women, in contrast with men, could skip part of a shift if they had to take care of a baby or urgent household tasks. What ensured women's participation in collective work was not coercion but the need to earn work points that could be converted into cash and grain. Commercial weaving, the main source of cash income for most families until collectivization, was increasingly curtailed and finally banned;[49] and while black market sales of handloom cloth continued, the state left too little cotton in the villages for weaving to remain a major source of income. It was the loss of textile "sidelines" (which in many parts of Guanzhong had been the main source of cash income) that made it necessary for rural women to turn toward collective work.

The transition from a situation in which the majority of women worked mostly indoors to one in which fieldwork was the norm was extraordinarily rapid. Based on Women's Federation records, Gao Xiaoxian estimates that women's participation in agricultural work tripled from 30 to 50 labor days yearly in 1955 to 140 labor days in 1956.[50] A report from the Beijingzhai cooperative in Zhouzhi shows that in 1955, women worked an average of only 9.6 days in the collective fields. Only very young women and those old enough to be free of household duties worked more than 10 days; women aged eighteen to fifty worked in the fields for 5.5 days a year.[51] Only four years later, however, women's labor input had risen to the same level as men's.[52] Women's mobilization for agricultural work took place in a context of general labor intensification. "Too little time and too much work" seems to have been a nearly universal complaint in newly collectivized villages. Some people compared the collectives to labor camps, or opined that "increased income under the collectives is a good thing, but working nonstop in all seasons is simply too much; we'll all end up flayed, with our skin stretched out on a frame" (*ba renpi jiu da zai gangan shang*).[53]

The Great Leap Forward, with its large infrastructural campaigns, further intensified labor demands. Women, like men, were mobilized to build roads, irrigation canals, and reservoirs. In Gedatou, women's teams competed with men's teams to flatten the hillock or "bump" (*geda*) that had given the village its name; deep plowing, close planting, and "fertilizing" fields with dredged river sand or rubble from torn-down houses further added to the workload. Many young women enthusiastically embraced the challenge of demonstrating that they could work as hard as men. As Kimberley Manning has shown, female activists and grassroots leaders during the Great Leap Forward were often indifferent or hostile toward aspects of CCP policy that stressed the reproductive role of women: health programs, sanitation, and protection from overwork and disease.[54] In Guanzhong too, women activists chose spectacular self-denial and punishing work, rather than protection from physical suffering, as their route to liberation.[55] Reproductive work in the household, whether it consisted of raising children or clothing a family, was difficult to reconcile with this role.

In the long run, however, it was the intensification of cotton cultivation that added most to women's workloads in the region. Cotton is a labor-intensive crop at the best of times; it was especially so in Maoist China, where fields were weeded, insect pests removed, and cotton picked by hand. Because cotton yields decline rapidly after several years of cultivation, teams had to mobilize more and more labor simply to keep output at constant levels. Traditionally, cotton cultivation in Guanzhong had been men's work, but it became almost completely feminized after collectivization. Tens of thousands of women participated in so-called "Silver Flower Contests," competitions to raise cotton output through improved—and, in most cases, more labor-intensive—cultivation techniques. As Gail Hershatter and Gao Xiaoxian have shown, these campaigns had a liberating effect on female activists and labor models, some of whom gained national prominence, albeit often at great cost to their health and private life.[56] However, women who did not aspire to activist or model status often experienced these contests as exhausting and badly remunerated production drives.

While women's participation in the fields increased dramatically, little was done to reduce domestic workloads. Most villages introduced canteens during the Great Leap Forward, and some experimented with forms of collective childcare, but these efforts, poorly thought through and hastily implemented, remained unpopular and were abandoned in the famine years that followed the Leap.[57] Women's textile work also continued unchanged. In theory, the introduction of rationing in 1954 should have ensured that every person received an adequate supply of factory-produced cloth. Cloth rations differed widely from year to year and from place to place, but rural rations were consistently lower than urban ones, by a ratio of about 1:2.[58] Rations were also set lower in historically poor mountain areas than in the wealthier plains. To counter accusations of unfairness, state publications explained that rationing was not an instrument of leveling but was designed to assure that people were supplied the quantity of cloth they were accustomed to.[59] Average rural rations in Guanzhong dropped from around 5 square meters in the early 1950s to less than 1 square meter in the crisis years of 1960 and 1961, and then gradually rose back to about 4 square meters per year.[60] Based on my interviews, I estimate a yearly *subsistence* minimum of 3 square meters of *tubu* cloth, or 4 square meters of factory cloth (which is lighter and wears out more quickly). This is enough for one suit of summer clothes, one suit of winter clothes, and a quilt and blanket shared between two, to be replaced every three to five years. Twice that amount (6 m² of *tubu* or 8 m² of factory cloth) would constitute a *social* minimum—the amount needed, according to local standards, by a person who is poor but not destitute. Ration supplies, in other words, were sufficient to keep people covered but not to keep them decently clothed according to the very frugal standards of the time.

However, rural people in Zhouzhi did not use their rations. All my informants agreed that only village cadres (who were expected to wear "urban" clothing when they attended meetings) and courting or recently married couples wore factory cloth. Most other people sold their ration coupons on the black market and continued to wear *tubu* until the 1970s. The reason was cash scarcity: high quotas and low state procurement prices for wheat and cotton depressed collective incomes and reduced the amount of cash and grain that was distributed at year's end to team members. In Gedatou, the average value of a male labor day was around 0.5 yuan, with substantial variations between teams and over time; women earned about 0.4 yuan a day. Assuming 300 workdays for a man and 250 workdays for a woman, a family with two earners earned 250 yuan a year. Since most of this income was retained by the collective to compensate for grain consumed by the family, disposable income was often as low as 50 yuan—barely enough to purchase salt, vinegar, schoolbooks, and other necessary items. By making cloth at home, households not only saved the money they would otherwise have spent on factory cloth (between 5 and 15 yuan per person) but also earned an additional 1.2 to 6 yuan from the sale of their coupons.

As mentioned previously, the main source for homemade cloth was the "self-retained cotton" (*ziliumian*) ration, set in most teams at 1 kilogram per person. One kilogram of cotton yields about 9 meters of *kuanbu* cloth (45 cm wide), or about 4 square meters—more than the subsistence minimum of 3 square meters. However, only part of the ration could be used for spinning: in an area where few people owned any wool or leather garments, warmth in the winter came from cotton padding. A warm winter suit contained about

1 kilogram of cotton padding; a large quilt required 1.5 to 2 kilograms. If quilts and padded garments were taken apart once a year and the cotton was washed and fluffed, the padding could be used for up to ten years, but some new cotton must be added every year. If we subtract the amount needed for padding as well as losses in spinning, we arrive at a yarn availability of 590 grams, equivalent to 2.5 square meters of cloth—somewhat below the subsistence minimum.[61]

People without additional sources of cotton would have reached the end of the collective period with their clothes not only patched (as indeed most rural people did) but in complete tatters. How, then, did people manage? Part of the answer was pilfering: while farmers I interviewed often maintained that taking cotton from the fields was "impossible," former team leaders said that the practice was widespread and joked about women "returning from the cotton harvest with big bellies" because they had stuffed so much lint in their jackets. Retired commune-level cadres also said that teams hid part of their harvest; in retrospect, they saw this as legitimate, even though they had once tried to stamp out the practice.[62] Teams sold cotton on the black market to finance necessary purchases of fertilizer, pesticides, and fuel. Many teams also maintained a social fund to help families defray the costs of marriages and funerals. Young men who were about to marry received 1 to 2 *kun* (5–10 kg) of ginned cotton to help them pay their bride price; some teams also gave 1 to 2 *jin* (0.5–1 kg) of cotton to help families clothe their dead. At year-end meetings, when teams distributed cash and grain income, many teams also gave out "secret" shares of cotton— sometimes as much as an extra kilogram per person.

Another source of cotton was the black market, fed by illegal sales of collective stocks. Cash-strapped farmers rarely bought cotton for their own clothing needs, but in a common pattern, women bought cotton, transformed it into cloth, and exchanged cloth for more cotton. By doing this repeatedly, they could earn cash income for everyday needs or accumulate cotton for a bride price or cloth for a dowry. Profits in black market weaving were relatively high, especially if one made the long trek to the cattle fairs of Dianzhen and Mazhao at the foot of the Qinling Mountains, where people from remote mountain villages exchanged livestock and forest products for cloth and winter stores. A woman who bought three *jin* of raw cotton for 4 to 6 yuan could produce one standard-length cloth (14 × 0.45 m) in ten to twelve days of work and sell it for 20 to 30 yuan, earning much more than what she would have earned in the fields. Several interviewees, including a former chairwoman of the village Women's Federation, admitted that they sold one or two pieces every year; one old lady even claimed that she had sold about ten pieces every year for several consecutive years. Most people, however, said that weaving for the market was too risky and that in any case they could not withdraw labor from the team to the extent necessary for commercial weaving.

The Experience of Work under the Collectives

Women in Zhouzhi, and elsewhere in rural China, participated in four distinct economic spheres: a planned economy in which the state was the first claimant to labor time and goods, leaving collectives and individuals only with what they needed according to state estimates; a household economy in which women provided for their children and performed labor for husbands and in-laws; a black market economy that siphoned resources such as cotton, cloth, and coupons out of the villages and into the cities; and a gift economy in which no marriage could be concluded, no newborn child accepted into the community, and no dead person buried without the ritual exchange of cloth. Demands from these distinct spheres converged on the bodies of women, who were forced to work triple shifts in collective agriculture, unrecognized and invisible home textile work, and bearing and raising unprecedented numbers of children. Under conditions of pervasive scarcity, to fulfill one obligation often meant to neglect another one. Each hour spent in the field was an hour not spent at the loom; more farmwork meant more cash and grain but also fewer clothes for the family and thus potentially a loss of social standing. Weighing fieldwork against textile work was not just a material consideration—full stomachs versus warmth—but a choice between obligations toward state and collective and those toward one's family. Both obligations were deeply felt: the leader of the women's agricultural team was not a remote functionary, but rather a neighbor and perhaps a relative; her demand that each able-bodied woman work three shifts a day could not simply be shrugged off.

For many women, the only way to square this circle was to work ever longer hours, up to the limit of endurance. Women rose before men and children and went on working long after men had gone to bed; in contrast to men, who took naps in the afternoon, women filled their short breaks with textile work. In busy periods, women routinely slept for only three to four hours every night. Many women I interviewed remembered falling asleep over their spinning wheels, and some said that the only rest they had for many years was when they fell sick; but even then, they went back to work before full recovery. Pregnant women often worked into the last few weeks of pregnancy and returned to the fields a few weeks after giving birth, not even sitting out the traditional month of postpartum confinement (*zuo yuezi*).

Intense collective labor, to be sure, had its joys. Gao Xiaoxian, in her work on the Silver Flower Contest, quotes the enthusiastic recollection of a former activist:

> At that time, we had such a bustling life working in the fields! Recalling those times, we had such a happy life. When we went weeding in the fields, each with a hoe working in a long line, we talked, laughed, and sang. Sometimes we gathered together and had great fun. It was really a carefree life—just wonderful![63]

How women experienced collective work depended largely on their work experience before collectivization. For women from poor families, farmwork was nothing new. Feng Jinlian, for example—a sprightly eighty years old at the time of the interview—learned to spin when she was six and to weave when she was twelve. Poverty forced her brothers to hire out as farmhands, so that she and her sisters had to do most of the work on the farm. She claimed, with some pride, that there was no task in the house or on the farm that she could not do; unusually for a woman, she knew how to plow and drive an oxcart. At the opposite end of the spectrum was Du Fengying, born into a landlord family in the same year as Feng. She learned to spin at age seven or eight, did not weave until she was seventeen, and did not do any farmwork before land reform; in fact, she hardly ever left her home. Her first experience of farmwork was in the early 1950s, when she and other women from well-off families began to work outside—driven more by the wish to remove the stigma of idle "landlord wife" than by economic need. She remembers farmwork as difficult and "awkward" (*bieniu*); initially, she and her fellow workers thought they would never learn the knack. Archival documents from the 1950s also mention women's lack of agricultural skill and enthusiasm for farmwork; one document speaks of the need to transform women's prevailing attitude of "if you have wine today, drink it today" into a spirit of "meticulous and precise farming, long-term advance planning, and thrift in food and raw material use."[64] Interestingly, reports by the Women's Federation are similar in tone, accusing rural women of "confused" or "muddled" attitudes toward production.[65]

Whether they grew up as poor peasants or as landlords, all women I interviewed worked from an early age. For them, the quality of work did not depend on whether it was hard or not; all work was hard in different ways. Bad work was lonely, isolated work; the worst work was that of a young wife harassed by a strict mother-in-law. Good work was work with peers, accompanied by jokes and laughter. Whether the work took place inside or outside the home was immaterial. Du Fengying, who grew up cloistered in her home, remembered her childhood as a happy one: there were nine girls in her extended family, and while they spun most of the day, they were allowed to take breaks in the garden, climb trees, play with marbles, or do paper cutting. Feng Jinlian, by contrast, experienced her work out in the fields as lonely and terrifying. Nobody, she said, spoke to a girl in the fields—not even other girls of the same age. Her most vivid childhood memory is that of encountering a wolf in the fields: a stark symbol of the danger, loneliness, and isolation of outdoors work. But the same work was good work if carried out with peers. All my interviewees described work in the teams as joyful (*renao* and *gaoxing* were the terms most often used) because it took place in the company of equals, free from the supervision of seniors.

Another source of work satisfaction was the learning of new skills. As Sigrid Schmalzer shows in Chapter 6, participation in the mass science movement had the potential to empower people who had traditionally been denied access to technology and scientific knowledge. Gao Xiaoxian describes the enthusiasm with which young women participated in the "Qiuxiang field" movement of mass experimentation, named after the model cotton cultivator Zhang Qiuxiang.[66] The women I interviewed, most of whom were neither activists nor grassroots leaders, had a rather more jaded view of mass experimentation. Qiuxiang fields, they recalled, did indeed produce higher-than-average yields, but they also required a very high input of unpaid volunteer labor. One woman laughingly recalled a competition between her all-female Qiuxiang team and an all-male "Wang Baojing corn-growing team" in which the women applied huge quantities of solid manure to the cotton plants while the men applied equally large quantities of urine to the corn. The initial results for both teams were encouraging, but in the end, the overfertilized plants collapsed and both teams lost their harvest.[67] Other women said that experimentation in the Qiuxiang fields consisted mainly in applying the extra rations of synthetic fertilizer that were made available by the agricultural extension station and that they did not learn any new skills.[68]

Despite these limitations, there can be no doubt that Silver Flower Contests and experimental fields gave a new visibility to women's work and that young women, in particular, embraced their new social role as socialist producers. However, the valorization of new types of women's work was mirrored by the devaluation of other types. While women became visible as agricultural producers, their textile work became invisible, despite the fact that it continued to underpin people's material and social lives. Rituals such as the Skill Fairy Festival on the seventh day of the seventh month were abolished as feudal superstitions, and the exchange of textiles for births, weddings, funerals, and other celebrations was delegitimized. The way socially necessary work was emptied of cultural meaning is most evident if we look at a brief episode in early PRC policies. For a short time in 1949–1950, local authorities encouraged women to form spinning and weaving cooperatives, partly to draw women into politics, partly to fill an urgent need for textiles at a time when most cotton mills were not yet operational.[69] Nie Yuzhen, the sole surviving member of Gedatou's only spinning co-op, remembers how this work raised her status in her family and gave her financial independence from her mother-in-law. She also stressed that her little co-op was the first seed of the collective economy in Gedatou, established long before the first agricultural cooperative. Textile work transformed her life: because of the success of her co-op, she was elected chairwoman of the village Women's Federation and later became a representative in the county-level People's Congress. Yet she emphatically denied that her work in the co-op had any political significance: spinning and weaving were "something outside production" (*shengchan zhiwai de shi*), a "remnant of the old society." Textile work could not be considered work (*gongzuo*), labor (*laodong*), or production (*shengchan*); her spinning coop was nothing but "a group of girls playing around together."

Revolution and Everyday Life

Echoing Joan Kelly's question if European women had a renaissance, Gail Hershatter asks if Chinese rural women had a revolution, and if so, when.[70] There can be little doubt that women's lives were radically transformed in the decades between 1949 and 1976, yet these changes were not neatly synchronized with the accepted chronology of mass movements and political campaigns. For example, 1966 was not a date of great significance for Guanzhong women: even though some villages saw vicious factional struggles, none of the women I interviewed mentioned the Cultural Revolution. When asked, one woman explained that "the Cultural Revolution was all about striking down landlords and rich peasants; this had nothing to do with us poor and lower-middle peasants. Those who participated were also landlords, rich peasants, and officials; we ordinary poor and lower-middle peasants didn't talk about who was right or wrong—we simply did not take part."

For women who came of age at the time of land reform and collectivization, the revolutionary changes of the collective period were filtered through the experience of scarcity and overwork. "Holding up half of the sky" came at a heavy price for women of this generation. In interview after interview, they recalled fatigue, sleep deprivation, and exhaustion from constant overwork, as well as the constant shortage of cotton, cloth, grain, oil, salt, and cash. There can be little doubt that these women worked harder than both their mothers' and their daughters' generations. Whether their material lives improved is hard to tell; average cotton cloth consumption—like average grain consumption—stagnated from 1956 to 1976 and was below pre-1949 levels for most of the collective years.[71] The extreme scarcity of textile, and with it extreme self-exploitation, came to an end only in the 1970s, due largely to the maturation of China's chemical industry.[72] From the early 1970s on, increased input of nitrogenous and phosphate fertilizers led to higher yields in the cotton fields, while diesel-powered irrigation pumps and improved pesticide sprayers reduced workloads in the fields.[73] At the same time, China began to produce synthetics: viscose rayon since 1959, rising quantities of polyamide and polyester since 1975.[74] By the early 1980s, the average rural person bought two meters of *diqueliang* (dacron) a year.[75] Since these garments were durable even under the harsh conditions of rural China, people were able, for the first time in years, to add new clothing to their wardrobe year after year. To a large extent, it was the advent of the age of plastics that ended a textile crisis that had lasted a quarter century.

Dacron was only the beginning: from the mid-1970s on, cheap, mass-produced goods began to flow to the villages. As late as 1970, the average rural household in Guanzhong contained very few factory-made goods— perhaps a thermos flask, a few enamel bowls, a mirror, and a few clothes made from factory cloth. The only foodstuffs that came from outside the area were salt, sugar, cookies, tea, and alcohol; all but the first of these were rare delicacies. Apart from woks, knives, and some simple farm tools, households owned few metal implements. Spinning wheels, looms, and other wooden tools were made by local carpenters. Houses were built with local clay and timber (kiln-fired bricks and tiles did not come into general use before the 1970s) and heated with local corn and sorghum stalks. Most villages in Guanzhong began to generate electricity in the 1960s, though private use remained limited to one light bulb per household. Bicycles and sewing machines began to appear in rural homes in the last years of the collective period, together with more plentiful supplies of cloth, metal goods, and plastics.

By the 1980s, one of the central promises of socialism—that of a mutually beneficial rural-urban exchange in which raw materials flowed from the countryside to the city and cheap manufactured goods back from the city to the countryside—was slowly becoming reality. Rural people who had grown grain and cotton for the urban sector but had remained too poor to purchase the products that were made with the inputs they provided were now rapidly replacing homespun with factory yarn, hand cloth with factory textiles, cloth shoes with rubber boots, etc. Buying factory goods brought release from household chores; at the same time, labor-saving technologies in agriculture reduced time spent in the fields. If women who came of age in the 1950s bore a double burden in household and collective agriculture, their daughters were free to join the swelling ranks of migrant workers because little work was left to do at home and in the field, and what was left to do could be done by their mothers. At the same time, they were compelled to leave, because new needs (for example, expensive schooling for their children) had arisen that could not be denied and could be satisfied only with money earned in wages. Rural people were now integrated in the polity as producers *for* and consumers *from* the national market, in ways that proved more lasting and more binding than those of the collective order. These transformations would not have been possible without the invisible and unpaid work of women in the collective period.

6

Youth and the "Great Revolutionary Movement" of Scientific Experiment in 1960s–1970s Rural China

SIGRID SCHMALZER

During the 1960s and 1970s, millions of young Chinese people moved to the countryside to be tempered by the "three great revolutionary movements." Originating in a May 1963 quotation from Chairman Mao, this became a stock phrase in the Cultural Revolution. But what were these three movements? The first two are familiar enough. Class struggle constituted political study meetings, criticism/self-criticism sessions, and violent and sometimes deadly assaults on people identified as "class enemies." The struggle for production was manifested in back-breaking labor that defined life for rural people and offered a profound, and often bitter, lesson for sent-down urbanites. But what of the third? Rarely discussed in secondary literature, the "great revolutionary movement" of scientific experiment was nonetheless a significant experience for millions of people in rural China, and especially educated youth. In some areas, as many as one-third of urban, sent-down youth participated in scientific experiment.[1] Whether cultivating bacterial fertilizer in makeshift laboratories, observing insect behavior to develop more effective control technologies, or designing new agricultural machinery, youth provided key support to the state's goal of transforming agriculture. And participating in scientific experiment presented opportunities for young people to pursue both intellectual and revolutionary dreams.

The idea that science should be pitched to youth is by no means unique to China, but the Chinese case stands out because of the degree to which science itself was characterized as youthful and youth themselves under-stood as agents of revolutionary scientific transformation.[2] Nor was Mao the first in China to link science, youth, and revolution: he inherited this from the May Fourth Movement, which called for youth to rise up from under the traditions that demanded their subservience and which understood science as a fresh, new system of thought struggling to sprout amidst the thick and constraining roots of tradition. Mao saw science as a liberating force—a "weapon in [man's] fight for freedom."[3] In his widely propagated essay *On Practice,* he defined "social practice" as "material production, class struggle, or scientific experiment,"[4] a notion he expanded on in 1963: "Class struggle, the struggle for production, and scientific experiment are the three great revolutionary movements for building a mighty socialist country. These movements are a sure guarantee that Communists will be free from bureau-cracy and immune against revisionism and dogmatism, and will for ever remain invincible."[5]

Youth, too, represented a revolutionary force for Mao. On the eve of his victory in 1949, Mao counted the "student youth" among his most important supporters.[6] And in 1955, he famously wrote, "The young people are the most active and vital force in society. They are the most eager to learn and the least conservative in their thinking."[7] These qualities became the basis for the leadership role that youth were encouraged to take during the Cultural Revolution. They were certainly "active and vital" in their efforts to destroy the old society, but the same qualities were also the basis for the far more positive, constructive vision of youth involvement in science. The courage and energy they were seen to possess made youth apparently well suited to the task of transforming science from a conservative, elite, bourgeois field of activity into one worthy of the new, revolutionary society.

Memoirs by former Red Guards dominate English-language literature on youth in the Mao era, such that our mental picture of young people in rural China collapses onto an image of the former Red Guard, urban, "sent-down educated youth" (*xiaxiang zhishi qingnian*).[8] But long before 1968, rural youth had begun traveling to county seats to receive secondary education, only to return to their villages to rejoin agricultural labor. These "returned educated youth" (*huixiang zhishi qingnian*) were the original targets of Mao's declaration (another Cultural Revolution stock quotation, but dating to 1955): "All such educated young people who can go and work in the countryside should be glad to do so. The countryside is a big world where much can be accomplished."[9] For the state, rural-to-urban migration of young people presented the twin problems of urban unemployment and rural brain-drain.[10] Hence the need to convince rural youth that a return to the farm would not constitute a waste of talent (*qucai*), but rather a great opportunity for accomplishment (*dayou zuowei*). And hence the significance of rural programs to encourage youth to engage in scientific experiment. When urban youth began their massive migration to the countryside, they joined a "revolutionary movement" already in progress: rural, returned youth out-numbered urban, sent-down youth manyfold, and returned youth almost certainly made up the majority of participants in scientific experiment.[11]

Already in the 1950s, youth were central participants in efforts to extend new agricultural technologies and methods in rural areas.[12] This is not sur-prising: after all, young people were most apt to have an up-to-date educa-tion, and having studied science in secondary school, they were in the best position to apply scientific knowledge to such perennial agricultural prob-lems as soil fertilization, insect control, and breed improvement. Moreover, training youth in new methods represented a better long-term investment than training older peasants. By 1965, what were now called "rural scientific experiment groups" (*nongcun kexue shiyan xiaozu*)—with youth participa-tion especially emphasized—had grown to more than 400,000 nationwide.[13]

Charting the history of this third "great revolutionary movement" requires careful, but also creative, interpretation of available sources, which include published books and articles, posters, archival documents, diaries, hand-copied fiction, memoirs, and interviews. Most of the books, articles, and even archival documents are easily identified as propaganda—that is, they were produced by state actors for the purpose of disseminating ideas the state wanted people to embrace. Despite their failure to portray reality, such sources are invaluable for the clarity with which they articulate the state's voice and thus allow us to recapture the vision of science that state actors disseminated to Chinese youth, which differed significantly from the per-spective dominant today. Today in China, as in the West, science is largely accepted as the province of professionals. Propaganda materials of the 1960s and 1970s present a very different perspective on science: as a "great revolu-tionary movement," scientific experiment was depicted as part of a larger effort to overturn the authority of experts in ivory towers and to break down the division between mental and manual labor.

Reconstructing the experiences of individuals who participated in scientific experiment constitutes a considerably more difficult challenge. Memoirs written in later years, along with oral history interviews, speak to the personal experiences of Mao-era youth in science. Freed of the need to conform to Mao-era politics, such sources are especially helpful in conveying the narrators' doubts and disappointments. However, they are also inevitably filtered through the ideas and values of the era in which they were produced and therefore cannot be accepted as wholesale correctives to Mao-era propaganda. Diaries produced in the Mao era and published later present their own set of problems: not only is there the potential for selection and alteration after the fact, but youth are known to have kept politically virtuous diaries with the hope that they would be found by Party officials. Nonetheless, some diaries offer insight into the ways youth actually experienced events; and in many other cases, they provide clear evidence of the degree to which youth had mastered the state's language and perceived the state's vision. I consider hand-copied fiction similarly, as a type of source that, used thoughtfully, provides rare evidence as to the values of Mao-era youth and their appropriation of meanings conveyed in propaganda.

Bringing all of these sources together, I seek to make several related arguments, but none of them involves a claim about the overall success or failure of the rural scientific experiment movement. The post-Mao secondary literature on Mao-era agricultural policies has typically painted a very grim picture.[14] Today some agricultural officials and scholars in China, along with a few scholars abroad, are seeking to revise that verdict as it relates to specific areas of agricultural science and technology, including agricultural extension and the scientific experiment movement.[15] That is not my goal in this chapter, though I will touch on the meanings ascribed to failure in the historical sources themselves.

More centrally, I argue first that science—and specifically youth participation in science—mattered deeply to the Mao-era state, both because it was needed for the socialist economy and because it was seen as a revolutionary force in society. The priority placed on science drove the production of propaganda materials aimed at recruiting young people for the "scientific

experiment movement" and convincing them that science should be practiced in revolutionary ways. I further find that science mattered to youth,
who often volunteered to participate in scientific experiment and saw in science various opportunities—including diversion, intellectual satisfaction,
revolutionary heroism, adventure, and future education and employment.
And although youth experiences by no means mirrored the vision projected
by the state, I find enough resonance in the sources to argue that state propaganda had a significant impact on how youth understood science and
their role in it. In the first four of the sections that follow, the goal will be to
capture as closely as possible what vision the state sought to project to youth
through its propaganda. I will then turn to the more challenging task of
reconstructing youth experience, which will in turn allow consideration of
the extent to which youth themselves embraced the state's vision of revolutionary science.

State Vision: Science as Opportunity

Youth participation in agricultural science was critical to the state's goal of
agricultural transformation. The ideal "three-in-one" structure of agricultural experiment groups—designed to insure a mix of technical expertise,
adherence to the Party line, and revolutionary legitimacy—called for the
involvement of trained agricultural technicians alongside local cadres and
"old peasants." However, when the movement took off in 1965, there were
simply not enough technicians to go around; the state needed to tap the
energies of educated youth, and especially rural educated youth. The copious
published accounts of urban youth settling successfully in the countryside
and rural youth happily returning to help socialism in their home villages
should be read at least in part as an effort to convince educated youth to view
scientific experiment as "a great opportunity."

An example of such an account can be found in a 1968 *People's Daily*
article on an educated youth from Shanghai, Mei Minquan. The story went
that young Mei went to the "Great Northern Wilderness" in response to
Mao's call to "achieve great things" in the countryside. Finding himself
assigned to a forested area with low productive value, Mei was said to have
hatched a plan to import from the Shanghai area the fungus delicacy known
as "silver ears" (or white tree ears) and let the forest "blossom with silver

flowers." When he told others of his idea, he met with opposition. Some objected that the climates were too different; others questioned whether a secondary school graduate had the necessary microbiological knowledge. But the poor peasants were reportedly very supportive, saying, "For years it's been obvious that the timber has not been worth cutting. You youth have ambition and culture: go for the gusto!" Mei felt encouraged by the peasants' support, and he also appreciated the words of caution from the others. After some additional training at the agricultural institute in Shanghai, Mei succeeded in growing beautiful silver flowers in the Great Northern Wilderness. The moral of the story was that "silver ears and educated youth alike could settle down in the wilderness, and alike they needed to undergo struggle" to make that transition.[16] The story thus simultaneously justified the rustication movement, celebrated struggle, and offered inspirational testimony of the opportunities available to youth in improving agriculture through science.

Stories about returned youth similarly asserted the tremendous ultimate worth of an educated rural life; the chance to participate in rural scientific experiment offered the potential to apply one's knowledge to an endeavor recognized as both politically revolutionary and culturally advanced. A Communist Youth League document from 1965 reported on the experiences of ten returned youth in Yangchun County, Guangdong. In the beginning, they reportedly thought that participating in agricultural labor would be a waste of their talent (*dacai xiaoyong*), but after they began participating in scientific experiment, they realized that in the countryside there was much they could learn (*dayou xuewen ke xue*) and much they could contribute. As a mark of how their thought had been transformed, the account highlighted that they had stopped talking about food and clothing all the time and had instead begun talking about science and studying technology.[17]

A 1974 collection of stories about Beijing-area youth involved in scientific experiment repeatedly highlighted this theme. One youth wrote:

> I recall that when we graduated some of my classmates were worried that in participating in agricultural production they would lose the knowledge they had learned—how incredibly funny! Now I think that not only was the knowledge I studied in the past not in danger of being lost, but it was really deficient. Take forecasting as an example. If you

want to forecast whether a certain insect pest is going to appear, you need to use entomological knowledge to research the insect pest's life habits and how climate, geographical environment, and other conditions affect it, and you need to do lots of survey statistics. When you control the pest using chemical pesticides, if you don't have the necessary chemical knowledge, then you'll have safety and usage problems. In sum, the physics, chemistry, and mathematics you study in secondary school are all needed.

Another wrote, "For educated youth, going to the countryside isn't the end of the study mission but rather the beginning of an important educational stage. The countryside is another big school, the poor and lower-middle peasants are our excellent teachers, and scientific experiment is one of the courses in this big school." Sending secondary school graduates back to the countryside was not a case of "using a talented person in an insignificant position," nor of "water buffaloes jumping into a well." It was not a "waste of talent," but a "great opportunity."[18]

Propaganda accounts typically presented participation in scientific experiment as not only a "great opportunity" but a choice that youth were free to take or leave. In a 1966 Women's Federation document, a model youth named Huang Chunlai reported that others had encouraged her to take a job as a worker at the state farm because the pay was good and the workday only eight hours long. But she remembered that the Party had sent her to an agricultural high school so that she could build the new countryside, so she continued to devote herself to the struggle for production and scientific experiment.[19] In a 1972 account, the opening of a new chemical fertilizer plant excited local people because the plant represented "modernization" and there was a real future in becoming a technician there. The returned youth Lang Yuping reportedly debated whether to head to the new factory or take the opportunity presented by the brigade Party secretary to study to become an insect pest forecaster. "That night I was restless thinking it over. *Which one should I choose?* Then before my eyes floated an image of the Party secretary carrying an insecticide sprayer and directing us to exterminate armyworm. He said that we can't let in armyworms just like we can't let class enemies wreak havoc in the fields. . . . I realized that the countryside needed me and decided to stay and do pest forecasting."[20] Presenting scientific experiment as a choice not only implied a certain amount of autonomy youth supposedly enjoyed but, more importantly, emphasized the nobility of individual commitment, especially when nobody could deny that other, more urban paths offered better chances for personal gain.

State Vision: Youth as Intellectuals

State dependence on experts presented an uncomfortable dilemma, especially for leaders committed to the radical agenda of overturning elite intellectual authority. Although they were hardly "ivory tower" elites, educated youth bore the politically ambiguous label "educated," and Mao and others frequently spoke of "the intellectuals and student youth" as a single category. The "little red book" even conflated the two by including in the chapter entitled "Youth" a quotation that dealt solely (and critically) with "intellectuals" and mentioned "youth" not at all.[21] Propaganda on the scientific experiment movement thus took pains to distinguish between scientific attitudes associated with bourgeois intellectual elites and properly revolutionary ones.

The first principle embraced at a 1965 national conference on youth in rural scientific experiment was that scientific experiment served the revolution and was not for the purpose of gaining fame or private profit.[22] The *People's Daily* reporting on the conference hammered this point home: where youth embraced revolutionary ideals, they succeeded, and where they pursued science for personal fame or profit, they failed.[23] In 1972, *People's Daily* introduced a group of youth sent down from Nanjing to a production brigade in rural Jiangsu: "At one time because some of the youth had been influenced by capitalist-class ideas about fame and profit, their experiment topics departed from the practical needs" of the production brigade. They were "seeking overnight fame" and kept "holding out their hand for chemical fertilizer" so they could achieve a high yield. The Party branch organized them to engage in revolutionary criticism so they would realize that "scientific experiment is not about making individuals famous, but about transforming the face of the countryside."[24]

Intellectuals were also allegedly prone to relying on books rather than immersing themselves in the politically more respectable form of knowledge that came through practice. The group of Nanjing youth sent down to Jiangsu reportedly discovered the hard way that what they read in books about seed germination would not necessarily hold up in practice.[25] Another story tells of a recently sent-down youth excited to improve crop production through application of cobalt chloride, which he had learned about in school. But the team leader gently admonished him that the coming heavy rains would make such efforts useless. At first the youth assumed that the team leader was merely ignorant of science, but when not long after a tremendous rain flooded the fields, he reportedly realized the truth of Mao's words: "If intellectuals do not unite with the masses of workers and peasants, then all they do will come to naught."[26]

Nevertheless, propaganda of the 1960s and 1970s apparently could not avoid endorsing books as a key resource for youth in the scientific experiment movement. The most important books, of course, were those containing Mao's own words. But books on science and technology also played an important role. The account of Deng Yantang, one of the participants in the 1965 national conference on rural youth in scientific experiment, explicitly emphasized this issue. Abstaining from smoking and tea houses, Deng saved his money to buy books and magazines. He would go to town intending to buy food, enter bookstores to flip through a few books, and end by buying the books and returning home with an empty stomach. He began by reading pamphlets, then later books on agricultural theory. If he needed to understand the meaning of a term, he would look it up in one of his books or write to an expert at the provincial agricultural institute. He concluded: "In [acquiring] knowledge of breeding, practice is the foundation and books are the path."[27] A story from the 1974 collection handled the practice/book-learning dilemma in an innovative manner. A returned youth, Wang Chunling, experimented by taking weak piglets and placing them on the front nipples to help them grow more quickly. However, she then learned from an "old comrade" that this had been described long ago in books; she had taken a "circuitous path." Criticizing Liu Shaoqi, Lin Biao, and the theory of innate intelligence (in 1974 a crucial ingredient for political legitimacy), she concluded that books are the "synthesis of earlier people's experience." And so, she emphasized, in addition to pursuing one's own practice, it was important to read books so as to minimize circuitous paths.[28] This was the kind of politically savvy approach that state propaganda encouraged youth to heed as they made use of the book learning that had earned them the title "educated youth."

State Vision: Science as Revolutionary

Like their counterparts in the humanities, scientists faced persecution in Mao-era China because of their status as "intellectuals," "authorities," and "experts." But scientists had several things going for them that substantially reduced their risk. First, science was seen as both essential to socialist construction and capable of disproving traditional ways of thinking. Second, science often involved physical work—sometimes dangerous physical work—and therefore had some claim to the privileged category of *labor*.[29] So it was never science itself that came under attack, but rather elite, bourgeois authority in science. This in turn shaped the way propaganda presented youth participation. Propaganda stories about model youth participants in scientific experiment thus took pains to highlight the political character of their efforts. It was not enough that their efforts should result in the implementation of more effective technologies and thereby increase production. Rather, scientific experiment had to be revolutionary. In propaganda accounts, revolutionary science often involved hard physical labor or braving dangers to life and limb, but most importantly it was explicitly rooted in class struggle and pursued through class consciousness.

Portrayals of the scientific work of educated youth typically highlighted the gritty, daring face of science in the field rather than science as pursued in laboratories and libraries. Youth possessed the energy and courage necessary to try new ideas and to withstand physical hardships. In 1959, the media celebrated the discovery of large deposits of minerals by a "young girl" and geologist "hero" named Liu Jinmei. Liu "traversed some 7,000 kilometers in the towering ridges of the rugged Changpai Mountains in Northeast China, the haunt of tigers and bears."[30] In 1973, Lang Yuping, a returned youth in Miyun County (near Beijing), sought to control a wheat virus with a highly toxic insecticide: "One time I really was poisoned, dizzy, nauseous, sweating. . . . I was scared to death that I . . . would lose the fall crop. I went to the clinic, got an injection, and continued work. The Party branch [official] told me to go to the hospital to get a checkup and rest a few days, but I didn't go."[31] Nominally self-critical, the account in fact emphasized the youth's courageous and willing self-sacrifice. Other examples abound of young people celebrated for braving cold, rain, mosquitoes, and sweat, and going so far as to refuse medical treatment when ill, all because of their dedication to science and to production.[32]

But no amount of grit could entirely remove the ambiguity surrounding the intellectual character of educated youth. Thus stories of youth in science also frequently framed scientific experiment within the larger narrative of class struggle. According to one story, published in 1974 about an incident in 1969, county leaders called on returned educated youth to hybridize sorghum, but many people were doubtful. When the initial experiments failed, "class enemies" reportedly took the opportunity to attack science. But, as the story went, the production brigade Party branch organized the youth with the commune masses to struggle against the class enemies and study Mao, with the result that the youth learned to sex the sorghum plants more accurately and ultimately achieved success.[33]

In most stories, opposition from reactionary forces was balanced by the enthusiastic support of the peasants—and especially the "poor and middle peasants." But sometimes poor peasants themselves were said to have opposed the research. Deng Yantang (from the 1965 conference) successfully created hybridized rice strains, but he reportedly encountered criticism from old peasants who said that the hybrids looked good but tasted bad, and that "high lanterns see far, but not close." The Party secretary affirmed the peasants' criticism and reminded Deng that scientific experiment must serve production. Deng reread Mao's "Serve the People," and his thoughts clarified: "Yes! Cultivating superior varieties appears to be a question of technology, but first is the political-orientation question of breeding for whom and serving whom. If the orientation is wrong, the experiment will go off track."[34]

The concern that youth follow the lead of peasants was very much in keeping with Mao's own statements and with the dominant policy thrust of the late 1960s and 1970s. Thus such stories almost invariably emphasized at least their cooperation with, and usually their reliance on, or even subservience to, peasants. For example, a group of sent-down youth in Hebei Province set up an experiment station with the support of the local Party branch. Instead of allowing themselves to be guided by the "old peasants," however, they pursued impractical ideas in an attempt to "startle" people with their innovation, such as hybridizing cotton and paulownia to create a perennial "cotton tree." And so the story continued, with local Party officials becoming aware of the problem and educating the youth about the importance of uniting with the masses, then the youth reportedly becoming very successful in designing new forms of pest control and fertilizer.[35]

In many cases, references to youth being led by the masses appeared merely ritualistic, with little evidence as to the relevance of the education they were supposedly receiving. But some accounts were more specific in this regard. In one story, a rural youth graduated from secondary school, returned to the countryside, and was assigned to a weather station where poor and lower-middle class peasants observed leech behavior to forecast the weather. At first he reportedly had a negative attitude and did not realize how much he could learn from the peasants. Then came a day when the youth carelessly lost his leeches. He found a new leech, but his next forecast failed. A peasant explained that there are three kinds of leeches and that he had collected the wrong kind. The youth then realized that old peasants had a wealth of experience watching weather patterns. He visited more than eighty old peasants to collect their knowledge of observing animals to predict weather.[36] Such stories underscored the Maoist class-based philosophy of science, in which "old peasants"—by virtue of their class status—possessed knowledge of critical importance to the pursuit of agricultural science.

Warnings about the potential for youth to become divorced from the peasant masses and acquire bourgeois attitudes about knowledge, fame, and profit existed in tension with encouragement to imagine themselves as revolutionary heroes. Propaganda often directly encouraged youth to aspire to heroism and so provided plenty of room for celebrating individual efforts and achievements. The books that came out of youth conferences on scientific experiment highlighted the experiences of notable individuals to offer models and inspiration. Young people who related their stories spoke of "my own personal practice" (*ziji de qinshen shijian*) as a source of knowledge.[37] And third-person narratives portrayed youth in highly individualized, even romantic ways. Deng Yantang "had a tanned face and short hair, wore a blue shirt with bare feet, and was dirty from head to toe." This exquisitely humble young man pursued new strains of rice "like a brave explorer finding the path." His "influence over youth throughout the county grew day by day," and he achieved a following of other young technicians, who continually sought him out to ask questions and learn from his experience.[38] A 1974 magazine celebrated an urban youth named Xin Wen, recently graduated from junior high school, who volunteered to be sent down to Yunnan to plant cinchona (the plant from which quinine is made). Elected unanimously as the leader of an experiment group, Xin quickly began demonstrating strong leadership qualities. She sacrificed her siestas to experiment with different ways of addressing evaporation and the cinchona plants' weakness in pushing through thick soil. Soon, the entire group began using her methods. When the weather turned cool and rainy, she determined that the group should heat soil in pots to keep the young trees warm. She worked the longest hours, shouldered the heaviest responsibilities, and made all the big discoveries. And she was honored for it.[39]

This was what we might call the "Lei Feng paradox." Lei Feng's claim to fame was his humble life studying Mao's thought, which ended in a suitably humble death under the weight of a fallen utility pole. He achieved recognition and glory, ironically, for being utterly commonplace and unprepossessing. The campaign to emulate Lei Feng crystallized a much broader tension in the state's mandate to youth, found also in the vision of revolutionary science that the state presented to youth. It called on them to be revolutionary heroes and simultaneously mere "bolts" in the revolutionary machine.[40]

State Vision: Failure as the Mother of Success

One of the most striking themes in the literature on youth and scientific experiment was that of failure. Far from blanket optimism, propaganda emphasized the difficulties associated with agricultural experiment and recognized failure as a common—almost universal—experience. The frequent return to this subject makes clear that experiments commonly failed and that the state faced a major challenge to convince people that failure was acceptable, even revolutionary. So soon after the massive famine that followed the experiments of the Great Leap Forward, rural people needed a lot of convincing if they were to overcome fears that new experiments would end equally badly, leading to loss of valuable land and consequent lack of sufficient food.[41]

A key cause of failure commonly identified in post-Mao critiques is the inappropriate application of models: celebrated, stereotyped practices were forced on local communities in defiance of on-the-ground realities. *Chen Village* relates just such a scenario: compelled to emulate Dazhai by leveling hills to plant trees, the village invested vast amounts of labor and resources and ended up producing acres of land with insufficient topsoil to support the new crop.[42] Such debacles—and they were undoubtedly common—are certainly worthy of criticism; and in fact, Mao-era propaganda accounts themselves are full of critical reports of just this type. Throughout the 1960s and 1970s, we find rural experiment groups dedicated to testing new seeds and methods to determine local suitability and producing new varieties and techniques on site that better matched local conditions. The second principle cited at the 1965 conference on youth in scientific experiment proclaimed the need for tailoring experiments to "suit local conditions" and "serve production in the here and now."[43] Propaganda frequently identified importation of unsuitable seeds or methods as a chief reason for initial failures.[44]

Failure was so common that the 1965 conference embraced this saying as a core principle: "When experiments fail, we must diligently analyze the causes and explain it clearly to the masses."[45] And in 1969 when Huarong County (Hunan) established a new model network for scientific experiment, the plan highlighted the need to "help people develop a correct understanding of the relationship between success and failure."[46] Most of the inspirational propaganda stories concerning youth and science included some degree of failure before the eventual success of the experiments. This provided opportunities for kindly Party secretaries and poor peasants to offer encouraging words such as "Failure is the mother of success" and reminders of Mao's wisdom, especially the "winding road" that led to the production of new things and the need to emulate "the Foolish Old Man Who Moved the Mountains" and who was not afraid of failure.[47] Initial failures supposedly only sweetened the feelings accompanying success. And youth were expected to grow as a result. As a story published in 1974 explained, "The failure was a loss for the collective's production, but for the science team, especially for us youths, it was a great education: it made us deeply experience the process of integrating theory and practice and the process of receiving reeducation from the peasants and changing our worldview."[48] Thus, according to the vision presented in state propaganda, even failure was beautiful when it imparted revolutionary lessons and planted seeds for future success.

Youth Experience: Science as Opportunity?

So much for the propaganda. How did youth really feel? The very existence of so much propaganda designed to convince them of the opportunities in store for them should alert us to the likelihood that urban and rural youth alike often had trouble reconciling themselves to the prospect of building their futures in the countryside. Indeed, for the "sent-downers," agricultural labor meant unprecedented physical challenges and rural life brought unprecedented physical hardships. Moreover, many urban youth landed in remote places where they had no family to help them adjust to their new lives. Rural, returned youth faced a different, but no less difficult, set of challenges. They had intimate knowledge of life in the countryside, but this in itself could be a problem, since they knew all too well the limited opportunities that faced them. Attending secondary school in the city offered the hope of urban employment; returning to the countryside meant picking up the hoe again, perhaps forever.[49]

Nevertheless, diaries and interviews offer evidence that at least some educated youth in fact did get to choose whether to participate in the scientific experiment movement, and they sometimes spoke of this decision with revolutionary sentiment worthy of the state's best propaganda. One interviewee remembers that when the call came for someone to attend a training session on scientific experiment, local peasants thought it would be a waste of time; it was her "own motivation" that led her to pursue this opportunity.[50] A young Nanjing man sent down to Inner Mongolia wrote in his diary in 1971 that at that time many youth were responding to the call for industrial workers by entering factories. He had decided not to join them because his work producing the plant hormone gibberellin (in Chinese, "920") would suffer. The production brigade had committed to scientific farming with investments of time and money; to abandon the scientific experiments at this early stage would be a big blow to the brigade. "So I have decided to subordinate my individual interests to the interests of the revolution; I will stay here and not go."[51] Another sent-down youth reported no such alternative, but he still savored his decision, which for him amounted to a deeply philosophical consideration. On November 26, 1971, he wrote, "Of course, I still haven't made up my mind, because the conditions are not yet ripe." On December 12 and 16, with passionate language, he committed himself to the project of producing gibberellin in the laboratory: "Whether I live or die, I'll do this work well."[52]

For these educated youth, the chance to participate in the scientific experiment movement offered a rare opportunity to choose a path for oneself; the choice itself gave a sense of autonomy and even liberation. One interviewee, Chen Yongning, remembers the meeting of the production team in which they discussed the need to improve scientific farming technology by creating an agricultural science group. He volunteered and was made the leader of the group. The group members still spent most of their time working in the fields, but when they had experiment responsibilities, they told the production team leader and went off to do the experiment work by themselves. When he entered college in 1978, he studied plant protection at the Guangxi Institute for Agriculture (Guangxi nongxueyuan). This was his own choice, an interest formed when he was a sent-down youth.[53]

Of course, "choice" and "opportunity" are relative terms. Volunteering to work in the scientific experiment group was a decision made when larger decisions about what to do and where to be were out of the question. (A comparison could be made here to the situations faced by migrant workers in market-era China: rural people may "choose" to move to the cities to work grueling hours in factories, but, as Anita Chan reminds us, their "apparent freedom of choice" must be viewed within the larger context—in many cases, extreme poverty—that compelled it.)[54] Another interviewee, Cao Xingsui, remembers the feeling of being torn between wanting to use his knowledge to help the very poor local people in the village to which he had been sent down and thinking about his own life ambitions. He told me, "We felt that if we had the opportunity, we would want to leave the village. But while we were still there and had no way out, we were very happy to have the chance to help the local peasants."[55]

Not everyone experienced even as much choice as these two sent-down youth. Many people who wanted to participate in the scientific experiment groups must have been disappointed. Cao recalls that "everyone, whether they were returned or sent-down educated youth, wanted to participate in the groups because of the opportunity to go to the commune or county level to receive training."[56] However, spots were limited: at Chen's site, leaders picked just twelve of the forty or fifty rural youth and twelve sent-down youth in the production team.[57] Moreover, some sent-down youth gained opportunities to participate in agricultural science and technology in the villages only to later find themselves shut out of the far more significant opportunity of attending college.[58] For rural returned youth, this experience was far more common, and just as disappointing. The story told by one man I interviewed exemplifies this. After he graduated from secondary school in 1974, he returned to his village, participated in the scientific experiment group, and in 1977 became the third of three "plant protection specialists" (*zhibaoyuan*) to serve his production team. When I asked him how he studied the material, he said it was not real "studying": he consulted some books, and he recorded every day what insects he saw and how many. When I asked whether as a student he had been particularly interested in science, he replied that because it was the Cultural Revolution, there was no point in being particularly interested in anything, since there was "no opportunity." By the time the college entrance exams started again in 1977, it was too late for him to apply.[59] The bitterness felt by educated youth who missed the chance to attend college overwhelms any sense that their earlier participation in scientific experiment represented "choice," "opportunity," or even real "studying."

Youth Experience: Science as Revolutionary . . . and Romantic

Evidence from recent memoirs indicates that youth were strongly attracted to science in the Mao era and that participation in scientific experiment was deeply meaningful to them. Even as intellectuals of their parents' generation were suffering humiliation, imprisonment, and physical abuse, a surprising number of youth dreamed of becoming scientists. Several contributors to a recent volume of memoir essays by Chinese women who grew up during the Cultural Revolution specifically recall positive memories of their engagement in science and aspirations to careers in scientific fields. One remembers how much she loved the children's encyclopedia collection *A Hundred Thousand Whys* (*Shiwan ge weishenme*). "I had learned from it why there are little holes in bread, why a zebra has stripes on its body, why hens lay more eggs in summer, and why I would have a different weight on Mars. I wanted to be a scientist or an astronaut so that I could ask more whys and publish the answers in books."[60] Another contributor remembered hoping to become a biologist.[61] A former Red Guard relates, "I believe many little girls and boys of my generation dreamed of being a geological prospector. . . . Propaganda for recruiting young people to work in this area was very effective. When my neighbor's daughter was accepted by the geology department of a prestigious university, we all envied her for her future prospects of an adventurous life."[62] She makes clear in her account that she considers such propaganda to have been generally a positive influence, or at least more positive than the propaganda that leads American girls to aspire to be cheerleaders.

It can be difficult to uncover through interviews or memoirs the extent to which the state's vision of revolutionary science resonated with youth: the very different politics of the intervening years often inhibit people's ability to recapture (or in some cases, perhaps, to admit) the political perspectives they once held. Evidence of any kind that youth embraced the idea of scientific experiment as class struggle is rare, and even the less radical notion that "old peasants" were valuable sources of knowledge is hard to uncover.

However, it is clear that youth were captivated by the romance of revolutionary heroism, and they shared with the state a notion that science could provide the framework for such a narrative. Evidence of this can be found, ironically, in their illicit, underground reading material. The memoirs of former Red Guards frequently emphasize the joy they found in reading, but with the exception of Mao's writings and technical manuals (such as those on scientific farming), there was little that was safe to read. Despite the danger, youth kept and circulated novels and other cherished books; many even copied such books out by hand. The most widely read of such hand-copied literature was an unpublished novel by Zhang Yang entitled *The Second Handshake* (*Di'erci woshou*). The story revolves around two patriotic young scientists who fall in love in the early decades of the twentieth century. Fate separates them when the woman, Ding Jieqiong, goes to the United States to study and then to work on the atom bomb project, which she eventually exposes as a weapon for killing civilians. In 1959, she is reunited with her old flame in the fatherland—but too late to pick up where they had left off.

In 1999, Zhang Yang published a book-length account of his writing of the novel. In it, he traces the childhood origins of his passion for science and his deep affection for scientists, though the memoir's tremendous resonance with the values of the post-Mao era—the adulation for Zhou Enlai, the bitterness about the treatment of intellectuals, the faith in science over politics—reminds us to use this source with caution. Zhang recalls following the political travails of intellectuals through the 1950s and 60s, suffering vicariously when the Anti-Rightist Movement crushed the hopes of the mid-1950s' "March toward Science" promoted by Zhou Enlai, and worrying about the fate of "regular scientists" when the Sixteen Articles on the Cultural Revolution called for "greater protection for scientists making contributions." As he explains his decision to write the story *The Second Handshake,* "Since I could not become a scientist myself, I used my pen to portray scientists, to represent them, to eulogize them so that my readers could understand them, respect them, and love them just as I did!" The scientists he chose to present were of his uncle's generation, educated in the "old society" but ready and enthusiastic to participate in revolutionary work—for example, by researching methods to combat the germ warfare allegedly waged by U.S. forces during the Korean War. Notable also is his decision to place a woman in the most prestigious scientific role: Ding Jieqiong inspired untold numbers of young women with scientific aspirations; in later years, an official with a similar name was driven to distraction by fan letters asking her advice and encouragement.[63]

The book's presentation of scientists as courageous, patriotic, and romantic clearly resonated with young readers. It also strikingly mirrored many themes found in state propaganda. But political leaders in 1975 saw too much that was threatening about the descriptions of American cities, the prominence of Premier Zhou Enlai (then out of favor with the radicals), and the risqué love scenes, which no doubt became more elaborate as copiers added their own details. Official critics blasted Zhang Yang for suggesting that science, rather than Marxism, would "save China," a charge Zhang did not deny.[64] Possessing the book brought the risk of imprisonment or worse, and Zhang Yang himself endured four years of prison. But in 1979, after the end of the Cultural Revolution and the birth of a new regime, China Youth Press printed 3.3 million copies of a cleaned-up version of the novel. By the late 1980s, it was "the most widely circulated story of any kind in the history of the People's Republic."[65] That youth in the Cultural Revolution would choose such a novel in defiance of political authorities—and that of all the novels circulated one featuring heroic scientists would be the most popular—speaks volumes about their internalization of the value of science.

The passion that some youth felt for science as a revolutionary practice, along with their struggles to reconcile their own values with those presented in propaganda, comes through vividly in the diary of Shen Dianzhong, who in 1968 was sent to a state farm in Liaoning Province. While waiting for news of his impending transfer, Shen seized the free time to read about science, especially the development of quantum physics. He wrote with interest on Marxist interpretations of the history of science, and he quoted Marx regarding the relationship between studying science and serving the people: "Science must not be a selfish pleasure. Those who have the good fortune to be able to devote themselves to scientific pursuits must be the first to place their knowledge at the service of humanity."[66]

In November 1971, Shen began discussing his thoughts on joining a scientific experiment group engaged in the production of the plant hormone 920. "The process of doing scientific experiment is in actuality a process of struggle. This kind of struggle is a struggle I love, a struggle I want to go for, a struggle I welcome, a struggle I support." He went on to list the three main reasons in favor of his participation: for three years he had been enthusiastic about the scientific experiment activities others were pursuing on the farm, he wanted to make a contribution to the "battle to transform Liaoning's agriculture," and it would be a learning experience and a way to transform himself.[67]

In an early diary entry, years before his participation in rural scientific experiment, Shen Dianzhong pondered an issue made familiar in propaganda materials: "Why do we do scientific experiment? Is it to 'make a name' for oneself as an individual, or do we do scientific experiment for the revolution? Does one close the door and do it by oneself, or do we go into the wide fields and unite with the masses?" Despite his stated concern, he later invited criticism by talking too openly about wanting to write a book: others were quick to chastise him for seeking fame. Shen wrote defensively that his critics were "focusing on the motivation question." But, he countered, "experience can offer profound warnings to people (for example the lessons from the 920 work experience)."[68] (Indeed, as we will see below, Shen's experience with 920 served, if anything, as a negative example.) Shen's diary thus provides invaluable insight not only into the ways in which youth shared the state's vision of science as revolutionary, but also of their active agency in wrestling over the meaning of revolutionary science and their own relationship to it.

Youth Experience: The Pain of Failure

The prettiness of the state's mantra "failure is the mother of success" contrasted poignantly with the experiences of youth involved in failed experiment projects. A Beijing youth sent down to Shaanxi, Ye Wa enthusiastically volunteered to join the scientific experiment team when offered the chance to get out of the village for a little while and go to the county seat. She learned to create bacterial fertilizers and acquired an improved breed of sorghum to introduce to the village. Upon her return, she was given a piece of the most fertile land on which to plant the sorghum. As the plants matured, she suspected the harvest would not be as good as expected—or even as good as an ordinary crop. Ashamed to have wasted the land that the peasants had given up for her, she strategically arranged to leave the village when harvest time approached. We should all be able to empathize to some degree with the shame of failure. However, to understand what it meant for this young woman at the time, we need to consider that sent-down youth were by no means sheltered from the realities of poverty around them. Not long before during a poor harvest, she had witnessed the death of three village children from illnesses associated with malnourishment. To her horror, she had even inadvertently directed the mother of one of these children to work in a field where the child's decomposed body lay abandoned—no one had had the strength to give her a proper burial. Today, Ye Wa remembers the episode with painful vividness; at the time, this and other experiences with extreme poverty undoubtedly did much to provide the framework within which she viewed any failure on her part, any waste of good land, any poor harvest.[69] This was a far cry from the youth in state propaganda who easily wrote off losses to the production team and declared their failure a "great education."

Shen Dianzhong's diary offers poignant evidence of how well some youth learned to anticipate failure, and how devastating that failure could nevertheless be. Shen's early entries about his decision to embark on 920 production are filled with words of self-warning and self-encouragement that could be taken straight from the pages of propaganda stories. "If I really do it, I may encounter setbacks and losses, and I may have to travel a winding road.

I must really make failure into the mother of success." He went on: "I deeply understand that the road before me will have many difficulties, including some difficulties I cannot even imagine and some that would give people thoughts of faltering."[70]

On January 22, 1972, Shen recorded his sadness upon the event of his first failure. More than a week later, he was still preoccupied with it. "Everything I have prepared for has come to pass. Now, only now, do I understand something; now, only now, have I been put to this real, solemn, profound, merciless test." Then on February 12, he wrote: "Another failure has come before my eyes. This kind of blow is really too severe—it just makes it hard for me to breathe, just makes me fall over. But I cannot, absolutely cannot. I must straighten up and move on, must stand and be steady, must coldly and tenaciously persevere, working without stop. If I fall I must crawl, if I fail I must do it anew."

Spring Festival came and went with no mention in Shen's diary of this most important of all Chinese holidays—just a short entry on enthusiasm and the need to persevere. The next day, he sought out the production brigade leader, who gave him a ray of hope about the future of the work but warned it would get harder, not easier. This turned out to be the case, and Shen plunged into increasingly despairing discussions of failure. In June he wrote a lengthy "summary" of the 920 work in his diary, and in July he composed a "report" to submit to the District Party Committee youth group, which subsequently discontinued the experiments and apparently offered Shen little in the way of consolation. Shen wrote: "Recent events have stripped me of any right to 'work.' . . . Who will work with me in the future, and whom will I be able to work with? Maybe nobody! . . . I had best face death calmly. Of course, this is not a death of the living flesh, but a death of my political life. Although I'll never be able to accept this death, I will ultimately find some significance in it and survive. . . . I will not be pessimistic or timid, but will pledge my life to upholding the truth."[71]

Was this making failure into "the mother of success"? Propaganda stories were never so sad or fatalistic. Still, the stark differences between Shen's account and those found in propaganda materials betray an underlying sameness. It is painfully clear just how deeply Shen had internalized the values associated with the state's vision for revolutionary science. The same passion that had inspired him to participate in scientific experiment in the first place left him susceptible to the shame of failure, and the harsh climate of political criticism did little to bolster his confidence for the future.

Epilogue: Bourgeois Science? The Post-1978 Transformation of Youth and Science

After the death of Mao and arrest of the "Gang of Four," urban sent-down youth and their supporters increasingly resisted the rustication policy. In 1978 and 1979, coinciding with the widespread prodemocracy actions throughout the country, great numbers participated in protests calling for a return of sent-down youth to their homes.[72] The leadership had no ready solution for the problem of the rusticated youth. On the one hand, Hua Guofeng and Deng Xiaoping had both condemned the travesties wrought by the Gang of Four. On the other hand, bringing 14 million young people back to the cities and finding jobs for them was no easy matter. The publication in 1979 by the Agricultural Press of a collection of stories about urban, sent-down youth, entitled *Young People Bravely Scaling the Heights: The Scientific Experiment Achievements of Educated Youth on State Farms,* reflected these political tensions.

In some ways, the stories in this 1979 collection were very much in keeping with earlier accounts. They celebrated the positive scientific contributions youth were making in the countryside. They also continued the familiar narrative in which youth faced opposition from politically suspect characters but flourished under the guidance and with the enthusiastic support of the peasantry and the Party (now represented by Chairman Hua). And they still emphasized the courage of youth in overcoming adversity and boldly trying new ideas. Whether skipping meals and sleep or braving bad weather to observe conditions in the fields, youth were participating in the same kind of heroic scientific endeavor that had been celebrated throughout the 1960s and 1970s.[73]

Nonetheless, the 1979 stories differed from those of earlier years. Not only did they identify the Gang of Four as the principal obstacle to scientific progress, but they emphasized book learning in a far more unambiguously approving way. In several of the stories, the youths in question were positive bookworms. In one story, a youth was celebrated for having resisted the "anarchism" of the Cultural Revolution and the political labeling of the

Gang of Four by continuing on his own to study math, physics, mechanics, and combine harvester theory and design.[74] The title story of the collection introduced a youth who since secondary school had loved to read science fiction stories and science magazines. When assigned to be a "plant pro-tector" (*zhibaoyuan*), he bought books from the bookstore on preventing plant diseases and pests. Once he sacrificed a bus ticket in order to buy books, even though it meant traveling back to the farm by boat. He read during every possible moment—while eating, instead of sleeping, and even while walking down the street. One day, lost in thought about the books he was studying, he walked right into a utility pole before coming to his senses.[75] This story resembles the 1965 account of Deng Yantang, who abstained from smoking and even went without lunch to buy agricultural books. But in Deng's time, an anecdote presenting an urban youth with such pronounced bookishness would undoubtedly have signified the need for intellectuals to put away their books, get their heads out of the clouds, and forge solid rela-tionships with peasants who had real experience in agriculture. Now, bookish leanings were unambiguously a point of pride, indicating a keen mind not distracted by such mundane things as buses or utility poles.

Young People Bravely Scaling the Heights was among the last gasps of sup-port for the rustication movement, a policy that could not be saved in the new political climate.[76] The tide was turning: intellectuals would no longer be called to be reeducated in the countryside. In keeping with this trend, in 1979 the popular science magazine *Scientific Experiment* (*Kexue shiyan*) suddenly but decisively accomplished a shift in orientation. Whereas in previous years agriculture along with other obviously "mass" sciences had filled the pages, it now disappeared as a category in the index. Instead, the magazine began publishing more articles of general interest to urban youth—for example, on breakthroughs in computer technology or new knowledge about Mars from NASA's Viking space probes. We can imagine youth curiously poring over the stories in their city homes, without thought of applying the knowledge in the here and now. Not only are these urban youth now returned to urban set-tings, but rural youth disappear almost entirely from the stage.

In the pages of a brand-new science magazine, *Science for Children* (*Shaonian kexue*), we can see still more clearly the changes that the post-Mao era would bring. Its inaugural issue, published January 1979, began with the reprinting of a letter Mao wrote to his sons in 1941 urging them to "take advantage of your youth to study more natural science and talk a little less about politics."[77] This was followed by a poem by the famous science popularizer Gao Shiqi entitled "Spring," which brought to children the theme China's top leaders had embraced for the beginning of the new era: "Springtime for Science" (*kexue zhi chun*).[78] The idea was that China would now move away from the political struggles that had dominated recent years and instead focus on modernizing the country by investing in science and technology—which, along with agriculture, industry, and national defense, constituted the "four modernizations" now enshrined as cornerstones of Deng Xiaoping's platform. "Where is spring?" Gao asked, and then answered, "Spring is you; you are the ancestral country's spring." He further elaborated: "Today you study science culture; tomorrow you'll turn around and realize the great responsibility of the four modernizations."[79]

The use of spring as a metaphor for science and youth was certainly not a dramatic break from the past. Rather, it strongly recalled the May Fourth legacy that had also infused the 1960s and 1970s, when young people were called to give their "youth" (literally, their "young spring") to their country, and when scientific experiment was contrasted with the old, dead knowledge to be found in the ivory tower. Nonetheless, there is a subtle but important way in which this "spring" was unlike that evoked during the Mao era. Instead of being called to transform the present with their energy and courage, young people after 1978 were portrayed as China's future. In issue after issue of *Science for Children,* distinguished scientists wrote articles encouraging children to study hard because "the future of science rests on your shoulders."[80]

This language is far more similar to the conceptualization of the value of youth and children found in capitalist countries: they are to be invested in for future dividends. It is no coincidence, then, that the shift occurred as the post-Mao leadership began to steer China in a direction dominated by the logic of a market economy rather than revolutionary politics. It was part and parcel of the more sober sense of planning that characterized Deng's economic program, which celebrated not the glory of struggle today but the possibility for a better tomorrow. Immersed in such political values and perspectives on science as we are (and as our informants have now been for decades as well), it requires considerable effort to understand the Mao-era state's vision of science and to appreciate the ways in which that vision shaped youth experience at the time.

7

Adrift in Tianjin, 1976

A Diary of Natural Disaster, Everyday Urban Life, and Exile to the Countryside

SHA QINGQING AND JEREMY BROWN

At 3:40 A.M. on July 28, 1976, in the city of Tianjin, a high school student named Tongshan was startled awake by a violent tremor. He wrote in his diary that the earthquake must have been as strong as "6 or 7 on the Richter scale," and that "60 to 70 percent of the buildings in the streets nearby have collapsed and 95 percent of buildings are damaged. I can see entire buildings that have turned into piles of rubble."[1] The Great Tangshan Earthquake of 1976 was one of the most devastating natural disasters in Chinese history. Although many memoirs and official accounts describe it, little work has been done to recreate the event using historical sources. Moreover, most memoirs about the earthquake tend to focus on the city of Tangshan itself, not on its lasting effects on individual lives. The quake's sheer destructive power not only flattened Tangshan, its epicenter, but also damaged large swaths of the surrounding area. The Tianjin area experienced seismic shocks measuring between 6 and 9 on the Richter scale. Over 140,000 people were killed or injured, and 67 percent of Tianjin's buildings suffered damage.[2] On July 29, 1986, the tenth anniversary of the quake, the Tianjin Earthquake Monument was officially unveiled. In the decades that followed, however, fewer and fewer people were remembering and talking about the earthquake.[3]

Because the scale of destruction was far worse in Tangshan than in Tianjin, Tianjin's experience has never received much attention, whether in the immediate aftermath of the earthquake or in the present day. Apart from general descriptions and numerical data related to the disaster, historians have not written about how the event and its aftermath affected the lives of Tianjin residents, nor have they connected the quake to the broader context of city life. Thanks to the recently unearthed private diary of Tongshan, it is now possible to see, hear, and smell Tianjin in 1976 and to learn how one young man attempted to cope with stress and uncertainty. The quake itself caused much anxiety. It also magnified other stresses in people's lives as the Mao era came to a close.

The single notebook in our possession, which is presumably one small part of a larger series of booklets filled with Tongshan's diary entries, contains entries that begin on July 25, 1976, and end on December 13, 1976. There are a total of 140 entries written on 178 pages. The diary's author was a Tianjin high school student who was about to become a sent-down youth in the countryside. His name was Tongshan, and he lived on Shengli Street in Heping District in the center of Tianjin.[4] Tongshan was one of a family of six, comprised of his parents, an older sister, and two younger brothers, one of whom had chosen a "life of crime" and had recently begun serving a fifteen-year sentence.[5] At the time of the quake, Tongshan was about to graduate from high school and had been assigned to become a peasant in a village in Jixian County, about seventy miles north of Tianjin.

Although diaries are personal in nature, they are still affected by ideology and power relationships. This was especially true in such extraordinary times as the Cultural Revolution, when authoritarian politics and Maoist ideology infused everyday life.[6] After 1949, elements of state ideology began to percolate increasingly into the diaries written by ordinary people. According to Wu Yanhong and David J. Knottnerus, there was a sharp rise in the number of news reports about diary-keeping after 1960, reaching a peak on the eve of the Cultural Revolution. *People's Daily*, for example, published a total of 110 headlines containing the word "diary" (*riji*) in 1965. In 1966, there were 128 articles with "diary" in the headline, meaning that *People's Daily* reported on diaries about once every three days that year.[7] Propaganda authorities celebrated the diaries of such model heroes as Lei Feng and Wang Jie. The propaganda intensified the public political nature of private diaries and reinforced ritualized behavior in everyday life. Keeping a diary during the Mao era became a means of political learning and self-reflection, to the detriment of its record-keeping function. With the increase in the number of so-called "diary crimes," many people worried that their diary entries would become "evidence" that would be used against them in the future. Many wrote nothing at all, or religiously copied Mao's quotations, or simply wrote about everyday events.[8]

Nonetheless, even in repressive times, diaries still reflect their authors' experiences. In the Mao period, private diaries were a way to express revolutionary fervor, but writing diary entries also turned out to be a way for people to unburden themselves of anxieties. Tongshan's diary is peppered with the militant and grandiose words typical of that period. When Mao died on September 9, 1976, for example, Tongshan wrote, "you cannot die; you will live forever in our hearts," and continued to mourn and eulogize the Chairman for the next five days.[9] In addition to such unsurprising political content, however, Tongshan's diary also contains his independent observations of society. He described street fights, shoplifting, and petty corruption. He bemoaned his fate as a sent-down youth, complained bitterly about some of his teachers and classmates, and cursed himself for his own shortcomings. His diary shows the many anxieties of urban life in 1976, exacerbated by a natural disaster and by the prospect of being exiled to the countryside. It also reveals yet another area in which official efforts to remold society during the Mao period had unintended consequences at the grassroots. Propagandists' constant celebration of diary-keeping was meant to foster a generation of self-critical, self-reflective revolutionary successors. As we shall see, young diary authors were indeed self-critical and were well versed in revolutionary language. But they also used their skills of critical analysis to ask why their lives were so full of stress and unfulfilled hopes.

The earthquake and the prospect of becoming a sent-down youth were not the only things that made Tongshan anxious. Like many others living through the summer and fall of 1976, he suffered from a sense of uncertainty about the future and an inability to control important aspects of his life. This chapter opens with Tongshan's description of the earthquake, then discusses his efforts to avoid his assignment to the countryside while coping with other stresses, and closes with his first month in a village. Months of sitting idle in the city agonizing about his impending fate as a sent-down youth turned out to be more stressful than the actual experience of living and working in a village.

Surviving the Earthquake and Its Aftermath

In the wake of the quake and facing fears brought about by the unprecedented disaster, Tongshan "risked death, which might come at any moment" because of aftershocks, "to write diary entries."[10] He insisted on writing down everything he saw or heard every day, thus preserving with his simple, unadorned language a record of his personal experience and observations. Because we have few other records about the quake in Tianjin, such first-person sources written in the immediate aftermath are extremely valuable, especially when used in tandem with archival and published materials.[11] For example, Tongshan's initial estimate of 95 percent of buildings being damaged was accurate. According to investigations by city authorities after the disaster, buildings in Tianjin did suffer heavy damage. Over 70 locations had more than 180 surface cracks of between a few dozen and several hundred meters. These were concentrated in Heping and Hexi Districts and in the southeastern parts of the city.[12] Damage to buildings was especially severe in Heping District, where Tongshan lived.[13] The number of collapsed buildings in Heping and Hexi accounted for 91.6 percent of the total number in the whole city.[14]

The human toll was even more serious than the damage to buildings and infrastructure. Because the earthquake occurred in the early hours of the morning when the city was asleep, people had no chance to take cover. In a state of shock, Tongshan wrote on the day of the quake that the shaking "occurred in the middle of the night, when it was least expected. The number of dead and injured was terrible."[15] Three days later, on July 31, he wrote, "I have not dared to face the facts about building damage and human injuries, and have not gone anywhere to take a look, but sometimes it is impossible not to look." When he dared to venture out, he saw soldiers pulling people out of the ruins. He also heard about a family of four that had been rescued, unhurt, after two-and-a-half days of being buried in the rubble.[16] Although there is no evidence to corroborate this rescue story, we do know that in Tongshan's district of Heping, 761 people died, 1,234 people were seriously injured, and 5,968 were slightly injured. This was the area with the second-highest number of dead and injured victims within the city limits.[17]

Cracks appeared in Tongshan's building, but it did not collapse, and there were no casualties in his family. Next door, however, "was a building that was endangering my house. Just one more tremor would cause it to crush my house, and everything would be a pile of rubble."[18] At the time, all the residents in the neighborhood were living in the streets for safety. Shengli Road near Tongshan's house was "full of tents." Most people "erected a tent and took turns sleeping and monitoring the situation."[19]

Similar scenes played out throughout Tianjin. Because so many buildings had been destroyed by the earthquake, about a million people in the city had to live in the streets.[20] For this reason, the Tianjin municipal government gave special orders to its commercial and industrial bureaus to distribute 90 tons of plastic cloth and thin plastic sheets, 1.95 million straw sacks, 8,700 bamboo poles, 18,800 wooden poles, 92,000 straw mats, and 50,000 tons of wires.[21] Shelters made of plastic covering bamboo or wooden poles filled the streets almost overnight, snaking over dozens of kilometers like a massive military encampment.[22] In the first few days after the earthquake, temporary shacks throughout the city covered an area of up to one million square meters. By the middle of August, the number of makeshift structures erected in Heping District was over 11,200.[23]

Tongshan wrote on July 29 that the previous night a policeman had announced to people living on the streets that "there will be a big earthquake tonight. I urge my comrades not to go back to your homes. Remain calm and keep away from tall buildings."[24] People whose houses had not already collapsed did not dare go home and could only "wander in the streets like disembodied spirits." In Tongshan's retelling, people's lives lost all semblance of order and normalcy. They were constantly on tenterhooks about aftershocks and could not even recall how many meals they ate each day.[25]

Another problem arose when people who could not return to their homes had to answer the call of nature in public. Mounds of excrement could be seen everywhere along the streets. To quote Tongshan, "in order to survive, the people cannot be bothered with anything anymore—revolution and all the rest of it. They no longer even care about shame."[26] After several days, entire roads and alleys were covered in excrement. Because the weather after the earthquake was hot, rainy, and humid, hygiene conditions worsened, and infectious diseases such as dysentery, enteritis, and encephalitis broke out. On the afternoon of July 31, the street committee asked each household to send someone for cleanup work. Overcome by his neighborhood's "overwhelming stench," Tongshan wrote that he "unconditionally accepted" the call to join a sanitation team. "For me, labor is a pleasure," he wrote, adding that he hoped the authorities would look favorably on volunteer laborers' applications to join the Communist Party. He concluded his diary entry for the day with the thought that "deep in my heart" the dream of Party membership "has been planted." Tongshan viewed labor as a performance. The pleasure he took in accepting an assignment to shovel excrement was not as unconditional as he claimed.[27]

On the morning of July 30, a delegation sent by Party Center to console the victims arrived in Tianjin. The team leaders included Guo Yufeng, head of the Central Organization Department, and Zhang Zongxun, director of the People's Liberation Army General Logistics Department. The following day, Tongshan recorded that "Premier Hua Guofeng came to our city to offer his condolences to victims of the disaster. I did not see him, but I saw the slogans posted on the streets."[28] Not long afterward, however, he wrote that Hua Guofeng had not come on that day but on August 2, and had stopped at the city's general hospital to visit the injured.[29] Those rumors were incorrect. In fact, it was on the evening of August 4 that Hua Guofeng finally arrived in Tianjin. On the afternoon of August 5, municipal-, county-, and district-level cadres were all summoned to the Tianjin Cadres' Club to hear Hua Guofeng convey a message from Party Center.[30] In the absence of accurate, up-to-date information, people in Tianjin relied on rumors.[31] Most Tianjin denizens, including Tongshan, were not immediately aware of the colossal damage brought about by the quake. Some even thought that Tianjin was the epicenter. For instance, Tongshan went downtown to run errands on August 5, and it was only then that he realized that "Tianjin, despite the seriousness of the damage, was in fact only an indirectly affected area. The epicenter was Tangshan."[32]

While Tianjin residents lacked accurate information, the rest of China was even more in the dark about the disaster. Tongshan wrote that Tianjin was "strictly sealing off the earthquake situation from the outside world," noting that incoming telegrams could get through but that outgoing messages were prohibited.[33] By August 5, the lockdown had been lifted and Tongshan saw huge queues of people waiting to send telegrams when he went to the post office to mail a letter. Postal clerks were telling customers that letters would be delivered more quickly than telegrams, a claim that Tongshan dismissed as "sheer nonsense."[34]

In a climate where politics came first, disaster relief efforts were inevitably delayed and difficult to carry out. This was especially the case because Tianjin was not the area most seriously affected.[35] Thus, feelings of dissatisfaction began to spread at the grassroots. On July 28, Tongshan wrote, "Society became anarchic. No one came to intervene, and leaders have not arrived . . . no words of consolation were heard."[36] The next week, he vented his frustration in his diary, writing, "Party Center instructed the people in disaster areas to stand on our own feet. The fact is that we have stood on our own feet for several days living as refugees, and we have not even seen the slightest assistance provided by the state."[37] In addition, he even heard rumors that because his home district of Heping "is where many cadres live, they have all fled and there is no one around to take care of the common people."[38]

Although Tongshan did not see or hear of officials providing assistance in the aftermath of the quake, he did note that the police were still on duty. The week after the quake, a Communist Party member was caught stealing string beans from the vegetable stand outside Tongshan's home. The culprit was punished as an "active counterrevolutionary" and was subjected to struggle sessions. "Some people are saying that thieves should be shot on the spot, but I'm not sure about that," Tongshan wrote. "The severity of the situation should be considered, and in general they should not be shot."[39] Later in August, Tongshan saw a thirty-year-old woman "replaying the 'string bean' tragedy" by stealing a winter melon from the same vegetable stand. When the woman was discovered in her tent with the melon, she denied having stolen it. Only when the vegetable seller confronted her and mentioned the fate of the bean thief who was "paraded on the streets with a sign around his neck" did the woman admit her crime. In Tongshan's analysis, hoarding and panic buying in the days after the quake caused chaos in the marketplace, "giving class enemies an opportunity to sabotage and make trouble."[40] Tongshan saw himself in a different league from those accused of petty crimes after the quake, as shown by his detached musings about class enemies stealing vegetables and possibly being executed. Little did he imagine that he himself would be accused of stealing state property two months later, during his long wait to learn about his assignment to the countryside as a sent-down youth.

Waiting to Leave for the Countryside

Tongshan appears to have cracked open a brand new notebook for his diary because of a major change in his life: the news that he would become a sent-down youth. The very first page, dated July 25, 1976, tells us the author's name because he refers to himself in the first person: "Oh Tongshan, stand up bravely, don't fear hard work, climb to the summit along the rugged road of life." It also states that "today is a turning point, my new life will begin soon . . . becoming a peasant is the first step in forging ahead."[41] This first entry makes it clear what would be occupying most of Tongshan's thoughts in the weeks and months to follow. Tongshan's hopes and anxieties about becoming a peasant were only briefly interrupted by the trauma of the great earthquake.

In his diary entries, Tongshan was typical of Chinese youth, who liked putting down impassioned revolutionary slogans on paper. He also attempted to calm himself, however, with pragmatic aphorisms such as "only after several years of practice in the village might I get an opportunity to continue studying."[42] His long-term goal was higher education, not a lifetime of agricultural labor. Although he had not yet gone to the countryside, he was already beginning to think seriously about how he "should treat the poor and lower-middle peasants" after his arrival. At the same time, he wondered "how to make the poor and lower-middle peasants trust" him.[43] Perhaps based on what he had heard about the experiences of older sent-down youth, on July 27 Tongshan told himself that "it is not permitted to treat the poor and lower-middle peasants with arrogance, for there is nothing they hate more than people who are arrogant and look down on them." He continued: "They loathe sent-down youth who loaf on the job, and what they hate most are those who get involved in romantic attachments."[44]

As an earthquake survivor, Tongshan had to endure tough living conditions and live in fear of aftershocks, but very soon his thoughts turned to his impending departure to a village. On August 3, he wrote with unhappiness, "after this earthquake, I am even more worried and feeling more unhappy about going to the countryside!"[45] A week later, he was even more pessimistic, writing, "Recently I am thinking that I'm done for. Even though the earthquake did not crush me to death, my future will destroy me."[46]

Tongshan and his peers were different from the first generation of Red Guards, some of whom threw themselves eagerly into the movement in the early years of the Cultural Revolution. Later waves of sent-down youth lacked the revolutionary zeal of "destroying the old order." In contrast to earlier peers, after they had witnessed the social disorder of the Cultural Revolution, they tended to develop a sense of disconnection or even dissatisfaction with such revolutionary movements.[47] Tongshan showed none of the enthusiasm some urban youth had for conducting scientific experiments in the countryside (as described in Chapter 6, by Sigrid Schmalzer). Instead, Tongshan worried that going to a village was akin to being sentenced to reform through labor. For example, on August 3, Tongshan wrote: "Having to go to Jixian County has made me very scared. It is a kind of pressure. I don't even mind that people are saying 'going up to the mountains and down to the countryside is the same as *laogai*.' Perhaps such thinking is what is closest to people's hearts."[48] The phrase "going up to the mountains and down to the countryside is the same as *laogai*" is from "The Summary of Project 571," a document detailing former vice-chairman Lin Biao's purported "counterrevolutionary coup."[49] It is striking that Tongshan would portray this "counterrevolutionary" idea so favorably, even in his private diary.

On August 11, Tongshan's teacher visited him to find out how he had been affected by the earthquake. Tongshan learned that the quake had killed students from his grade. He also figured out why his teacher had come to see him: on the one hand it was to confirm that he could still go to the countryside; on the other the teacher was worried that he could not find anyone when it was time to assign students to urban jobs after graduation.[50] Although he was resentful, Tongshan understood that the policy of sending people to the countryside would not change in the short term. "The policy is the same for me as it is for others—you can't get around it."[51] People around him suggested that he fake the extent of the damage inflicted on his home and play up his family's poverty to get out of going to the countryside. Tongshan thought carefully about this option, but his chances of finding a way to stay in the city were slim because he had already relinquished his urban *hukou* before the earthquake. His only hope was for there to be so many casualties that schools would change their quotas for urban job assignments. Tongshan found out in conversations with his classmates that his friends, who like him had canceled their *hukou*, were all hopeful. He reckoned, "we will never leave. All of us will remain in the city, and the *hukou* problem will be resolved with ease."[52]

Soon afterward, however, Tongshan got the runaround when he tried to restore his city *hukou*. He went to his school to seek the help of the leaders there, but they refused to get involved. He felt as if he had "walked up to the

guillotine feeling very bad inside. The teachers seemed like maniacal murderers—you could see the contempt in their eyes." The teacher who had previously forced the students to give up their *hukou* slunk away with the excuse
of buying cigarettes.[53] Tongshan wrote, "It was you who forced us to cancel
our *hukou,* but now you are washing your hands of the matter. Aren't you
driving us to our deaths?" Tongshan's diary entries in mid-August are full of
resentment: "I used to think that there were not any bad people around. I
was wrong. Some people are just plain bad, and some have turned bad, but
bad guys never turn into good guys."[54] After surviving the earthquake,
Tongshan could no longer convince himself to willingly accept his fate of
being sent to the countryside. Instead, the sent-down youth program had
become a fuse for various dissatisfactions that were plaguing him. He wrote
in his diary: "When even the lowest standard of living cannot be guaranteed, how are sent-down youth going to survive?"[55]

A month after the earthquake, Tongshan's high school announced that
postgraduation urban job assignments would continue.[56] The school convened a meeting on August 23 about the new plan. Originally, 13,000 out of
46,000 graduates had been eligible to remain in the city. Because of the
earthquake, of the 33,000 youth who had been told to settle in the countryside, 10,000 would now be allowed to remain in the city, where they would
be assigned to the construction bureau. If there were any among them who
had canceled their Tianjin *hukou* and if they met the criteria, then they could
get documented proof from their districts and neighborhoods and restore
their urban residency.[57] A neologism was coined among the graduating students that year: *zhenliu* ("to stay behind due to earthquake"). Tongshan's
diary is confirmed by the memoirs of other Tianjin residents who recall that
their city *hukou* were restored in late August 1976; by September 1, they had
to report to construction companies.[58] Tongshan, however, did not make it
into the *zhenliu* cohort. He could not get his *hukou* back and could only wait
for the day when he would be sent to the countryside. Of the thirty-seven
students in his class, twenty-four were assigned urban industrial jobs, one
was recruited for a job outside the official employment assignment system,
two were sent back to their original hometowns, and the remaining ten
became sent-down youth. Tongshan became despondent: "I am powerless to
change my fate," he wrote.[59]

During the excruciating wait before his departure, Tongshan lived through Mao Zedong's death and the fall of the Gang of Four. After copying newspaper editorials in his diary for several days, Tongshan made a bold conjecture about the political situation after Mao's death. "It is such a difficult task to choose a leader now. It is not good for the old-timers to take over, but no new people have been nurtured," he wrote. "Among the mature ones, there is only Hua Guofeng."[60] In the month that followed, similar sentiments appeared in Tongshan's diary. "There is no word on who the Premier will be," he wrote. "It looks like it may be Zhang Chunqiao, but that is uncertain. It may even be Li Xiannian."[61] On October 17 he wrote: "People say that there is yet another failed coup in Party Center. Several central leaders have engaged in intense struggle over the issue of who will succeed Chairman Mao Zedong."[62] Tongshan was lucky his diary did not fall into the hands of the police, who would be investigating him the next week. As Daniel Leese shows in Chapter 4, seemingly innocuous musings about elite politics after Mao's death was enough to earn someone a label of counterrevolutionary.

Although the political situation at the top was turbulent, the mobilization of students to the countryside went on as usual. "In order to be assigned to good jobs," Tongshan's classmates "were tireless in their efforts and visited the homes of all their teachers." Because of a combination of pride and timidity, however, Tongshan found it extremely hard to "use the backdoor."[63] And he had no other choice but to take part in the physical labor that his school organized. Tongshan wrote that he was "more enthusiastic than those classmates who were going to the factories," in the hope that his good work performance would "win the school's favor and get an assignment to somewhere nearer and better."[64] He did not want to go to Jixian County. Instead, he hoped to go to a suburban village on the immediate outskirts of the city, where he thought he would have a better chance of eventually getting a factory job. A few years earlier, a youth from Tianjin would have considered himself very lucky to go to Jixian instead of to faraway Inner Mongolia. In fact, he would have had to "use the backdoor" to get sent to a village so close to home. Jixian, which used to be part of Hebei Province, came under the jurisdiction of Tianjin Municipality in 1972, but Tianjin residents continued to regard this region as a "different place" and not part of the city's suburbs.

On September 24, Tongshan was surprised to discover that he and his classmates had been assigned to help rebuild the homes of two cadres at his school, Secretary Jia and Mr. Tian. Rather than complain about the officials' petty corruption, Tongshan embraced it. "If I had known that we would be working for the leaders, I would have been more enthusiastic and would have gone all out," he wrote. "I know that Mr. Tian is in charge of postgraduation assignments, and Secretary Jia is even more influential. If they say they'll take care of you, it means they'll send you to a better location."[65]

Tongshan was deluded if he thought that enthusiastic participation on volunteer labor projects would get him special treatment. Although he visited his school repeatedly to plead for an assignment to the suburbs, his sob stories never did him any good. He realized that going through the backdoor required giving gifts or favors, but he was unable or unwilling to take that step. His parents lacked money or influence. Tongshan also saw his brother's criminality as an obstacle in his attempt to get a favorable assignment. He blamed his brother's life of crime on his parents' "incompetence," writing that "my family saw him making mistakes and didn't address them."[66]

Tongshan's frustration with his inability to change his situation took a toll on his psyche, and he began to lash out. In his diary entry dated September 29, he blamed Mr. Huang, a teacher at his school, for persuading him to relinquish his urban *hukou*. Tongshan got so mad agonizing over his *hukou* that he threw a rock at his neighbor's window, shattering the glass. After breaking the window, he wrote, "I couldn't help being a bit surprised, but it's no use having regrets." He made no mention of apologizing to the window's owner or offering to fix it, so we can assume that he kept his offense a secret.[67]

In mid-October, Tongshan's mood got even worse. He recounted cursing at a fellow Tianjin resident wearing eyeglasses who had cut him off while bicycling, saying, "You've got four eyes and you still can't see—how can you be so blind?"[68] Two days later, after another fruitless visit to his school during which he tearfully begged for an assignment to a nearby suburban village, Tongshan mentioned the possibility of suicide in his diary. He reminisced about a classmate who had killed herself after bullies taunted her for being poor. "I'm always afraid that I will replay her tragedy," he wrote.[69]

Although Tongshan did not return to the theme of suicide in his diary, his anxiety deepened and turned into paranoia. Twice in late October, a neighborhood police officer came to Tongshan's home to investigate his carpentry work. The police even paid a visit to his school to ask school officials what they knew about the matter. Tongshan had been passing the time and earning a bit of money by building a cabinet, stool, and cutting board. The police were suspicious about the provenance of the wood and thought that Tongshan might be stealing state property in order to resell it. The first police visit prompted Tongshan to write, "I don't get why they don't trust me."[70] After the police officer's investigation caused Tongshan's school to ask neighborhood officials about the matter, Tongshan began to see a conspiracy. On October 27, he wrote, "I am sick and tired of the *hukou* police supervising me . . . it's undermining my request to go to the suburbs. But even so, I'm still going to ask to go to the suburbs, no matter what."[71]

Tongshan never mentioned how he obtained the wood. If he had scavenged it from the post-quake rubble—in other words, from the ruins of state-provided housing—the police accusations against him might have been technically accurate. But it rankled him that, after sitting around for three months after the quake, his attempt to build a few pieces of furniture had sparked police surveillance and potentially damaged his attempt to curry favor with officials at his school. Because harsh sentences for minor offenses were commonplace during the 1970s, as shown by Daniel Leese in Chapter 4, and because his brother was already serving time, Tongshan's nervousness is understandable. Not only did he lack control over where he would end up, he could not even feel secure while hammering wood in his own home.

Tongshan's pledge to continue seeking an assignment to the nearby suburbs "no matter what" died a quick death. On October 29, 1976, the school and Jixian County notified Tongshan that he had been assigned to Malonggang production brigade in Yangjinzhuang Commune. For Tongshan, the hope of being sent "somewhere nearer and better" was "like a bubble that was popped by the school."[72] The next day he went to his school, looking for a confrontation. First he offended a "leading comrade" from Jixian. "I was very impolite," Tongshan wrote. "As soon as I met him I refused to go to Jixian. I kept emphasizing that I would not go." Next he rushed up to Mr. Huang, saying, "You're really hard to find—are you hiding from us?" and accusing Huang of forcing him to give up his city *hukou*. According to Tongshan, this threw Huang into a "rage." The two got into a shouting match, with Huang demanding three or four times that Tongshan repeat to his face who he was accusing. Tongshan, however, was happy that he got the last word: "I responded each time with a crisp 'You!'"[73]

Tongshan's resistance disintegrated, however, as he realized that there was nothing he could do to prevent his departure. On November 4, he not only told another teacher, Mr. Tian, that he was willing to go to Jixian, but he also went out of his way to cooperate with school officials, spilling the beans about his classmates' "character problems" during a meeting with three teachers who were deciding which sent-down youth would become group leaders in Jixian. The detailed recounting of his classmates' individual strengths and weaknesses in Tongshan's diary makes that day's entry one of the longest in the entire booklet.[74] Teachers rewarded Tongshan for his gossiping by putting his name at the top of a list of students going to the countryside. He wrote that when he saw the list posted at his school, he "felt like a stooge . . . it makes me really guilty and unsettled."[75] By reporting about his classmates' problems to school officials, Tongshan had finally done something to break through the sense of powerlessness and uncertainty that had dominated his diary entries in the months after the earthquake. He had finally resigned himself to his fate and tried to make the best of it. But he hated the way it made him feel.

Tongshan in the Countryside

On November 8, 1976, Tongshan finally took the train to Jixian. This was to be his "second school," where he would study and reform his thoughts.[76] Tongshan found that although his first month in the countryside was not free from turbulence, it was not as terrible as he had expected it to be. Life in Jixian was both more predictable and more interesting than his troubled summer and autumn of rock-throwing, yelling, and illicit carpentry in Tianjin had been.

Shortly after arriving in Jixian, the two teachers who had accompanied them gave Tongshan and his school friends a list of five demands: (1) work more, talk less; (2) obey the local leaders; (3) strengthen your unity and think as one; (4) do not promote disunity and raise complaints; (5) do not gossip about others in private. In addition, they specifically cautioned Tongshan "not to get mixed up in conflicts involving personal complaints" and in no circumstances to "get mixed up in factionalism among the villagers."[77] This tough, practical advice on how to survive was more useful to Tongshan than a vague speech the next day by the village Party secretary about the area's "class struggle history."[78] Even so, after a week Tongshan came to respect the Party secretary, writing that he had been mistaken to look down on him: "Even though Secretary Su is only three years older than us, he is way more mature than us in his thoughts . . . he is extremely talented."[79] Tongshan was especially impressed by how Secretary Su had handled a fistfight between two villagers on the sent-down youths' second day of collective labor dredging a river. Su broke up the fight on the spot and later convened a meeting, with the entire village in attendance, to criticize the brawlers.

Although Tongshan found much to admire in Secretary Su, he was surprised to see that many other villagers had succumbed to what he called "bad ways." He wrote that "their hands and feet are inextricably fettered by their private ownership mentality."[80] It did not occur to him to comment that his carpentry in Tianjin might leave him open to a similar line of criticism. Although he had only recently arrived in Malonggang, Tongshan had already observed that "the communist spirit of cooperation cannot be found among the members; instead there are undisguised commodified relationships. No one is willing to put in even a little extra work and everyone defends their personal interests with their lives."[81] As Michel Bonnin writes, many sent-down youth were shocked to discover that "real peasants bore no resemblance at all to the idealized ones vaunted in propaganda."[82]

Although it was not as poor as other rural areas in north China, working life in Jixian was not easy. It was also fraught with many things that the urban youth had not expected. Having heard that "the brigade will judge us using work points," Tongshan and the other newly arrived youth were somewhat nervous. "The work points we earn are based on the work that we do right now. If we do not perform well right away, earning work points later on will be practically impossible."[83] Like sent-down youth in other parts of China, most of them found it very difficult to be self-sufficient. This was because their incomes from collective farmwork would always be lower than those of local villagers. When work points were calculated, the inexperienced outsiders got less. Those who worked hard felt they were being unfairly treated, while the local cadres thought that it was the most natural thing in the world. In time, the inability of sent-down youth to achieve self-sufficiency became a vicious cycle, giving rise to despondency and foot-dragging.[84]

Just as the youth were mulling over their hardships in the countryside, they experienced another earthquake. On the night of November 15, a strong quake measuring 6.9 on the Richter scale occurred in the areas of Ninghe and Nanfeng.[85] Tongshan was writing a letter to a classmate when the earth-quake struck. "Suddenly, the earthquake happened." He "quickly woke up his comrades, who had been sleeping soundly, and all of them ran out in their underwear." The Ninghe aftershock exacerbated the damage in Tianjin and also stirred up "waves of emotions" among the urban youth.[86] When they heard that parts of Tianjin had been badly damaged, some of them burst into tears and were adamant to go home and take a look. The Party branch gave in to their demands and permitted the youth to send five repre-sentatives to Tianjin to check if their family members were safe. Tongshan himself declined to go back to the city, writing that it would look bad for him to visit home so shortly after arriving in the countryside.

Tongshan's resolve wavered, however, when he heard an announcement that universities and technical schools were recruiting new students. He admitted in his diary, "I definitely need a few years' training in the country-side, but putting down roots for my whole life in a village does not suit me." But because he had not completed two years of agricultural labor, he was ineligible to apply for the schools. This setback caused him to speculate that his frustrated ambitions might eventually drive him crazy. Friends told him that two main things caused sent-down youth to become mentally ill: trying to get a girlfriend and not getting into university. "My personality does lend itself to the possibility of becoming mentally ill. . . . Aiya! How could I think of such a terrible thing!"[87]

In addition to stressing out about his future, Tongshan was also bothered that since coming to the village, his fellow sent-down youth were becoming apolitical—meaning that they had no enthusiasm for officially approved political discussions or study sessions. Tongshan felt obligated to cooperate with the village Party secretary in keeping the youth involved in politics but wrote that "It seems like the hope of creating a deeply political environment has burst like a bubble. . . . Our lives will be so boring if we detach ourselves from politics."[88]

Tongshan wanted mental stimulation as well as praise from the village Party secretary, but at the same time he welcomed a respite from the pres-sure of always acting in politically correct ways. In the village, for the first time in his diary he reflected on the beauty of his natural surroundings and the simple routine of waking up early and walking to work. "We saw the splendid colors of dawn, lifting our heads toward the rosy clouds and walking toward the red sunrise," he wrote. "I then had the thought that this would be difficult to see in the city. Only in the vast countryside can those who do not fear the frigid cold experience such a limitless, lovely scene. And when the walk was over, we got to work."[89]

We do not know whether Tongshan's appreciation for rural sunrises eventually dampened, nor do we know how long his residency in Jixian lasted. The last entry in his diary is dated December 13, 1976. Like most sent-down youth who returned to cities as the rustication program was phased out in the late 1970s and early 1980s, he probably went back to his home. He may have even achieved his dream of attending university. His diary is a snapshot of an uncertain and anxiety-laden time when a lack of individual control over housing, schooling, and work took a psychological toll on many young Chinese people. Natural disasters exacerbated this sense of powerlessness and added new uncertainties.

After 1949, when the Chinese Communist Party came to power, and especially in the years after 1960, diary writing became a political ritual endorsed by the Party-state. Even though model diary entries published in *People's Daily* told people what they were supposed to write, authors were unable to hold back from deviating from official prescriptions. In this way they were similar to the rural "rightists" in Henan who could not keep their critical thoughts to themselves during the late 1950s, as described by Cao Shuji in Chapter 3. Within the pages of diaries, highly politicized, standardized slogans competed for space with a diverse array of personal thoughts and painful experiences as complex and unique as the individuals who wrote them. By the end of the Mao era, the harsh living conditions, collapsing revolutionary ideals, and uncertain political situation confused and stressed out young people. Keeping a diary, which was supposed to be a revolutionary political ritual, had become an individualized outlet for expression and even part of a process of disenchantment. By the end of the Mao years it had become one of the few aspects of everyday life in which young people had the freedom and space to do as they pleased. Diary writing therefore reflects a broader theme in the history of the Mao era: people at the grassroots were profoundly affected by official efforts to reshape their lives, but the result looked different from what authorities had intended.

Part III

CULTURE AND COMMUNICATION

8

Beneath the Propaganda State

Official and Unofficial Cultural Landscapes
in Shanghai, 1949–1965

MATTHEW D. JOHNSON

The creation of the People's Republic of China began a new period of mass cultural experiment, one in which the Communist Party–led state sought to become society's sole cultural provider and regulator of leisure. In the context of socialism, culture was an enormous and costly undertaking, a "social wage" guaranteed and paid for by the state.[1] However, the administrative systems through which state culture was produced from the 1950s onward showed signs of severe strain before the end of the decade. The new political culture of the early People's Republic of China was, almost from the outset, undermined by economic crisis and participant fatigue. Unrealistic economic planning—notably, though not exclusively, the Great Leap Forward—and organizational corruption fostered limitations to state cultural reach at the level of local, or grassroots, society.[2] This chapter, which is based primarily on sources drawn from the archives of the Communist Party Shanghai Municipal Committee (*Gongchandang Shanghai shi weiyuanhui,* hereafter Party Committee) and Shanghai People's Government (*Shanghai shi renmin zhengfu,* hereafter municipal government), argues that state-created official culture was only one of numerous cultural landscapes that existed during the 1950s and 1960s.[3] Like other chapters in this volume—and especially those by S. A. Smith, Xiaoxuan Wang, and Michael Schoenhals—it shows that significant conflict and competition over cultural meaning and, in a general sense, information lay at the heart of the high socialist state-building project.[4]

The political use of mass culture to create communality and legitimize authority is a theme that has become central to how historians explain successful instances of revolution or regime change. As suggested by use of the term "cultural landscape," this chapter represents a preliminary study of how the physical and human geography of the People's Republic was, and was not, integrated into a distinct pattern shaped by Communist political culture and propaganda. The content and planning of China's post-1949 political culture has already received extensive treatment through recent studies of archival sources, oral histories, and rediscovered ephemera such as plays, films, and posters. However, a spatially informed perspective has largely been missing. Where did political culture go once it was produced? Who did it reach? What impact did it have on existing forms of cultural production and the social organization of leisure? Answering such questions, though difficult, is necessary for explaining whether, in the case of the People's Republic, a culturally unified country was indeed created along with the establishment of a new, Communist Party–dominated national state in 1949.[5]

The evidence presented in this chapter suggests that political culture, as disseminated through the activities of Communist Party propagandists or via state-sponsored cultural production (for example, films, plays, musical performances, and print media) and referred to here as "official" or "state" culture, was by no means uniform or uncontested at the grassroots. Unsanctioned, unofficial culture was never fully excluded from everyday life. Particularly in the wake of the Great Leap Forward (1958–1961), Communist and non-Communist members of society alike modified, subverted, challenged, and criticized local systems of state cultural dominance and information control.[6] Grassroots institutions and interstitial zones between city and countryside became sites of independent activity, some of it profit-seeking, which foreshadowed the post-Mao resurgence of local alternatives to state-produced culture endorsed by the Party Center. Indeed, viewed from a geographic perspective, one of the unexamined legacies of the failure of Great Leap Forward economic planning was the halting of state cultural expansion into the countryside and urban slums that surrounded major cities such as Shanghai. Moreover, early 1960s mass attitudes toward culture, including those of grassroots Communist Party cadres themselves, indicate that serious questions had begun to arise within core urban areas concerning the legitimacy of Communist visions of the "good life" and the role the Party Center should play as cultural provider and censor for society as a whole.

As a result, what happened after the Leap is not simply that the state retreated, creating a vacuum later to be filled by nonstate forces, but also that state institutions followed a path of involution and corruption. Factories engaged in illegal publishing and imported popular foreign films. Film projectionists and other low-level cultural workers used their positions for profit. Rural residents left their communes and set up stages and book stalls along urban peripheries. In the resource-constrained landscape of post-Leap China, people leveraged what resources they had—including their positions within the system—to more intensively pursue their own pathways toward self-interest at the expense of central and municipal policy. This outcome was not planned and cannot be associated with state "loosening" in the cultural realm, although less zealous oversight from higher-ups was certainly an enabling factor. Grassroots semiprivatization coexisted with the planned economy throughout the period of high socialism, and it could not be eradicated through the bolstering of existing institutions and organizational forms because grassroots Communist Party members themselves were beneficiaries of the informal and illegal cultural marketplace.[7] Thus, paradoxically, state institutions themselves became bearers of unofficial culture, creating unresolvable internal contradictions that later movements such as the Socialist Education Movement and the Great Proletarian Cultural Revolution attempted, with paroxysmal futility, to address.

State Culture at the Grassroots

Shanghai, with its large industrial and commercial sectors, occupied an important place in the economy of the People's Republic. Following Communist Party takeover of the city in 1949, Shanghai's factories came under military and, ultimately, state control.[8] Social welfare provided for workers included housing and other attempts to ameliorate living conditions, as well as cultural services. In addition, Shanghai's theaters, stages, book markets, parks, and other spaces of leisure were incorporated into Communist Party

propaganda systems and Party-controlled cultural bureaucracies. Geographically, much of the existing cultural infrastructure was clustered within the
formerly foreign-controlled concession and settlement areas at the center of
Shanghai. Urban slums with relatively few built amenities were clustered in
the north and south, and beyond these lay villages and countryside with
no notable urban development.[9] Shanghai's size and administrative divisions changed throughout the 1950s and 1960s, but in general one constant
remained: the city's official cultural geography was concentrated in the city
proper and factories, while poor neighborhoods, slums, and villages represented the edge of the Party-state's cultural reach.

For this reason, state cultural management consisted of two intertwined
projects that directly impacted the ways in which Shanghai residents experienced everyday life and leisure. The first project was to administer Shanghai's
existing state-controlled cultural infrastructure. In Shanghai, as in other
municipalities, the main hubs of cultural administration were Culture and
Education Committees (*Wenhua jiaoyu weiyuanhui*) that governed a wide
range of areas related to culture, education, hygiene, publishing, news, religion, and the education of cadres.[10] The Culture and Education Committee
was, in turn, directed by the propaganda organs of the municipal Party
Committee; this chapter refers to the Party-created fusion of cultural and
propaganda policy, institutions, and functions as the *propaganda-culture
system*.

At its apex, the system was directed by the Chinese Communist Party
Central Committee Propaganda Department and the Central People's
Government cultural and educational bureaucracy, whereas the system's
grassroots manifestations included local cultural institutions such as clubs
(*julebu*), cultural halls (*wenhua guan*), film theaters (*dianying yuan*), and
film projection teams (*fangying dui*).[11] Administrative duties within the
system were divided according to a similar hierarchy, with the Party Center
setting general parameters of cultural management and guidelines concerning content, while grassroots Communist Party members organized
and carried out everyday propaganda-culture work. The second project, also
centrally directed, was thus to increase the propaganda-culture system's
social presence through expansion of its institutions and personnel.
Recruitment of performers and non-Party intellectuals into the system was
an important factor in the system's local growth during the 1950s.[12] Political

education and training of personnel constituted another critical area of policy implementation.[13] In essence, the Party Center, and more generally the Communist Party itself, attempted to not only control the cultural market, but also to create it—to administer in the name of "culture" the wide range of less easily categorized performers, venues, folk arts, and other social practices of popular entertainment that comprised leisure, or culture in the unofficial sense, prior to the arrival of state regulation and management. As a result of this process, the Party-state became the patron of grassroots cultural production as well as the administrator and provider of culture-as-social-wage.[14]

Effective dissemination of mass culture depended upon a combination of infrastructure, fiscal support, organization, and personnel. Yet though the aims of the propaganda-culture system were totalizing, its reach was not total. While the institutionalization of the system began in earnest in 1951, by 1958 the central Propaganda Department was forced to report that across the country "the propaganda network (*xuanchuan wang*) has disappeared in all but name."[15] This complaint alluded to two persistent obstacles to propaganda work and, by extension, cultural work more generally. First, the reality of finite resources meant that the propaganda-culture system did not operate as regularly as its planners would have liked, nor did its reach extend uniformly throughout society. Second, the Party-organized system of discipline and training for cultural work that the propaganda network entailed was not easily reproduced; even within the system itself, corruption existed in the form of state officials and cultural workers engaging in corrupt practices by not doing exactly what they were told to do by superiors.[16]

What these obstacles meant in practice was that post-1949 local cultural landscapes remained heterogeneous, even in the context of ongoing state expansion into previously unorganized leisure time or amidst efforts to export urban-produced cultural templates from city core to periphery and countryside. From this perspective, the Communist Party "propaganda state" was in perpetual crisis throughout the 1950s and 1960s due largely to pre-1949 inequalities—most notably the gap in standards between urban and rural—that were not significantly ameliorated during the Mao era.[17] Although claims that Party-state "reach" was always limited, particularly in rural areas, have been proposed and validated by numerous studies of both urban and rural China, far less has been said concerning how official culture was challenged by forces internal to the propaganda-culture system, or how popular attitudes continued to show support for unofficial or marginal alternatives to mainstream state culture. This chapter, accordingly, focuses on what official statistics, institutional reports, and the recorded testimony of both state and nonstate historical actors can tell us concerning Shanghai's divided cultural landscape.

Official Culture: The Institutional Perspective

The history of 1950s Shanghai is partly a history of the expansion of centralized state culture at the expense of dispersed nonstate alternatives. Local cultural control effectively began with the occupation of Shanghai's news, arts, publishing, and education institutions by members of the East China Military Region Cultural Work Brigade (*Huadong jun qu wen-gong tuan*).[18] During the first months of occupation, the center of Communist cultural power in Shanghai was symbolized by the Pudong Tower (*Pudong dalou*), headquarters of the Military Control Cultural and Education Handover Committee (later known as the Culture and Education Management Committee).[19] Below the municipal level, district committees were established across nine urban districts (*qu*) of twenty total as well as ten surrounding suburban districts. After 1954, cultural policy was directed at the municipal level by the Party Committee Propaganda Department and its Literature and Art Work Committee (*Wenyi gongzuo weiyuanhui*), whereas district and county governments played a more active role in planning and overseeing state cultural activities by the 1960s.[20]

Municipal literary, artistic, and other cultural work consisted of a combination of inspection and registration, organization for production, and reporting and censorship. Artists and painters were organized into associations. Newspaper and magazine publishers were registered or closed, and the Xinhua Bookstore established as the region's principal vendor and publisher, while union and institutional publishing organs were created to serve more specific functional goals, such as youth education.[21] By 1953, Shanghai was home to 34 Xinhua Bookstore branches, 201 privately managed bookstores, and 181 small vendors of books and newspapers (*shubao tan*); in 1959, 91 bookstores were scattered throughout the city and its outskirts, all of them Xinhua-owned. Former Nationalist Party and state radio stations became Shanghai People's Radio on May 27, 1949, and the registration of private station owners on June 13, 1949, led to complete state control of the broadcasting industry by December.[22] Within the film industry, a Theater and Film Workers' Association was formed in June 1949, after which censorship and exhibition controls were established by the central government and implemented through the centrally directed East China Film Management Company (*Zhongyang dianying shiye guanli ju Huadong yingpian jingli gongsi*).[23] Policies and offices for the reform of local theater coincided with the registration of performers as municipal association members—a lengthy process that lasted until at least 1958.[24] Mass organization culture and arts backbone cadres (*she yuan wenyi gu gan*) attempted to implement new, revolutionary models of performance, such as the *yangge,* waist drum performances, and the singing of revolutionary songs.[25]

Postliberation cultural production was not only a matter of ensuring the right messages, but also one of expanding existing media and other channels of dissemination. The East China People's Painting Press (*Huadong renmin meishu chubanshe*), established in August 1952, was the main publisher of propaganda prints intended to celebrate liberation, sell national bonds, and promote ongoing political campaigns.[26] The Shanghai United Press, nearly 80 percent privately managed at the time of its establishment on July 21, 1949, was the most important producer of printed material in urban and rural areas.[27] Rural loudspeaker systems provided electrified (*dianhua*) conduits for political information and entertainment, and fostered research in the emerging field of public opinion.[28] Film distribution was likewise managed and controlled in vertical fashion, with local East China and Shanghai offices of the state-owned China Film Distribution Company (*Zhongguo dianying faxing gongsi*) exercising authority over dissemination and screening of officially sanctioned productions.[29] Creation of a wider projection network (*fangying wang*) was effected through municipal government, district government, and private "social" investment (*shehui jizi*) in six new cinemas between 1952 and 1956, which also led to the construction of four fixed outdoor screening locations; another five cinemas and four multipurpose theaters with screening facilities were constructed between 1957 and 1966.[30]

Nonetheless, many of the new cultural institutions "created" by the Communist Party-state after 1949 were former Nationalist Party facilities or formerly private enterprises. While some new inroads were made, particularly in the areas of mobile film projection and commune-level cultural station (*wenhua zhan*) construction after 1958, official culture was most available on a per capita basis within Shanghai's urban core.[31] Expansion of Shanghai's cultural infrastructure meant, primarily, the appropriation or closure of existing institutions, accompanied by increases in managerial and culture-, education-, and propaganda-related personnel. Some cultural professions, such as theater, actually experienced a rapid downsizing during the years immediately following 1949, due to a combination of budgetary constraints and the allegedly "feudal" or "backward" nature of performer repertoires.[32] Following registration or disbandment, Shanghai's stage performers were likewise concentrated within the city proper, with a total of 79 registered professional troupes active within urban districts and 37 in suburban (*jiaoqu*) administrative areas along the more rural periphery. Foreign performers also filled the gap created by initial downsizing in the cultural ranks; between 1949 and 1966, more than 130 foreign cultural and artistic groups performed in Shanghai, including the Soviet Circus.[33]

Throughout this course of events, nonstate cultural production was very nearly eliminated. The 1951–1952 reorganization of the publishing industry, for example, resulted in a dramatic decrease in the number of Shanghai's booksellers, printers, and distributors, and their replacement with state-managed enterprises such as the East China People's Press (established in August 1952).[34] Private radio broadcasting ceased.[35] Early restrictions on the import of Hong Kong and U.S. films coincided with a crackdown on itinerant motion picture projectionists ending in 1953.[36] Foreign-funded religious organizations were registered, taken over by state-appointed managers, and reorganized, while "reactionary" sects (*fandong huidaomen*) were investigated and attacked by public security forces and the military.[37]

Although cultural infrastructure and control mechanisms gained the upper hand during the 1950s, so too did the Communist Party itself. By 1960 there were 335,056 CCP members in Shanghai, in part the result of rapid Party expansion during the periods 1952–1955, 1956, and 1959–1960.[38] (In 1954, CCP members accounted for 1.85 percent of the total urban population, with concentrations particularly high in the government and industrial sectors.) Although the number of district and sub-urban (county) committees

remained in flux from 1949 onward, in general the trend was toward a consolidation of urban administration and the expansion of administrative
units on the city's outskirts. Numbers rose steadily in the area of Communist
Party cultural organizations, with a separate Culture Bureau Party Group
established in March 1953 and increasing numbers of grassroots Party organizations in the fields of education, hygiene, culture, athletics, and science
and technology.[39] The result was an explosion in urban propaganda work,
which took a range of forms, including large and small criticism sessions,
demonstrations, newspaper and media propaganda, and agitprop performance.[40] Such activities primarily targeted places of entertainment, work
units, and public transportation, and were supplemented by organized political study of state-published documents, such as Mao Zedong's writings or
People's Daily.[41] Other, more leisure-oriented forms of culture, such as film,
were used primarily as an attraction, and free screenings on national holidays represented one means by which propagandists attempted to increase
the reach of their message.

Although cultural production and dissemination were overseen by the
Communist Party, and particularly its propaganda system, propaganda as
an activity was distinct from the activities of film studios, artists' organizations, and other state-managed institutions. Propaganda itself was the
domain of state-employed propagandists or report-givers (*baogao yuan*),
whose ranks in May 1950 included 820 propagandists and 766 mobilizers
(*gudong yuan*).[42] The propaganda network, established by central resolution
on February 1, 1951, and rapidly expanded during the Three and Five Antis
campaigns, consisted primarily of propagandists, report-givers, military-
style propaganda teams (*xuanchuan duiwu*), newspaper reading groups, and
public poster and blackboard displays. By the end of 1952, Shanghai's propagandists numbered 32,543 individuals; with the establishment of new state-
run institutions, propaganda activities became increasingly located within
workplaces and sites of cultural entertainment.[43] From 1953 onward the
Party's Shanghai Committee Propaganda Department also devoted considerable effort to the reform of mass cultural and entertainment activities, culminating in a proliferation of official cultural teams (*wenyi duiwu*), organized
singing activities, mass publications, and local cultural facilities during the
Great Leap Forward.

Limits to Growth, Profit over Politics, and the Defiance of Cultural Management

The propaganda-culture system was not absolute or uniform at any point after 1949, despite early successes in co-opting or suppressing unofficial modes of cultural production. Moreover, additional forms of internal cultural management were required to ensure that propagandists and cultural workers themselves consistently adhered to policies set by higher-level officials. From 1951 onward, Shanghai's theater world was reshaped by Communist Party–led efforts to "reform plays, reform people, and reform the system" (*gai xi, gai ren, gai zhi*). Cinema and theater management underwent "democratic reform" (*mingai*) between 1952 and 1954. Between 1951 and 1956, media and other cultural institutions experienced five rectification (*zhengdun*) periods. In addition, the Communist Party also attempted to improve cultural administration through education, launching a Propaganda Work Committee (*Xuanchuan gongzuo weiyuanhui*) for research on grassroots issues in 1952, and later a Shanghai Municipal Cadres Cultural School (*Shanghai shi ganbu wenhua xuexiao*) in the fall of 1956.[44]

Nonetheless, the local impact—even the presence—of the propaganda-culture system depended on context, and particularly on location. Activities and cultural resources were concentrated in factories and areas surrounding the city; areas where local institutions and officials were not devoted to cultural work remained comparatively underserved. Expansion was not an irreversible trend during the 1950s and 1960s, and variations persisted between localities and across time periods. Responsibility for managing local cultural activity fell to provincial and municipal, rather than county, governments, creating limitations on budgets and personnel available for the promotion of state culture in rural areas.[45] Internally published statistics indicate that by 1960 there was still a gap between the level of cultural services offered to urban audiences and those offered to audiences in the countryside, despite the fact that cultural dissemination became more regular at the county and subcounty level after 1958.[46] In addition, local cultural access varied between districts and counties, as well as between different subnational units such as provinces and major municipalities. As a result of the economic and human catastrophe created by the failed developmental policies of the 1958 Great Leap Forward, 1,200 of Shanghai's rural cultural facilities and nearly all rural "amateur" drama troupes (*nongcun yeyu jutuan*) were eliminated from state budgets in 1961, along with more than 1,600 urban district cultural stations and offices.[47] The pattern of decline was not reversed until 1963, when commune and urban street-level (*jiedao*) cultural stations began to reappear in more modest numbers.

Both Party and non-Party personnel employed by the state to promote and supervise state culture were, at times, also resistant to the official line that cultural work was, first and foremost, political. Early 1950s efforts to reform Shanghai's theaters found employees unenthusiastic about ideological education and propaganda work.[48] Workers in these institutions were as likely to quarrel with one another as they were to criticize their former "capitalist" managers in carefully organized, Party-led democratic reform meetings. Even as the reform process drew to a temporary close, Communist Party team members reported a range of what can only be described as "attitude problems" among theater staff: unresolved political problems, concern for wages, lack of class consciousness, bad work ethics, dissolute lifestyles, and troubling "worship" of the United States and the defeated Nationalist Party. Certain theaters were known to "not support propaganda activity, and avoid carrying it out."[49] The need to manage the propaganda-cultural system internally never disappeared, because it was a necessary part of the process of cultural expansion, as was the management of cultural audience. As public outdoor film screenings began appearing regularly in more rural environs, for example, enormous numbers of onlookers created higher risks of injury, and even death, due to overcrowding; this situation occurred several times during 1952.[50] Lack of policy coordination between district- and county-level cultural sections (*ke*) left remote villages underserved and posed an obstacle to the uniform monitoring of local cultural employees.[51] Even as the private entertainment sector withered, some state cultural institutions and enterprises continued to exhibit profit-minded behavior by focusing their efforts on maximizing attendance, rather than on correct propaganda and enforcement of high ideological standards among employees.[52]

From 1949 to 1958, the continued presence of "economism" in the cultural sector allowed officials, managers, and workers alike to pursue profits, as opposed to universal access, during the course of expansion. From the perspective of the population, state-produced culture was not always regularly available, particularly for those residing in remote, or fiscally impoverished, locations. By contrast, municipal cadre-officials and their families were reported making free use of the system and its resources, including tickets to performances and private screenings of foreign films.[53] Military personnel and union members were entitled to discounts and other forms of preferential treatment, such as exclusive and air-conditioned facilities and leisure clubs.[54] Even beyond the Shanghai-based ranks of the Communist Party, urbanites were, on average, more regular attendees of cultural activities. Thus, though rural cultural construction continued to accelerate during the First Five-Year Plan and early Great Leap Forward periods, the state never succeeded in closing this persistent urban-rural gap.

The Great Leap Forward Crisis

From the perspective of Shanghai's cultural planners, persistent shortcomings in the propaganda-culture system included the fiscal and material issues of inadequate infrastructure and insufficient cultural "goods" to be circulated as well as the organizational issues of political guidance at the local level and the standardization of cultural and propaganda work. Their complaints—which show up in archived internal reports produced throughout the 1950s—went hand in hand with the state-managed and state-owned culture-propaganda system's expansion at the expense of nonstate cultural production; illicit leisure and pleasure-seeking; and other activities, such as religion, not directly related to participation in the state economy.

Following the utopian developmental surge of the Great Leap Forward (1958–1961), critiques of state cultural construction and propaganda work took on a palpable sense of urgency. Even as the Leap was being launched, the Party Committee had expressed concerns over lack of coordination between local Party organizations at the district, county, and municipal levels—a response, in part, to the emphasis on local decision-making embedded in Leap policy, but also an indication that the Leap itself was placing considerable strain on personnel and other resources upon which cultural management, among other state activities, depended.[55] By July 1962, Shanghai's leaders were already engaged with an investigative and disciplinary campaign intended to reassert control over grassroots decision-making and to stamp out illegal, independent, and politically heterodox behavior within the Communist Party itself.

Initially, the primary focus of the Party's attempt to combat more localized forms of autonomy that had sprung up during the Leap was the countryside. Personnel were shifted away from urban areas and back toward the rural sector and "third fronts" of defense mobilization in Anhui, Jiangxi, and northwest and southwest China.[56] (Urban-to-rural downsizing had initially represented an attempt to cope with the straightened budgets and inflation confronted by urban leaders, and triggered by a sharp decline in national economic productivity as a result of the Leap's failed developmental policies. At the same time, China's relations with the Soviet Union had also begun to sour during the early 1960s, adding to the importance attached to domestic stability and recentralization as matters of national defense.) From 1962 to 1963 onward, Party rectification in rural areas gained momentum, taking the form of the rural (Small) Four Cleanups and, by 1964, the Socialist Education Campaign. Urban areas, however, were also affected by the Communist Party's renewed focus on rebuilding ideological and administrative control, as evidenced by the concurrent Five Antis Campaign, national expansion of the Socialist Education Movement, and the Socialist Education Movement's subsequent transformation into a broader program of "cultural revolution" in 1965–1966.

Nonetheless, post-Leap Communist Party downsizing, diminished economic resources and organizational discipline, and loss of legitimacy resulting from the failure of the Leap resulted in a surge of threats to state cultural authority at the institutional margins, and even within institutions themselves.[57] Since 1949, the area of greatest Party expansion had been Shanghai's nonindustrial commercial sector; yet as late as the early 1960s, grassroots-level Party organizations were primarily clustered in industrial and bureaucratic settings.[58] What went on at the populous organizational margins—the urban neighborhoods, rural townships, and villages in which much of Shanghai's population resided—was not always clear to urban cultural planners. In the context of post-Leap rectification and retrenchment, however, the relative opacity of grassroots society had become a political liability. As part of their efforts to reassert local control, Shanghai's officials launched a wave of investigations into grassroots cultural institutions, revealing in turn the extent of Leap-created damage to state cultural control, as well as the spread of new, unofficial forms of culture within official spaces and throughout society as a whole.

The Resurgence of Unofficial Culture

From 1962 to 1963, the Municipal Culture Bureau Party Committee conducted investigations of Shanghai's cultural halls—urban district–level centers for entertainment activities such as music, games, and stage performance. Their findings included evidence of popular dissatisfaction with the state cultural system; illicit, for-profit cultural enterprise; subversion of political norms by grassroots cultural performers and employees; and the weakness of Communist Party cultural leadership at the grassroots level. Although these accounts reflected conditions in a particular type of cultural venue, they suggest that grassroots cultural life remained difficult to manage even after a decade of institutional expansion.

The reports on the breakdown of cultural management unmistakably filtered mass attitudes through the Party's own formulaic ideological language of political correctness. In the Huangpu District Cultural Hall, Communist Party investigators found that hall administrators—themselves also Party members—ignored propaganda work and central policies in favor of promoting more entertaining activities.[59] (One of the administrators was a former Shanghai Propaganda Department deputy department head, demoted following the Oppose Rightist Tendencies Campaign; the other was a former head of a local workers' leisure club.) As a comment on their disinterested and apolitical leadership, it was noted that the cultural hall's record player had become a source of attraction for youth with "unhealthy" ideological tendencies, who preferred to listen to love songs rather than revolutionary recordings. In other instances, "unorthodox" sung accompaniment to the records was provided by actors, described by investigating officials as "indecent and low class" (*huangse xialiu*). During stage performances, actors could be observed behaving in a "comical or frivolous manner, and making strange sounds and intonations," whereas the hall's harmonica (*kouqin*) group had taken to performing in a "foreign jazz" (*yang qin gui*) style. Such deviations were attributed to the "seriously impure class statuses" of many of the performers and of leadership; two hall employees were turned in for having attempted to hire a nude female model for a painting class. As a result, the investigators' report concluded that class struggle was brewing amidst the cultural ranks and expressed concern that "our political noses were not sharp enough."

Findings from other halls indicated that the lax behavior of grassroots cultural officials and performers was at least partly attributable to mass dissatisfaction with state-sanctioned cultural activities and to the pursuit of profit. In Xuhui District, local Propaganda Department members found that cultural halls and other facilities frequented by workers were characterized by a "neglect of political thought" and the presence of "pleasure-seekers and opportunistic profiteers."[60] Significantly, this declining fidelity to politics in grassroots cultural institutions was perceived as a recent phenomenon: "in the past, the cultural halls, leisure, and cultural work units were good units, but now they are lax and unenthusiastic." Performance styles and themes had become increasingly "feudal," harkening back to pre-1949 society and values; of thirty-three productions staged by Xuhui's Amateur Cultural Work Troupe, only three focused on socialist policies and the recent past. Instead, amateur performers wrote their own pieces, some of which made positive reference to life in the United States or contained "immoral" elements. Younger female troupe members later stood accused of joining in order to solicit male companionship, or as a cover for prostitution.

The sharpening critique of organizer laxity and performer debauchery was echoed at higher levels in reports from the Party Committee Mass Arts Work Committee Office. Cultural officials observed that, throughout the city, local cultural performances revealed a preoccupation with themes of hardship and powerlessness, were filled with "backward characters," and showed a preference for "old" themes over official motifs highlighting the contemporary achievements of proletarians—workers, peasants, and soldiers.[61] Actors and other cultural producers were confirmed to be a principal cause of cultural deviance:

Some people feel that the One Hundred Flowers policies mean that the only restrictions should be on reactionary or licentious content. The content of their plays is nostalgic, foreign, satirical, and unhealthy. For example, singing "A Spanish Lady" and shaking their hips. Or, when performing in the role of a drunkard, drinking alcohol in order to better "experience" the part, then showing up drunk to work. Other actors perform in a low-class fashion, sing in an exaggerated manner, and put on airs. These problems are also common in regions around the city.[62]

Moreover, members of cultural organizations not only defied official conventions for the production and performance of official culture, but also sought to profit from their heterodox, and popular, work. Party Committee officials labeled the behavior "capitalist," alleging that it stemmed from the questionable political backgrounds of those involved.

In general, however, grassroots cultural officials, producers, performers, and audiences alike seemed to exhibit a lack of interest in politicized culture after the Leap. For the culture-propaganda system, the year 1962 marked a return to big-budget cultural extravaganzas intended to create a celebratory atmosphere during national holidays such as May First, the Spring Festival, and Communist Party anniversaries. Yet in Shanghai, officials in artistic organizations reported that performers under their supervision exhibited declining enthusiasm as well as disinclination to study Mao Zedong's *Talks at the Yan'an Forum on Literature and Art*—then celebrating its fortieth anniversary as the ostensible cornerstone of Communist Party cultural policy. Declining economic conditions were blamed for the malaise. Many performers were personally faced with material hardships and the specter of reduced employment prospects. As a result, officials reported, "no one cares about participating in artistic brigades."[63] Audiences registered their disinterest by foregoing tickets to official cultural events, leaving cultural institutions in the red. Theaters, book markets, and amusement facilities (*youle chang*) in Shanghai all lost money, leaving films the sole source of culture-propaganda system profit.[64] Licensed booksellers stocked fewer and fewer books; new dramas bombed at the box office; and eight theaters were on the verge of closure in July 1962.[65]

As municipal investigators also learned, audience disinterest in state culture was not limited to urban environments, and this downturn had created profitable opportunities for those willing to operate illegally at the city's institutional margins. In October and November 1963, members of the

All-Cultural Circles Federation (*Wen-lian*) were dispatched to Jiading County to "investigate and enrich" rural cultural life.[66] As indicated by their reports, no permanent cultural institutions could be located, and the majority of official culture consisted of periodic film screenings and "lively" local performances—singing, storytelling, and putting on locally produced plays. Moreover, most rural cultural performers had migrated to the margins of the city proper, where they had established unregulated "big-awning drama troupes" (*dafeng jutuan*) and "small drama troupes" (*xiao jutuan*). The stock-and-trade of these itinerant performers was highly illicit, fanciful, and satirical, as conveyed by the titles of several productions: *The Zombie Opens a Store* (*Jiangshi kai dian*), *The Zombie Pays Respects to the Moon* (*Jiangshi bai yue*), *The Red-Haired Zombie* (*Hong mao jiangshi*), *Hooligan Factory* (*Afei zhizaochang*), *Hooligan Commander-in-Chief* (*Afei zongsiling*), and plays that depicted murderous crimes.[67] Other troupes performed within factories, where it was reported that "illegal troupes are invited to perform for 20 or 25 yuan per performance," with one troupe allegedly earning 5,645 yuan in a three-month period.[68] The report also stated that unemployed workers themselves joined the growing shadow cultural economy, drawn by the allure of extra income.

Illegal cultural production was thus symbiotic not only with laxity in cultural administration, but also with the unemployment created by a downsized post-Leap economy. As in the case of illegal drama troupes, the proliferation of unlicensed book vendors also reflected a reality of contracting rural and urban economies. In the course of investigating Shanghai's book markets, cultural officials discovered that some rural-to-urban "temporary" residents, together with the urban unemployed and a handful of recently released convicts, were operating openly as vendors of prohibited published material. In Putuo District, unlicensed book stalls outnumbered licensed stalls by 71 to 48 during July 1962.[69] Pictorial series (*lianhuan*, somewhat akin to comic books) were the largest source of revenue, typically rented rather than purchased; renters were primarily children, youth, and some adults. Some print material was illegal in the sense that those selling it had no licenses, whereas other publications consisted of books prohibited after 1949—"fantastic" and "licentious" titles concerning knights-errant, Qing dynasty detectives, and tales of the strange. (Many of these were undoubtedly classics of Chinese popular literature or magazines produced during the Republican era.) Cash generated by such transactions was relatively minimal, averaging perhaps 6 to 8 jiao per day, or 2 to 3 yuan at best. However, and more worrying from the perspective of investigators, the numbers of those engaged in this business of "small capital, decent profits" continued to increase, and with them the influence of "unhealthy" publications on young people and the general public.

An unexpected revelation emerging from these early 1960s investigations was thus the precarious state of control over urban youth culture. *Samizdat*-type publications, labeled "pornographic" by investigators, circulated in factory reading rooms, where they were reportedly introduced to young male workers by female staff.[70] The production of such materials was traced back to regional paper factories; illegal publications were also reportedly obtainable on the street to those who uttered a secret password to vendors. Male workers and students were allegedly the primary readership for proscribed books; this taboo mixture of youth, sex, and illicit culture lent reports an air of moral panic. Concerning behavior observed in factory cultural institutions, officials complained that

> Young people object to the cultural club atmosphere, want foreign records, and borrow these from outside the factory. Few workers visit the club anymore. Friday and Saturday evening group singing activities attract all kinds of dubious [*bu san bu si*] people. As a result, female students who attend are corrupted by hooligan [*afei*] types. This has a negative effect on political thought, and hairstyles, and diminishes participation in group singing and other healthy activities. Other for-profit, low-class performances take place on the hills [surrounding the factory]. These traveling performers move from town to town.[71]

Factories were not the only environment impacted by restive youth and social undesirables. In Xuhui District, it was also reported that local tearooms—once reserved for older community members—had been taken over by younger gamblers and card players. Grassroots propagandists blamed the transgressions on popular resentment of Communist Party cultural dominance and poor local leadership but had little to say concerning how the proliferation of unsanctioned culture and leisure activities might be stopped.

Cultural Manias and Youth Culture: The Hong Kong Film Craze

During the early 1960s, motion pictures became increasingly popular among Shanghai's citizens, due in part to declining funding for other sectors of the culture-propaganda system. Cultural personnel were reduced by nearly 10 percent in 1962, with some returned to their home villages to engage in production (*huixiang shengchan*), others sent to more economically dire regions as external labor and aid (*waidi zhiyuan*), and still others considered for military service.[72] Within city districts, theaters and cultural halls were shuttered or downsized, and employees dispersed or forcibly retired. Stage performers and noncinematic theaters were hardest hit by the closures, and unpaid unemployment was often the fate of those who remained in the non-state (*minying*) cultural sector. Audience disinterest and constrained household economies were other key reasons for the decline in stage performance as an element of official state culture, with one survey citing unsettled states of mind (*xinsi bu ding*), lack of money, and concerns about public security as reasons why attendances had fallen. It was also noted—echoing factory reports—that audiences had little interest in official depictions of contemporary realities. By contrast, time-tested cultural modes such as opera, acrobatics, and comedy garnered robust crowds; however, these could not halt the theater industry's slide toward unprofitability.

According to the Shanghai Propaganda Department, film represented the sole source of profit within the cultural system as a whole. (In addition to theaters, book markets and amusement facilities had also become economic liabilities.) Income provided by film showings not only supported cinemas but other cultural institutions throughout the city as well.[73] This was in spite of the fact that Shanghai, like the rest of China, was facing a film shortage due to slowdowns in the studio system and the removal of older titles from circulation due to their politically erroneous content.[74] To compensate for this shortfall, films were imported from Hong Kong studios; the new Hong Kong features soon became among the most popular forms of officially sanctioned culture available to Shanghai urbanites during the early 1960s. Reports indicated that, in contrast with the "serious and stiff face" (*yi ben zhengjing ban miankong*) of domestic filmmaking, Hong Kong films were seen as "lively" and "humorous."[75] The reason was clear: with economic worries mounting, "stories about the center are dry and boring, no one wants to see them" (*xie zhongxin gan baba, sha ren kan nide*).

Imports of Hong Kong films began in 1958, supposedly as a means of supporting the colony's leftist film industry, but with the more obvious purpose of supplementing domestic cultural output. Approximately twenty titles had been imported per year thereafter, but few had been circulated and screened prior to 1960, when more than half of the imported titles were shown in large- and medium-scale cities, most notably Shanghai.[76] Circulation was accompanied by restrictions, and advertising and screening venues were purposely limited by cultural authorities to minimize the films' popularity and social impact. For Shanghai officials concerned with the appeal of Hong Kong culture and its effect on theater-goers, concern was warranted. During 1959, the presentation of Hong Kong films had reached 3,452 screenings and yielded 3,300,290 attendances, or 13.2 percent of yearly audience.

Subsequent measures taken to "reduce negative influence" of the films created other problems. In 1960, a mere 442 screenings yielded 537,764 individual attendances, averaging approximately 1,200 attendees per screening.[77] Unsatisfied demand led to social unrest. Ticket sales for the films were described as "chaotic," with theater doors broken and filmgoers harmed in the commotion. The stark social realism of some films, described by authorities as "depressing" and "harmful," was reported to inhibit feelings of happiness, or even willingness to marry. Indeed, with the majority of Shanghai's Hong Kong film fans consisting of younger people, including students and workers, their danger lay in the fact that such images made "pleasurable and corrupt lifestyles" appealing by contrast to the norm, thus "confusing" their audiences and causing them to "suffer harm unknowingly." Enjoyment of the films was not limited solely to young people, however. City cadres were also reported to enjoy the films, using their privilege and influence to obtain tickets through back-door channels, which presumably contributed to pent-up demand among those who could not obtain tickets through official means.[78] As in other areas of the cultural economy, profiteering ran rampant, with some factories alleged to be importing the films illegally and creating cartels (*jituan*). The spread of Hong Kong cinema culture was attributable not only to state decisions regarding cultural imports, but also to coastal trade, which flouted commercial controls.

As Hong Kong films became more popular, official concern with their pernicious effects mounted. At the base of this concern was a fear that cultural work at the grassroots had become almost wholly inadequate to the task of shaping social values, particularly among ideologically vulnerable segments of society. One November 1962 observation of district-level mass culture ascribed the popularity of Hong Kong films to their "liveliness, flavor, and humor."[79] Films such as *The Wedding Night* (*Xinhun diyiye,* 1956), *The Lady Racketeer* (*Meiren ji,* 1961), and *Tonight and Every Night* (*Yeye pan lang gui,* 1958) sold out theaters and resulted in crowds, chaos, and damage to theater property due to the frenzied excitement they generated. By January 1963, the fad and its attendant disorder had reached the attention of the urban Party Committee when it was reported by the Propaganda Department that, as a result of long and disorderly lines for the films,

> Traffic has been obstructed, shops cannot open, and there are lines of ticket-buyers at the entrances of some theaters both day and night. Some theaters report that when they open the doors crowds burst into the theater, smashing seats. This has reached the point of emergency, with some people sent to the hospital after being crushed and injured. Block bookings are controlled and monopolized; individual tickets are exchanged on the black market. There are repeated incidents of illegally high prices [for the tickets].[80]

The business had become so lucrative that, in addition to corrupt factory cadres, congee sellers and shoe repairmen were observed plunging into the black market for tickets, which were valued as high as 1.6 yuan.

Initial official reactions were mixed, with some finding the films harmful and others believing that the films could be considered instructive, insofar as they exposed the darkness (*hei'an*) of capitalist societies. This latter view was a minority position, however, especially as evidence mounted concerning their impact on filmgoers—primarily young students and workers, housewives, and unemployed youth. As noted by officials within the Propaganda Department, the films also had a distinctly young and female audience, which was comprised of middle school–aged female students, nurses, and other young employed women.[81] These female filmgoers appeared captivated by the clothing, elegance, and luxurious lifestyles depicted in *The Lady*

Racketeer; one young student was alleged to have claimed that "she would rather be a prostitute in Hong Kong." In general, both male and female audience members were noted to express the belief that life in Hong Kong was better than in Shanghai, to wear their clothes in a "Hong Kong style," and to imitate the "immoral" behaviors of villainous characters depicted in the films. A distinct youth culture was taking shape. Or, as viewed by the Party, "incorrect viewpoints" were being spread among youth, requiring further "education."

Hong Kong films came in a variety of genres. Lighter fare concerned family issues and love stories, while social realist films depicted gangsters and crime. In all cases, though, the aesthetic qualities of the films and performers, along with the luxurious lifestyles that they inhabited on screen—as well as the films' own glaring lack of overt political ideology—were the key elements that attracted those swept up in the craze. Propaganda Department officials attempted to capture this appeal in a variety of ways. The youth who embraced Hong Kong films were "naïve and weak-willed."[82] They found the actors and actresses attractive. They enjoyed the quick pace, big sets, good music, and charismatic acting that Hong Kong films provided. They were attracted by, and addicted to, images of capitalist life as well as by the fact that the films were "like nothing produced in our country." More disconcertingly, wrote investigators, the number of such "addicts" seemed to be growing. Between 1961 and 1962, Hong Kong film screenings in Shanghai increased from 7,233 to 7,792, but audience increased from 640,000 (an approximate figure) to a staggering 6,145,971.[83] Each screening was a sellout. Those involved in fueling the soaring ticket prices included Party, municipal, union, and Youth League cadres. Although continued screenings were justified on the grounds of "exposing the corruption of capitalist society," they were also creating the desire for imagined material living standards in Hong Kong, especially among the young.

Both the Party and the Youth League viewed the early 1960s Hong Kong film craze as a threat to social order. In one report on the influence of Hong Kong films, young workers in a Shanghai machinery factory were described as

Upset that they still need ration coupons to eat when Hong Kong people eat whatever they want. [They also believe that] even poor people in

Hong Kong wear Western clothes. They want to know when China will look like this. They believe that Hong Kong people are smart and get ahead in life despite oppression, while in China wages always remain the same.[84]

Similar attitudes were observed among Shanghai's student population. Male students described Hong Kong girls as "pretty" after viewing the films and envied Hong Kong's thrilling nightlife. One student was reported to have quit school to stay home and study English, another to have expressed a desire to move to Hong Kong and shine shoes. A female student of sixteen *sui* wore her clothing in a "strange style," cultivated friends with foreign connections, and refused to attend school regularly. A female factory apprentice was caught stealing money for clothes. Another factory worker exposed to the films suddenly quit the Youth League; yet another described capitalist lifestyles as "interesting," adopted "hooligan" attire, and was frequently overheard telling coworkers that life in Hong Kong was "good."

The threat that these films posed, as noted in internal Party communication, was that they caused people to disdain domestic culture, and films, as "warlike" and "monotonous," and that they encouraged younger people to envy Hong Kong lifestyles while also becoming bored and frustrated with their own circumstances. Other perceived threats to social order were economic rather than ideological. Ticket scalpers siphoned money and other goods into the black market, where tickets could be obtained in exchange for cash, sick leave, cigarettes, food, and cooking oil. Fights broke out in front of theaters over tickets. Enormous crowds caused damage to theaters, where particularly energetic fans would even force their way in through the windows. Public security forces were dispatched to manage crowds of 3,000 to 4,000 filmgoers per single screening—or to manage other film-related crises. One young girl's parents called the police because they believed that their daughter, in an agitated state as she waited to obtain tickets for *The Lady Racketeer,* was suffering a nervous breakdown.

It is important not to overemphasize the ubiquity of the Hong Kong film craze as a cultural phenomenon. In 1962, attendances for Hong Kong films accounted for nearly six percent of the annual total for all film attendances.[85] In other words, though the films were popular, they were perhaps far from mainstream. However, the very fact of their popularity, and the Party's reaction by 1963—which included Public Security Bureau break-ups of illegal film import and scalping rings, arrests, and a subsequent wave of "thought work" carried out in unions and schools—indicates that China's cultural system was not closed or centrally regulated after 1949. And that public frustration with stalled post-Leap development, particularly among young people, found cultural expression in ways that co-opted and fetishized depictions of societies outside of China. In this sense film culture, like the subversive and illegal cultures detected by Party officials in cultural halls, book markets, and other spaces of leisure, betrayed a subaltern but visible, and even fashionable, sense of alienation toward the state. At the same time, others simply turned their backs on state culture by refusing to attend or engage.

Involution and Corruption in Projection Work

In cities such as Shanghai, attempts to restore order to the post-Leap cultural system were important aspects of the Socialist Education Movement and related Four Cleanups Movement in the countryside. In each case, the strengthening of Communist Party authority went hand in hand with renewed focus on effective dissemination of state culture. As early as 1963, cultural workers were dispatched to rural areas to investigate conditions of cultural life, better understand audience preferences, and provide guidance in cultural work to low-level rural cadres.[86] Their findings concerning rural film dissemination and exhibition indicated that two trends had taken hold since 1961. First, cultural activity was on the rebound, with activities and audiences increasing. However, a second set of findings indicated that corruption and official laxity were endemic features of the cultural system and that an overall sensitivity to economic, rather than political, incentives limited the reach of state culture primarily to those locales whose residents and local state institutions were already able to afford the cost. Inequality thus persisted, while state cultural reach remained outwardly unpredictable and uncertain. Since 1957, rural film distribution had been controlled locally as a commercial cultural product (*xiaoshouxing de wenhua shangpin*), with subnational distributors responsible for the planning and expansion of the dissemination and exhibition network.[87] Culture was an enterprise, and this meant that cash- and infrastructure-poor rural areas were rarely targeted for revenue-minded cultural activities.

Another familiar issue concerned whether or not films were being screened by politically educated, and reliable, cultural personnel. In one 1965 study of rural exhibition, investigators found that increases in the circulation of political films had not been accompanied by enhanced political oversight of the exhibition system.[88] In Jinshan County, Zhujing Township possessed its own theater, while each of the county's five 16mm film teams served approximately twenty-six village-sized production teams. Average annual exhibitions per person had increased from 4.4 in 1962 to 7.7 in 1964. Nearly one-third of the county's thirty film workers were assigned to the Projection Management Station or to the township's theater. Resources remained concentrated in townships rather than villages; projectionists continued to neglect the countryside.

The issue of village-level exhibition was tackled head on during the Socialist Education Movement, in which projectionists were required to study Mao Zedong's writings and encouraged to apply for Youth League or Communist Party membership. Early returns were promising. Projectionists became more punctual and more willing to travel to remote locations without asking for "hardship bonuses" as incentive.[89] The films they screened—such as *After the Harvest* (*Fengshou zhi hou*, 1964), *The Life of Lei Feng* (*Lei Feng*, 1964), and numerous science education films and newsreels—likewise appeared to have a positive effect on commune and militia morale. Drama troupes and film exhibition teams conducted pre-exhibition propaganda using slides, sung and spoken entertainment, or the film itself.

At the same time, as the Four Cleanups Movement gained momentum, politically reliable cultural workers were often transferred away to politically sensitive areas, leaving behind a less reliable corps of personnel, who in turn became targets for ongoing local investigations. In Songjiang, those remaining were criticized for being "politically backward," meaning that they avoided the countryside, shunned contact with Communist Party organizations, and rarely engaged in organized propaganda work. Five generators purchased for exhibition work in areas with no wired electricity remained in storage—the projectionists would not take then into the field, which meant transporting the bulky equipment by boat. It was discovered that there was no regular contact or communication between county cultural institutions (e.g., the film station, Xinhua bookstore, broadcast station, cultural hall, library, children's palace, athletics committee, theater, and musical performance team) and local Communist Party branches. Because of the expense of running a full-time exhibition station—transportation alone totaled 7,680 yuan per year—leaders ignored political study and rural work—presumably in favor of managing the more profitable theater. Nor did Party committees regularly supervise film exhibitions, which often took place with little accompanying lecturing or other propaganda work. Often the films shown were those popular with regular filmgoers, and not intended to propagandize the "three great revolutions" of class struggle, production, and science.

The result was that even at the height of the Socialist Education Movement, some villages had gone more than eight months without a single screening, whereas up to 80 percent of screenings took place in county townships. Peasants who did seek tickets for popular films could not obtain them; others were turned away at the door after tickets had sold out. As Party branch secretary Cao Wenqi of the Xingfu production team reported: "Commune members complain that they can't see films and say that although the production team has a good reputation, it can't book a screening." The reasons were primarily economic, as projectionists and station managers did not believe that commune production teams were capable of generating enough ticket sales to cover the cost of the bookings. Increased exhibitions did not necessarily mean increased rural access or political content.

In 1965, a general investigation carried out during the Socialist Education Movement highlighted the disconnect between Communist Party propaganda goals and actual work carried out by exhibition teams, much to the consternation of the Shanghai municipal committee's Culture and Education Office. Such problems were not specific to the countryside, but existed anywhere film exhibition teams operated. As of February 15, 1965, all of Shanghai's 143 exhibition teams had recently been evaluated for evidence of the "four uncleans" (*si buqing*) and compliance with a central directive stipulating that distribution and exhibition work "tightly coordinate with the demands of the Socialist Education Movement and Socialist Cultural Revolution Movement."[90] Measured against such standards, Shanghai fell short. As the investigators found,

There is little leadership of exhibition teams; work does not serve the propaganda needs of the Communist Party. Projectionists are not aware that they are the "light cavalry of the literary and artistic line" and "red propagandists." Problems are particularly acute in rural areas.

> Film exhibitions are only given at night; during the day projectionists gather on the ferry or return home. They do little propaganda work and rarely listen to mass opinion.[91]

This behavior, they continued, had become notable starting in 1961 and 1962, when Shanghai's distribution company had emphasized profit over politics, justifying the import of commercially oriented Hong Kong films as "support [for] progressive Hong Kong filmmakers" and "united front action." These films, which included renderings of traditional operas (e.g., *Luan dian yuan-yang pu*, a tale of mismatched couples), accounted for 50 percent of all films shown in Jinshan County. Projectionists deliberately evaded responsibilities to show state-produced rural education films, falsifying their logs to mask the deception. In Yangpu, cultural officials authorized the use of bicycles and automobiles in order to keep pace with mass demand for the popular Hong Kong features. The trend only subsided in 1964, when imports again slowed to a trickle. Within the city proper, film teams continued to show popular 1950s thrillers such as *Night Sentry in Yangcheng* (*Yangchang anxiao*, 1957). More contemporary state films were, by contrast, far harder to locate, not only because they were difficult to obtain, but also because they were unpopular with audiences.

The use of motion pictures for political education was hampered by a variety of factors in addition to profit-seeking. State-produced films on rural topics, such as *After the Harvest* and *Beside the Jian'gan River* (*Jian'gan he bian*, 1964), could not be shown simultaneously in urban and rural settings because not enough copies were available. Only two counties, Jinshan and Fengxian, were able to coordinate their exhibition schedules with the ongoing Socialist Education Movement. Political and personal wrongdoing on the part of exhibition team members also reared its head. Some were transferred to the job after having committed errors in other work units. Others were already known to public security authorities for various crimes and infractions:

> In Chuansha County a projectionist Zhang XX has attempted to escape to Hong Kong, and talks like a reactionary, opposes leadership, and has organized a corrupt cartel. Zhu X has problems with his political history, raped a woman after Liberation, and has also corrupted (*cuican*)

twenty-one younger women. Qiu XX has engaged in sodomy since 1945. All three of these men have been detained, and two removed from their posts. In Fengxian County a rightist who used to work at the broadcasting station has recently been transferred to a film team to keep him away from the station.[92]

A persistent problem facing the exhibition network, in the eyes of cultural authorities, was that it lacked oversight (e.g., leadership, precise reporting) and deemphasized political education. "The problem is the system," they wrote. The need for reform was most dire at the county level, where temporary labor was still used and professional projectionists with reliable ideological tendencies lacking.

One of the most persistent obstacles to effective political control of film exhibition was that projectionists were so rarely supervised. Films and projectors could easily be obtained to conduct for-profit screenings. This form of local autonomy also permitted additional opportunities for engagement in black market activities. Of seven active projection team personnel in Nanshi District, five were believed to be participants in corruption or theft, embezzling amounts ranging from 100 to 5,000 yuan:

> Some individuals collude with external cliques to peddle watches, gold, etc., and have accumulated illegal profits of more than 1,000 yuan. In August of last year, the group was put under investigation and its exhibition activities ceased. In Nanhui County, of forty-eight personnel, including those in the theater and film station, thirty-two were involved in embezzling more than 3,000 yuan, in amounts ranging from 20 to 800 [at a time]. Of nine Communist Party members, six are corrupt. Among thirteen personnel in Yangpu District, most are engaged in some corrupt activity. Of twelve Communist Party members from the all-Shanghai union engaged in district-level projection work, nine are found to have engaged in some form of corruption.[93]

Most illicit earnings came from reselling tickets, underreporting ticket sales (and pocketing the difference), underreporting screenings, accepting money without issuing tickets, and raising ticket prices above local standards. Corrupt local officials also involved themselves in the schemes for a cut of the profits. The exhibition network had, for the unscrupulous within its ranks, become a cash cow. State-owned equipment created personal wealth.

Nonetheless, socialist mass culture did undoubtedly reach the countryside. However, it did so in ways that met with upper-level approval only when the state culture industry and Party institutions had already thrown considerable resources into making current, politically focused material available. This was indeed the case at the outset of the Socialist Education Movement, when plays were performed and films screened to accompany the movement and inculcate popular support for Party-state efforts to reform the rural commune system. Plays about class struggle, such as *Stealing the Seals* (*Duo yin*), *Yang Libei,* and *Xi Wang saozi,* or films on similar themes (e.g. *Li Shuangshuang, Locust Tree Village*), attracted large attendances—an average of roughly 561 audience members per exhibition of *Li Shuangshuang* and 524 audience members for *Locust Tree Village* (*Huaishu zhuang*).[94] Yet they appear to have been exhibited free of charge, and on the direct orders of those responsible for coordinating the Socialist Education Movement in Shanghai. Thus, they represented the exception and not the rule.

The rule was that villagers possessed discernment and displayed clear preferences when it came to film consumption. Not all exhibited titles were widely enjoyed or attended. "Fighting and singing" (*yi da er chang*) in war and opera films garnered far more in revenue than did narratives highlighting national policies or foreign films depicting unfamiliar social settings and incomprehensible plots.[95] However, as the Socialist Education Movement and the Four Cleanups Movement revealed, lack of popular film offerings in the countryside drove rural projectionists and county-level cultural sections to avoid taking losses by minimizing the exhibition of unpopular political and imported films, or by avoiding poor villages entirely. As a result, only in moments of intense scrutiny did politics trump profits in determining what was shown and where it was exhibited. According to one 1962 report,

> Half of production teams have yet to see a film this year or have seen very few, because audience members are now expected to pay. Teams are overworked selling tickets and rarely go to more remote areas. . . . Peasants don't like to see certain films, so ticket sales [for those films] are low. Some projectionists only work six days a month instead of the

required twenty-two, only arrange seven screenings instead of twenty-five, and don't know how to care for films. Some commune leaders don't pay much attention at all to film exhibition, or to propaganda.[96]

In both rural and urban settings, weak supervision over the culture-propaganda system and the tacit sanction of rent-seeking activity in the cultural sector as means of supplementing meager institutional budgets were two key factors that eroded the foundations of a unified state culture. Corruption, shirking, and co-optation crept in. Two cultural landscapes existed, one of which was based on policy, the other based on the less easily anticipated and organized preferences of people, including local state agents. The features of these two landscapes were almost entirely dissimilar.

*   *   *

This chapter has argued against the view that a single national culture, or even a coherently organized state culture that included spaces of sanctioned pluralism, was socially pervasive throughout the Mao era. Following a period of rapid expansion during the 1950s, a key decade of propaganda-culture system expansion that proceeded in spite of low-level resistance, the PRC economy's post-Leap crash dealt a serious blow to institutions and morale at the grassroots level. Even during the Socialist Education Movement and Cultural Revolution, rural areas remained fiscally unable to support the costs of maintaining a strong official cultural presence on behalf of the central Party-state. (To this day, the Cultural Revolution–era countryside is remembered as a space of personal and intellectual freedom by former sent-down writers and memoirists.)[97] As a result, deideologized urban and rural conditions widely attributed to post-Mao cultural reforms must instead be seen as inevitable and unplanned consequences of fiscal and organizational contraction beginning in the early 1960s.

Furthermore, while the "organizational involution" of the Communist Party is often blamed on cadre corruption, this chapter also suggests that grassroots cadres and low-level functionaries ignored directives in moments of state crises in order to maintain their legitimacy via a restive populace.[98] To be sure, corruption was evident within the post-Leap propaganda-culture system. However, authorities in cultural halls and theaters also turned a blind eye to apolitical drift because, like performers, audiences, and others whose relationship to the dominant political values of the moment was strained by circumstance, they shared the same sense of fatigue and frustration concerning central *diktat*. Finally, economic and organizational obstacles to effective state cultural transmission returned with a vengeance following the Leap, thus increasing the available space for imported and homegrown nonstate cultures to return.

In comparative and cross-temporal terms, the early 1960s birthed a new cultural moment in the history of the People's Republic of China—a moment of deceleration in the advance of grassroots cultural institutions during which viable rural and youth countercultures emerged and cultural policy became less supportable in the eyes of grassroots cadres pressed to maintain their own political authority. Likewise, officials were forced to acknowledge that the PRC populace, and indeed many within the Party itself, remained as deeply committed to "feudal" and "bourgeois" culture as ever. Viewed through the eyes of municipal Shanghai elites, these trends were often over-represented and labeled as "problems," but this does not mean that historians should downplay their significance, for the persistence of such problems signaled the end of the Communist Party's ability to make further cultural gains. Instead, what emerged was an uneasy standoff between a municipal bureaucracy charged with passing down directives and conducting investigations, and a branch grassroots bureaucracy that managed state-society relations under conditions of fragile legitimacy and scarce resources—and, as a result, a division between official and unofficial cultural landscapes.

9

China's "Great Proletarian Information Revolution" of 1966–1967

MICHAEL SCHOENHALS

Ubiquitous in historical scholarship on Mao Zedong's Cultural Revolution and final decade at the helm is a focus on violence and chaos. For this, the Chairman himself is not the least to blame. Even students of his thinking—as opposed to his practice—confront, again and again, a remarkable inclination toward chaos as a catalyst for change and love of struggle as a motor of development. But buried in the raw record from the period are also not necessarily "lesser" but less violent histories. Indeed, obscured by the chaos are dimensions of the Cultural Revolution still awaiting the arrival of the first arrogant inquisitor from the future. One reason this merits attention was made explicit years ago by intelligence historian Christopher Andrew, who noted in a general Cold War context that the "great danger of any missing historical dimension is that its absence may distort our understanding of other, accessible dimensions."[1]

One dimension of the Cultural Revolution still missing from scholarly as well as nonscholarly histories involves the "organizations of the revolutionary masses" that proliferated after the summer of 1966. That these organizations enjoyed varying degrees of autonomy from state and Communist Party structures is generally accepted, as is the role played by Mao Zedong in making their existence possible.[2] Their development and demise has already been chronicled, their political raison d'être probed, analyzed, and explained.[3] But despite the degree to which, in today's digital era, we believe ourselves to have developed an acute sensitivity to the *informational* aspects of just about everything, historians have yet to give *that* particular dimension of these organizations its historical due. As it turns out, they all shared a remarkable appreciation of the degree to which their own empowerment and autonomy was predicated on a capacity to independently collect, process, internally disseminate, and exchange information. And unless we add this to our understanding of the Cultural Revolution, our social and political histories will remain distorted.

To illustrate how much the informational dimension of the involvement by "revolutionary mass organizations" in the Cultural Revolution entailed, one need only look at the Revolutionary Rebel Headquarters of University Red Guards in the Capital (aka, the 3rd HQ), led by Beijing Geology Institute student Zhu Chengzhao. Its members may not yet have been armed with mobile phones, internet connections, Twitter, and SMS software; what counted to them as advanced communication technology were hand-cranked mimeograph machines, motorcycles, and occasional access to somebody else's switchboard-operated telephone (on which getting connected from Beijing to Shanghai might take the better part of a day). But at the height of the 3rd HQ's five-and-a-half-month existence in the winter and spring of 1966–1967, it boasted its very own dedicated network of information officers staffing quasi-permanent "liaison-stations" in close to fifty cities across China.[4] News of everything from the progress of armed clashes in faraway Qinghai Province to the word in the street in downtown Shanghai, not to mention what was going on in and around Beijing, reached the membership of the 3rd HQ sometimes once, sometimes twice, sometimes even three times daily in mimeographed current information (*dongtai*) newsletters. Other organizations with fewer human and material resources may have run less impressive operations, but even a historically insignificant one such as the East Wind Revolutionary Rebel HQ of workers and staff in the industrial machine industry sector in Beijing ran its very own *Internal Reference*, with news for members about significant local, national, and even international events.[5]

The *purpose* for which informational and other mediated resources were brought into play by the "revolutionary masses" after August 1966 was to confront China's local state and officialdom—to purge it of "hidden representatives of the bourgeoisie" and "persons in power taking the capitalist road"! Up to the point when prior restrictions on organization were rendered inoperative in the name of the Cultural Revolution, attempts by ordinary citizens to open up and manage their own channels of current information for even modestly political purposes had been illegal. But between August 1966 and the seemingly inevitable return to the status quo ante in 1968, nothing less than a Great Proletarian Information Revolution played itself out in China. Its duration may have been brief, but as the present chapter seeks to illustrate, it is significant enough to deserve its own place in the history of the People's Republic.

1949–1966: Organization as "Spontaneous Counterrevolution"

In what sociologists in due course came to call "real socialism," groups of Chinese who congregated regularly under circumstances deemed in any way unusual ran the risk of ending up on watch lists maintained by the operational departments of the People's Democratic Dictatorship. Such lists—broadly similar in their overall design but with some categories of persons of interest amended or modified to suit local conditions—included in the national capital the No. 4:b subcategory of so-called "elements suspected of spontaneous counterrevolution" (*zifa fangeming xianyi fenzi*). These were described as individuals who "often gather in the company of some reactionary elements or gravely dissatisfied persons to spread reactionary utterances, or gather under circumstances or for purposes the details of which are unclear or suspicious, and who show signs indicative of the active formation of a counterrevolutionary group."[6]

How "elements" such as these were dealt with depended on the circumstances. Normally, they were not denied any rights merely based on the nature of transgressions they were *suspected* of committing, but that could change quickly if and when the Communist Party declared that extraordinary circumstances prevailed. That happened, for example, in the summer of 1957, when Mao Zedong anticipated a "big battle (with the battleground both inside and outside the Party)" to "repulse the rightists' wild attacks."[7] Each elevation of the national threat level triggered specific actions by national, provincial, and lower-level public security organs, including the closer monitoring of some categories and subcategories of "elements" and the possible preemptive detention of others.

Each year, the branches of China's public security organs responsible for political, economic, cultural, etc., "protection work" claimed to have put a number of "counterrevolutionary" groups out of action. In April 1958, the 2nd (Economic Protection) Bureau of the Central Ministry of Public Security (CMPS) reported as follows in its classified serial *Economic Protection Work:*

> A total of eleven cases of counterrevolutionary banding together were cracked by the finance and trade protection organs in Zhejiang, Yunnan, Hunan, Guangxi, Hubei, Jilin, Shandong, Shaanxi, and Tianjin in 1957. Eight of these cases alone led to the arrest of some eighteen prime culprits. They also resulted in the seizure of significant quantities of counterrevolutionary identification papers, chops, symbols, counter-revolutionary propaganda, and other criminal evidence.[8]

The CMPS 2nd Bureau added that not only did these "counterrevolutionary" organizations and networks have action programs and long-term plans to expand, but some of them also "put out publications" of their own.[9]

Detailed descriptions of *how* a specific "case" of illicit networking or "banding together" had been solved were presented only to senior public security officers. Sanitized accounts were given wider circulation, however, including to ordinary police. In the winter of 1963–1964, the Beijing Bureau of Public Security had the capital's police force study the story of a network of disgruntled young factory workers and staff who, it was said, had strayed off the socialist path, self-radicalized, and become "eager to see capitalism restored" in China. For two years, from 1961 to August 1963, the man identified as the leader of the network, a twenty-six-year-old technician in the Beijing Electric Meter Factory by the name of Sun Ruisheng was alleged to have

> employed such means as "sounding people out politically," "roping them in, in terms of their everyday lives," and "inciting them ideologically." Among fellow students and colleagues, he developed sixteen members of his counterrevolutionary organization. He organized a "six-member mass movement leadership nucleus," wrote reactionary articles altogether more than 300,000 characters in length, formulated

more than a dozen reactionary slogans (*kouhao*), as well as plotted to start an "underground publication" and to print reactionary handbills and slogans (*biaoyu*).[10]

It mattered little that a fair number of people categorized by public security organs as persons of interest by the 1960s were from so-called "good" class background. If they networked in any way that could be construed as politically motivated, they too ran the risk of being seen as "objectively" posing a threat to the socialist order. Hence the Beijing students from elite backgrounds who, in May and June of 1966, met among the ruins of the old imperial Summer Palace to, as they themselves put it, "debate the domestic and international situation" and "draft articles denouncing our school's black Party Committee" soon found themselves charged with having formed an "illegal organization."[11] Before the end of the summer, however, in an unanticipated development, the charges against them would be dropped.

August 1966: "It Is Right to Rebel against Reactionaries"

At the highest levels of the Communist Party, the Cultural Revolution had already been well under way for some time when a session of the Politburo, in May 1966, denounced—in a circular, the text of which would not be made public in the *People's Daily* until a year later but whose content was immediately disclosed to Party members—so-called "restrictions on the proletarian Left" and imposition of "taboos and commandments in order to tie its hands."[12] During the summer months, the movement engulfed ever wider spheres of society, picking up speed and gaining in intensity in the process. In Beijing, the municipal Party Committee sought to micromanage this movement at the grassroots by dispatching so-called "work teams" to schools and universities, but on July 28, it was forced to agree to the withdrawal of those teams. The order to withdraw had been drafted by members of Mao Zedong's inner circle, who now explicitly affirmed for the first time the rights of teachers and students to form "mass organizations of the Cultural Revolution" (*wenhua geming de qunzhong zuzhi*).[13] Such organizations were "entirely legal," they declared on August 1.[14] A week later, an enlarged plenary session of the CCP Central Committee exonerated the Beijing students who had met in May and June to "debate the domestic and international situation" and called such young people "courageous and daring path breakers" whose "general revolutionary orientation has been correct from the beginning."[15]

Suddenly it seemed as if everybody under twenty-five wanted to "Get Organized!"[16] Beijing's first five hundred or so new "Red Organizations" (the term was Premier Zhou Enlai's) were officially recognized by the authorities in the final week of August 1966. Their membership, leadership, names, and further particulars were duly recorded by the staff of a state-run ad hoc General Liaison Station just off Tiananmen Square. An absolute majority was composed entirely of "revolutionary teachers and students," but it did not take long before this began to change and organizations representing other constituencies began to emerge. A twenty-five-year-old woman by the name of Tan Houlan who helped found and lead the "Jinggangshan Combat Regiment" based in China's foremost teachers training college, Beijing Normal University, explained what drove her and many like her:

> There cannot be any proletarian dictatorship—or at least not any con-
> solidated proletarian dictatorship—without the criticism, supervision,
> and active support of the masses. . . . Chairman Mao has taught us that
> democracy is a means and not an end in itself. We use this means to
> reach our goal of making a success of the Great Proletarian Cultural
> Revolution, of consolidating the dictatorship of the proletariat, and of
> promoting the socialist cause.[17]

Tan, as it happened, was well connected and had an inside track to Mao's inner circle via a close friend who worked for *Red Flag*, the Party's theoretical journal. Again and again in the months that followed, such contacts would prove indispensable to all who had them. Without them and the access they provided, navigating the treacherous political currents of the Cultural Revolution proved both difficult and dangerous.

"Exchange of Intelligence"

From the outset, university-based organizations in particular put a premium on the "exchange of intelligence" (*hutong qingbao*)—an activity described by Mao as a crucial aspect of "exercising leadership" in a text that the Communist

Party now called on members to study "conscientiously and in a creative way."[18] Tactical concerns about current information were first voiced by students and junior faculty representing these organizations in the context of identifying, discrediting, and purging campuses of so-called "anti-Party and antisocialist rightists." In order to successfully manage this "question of first importance for the Cultural Revolution," one organization based on the campus of Peking University stressed, one had to set up specialized groups to manage *dongtai*—news on trends and unfolding developments.[19]

Most of the time, it was information about events close to home that was most eagerly sought. But there was also a thirst for news about what was happening elsewhere in China, especially among activists with friends in faraway places. The following excerpt from a request for information illustrates this point—a letter, dated August 20, 1966, from a student at Tsinghua University in Beijing to a friend at the Forestry Institute in Kunming, Yunnan, some 3,562 kilometers by rail from the capital. Note the use of the pronoun "we," suggesting that here was someone already asking not just for him/herself, but with the intention of sharing the answer with a wider body of people:

> What we're looking forward to from you is a detailed presentation of the situation in Kunming's universities in the Cultural Revolution, with particular stress on the following: (1) How's the mobilization of the masses proceeding? Does everybody dare to strike out, charge, and touch the tiger's arse? What about big-character posters (numbers, contents, etc.)? . . . (2) How are you doing bombarding of the headquarters? Has the lid on the Party Committee been removed altogether or not? . . . (3) What about contacts among the universities in Kunming? Are the universities trying to maintain a news blackout? What's the situation like at other schools? Is it noisy and boisterous or cold and cheerless?[20]

Selected phrases employed by the letter writer suggest that he (or she) was, on the whole, very much au fait with some recent and remarkable developments at the very highest levels of the Communist Party. The reference to "bombarding the headquarters," for example, was clearly lifted from Mao Zedong's blistering attack on Liu Shaoqi entitled "Bombard the Headquarters—My Big-Character Poster," the text of which had only just been disclosed to Party members in the form of Central Document *Zhongfa* [1966] 405 (dated August 17).[21] The letter as a whole was full of what counted as the "politically correct" language of the day—from "removing the lid," to "noisy and boisterous" and "cold and cheerless." In a recent speech, the text circulated on the same day as Mao's "Bombard the Headquarters," Party Vice-Chairman Lin Biao said he hoped the Cultural Revolution would become *so* "noisy and boisterous . . . neither the bourgeoisie nor the proletariat will be able to sleep."[22]

Innocent as they may appear today, communications such as the Tsinghua student's letter to Kunming were seen by the local Communist Party apparat as highly subversive (elsewhere in it, the writer sums up how far things had developed in Beijing). Although obviously framed in the form of questions, the requests for an update on what was "happening" could easily be interpreted as transparent agitation (*"Touch* the tiger's arse!" *"Lift* the news blackout!"). In the summer of 1966, attempts had still been made locally to impede the horizontal flow of information by banning certain forms of person-to-person contact in the absence of letters of introduction issued by the competent authorities. But these efforts ultimately proved futile. A major hurdle preventing the organized and independent nationwide collection and spread of news was removed at a mass rally in Beijing on August 16, at which Director of the Central Cultural Revolution Group (CCRG) Chen Boda announced that "revolutionary comrades and revolutionary students" across China were "very much welcome to travel to the capital of the revolution, to the capital where Chairman Mao is, to exchange experience."[23]

The full text of Chen's speech appeared on the pages of both *Red Flag* and the *People's Daily* within a couple of days, but it was on the whole rare for the words of senior political figures to made public. Indeed, the most sensitive information that the "organizations of the revolutionary masses" would now attempt to lay their hands on concerned what senior political figures said, including off the record or to restricted audiences. Savvy political operators, in turn, sought to retain a high degree of control over by whom, when, and how they were quoted. On one occasion in September 1966, CCRG Advisor Tao Zhu stated bluntly: "I'm not permitting you to go public with what I have just said. If you do, I will claim you made it all up."[24] A strong desire to maintain deniability was one reason for the suspicion with which Tao viewed attempts to tape-record what he said:

TAO ZHU: Is it OK if we don't tape? . . . The Premier has ruled that there should be no tape recording of speeches by comrades from the Center . . .

STUDENT: There is no way we're not going to put this on tape!

TAO ZHU: (*furious*) Why is that?

STUDENT: We've just explained why!

TAO ZHU: (*furious*) And I explained why not!

STUDENT: You're not going to prevail.

TAO ZHU: Neither are you . . .

STUDENT: Every time we produce a record of what's been said and Comrade Tao Zhu gets into trouble, he says those are rumors and makes a denial.[25]

In June 1967, a CCRG staffer remarked that he had once been present when his boss spoke, and he later heard a tape recording made on the same occasion. The recording, he said, was a gross distortion of the "spirit and tone" of the speech: "The practice of playing back a tape recording to other audiences," he insisted, "is very vile."[26]

Much of the collecting and sharing of information that was such a striking feature of the unfolding movement was ad hoc and short-lived, as the political fortunes of organizations shifted and the degree of activism and *engagement* of individual members fluctuated.[27] But some of the larger organizations quickly began contemplating operations far more ambitious than anything even Mao Zedong and the CCRG are likely to have anticipated. Beijing's 3rd HQ, for example, announced plans to launch a "Red Guard News Agency of the People's Republic of China." On January 1, 1967, its core members on the campus of the Beijing Geology Institute put out a "press release" explaining that

the Red Guard News Agency [will be] a combat news organ serving revolutionary rebels and organized by Red Guards who dare to make revolution and dare to rebel. The responsibility of the Red Guard News Agency [will be] to provide news and current information about the Great Cultural Revolution nationwide to red rebel newspapers nationwide, in particular news and current information from the capital and from other localities central to the movement. . . . We hope red rebels all over the country will fully consider and discuss this proposal of ours and share with us your opinions.[28]

This plan never materialized, but what did was the nationwide no-name network mentioned at the beginning of this paper: a veritable army of 3rd HQ members and affiliates collecting and passing on the news, by whatever medium of communication happened to be available, to their very own "head office" in Beijing.

Collecting and Processing Current Information

Historians would be exaggerating the professionalism of the organizations that ran the operations described here if they were to apply a fully fledged intelligence or news agency terminology to describe and analyze their collection, processing, internal dissemination, analysis, and exchange of information. Some "field collectors" were, by their own admission, little more than inquisitive activists with a nose for gossip. This is how one of them—who must have had a knack for what she was doing, since she quickly ended up being drafted onto the official Current Information Group of the new Beijing Municipal Revolutionary Committee in April 1967—explained what made her suited to the job:

> While attending the middle school for girls attached to Beijing Normal University, I came into contact with—and became a close friend of—many daughters of department heads, ministers, and Party secretaries (many of whom I now realize had serious [political] problems). When we got together, we would always exchange and comment on the latest gossip and news picked up at home. . . . Important matters and crucial developments about which [ordinary] cadres inside the Party might not yet even have been briefed were to us simply popular subjects of chit-chat after dinner or over tea. The outcome of all this was that I developed, at an early age, a reactionary bad habit of defying the Center and of not paying any attention to [the protection of] Party secrets. In all of this, actually, one sees the first sprouts of what happened later in the Great Cultural Revolution when I teamed up with the likes of XX and XXX to gather intelligence and attack the proletarian headquarters.[29]

This self-critical account, of course, dates from a point in time (February 1969) when the Cultural Revolution was winding down and information-gathering activities such as these were once again viewed with suspicion by the authorities.

To work effectively "in the field" collecting current information and news required resourcefulness and daring. A young man from the Beijing Geology Institute's East Is Red organization who for a time served as a liaison officer for the 3rd HQ in the city of Guangzhou boasted years later of what it had been like:

> To get a hotel room, you simply needed to produce a letter of introduction. For meals, I had national grain ration coupons and cash. I had no shortage of blank letters of introduction, and in my pocket I carried chops. At that time, you could have a "Geology Institute East Is Red" chop carved just about anywhere. Wherever you went, they would ask you for a letter of introduction, so you just stamped a letter with your chop and that was it. . . . At the time, I carried all sorts of letters of introduction. Every conceivable sort! From the Beijing Municipal Revolutionary Committee, from the Capital 3rd HQ, from our institute's Revolutionary Committee, as well as from Red Guards. I would just invent a name for myself and produce my own identity papers. It was easy![30]

A glance at the pages of a notebook kept by another member of East Is Red hints at the existence of vast "networks of networks." Scribbled down are telephone numbers to contacts in organizations the names of which have long since faded into obscurity ("Condemn Toxic Movies Liaison Station: Chen Jiageng 664 359 or 664 527 or 666 168"); names and telephone numbers of contacts in the armed forces next to extraneous information ("A Single Spark Can Start a Prairie Fire Revolutionary Rebel Team: Wang Jinshan and Li Beili 893 034 ext. 138. Unit 8201 supports the Million Heroes, 8199 supports the Left, airborne division and a dozen warships"); and countless other faded, altered, updated and crossed-out names, organizational affiliations, and telephone numbers.[31]

In November 1970, in a deposition submitted to the Beijing Municipal Revolutionary Committee, a former member of East Is Red summarized as follows "the ways and means by which we collected current information." Firstly, she explained, it was obtained from persons who "came to our institute to exchange revolutionary experiences." In the same way, the group's own members would obtain information through "visits to other units and *dongtai* exchange stations" (to be discussed later) in Beijing. Secondly, information about what was happening outside the capital was the subject of "mutual exchanges, through the mail, of *dongtai* from organizations outside Beijing and in other provinces and municipalities." Thirdly, there were "telegrams" and "long-distance telephone calls."[32]

In order to frustrate those who might be listening in on their telephone calls, "revolutionary mass organizations" devised their own homemade codes. In early September 1967, a cadre at Beijing Normal University leaked the following codes being used by members of one organization: the Beijing Geological Institute was represented by the number "01," the Beijing Iron and Steel Institute "Yan'an Commune" by 04, the Tsinghua University "414" organization by "33," and so on. Feigning surprise and outrage, the Tsinghua Jinggangshan Regiment Combat Operations Department (who almost certainly employed similar codes of their own) commented on the revelation: "Think about it comrades, what kind of organization would choose to employ codes like these? What kind of sinister schemes are they up to?"[33] CCRG advisor Kang Sheng called on all organizations implicated to "make thorough self-criticisms. This is no joking matter. [In addition to tapping phones] some of you have even created your own codes, a matter even more serious."[34]

Very little is known in detail about the internal finances of "revolutionary mass organizations," including budgets for collecting, processing, and disseminating information. Many organizations are unlikely to have kept any accounts in a professional or orderly manner, but some must have done so. A Five-Point Agreement (see appendix) between a Nanjing "revolutionary mass organization" and the employer (which in this case just happened to be a state-owned bank) of the core membership of that same organization illustrates one kind of arrangement, whereby operating funds and basic resources were made conditionally available. When an organization went over budget for reasons in keeping with the overall aim of the Cultural Revolution, the CCRG is known on occasion to have stepped in and covered the loss. During a meeting devoted to developments in the Xinjiang Uighur Autonomous

Region in March 1967, Zhou Enlai (who chaired the meetings of the CCRG) told representatives of the Revolutionary Rebel Headquarters of Xinjiang Red Guards—whose close contacts with Red Guards at some of Beijing's key universities served as an important conduit of information between Ürümqi and Beijing—that so far, to the best of his knowledge, they had run up a 30,000-yuan phone bill. "That's how much you've cost the state, and we write it off at one stroke," Zhou said. "That's freedom given you by Chairman Mao. [To live in] the era of Chairman Mao's leadership—oh how lucky you are!"[35]

Sample Contents 1

What, then, did the contents of a newsletter published by a "revolutionary mass organization" look like? At a point when their aim was to make it appear as if they were doing little else than hemorrhage state secrets, on-campus *critics* of the Jinggangshan Regiment Combat Operations Department described the contents of its *Current Information* as follows:

> Special sections on our central leaders; the overall distribution of our nation's industries; daily outputs of iron and steel; industrial and military installations along the Third Front; [classified] designations of military units everywhere; details surrounding garrisons at major airports; cryptonyms and careers of officers above the regiment level; activities at nuclear and missile test sites; and even detailed maps [showing the deployment] of our military.[36]

Had this characterization been accurate, the recipients of *Current Information* might well, at the end of the day, have suffered from information overload. But careful study of the contents of close to a hundred issues from between May and September 1967 proves the characterization to be grossly misleading, because it exaggerates by far the degree to which "state secrets" appeared on its pages.

Some *dongtai* were obviously better managed than others, which makes generalizations about contents difficult. The volume of information deemed suitable for wider dissemination by a particular group also varied over time. The following translation of page 3 of issue No. 94 (dated July 22, 1967) of

Important News is meant to illustrate what might appear in a newsletter at a time when a major event of national import was unfolding. *Important News* was put out by an organization of factory workers called the "General Headquarters of Revolutionary Rebels in the Fengtai Rolling Stock Plant." These workers from the southwestern outskirts of Beijing are *not* known to have had any information-gathering resources of their own outside the greater Beijing region, yet they managed to maintain fairly good coverage of the rapidly developing story that historians would one day call the "Wuhan incident":

Telegrams dated July 20, A.M.:

• On July 20, PLA Unit 8201 issued an appeal, citing the Supreme Instruction "Political Power Grows Out of the Barrel of a Gun" and saying "The Million Heroes is a no-nonsense and tough organization of rebels, and Unit 8201 swears it will back it up. Whoever touches even so much as a hair of one of the Million Heroes will be killed: there'll be nothing left of him. Knock the 'Worker's General HQ' to the ground and get rid of this pest for the sake of the people." PLA Unit 8201 says: "If the Center's ruling [here referring to Vice-Premier Xie's attitude] is correct, then we'll not stay soldiers any more, but go and join the Million Heroes." It also says: "No matter how senior Premier Zhou may be, no matter how exalted his position, we're going to drag him off his high horse all the same!"

• Railway traffic on the north to south Beijing to Guangzhou trunk line is no longer possible, and control of the bridge across the Yangzi river is in the hands of PLA Unit 8201.

Telegrams dated July 21, evening:

• At 10 A.M. on July 21, two girls from the Beijing Aeronautics Institute who managed to get out of Wuhan said: A lot of comrades are stuck in the Wuhan Guesthouse, and Vice-Premier Xie is injured after having been struck on the head and waist.

• PLA Unit 8201 has already delivered Wang Li into the hands of the Million Heroic Bandits.

• Last night (July 20) at 7 o'clock, the Wuhan office of the *Liberation Army Daily, Red Flag,* and New China News Agency was raided. 250 yuan in cash were stolen from Comrade Yang Ligong from *Red Flag,* together with documents and classified materials of interest. Only one person managed to escape, while the whereabouts of the others is unclear.

• In the afternoon of July 21, officers and men of the PLA in Wuhan said to Wuhan University: "If you make one more move, we will shoot you!" The loudspeaker vans of the Million Heroic Bandits spread a forged instruction of Chairman Mao's, "The Million Heroes are big! Good!" They also said the Wang Li was a time bomb buried right by Chairman Mao's side.

Telegrams dated July 21:

• The security of the leaders from the Center can at present not be guaranteed. It is still unclear whether the two people from the Beijing Aeronautics Institute and Jinggangshan have been killed or not.

• The PLA Units 8201 and 8199 specialize in beating up fighters from the 2nd HQ. In secret, they are deploying large numbers of troops to encircle and suppress the Wuhan Institute of Surveying and Mapping and Institute of Hydroelectric Engineering.

• Slogans of the Million Heroic Bandits: "Army, navy, and air force; ships, vehicles, and aircraft—we control all of them! There's no way you will be able to escape, Wang Li. Who do you think you are?"

• The 2nd HQ is right now preparing a mission to rescue the central leaders, and is ready to make whatever sacrifices will be called for. But in order not to interfere with any operations conducted by the Center, we hope the Central Cultural Revolution Group will provide us with instructions.

• Premier Zhou has already returned safely to Beijing after visiting Wuhan.

• At 5:25 P.M. on July 20, the Center issued a directive to the Wuhan Military Region, declaring that it had been as full representatives of the

Center that Xie Fuzhi and Wang Li went to Wuhan to resolve problems.

• At 2 P.M. on July 20, Wuhan University was attacked and taken over by the Million Heroic Bandits, and then the New Hubei University as well. Later, they went to surround and attack the Institute of Hydroelectric Engineering.

NOTE: PLA Unit 8201 is a military unit controlled directly by Chen Zaidao and his clique of counterrevolutionary elements that from the very beginning backed conservative organizations such as the "Million Heroes."[37]

The above is but the final third of the coverage of the Wuhan incident in *Important News* that day: the first two pages of issue No. 94 contained more of the same. On the bottom of page 3, there was background information on the leadership of the "Million Heroes," while page 4 was devoted to other news, including on a major sit-in outside the Zhongnanhai leadership compound in downtown Beijing, a confrontation on the campus of the Beijing Film Academy, and a series of recent events in Shanghai.[38]

Sample Contents 2

When no single "story" in particular outweighed all others in importance, the contents of a newsletter would have a wider scope. Translated below is the first page of *Current Information Newsletter* No. 26 (dated February 3, 1967), produced by a group attached to the on-campus "reception station" of the Tsinghua Jinggangshan organization:

HAPPY NEWS—

Premier Zhou says: In 1966, some 30 million sets of Mao's *Selected Works* were printed nationwide, and in 1967 the plan is to print 80 million sets. We ask everyone to use paper sparingly and to print more of Chairman Mao's works.

Telegram from Nanjing: Chairman Mao's third child Mao Anlong, whose disappearance during the White Terror of 1932 is mentioned in

"We Were Brave and Sacrifice Was Easy, and We Asked the Sun, the Moon, to Alter the Sky: Record of Visit to the Older Brother and Sister-in-Law of the Martyred Yang Kaihui," has recently been found in the Crossroads Brigade of Likou Commune in Wu County, Suzhou Prefecture, Jiangsu Province, where he is the current brigade accountant. He has already gone to Shaoshan to see his aunt.

PREMIER ZHOU'S INSTRUCTIONS ON JANUARY 28, PROMPTED BY THE "XINJIANG MASSACRE"—

1. Send a telegram to the CCP Committee of the Xinjiang Production and Construction Corps, telling them to suspend fire and withdraw immediately.

2. The Center organizes an investigation group that will carry out an investigation.

3. Send people to Xinjiang to understand the situation, resolve problems, and send Wang Enmao back to Xinjiang to resolve matters.

4. Counterrevolutionary elements in the corps, as well as armed and local units are to be suppressed. Counterrevolutionary organizations are to be arrested, but one must not open fire and shoot at people.

XINJIANG SPECIAL REPORT—

(This paper's special report) Recently there have been extremely serious developments in the situation in Xinjiang, and all revolutionary comrades must keep a very close eye on this. We thank the comrades manning our stations in Xinjiang for providing us with the information below:

Soviet Revisionists on the Border. It is reported that after the January 26 Mutiny in Xinjiang, the Soviet Revisionists reinforced their troops on the border with a rapid deployment force of some 200,000 fully armed men, ready to start trouble.

United Action Committee in Xinjiang. Recently elements from the United Action Committee have run wild across Xinjiang, everywhere disseminating copies of their "Three Questions to the Central Cultural Revolution Group," "Sons of High-Level Cadres Unite!" "Smash the Dog's Head of Whoever Opposes Wang Enmao" (1st Secretary of the Autonomous Region Party Committee and the Embodiment of the Liu-Deng Line in Xinjiang)," and other reactionary broadsheets, as well as madly shouting stuff like "We'll smash the dog's head of whoever tries to arrest us!" and "Certain leaders of the Central Cultural Revolution Group should not be too arrogant!"

They have joined forces with a handful of rotten eggs from the Xinjiang August 1 Middle School, and it is reported that they have guns and knives and say they're going to kill the rebel faction.

The rebel faction in Xinjiang is keeping a close watch on their movements, and recently rebels in the school for children of employees in industry and transport raided one of their liaison stations, where they found a big rubber stamp of the "Capital August 1 Regiment," a pile of letters of introduction from the Beijing West City Pickets, and an armband from the pickets.

Ethnic Current Information. Xinjiang recently witnessed the foundation of a "Grand Alliance of All Nationalities Rebel Headquarters." Most of its members are Hui, in addition to which some Uighurs have joined. Its manifesto urges a "revival of religious activities in the Mosques" and says that "the state should print new copies of the Qur'an to replace those burnt and destroyed during the 'destruction of the four olds.'" Four Imams involved in counterrevolutionary riots in Qinghai are alleged to previously have been in close contact [with the Headquarters]. At one point, it forcibly occupied the premises of the [Urümqi] municipal Association of Industry and Commerce and Political Consultative Conference, but political power has now been wrested from it and is once more in the hands of the Revolutionary Rebel Headquarters of Xinjiang Red Guards.[39]

The mimeograph technique widely employed to produce newsletters such as this one limited "print runs" to about four hundred for a single stencil: after that, copies were no longer legible. This particular copy of No. 26 of the

Current Information Newsletter shows how organizations devised simple, albeit labor-intensive, ways of getting around this problem: it is actually a "reprint," made from a new stencil cut a few days after the original's appearance. At the end of the (original) text on page 6, the following note has been added: "Reprinted by the Propaganda Group of the branch regiment of teachers and staff belonging to the Jinggangshan Regiment of Tsinghua University, February 6, 1967."[40]

Stories that had an international component were, for obvious reasons, rare. But now and then, bulletins would carry their very own reports on foreigners' suspicious or otherwise newsworthy activities in China. For instance, on May 6, 1967, under the headline "Be Vigilant!" the Jinggangshan Regiment *Teachers and Staff Current Information* reported that one member of a group of seven West German tourists (!) visiting Tsinghua University on April 28 had bragged about how "In West Germany, it is possible to criticize Adenauer in public."[41] On June 11, Jinggangshan organization sister-publication *Current Information* revealed that "a group of Swedish students have come to China and are running around everywhere taking photographs. Late at night on 5 June, they even tried to enter the campus of the Beijing Mining Institute to attend a rally at which Pan Zinian was being struggled."[42]

Dissemination

Newsletters such as those excerpted here were meant first of all to satisfy the information needs of members of the organizations that produced them. As has already been noted, however, they also gained wider circulation by way of informal exchange agreements with other organizations. In some cases, it was a matter of one-on-one exchanges, as a onetime member of the "Red Alliance" based in the Chinese Academy's Institute of Physics recalled decades later: "The 'June 16' group in the Beijing Foreign Languages Institute would send someone to our Academy's United Power Seizure Committee to pick up material (such as the tabloids and current information newsletters we put out). This was a regular occurrence among mass organizations."[43]

In Beijing, and in all probability in other large cities as well, dissemination and distribution eventually became more organized, and centered in practical terms on *dongtai* exchange stations. One such station was set up and run in the Haidian suburb of Beijing (where most of the universities in the capital were located) by one of the city's two quasi-official umbrella organizations for campus-based mass organizations, the so-called Capital University Red Guard Congress.[44] "After our *dongtai* group had been set up," a woman who worked in central Beijing at the time explained, "we would send someone every day to the offices of the Capital University Red Guard Congress (on the Peking University campus), to pick up a stack of that day's current information newsletters from the various schools. It took a lot of time and effort."[45] At the exchange stations, organizations would have their own "pigeon holes" and be able to deposit copies of their newsletters and publications, as well as pick up (assuming they had the right credentials) copies of those produced by other organizations. For example, an identity card—a Paper Pick-Up Permission (*lingbaozheng*), as it was called—marked "not transferable" was issued to a student (representing the Jinggangshan organization in the Beijing No. 3 Middle School) by another municipal umbrella organization, the Capital Middle School Red Guard Congress, managing the *dongtai* exchange station for mass organizations based on the campuses of middle schools.

In many cases, the inaugural issue of a particular newsletter would carry a mission statement specifying the purpose and readership for which it was being produced. For a time in 1967, Tsinghua University's Jinggangshan Regiment produced not just one but many different newsletters, each with its own unique focus and coverage, and here is what was said in the inaugural issue of the one called *Teachers and Staff Current Information,* devoted to developments on campus:

> The present publication is an internal publication. . . . It mainly reports on what is happening among the teachers and staff of our school in the Cultural Revolution and is meant to serve the relevant research conducted by the Regiment as a reference tool. What has to be explained is that in order to facilitate the work of those engaged in analysis, the reports published [on its pages] reflect a variety of aspects [of what is happening]. Hence the viewpoints expressed do not [necessarily] represent those of the [Regiment] General Headquarters. Please keep this publication in a safe place and refrain from circulating it.[46]

Interesting in this context is the separation between the reporting and analysis functions, reminiscent of the higher echelons of the Communist Party, where the task of the flagship *Internal Reference* produced by the New China News Agency was to report, while on the basis of its contents (as well as other information) other, specialized entities were tasked with analysis.

Here it is worth noting that few "revolutionary mass organizations" appear to have given much thought to problems of information retrieval and archiving. In technical colleges and universities, organizations sometimes confused a truly scientific and therefore convenient information retrieval system with one that simply had a high "gee whiz" coefficient, such as the unique string of more than twenty digits, hyphens, Roman letters, and numerals that identified an issue (and the contents) of the mimeographed series of transcripts of central leaders' speeches produced by the Tsinghua Jinggangshan Regiment 3rd *dongtai* Group.

Newsletter distribution could be remarkably organized and controlled. Copies came at no cost, but this did not mean that they could be had by just anybody (not the least because of the practical limit on print runs). On the campus of the Beijing School of Chemical Engineering, the East Is Red Commune employed a system of special "provision permits" (*dongtai fafang zheng*; see page 251), valid for a period of between six and seven weeks, that entitled the privileged holder to one or more copies of each issue (the exact number to be written on the permit at the time of its issue and validation). Printed on the permits were the following points for attention:

(1) Passing on to outsiders strictly forbidden; only for reference purposes; (2) may not be cited, relayed, copied, or pasted up in public without prior consent; (3) may be picked up daily at the *dongtai* distribution point, between 6 and 7 P.M.; (4) timely comments are welcome, as is the submission of material and information; (5) does not appear on Sundays.[47]

Preprinted on the back of the permit were the running numbers of the issues it entitled the holder to pick up. Once a certain issue had appeared and been picked up, its number would be crossed out, so as to make it impossible for the permit holder to get more than one copy of it with the same permit.

最高指示

　我们的责任，是向人民负责。每句话，每个行动，每项政策，都要适合人民的利益，如果有了错误，一定要改正，这就叫向人民负责。

毛主席万岁！

北京化工学校
革命委员会　东方红公社
红代会　动态组
No. 000005

单位：工农兵46
领取人：
份数：2/3

动态发放证

58	59	60	61	62	63
64	65	66	67	68	69
70	71	72	73	74	75
76	77	78	79	80	81
82	83	84	85	86	87
88	89	90	91	92	93
94	95	96	97	98	99

注意事项

(1) 严禁外传，仅供参考
(2) 未得允许，不得引用、转抄、张贴。
(3) 每天晚6•00～7•00到动态发放处领取。
(4) 及时提出意见，提供材料、情况。
(5) 星期日休息。

A "provision permit" (*dongtai fafang zheng*) from the East Is Red Commune at the Beijing School of Chemical Engineering (author's collection).

Once a copy of a newsletter had been read by the intended recipient, he or she might share it with others or even attempt to trade or sell it on the "open market"! The latter act of "spontaneous capitalism" was highly controversial. On April 17, 1967, an anonymous reader of a newsletter produced by the Shanghai Jiaotong University "Resist All the Way" Regiment Current Information Group, wrote to the editors telling them of how he had recently observed "some people (mostly middle school students) trading documents in public places, some even exchanging internal ones for [Mao] badges, which is a very bad thing and easily exploited by the class enemy."[48] At the end of May, the Liaison Group of the Resist All the Way organization issued the following statement:

> We have recently discovered that some people are making and selling unauthorized copies of our newsletter and therefore we issue this severe warning to these economic and political pickpockets: revolutionary action will be taken to deal with further incidents of this sort, should they occur. We ask other revolutionary organizations to assist us. Should anyone encounter persons making and selling unauthorized copies of our newsletter, please either escort them to our regiment or contact us by telephone immediately [at 370 147 ext. 408].[49]

At the same time, the distributors of the *Resist All the Way Bulletin* announced that all its current recipients would have to reregister and that, for the time being, registration of any new recipients was halted. Earlier, the editors had threatened anyone found copying its contents without authorization with the immediate suspension of readers' privileges.[50]

Rumor had it that current information newsletters were much sought after by foreigners and that hostile intelligence agencies in particular were prepared to pay large sums of money for them. In Beijing on the evening of April 5, 1967, two children aged nine and twelve were caught stealing "a huge amount of internal current information newsletters" from unlocked premises on the campus of the Beijing Mining Institute. Because of the age of the two thieves, the institute authorities at first did not take the incident very seriously, but reported it to the local police station all the same. When the police visited the children's home, they discovered to their amazement between 15 and 20 kilograms of mimeographed current information newsletters, transcripts of CCP leaders' speeches, and handbills, apparently stolen on the campuses of surrounding universities. The father of the children, an unemployed former major in the Nationalist army and foreign-language translator, was immediately detained on suspicion of having intended to pass the material on to foreign intelligence agencies.[51]

No information has come to light showing that foreigners actually managed *at the time* to get ahold of any current information newsletters produced by China's "revolutionary mass organizations." But the belief that they were was reinforced by reports put out by the organizations themselves. In May 1968, a rumor on the Tsinghua University campus had it that copies of the Jinggangshan Regiment Combat Operations Department *Current Information* were "regarded by the imperialists and reactionaries of the world as priceless treasures" and that "American spies have been paying 40,000 U.S. dollars per copy in Hong Kong."[52]

September 1967: Enforced Dissolution

In the overall scheme of things, the Cultural Revolution "had come full circle" by August 1968.[53] That was the time when high-powered task forces similar to those with which the local Communist Party apparat had attempted, but failed, to micromanage the movement two years earlier finally fanned out into society—this time on orders from Mao Zedong himself. In the second half of 1968, all "organizations of the revolutionary masses" were forced to disband. The beginning of the end of the collection and exchange of information discussed in this paper, however, had in fact occurred a full year earlier, in September 1967.

Already in late summer of 1967, members of Mao's inner circle had started to voice concerns over the independent information collection by the "revolutionary masses." One important reason for this was that the best *dongtai* groups were simply getting to be *too* good at what they were doing and were weakening the CCRG's hold on the national political agenda. In July 1967, representatives of "organizations of the revolutionary masses" from twenty-eight provinces and cities across China met informally at the HQ of the Tsinghua Jinggangshan Regiment in Beijing to debate the "current situation."[54] On the basis of the information available to them, the meeting participants made their own informed assessments. A note in *Current*

Information after the meeting painted a bleak picture of the progress and direction of the Cultural Revolution, arguing that "numerous signs" showed very plainly that "a small handful of persons in power taking the capitalist road in the Party *and in the military* are currently joining forces and encircling Beijing in a vain and frenzied attempt to counterattack." In response, *Current Information* suggested, it was imperative to make preparations to "take up arms to defend Beijing."[55]

This did not tally with Mao Zedong's assessment at the time, the gist of which was said to be that "the situation in the Great Proletarian Cultural Revolution nationwide is truly excellent, not merely OK. The situation now is better than it has ever been. . . . In another couple of months, the situation as a whole will have changed and be better still."[56] The failure of those who had their own sources of information and news to "fall into line" with this view irritated members of Mao's inner circle. The reaction of someone such as Chen Boda, the head of the CCRG, was to order them to study Chairman Mao's instructions and substitute his views for their own "self-centered" ones.[57]

Minister of Public Security Xie Fuzhi chose to concentrate on the information sources as such, rather than on the views of the "situation" they allowed. At a rally in Beijing on August 11, 1967, he pointedly asked leaders of major organizations in Beijing whether it really was right to allow oneself "to be guided by the assessment of the situation made by one school, by one organ, by one particular person, or by one *dongtai* group?"[58] Jiang Qing indicated where the real problem lay when she, on the same occasion, claimed to have heard that

> Peking University has between one and two thousand people out there gathering intelligence. (Turning to Xie) What are they called? (Xie responds: "Current information groups.") That's going too far. Have they been recalled yet? (Peking University representative Nie Yuanzi stands up and responds: "We've already recalled them. There are not as many as that.")[59]

A few weeks later, on September 1, Chen Boda reiterated the point Jiang had made, calling on Nie Yuanzi to do something about the "current information groups of more than 1,000 people nationwide" who worked for her Xin

Beida organization: to either "withdraw" them, "disband" them, or simply "get rid of" them.[60]

By mid-September 1967, the "organizations of the revolutionary masses" had begun to take action. On September 12, the East Is Red organization on the campus of the Beijing Geology Institute announced that it was "dissolving all combat operations groups and current information groups (in Beijing and outside the capital) and suspending further publication of current information newsletters."[61] On September 17, Jiang Qing kept up the pressure at a meeting with university students:

> The movement has ended up in the hands of you intellectuals. You've had a bourgeois education, right? (Response: yes!) You've had a bourgeois education, so you're trying everywhere to find things out, and every time the wind blows one way or the other, you bend with it. These *dongtai,* combat, and bugging operations—get rid of all of them![62]

On September 20, the Politics and Law Commune organization released the final issue of its *Important News in Brief.*[63] On September 21, the Tsinghua Jinggangshan Regiment announced the suspension of activities of its 3rd *dongtai* Group, responsible for the production of *Current Information.*[64] On September 22, the Liaison Station of Red Rebels in Finance and Trade announced that "in accordance with the spirit of instructions from the central leaders," it was dissolving its *dongtai* group and that its *Current Information Newsletter* would no longer be appearing.[65]

The September 1967 clampdown was of course not really the complete end of all of the current information groups. Some leaders of the "organizations of the revolutionary masses" that they had served, rather than truly disband the groups simply opted for leaner, meaner, and altogether *covert* means. This was not something that went unnoticed by the authorities, as evident from repeated critical remarks by the Minister of Public Security in the winter of 1967–1968. So, for example, on December 16, 1967, Xie Fuzhi told an audience of university students:

> I've heard that your *dongtai* groups are six in number and that groups 1 and 2, in particular, are covert. Compiling materials on central leaders, eh? All of them copied. . . . And I hear the fifth group deals with the

military? (Kuai Dafu: On September 17, Comrade Jiang Qing called for the dissolution of *dongtai* groups, so after that we dissolved them.) I am not talking specifically about your Tsinghua University. I am asking, are there still *dongtai* groups out there of one kind or another?[66]

When a member of his audience responded, saying that any groups still in existence had no other purpose than "to exchange experiences and to study leaders' speeches," Xie admitted that "To exchange experiences is of course permitted."[67] It was the running of translocal news and current information networks that was once more raising suspicions of "spontaneous counter-revolution."

*   *   *

Almost five decades have passed since the subject of this paper was in and of the present. Today, the politics that briefly embroiled so many ordinary citizens in a Great Proletarian Information Revolution are no longer relevant: the precepts set in boldface that spelled out "Serve the People" and "The Working Class Must Exercise Leadership in Everything" have since been turned from guides to revolutionary action into slogans that sell T-shirts and overstuffed pillows. The medium that spread the message then has today become an archaeological curiosity: mimeograph machinery now prompts not the question "How do you use it?" but "What is it?" The dialing instructions on the inside back cover of the 1967 Beijing telephone directory ("Insert your finger into a hole in the dial, turn clockwise until you hit the copper hook, pull your finger out, and let the dial return automatically.") no longer convey useful information.

Reduced to its bare essentials, the organizers of a conference on the subject at New York's New School in February 2010 stressed that "free access to knowledge and information are the bedrock of all democratic societies." But, they went on to add, "there is no need to be a student of history to know that the kinds and severity of limits [on what can be known] wax and wane over time."[68] In the People's Republic of China too there has been a palpable waxing and waning of limits. Access to knowledge has been hampered by a culture of secrecy and information curtailment: "Don't enquire about secrets you're not meant to be privy to," CCP members were reminded under Mao Zedong, "and don't share secrets with those who are not meant to know them!" But in 1966–1967, at Beijing's "Democracy Wall" in the winter of 1978–1979, and in the streets of the capital for an all-too-brief spring in 1989, almost anything seemed permissible and briefly possible as citizens were able to challenge the state over the "right to know" (as distinct from the right to know some specific thing). Since the end of the 1990s, China's internet has become *the* theater where "information warfare" is waged 24/7.

For historians who write about how patterns from the past continue to impact contemporary China, the history of the "information networks" managed by the Cultural Revolution's "organizations of the revolutionary masses" should provoke a rethink on the conceptualization level and make us question our habitual equation of so-called legacies of the Cultural Revolution with "ever-more-simplistic slogans" or "violence and anarchy." There was far more than slogans and chaos to the thirteen months from August 1966 to September 1967: they saw a genuine waning of limits on access to, and sharing of, knowledge and information. Today's Chinese civic and social organizations may grapple with their own problems of autonomy, empowerment, and information access, and are unlikely to be aware of—or even care very much about—the experiences of the 3rd HQ or the "East Is Red." And given that new information and communication technologies always alter information flows and relationships, perhaps this is just the way it should be. Students of civil society may well shun the organizations of the Cultural Revolution altogether, because few of these espoused the kind of muffled democratic sentiment that scholarship likes to identify as a corollary of genuine social organizations "under communism." But there are undoubtedly strands in the present age of social changes and political transformation in China that can be drawn back to an entirely different era in the history of the People's Republic.

Appendix: Five-Point Agreement

1. In accordance with the spirit of the Center's *Ten-Point Regulations* on the unfolding of the Great Cultural Revolution in industrial and mining enterprises, the Party Group of the [Nanjing municipal] Sub-branch [of the China People's Bank] recognizes the Jiangsu Workers' Red Rebel General Command Nanjing Area Banking System General Department as a revolutionary organization of mass character.

2. The Sub-branch will actively assist in providing the necessary funding for the activities of the General Department and is furthermore at once allocating [to the General Department] 500 yuan in working funds. In the future, [the General Department] will be reimbursed for outlays in accordance with the [CCP] Chairman's principles that state that all undertakings should be run industriously and thriftily.

3. In order to facilitate the activities of the General Department, the Sub-branch provides the General Department with two vacant rooms to use as offices and furthermore allocates to it one telephone, two bicycles, and one moped. The right to priority use of cars belonging to the Sub-branch is granted the General Department as long as such use does not interfere with regular money transports.

4. [The Sub-branch] agrees to free five comrades from the General Department from their normal production duties. With the active support of the Party Group of the Sub-branch and the Party Branches of the various sections and offices, the General Department has the power to free from their normal production duties the personnel needed [to manage the activities of] the Red Rebel Teams in the various sections and offices [of the Sub-branch].

5. Exclusive control and use of the broadcasting stations and broadcasting and propaganda equipment in the various sections and offices [of the Sub-branch] is granted the Red Rebel Teams in those same sections and offices in accordance with the Provincial Party Committee's *Eight-Point Agreement* and the Municipal Party Committee's *Ten-Point Regulations.*

Signed on behalf of the Party Group of the [Nanjing municipal] Sub-branch [of the China People's Bank]: Xu Zhaowu

Signed on behalf of the [Jiangsu Workers' Red Rebel General Command Nanjing Area] Banking System General Department: Qiu Rongsong

January 5, 1967

10

The Dilemma of Implementation

The State and Religion in the People's Republic of China, 1949–1990

XIAOXUAN WANG

The 1949 revolution ushered in a period of unparalleled repression of religion in China. Over the course of the first half of the twentieth century, the government and various interest groups attacked communal religion as "superstition" (*mixin*).[1] The "temple to school" (*miaochan xingxue*) movement, starting in 1898 with Zhang Zhidong's essay "Exhortation to Learning" (*Quan xue pian*) and recurring sporadically through the 1930s, considerably squeezed the land and space of communal temples and Buddhist monasteries. Following the victory of the Communist revolution, however, was a systematic seizure in the 1950s of the properties of all religious traditions—Protestant and Catholic churches as well as communal temples and Buddhist monasteries. Most religious activities were also forcibly restricted. The situation further worsened in the 1960s and early 1970s, when virtually all religious activities were criminalized. The repression of religion seemed to have profoundly secularized society itself until the unexpected resurgence of religious life in the 1980s, which called into question the long-term effectiveness of the government in transforming religious beliefs.

Recent studies, using newly accessible government archives and fieldwork in villages, reveal a rather different contour of religious life than was previously believed to exist in the Chinese countryside during the first thirty years of the People's Republic. These studies have demonstrated that the government was far less successful in controlling religion than we used to believe. Religious beliefs and practices continued to exert significant influence over village life and peasant behavior despite the intensive propaganda and political pressures in this period.[2] Why then did the government fail to effectively keep religion under control in the long run?

To answer this question it is necessary to reconsider the gap between policy and implementation, between official claims and local realities. Most previous studies on state and religion in modern China, whether emphasizing continuity or discontinuity, have highlighted the continued interest of the Communist government in controlling religion.[3] However, these studies not only tend to ignore the local enforcement of religious policies and focus instead on the macro policies of the central state, they also overlook the vacillation of the Communist Party's approach to religion while stressing its ultimate goal of controlling it. One aspect of this lack of a uniform plan is the juxtaposition of suppression with limited tolerance. Despite the government's many measures to repress religious activities, the Constitution of the People's Republic of China stipulates that religious freedom must be protected. Even in the 1960s, the government claimed to support to a certain degree so-called legal religious activities. Another facet of vacillation, integrally related to the first, is the instability and indeterminacy of the categories and discourses used in the government's religious policies, such as "religion," "superstition," "normal religious activities" (*zhengchang de zongjiao huodong*), and "counterrevolutionary activities" (*fangeming huodong*).[4] Changing policy thus created more space for both sanctioned and unsanctioned religious practice than has previously been evident in the PRC government's secular stance or survivors' testimony concerning religious persecution under Mao.

This chapter surveys religious life in Ruian County (a county-level city since 1987) in southern Zhejiang during the Mao and post-Mao eras.[5] In this study, I aim to demonstrate how policy created by the Communist government's vacillating approach to religion played out locally and to assess the consequences of policy ambiguity for local religious practices. I argue that the reason for the government's inability to bring religious activities under control in the long run was not only the lack of effective administrative institutions but also the less than full support of cadres at the grassroots level. The mutually reinforcing interactions between the inconsistent commands of suppressive and tolerant religious policies and the instability and indeterminacy of discourses and categories pertaining to religious policies had two consequences: first, to confuse local cadres, who therefore fluctuated between brutal crackdown and no interference; and second, to leave room for cadres to manipulate the commands from their superiors—especially those cadres who were themselves involved in religious activities in one way or another. Even today, the implementation of religious policies in China lacks the support of local cadres, despite efforts by the government to improve its relations with religious communities.

These findings will help us understand why religious activities never disappeared and even expanded from an institutional perspective in some places during the Maoist era. The religion issue in the People's Republic, especially during the Mao years, is often framed as a zero-sum game with state repression on one side and local resistance on the other. But my study will help look beyond religion simply as a state-society matter. It instead looks into the religious issue from the dynamics of different arms of governments at all levels. In this light, it might also help us understand other issues in everyday life at the grassroots level during the Maoist era.

State and Religion in Pre-1949 Ruian

Ruian is an administrative unit in Wenzhou Prefecture. It had a population of 456,900 persons in 1949 and a total area covering 1,360 square kilometers of land.[6] As recorded in an annual government report, the county had 115 churches and gatherings spots (Protestant and Catholic) and 317 Buddhist temples in 1957.[7] During the Maoist era (1949–1976), Christian communities in Ruian continued to proliferate. In 2012 there were 595 registered religious sites and more than 1,200 unregistered temples for the worship of local deities.[8] Throughout Ruian, as typical in south China in the late imperial era, territorial cults and rituals created an elaborate religious network that was vital to village life and politics. Annual festivals were held to celebrate birthdays of deities and communal rituals to deal with seasonal calamities. Two rituals were particularly important in Ruian before 1949. The *taifo* (literally, "touring the Buddha") ceremony was performed to make rain during drought periods and to bring "blessings with great peace" (*bao taiping*) in the new year. The other highly significant ritual was the annual dragon boat racing, or *hualongchuan,* performed during the Dragon Boat Festival.[9] This observance was not merely a rowing competition as its name suggests, but a series of rituals of which the competition was only one part. Such rituals were mainly held to prevent plagues and bring blessing to the community. Ruian, as elsewhere in Wenzhou, was a destination for waves of migrants from outside the region. Dragon boat racing therefore also served as a platform to confirm the boundaries between villages and stratify access to resources. The imperial authority basically treated communal rituals as "customs" (su)—antonyms of "standard" (zheng).[10] A su such as dragon boat racing might cause disputes and conflict. With the management of the state and the local elites, however, they rarely posed a threat to Confucian ideology or a political challenge to the dynasty. Therefore dragon boat racing was generally tolerated.

However, the turn of the twentieth century coincided with a critical change in the classification of, and discourses on, religion. Under the new system, communal religion was categorized as "superstition," as opposed to legally protected "religion."[11] Prohibition and surveillance of saihui (religious parades and fairs) such as dragon boat rowing were routinized and "naturalized as a scheme of governance."[12] These changes in the government's attitude toward communal rituals could certainly be felt in Ruian.[13] However, they were rarely effective and "only lined policemen's pockets," because local Nationalist Party committees did not gain enough support from local elites.[14] Some elites moved out of temple activities to new power arenas, such as modern education, but only a small number of temples were consequently converted into schools or other institutions.[15] Temple activities remained prosperous. About 40.6 percent of Buddhist temples and 11.8 percent of communal temples experienced reconstruction from 1900 to 1937, and in most cases reconstruction took place after 1911.[16] As for Christian churches, it was certainly a period of tremendous growth: the number of churches and gathering spots (juhuidian) increased from 28 to 108 between 1911 and 1937.[17] Ruian County and the whole Wenzhou region represent a traditional stronghold of Christianity. Ever since the arrival of Protestantism and Catholicism in the late 1860s, Christian churches kept growing in the county despite significant setbacks in the Maoist era. (The economic "miracle" in contemporary Wenzhou has sometimes been attributed to this Christian presence.)[18] Religion was a vital source of community meaning and organization.

Land Reform, the Conversion of Religious Space, and Resistance, 1949–1957

The Communist Party, unlike the Nationalist Party, did not launch campaigns directly targeting communal religious activities after taking power in 1949, though it did launch the campaign against new religious movements—"counterrevolutionary" redemptive societies. In its attitudes and policies toward communal religious practices, the Communist Party was initially more cautious than the Nationalist Party. As David Holm writes, the Communist Party "seemed to have recognized very early the dangers of high-handed government action after the Nationalist Party's fashion."[19] From its early stages, the Party understood the great practical importance of "local flavor" in carrying out propaganda. Before taking over the whole nation, the Communist Party appropriated and reconstructed local folk customs such as *yangge* (rice-sprout songs) and *nianhua* (new year painting) in its liberation zones to implement Communist ideology, mobilize the masses, and transform and control cultural life.[20] From 1938 to 1942, in a series of speeches, including the famous "Speech at the Yan'an Forum on Literature and Art," Mao Zedong advocated the adoption of "national forms" for ideological propaganda, which would include the "use of old forms."[21]

Land reform, however, severely devastated communal religion in Ruian, as it did elsewhere in the country.[22] Not only was the land of communal temples seized, the temples themselves were also either shut down or, more often, taken for secular purposes.[23] Village elites who traditionally dominated rural life were purged from the local leadership. Zhang Junsun recalled that his family had been for generations a major patron of a local temple, Lord Jiang's Palace, in Dingtian, Xincheng District. Land and properties owned by his family were confiscated and redistributed to poor villagers.[24] His father, once a township head before 1949, was executed soon after land reform. Ying Qiancheng was a Daoist master and a successful businessman at Meitou Town, Tangxia. He had been a constable (*baozhang*) for twelve years and was also a major patron of the East Peak Pavilion (*Dongyue guan*) at Meitou. Ying was classified as a businessman landlord (*gongshangye dizhu*) and a head of superstition (*mixin touzi*) and lost all lands he owned and most of his houses.[25] Those members of the traditional elite who were

not executed or put into jail became social outcasts. They could not participate in the new power structure and continued to be the target of various
campaigns in subsequent years. Land reform created an ostensible vacuum
in religious leadership and a shortage of physical space and revenue for religious practice in Ruian. Local authorities, however, soon realized that they
were put in the position of confronting religious activities led mainly by
revolutionary masses (*geming qunzhong*), the landless peasants, poor peasants, and middle peasants on whom the Chinese revolution and socialist
construction relied. For many cadres, dealing with the religious behaviors of
revolutionary masses was no easier than dealing with those of traditional
elites.

The attitude of the Communist Party toward peasants' participation in
communal religious activities was not clearly formulated around the time of
land reform. In the 1950s the Party had not begun to differentiate "superstition" from "religion."[26] The Party considered communal religious activities
superstition that should be opposed in principle. But superstition was
believed to be a thought issue (*sixiang wenti*) that could only be solved gradually, as exemplified in Mao's famous judgment that "peasants themselves
erected *pusa* [literally, Bodhisattva, but in this case it refers broadly to all
sorts of deities, including Bodhisattva] and they would use their own hands
to cast aside *pusa* at some point."[27]

The handling of communal religious activities therefore often depended
on the needs of local officials. When the issue of suppressing superstition
was low on their list of priorities, they could choose to make a concession, as
they did during the rainmaking riots of the summer of 1953. A prolonged
drought ravaged Ruian as well as the rest of the province between June and
mid-August of that year. Rainmaking and other ritual activities emerged
and quickly spread throughout the county beginning in late June. Villagers
openly criticized the Communist Party for "destroying the statues of gods"
(*daofo*), ascribing the drought to the conversion of temples and the demoli-
tion of sacred statues of divinities.[28] Rainmaking ceremonies quickly turned
into an attack on cadres and the village and town government. To deal with
the surge of rainmaking ceremonies, in addition to sending cadres to help
irrigate land and pump water, the county government ordered first to "educate" (*jiaoyu*) villagers and, if persuasion turned out to be futile, then to let
people do the ritual.[29] County officials stressed that the cadres should not

impose uncompromising prohibition but should try to illustrate that "there is no prohibition on the belief in deities and there is also freedom not to believe in religion."[30]

The county government's equivocal attitude toward communal religion was more clearly manifested in the case of dragon boat racing. Land reform and other political campaigns disrupted dragon boat racing between 1949 and 1952. In many villages, cadres dismantled dragon boats to build houses for schools and the village government. When dragon boat racing reappeared in 1953, however, local residents in many districts reportedly poured into the commune, schools, and town governments to demand compensation for their dismantled boats. Village cadres were attacked for actively prohibiting dragon boat racing.[31] In 1954, the county government's policy took a dramatic turn. The ritual, instead of being condemned as superstition, was interpreted as the people's traditional cultural recreation (*wenhua yule*), created for commemorating the great patriotic national poet Qu Yuan,[32] and in 1957 it was treated as "an opportunity for our Party to lead the masses to develop cultural recreation."[33] Consequently, educating the masses and inventing new forms to replace old forms became the theme of the county government's policy.

Attempts to transform dragon boat racing to serve the government's own agenda were often *pro forma* and tentative—that is, selectively enforcing certain inconsequential directives without any substantive effort to transform the ritual itself. Following the policy change in 1954, several new institutions, including district and township cultural entertainment committees and small groups, were set up to lead and supervise dragon boat racing.[34] But the idea of "developing new forms" (*fazhan xin xingshi*) introduced in the 1954 policy was no more than an empty slogan. During the Dragon Boat Festival, town and village cadres organized cultural and artistic activities (*wenyi huodong*) and sporting events at the request of their superiors but also turned a blind eye to dragon boat racing. Traditional religious consciousness still informed the event to such an extent that in 1961 the local government had to prohibit practices such as eulogizing the god (*changsheng*) and holding incense baskets (*duan xiangdou*).[35] In addition, uncondoned display of the images of Party leaders was prohibited in boat competitions.

The new regime ran into similar difficulties in dealing with Buddhism and Christianity in Ruian in the 1950s. The Communist Party, though lacking systematic policies, had some general principles for controlling state-sanctioned religion as part of the broader united front policies (*tongzhan zhengce*). These policies emphasized the importance of differentiating "major contradictions" (*zhuyao maodun*) from "minor contradictions" (*ciyao maodun*) and "contradictions among the people" (*renmin neibu maodun*) from "contradictions between the enemy and us" (*diwo maodun*).[36] The question of Buddhism and Christianity was primarily regarded as one of "contradictions among the people" but sometimes also considered as "contradictions between the enemy and us," for religion had been exploited by feudal landlords and imperialists to oppress the people and threaten the socialist regime. Hence, the government required the suppression of counter-revolutionary activities under the cloak of religion (*pizhe zongjiao waiyi de fangeming huodong,* for instance, cutting connections between religious organization and foreign imperialist powers), while also mandating the protection of limited "religious freedom."[37]

Although the Party claimed to protect religious freedom from the very beginning of the People's Republic, the pressing task of regime consolidation made it impossible to do so. Thus, even limited religious freedom could not be guaranteed while political campaigns prioritized suppression of religion, because religious organizations were purportedly tied to feudal landlords, class oppression, and imperialism. All Buddhist temples and churches in Ruian were asked to cease activities during land reform. Although the reform did not directly target Buddhism, Buddhist temples, traditionally relying on the land they owned for income, encountered an unprecedented crisis. Most land and some buildings belonging to Buddhist temples were reallocated to villagers, though Buddhist monks and nuns who resided in the temples also received a small portion of land.[38] The situation for Buddhists in Yueqing, another county in Wenzhou, was perhaps even worse. Jiaoxuan, the first head of the Buddhist association in Yueqing, printed the land reform law for the purpose of helping monks and nuns learn the law and therefore better protect Buddhist temples and properties. He was consequently sentenced to five years in prison for undermining the reform. Baihe Temple, where the association was located, was sealed up on governmental orders. Throughout the county, most Buddhist temples were confiscated.[39]

One legacy of land reform was that the encroachment on the religious space of Buddhism and Christianity became routine during the next two decades as religious activities were further stigmatized and attacked. All churches in Tangxia and Xianyan were closed during the land reform period and occupied as schools, offices, or private residences thereafter.[40] The Wenzhou prefectural government, responding to mounting cases of unauthorized occupation of churches, had to issue a command in March 1956 stipulating that there would be "no occupation of churches without permission from now on."[41]

Another problem emerged when the provincial and regional authorities attempted to rectify local violations of religious policies, leaving local cadres reluctant to cooperate. In 1952, there were growing concerns of "violation of religious policy" (*weifan zongjiao zhengce*) among provincial and prefectural government officials during the peak of the land reform movement. In the meantime, some Christian communities in Ruian resumed regular gatherings without state authorization, while still more petitioned to reopen churches.[42] Buddhists also petitioned to organize a new Buddhist association.[43] In reply, the civil affairs offices of the provincial government and Wenzhou prefectural commission gave orders to permit those churches that had petitioned to reopen and those that had proved not to have political issues to resume regular gatherings. The Ruian County government, however, did not fully comply and instead asked district and town governments not to give permission to reopen churches. The county government asked groups that had restored regular meetings without authorization to wait for further instructions from the prefectural government.[44] In this way, the county procrastinated instead of replying to the Buddhists' petition to form an association and, more generally, stymied provincial and regional policies.

The provincial government ascribed this type of unwillingness to cooperate to the local cadres' inadequate understanding of the importance of religious affairs and religious policies. In a December 1952 report on the first provincial meeting on religious affairs, provincial officials noted that there were pervasive sentiments of avoidance and reluctance (*qingshi he weinan qingxu*) caused by the difficulty of managing religious affairs. "Most of the Party Committee propaganda departments do not pay attention to or examine this work. They also do not designate officials to specifically take charge of this work ... which is widely considered unimportant ... but tough to do. They prefer not to do it."[45]

Although religious affairs may have been a low priority for local cadres, grassroots officials were made to bear the blame for a more systemic issue. The government's two-pronged strategy itself created confusion and difficulties among local cadres, who were basically being asked to distinguish normal religious activities from a more serious political concern—counterrevolutionary activities carried out under the guise of religion. Therefore, the government appears to have handled state-sanctioned religions, particularly at the town and village level, and communal rituals with a similar kind of tentativeness. According to a report made by the Ruian government in 1955, "for most of the time, [village and town cadres] either do not know what to do or feel impatient"; indeed, "their mastery of religious policies is very limited," and "they sway between 'leftism' and 'rightism,'" but more frequently toward the right.[46] "Leftism" meant the repression of religious activities with harsh measures, such as closing temples and churches and direct interference in religious life. "Rightism" referred to the inclination not to interfere. Village cadres, well aware of the existence of religious activities, often did not report on them until a command came from their superiors.

The vacillation and half-heartedness evident in the enforcement of religious policy may explain why the number of religious believers in Ruian did not drop significantly between 1952 and 1957, when state control of religion gradually intensified. More preachers and catechists were arrested and more monks and nuns were forced to give up monastic life and to participate in cooperative agriculture. Official statistics, however, indicate that the number of monks and nuns only dropped from 480 in the early years of the liberation to 410 on the eve of the Great Leap Forward, and the number of Christians (not including the number of the Assembly [Juhuichu], a Christian association, which had about 4,100 members in 1956) only dropped from 11,102 to 10,602.[47]

Intensified Coercion and the Clandestine Advance of Religion, 1958–1978

The Great Leap Forward in 1958 further squeezed the space of communal religion as more temple properties in Ruian were seized for agricultural and industrial production. Many temples were torn down, and statues of divinities were taken as raw materials to be used in the iron-smelting movement. Yet an astonishing surge of religious activity swept through not only Ruian but also the entire Zhejiang Province after the Great Famine (1959–1961). In the middle of the famine, "rumors went around in some places: 'Backward people' (*luohou qunzhong*) have started superstitious activities such as reciting scriptures, worshiping deities, building temples and statues of divinities."[48] After 1961, official investigations showed that many "superstition professionals" (*mixin zhiye fenzi*), including witches, sorcerers, and diviners, had taken up their former profession in Zhejiang. In Pingyang, a neighboring county of Ruian, as well as in other counties in southeastern Zhejiang, investigators estimated that almost 100 percent of superstition professionals had resumed their former roles.[49]

In 1964, the Zhejiang provincial government issued a special antifeudal superstition notice, addressing the fear that "superstitious activities" could affect social stability by providing cover for the activities of counterrevolutionaries. The notice called for banning "superstitious activities, carrying out antifeudal superstition education among the masses, and reducing, until completely annihilating, all superstitious activities."[50] In Ruian, the county government reiterated the ban on dragon boat racing in May 1963, after an unsuccessful attempt to stop the ritual's reemergence in 1961.[51] It appears that the effort was unsuccessful, as the county government again prohibited dragon boat racing in spring 1966, citing it as "rampant feudal superstitious activities in the guise of dragon boat races, which have caused multiple disputes and even fights between villages."[52]

In the early 1960s, the government also became concerned about the engagement in "superstition" and lineage activities by cadres, on whom the government relied in its efforts to suppress communal religious activities and other traditional activities.[53] During the Socialist Education Movement of 1962–1966, many town and village cadres in Ruian were reported to be either directly organizing or participating in religious activities such as temple reconstruction and genealogy compilation. In one case, Zhang Buwang, the Party secretary of the embroidery (handicraft) brigade in Tangxia Commune, arranged a large-scale funeral for his mother, who had passed away on December 28, 1965. Zhang invited a group of vocal liturgists and Daoists to host a complete set of elaborate rituals, some of which had allegedly only been seen before liberation. Hundreds of relatives and neighbors—including "landlords, rich peasants, counterrevolutionaries, and bad elements"—attended the funeral and a huge banquet afterward.[54] In another case, Shao Yongsheng, who was the vice-head of Zi'ao Brigade in Tangxia, was invited to organize the compilation of a new genealogy of the Shao lineage in the entire Tangxia District by other Shaos in Shaozhai Brigade of Tangxia Commune.[55] In the new genealogy, which I was able to see in 2012, Shao's name was listed alongside that of chief editor Shao Yanliu, a former landlord who was also the chief editor of the previous genealogy. Both cases were targets of criticism in cadre meetings supposedly held to educate other cadres and to teach "correct" attitudes and an understanding of such issues as feudal superstition and lineage.

Many cadres, however, explicitly expressed sympathy toward Shao and Zhang in meetings. In Shao's case, for instance, some believed it was necessary to compile a genealogy because without it "the five relations [wulun] would get messy. We would not be able to recognize our ancestor, and a grand-aunt would not realize that she had married her grandnephew.... everything has its order. A nation is constituted of the center, province, county, and commune, level by level. So human relations should also be sequenced generation by generation."[56] In Zhang's case, someone said: "Funeral rituals have been our custom for thousands of years. Zhang's mother, she was long-lived and senior in genealogical ranking [beifen]. [She also had] good fortune for four generations [in her family] living together in a house [sishitongtang]. Her son is Party secretary, and her grandson is the head of a cooperative. They have money, and there is nothing wrong with making the funeral boisterous [renao]." The observer continued, "if funeral is class struggle, then everything in villages is class struggle. It is an old custom handed down from the old generation. If somebody's funeral is cold and cheerless [lenglengqingqing], what taste does it have?"[57]

Increased engagement by village cadres in religious and other traditional practices and their continued equivocal attitudes indicated that the dilemma of suppressing superstition persisted in Ruian in the 1960s. When village affairs after collectivization became more dependent on cadres, they turned out to be an obstacle in clamping down on superstition. The new leaders of the villages were both the target and the enforcers of antisuperstition policies. Although there was a considerable gap between the village cadres' perceptions of religious and lineage activities and the politically correct notions that superior officials were at pains to inculcate in them, there was not such a wide gap in perception between village cadres and ordinary villagers. Village cadres might take actions to suppress communal religious and lineage activities, even if they actually considered those activities harmless customs, but they might secretly permit, support, or even directly participate in religious and lineage activities, just as the county government discovered in its investigations.

Local authorities in Ruian seemed to be less concerned about town and village cadres' involvement in Christianity and Buddhism between 1958–1966, but they continued to see passivity in local cadres' handing of Christianity and Buddhism. In April 1958, the county government took greater strides in suppressing religious affairs (*zongjiao gongzuo*) in line with the spirit of the Great Leap Forward. Hardcore religious professionals were gathered to debate atheism and theism, on such topics as "whether the Bible is milk or opium." Churches were shut down, and Christians were forced to surrender their Bibles.[58] Most religious leaders were forced to publicly renounce their faith under tremendous political pressure. Those who refused to do so were arrested. "Ninety percent of temples and churches were voluntarily donated to brigades."[59] On Daluo Mountain in Tangxia, some monks and nuns even "voluntarily" destroyed statues of Buddha, and more chose to abandon monastic life to become laypersons.[60]

These actions were precisely what the Ministry of United Front Work intended to prohibit in its 1957 command on socialist education. The ministry's goals were to persuade, through debate, religious leaders to follow the socialist path and to accept the leadership of the Communist Party. Yet the Ministry of Public Security and the National Bureau of Religious Affairs apparently favored the extremism displayed by the county government. Officials from the two departments, without the presence of United Front Work officials, held a special on-the-spot meeting in September in Pingyang, a neighboring county where the county government had launched an identical "great leap forward in religious affairs," to praise and popularize the Wenzhou experience. Later on, Pingyang and Hongdong, a county in Shanxi, were selected as model areas for "eliminating religion." Following Wenzhou's "great leap forward in religious affairs" in 1958, the Zhejiang Provincial United Front Work Department ordered an investigation in 1959 on the implementation of religious policy in Wenzhou, after considering the campaigns to stamp out religion in Wenzhou a deviation from normal religious policy and requesting rectification.[61]

In the following years, there were similar disagreements between different government departments. Principles such as protecting religious freedom or differentiating illegal religious activities from normal religious activities were at times emphasized in the commands to local cadres, though the suppression of religious activities intensified further.[62] But the disagreement between offices at higher levels and the different policies they generated only deepened confusion among cadres at the grassroots level and did not necessarily improve their capacity for discerning "the boundary between political issues and the issues of thought and faiths, the boundary between illegal activities and normal religious activities," as they were so often requested to do.[63]

"Letting things drift" (*fangrenziliu*) and crude actions (*cubaozuofa*) were typical attitudes of town and village cadres in the early 1960s. Reluctance and vacillation similar to that of the 1950s were seen in some religious strongholds in Ruian. Cadres in Mayu District, for instance, either did not interfere or "simply called together Christians to force them to write confessions or to educate them together with those thieves, landlords, or counter-revolutionaries and asked them to write guarantees" promising not to participate in religious activities anymore.[64] County officials criticized town and village cadres for "being short of methods" in dealing with religion.[65] The town and village cadres, however, complained that religious affairs were not easy to handle. The head of Xincheng Commune said in a meeting that "if we do not handle religious affairs well, it will affect religious freedom. However, if we do not interfere, religious activities will gradually expand, which would affect production and the development of socialism. We are caught in the middle. It is better for superiors to provide us with some solutions [*chuzhuyi*]."[66] The cadres were right to fear expansion. In view of the passivity of local authorities in carrying out religious policies, Christian and Buddhist activities were able to find new niches by going underground. According to an official estimate, after the Great Leap Forward of 1958, approximately 760 devout Christians moved their worship from churches to underground family gatherings. Similarly, it was estimated that 73 Buddhist monks and nuns continued to secretly practice even though their temples were closed.[67]

Soon after the beginning of the Cultural Revolution, the Zhejiang Provincial Commercial Bureau ordered the cessation of temple fairs (*miaohui*), which had been held in the form of secular commodity exchange meetings for more than a decade. In October 1966, Red Guards in Ruian went to the streets to "destroy the Four Olds." In Mayu alone, within one month Red Guards confiscated 7,484.5 taels of tin and 57,698 incense holders, while destroying 180 statues of divinities and burning 1,060 volumes of genealogical records.[68] Christianity and Buddhism were attacked as "religious superstitions" (*zongjiao mixin*). Shu Chengqian, a prominent preacher of the Seventh-day Adventist Church (*Anxirihui*) who was in Mayu at the beginning of the Cultural Revolution, was taken to the struggle meetings, where he was insulted and beaten.[69] According to Shu's memoir, his brother-in-law in Wenzhou saw church leaders being paraded through the streets with placards hanging on their chests and forced to shout anti-Christian slogans; they were holding Bibles and other religious texts that were then burned at the end of the parade.

As the political campaign incapacitated regular government functions, the attitudes of cadres at the grassroots level became extraordinarily important to the control of religion. The whole county fell into collective "armed fights" (*wudou*) between two major factions after January 1967. All government institutions—the county government, the county Party Committee, the Public Security Bureau (PSB), and others—were completely paralyzed. The PSB was not reestablished until April 1973.[70] The entire area of the Wenzhou-Ruian plains suffered another drought, the greatest since 1953, just as the frenzy of armed fights reached its climax in the summer of 1967.[71] Senior villagers from surrounding villages poured into the East Palace Hall, Lower Village, Xincheng, to pray for rain. One faction surprisingly agreed that the ceremony could continue, though the other faction did not agree, causing violent conflicts. Two people were killed.[72]

Additional cases of cadre involvement in religion emerged during the early 1970s, following the Lin Biao incident (an attempted coup against Mao that resulted in Lin's death) in September 1971 and Nixon's visit to China in February 1972.[73] A report of the Zhejiang Party Committee in 1973 stated that nineteen village Party secretaries and heads of the Communist Youth League, all of them attached to brigades in nine counties where Christianity still held deep historic roots, had converted to Christianity. Authorities accused Christian churches of attempting to usurp the leadership of grass-roots organizations by infiltrating local Party organizations. For instance, in Pingyang County's Huli Brigade, a once-famous Christian village that had been set up as a model for the elimination of Protestantism in 1958, the Party secretary of the brigade turned his home into a meeting place for church activities.[74] In other cases, religious activities were legitimized through indirect connections to grassroots cadres. Zhushan Village in Huling District had just over twenty Christians in the early 1970s, but the village eventually became the district's new center of church activities. Part of the reason, it was said, was that a town cadre's wife who had been "possessed" for years converted to Christianity in 1974, after which she became an activist and opened her home to other Christian families for religious activities.[75]

By the early 1970s, Buddhist and communal religious activities were once again flourishing on Daluo Mountain of the Wen-Rui coastal plains—traditionally the center of Buddhism in Wenzhou. The same was true of inland Shengjing Mountain and Baiyan Mountain, allegedly the birthplace of Lord Yang, the most famous local deity in Wenzhou.[76] There were also signs of the restoration of temple and lineage activities in some villages.[77] The number of Christians—and Protestants in particular—exhibited a remarkable increase during the Cultural Revolution: available statistics show that there were a total of 71,185 Christians (11,000 Catholics and 60,185 Protestants) in 1981, more than four times the number in 1956.[78] The growth of the Christian population during the Cultural Revolution was surprising even in light of the total population growth in the county (about 2.2 times the 1956 figure) and the growth of the Christian population between 1978 and 1981.[79]

The Boom of Religion and the Accommodative State

Religious activity in Ruian increased dramatically after 1978, as the Wenzhou region changed from one of the most impoverished regions in Zhejiang into one of the wealthiest in the nation. Christian populations climbed to 71,185 in 1982 and to 81,900 in 1990.[80] During this same period, the number of churches and household meeting places increased from 276 to 299 and Buddhist temples from 44 to 148.[81] Communal religious activities also flourished, with dragon boat racing restored on a countywide basis after 1980. The number of registered dragon boats increased from 157 in 1981 to 605 in

2005,[82] even though the total population of the city only grew by about 6 percent in the same period.

In March 1982, the central government issued "Basic Viewpoints and Policies on the Religious Question during Our Country's Socialist Period" (*Guanyu woguo shehuizhuyi shiqi zongjiao wenti de jiben guandian he jiben zhengce*), the Communist Party's guidelines for religious work after the Maoist era. This document, most commonly known as "Document 19," authorized "selectively" and "gradually" reopening sites for legal religious activities for the dual purpose of improving the Party-state's relationship with religious communities and China's image in the eyes of the international community. In Ruian and the Wenzhou region, however, the process of reclamation and restoration of temples and churches had been initiated even earlier than the timing of Document 19 suggests. People had already started to reclaim and rebuild temples and churches at the end of the 1970s, when they felt that the political climate was rapidly changing. The Ruian County government was slow to change, however, only permitting the reopening of two churches by the end of 1982, while entirely denying formal permission to Buddhist temples. Nor was the new policy described in Document 19 widely disseminated.[83] Nevertheless, at the grassroots level during the same period, 36 churches and 44 temples were restored after religious communities negotiated with or gained the tacit consent of district, town, and village cadres.[84]

In the 1980s, there was still no clear sign that the central government would more fully accept communal religious activities—those that took place outside formally recognized institutions. Instead, these activities were singled out in Document 19 as not belonging to the category of religion and were thus targeted for suppression. The Ruian County government launched several campaigns to suppress "superstition" at the request of the municipal, provincial, and central governments. However, the campaigns were futile. "We demolished the temple today, they built it the next day" was how one report characterized the situation.[85] While communal religious activities proliferated, cadres had no incentive to "implement the religious policies" (*luoshi zongjiao zhengce*), but instead "turned a blind eye to feudal superstition, feudal lineage, and ancestral halls, or just let them go. . . . Many town and village cadres also participated in or secretly supported them."[86] County officials believed the situation to be critical, but also beyond their ability to control.

The Empress Palace of the Yantou Brigade in Mayu was confiscated and turned into an elementary school in the 1950s and was later used as the offices of the district government in the 1960s. This monopoly ended when a group of elderly women led by the mother of the brigade head eventually occupied a part of the school and established a shrine after 1980. Brigade cadres did not interfere at all, and many directly participated in the reconstruction of the temple. The Mayu district government, just across the street from the temple site, received numerous complaints from the school that classrooms were occupied and school activities were disrupted by the new religious activity. The district government's attitude, however, was as half-hearted as ever. Though they tried to persuade people to remove the temple, they did not directly interfere in its operation. Not until the national campaign to "clean up spiritual pollution" in 1983 was the temple finally demolished.[87]

Even more conciliatory measures in Ruian have been evident since the 1990s, though not without occasional and brief campaigns against communal religious activities.[88] Since 1992, the city government has gradually legalized more than 150 communal temples by allowing them to register as members of the city Daoist association, citing a Zhejiang provincial regulation about temples and pavilions issued that same year. City authorities had tried to quell dragon boat racing when the ritual reemerged in the early 1980s, but when prohibition turned out to be futile, they soon adopted a different strategy. In a notice from 1984, the government proposed to "positively guide and actively regulate" and "take effective measures to guide dragon boat racing to a healthy track of physical cultural activity."[89] This was a clear appropriation of the National Committee of Physical Sports' decision to include "dragon boat competitions" (longzhou jingsai) as a formal program in sports events. In 2003, the Wenzhou municipal government permitted dragon boat racing once again, in reaction to multiple appeals of local communities after a long ban from 1991 to 2002.[90] This time dragon boat racing was reinterpreted as "traditional culture" (chuantong wenhua) and was thus rendered immune from the ban; the official slogan used to authorize the decision was "carrying forward traditional culture, strengthening the people's bodies, enriching the life of the masses, and promoting spiritual civilization."[91]

*   *   *

During the Maoist era, the Communist Party greatly weakened the economic foundations, leadership, and political functions of religion through various state campaigns in rural Ruian. The land reform of 1950 and 1951, the Great Leap Forward in 1958, and the onset of the Cultural Revolution in 1966 all stripped religious communities of sites for practice and worship. Religious leaders were subject to severe persecution; some were put in jail and even killed. The government, however, never fully succeeded in its aim of subduing religious activities. Campaigns to eliminate religious activities since 1958 only intensified the tension between the government and religious communities, especially Christian congregations, which even witnessed considerable growth during the Cultural Revolution.

The combination of suppression and limited tolerance seemed a sensible approach, but it ran into insurmountable difficulties in practice, making it impossible for the government to prevent religious activities from resurgence over the long run. First, when different arms of the government attempted to implement religious policy, the result was often inconsistent orders concerning which religious activities were to be suppressed and which tolerated. Second, the categories essential to the state religious policy—such as "religion," "superstition," and "normal religious activities"—were never clearly defined, whether intentionally or not. Under these circumstances, religious communities were still able to carry on their practices intermittently, even during the Cultural Revolution.

The space for religious practice was created by the mutually reinforcing dynamics of inconsistent orders, the instability and indeterminacy of discourse and categories, and the inevitable unwillingness of local cadres to risk their own necks one way or the other by forcibly implementing religious policy. On the one hand, local cadres who directly controlled and regulated religious activities were often bewildered because they did not know how to apply the constantly changing language of religious policy to the realities they faced; on the other hand, they felt obliged to comply with requests from above. As a result, village and township cadres often moved back and forth between blunt crackdowns during political campaigns and less interference at other times.

Finally, the vacillating nature of religious policy left considerable room for manipulation, obfuscation, and deliberate avoidance with respect to the control of religious behavior. Local cadres could shirk their responsibilities by shifting blame onto the policies' vague wording or could even take advantage of semantic confusion to shield religious activities. Because the government could not fundamentally transform cadres' traditional conceptions of religion, which were similar to those of ordinary villagers, cadres became not only the targets of but also obstacles to religious control, as they were often themselves involved in religious activities. This tendency became more and more apparent over time during the Maoist period. Since 1978, the government has taken more conciliatory measures, such as returning and reopening temples and churches as well as permitting certain communal religious practices. In the process, the central government's capacity to mobilize local cadres to regulate religious activities has become even weaker as increasing numbers of incumbent and retired cadres engage openly in religious activities, including some who have even resisted government interference in religion.

Part IV

DISCONTENT

11

Radical Agricultural Collectivization and Ethnic Rebellion

The Communist Encounter with a "New Emperor" in Guizhou's Mashan Region, 1956

WANG HAIGUANG

The rapid socialist transformation of China's rural economy created discontent throughout the country. In the summer of 1955, Mao Zedong excoriated other Communist Party leaders who wanted a more gradual transition to socialism. Mao sought speed, not moderation, so he took charge and mobilized the entire Party to hasten agricultural collectivization. As a result, China's socialist reform of agriculture was achieved in the short span of half a year through harsh and heavy-handed measures. By the end of 1956, 97 percent of agricultural households had joined upper-level cooperatives.[1] This movement to radically transform China's countryside sparked widespread resistance. Peasants expressed their opposition to the collective takeover of personal property by cutting down trees, killing livestock, or simply withdrawing from cooperatives.

In areas heavily populated by ethnic minorities, socialist agricultural reform also inflamed resistance to Han rule. About 28 million of the more than 35 million members of ethnic minorities nationwide were also pushed into collectives.[2] In regions home to these minorities, resistance against collectivization was particularly intense because it was colored by ethnic tensions between Han officials and minority villagers. Agricultural collectivization not only went against the Party's policy of "cautious and steady advances" (*shenzhong wenjin*) in reforming minority areas, it also destroyed ethnic minorities' traditional way of life by forcing them to assimilate to a Han lifestyle. The grievances that had been mounting ever since the implementation of the state grain monopoly finally exploded, and the extent of open resistance in minority areas exceeded that occurring in Han districts. Almost all parts of China with concentrated populations of ethnic minorities experienced disturbances and even armed rebellions.

Frontier provinces were especially vulnerable to minority-led resistance and conflict. In Guizhou and Yunnan, ethnic Miao and Yao villagers responded to collectivization by searching for holy water and magical herbs,[3] by withdrawing from cooperatives and moving away, and by taking part in armed uprisings. Some members of the Dai and Jingpo ethnicities who lived in Yunnan's border regions fled to neighboring countries. In Gansu and Qinghai, minority elites assembled armed groups to oppose the transition to socialism. And in many parts of Xinjiang, people used weapons to attack local government offices.[4] At the time, the largest armed rebellions were led by ethnic Tibetans in Sichuan's Ganzizhou region and by Yi people in Yunnan's Daxiao Liangshan area.

Party leaders moved quickly to forcibly suppress the uprisings in Sichuan and Yunnan but soon realized that radical agricultural collectivization had deeply strained ethnic relations to the point that more moderate methods were required to reduce conflict between Han and ethnic minorities. Starting in spring 1956, many uprisings took place in the minority regions of Guizhou Province, most notably when an armed rebellion shook the Mashan area of Wangmo County. In handling the Mashan rebellion, Guizhou provincial officials followed Party Center's call for moderation and sought a nonviolent resolution. They attempted to put down the rebellion peacefully.

A broader policy background undergirded the Party's attempt to use politics instead of force to quell the Mashan rebellion. Throughout its history, the Party had more often than not relied on violence to eliminate threats rather than seeking political solutions. In early 1956, Mao and other central leaders recognized that during the course of collectivization, the Party had made the mistake of applying experiences from Han areas to minority regions, failing to take into account ethnic minorities' unique characteristics and disrespecting their customs. In his famous speech "On the Ten

Great Relationships" on April 25, 1956, Mao said, "We should emphasize opposing Han chauvinism. Local nationalism should also be opposed, but it should not be the main focus." Mao ordered a large-scale reinvestigation of ethnic relations, saying, "if relations are abnormal, they must be taken care of conscientiously."[5] In April 1956, Party committees in ethnic minority areas began assessing ethnic relations, focusing particularly on overcoming Han chauvinism. At the Eighth Party Congress held in Beijing in September 1956, addressing recent ethnic tensions was high on the agenda. In his political report, Liu Shaoqi called for a cautious approach to minority relations, which would include consulting with ethnic leaders and "doing things according to ethnic groups' own wishes. We must undertake reforms peacefully and should not use coercive methods."[6]

As part of the review of ethnic minority policy in 1956, on December 26, Party Center pointed out that minority cadres "have the right to bravely criticize Han chauvinism."[7] Mao followed up on this in February 1957 in his famous "On the Correct Handling of Contradictions among the People" speech, saying that "the key to getting Han-minority relations right is overcoming Han chauvinism."[8] In essence, all the talk about correcting the mistakes of "Han chauvinism" was targeted at solving the ethnic problems that had been exacerbated by agricultural collectivization. Mao was calling for nonviolent political solutions to uprisings in minority regions. The problem was that leaders from Party Center all the way down to the grassroots lacked experience in handling ethnic problems peacefully. For this reason, Party Center put great importance on quelling the Mashan rebellion through political means and ordered Guizhou Party leaders to handle the conflict with great caution. The management of the Mashan rebellion was a significant instance in which the Party actually attempted to resolve an ethnic armed uprising through conciliatory tactics.

Local historians from Guizhou have analyzed the reasons for the Mashan uprising and narrated its rise and fall in gazetteers, official chronologies, and journals.[9] While these accounts are valuable, they only provide a rough and sometimes contradictory picture of the event. More recently, young scholars have begun to pay attention to what happened in Mashan in 1956. Two articles by Wu Xiaotao, a researcher at the Guizhou Provincial Party School, have been particularly influential, despite certain limitations.[10] Other notable works that many people in Wangmo County consider reliable include Wang Fengchang's *Eagle of Mashan* and Wei Rang's *Dense Fog of Mashan*.[11]

This chapter analyzes the Mashan uprising and its consequences from a perspective that considers links between collectivization and the Party's adjustment of policies toward ethnic minorities.

Ethnic Relations in Mashan

To understand the Mashan rebellion, it is first necessary to introduce the history of Han-minority relations in this geographically isolated area. Wangmo County, located in southern Guizhou on the border with Guangxi, has 104 mountain peaks, and 76.8 percent of the county's land is mountainous. In 1955, the county had five subdistricts and sixty-eight townships (*xiangzhen*). Nineteen different ethnic groups reside in the county, and at the time of the uprising 78 percent of the population was non-Han—primarily Buyi, Miao, Yao, and Zhuang. Buyi settlements are concentrated in Wangmo's fertile river valleys, whereas the Miao live in the high mountains.[12]

The Mashan region is in the eastern part of Wangmo County, near the junction of Ziyun and Luodian Counties, and is dominated by the rugged Miao mountain range. Water is scarce, and most slopes are so steep that oxen cannot be used for farming. One Republican-era travel journalist was not exaggerating when he wrote that Mashan's "precipitous cliffs and deep valleys" made it "difficult for outsiders to climb up there" and that "the oxen are carried in on people's backs as calves; otherwise they would not be able to get there."[13] Historically, Mashan was so isolated that it was barely affected by state authority. The Miao people were considered "raw" (*sheng*) because they remained relatively untouched by Han ways, unlike "cooked" (*shu*) Miao in other areas who had assimilated.[14] Economic, religious, and cultural practices in Mashan developed independently from other areas, even nearby ones.

Mashan's poverty also set it apart. According to an investigation conducted in 1957 about the Mashan economy, 978 people in 179 households were spread out across twenty-eight separate stockaded villages (*zhaizi*). An average of 6.4 households lived in each village. Farmers had to walk as far as fifteen kilometers to get to their fields and almost as far to get water, which they carried home in buckets. Each *mu* only yielded an average of 60 kilograms of grain annually. It is therefore not surprising that during land reform, only 3 households in Mashan were categorized as "rich peasants," while 41 were "middle peasants," and 135 received the label of "poor peasants." In 1955, the average annual income was 21.5 yuan per person, and the average amount of unprocessed grain per person was 150.5 kilograms. Almost one-quarter of the families in Mashan were short of grain for more than three months per year. In stark contrast to the cotton-spinning villagers in Shaanxi discussed by Jacob Eyferth in Chapter 5, nobody in Mashan had any cotton clothing, and about a quarter of households had no quilts.[15]

Mashan was even more isolated and impoverished than other Miao districts. Through 1957, not a single person in Mashan Township was considered literate. The Miao people in Mashan were polytheistic animists who believed that the world was controlled by invisible spirits.[16] Every year the villagers would offer sacrifices to the god of the earth and to their ancestors. They also believed that properly avoiding taboos would bring bumper harvests and stability. Even after 1949, village cadres feared the powers of "medicine women" (*yaopo*), who could magically poison humans and livestock. One local official said that in 1955 his young son died shortly after he cursed people in his village, implying that the medicine woman was to blame. To appease the spirits, people in Mashan often sought out fortune-tellers and exorcists. Getting rid of the evil influence of ghosts and medicine women frequently gave rise to jealousy and feuds among villagers.[17]

During the Republican era, the central government in Nanjing could only indirectly administer Mashan. Power on the ground belonged to local elites, who battled for influence. The Nationalist government's lack of influence in the area was actually beneficial to the Communists, who passed through Wangmo County during the Long March. In addition, the Red Seventh and Eighth Armies had long been active in the nearby Guangxi Zuoyoujiang Base Area.[18] When the Nationalist government attempted to increase taxation on Mashan residents after the outbreak of the war against Japan, locals responded by opposing the "three levies" (*sanzheng*) of grain requisition, monetary taxes, and conscription. Of the more than ten antitax rebellions, the largest and most significant was led by Xiong Liangchen.

Xiong Liangchen was born into a poor Miao family in Mashan and made a living as a laborer. In 1939, influenced by the Communist revolution, Xiong organized the "Mashan Antityranny Civil Corps" (*Mashan kangbao min-tuan*) by uniting thirteen armed groups to oppose conscription and taxation. After the Communist Party sent agents to meet with Xiong, he accepted their suggestions and turned his armed group into a "peasants' self-defense corps." At its peak, the corps boasted more than 10,000 soldiers and between 200 and 300 guns, and controlled most of the Mashan area.

To suppress the antigovernment rebels, Nationalist authorities in Guizhou sent troops to Wangmo in 1940. But the rebels took advantage of their familiarity with the local landscape and evaded capture. During the Nationalists' encirclement campaign of 1944, government officials realized that a purely military approach would not work. They attempted to divide and conquer the rebels, using such slogans as "attack Miao but not Buyi," "only attack Red Miao but not other Miao," and "only attack the Xiongs of the Red Miao." In response, many rebels surrendered; the six-year-long Mashan rebellion was finally defeated in 1945. More than 400 rebels and other Mashan natives were executed, but Xiong Liangchen, who had been wounded in battle, managed to slip across the provincial border to Guangxi, where he, his brother Xiong Liangbin, and their comrade Yang Shaobin joined up with a Communist guerrilla unit.[19] In Guangxi, Xiong became a Communist Party member and assumed a leadership position. In 1949, he led a team of guerrillas back home to assist in the People's Liberation Army's (PLA) takeover of Ziyun and Wangmo Counties.[20]

As an impoverished place with a long history of anti-Nationalist rebellions, Mashan seemed like a place where Communist control would quickly take root and gain support. It is therefore somewhat surprising that the region became a bastion of anti-Communist resistance after 1949. Following a pattern common in many Guizhou counties, Nationalist authorities in Wangmo County first pledged allegiance to the Communists, then revolted and resisted the new regime.[21] Anti-Communist guerrilla groups that had been dispersed by the PLA in other parts of Guizhou fled to isolated Wangmo, which filled up with "a city of soldiers and half a city of officials." Wangmo and neighboring Ceheng County were the final sites of stubborn resistance in Guizhou. In May and June 1951, the PLA wiped out 5,679 guerrillas and occupied the two county seats, ending a civil war that had lasted a year and a half.[22]

After occupying minority areas, the Communists tried to win over ethnic elites. Local leaders such as Xiong Liangchen who had proved their mettle in opposing the Nationalists were rewarded with official posts. Xiong himself served as a township head, district head, and then vice-magistrate of Ziyun County. His younger brother, Xiong Liangbin, became a peasant association cadre and later rose to vice–district head. The three Xiong sisters also received positions. But few followers of the Xiongs were well suited for government work. They were warriors, not administrators. Shortly after land reform, most of the former anti-Nationalist rebels returned to their villages to farm. The families of Mashan self-defense corpsmen who had been killed in battle received no compensation or official recognition as revolutionary martyrs from the Communists, which led to complaints and resentment. Yang Shaobin, who served with Xiong Liangchen in the Self-Defense Corps, once privately complained: "My contributions to the revolution were at least as great as the Xiongs'. I conquered the land, but you became big officials. The way the government handled it was so unfair."[23]

The Communist occupation of Mashan was also complicated by the outsider identity of takeover cadres, most of whom came from the Hebei-Shandong-Henan Base Area (*Ji-Lu-Yu genjudi*) in north China. They were district-level officials who were dispatched to govern an entire province. They were committed to the revolution and good at following orders but were not well educated. Han cadres simply imported work methods from north China to Guizhou and did not make an effort to understand ethnic minorities' traditions and religious beliefs because they considered them ignorant and superstitious. And after land reform, outsider cadres did not pay as much attention to older ethnic elites, instead choosing to foster young minority activists who depended on the Han cadres for their positions and who repaid the outsiders with loyalty. This helped Han authorities govern ethnic minority areas but meant that young Miao and Buyi officials became increasingly alienated from their own communities.

Communist governance in Wangmo County began later than in other areas of Guizhou and did not penetrate to the grassroots. In May 1951, Wangmo's county government was made up of thirty-seven officials from the Zunyi prefectural Party Committee and twenty-three minority cadres sent by the Xingren prefectural commissioner's office.[24] The officials spent more time satisfying the demands of superiors in Xingren than they did investigating conditions in villages. As a self-criticism report noted after the 1956 Mashan uprising, "in the years since liberation, not one responsible cadre from the county or district came to the interior of Mashan. The masses in some villages have never even seen a comrade at work."[25]

Newly arrived Han cadres in Wangmo were so unfamiliar with the territory that the language in their reports failed to distinguish between Buyi and Yi people.[26] Even worse, Han officials were unwilling to let minority cadres have any real authority. A Han cadre named Jiang ordered around Xiong Liangbin, a Miao man who was serving as vice–district head, and required Xiong to constantly report to him. When Xiong was ill and wanted to use his own money to buy a horse for transportation, Jiang criticized him, saying, "What qualifications do you have to ride a horse?" Han cadres behaved arrogantly and disregarded minorities' customs. Some even made comments such as "the only thing that's special about the ethnic minorities is their backwardness" and "their customs are nothing more than superstition." Many minority villagers were extremely unhappy with Han cadres, saying that they were the "devil incarnate."[27]

These problems were all exacerbated in the mid-1950s by the forcible implementation of the state grain monopoly and the collectivization of agriculture, neither of which were well suited to Mashan's natural setting, economic conditions, and cultivation techniques. In fact, locals equated the Communists' radical reforms of the 1950s to the "three levies" the Nationalists had imposed in the 1940s. It is therefore not surprising that people in the Mashan region rose up in a rebellion that lasted ten months and spread to fifty townships in Guizhou's Wangmo, Ziyun, and Luodian Counties and extended to Leye and Tian'e Counties in Guangxi. Altogether more than 5,000 people took part in the uprising, 90 percent of them Miao. In Wangmo County alone, more than 3,300 people counted themselves among the rebels.[28] It is particularly notable that many of the rebels were originally followers of Xiong Liangchen in the armed anti-Nationalist uprisings of the 1940s. In the 1950s, these rebels had received positions as local cadres, and many had joined the Communist Party or Communist Youth League.[29] Their positions within the system, however, did not stop them from rising up to resist the socialist policies forced on them by outsiders.

How Collectivization Assailed Ethnic Minority Lifestyles

Just as Communist control and land reform came to Guizhou later than in other parts of China, so too did the organization of farmers into cooperatives.

At the end of 1953, Guizhou provincial leaders authorized a single pilot lower-level cooperative of twenty-two households. In 1954, the number of cooperatives grew to 6,000, but Guizhou leaders scaled back plans for continued cooperativization, changing the original target from 18,000 to 10,000 cooperatives. They also noted that in minority areas it would be preferable to organize fewer cooperatives and that plots where minority farmers traditionally planted cotton, chili pepper, indigo, and hemp would be exempt from cooperativization, as would "bride land" (*guniang tian*), which in Buyi society was traditionally part of the package of gifts given by a groom's family to a bride's family. All of these policies were aimed at "respecting ethnic minority customs."[30] But when Mao Zedong likened the pace of cooperativization to the hobbling of a woman with bound feet in summer 1955, Guizhou leaders hurried to catch up. By autumn, 30,000 cooperatives had been established in the province, while "cautious advance" in minority areas was criticized. The Guizhou Party Committee said that the movement to organize minority farmers into cooperatives had in fact been "cautious without advancing" and was "rightist."[31] By the second half of 1956, 93.4 percent of rural households had joined cooperatives.[32]

In Wangmo County, where land reform had not been completed until the late date of February 1954,[33] authorities did not want to lag behind in becoming socialist. In September 1954 the county implemented a monopoly on cotton cloth, and in February 1955 the "three fixed quotas" (*san ding*) for production, purchase, and sale of grain went into effect. During the "high tide of collectivization," Wangmo County leaders, under intense pressure from superiors in Guiyang, criticized themselves, saying that their "leadership lagged behind the masses" and their "ideology lagged behind reality." They vowed to organize peasants into cooperatives within two months. In the end, the cooperative movement in Wangmo took almost three months, but forcing peasants into cooperatives was hasty (taking only three days in some villages) and ignored ethnic minority interests. Sacrificial, ritual, and bride land, along with hemp and indigo fields, was taken for cooperative use. In addition, farmers were compensated at low rates for the tools they contributed to the cooperatives, and barely any land was reserved for private plots (*ziliudi*).[34] Authorities organized cooperatives based on standardized numbers of households, even though some families in mountainous Wangmo lived so far apart that it was unrealistic to expect them to work together. For example, some communities fifteen to twenty kilometers apart

and separated by steep mountain ranges were placed in the same cooperative. People complained that "working in the cooperative is like being a labor
convict; you put in tons of effort but have no way to make a living."[35] Wangmo
residents bemoaned the loss of land and livestock for sacrificial purposes.
An elderly Miao man said, "It would have been better to have died two years
ago, when there were oxen to sacrifice. If I die now, we're not allowed to sacrifice oxen." He was correct. When an ethnic Yao farmer asked a cadre if he
could sacrifice an ox for a funeral, the official retorted, "If you kill that ox, I'll
cut off your head."[36]

Some officials in Wangmo forced people to join cooperatives by issuing
the following rules: (1) whoever does not join the cooperative will not
be allowed to buy salt; (2) if items are stolen from cooperative members,
nonco-op households will compensate them; (3) if people quit the cooperative, nonco-op households will be held responsible; (4) whoever does not join
the cooperative does not support Chairman Mao; (5) if you do not join the
cooperative, you must do road repair work without receiving work points.[37]

Wangmo residents were also overburdened by excessive grain requisitions
and taxation. Striving to satisfy their superiors, county officials exceeded the
quota of grain to be handed over to the state by more than 40 percent in 1954
and 1955.[38] The grain bureau also disrupted ethnic minorities' traditional
ways of using grain by restricting alcohol distillation and cake-making, and
families that grew rice were not allowed to keep it for themselves. Miao
farmers expressed their dissatisfaction in song, singing, "Face to the ground,
back to the sky, handing over 430 kilos every year, the Miao won't be well fed
until a new emperor arrives."[39]

By 1955, taxes on commerce in the four counties of Anlong, Zhenfeng,
Ceheng, and Wangmo were eighteen times higher than they had been in
1950. An audit of unpaid taxes in Wangmo in 1954 was particularly harsh,
earning county officials severe criticism from the prefectural commissioner's office in Xingyi because it had "negatively affected the worker-peasant
alliance and the Party's relationship with the people."[40] The main sources of
tax revenue in southwestern Guizhou villages were butchering, local wine,
and logs. Before 1953, butchering meat and making wine for personal use
had been tax exempt. Starting in 1953, these activities began to be taxed.[41]
The tax on slaughtered pigs was calculated at 8 percent in 1954, rose to 12
percent in 1955, and was up to 15 percent in 1956. Locals said that the annual

tax increases were worse than when the Nationalists were in charge.[42] Many peasants reported that "the Nationalists only collected one tax for the entire year. Now there are all kinds of different taxes, and the overall burden is heavier."[43]

Onerous taxation and coercive collectivization were exacerbated by other policy blunders, including low state-mandated prices for pork, the sale of which had been the primary sideline income for many in Mashan.[44] These issues added up to a volatile situation, especially in a region that had a long history of opposing outside schemes to change lifestyles and extract resources. It was therefore no surprise that armed revolts occurred in twenty-two minority counties in Guizhou's border regions starting in February 1956. The uprising in Wangmo was the most serious of all the revolts.

The "Empress Mother" Spreads Rumors
That an Emperor Will Emerge

On March 3, 1956, Yang Shaobin departed his home village of Haimengzhai in Mashan along with Zhang Laomao and five others. The men were headed to Luodian County to help Yang's brother-in-law move to a new house. Along the way, they made a rest stop at the home of an acquaintance named Xiang Laoxiang. During a meal, Xiang's mother said that an emperor had arisen in Ganpengzhai. Yang and Zhang were curious and asked Xiang to lead them there.

When they got to Ganpengzhai, Yang encountered a sixty-year-old woman known as Dog Granny Xiong (Xiong Gounai). People in the village said that she had been crazy for many years and sometimes walked around without her pants on. Yang and the others heard the woman raving that an emperor would ascend to the throne, that the emperor was her son, and that Chairman Mao and Chiang Kai-shek were also her sons. She instructed her audience to spread the word about the emperor and vowed to punish those who did not publicize her story. She also demanded that they call Mao to Guizhou so that he could see for himself how much locals disliked the People's Government and military conscription.[45]

Yang Shaobin was a skilled marksman who had served as an officer in Xiong Liangchen's Peasant Self-Defense Corps and had fought against the Nationalists for more than ten years. His elder brother and cousin had been killed by Nationalist authorities. When the Communists took over southwest Guizhou, Yang followed Xiong Liangchen and assisted with the occupation of Wangmo, Ziyun, Luodian, and other counties. He had been active in fighting against anti-Communist guerrilla groups in the early 1950s and became chair of a village peasant association. But in 1953, he was removed from his position after being caught smoking opium that he had purchased with public funds. He returned to his hometown and made a living as a fortune-teller. After cooperativization, Yang had to walk many kilometers to the fields, which angered him. He had always considered himself a sorcerer who had special powers, so he felt especially inspired by Dog Granny Xiong's prophesy. This was too good an opportunity to pass up, he thought.[46] Yang and his friend Zhang Laomao returned to their home village and enthusiastically spread the news that an emperor had arisen.

Between March 7 and March 10, Yang Shaobin decked himself out with a red sash and beat gongs and drums as if he were in a trance. He proclaimed that the "Empress Mother" had descended to earth to decree that an emperor had arisen and would ascend to the throne on June 6. Yang himself had been named as an imperial senior general, while Zhang Laomao was his "flying tiger." Yang said, "When the emperor comes, peasants will have food and clothing without having to do work. There will be ten thousand years of food, one grain of rice will be enough for ten thousand years—once you've eaten it, you'll always be full." There would be no more grain taxes or money, and everyone would be housed in mansions and would wear silks and satins, Yang claimed.[47] His promises attracted almost one thousand followers in six townships in the Mashan area. Some followers were Party members, cadres, and militia members. Encouraged by the support, Yang Shaobin and two others wrote "Empress Mother's Proclamation of Peace under Heaven" (*Huangmu niangniang gao tianxia taiping shu*) and posted notices about the founding of a new "Peasant's Republic" (*Nongmin gongheguo*) headquartered in Yang's home village of Haimengzhai.

On March 9, 1956, the Wangmo County Party Committee received a report about Yang's activities from the Lewang Township public security office. Yang Shaobin, Zhang Laomao, Yang Guangcai, and Kong Huazhen were arrested (the last two had helped to draft the "Proclamation of Peace"), and a work team was sent to the area to publicize the Party's ethnic minority policy and the superiority of cooperativization, and to convince people to go back to the fields. At the time, the Party Committee considered the incident a simple example of "mass superstition." In the eyes of the authorities, Yang Shaobin had a history of resisting the Nationalists but smoked opium and made a living through superstitious activities that tricked the masses; Zhang Laomao was a sincere peasant and militia member. After "educating" the detained men, their release was approved by the Xingyi prefectural Party Committee in May 1956.[48] At the same time, Wangmo County authorities set up a secret intelligence presence in Mashan.

Releasing Yang Shaobin and his friends would eventually come back to bite Wangmo authorities and their prefectural superiors. But the relatively lenient handling of the men had to do with the broader context of shifting policies toward ethnic minorities. In early March 1956, more than three hundred non-Han people had protested in Guizhou's Nayong County, killing a militia leader and two others. Guizhou provincial leaders demanded a report about whether the incident had been caused by coercing people to join cooperatives or by violations of policies toward ethnic minorities. On April 14, 1956, Party Center issued an "Order about Investigating the Implementation of Ethnic Minority Policy," asking officials in areas where protests had occurred to analyze their causes and to learn from them. In response, Guizhou provincial leaders criticized localities that had experienced problems with forced cooperativization and mistreatment of ethnic minority cadres. Wangmo County authorities had this in mind when they let Yang Shaobin out of jail.

From Rumors of an Emperor to an Armed Uprising

On May 18, Yang Shaobin and Huang Buzhi, a Miao man with poor peasant status, convened a meeting of more than seventy resisters in Jiaopaozhai. Many of the men present at the meeting had taken part in anti-Nationalist uprisings during the 1940s. They decided to use similar methods in taking up arms to resist cooperativization and grain requisition. Yang Shaobin declared that he was the "senior general" and then bestowed honorary titles on Huang Buzhi and others, including a propagandist who was called the "immortal" (*shenxian*). The leaders of the uprising decided to seize weapons from Communist Party militia members and local cadres. They brandished three guns already in their possession, saying that "the first gun will knock down cooperativization, the second will knock down government bonds, the third will knock down the state grain monopoly."[49]

Fueled by rumors, the rebellion spread from Miao areas to Han and Buyi regions. There were a number of rumors and remarks: "When the emperor takes the throne on June 6, half of the Buyi and all of the Han will be killed, but white and black Miao will not be killed. The Miao will wear imperial robes instead of burlap." "The Communists forced us to plant grain and labeled us landlords and rich peasants." "We will not be allowed to eat if Mao Zedong is still around. We must fight our way to Beijing. There is a millet tree in Beijing that still provides food even after ten thousand people have eaten from it. In Beijing there will be food to eat, clothes to wear, and books to read, and each man can have eight wives." "Chairman Mao was killed by a hailstone one year after Stalin died, and nobody is in charge of the Communist Party anymore." These rumors expressed ethnic discontent and unhappiness with the Communists' agricultural policies. Quite a few people stopped working the fields and simply waited for the emperor's ascent to the throne. Some families disrobed and knelt as if before the emperor, begging him to give them silks and satins.[50] The rumors also led to panic buying and hoarding. After someone in Sanglang claimed that people who did not have their lamps lit when the emperor ascended would be killed, families rushed to buy lamp oil, and the supply depot sold six times more than usual. Sales of white cloth also skyrocketed.

A work team comprised of members from the Wangmo County Party Committee and the prefectural committee arrived in the center of the uprising to try to counter the rumors and get people farming again. Locals, however, ignored the work team's propaganda and refused to attend meetings. Huang Buzhi proclaimed that the work team's banners could be used as medicine and ordered everyone to tear them down. Starting on June 3, Huang refused to meet with the work team and instead led an armed group of thirty or forty into the mountains. The group called itself the Sickle and Hatchet Army. On June 9, Huang ordered armed followers to gather in Shuli, where on June 14 the vice-county secretary met with PLA soldiers nearby. Huang said that there were many imperial troops "upstairs" and that there would be many large tigers in the mountains the next day. He told his followers that they were allowed to join but not to leave. Anyone who revealed information about the uprising to the authorities would be turned into a stone, he said.[51]

Huang Buzhi and Yang Shaobin split up and tried to get militia members to surrender by proclaiming the establishment of a peasant republic, a Taiping army, an imperial army, a Chinese youth political corps, and a scientific research academy.[52] Yang also held training sessions to teach young women how to stop PLA bullets by casting spells and waving towels. The women were headed by Big Sister Tao, who led them in a chant: "Collectivization, collectivization, double-planting wheat and corn is a fraud. Collectivization, collectivization, the heavens and earth will collapse. When the emperor comes, we will have rice, mansions, and silk for ten thousand years."[53]

These promises sounded attractive to local residents, many of whom preferred an emperor to the Communist Party. Convinced that the PLA's guns would not fire, Mashan residents took up knives against the government. Many also believed that because food would be limitless in the new dynasty, there was no need to work the fields. They dug up the grain they had already planted and slaughtered their pigs to give to the imperial army to eat. They expressed their loyalty to the emperor by offering bullets, silver dollars, and opium. Sensing the rebellion's momentum, many Party members, local cadres, and militia members joined the "imperial" troops. More than two hundred militia members in Wangmo County defected.[54]

By late June 1956, spurred by rumors that an ox had given birth to a human who quickly grew into an adult emperor, the rebellion had spread to twenty-nine townships in Wangmo, Ziyun, and Luodian and also gained followers in Guangxi's Tian'e and Leye Counties.[55] Armed rebels sought out grassroots officials, killing a grain management cadre, a supply depot clerk, and a postal carrier. One rebel group led by Huang Buzhi attempted to assassinate a vice–township leader and seize his weapon, but the cadre was able to escape. Local governments fell into paralysis.

Forcefully Suppressing the Uprising

Provincial authorities in Guiyang were troubled by the spread of the Mashan rebellion. Xiong Liangchen, the vice-magistrate of Ziyun County who had led anti-Nationalist uprisings during the 1940s, happened to be studying at the Guizhou Nationalities Institute in the provincial capital. He was sent back home to work on suppressing the Mashan rebellion. The Ziyun Party Committee learned that rebels were planning to attack the township of Baihua on June 23, 1956. After Xiong Liangchen led a group, dubbed the Ziyun Baihua Disturbance Suppression Work Team, to guard the town, rebels opted not to launch the attack. Meanwhile, prefectural leaders sent armed police to occupy the county seats of Wangmo, Ziyun, and Luodian. On June 28, a prefectural work team stationed in Sanglang asked for armed reinforcements.

On July 1, Meng Guanyi, regimental commander of the 3505th Army (Internal Security 59th Regiment), led a reinforced company to Wangmo County. In addition, a platoon from the Anshun Military Region was sent to occupy Baihua, and armed forces from the provincial Public Security Bureau were assigned to Mashan. Weapons were distributed to most local cadres in Wangmo. A few of them stayed in the county seat, while the rest entered the heart of the rebellion in Mashan. An additional 644 militia members and demobilized soldiers were given the task of suppressing the rebellion. Meng Guanyi, Wang Gangzheng (vice-head of Xingyi Prefecture), and Li Muzhen (Wangmo Party secretary) led all of these forces from the Wangmo Front Headquarters. They issued a strict order to all of the troops under their command: "Do not fire the first shot."[56] Huang Buzhi made it easy for troops to obey this directive. On July 7, 1956, Huang and his followers ambushed a group of officials on the road from Baiyi Township to Angwu Township, severely injuring Liang Xianzhuang, vice-director of the Wangmo County Public Security Bureau. The rebels had fired the first shot.

Shortly thereafter, Di Shunguo, a twenty-eight-year-old militia leader from Shuiyang Township, made matters worse for officials trying to calm the area. Di, a demobilized soldier and Miao of poor peasant background, fervently endorsed Yang Shaowu's call to oppose grain rationing and collectivization and recruited a group of young toughs to join the uprising. Local officials sneaked into Di's home and confiscated his militia-issued gun when he was out of the house, but that only made him angrier. On July 8, Di and more than one hundred followers blocked two local Party leaders and fourteen militia members who were passing through. The rebels seized eight rifles and extra ammunition from the outnumbered group. The next day, an armed work team went to Shuiyang to try to get the weapons back from Di, but Di and his band ambushed the work team, killing three and wounding many others. By mid-July, the rebel force had grown to approximately four hundred, divided into six groups. They had well over one hundred guns.

Since disturbances began in Wangmo, officials at various levels had shifting and conflicting understandings of the situation. The specific language they used to characterize events conditioned their responses. At first, Wangmo County Party leaders believed that opposition to collectivization in Mashan was not counterrevolutionary in nature. It was simply a matter of ethnic minorities spreading rumors, county authorities reasoned, but there was always the possibility that class enemies could take advantage of the situation.[57] Starting in mid-May 1956, as local discontent grew, county leaders changed their minds, saying that "hard core counterrevolutionaries may have instigated the incident." A prefectural work team stationed in Wangmo reported that "this is a case of counterrevolutionaries taking advantage of minorities' feudal superstitions by spreading rumors and inciting them to engage in counterrevolutionary activities. It's just that we have not yet ferreted out the behind-the-scenes backer."[58]

Confusion about the origins of the uprising persisted through July 1956. Because county officials were receiving conflicting reports, some thought that the situation was dire, while others did not think it was especially serious. After the Wangmo Front Headquarters was established, officials on the ground found it difficult to believe that high-level enemy agents had instigated the uprising. They decided to investigate further while pursuing the forces led by Huang Buzhi. Commander Meng Guanyi issued an order to cut off Huang's escape routes to Guangxi. The plan was to encircle Huang's men and try to convince them to surrender. If the rebels continued to resist, however, they would be "exterminated." After taking care of Huang, Commander Meng planned to take the fight to Ziyun County.[59]

Even though local officials knew early on that the appearance of an emperor in Mashan had been fueled by ethnic resentment against grain requisitions and collectivization, they had not expected armed resistance. At a meeting of the Wangmo Front Headquarters and county Party Committee on July 11, 1956, leaders had a heated debate about how to handle the uprising. One group, mainly Party and government officials, argued that the incident was simply an ethnic problem that could not be solved by armed intervention. Another side, mostly made up of military cadres, felt strongly that opposition in Mashan was counterrevolutionary in nature and that anyone supporting the new imperial dynasty should be regarded as an enemy bandit. Miao leader Xiong Liangchen offered a third interpretation: the uprising was an ethnic problem, but not entirely, because counterrevolutionaries and bad people had manipulated it. Xiong argued that the rebellion was not a counter-revolutionary incident—it had been sparked by the Communist Party's poor work methods. The masses were using guns to express their unhappiness with the Party, Xiong said, but it would be wrong to call them bandits and to attack ordinary people who got caught up in the turmoil.[60]

On July 19, 1956, the Xingyi prefectural Party Committee weighed in with an order to the Wangmo County Committee, saying there were problems with the Party's ethnic policies, but the main problem was that the county's suppression of counterrevolutionaries earlier in the decade had been incomplete. According to the prefecture, "only" 139 people had been executed since the campaign to suppress counterrevolutionaries began in the early 1950s. Hidden counterrevolutionaries had seized on ethnic discontent to sow chaos. Prefectural leaders criticized those who saw the rebellion solely through an ethnic lens. This had led to a "rightist deviation" of limiting military engagements and not daring to wipe out the enemy. The prefectural order concluded by noting that low-level rebels who had been captured could be released on bail after undergoing interrogation and education and should publicly confess their mistakes to the masses. Bandit leaders, however, should be punished at large public trials. On approval from the provincial Party Committee, rebel ringleaders could be executed.[61]

The Guizhou provincial officials who would be expected to sign off on the executions of captured rebel leaders could not agree on how to characterize what was happening in Mashan. One group, represented by public security chief Song Zijian, wanted to wipe out opposition in Wangmo by any means necessary. Another group hoped to resolve the matter without resorting to force. On July 18, 1956, it seemed that Song Zijian's group had prevailed: the provincial Party Committee circulated a new report that it had sent to Party Center. This report stated that "counterrevolutionaries who had slipped through the net took advantage of shortcomings in our ethnic work to carry out a counterrevolutionary restoration by inciting ethnic minorities and backward Han masses." Provincial officials reported to Party Center that the uprising was not spontaneous—it had been carefully organized and planned.

Provincial leaders also claimed that "major secret agent bosses" (*zhongyao tewu touzi*) dispatched by the Nationalist Ministry of Defense had been participating in the incident. The policy of "not firing the first shot" against the rebels was a mistaken rightist tendency, according to Guizhou leaders.[62]

The road to a violent suppression of the uprising was now clear. An initial skirmish had already occurred on July 16, 1956, in Mashan. Seven rebels were killed, five injured, and four captured, but the rest escaped the government's net. These casualties dispelled rebel followers' belief that the PLA's guns did not work. After this bloodshed, young women chanting spells no longer appeared on the front lines. An even bigger engagement took place on July 23 in Shuiyang, which troops had encircled after learning that Yang Shaobin and Di Shunguo might be there. PLA forces surrounded one hundred rebels, killing and injuring more than fifty. The rest escaped and formed small, uncoordinated groups. Xingyi prefectural leaders reported that after the battle in Shuiyang, the only remaining significant opposition was in Mashan. By the end of the month, government forces' victories had convinced some participants in the uprising to turn themselves in. By July 29, more than forty people had handed over their weapons. But Yang Shaobin, Huang Buzhi, and Di Shunguo were still at large and continued to stage ambushes. The uprising was far from over, and discontent was still widespread.

Attempting a "Peaceful Resolution"

Guizhou provincial authorities' hard line lasted less than a month. The title of a directive sent from the provincial Party Committee to prefectural committees on July 27, 1956, and also reported to Party Center in Beijing, made the new direction clear: "Urgent Directive on the Peaceful Resolution of Riot Incidents in Ethnic Minority Regions." The document characterized the "riots" (*saoluan*) in Mashan as "basically an ethnic problem that is extremely destructive but in the end is not the same as the armed bandit uprisings that occurred immediately after liberation." To "peacefully resolve" the situation, provincial leaders revived the policy of "not firing the first shot" and ordered the army to "try its best to not resort to force, and to strive to not shed blood." On August 9, 1956, Party Center called the directive "correct" and circulated it to provincial and autonomous region Party committees in Tibet, Xinjiang, Gansu, Qinghai, Sichuan, and Yunnan.[63]

Why the sudden shift? Scholar Jiang Shifei claims that the provincial Public Security Bureau's Party group proposed a new, peaceful path and that the provincial Party Committee agreed to report the matter to Party Center, which approved circulating the new plan to localities.[64] In my view, this sequence seems improbable. It is more likely that the impetus for a peaceful resolution came directly from top central leaders, who had adopted a more conciliatory approach toward ethnic relations in spring 1956.

Wangmo County officials moved to implement the new policy by focusing on stopping the spread of rumors about the appearance of an emperor, stabilizing prices, offering economic compensation to victims, and no longer labeling people as "bandits" and "counterrevolutionaries." The county sent work teams into the areas where resistance was still strong to publicize its new policy of "letting bygones be bygones" and to offer a self-criticism of the mistakes it had made during collectivization and in ethnic work.

Military operations had been halted, but local people were unsure what to think of the sudden change in policy. Followers of the rebels were suspicious that the lull in violent suppression might be a trap, while the leaders of the uprising took the opportunity to recuperate and prepare a comeback. Between August 11 and 31, 1956, there were more than twenty battles in Wangmo; nine officials were killed and three were wounded. The rebels started all of the skirmishes. County leaders asked their prefectural superiors for permission to respond with military force but were denied. The prefecture responded: "The army's remaining task is to protect the work of local cadres and to reduce the scope of the riot. . . . It is not permitted to proactively launch an attack. If the two sides should meet, under no conditions fire the first shot."[65]

This new approach allowed a rebellion that had been flagging to gain new energy in late August and early September 1956. The rebels occupied new territory and attracted new followers, including Xiong Liangchen's brothers, sons-in-law, and nephews.[66] All of the Miao residents of Maozhai joined the imperial troops. Unable to fight back, government forces took heavy losses. Lieutenant Du Jinshan, political commissar of the Internal Security 59th Regiment, was killed by rebels in Bajiaoping.

On the evening of September 5, 1956, Yang Shaobin led a force to attack the Wangmo County seat. His plan was to release approximately eighty rebels from captivity, but more than sixty militia members blocked his men's path to the county seat, killing some rebels and driving others away. On September 8, Di Shunguo led around three hundred rebels to Fukai, where they met with Yang Shaobin and made plans for another siege on the county seat. The next day, officials met in Wangmo and set up a temporary head-quarters led by Meng Guanyi, with Xiong Liangchen as the vice-commander. Meng asked provincial officials for permission to "surround the armed rebels and take the initiative in attacking." The province responded, "You may sur-round, but do not attack." After continued pleas from Meng, the province allowed him to deploy troops for a siege against the rebels but told him not to move until he had a clear order from Governor Zhou Lin.[67] The rebel force, buoyed by knowledge of the army's policy to not open fire, grew to more than a thousand. After repeated SOS calls from forces on the front lines, Zhou Lin finally approved a military attack. It looked like the uprising would not be quelled peacefully after all.

The assault came on September 11, 1956. Almost one hundred rebels were killed or injured, more than one hundred were captured, and almost one hundred fifty weapons were confiscated.[68] Shortly thereafter, in a battle at Lishuwan, PLA troops attacked even more broadly, even killing and injuring some locals who were caught in the crossfire. Military officials Wang Yancai, Meng Guanyi, and Shan Yangshan were punished for the excesses. The Fukai and Lishuwan battles were a turning point. Rebel forces mostly collapsed; many participants turned in their weapons and said they repented. Yang Shaobin, Huang Buzhi, and Di Shunguo led small groups of followers into the mountains, but they had lost their power to influence local people. The military siege had laid the groundwork for what the government called a "peaceful resolution" that would placate the region.

In mid-September 1956, provincial and prefectural officials went to Mashan to direct pacification efforts. On September 17, Wangmo Party Secretary Li Muzhen ordered that ritual livestock and certain types of land that had been collectivized could be returned to their original owners, in consideration of the region's ethnic characteristics.[69] Then, in early October, more than two hundred provincial officials arrived in Wangmo. They split up, traveled throughout the county, and held meetings to listen to locals' opinions, publicize provincial policy, screen films, offer medical treatment, and provide relief to impoverished families. This work lasted for two months.

In late October 1956, Vice-Governor Wu Shi and Duyun prefectural Party secretary Jin Feng arrived in Wangmo and proclaimed that the uprising "was neither a counterrevolutionary riot nor economic banditry." On the contrary, they said, most participants were ordinary citizens. In an effort to convince people to return home, the officials announced the end of military actions and released eighty-three people who had joined the rebellion. Wu and Jin said that even rebel leaders should return home. They too would be treated mercifully. Returning cadres would keep their original positions, and Party members could retain their membership. Locals who had been wounded would receive medical treatment, relief payments, and compensation for their injuries.[70]

After this, most participants in the uprising overcame their fears and surrendered to the government. By the beginning of December 1956, 3,250 people had returned home. Altogether they handed over 833 guns, 11 grenades, 5,231 bullets, 4 homemade cannons, and 327 knives. As for the rebel leaders hiding in the mountains, their days were numbered. Huang Buzhi was the first to succumb. On October 27, he was severely injured by troops who stormed the cave where he was hiding. He died while being transported to the county seat. The next month, after Di Guocai was convinced to surrender, he apologized through tears at a mass meeting. Yang Shaobin and more than twenty diehards lasted until January 11, 1957, when they were finally surrounded by the army. Xiong Liangchen rushed to the scene, where he successfully convinced Yang and his men to give up. This event marked the end of the ten-month uprising.[71]

Temporary Resolutions

The Mashan uprising included 110 battles and caused 194 casualties between the assault on a vice–public security chief on July 6, 1956, and the end of military action on October 27, 1956. Government forces suffered 21 deaths and 23 injuries. The uprising was costly in other ways too. Locals slaughtered 180 oxen, 1,840 pigs, and countless chickens. Agricultural production came to a halt in more than twenty townships, and the grain yield dropped by almost 6,500 tons. Economic damages reached 12,700 yuan, and the state grain tax loss was of 34,500 kilograms. Authorities responded to Mashan residents' difficulties by reducing the grain quota; abolishing certain taxes;

providing 150 oxen, 800 pigs, and 2,200 bolts of cloth; and distributing 100,000 yuan and 750,000 kilograms of grain.[72] In the aftermath of the rebellion, Wangmo County leaders also backpedaled on cooperativization, allowing some cooperatives to downsize to mutual aid societies. Half of the cooperatives that had been formed in the county fell apart.

The Mashan uprising contained elements of two common trends in China in 1956: resistance to collectivization and violence in ethnic minority regions. Although the violent uprising in Mashan was part of a larger pattern, the Communist Party's attempt to resolve it peacefully was unique. In a report sent to Party Center on February 23, 1957, Guizhou provincial authorities reflected on the lessons they had learned from the Mashan uprising:

> When handling ethnic minority riots, we should strive to resolve them peacefully and do our best to not resort to force. It is dangerous to believe in the superstition that armed force can bring peace to the land. Using force not only does not eliminate the grievances of the ethnic minorities, but it also increases tensions, allows counterrevolutionaries to gain advantage, and lets the situation get out of control. Even if it temporarily suppresses an uprising, it causes endless trouble. The facts prove that only peaceful resolution wins over a majority of the masses, isolates a minority of bad people, and puts us in an advantageous position. Even if we are forced into self-defense, we still have the initiative politically.[73]

Much blood had been shed before provincial authorities arrived at this conclusion.

For a party that had come to power through war and revolution, being able to handle an armed uprising through negotiation—rather than resorting to violence immediately—would have represented major progress, a significant enhancement of its governing ability. But it turned out that the situation in Mashan was too complex to fit into Mao's evolving conception of "people" and "nonpeople." Conflict in Mashan extended beyond the masses (people) versus class enemies and counterrevolutionaries (nonpeople). It also pitted local people against the government, ethnic minorities against Han, and policy implementers against policy-makers. These complexities, along with Guizhou authorities' vacillation and a tendency to push responsibility down the administrative hierarchy to the grassroots level, made the attempted peaceful resolution of the Mashan uprising, although promising in theory, fall short in practice.

Prefectural and county cadres in Guizhou were distinguished more by their firmness in following orders than by their flexibility in adapting to circumstances on the ground. This was especially evident when we compare July and August 1956. In July, authorities used violent force to suppress the uprising. In August, government forces were not allowed to fight back against rebels. This sudden shift allowed the rebellion to make a comeback. By September, beleaguered military and armed police units were begging for permission to defend themselves. When they were finally allowed to use force, the rebellion was quashed, but most followers were forgiven and authorities backed away from the harshest elements of collectivization. In the end, "peaceful resolution" did not mean the total absence of force; it meant a flexible approach that allowed local officials to moderate policies that had driven people to take up arms. It was also an approach that did not condemn all resisters as counterrevolutionaries.

It is unfair, however, to blame grassroots officials for being inflexible. Not only were they following policies from above that varied widely from month to month, but they were being blamed for problems that were not of their own making. After provincial policy documents traced the origins of the Mashan uprising to problems in implementing collectivization, local officials made self-criticisms and some were punished. But coercive collectivization did not originate with frontline cadres setting up cooperatives in the mountains of Guizhou. Responsibility lay primarily with Mao Zedong and secondarily with Guizhou provincial officials. People caught up in the uprising assessed culpability for coercive collectivization more accurately than Communist authorities did. As recognized by the rebel who proclaimed, "We will not be allowed to eat if Mao Zedong is still around," the movement to install a new emperor in Mashan ultimately targeted Mao.

By the mid-1960s, of the authorities involved in promoting peaceful approaches toward the Mashan uprising, only Mao was left standing. The policy of promoting a peaceful resolution—promising on paper but flawed in execution—had been repudiated entirely. Conciliatory approaches toward people who opposed Party policies were only possible for a brief moment in 1956. That fleeting atmosphere of political compromise was quickly subsumed in 1957 with the Anti-Rightist Movement. As Zhe Wu's chapter in this volume (Chapter 12) shows, in ethnic minority regions the movement became a crusade against "local nationalism." Mashan was no exception in this regard. For example, Yang Shaobin had been rewarded with a government position after he surrendered in January 1957 and apologized for his role in the uprising. But after the Anti-Rightist Movement began, he was arrested. In December 1957, Yang was sent to prison, where he would remain for twenty years. In the wake of the Anti-Rightist Movement, rebellions such as the Mashan uprising were no longer understood as responses to coercive collectivization or the trampling of ethnic minority customs. They were considered counterrevolutionary incidents, plain and simple.

This post-1957 understanding of what had happened in Mashan eventually led to the downfall of others who had been involved in quelling the uprising. So too did continued violence and discontent, including a rebellion in July 1958 in which more than ninety people took up arms to support the imminent appearance of a new emperor, and also a deadly armed standoff in April 1960 that was sparked when hundreds of people ransacked a granary in Leyuan Commune.[74] In 1964, the Guizhou provincial governor and Party secretary, Zhou Lin, was removed from his position. One charge against him was that he had engaged in "class capitulationism" (*jieji touxiang*) by attempting a peaceful resolution in Mashan. The Xiong brothers did not escape punishment either. During the Four Cleanups in 1964, Xiong Liangbin was incarcerated for fourteen years for his role in the "Mashan murder gang case" (a euphemism for the 1956 uprising). And during the Cultural Revolution, Xiong Liangchen was labeled a "bandit" who was the behind-the-scenes leader of the rebellion—he was incarcerated for two years. The Wangmo County Revolutionary Committee labeled the Mashan uprising a "counterrevolutionary incident" and ruled that not enough people had been punished for their role in the rebellion; more people would have to be arrested.[75] The idea of peacefully resolving problems in minority areas such as Mashan had become unthinkable.

12

Caught between Opposing Han Chauvinism and Opposing Local Nationalism

The Drift toward Ethnic Antagonism in Xinjiang Society, 1952–1963

ZHE WU

Establishing a new, Communist government in Xinjiang after September 1949 required considerable assistance and cooperation from local, non-Han cadres, primarily Uyghurs. However, the reassertion of Chinese dominance in this formerly Soviet-controlled region only intensified ethnic tensions, resulting in repeated efforts by Party Center to introduce local ideological and political correctives. Within Xinjiang's outwardly multiethnic government and Party organization, non-Han "local nationalism" and its opposite, "Han chauvinism," were criticized throughout the 1950s and 1960s as divisive, even counterrevolutionary, mentalities.[1] While the Communist Party thought it could more easily restrict or contain local nationalism, it also saw Han chauvinism as an exceedingly dangerous trend that could destroy the Party's carefully cultivated image as a liberator and harm Beijing's long-term interests in the Northwest.

Warnings against Han chauvinism were not often heeded, leading to the reappearance of local nationalism as a counter to Han authority and its abuses in Xinjiang. Han cadres, whether inside or outside the Communist Party, had been warned that they should respect the customs of Xinjiang's ethnic minorities and listen to the opinions of their non-Han colleagues and were strictly forbidden from employing strong-arm tactics and "commandism."[2] Nor were they to engage in bureaucratism, "alienate themselves from the masses," or blindly introduce policies already being implemented in Han areas into Xinjiang. Instead, Han cadres were exhorted to conduct "democratic consultations" with non-Han cadres and citizens, take into account the special features and objective conditions of various localities, and exercise flexibility in policy implementation. Cadres who did not pay sufficient attention to ethnic differences and who did not work in close consultation with non-Han cadres were periodically criticized by the authorities for their "Han chauvinism."

At the same time, non-Han cadres within the Party—some of them former elites of the pre-1949 Gulja (Yining) government of the second East Turkestan Republic—worked strenuously after 1949 to consolidate their own power. The Turkic "Gulja regime," established in 1944 following the Three Districts Rebellion, was closely linked to the Soviet Union until 1949, after which its territories were absorbed by the People's Republic of China as part of northern Xinjiang. During the 1950s, former Gulja elites' political maneuvering yielded surprising results. First, former elites such as Saifudin Azizi, who in 1955 became Xinjiang Uyghur Autonomous Region (XUAR) regional government chairman, were able to convince other Communist Party officials that anti-Han nationalism in Xinjiang, and even within the Party itself, was primarily an isolated or individual phenomenon.[3] This allowed them to deflect attention from more organized forms of anti-Han behavior and, at least in the short term, to protect their own political positions. Second, by minimizing perceptions of unrest, they provided support for Party policies of expanding minority privileges in Xinjiang, mainly in the form of salaried government positions and economic compensation; this approach may also have forestalled more punitive Party and army activity directed against the antigovernment, anti-Han rioting that occurred periodically in the region throughout the 1950s and 1960s.

Nonetheless, this chapter demonstrates that both Han chauvinism and the organized resistance it inspired were fundamental to the nature of Xinjiang local politics after 1949. When both Han and non-Han efforts to defuse this tension failed, culminating in the unsuccessful conclusion of the 1957–1962 Movement against Local Nationalism, Xinjiang was swept by widespread crackdowns and even more drastic forms of ethnic unrest that included violent attacks and mass border crossings into the Soviet Union. In short, Han chauvinism and its responses fostered a general state of insecurity that permeated post-1949 Xinjiang society. Rather than focusing, as other scholars have done, on how Soviet influence and strained Sino-Soviet relations in the Northwest contributed to Xinjiang's early-1960s frontier uprisings, this chapter reveals the region's long history of local ethnic politics, riots, and anti-Han unrest.[4]

Han Chauvinism and Its Opponents, 1952–1955

One of the first major instances of Han chauvinism in Xinjiang involved radical redistribution policies implemented in pastoral areas between July and August 1952 by Wang Zhen, the First Party Secretary of Xinjiang. These were severely criticized by the Northwest Bureau and Party Center. The Communist Party Northwest Bureau Xinjiang Sub-Bureau accused Han cadres of

> Not giving consideration to the current stage of political, economic, and cultural development of the various nationalities, but blindly adopting the experiences of Han agricultural and even military areas; not paying attention to the finer aspects of history, culture, and traditions of the various nationalities, but focusing instead on their backwardness; emphasizing in an inappropriate way their opposition to narrow nationalism among local non-Han cadres and resolving problems in a rigid manner.[5]

As the Xinjiang Sub-Bureau stressed, only by focusing on overcoming chauvinism could Han cadres gain the trust of non-Han Party members.

From April 8 to April 17, 1954, Xinjiang leaders once again discussed the issue of Party unity. In their view, the main obstacle to unity in the province and Party was residual chauvinism among Han cadres and local nationalism among non-Han cadres. In a speech on the topic, Xinjiang Communist Party leader Wang Enmao stressed that inequality and mutual discrimination still existed between the different ethnic groups in Xinjiang, especially between Han and non-Han peoples, and that these were caused mainly by Han chauvinism. Wang also mentioned that there were certain people among the ethnic minorities who "continue in their attempts to destroy unity, distort the spirit of religious freedom, generate rumors, rouse the people, destroy production, and disregard the authority of the law in the name of religion."[6] Radical land reform—the seizure and redistribution of land formerly held by local, non-Han elites and others—was one source of tension. Religion was another.

Following his replacement of Wang Zhen as the top leader of Xinjiang, Wang Enmao continued to guard against the development of Han chauvinism and local nationalism, with emphasis on preventing the former. After Mao Zedong received reports from Wang Enmao and other key Party and government personnel working among minority peoples at the borders and from the Party's United Front and Minority Affairs departments, he stressed, during three separate Party congresses between 1953 and 1955, that Han chauvinism was obstructing the unity of the Chinese people and preventing China from exploiting the rich resources of over 60 percent of its landmass.[7] According to Mao, the Party was to train more non-Han cadres and respect their use of their native languages.

Mao's instructions had an immediate effect. In the middle of 1955, the Xinjiang United Front Work Department sent a notice to all administrative offices and Party committees of prefectural commissioner's offices, instructing them to review the implementation of regional autonomy of ethnic minorities. The notice expressed anger over the negligence of ethnic minority interests within the Party and government, stating that "in the use of written languages, most autonomous regions do not have native translators; most written documents are in the Chinese or Uyghur languages, while the Mongol and Kyrgyz languages are insufficiently used." Furthermore, "in the areas of culture, education, and public health, the problems of film [projectors] and cultural troupes have yet to be resolved, while itinerant medical teams should be set up in Qapqal and the Mongol areas where diseases are widespread."[8]

Another internal document, issued in August 1956, provided further direction concerning work on nationalities and United Front work. Its contents stressed the importance of "strengthening the unity of non-Han cadres by, first and foremost, opposing Han chauvinism and, at the same time, conducting ideological education with regard to local nationalistic tendencies among certain ethnic minority Party members." In addition, it provided detailed examples of Han chauvinism's manifestations on the ground, including Han cadres looking down on non-Han officials; inadequate support for local languages in official documents, commercial signage, and law courts; as well as other insults and slights. For example,

> The process of private industry reforms is ongoing in some places, and little consideration has been given to features that are characteristic of ethnic minorities or convenient to them. Following the transformation of Muslim canteens into joint state-private ownership concerns, the word "Muslim" (*qingzhen*) is removed. In some shops, pork is sold together with beef and mutton. Some Han cadres are thoughtless in saying things that hurt the feelings of ethnic minorities, such as, "Why believe in Huda [Allah] when you believe in Marxism-Leninism?" and "Eating pork is progress; not eating pork is backward!" Some businesses require their non-Han cadres who are Muslims to sell or transport pork, even threatening them by saying, "If you don't do it, you'll be fired."

The document by the Uyghur Autonomous Region Communist Party Committee (hereafter the Xinjiang Party Committee) only noted two brief instances of local nationalism as a source of friction: "There are those among ethnic minorities who say Han cadres are 'imperialists'" and others who "refer to workers who get along well with Han workers as 'traitors.'" Its conclusion, however, was clear: further attention would be required in handling differences in Han and non-Han customs such as food restrictions and taboos on intermarriage, and the Party would need to repair damage done to its image by Han chauvinism.[9]

1956: Saifudin Azizi Strikes a Delicate Balance

Between 1949 and 1956, monolithic leadership of the Party over government bodies meant the institution of Han advantage and power. At the same time, both Han and non-Han cadres worked to implement the national policy of "regional autonomy of nationalities," which worked to contain ethnic friction by compartmentalizing culture from politics and protecting minority interests. Because the Party did not wish to be accused of exploitative practices, particularly by minority peoples, its leaders adhered to the basic principles of the regional autonomy system—at least formally. For this reason, Party policy before summer 1957 was focused more on combating Han chauvinism than on addressing local nationalism.

Such policies, however, did not mean that relations between Han and non-Han in Xinjiang were characterized by an early-1950s "honeymoon" or that the Party tolerated expressions of what it labeled local nationalism. During the early days of the Communist takeover of Xinjiang, the Party severely repressed anti-Communist and anti-Han activity. The Xinjiang Peacekeeping Democratic Alliance, a left-wing organization that had carried over from the former Gulja regime and remained an ambiguous Communist ally, albeit a somewhat shaky one, was targeted for neutralization.[10] It was disbanded, and its Turkic-speaking members were removed from the political scene.[11] In practice, implementing regional autonomy for ethnic minorities in Xinjiang between 1951 and 1955 meant establishing, along lines drawn up by Beijing, a province-level "Uyghur Autonomous Region" government that contained numerous non-Uyghur autonomous counties and prefectures.[12]

Although the political power of non-Han groups had been diluted during the first half of the 1950s, local nationalism once again became a prominent issue in 1956, with the launching of the national Hundred Flowers campaign. In Xinjiang, the campaign's call for intellectuals to constructively criticize the Party's work elicited little response. Instead, non-Han loyalists of the formerly independent Gulja state—including those, such as Saifudin Azizi, who occupied positions within the Communist Party and Xinjiang government—sought to advance their interests by fighting for Muslim identity through existing Party frameworks. In a bold move, they adopted the strategy of leading the charge against "narrow nationalism" and local nationalism revivals within Xinjiang. By spearheading a search for internal, anti-Han dissent—rather than taking the issue of Han chauvinism head-on—they apparently hoped to protect anti-Han activists within their own ranks by seizing the initiative in labeling narrow and local nationalist manifestations as noncounterrevolutionary "contradictions among the people." Though daring, the initiative unfolded in ways that were difficult to control.

In February 1956, the Xinjiang Party Committee organized a conference for all subordinate departments. At the conference Azizi pointed out that

some non-Han cadres manifested "narrow nationalist" and "local nationalist" tendencies. Xinjiang Party Committee member Shu Mutong (Sibe
nationality), however, went a step further and made specific accusations
against "undercover counterrevolutionaries" within the Party's own ranks.
In January 1956, Shu alleged, a counterrevolutionary organization called the
East Turkestan Party had emerged in Turpan, where it attempted to "organize riots." Led by Muhemmet Sayidin, a Turpan County high school teacher,
the organization's membership included seven Communist Youth League
members and one Party cadre. Shu also claimed that certain Urumqi cadres
had joined a "counterrevolutionary clique" led by Isa Alptekin that spread
rumors and reactionary slogans, pamphlets, and letters. His allegations were
echoed by Xinjiang education director Anivar Khan Baba (an Uzbek), who
accused history and geography students in Xinjiang's colleges and universities of "distorting the Revolution of the Three Districts" by depicting the Ili
Rebellion as an uprising against brutal Han colonization and of inciting
anti-Communist and anti-Han riots in the spirit of the Three Districts/Ili
rebellions. Following Baba, Director of Health Yaqub Beg recalled a Uyghur
cadre who, while studying medicine in Lanzhou, referred to the Lanzhou-
Xinjiang railway line (then under construction) as a Han tool for the invasion of Xinjiang.[13]

Azizi attempted to dampen the allegations of counterrevolutionary activity
within the Party by submitting a report to Party Center about ideological
trends among non-Han local cadres. As an example of the "narrow nationalism" that was turning into counterrevolutionary activity, Azizi singled out
"a reactionary pamphlet that was found in Ili last year that advocated opposition to the Communist Party, the Central People's Government, and Chairman Mao." One of the three people arrested, "Akli," graduated in 1954 from
the history department of the former Institute of Nationalities, where he led
a students' strike, saying, "We do not want to study Han history; we want to
study Uyghur history." Akli advocated revolution and independence, calling
for the foundation of an independent East Turkestan state.

Azizi subtly depicted such counterrevolutionary behavior within the
Party as the work of individuals, rather than groups. He tried to divert attention away from new incidences of activity beyond already-known events
unfolding in Hotan and Turpan. The problem, according to Azizi, was not
one of conspiring cadres, but of lingering resentments: "These problems can

be summed up in one phrase: ideologies of the old society—the remnants of capitalist nationalism, pan-Islamism and pan-Turkism. As a result, our political and ideological education work should be improved."[14] In addition, Azizi advocated cultural integration. In February 1956, in a speech given at a symposium for non-Han cadres, he proposed that non-Han schoolchildren should start learning how to read and write in Chinese, as well as Russian, from their fourth year in primary school onward.[15]

Preludes to Conflict

On June 30, 1956, the Xinjiang Party Committee convened a standing committee meeting to discuss the Hotan riots—a series of eight violent protests that had shaken the region between December 31, 1954, and May 4, 1956. These were, in turn, part of a larger pattern of approximately forty outbreaks of violence around Hotan since the founding of the People's Republic. Total participants in these incidents numbered "several thousand," most of whom were peasants protesting collectivization.[16] In confronting the Hotan riots, Xinjiang leaders maintained a moderate tone, stating that "lessons from the Hotan Incident should include stressing training and promoting local non-Han cadres and economic and cultural development of the Hotan region to prevent similar incidents from occurring again."[17] Because the ethnic situation in Xinjiang was already highly sensitive by 1956, local minority elites were unlikely to take further political risks by directly confronting the Communist Party.

Still, the protests continued. During 1956 and 1957, a "socialist upsurge"—collectivization of farmland and pastureland, coupled with linguistic reforms—resulted in many new protests in Xinjiang. The Party blamed ethnic differences and intrigue, insisting that "counterrevolutionaries had made use of ethnic and religious issues to incite unrest among backward peoples in places such as Hotan, Kalikash, Lop, and Yengisar." On many occasions, protesters attacked units involved in agricultural compounds, "killing and injuring our cadres, soldiers, and comrades." Following these acts of violence, the Xinjiang Party Committee dispatched standing committee member Lü Jianren, who was responsible for United Front work, to investigate, with instructions stating that "political disintegration should be the main line of approach, supplemented by military deterrence." Protesters were to be dealt with according to the following formula: "leaders are to be punished; those who became accomplices under duress should not be penalized; those who render meritorious services are to be rewarded."[18] The goal was to prevent further protests, while at the same time avoiding the instigation of further unrest.

At this juncture, the Party and the army continued to avoid looking too deeply for signs of counterrevolutionary activity; the policy was to identify but also minimize conflict. For example, the People's Liberation Army, Xinjiang Military Region command, issued an order requiring its troops to differentiate between "disturbances created by local people" and "counter-revolutionary riots." Soldiers were to avoid the use of repressive measures in response to the disturbances that were considered "conflicts within the masses."[19] Likewise, in 1956 the Xinjiang United Front Department issued several circulars ordering local authorities to appease non–Party members and provide economic compensation to ethnic minority elites who had suffered economic losses as the result of socialist reform of the livestock industry. In addition, more political consultative conference positions were allocated to non-Party ethnic elites. The new positions of vice-chairman, standing committee member, and committee member came with government salaries; appointments were overseen by the United Front Department. More than 2 million yuan was budgeted for the 3,011 ethnic non–Party members and other elites who were eligible for these forms of compensation—an average of some 60 yuan per person each month.[20]

The calculated risk taken by Saifudin Azizi and other former members of the Gulja regime had paid off. By condemning "narrow" nationalism and local nationalism, while at the same time seeking to minimize interethnic conflict and a wider hunt for counterrevolutionaries within Xinjiang—a search they feared that they themselves might fall afoul of—they had given the Party room to expand its United Front work among non-Han ethnic groups. The result, at least briefly, was a reconstituted political order in which local elites were allowed an increasingly visible consultative role.

1957: The Turning Point

The Hundred Flowers came suddenly to Xinjiang. A December 2, 1956, *People's Daily* editorial titled "Are there really no problems?" signaled that the Communist Party itself would be subject to criticism and attack. Soon thereafter, *Xinjiang Daily* articles denounced government officials who used Chinese exclusively and Han cadres who displayed arrogance toward ethnic minorities. Xinjiang Party boss Wang Enmao announced the need to strengthen unity between all ethnic groups in Xinjiang and to treat Han chauvinism as the "main contradiction."

Han cadres within the Xinjiang Party hierarchy, particularly those close to the Xinjiang Party Committee, followed Wang's lead by firing the first critical salvos against ethnic prejudices. Non-Han cadres then gradually cast aside their typical caution and reserve, venting grievances concerning Han chauvinism. Both trends were encouraged by the Xinjiang Party Committee, which issued written directives requiring Party and government bodies at all levels to rectify "bad ways" and "bad ideological tendencies" in their work. In conjunction with the rectification movement, a document issued by the Xinjiang Cultural and Education Department featured a list of "opinions of the masses." One of the most cited complaints having nothing to do with ethnic differences was that "Communist Party members are prejudiced against nonmembers." In the cultural, education, and public health departments, non-Han cadres complained about the chauvinism manifested by their Han colleagues, teachers, and students.

The range of complaints was notable for the acrimony it revealed on both sides of the ethnic divide. Han students at the Xinjiang Petroleum School resisted the mandatory study of the Uyghur language. Non-Han instructors at the Xinjiang Medical College were barred from participating in daily work or appearing in the classroom on the grounds that their training was out of date. One Muslim cadre was made to "dig graves"—a reference to the dismantling of a religious cemetery. Workers in the medical college canteen used the same knife for slaughtering both goats and pigs.[21] The criticisms also revealed anti-Han sentiments among the Party rank and file. Muhemmet Sidik, a cadre of the Urumqi Public Security Bureau, was quoted as openly resisting efforts to root out prejudice on both sides: "Do all the checks you want; it all boils down to our oppression by the *Kitai* [a pejorative name referring to Han people—literally, "black lords"]. If the Hungarian Revolution occurs in Xinjiang, I will be the first person to join."[22]

Xinjiang leaders' initial response was to turn to education. On February 22, 1957, the Xinjiang Party Committee lamented that "Han comrades have been less enthusiastic than minority comrades" in learning new languages and recommended that "ideological mobilization should be earnestly intensified." Language, the committee's members continued,

> Is the most crucial key to connecting the different nationalities in various places, communicating thoughts and emotions, and implementing policies. . . . Every Han cadre arriving from outside Xinjiang should strive to master the language and script of the local people within two to three years; . . . the specific requirement is for them to be able to read and understand general documents written in the Uyghur language within three to five years. As for local non-Han cadres in the Xinjiang Autonomous Region, their level of Chinese proficiency should improve within three to five years (for autonomous region–level cadres) or five to six years (for prefecture- and county-level cadres) to allow them to have conversations and read Chinese newspapers and general documents.[23]

Within two months, however, emphasis had shifted from education to rectification. At a meeting of the Xinjiang Autonomous Region People's Congress, held from April 14 to 25, 1957, Burhan Shahidi read aloud Mao Zedong's speech "On the Correct Handling of Contradictions among the People." Thereafter, the Xinjiang Party Committee convened an enlarged meeting from April 26 to May 24 and established a special rectification group led by Wang Enmao and Saifudin Azizi. Wang's first step was to notify all Xinjiang Party organs of an upcoming conference for airing "free discussions and criticisms" of contradictions, with a focus on issues of local nationalism and Han chauvinism.[24] In preparation, Mao's speech was circulated in both Chinese and minority language versions.

During the conference itself, participants indicated an increase in the frequency and severity of criticisms leveled against Han Party members, cadres, and civil servants. These views were recorded and collected by the Xinjiang Autonomous Region's propaganda office; it is noteworthy that they included many Han voices critical of Party rule. Han intellectuals, for example, used sarcastic language to criticize the Party's absolute right to rule China, as in the case of one member of the Geological Bureau No. 519 Prospecting Team

Party Committee, who gibed: "The Party says, 'The democratic parties will coexist permanently.' I don't believe this. When the people get old and nobody joins the democratic parties, they won't exist anymore, will they?"[25]

Far more serious were the criticisms of the Party's ethnic policies by non-Han cadres and intellectuals. Borrowing communist concepts, they argued that Party members of one ethnicity could not possibly guarantee the happiness and welfare of those belonging to other ethnicities and advocated for the right of non-Han ethnic groups to set up their own Party organizations. As one cultural cadre posed the question: "Why do we need Han people's help to become socialist? The Soviet Union has a federal system, and every ethnic group became socialist, didn't they?"[26] Others, including a worker from the Cultural Department ethnic minority drama company, could no longer keep their frustration with everyday discrimination under wraps: "Chairman Mao's report was correct. Although Xinjiang is autonomous, 70 percent of the power is in the hands of the Han people. The Han drama company installed electricity in their rooms, enabling them to turn on the lights even when they are in bed. If an ethnic minority drama company wants to do this, it will not be allowed."[27] From a non-Han perspective, local national identity, Han chauvinism, and the inability of the Party to guarantee equality among its members were intertwined. Such experiences created a volatile situation.

From Attacking Rightists to Combating Local Nationalism

Mao Zedong's response to the widespread criticisms of the Hundred Flowers was decisive: cleanse and purge through the Anti-Rightist Movement. In Xinjiang, the first to fall as a result of the new policies were the Han editors of the *Xinjiang Daily*, whose alleged crime was that they had complained, either in their own published writings or in articles sent to Shanghai's *Wenhui Bao*, that Xinjiang lacked freedom of speech in comparison with the rest of China.[28] Starting in August 1957, various units of Xinjiang's Production and Construction Military Corps also launched their own anti-rightist movements, identifying 190 rightists within their ranks by the end of 1958. The corps also absorbed an additional 300 rightists deported from Beijing, Shanghai, and other coastal cities, and 316 more who had fled to Xinjiang from the hinterland, only to be apprehended upon arrival.[29] The organization accounted for approximately one-quarter of all 3,246 people labeled rightists in Xinjiang.[30]

During roughly the same period, beginning in May 1957 and lasting until the end of the year, the Xinjiang Autonomous Region Public Security Bureau also stepped up its search for "hidden counterrevolutionary cliques." Alleged counterrevolutionary organizations included the "United Party of Nationalities of China"—concealed within the Xinjiang Nonferrous Metals Mining Company (a former Sino-Soviet venture)—and the "Agriculture and Labor Party of China," formed by Han deportees to a labor camp operated by the already rightist-prone Production and Construction Military Corps.[31]

The focus of Xinjiang's Anti-Rightist Movement shifted toward non-Han people. This was a significant development; the movement in Xinjiang shifted away from what was happening in the rest of China and transformed into an effort to combat local nationalism. Efforts to combat Han chauvinism, prevalent in earlier years, evaporated. Instead, the Party reprimanded cadres for having slackened in their struggle against local nationalism. Newspapers and magazines in Xinjiang began to expose "attacks" by non-Han peoples against the Party. These reports included accusations that some ethnic groups nursed grievances against the Production and Construction Military Corps, which had caused environmental degradation in its project to "open wastelands."

Other complaints were that Han people occupied all key Party posts—so that the region was autonomous in name only—and that in the construction industry Han people occupied all the managerial positions, leaving all the heavy work to their non-Han subordinates. Others were alleged to have said that they would prefer to cast off the dictatorship of the Communist Party by joining their own people in the Soviet Union. Some non-Han cadres were accused of "harboring enmity toward the motherland" and attempting to reestablish an independent East Turkestan Republic, which would rid Xinjiang of all Han people. Other "local nationalists" insisted that there were too many Han cadres and that non-Han cadres feared expressing their opinions in meetings and were frequently passed over for promotions.

Responses were swift. Pro-Soviet publications and ideas were among the first targets of censure; non-Han cadres and others believed to have shown pro-Soviet tendencies were eliminated from positions of authority.[32] On December 16, 1957, a meeting of the Xinjiang Party Committee aimed at "resolving local nationalism" was convened in Urumqi. At the meeting's opening, Saifudin Azizi read a report titled "Firmly Oppose Local Nationalism and Struggle for the Grand Victory of Socialism," which stated that, since 1956, levels of local nationalism among ethnic minorities had reached critical levels. Following "raving attacks" by these rightist intellectuals on the Party, local nationalism now represented the most dangerous ideological tendency in Xinjiang. Azizi further stressed that Xinjiang was an inalienable part of China, that China's revolution took precedence over local revolutions, and that opponents of China's socialist transformation, Communist Party leadership, and the role of the Han people in helping Xinjiang were extremist counterrevolutionary nationalists. Finally, Azizi warned that anyone interfering with Han workers and Party members in Xinjiang would be labeled a saboteur, and anyone calling non-Han cadres and Party members "running dogs of the Han people" would themselves be considered an enemy of the people.

Saifudin Azizi and Wang Enmao—who echoed Azizi's remarks—were also fighting back against the argument, now being loudly voiced among non-Han cadres, that the Party should be made more suitable to Xinjiang's "local conditions" by rapidly promoting non-Han Party members and creating a non-Han majority within the upper echelons of Party leadership.[33] Instead, they moved to expose and criticize current non-Han leaders within the Party as local nationalists. A *People's Daily* editorial from April 26, 1958, also accused local nationalists of attempting to detach Xinjiang from the rest of China. Wang Enmao reminded Xinjiang officials to oppose rightists within the Party who were secretly helping the independence movement and expressed his belief that there were still people in the Party loyal to the former (and pro-Soviet) East Turkestan Republic who took encouragement from the 1956 Hungarian revolt.[34]

Rectification and Assimilation, 1958–1959

On May 14, 1958, the Xinjiang Party Committee promulgated its "Plan for Carrying Out Rectification among Non-Han Cadres and Intellectuals," which instructed all subordinate Party committees to combat local nationalism by focusing on non-Han cadres and intellectuals and "persons who sabotage the unity of the motherland and its peoples." This campaign lasted from late May 1958 to March 1959.

Rectification was widespread. In Ili Kazakh Autonomous Prefecture, a former Gulja regime stronghold, 1,423 people were labeled rightists between late February and early March 1958.[35] The Qeshqer prefectural commissioner's office and Party Committee held a meeting between May 25 and August 8 that resulted in the identification and criticism of 232 local nationalists. Punishments followed. Those known to have played prominent roles in the Gulja government were denounced and labeled local nationalists at yet another Xinjiang Party Committee meeting. They were dismissed, demoted, suspended, and ordered to undergo ideological reform. Non-Han Party and government leaders in Urumqi, Qeshqer, Qizilsu, and Ili were also publicly denounced as local nationalists. In general, the areas targeted were those believed to harbor residual Soviet influence. In the Xinjiang-wide movement to combat local nationalism, a total of 1,612 people were labeled local nationalists.[36]

Between 1958 and 1960 the Party searched high and low for local nationalists. The main targets were Uyghurs and Kazakhs who had served under the pro-Soviet Gulja government. The Party also dealt harshly with those who had been vocal in their opposition to Party and Han rule, as well as those known to have pushed for independence or a return to the Soviet sphere of influence. Those who represented local ethnic interests, stressed Xinjiang's special circumstances and characteristics, and wanted the Party organization to be "ethnicized" were also exposed and attacked. Ethnic policies became increasingly radicalized in the course of the campaign. As the Great Leap Forward began, the Party attempted to advance acculturation of non-Han peoples by implementing policies designed for Han areas and Han populations. These measures can be traced back at least as far as June 1957, when the Cyrillic-based writing systems used by Uyghur, Kazakh, Mongolian, Sibe, and Kyrgyz peoples were replaced with the Latin alphabet–based Hanyu Pinyin system.[37] This included the Pinyinization (i.e., phonetic standardization) of Uyghur and Kazakh words and the introduction of Chinese prepositions into the written language. In a July 20, 1959, speech on the language reforms, Saifudin Azizi stated that the goals of the reforms were development, integration, and assimilation. As Abdul Zakirov,

Chairman of the Committee for Language Reform of the Xinjiang Uyghur Autonomous Region, added, "Based on actual work situations and current, specific circumstances, we have found that the most suitable alphabet is not the Slavic alphabet but the Latin one."[38] The ultimate aim of the new initiative was to gradually make Chinese the common language of Xinjiang.

Sinification of non-Chinese languages had another goal as well: breaking the hold of Islam over local people, especially youth. The history and cultural heritage of minority peoples was to be relegated to museums or destroyed. In their stead would appear Chinese-style socialism and Mao Zedong Thought. Sinification also aimed to obliterate the Soviet Union's influence over Xinjiang and sever ties linking Turkic Muslims on both sides of the Sino-Soviet border. Implementation of the reforms was delayed until 1960, however, which suggests that the Party was wary of the discontent that the reforms would inevitably cause. Turkic-language textbooks, published in the Soviet Union, remained in use in areas such as Ili; the new writing system was not popularized until 1965.

Local and Party Responses

Between 1958 and 1959 many uprisings involving ethnic minorities were reported in Xinjiang. These were caused by various factors: assimilationist minority policies, economic turmoil caused by the Great Leap Forward, Han migration into Xinjiang, the breakdown of Sino-Soviet relations, news of armed revolt in Tibet. In October 1958, the Danzeng Jiamucuo rebellion—which was directly connected to Tibetan resistance in Tibet, Qinghai, and Sichuan—erupted in Wusu County, only to be swiftly put down by the People's Liberation Army. Uprisings in Koktokay (north Xinjiang), Hami (east Xinjiang), and Bay (located on the northern rim of the Tarim Basin) flared up as responses to the Great Leap Forward and the intensified competition for land caused by policies accelerating Han migration.[39]

These challenges put the Party on the defensive. The November 1957 concern over minority intellectuals inciting "racial chauvinism" and slandering Party ethnic policies among the masses indicated that control of Xinjiang was far from assured. Later, the Xinjiang Islamic Association was criticized for placing religious interests above national interests. The Party accused ethnic minority dissenters of preferring their own native languages, refusing to learn Chinese, and referring to Party cadres as "Han colonizers." In May 1959, the Xinjiang Party Committee notified all higher education institutions that graduation of minority students was to be postponed by a year, during which time the students would be made to study Chinese; the Committee also demanded more intensive Chinese courses in junior and senior high schools.[40] These reforms, however, failed to mitigate perceptible pro-Soviet and anti-Han sentiments in the region and to stem the increase in Soviet propaganda and subversion among local people in Xinjiang.

In July 1960, the Xinjiang United Front Department promulgated a policy document titled "Several Questions Regarding the Further Reinforcement and Development of Socialist Ethnic Relations," which summarized ethnic policies of the past three years, while calling for mitigation of ethnic antagonisms. One version of the document, personally revised by Wang Enmao, read as follows:

> Over the past ten years, [Wang: at the same time as we actively pursue the socialist construction of the socialist revolution, in our work among the nationalities] we have censured Han chauvinism most resolutely. When local nationalism became the main source of danger, we also firmly censured local nationalism. The Second Xinjiang Party Congress in 1952 also strongly condemned Han chauvinism. From 1957 to 1959 there were struggles against local nationalism both within and outside the Party in the autonomous region, which resulted in a total victory. [Wang: Currently we are still primarily fighting local nationalism.] To understand and to completely resolve the ethnic issue, we must develop the economies and cultures of ethnic minorities in a big way. This should be so in the past, in the present, and in the future.
>
> Only a small number of people are opposed to these new socialist ethnic relations. They do not know the developmental laws of ethnic groups and harbor local nationalist ideologies. On the pretext of "maintaining the distinctive features of their ethnic group," they are opposed to the Three Treasures of socialist development. Where there are certain aspects of integration between ethnic groups, they malign them as "forced assimilation of ethnic minorities by the Han Chinese." They are opposed to incorporating the advanced culture of the Han people and attempt to preserve all the backward elements of their own people. They

even revive archaic and obsolete things to manufacture ethnic characteristics, and artificially magnify the differences between ethnic groups.
On the pretext of "preserving the purity of the languages and scripts of
ethnic minorities," they are opposed to learning Chinese and the
reforms of ethnic minority scripts based on the Hanyu Pinyin system,
and they refuse to incorporate Han vocabulary into their own languages. They are adamant in preserving indigenous habits and customs
that are detrimental to the development of socialism. Using so-called
"religious customs" as an excuse, they are opposed to ethnic minorities rearing pigs voluntarily and being engaged in active production.
They are opposed to minority women marrying Han men voluntarily,
and so on.

As for the issue of intermarriage between nationalities, there are not
many problems associated with Han women marrying ethnic minority
men. In cases where ethnic minority women marry Han men, however,
there exist certain erroneous perceptions. In the past, we stipulated
that Han men must not pursue minority women. This stipulation was
correct. Circumstances are different now. People of all ethnicities work,
live, develop, and prosper together; people of all ethnicities have closer
links with one another. Therefore, if the relationship between two individuals is genuine and voluntarily entered into, then it is to be given full
support in accordance with the constitution.

Over the past ten years, there is a group of people that still does not
have the notion of the motherland. There are even those who deny that
China is their motherland. Instead, they place their ethnicity high
above the motherland. Therefore, we must emphasize patriotic education, completion of the communization of cadres, and abandonment of
religious beliefs. We must increase cultural interactions between ethnic
groups, set up joint schools, and learn each other's languages.[41]

The document indicated that the Party would uphold new ethnic policies
that had been in place since the second half of 1957 and that it was also
willing to pursue the "communization" of society in order to eradicate Soviet
influence. In practice, communization meant that the Party would seek support from local ethnic groups and take a more moderate approach to handling ethnic relations in the long run.

Communizing and Desovietizing Xinjiang, 1958–1962

The movement to combat local nationalism can be considered the first step toward the goal of eradicating pro-Soviet sentiment in Xinjiang. Between 1958 and 1962, the Party attacked individuals suspected of opposing the Party or Chinese rule. The range of labels applied to those who were targeted indicates that opposition to the Party's presence in Xinjiang was a cross-class and cross-ethnic phenomenon: "local nationalists," "rightist conservative elements," "decaying and degenerate elements who have not been properly reformed," "reactionaries who are landlords, rich peasants, and capitalists," and "criminals" were all included under the broad umbrella of political opposition. Even in the midst of successive purges and rectification campaigns, however, the Party attempted to maintain a base of support among non-Han ethnic groups. But policies enacted during the Great Leap Forward made tensions inevitable, and it is against this background that the Party's 1960 policy of "moderation" must be understood.

During the 1957–1959 Anti-Rightist Movement to combat local nationalism, intense criticism of bureaucratism, capitalism, and separatist tendencies among non-Han ethnic peoples became standard features of Xinjiang politics. At the same time, the Great Leap Forward began to unfold in Xinjiang. In July 1958, Wang Enmao outlined priorities for the Leap: completion of the Lanzhou-Xinjiang Railway, introduction of large-scale industrial production, and communization of agriculture.[42] By the end of 1958, several signs indicated that the Great Leap Forward had plunged Xinjiang's society and economy into chaos. Implementing communization was most difficult among non-Han ethnic groups, who—much like the Miao people in Guizhou who resisted collectivization, as described by Wang Haiguang in Chapter 11 in this volume—believed that what was being imposed was simply another form of Han domination.[43] In early 1960, propaganda messages urged the population to reduce food intake; the seriousness of China's food crisis was readily apparent.[44] From 1960 to 1961, cadres throughout Xinjiang desperately sought to meet targets set by their superiors for increased food production. In practice, this meant putting the rest of the region on a program of forced austerity to "help [our] brother provinces."[45] Social and economic disorder continued to mount. Faced with severe opposition along ethnic lines, the Party moved to elevate elite members of the pre-1949 Gulja government to positions of visible political authority. These individuals had value as symbols of Party accommodation of non-Han ethnic interests; moreover, each had stood with the Party during the campaigns against rightists and local nationalism. Also promoted at the same time were younger non-Han cadres from the grassroots level, who replaced the purged, allegedly pro-Soviet faction within the former Gulja elite.

In February 1960, to counter the "severe local nationalism, separatist notions, animosity toward Han cadres, and sympathy and assistance rendered to local nationalists" among non-Han cadres, the Central Party School added new political classes for non-Han cadres from Xinjiang. The autonomous region also moved to expand the non-Han cadre ranks. At the First Xinjiang Party Congress during February and March, former Gulja supporters Ismail Yasinov, Anivar Zhakulin, and Abdul Zakirov were added as standing members of the Xinjiang Party Committee—a reward for their opposition to local nationalism. Sultanov Zayir became an alternate member of the Xinjiang Party Committee; Tömür Dawamet, a Uyghur veteran of several post-1949 political campaigns, was also added.[46]

The most important political transformation to take place during the Great Leap Forward was the "desovietizing" of the Xinjiang Party. This event was directly tied to the deterioration of PRC-Soviet relations. Within this context of worsening international relations, the Party's policies concerning cadres and ethnic minorities in Xinjiang focused on eradicating Soviet influence within China's borders. Some veterans of the former Soviet-backed Gulja government, such as Saifudin Azizi, Ismail Yasinov, Anivar Zhakulin, Abdul Zakirov, and Shu Mutong, survived, perhaps because they had been "early" joiners of the Communist Party between late 1949 and early 1950. Others, such as Iburayim Turdi, Uygur Shairan, and Aishait Ishakov, did not politically survive the purge. Both Saifudin Azizi and Aishait Ishakov were former members of Abdul Karim Abasov's pro-Soviet revolutionary movement before 1949, and the difference in their fates indicates the sensitivity surrounding issues of Soviet influence within the Party. While Azizi retained his positions, Ishakov was labeled a "local nationalist" and "rightist opportunist." This disparate treatment can be ascribed in part to backstabbing among non-Han cadres with Gulja and Soviet connections. Uygur Shairan, a former propagandist and organizer for the pre-1949 Xinjiang Peacekeeping Democratic Alliance, had a lengthy career in political publishing and journalism before accusations of local nationalism ended his tenure as chief editor of the *Xinjiang Daily* and deputy director of the Xinjiang Academy of Social Sciences. One of his chief critics was former Gulja comrade Abdul Zakirov. Later, a panicked Aishait Ishakov added to the accusations in confessions intended to save his own career.

Further evidence of ties between the Soviet Union and non-Han cadres came in the form of reports and confessions delivered by Azizi, who in April 1960 entered the Central Party School to undergo further political training. In one report, dated November 1960 and addressed to the Secretariat of the Xinjiang Party Committee, Azizi wrote:

> Dear Comrade Wang Enmao and other comrades in the Secretariat,
>   I salute you as a comrade and a revolutionary!
>   It has been over half a year since I came to study at the high-level Party school. In addition to working hard at learning Chinese and Chinese history, I have spent most of my time focused on the in-depth study of antirevisionism, from which I have gained much. I have abandoned my blind faith in the Soviet Union and reflected thoroughly upon my local nationalist error. If you have no objections, I wish to copy this letter to the cadres in the Party Committee who are in charge of minority affairs, for their perusal: Ismail Yasinov, Muhemmet'imin Iminov, Anivar Khan Baba, Ablimit Hajiyev, Sultanov Zayir, and Patikhan Sugurbayev.
>   —Saifudin Azizi, November 3, 1960[47]

The "error" to which Azizi referred had been addressed in an earlier report to Party Center. This document, titled "Report and Opinion about the Soviet Union's Attitude toward Our Party in Xinjiang," was intended to highlight Azizi's antirevisionism and abandonment of "blind faith in the Soviet Union." Its contents included the following:

> On the issue of national unification. On the eve of liberation, intellectuals in Ili put forward and debated the issue of "Xinjiang's future." There were three opinions: (1) become a province of China, (2) join the Soviet Union, and (3) independence. We adopted the first opinion.

During the debate in 1949, the Soviet Union adopted a neutral position, but in fact it encouraged the second and third opinions.

The Soviet Union was protective of Xinjiang's local nationalists in their opposition to the Party, the motherland, and the Han people. For example, Uygur Shairan proclaimed that "Xinjiang has always been an independent state." In a conversation with the autonomous region vice-chairman, Abdul Zakirov, the Soviet vice-consul in Urumqi said, "Isn't it true that Xinjiang was independent in the past? I am not saying this from a political point of view, but from a historical and scientific one."[48]

The impact of Azizi's report was to suggest a clear connection between pre-1949 supporters of the Ili-based Gulja government, current non-Han cadres with ties to former Gulja circles, and past and present Soviet schemes to pry Xinjiang away from China.

Another significant testimony indicates that not all purge victims met their political fate with meek submission. Aishait Ishakov had been disciplined by the Party in April 1958, sent to a labor camp for reeducation, and later recalled by the Xinjiang Party Committee in late 1959. Thereupon, he was ordered to "assist" Uygur Shairan in correcting the latter's serious errors and uncooperative attitude. The details of a December 25 conversation between the two were recorded and later submitted to the Party:

> In the course of the conversation, Uygur Shairan's attitude was one of total rejection of both the punishment meted out to him and the cadres' opinions given during the struggle sessions. His words included the following: "People with knowledge would laugh at these proceedings." "The nature of the errors was inflated by Abdul Zakirov." "The ability of the lower-ranked cadres is too low." "Before I was dealt with, I was not allowed to see any specific material, and my opinions were not accepted." "My mistake was referring to the 1930 Hotan Incident as a riot or a rebellion. . . . I did not know what the new word was for it." "It was inappropriate to 'criticize my view on Xinjiang's history as a capitalist view.'"[49]

Uygur Shairan was betrayed by former comrades such as Aishait Ishakov, who continued to insist on the seriousness of his political errors. But his biggest miscalculation was not his pro-Soviet stance, but rather his opposition to the policies of the Great Leap Forward and support for a more moderate approach to collectivization.

That the purging of Soviet influence from the Party was intertwined with eradicating opposition to the Leap is obvious from Aishait Ishakov's further self-criticisms in March and April 1960. Uygur Shairan had been disposed of, but Ishakov's own "errors" remained. As he wrote on March 18: "One, I believed that rations were insufficient, and two, I suggested that people eat at home and that food supplies should be given directly to the people instead of being kept in the public canteens. . . . I am a rightist. I also felt that the superiority of the people's communes was exaggerated. . . . I thought that industry had squeezed out agriculture."[50]

Xinjiang Party Committee members did not believe that Ishakov's criticism of his own rightist errors during the Great Leap Forward fully addressed the more serious issue of local nationalism:

Comrade Aishait Ishakov committed the error of local nationalism. Following the struggle against local nationalism, he did not recognize his own errors, nor did he take the initiative to reform himself. In a speech given at the Xinjiang Autonomous Region People's Congress last year, he said that he "did not struggle against nationalists in the culture and education sector," as though he himself was not a nationalist. He even said, "My local nationalist error has not grown to a level where it would split the motherland and damage the unity between the nationalities."[51]

Ishakov, a former member of Abdul Karim Abasov's pro-CCP Chinese Democratic Revolution Party, may have felt unjustly persecuted by allegations of local nationalism. In his self-criticism of March 23, he instead continued to focus on recounting his rightist errors, and even defended his past actions, adding: "With regards to production, I did not doubt that the goal of 'catching up with the United Kingdom' was attainable. We are a big country, and only by catching up in terms of production per capita could we be considered victorious."[52] As an ethnic Tatar and former dual citizen, however, Ishakov could not shake the Communist Party's suspicion that his loyalties lay elsewhere. On April 2, 1960, as requested by the Xinjiang Party

Committee, Ishakov submitted a document titled "Report on Certain Circumstances and Certain Personal Opinions about Relatives and Cadres Who Are Soviet Citizens Remaining in China." In his report, Ishakov affirmed that "by 1956 we [referring to Ishakov, his relations, and other clan members] had already made applications to renounce our Soviet citizenships. I had decided not to return to the Soviet Union but rather to adopt a proletarian position and worldview in order to overcome local nationalism and individualism."[53]

High- and middle-ranking cadres who, like Aishait Ishakov, possessed apparently inextricable ties to the Soviet Union were thus the focus of desovietization during the Great Leap Forward. By contrast, non-Han cadres at the grassroots level were treated more moderately by the Party; as many Leap plans were abandoned by 1961, they received only instructions to report to the Party "faithfully" and to relay the opinions and demands of the masses "in their purest form." Non-Han cadres were seen as key links between the Communist Party and mass society. In addition, ethnic markers such as language were allowed to coexist with the increasingly dominant Han culture.

At the same time, elite non-Han cadres such as Saifudin Azizi still publicly stated that non-Han cadres at the grassroots remained deficient, particularly in terms of ideological standpoint and professional competence. They should reform themselves, he urged, and welcome assistance from Han cadres, while remaining firm and resolute in their support for the Communist Party, Chairman Mao, and the People's Republic of China.[54] Moderation, in this context, meant supporting the "grand unity of ethnic groups under the leadership of the Han people" and devotion to socialism and the communist cause.

1962: The Ili-Tacheng Incident and an End to Moderation

The Great Leap Forward had a profound effect on PRC government control over Xinjiang and transformed economic and ethnic policy in the region. Among the more notable long-term consequences were the disruption of Islamic political and cultural influence on local politics, and the division and further disintegration of left-wing alliances that had formed during the mid-1940s and taken root among Turkic-speaking Muslims. Communization led to the penetration of centralized state power down to the grassroots, including pasturelands. Xinjiang's economy was incorporated into China's economic system, even though the failure of the Leap had dealt that system a serious blow. In the end, Beijing's rule over Xinjiang was consolidated through the Leap.

In the short term, however, the Great Leap Forward exacerbated mutual antagonism between Han and non-Han. Amid mistreatment at the hands of Han Chinese, many ethnic groups in Xinjiang fondly recalled their ties to the Soviet Union. Against the backdrop of the looming Sino-Soviet split, political uncertainty caused by PRC leaders' perceptions of lingering Soviet influence in Xinjiang, and socioeconomic upheaval caused by the Great Leap Forward itself, the I-Ta [Ili-Tacheng] Incident unfolded in the middle of 1962. The incident and its resolution marked an end to moderate ethnic policies in Xinjiang.

During 1961 and 1962, many students from Xinjiang who had been educated in the Soviet Union during the 1950s chose to remain on the Soviet side of the border. Their decision signaled a return to a state of affairs that had briefly faded during the Sino-Soviet "honeymoon" period—the sheltering of non-Han political groups by Soviet authorities during a period when relations between the two fraternal communist parties were strained. As Sino-Soviet tensions mounted, the Soviet Union once again began to tacitly allow Chinese students to remain in areas close to the Sino-Soviet border. This group of students was drawn primarily from Xinjiang's Turkic-speaking Muslim population, had spent a long period of time in the Soviet Union, and had relatives on the Soviet-controlled side of the border. Some even held, or were alleged to hold, dual citizenship. The catalysts in their decision were the Leap-caused famine and fear generated by the three years of continuous campaigns against local nationalism. Enmeshed in an intensifying dispute with the PRC, the Soviet Union was happy to capitalize on the students' rising resentment.

Official response to the students' decision was initially passive. In May 1961, with Soviet approval and encouragement, a number of Turkic Muslims who were connected with the 1940s Gulja regime and had resided in the Soviet Union from the late 1940s until the early 1950s joined forces with Xinjiang Muslims who were living in the Soviet Union.[55] The group gathered before the PRC consulate in Tashkent to protest against China's persecution of their Xinjiang compatriots and founded a new anti-CCP organization. A number of Xinjiang students in the Soviet Union participated in this protest and joined the new organization.[56] By 1962, the number of Xinjiang students staying in the Soviet Union and not returning to China had increased. As a result, the Chinese government ordered educational and research institutes to stop sending students to the Soviet Union.[57] As Sino-Soviet relations worsened, the Xinjiang Party Committee, acting on the orders of Party Center, issued a directive on February 17, 1962, that directed all subordinate committees to guard against pro-Soviet activity.[58] Non-Han individuals suspected of harboring pro-Soviet sympathies were placed under surveillance; others were sent to labor camps for reeducation.

The first to bear the brunt of these new policies were ethnic Russians in China, who were immediately singled out for discrimination by grassroots cadres. Many were afraid to speak in Russian or use their Russian names in public. One ethnic Russian female employee at an Urumqi post office was transferred and placed under surveillance because she spoke Russian with a foreign tourist. To escape the new circumstances, some ethnic Russians applied to return to the Soviet Union or migrate to Australia. Others attempted to change their ethnicity on their household register, identifying themselves as Tatar or Uzbek.[59]

The anti-Russian policies soon incurred a response from the Soviet Union. From 1961 onward, pro-Soviet Muslims and radio facilities in Soviet Central Asia were mobilized to promote Soviet ethnic policy. These efforts targeted Xinjiang's non-Han population and attempted to bring more local ethnicities under Soviet influence.[60] Chinese authorities' treatment of the targeted minority groups did not immediately change, though there was an increase in surveillance. Following the initial wave of arrests, even suspected pro-Soviet agents, students who had studied abroad in the Soviet Union, and returned students who openly expressed discontent with Xinjiang's Chinese authorities were not treated harshly.

These events took place against a backdrop of relative moderation and stability in PRC policy toward minority ethnicities. As a result of CCP Central Committee United Front Ministry decisions reached in late 1958 and early 1959, Xinjiang had begun to recover from the acrimonies generated by the attacks against rightists and local nationalists. The Eleventh National United Front Working Conference, held in Beijing from December 1958 to January 1959, reached the conclusion that while local nationalism and calls for the merging of autonomous counties with neighboring ethnic territories should be opposed, criticism of local nationalism had been unduly "amplified" during previous years. In this context, Xinjiang United Front leader Wang Feng defended the Party's earlier policies of "no struggle, no division, and no drawing of class lines" in non-Han pasturelands and of recognizing the existence of religion. Wang added that only through preventing and overcoming Han chauvinism could local nationalism itself be overcome:

> Administrative orders will not really get rid of religion. When educating the masses about atheism, never demand that everyone renounce their faith, because this will only create false appearances. People with no religious beliefs should not be mobilized to struggle against those who hold religious beliefs.[61]

Cadres such as Wang Feng represented a fleetingly resurgent moderate voice in Xinjiang ethnic politics.

The new policies took over a year to implement. Even in late 1960, the Xinjiang Party Committee continued to rail against those who "held fast to local nationalist ideas" and "overemphasize the uniqueness of their ethnic groups." Monitoring and surveillance remained the norm. Yet during this same period, the Communist Party also began to stress preserving ethnic forms, traditions, and customs that did not inhibit development along socialist or Chinese lines.[62] In this sense, the policies of 1960 also embraced the fundamental goal of Communist Party ethnic policy: to dilute ethnic difference and assert the dominance of the Han people. From July 1960 onward, the strong-arm tactics that defined the 1957–1960 period were slowly replaced by more moderate methods. Mosques recognized as having historical importance were placed on a list for permanent preservation.[63] On December 14, 1961, the Xinjiang Party Committee instructed Party branches above the commune level to review their implementation of minority and religious policy and to prohibit actions that violated this moderate approach.

In January and February 1962, key Xinjiang cadres from all levels of the Construction Military Corps returned from Beijing after attending the "Seven Thousand Cadres' Conference," where the Great Leap Forward's failure was reviewed. This influential group then convened a meeting, led by

Wang Enmao, to discuss Xinjiang's own experience of the Leap. The outcome was a renewal of the language of ethnic unity. On the first day of the Lunar New Year, regional newspapers and magazines once again urged that special customs of minority peoples should be protected and even supported. Forced assimilation or eradication of ethnic differences was publicly condemned. Cadres and the masses alike were warned to respect these differences; shared interests, rather than class conflict, were put at the forefront for all ethnic groups. Lü Jianren assured religious figures and non-Han ethnic leaders that their living arrangements and political status would be protected. But Lü also warned that counterrevolutionaries who attempted to hide behind the cloak of religion would be eradicated.[64]

Nonetheless, in February 1962, the Party's primary goal was apparently to ease dissatisfaction among non-Party elites by remedying the effects of hunger and material deprivation produced by the Leap. In advance of Spring Festival, the Xinjiang United Front Department ordered a direct transfer of consumer goods and luxury items to these ethnic elites. Sixty-eight people in Xinjiang were selected to receive a modest "basket" that contained "1 kg of fruit candy, 1 kg of dried fruit, one bottle of ordinary liquor, 5 kg of vegetables, two cartons of grade A or B cigarettes per person (for smokers), 1 kg of pork (for Han recipients), and 1 kg of mutton (for Muslim recipients)."[65] In the aftermath of the famine, this represented a notable gift. By contrast, among Xinjiang's nonelite population, the reduction of food rations and forced requisitioning of food for transfer to the hinterland had resulted in many people moving near the Sino-Soviet border or crossing the border into the Soviet Union in search of food and shelter.

The situation in 1962 was thus characterized by Sino-Soviet tensions; moderate Chinese policies toward Xinjiang's non-Han populations; and increasing intellectual, popular, and political resistance to Han rule over Xinjiang. At the forefront of the latter trend were cadres from various levels in the pre-1949 Gulja government, all of whom had at one point possessed Soviet citizenship. The most influential leaders were Major General Zunun Taipov, deputy chief of staff of the Xinjiang Military Region and minister of military affairs in the former East Turkestan, and Ziya Saimaiti, director of the Cultural Office of the Xinjiang Autonomous Region. The rest of the leaders were middle- and low-ranking cadres.[66] Local nationalism and Soviet influence remained intertwined.

Indeed, Soviet influence reinforced local nationalist feeling, which was in turn exacerbated by frustrations created by Chinese policy concerning the issue of citizenship. From 1954 to 1959, China and the Soviet Union had cooperated on issues related to nationals residing abroad and citizenship. Dual citizenship was no longer legally recognized, and Soviet citizens in China, along with their Chinese family members (some 130,000 people in total) who wished to live in the Soviet Union, were allowed to emigrate. China also demanded that newly minted, high-ranking cadres in the Xinjiang Party and government organs with dual PRC-Soviet citizenship choose one or the other. In theory, there were fewer than 10,000 Soviet citizens residing in Xinjiang. But during the early 1950s, middle- and low-ranking non-Han cadres retained their old Soviet passports with tacit consent and even encouragement from the Soviet Union. Approximately 8,000 people belonged to this category. As PRC-Soviet relations worsened during the early 1960s, China refused to recognize the citizenship claims of individuals "illegally" possessing Soviet citizenship and refused them the right of travel to the Soviet Union. Instead, Beijing demanded that these cadres unequivocally renounce their Soviet citizenship.[67]

Soviet policies, also related to the split, took advantage of public discontent with the Great Leap Forward, as well as the anger of local nationalists, to further undermine China's position in Xinjiang. Beginning in 1961, Soviet consulates in Xinjiang began disseminating certificates that identified bearers as Soviet residents abroad and offering backdated Soviet passports to Chinese citizens who were Turkic-speaking Muslims; the number of backdated passports alone came to several thousand.[68] As a result, increasing numbers of "legal" tourists began crossing the border into Kazakhstan, where they were settled in collective farms. Those who fled Xinjiang were mostly Kazakhs, but their numbers also included Uyghurs and other Muslims. Ethnicity aside, the sojourners could be classified into two groups: intellectuals who were either pro-Soviet or anti-Han, and farmers and herders who fled for survival reasons. Although China's Xinjiang authorities tried to stem the migration using administrative means and propaganda, these attempts failed. Between May and July 1962, before the border was finally sealed by diplomatic agreement and military patrols, 61,361 people fled Xinjiang.[69]

Crisis and Aftermath

The brewing crisis in Ili-Tacheng had reached a nearly uncontrollable point but did not develop further, in part because of the earlier reversal of the radical policies of the Great Leap Forward and in part because of the persuasive force of Saifudin Azizi, who still maintained considerable political clout in Ili.[70] The outcomes of the crisis, however, were significant nonetheless. As a result of the Soviet-sponsored flight of border inhabitants, both sides sealed off and increasingly militarized their borders, and direct Soviet involvement in Xinjiang's internal politics, especially in the Ili Kazakh Autonomous Prefecture, ceased. In the name of national defense, the People's Liberation Army sent reinforcements to Ili from the Lanzhou Military Region. The Production and Construction Military Corps now controlled the entire border area, and people living nearby who had not crossed into the Soviet Union were forced to move further into the interior. Sino-Soviet trade in Xinjiang plummeted, and the planned railroad that was to connect Urumqi with the Soviet border city of Aktogay was abandoned.[71]

In 1958, key goals of the Great Leap Forward in Xinjiang had included the removal of Soviet interests in the region and pro-Soviet influences among local ethnic minorities, and the solidifying of China's claims to natural resources in the region. The 1962 I-Ta crisis pushed these goals forward, insofar as they led to Soviet withdrawal; they also brought about a final end to the independent revolutionary goals of the former Gulja regime. From this point onward, Beijing could claim undisputed Han rule over Xinjiang. Control of the Ili Kazakh Autonomous Region, long considered a stronghold of pro-Soviet sympathies, was no longer an intractable problem. Nonetheless, measures used to overcome the forces of discontent unleashed at I-Ta had their own violent repercussions.

Following the crisis, Xinjiang Party leaders began to step up their struggle against "modern revisionism" in Xinjiang. Non-Han cadres were once again investigated on the grounds of suspected anti-Han and anti-CCP sympathies. This time, those so identified were labeled not only "local nationalists" and "capitalist nationalists" but also "counterrevolutionaries" and "revisionists."[72] Revisionist, anti-Party, and local nationalist activities were still purportedly being carried out in late 1963. One person accused of killing a Han cadre in

Turpan was quoted as saying after his arrest, "I am a citizen of Huda [Allah], not a citizen of the People's Republic of China." Sixty-one people, including Imin Muhemmet, attempted to blow up the Kunlun Guest House, a landmark building in Urumqi. And rumors abounded, including the claim that the government wanted to expel all *erzhuanzi* (a word used by Han people in Gansu and Xinjiang to refer to people of mixed ethnicities) from the country.[73]

As a result, in 1963 the number of people fleeing Tarbagatay, which bordered the Soviet Union, began to increase once again. According to the Tacheng District Party Committee, there were "many groups fleeing the country," including four groups totaling over 110 people, all of whom were finally apprehended crossing into the Soviet Union through pasturelands. In Hoboskar, a town near the border, six groups attempted to flee. Additional reports testified to the continued prevalence of local dissent. In the Wusu County Geological Team,

> An ethnic [minority] worker publicly shouted, "Long live the Nationalist Party!" . . . [And] 22.5 percent of commune members want to flee China. Among the 128 non-Han cadres in Tacheng County, 28 want to flee. Certain commune members in Toli publicly said, "Didn't you say we must love the motherland? Well, I am a Soviet citizen. I came here in 1933, and now I want to go back there." Some said, "China is not great. It has three characteristic features: lots of thieves, no firewood, and no shoes for the feet. China will not catch up with the Soviet Union even in a hundred years!" Others said, "The houses of those who fled to the Soviet Union are better than those of Chinese officials."[74]

The crackdown on dissent among non-Han cadres could not stem the tide of dissatisfaction coming from below.

Despite the closure of the border to migration, letter and parcels sent from the Soviet Union by relatives of those living in Xinjiang added force to this second wave of unrest, especially in Ili. Ili residents demanded through legal channels to visit relatives or reunite with their families in the Soviet Union.[75] Party and government units resorted to seizing and opening letters sent to their employees, generating additional complaints and anger. To prevent further deterioration of the Communist Party's image, the Xinjiang Party

Committee issued a sternly worded directive prohibiting the "unlawful inspection and seizure of private mail."[76]

These comparatively moderate policies seem incongruous given that dissent among non-Han intellectuals was even more intense than during the "local nationalism" scare of 1957. According to a report received by the Xinjiang Party Committee, a student in the Xinjiang University chemistry department was overheard saying, "The Han people in Xinjiang are colonialists. If we do not get rid of the Han, ethnic minorities will not be liberated." Other accounts provided a more chilling vision of ethnic conflict: "Last year a Uyghur-language editor of *Xinjiang Daily* on a public bus beat up a Han passenger for no apparent reason. When others intervened, he shouted and called on other ethnic minorities to beat up Han people. A student in Xinjiang University's biology department publicly said, 'If I had seven atomic bombs, I would use six to kill the Han and the last one to kill myself.'"[77] More than a decade of joint Han-minority rule had exacerbated rather than erased mistrust and hatred among the populace.

Eventually, the Xinjiang Party Committee took action. To deal head-on with interethnic tensions and counter Soviet propaganda, the government again began to advertise its concern for the livelihood and prosperity of ethnic minorities during the second half of 1962. According to one planning document, Xinjiang leaders noted that Chairman Mao had stressed that the economy should be the primary focus of the antirevisionist struggle in Xinjiang. "Not only must production levels be higher than in the past, when Xinjiang was under Nationalist rule, they must be higher than production levels in the Soviet Union under the revisionist regime. [Mao] also told us that, while we must accumulate resources for the development of socialist enterprise, we must not overdo it. We must lessen the people's burden and improve their lives. The supply of goods to the various nationalities in Xinjiang is to be more generous than in other regions."[78] This signaled a tacit admission that the Great Leap Forward had been a disaster politically as well as economically. Publicly, the Xinjiang Party Committee stated that there would be "care" for the "distinctive features and special needs" of Xinjiang's ethnic minorities, and it reiterated that local people should be allowed to use their own languages in writing and speaking, and to preserve their customs and traditions. Tolerance, however, required separation from the Soviet Union and from agitators within. Ethnic minorities were also cautioned to "increase their political awareness and revolutionary watchfulness" and to "make every effort to oppose any erroneous actions and conspiracies hatched by imperialists, foreign reactionary cliques, and modern revisionists." Within the spaces of China's frontier regions, "struggle against class enemies" was actually a struggle to separate populations under Han rule from connections to kin and other states on the other side of the border. Failure to effect this change completely was a significant cause of persistent unrest and animosity.

*   *   *

After 1949, the Communist Party succeeded in bringing over members of the former Gulja regime as political partners in establishing a new regional government. As a result, Ili-based nationalism was temporarily dispelled, and the dominant policy of restricting Han chauvinism aimed to avoid its resurgence. This did not mean, however, that Han authorities and non-Han masses, or even political leaders, enjoyed a real honeymoon. During the Hundred Flowers campaign in Xinjiang, local non-Han elites complained about Han cadres' arrogance, ignorance, and obtuseness in handling non-Han affairs. They also criticized severe damage to the environment and economy created by the Xinjiang Production and Construction Military Corps, which mobilized former People's Liberation Army soldiers and personnel to "develop the wasteland" but in fact replaced existing local modes of production with those sanctioned by Beijing. Still others demanded genuine autonomy and the elevation of non-Han peoples to positions of real political power. The most confrontational demands called for expulsion of the Han and establishment of an independent, non-Chinese state.[79]

Many of the local non-Han elites who made these complaints were connected with the former Gulja regime or the Soviet Union or were high-ranking Islamic clerics. As a result of their intransigence on the issue of self-determination, they were labeled "local nationalists" and attacked. During the late 1950s, local nationalism was linked to revisionism, with the consequence that movements launched against rightists and local nationalism in Xinjiang developed into campaigns against Soviet influence among non-Han government elites. Some of the principal leaders of the campaigns were themselves non-Han, which may have increased their efficacy, as when Saifudin Azizi helped Wang Enmao "rectify" many of Azizi's ex-colleagues from the former Turkestan republic. According to accounts given by China's official historians, 1,612 cadres were labeled local nationalists during the movements against rightists and local nationalists; of these, most were sent to labor camps for reeducation. Many in the camps died during the Great Leap Forward. Some were only freed in 1979.[80]

The movements against rightists and local nationalists were also directly linked to political dissent caused by the economic and social consequences of the Leap, and of the establishment of people's communes in Xinjiang. Between 1957 and 1958, purges of non-Han local nationalists and pro-Soviet individuals, coupled with the establishment of communes in existing pasturelands—in other words, the forced imposition of sedentary lifestyles on pastoral peoples—generated intense opposition from former Gulja-regime elites and among the broader local populace. It was this opposition that provided the backdrop for Soviet-sponsored agitation as the Sino-Soviet split worsened; had it not already existed, it is difficult to imagine that Soviet influence alone could have led to the Ili-Tacheng incident. Ultimately, Beijing consolidated control over the region by replacing Uyghur farms and Kazakh ranches with an agricultural and resource-extraction empire under the direct control of the Xinjiang Production and Construction Military Corps, thus consolidating Chinese rule over Ili and the rest of Xinjiang, while further marginalizing non-Han peoples from the government and mainstream economy. Consolidating power, however, cannot be equated with the achievement of ethnic harmony, despite the Communist Party's avowed dedication to this cause in the years after 1949.

Translated by Wee Kek Koon

13

Redemptive Religious Societies and the Communist State, 1949 to the 1980s

S. A. SMITH

There is a now substantial literature on the redemptive religious societies[1] in the Ming and Qing dynasties, a small literature on these societies in the Republican era, and the beginnings of a literature on their revival in the People's Republic of China during the reform era—one focused mainly on Falungong.[2] As yet, almost nothing has been written on the fate of what the Communists called the "reactionary sects" (*fandong huidaomen*) in the Mao era, following their putative suppression in the violent campaigns of the early 1950s. The past two decades, however, have seen the publication in the PRC of a limited amount of primary source material, and this, together with increased but still restricted access to archives, allows us to begin to reconstruct their history from the 1950s through to the 1980s. Given the absence of a body of documentation generated by the redemptive sects themselves in this period—in contrast to the Republican era—we are still reliant mainly on official propaganda and police investigative sources. The present chapter uses this material to explore the conflict between the redemptive societies and the Party-state.[3] It examines Communist perceptions of and policies toward the societies, concentrating on the period after 1952, when the societies had supposedly been suppressed in perpetuity; it asks how far the societies represented an objective threat to the regime; it explores the extent to which the societies perceived themselves as being locked in battle with the state; and, finally, it investigates how the societies managed to survive intense persecution so as to revive with astonishing speed in the 1980s.

The redemptive societies, which blossomed in the second half of the Ming dynasty (1368–1644), were labeled by the Ming and Qing authorities as "White Lotus teachings" (*bailian jiao*). This label homogenized what in reality were highly variegated traditions of belief and practice, which included Pure Land Buddhism, the Luo teaching, the Yellow Heaven (*Huangtian*) teaching, the Great Yang (*Hongyang*) teaching, the inner alchemy (*neidan*) of the Eight Trigrams (*Bagua*) tradition, and the Three-in-One teachings.[4] Despite enormous differences in ritual and belief, redemptive societies by the Republican era shared certain common features: They were committed to an ideal of universal salvation, regardless of family, lineage, or place of residence, and it was this emphasis on salvation that distinguished them from family- and temple-based religion. In general, they explicated doctrine through "precious volumes" (*baojuan*), they were relatively open to new members, and they tended to be doctrinally syncretic and structurally fissile. Many believed in a creator deity and in three cycles of creation and destruction (kalpas) that would terminate in the third kalpa, when a savior would appear on earth to deliver the faithful from worldly torment. Many, but not all, put their faith in a female deity, the Unborn Venerable Mother (*Wusheng laomu*), who was not a figure found in orthodox Buddhism. She was believed to have given birth to a man and a woman whose union had produced the human race. After being sent to live in the Eastern World, humanity had fallen into wrongdoing and confusion, so the Unborn Mother had first sent the Lamplighter Buddha and then the Sakyamuni Buddha to teach her children how to return to the Pure Land. But to no avail. She was now about to send—or had already sent—a third Buddha, the Maitreya, who would guide believers to the Homeland of True Emptiness (*Zhenkong jiaxiang*), a paradise on earth free from war, hunger and tyranny.[5]

The Ming and Qing authorities regarded the so-called "White Lotus" sects as inherently "heretical" (*xie*), since their teachings described the existing state of human affairs as hopelessly corrupt. This was tantamount in official eyes to a denial of the fundamental Confucian values of political order and social harmony.[6] In reality, the majority of redemptive societies shied away from confrontation with the authorities, their sights being fixed on the supernatural rather than the secular world. As Daniel Overmyer shows, only a minority of sects ever became involved in popular rebellions, and though belief in a Maitreya Buddha, who would redeem the world through a process of violent destruction, was intrinsically apocalyptic, this did not in itself predispose believers to rebellion or preclude long periods of political quietism; nor was the popularity of the sects confined to periods of social strife. Nevertheless, as he points out, the sects possessed "deeply imbedded" political elements insofar as they made no clear distinction between the spiritual and worldly realms.[7] Expanding on this, Robert Weller suggests that it was the social and political context rather than the content of their beliefs that determined whether the sects would orient toward political quietism or collective resistance.[8] Thus, when the Communists came to power in 1949, some networks of the Yiguandao (the Way of Pervading Unity), the largest of the redemptive societies, did become involved in armed resistance and justified this by claiming that the "three disasters and eight difficulties" (*san zai ba nan*) that heralded the third kalpa were now at hand. In general, however, the Yiguandao interpreted the three disasters and eight difficulties metaphorically, understanding them more as tropes of suffering that members must undergo in order to achieve salvation, rather than a signal to rise up against the new Communist order.

In what appears to be a conservative estimate, Shao Yong calculated that by 1949 there were more than 300 redemptive societies in China with a total of 820,000 ritual specialists and more than 13 million disciples. This represented roughly 2.4 percent of the population.[9] It is now clear that the number of societies—together with the estimated number of members—was considerably greater than this, since typically they were small, village-level associations, occasionally integrated into communal life, that never came to the attention of the authorities.[10] The redemptive societies had grown rapidly in the unsettled conditions of the 1920s and 1930s, when millions of peasants were exposed to economic insecurity and the depredations of warlords and bandits, and starting in 1937 a devastating war with Japan. The biggest societies that developed in this period were the Yiguandao; the Society for Common Good (*Tongshanshe*), essentially a philanthropic association; the Way of Former Heaven (*Xiantiandao*); and the Nine Palaces Way (*Jiugongdao*). These groups offered their members social support, spiritual solace, and protection. With the Sino-Japanese War, they expanded apace, an expansion that continued through the civil war of 1946–1949. By the time the

Communists came to power, redemptive societies were to be found in every corner of the land, though they were strongest in the cities and villages of north China that had been behind Japanese lines.

By far the largest of the societies, the Yiguandao is held to have been founded by Wang Jueyi (1821–1884), who was understood to be an avatar of the Maitreya Buddha. The true founder of the modern society, however, was Zhang Guangbi (1889–1947), an incarnation of Living Buddha Jigong, who recast the organization and doctrine of the movement on modern lines starting in the late 1920s.[11] In accordance with the republic's law on religious freedom, the Yiguandao registered with the authorities and set up "altars," usually in homes in a semipublic fashion, and spread its message via spirit writing (*fuji*). This was a ritual in which a medium, usually a young boy in a trance, communed with the gods and wrote words in sand that were then interpreted by specialists. Initiation into the Yiguandao was informal, although some underwent a formal ceremony in which they received the "three treasures": a mantra, a hand gesture, and the opening of a mystic portal between the eyes through which divine power could pass. The sect saw its task as being to recruit as many members as possible to save them from the "final cataclysm of the three kalpas" (*san qi mo jie*), or to "join the teaching and escape the impending calamity" (*ru jiao bi jie*).[12] During the Sino-Japanese War, Zhang developed close ties to the Japanese, and he persuaded a number of officials in Wang Jingwei's government to join the sect. This drew obloquy from both the Nationalists and the Communists, and at the end of the war Zhang was arrested as a "national traitor" and the Yiguandao was banned.[13]

The Survival of the Societies

The Communists always distrusted the redemptive societies. Yet, like the Nationalists, they tried during the war and civil war to differentiate between societies, such as the Li sect (*Zaili jiao*), a temperance organization modeled on monastic Buddhism, or the Red Swastika Society, a relief organization modeled on the Red Cross, from the Yiguandao or Nine Palaces Way, which were compromised by their association with the Japanese. In newly liberated areas especially, the Communists, recognizing that the societies had certain "mass" characteristics, ordered some members to infiltrate the societies with a view to seizing political leadership. In the course of the civil war, however, the Yiguandao and the Nine Palaces Way became increasingly anti-Communist, partly as a result of infiltration by Guomindang special agents and partly as certain leaders took umbrage at Communist attacks on land-lords and "reactionary" (*fandong*) forces.[14] In the old liberated areas of the north, a campaign to suppress the societies began as early as 1948, and it escalated in January 1949, when the North China People's Government issued the decree "Dissolve All Sects and Feudal Superstition Organizations." There is no doubt that elements in some societies became involved in rebel-lions against the Communists, and those in the southwest in the early 1950s were quite large.[15] According to the Public Security Bureau (PSB), between April 1949 and the end of 1952, the ten biggest sects in Henan organized fifty-two "counterrevolutionary uprisings," an average of one a month, and their counterparts in Hubei organized the same number. Special agents (*tewu*) of the Nationalist Party and bandit chiefs were said to be behind these.[16]

The relentless energy of the new regime was nowhere more evident than in the campaign to punish the leaders of the redemptive societies and force their members to withdraw from the organizations.[17] Only in 1950, however, following the outbreak of the Korean War, did a national campaign get under way. In the wake of the speech by Mao on October 10, 1950—which called for the stepping up of the campaign against counterrevolutionaries— "reactionary huidaomen" were identified for the first time as one of five counterrevolutionary groups.[18] Official policy was to execute the most noto-rious leaders, especially those who had collaborated with the Japanese and Nationalists or who had betrayed Communists to the secret police; to imprison those guilty of serious offences; and to put ranking leaders not guilty of crimes under some form of surveillance. The millions of rank-and-file disciples were required to "repent" and publicly withdraw from the sects (*tuidao*). In Hebei, where nearly 200 societies were operative, 4,455 leaders were arrested and 5,961 required to register with the police.[19] In Cang County, a hotbed of sectarianism, the suppression was particularly harsh: all 5 of the highest Yiguandao leaders, 33 out of 47 transmitters of rites, and 52 others were sentenced to death in spring 1951.[20] In Shanghai, 768 altars had been suppressed and 3,974 leaders punished by 1953, of whom 65 were sentenced to death, 942 imprisoned, and 819 put under surveillance; 10,621 minor leaders were registered with the police, and 322,400 members withdrew from the societies.[21]

Accompanying this policy of repression was a large-scale propaganda campaign to educate the masses about the danger posed by the societies. PSB officials in the southwest complained that many disciples refused to accept that they were members of counterrevolutionary organizations and so show trials were staged in which leaders confessed to all manner of criminal and subversive activity.[22] In March 1951, according to incomplete statistics, 2.2 million people attended exhibitions exposing the "crimes" of the sects. Staged confessions by former sect members, demonstrations of the tricks used to deceive the gullible, and incriminating photographs—such as that of a U.S. flag hidden by an altar master—were said to have proved especially effective in encouraging visitors to overcome their fear of being "struck by heaven and the god of thunder."[23] In Tianjin, the Yiguandao Criminal Evidence exhibition was visited by 260,000 and featured money and goods fleeced from ordinary disciples.[24] In 1952, the Central Film Bureau produced a film, *Yiguan hairen dao* (The harmful way of pervading unity) ,and the national campaign was backed up by thousands of newspaper articles and cartoons, theatrical performances, and radio cross-talk sketches that dramatized the cases of those who had been duped by the sects. The lesson that the rank-and-file sectarians were expected to draw was this: "We thought to worship Buddha, but it turned out only to be special tricks."[25]

The ruthless campaign to suppress the societies shattered their networks, removed their leaders, and subdued the mass of followers. Yet though battered by the *tuidao* campaign, the societies were by no means destroyed. Indeed, the tumultuous changes set in motion by land reform and cooperativization created conditions of fear and uncertainty highly conducive to the revival of the societies. As early as 1953, a few societies became involved in resistance to the new program of grain procurement. In Baoding County in Hebei Han Chaobin, the leader of the Great Judgment Teaching (*Andadao*) gathered together 120 followers from more than fifty villages and urged his followers to give grain to Buddha but not to the state.[26] In Weinan and Shangluo Counties in Shaanxi, the Middle Way (*Zhongdao*) preached that "To enter a cooperative is like going to hell; to enter the Zhongdao is like being in Paradise." "If you enter a cooperative, you have to give up all your animals, trees, and utensils to the public authorities."[27] In Anhui Province, the PSB reported 822 attempts to "restore the old order" (*fubi*) between 1956 and 1958, many apparently designed to stop the drive to collectivization.[28]

Until recently, scholars assumed that popular resistance to the Mao regime was virtually nonexistent, either because of the might of the state or because of the support the Communists enjoyed. Partial access to archives suggests that still-substantial support for the regime notwithstanding, rapid collectivization, the Great Leap Forward, and the famine provoked a range of grassroots challenges to the political order, including some that involved the redemptive societies. The sources concerning the latter are problematic, since any action designed to revive or maintain a redemptive society—for example, a secret meeting in someone's house—was likely to be seen by the PSB as a "counterrevolutionary" act. Anything more substantial was likely to be classed as *fubi*—i.e., an act to restore the old order. In Jiangsu between 1954 and 1960, the security organs claimed to have uncovered 217 acts by the societies to restore the old order, 88 of them in 1958. These involved 1,385 sect leaders, 401 altars, and 16,363 followers.[29] How far sect leaders actually sought to overthrow the regime is unclear. Only rarely did the PSB differentiate types of action—i.e., violent uprisings from peaceful activities such as reestablishing an altar. In Shandong, the security organs dealt with 2,503 cases involving the societies between 1954 and 1984, but they described only 14 as rebellions (*baoluan*), although in a further 217 cases the societies are alleged to have sought to install a new emperor (discussed below).[30] Moreover, when there was some element of organized or violent opposition to the political order, this was generally on a small scale. In Zhangjiakou, Hebei, the PSB reported 118 acts to restore the old order in which 1,252 people were arrested; but it described only 3 as rebellions, and only a paltry four guns and ammunition were seized.[31] Nevertheless, there were a handful of rebellions that were by no means trivial. In Henan, the Regiment of Spirit Soldiers (Shenbingtuan) gathered 1,200 followers from Hubei, Sichuan, and Shaanxi and attacked government offices in Sizhuang County on February 2, 1959. The rebellion lasted twenty days.[32] In Gansu in August to September 1958, police and militia quashed an uprising in Yongjing County that led to the arrest of 855 people and the summary execution of 21 leaders.[33] In Fuzhou in Jiangxi, a rebellion by the Great Chariot sect (*Dashengjiao*) in April 1958 affected over nine counties and involved 109 leaders, 542 followers, and 24 altars. Ten leaders were arrested and 931 books, 159 seals, and 436 other ritual objects seized.[34] Ironically, the utopian rhetoric of the regime during this period may have catalyzed apocalyptic sentiment in the societies, spurring them to prepare for the final kalpa.

The appalling famine caused by the Great Leap Forward led to an upsurge in religious activity. This was a conjuncture in which the apocalyptic message of the sects resonated with a wider audience. Whereas the government referred cryptically to "temporary economic difficulties," some of the largest redemptive societies talked of the "calamity of starvation" (*ji'e jie*).[35] In 1960, the PSB calculated that nationally there were 900 actions by the societies to restore the old order, 42 of which involved would-be emperors claiming the throne.[36] This is likely to have been an underestimate, for in Jin Prefecture in Shanxi alone there were 26 such attempts, mobilized by the slogan "join the dao and tide over this lean year" (*ru dao duhuang*).[37] In 1962 in Xiaoyi County in Shanxi, the Buddha Way to Release the Mind and Suffuse the Body (*Shixin ruyi yishen dao*) assembled 1,673 disciples in fourteen communes, 600 of whom were said to be under fifteen years of age, in order to confront the "three disasters and eight difficulties." The sect predicted that June would see severe frosts and July rivers of blood: "People of the dao will be busy, the Communist Party will be driven out, and the country will prosper and the people live in peace."[38] It was in Hebei—long a stronghold of the redemptive societies—that the revival was most vigorous, with the societies said to have recruited more than 1.8 million followers.[39] In Jiangsu between 1960 and 1965, there were 195 attempts at imperial restoration, of which 42 were led by the Yiguandao, 20 by the Way of Former Heaven, and 12 by the Three Red Teachings (*Hongsanjiao*).[40]

It is unlikely that the rise in the number of "acts to restore the old regime" imperiled the security of the state. Yet the authorities were jittery. In spring 1960, as epidemic disease raged across Hubei, Yan Puzhen made contact with former Yiguandao leader Lü Zudao and "landlord element" Han Dating, and together they formed the New Star Society (*Xinxinghui*). Yan had been arrested by the police in 1958 but had feigned suicide by jumping into a river. Thereafter he lived clandestinely, disguised as a woman. The Society plotted to seize Laocheng in Yongnian County "because its city walls are intact and it is surrounded by water." On December 13, 1960, Yan and ninety-six followers set off from Nanzuoliang Village in Ci County in horse-drawn carts laden with primitive weapons. Arriving in Laocheng that night, they occupied the north gate, intending to seize the police station, the bank, and the grain store; to cut off the main road and electricity supply; and to publish an edict to "summon the virtuous to bring peace to the people." Once Laocheng was secured, their aim was to make Yongnian County a base from which to overthrow the government and inaugurate the white kalpa. The plot was rumbled by the local police, who arrested those involved and confiscated thirty-six rifles, many axes and knives, thirteen banners, and one seal.[41]

In April 1963, the Ministry of Public Security called for a merciless attack on the "attempts of the reactionary sects to restore the old order."[42] By this stage, however, the suppression campaign was taking its toll. In Hubei, the police reported 96 cases of sectarian activity between 1962 and 1966, an average of 24 cases a year, but this represented a significant drop from the 1950s. And between 1967 and 1976, they reported only 83 cases, an average of 8.3 per year.[43] In Henan, figures for the number of court cases involving the societies suggest a similar picture: out of 9,685 cases tried between 1950 and 1987, 92 percent were heard in the 1950s; 3 percent in the 1960s, 4 percent in the 1970s, and 0.7 percent between 1980 and 1987.[44] Such statistics are not without problems, since in part they reflect the intensity of activity on the part of the police, who were sometimes under pressure from higher authorities to be seen to be doing something and at other times—as possibly in the late 1980s—freer to relax their efforts. But the downward trend in the activities of the societies that the figures suggest does seem credible.

The effects of the Cultural Revolution on the redemptive societies were uneven and contradictory. In some places the frenetic attack on the "four olds" compounded their disarray, forcing them to disband clandestine networks or go deep underground. In some regions, low-ranking leaders of the societies, such as altar masters, were targeted for the first time: "although they are not the heads of reactionary secret societies . . . they continue to revive and develop sectarian organizations or undertake counterrevolutionary wrecking activity and so should be treated as counterrevolutionaries."[45] Elsewhere the societies exploited the fact that the PSB apparatus was crippled and would not become fully operational again until 1974. In Guizhou Yang Qingming, the head of the eastern altar of the White Sun sect (Baiyangdao), had escaped from a labor camp in 1962, where he had been serving a fifteen-year term, and returned to his native village in Weining County. Changing his name, he took up as a peddler in order to make contact with old members of the sect and collect "precious volumes" they had hidden. Between 1963 and 1968 he brought together several hundred members in Weining and Hezhang Counties, reviving eighteen old altars and establishing seven new ones. According to our source, officials of the PSB, the procuracy, and the courts were so busy attending study classes during the Cultural Revolution that they failed to notice this revival, and when Yang was arrested in August 1968 it was only because "the masses" took him to the military authorities for disrupting production. This, however, did not stop 147 officers in the White Sun Society from continuing their activities, which included holding 240 ceremonies during work time. Only in 1977, when the PSB was once again functioning properly, was Yang brought back from a labor camp and executed. Ten leaders were imprisoned, seventeen put under surveillance, twenty-nine subjected to mass criticism, and forty sent to reeducation, with two "changing hats."[46] Despite the severity of the sentences, it appears that the White Sun Society had done no more than take advantage of the paralysis of the PSB in order to revive religious activity. In this it may have been typical. In Huolu County in Hebei, the Way of Saints and the Virtuous (*Shengxiandao*), which practiced vegetarianism and meditation, reestablished a network of 145 leaders and 1,983 disciples and appears to have taken advantage of the disturbed situation to hold open meetings for worship.[47]

In some areas, the intense factional conflict, social tension, and psychological uncertainty fermented by the Cultural Revolution may have increased the receptiveness of the population to the apocalyptic rhetoric of certain societies. The Sino-Soviet border skirmishes at Zhenbao Island on the Ussuri River in March 1969 had a deeply unsettling effect, provoking fears of a Soviet invasion and nuclear attack. Millions were mobilized to build air raid shelters and train in the militia.[48] Fear of war was particularly intense in the northeast because this was the region closest to the Soviet border. In Jilin, sectarian movements appeared across the province, convinced that doomsday was at hand, and the revolutionary committees grappled to contain them. According to one report, the Nine Palaces Way tried three times to seize Changchun but each time was repulsed. In Shuangyang County, the Mount Wutai (*Wutaishan*) sect gathered a force of more than 2,500 people that was put down by the people's militia.[49] In Yanji County, Wang Guoqing, head of the Qiankundao (Heaven and Earth sect), declared himself emperor, appointing eight banner chiefs and five tiger generals (inspired by the fourteenth-century *Romance of the Three Kingdoms*). Even though the war scare dissipated in the course of 1970, this did not prevent mass suicides in Jilin in 1971. Thirty-three members of the Qiankundao allegedly drank agricultural chemicals in order to "ascend to heaven collectively." Of these, twenty-five died, their ages ranging from ten to seventy.[50]

One of the most remarkable features of the redemptive societies was their continuing ability to draw members of the CCP and the Youth League into their ranks. In 1950 in Shanxi, 18 percent of the 3,000 Communists in Dai County were members of the Yiguandao, which had affiliates in 74 percent of rural Party branches. In Chahar Province, no fewer than 500 out of 900 Party members in Yanbei District were in the Yiguandao. Moreover, when forced to withdraw, 200 opted to leave the CCP.[51] As Thomas DuBois suggests, this casts doubt on the claim that the organization was a tool of the Japanese. By the 1950s, Party members and local officials can have been in no doubt that membership in the societies was unacceptable, for they were regularly dragged into campaigns against the "reactionary sects" at the provincial and county as well as the national level. In Shouguang County in Shandong, campaigns were launched in 1953, 1956, 1961, 1973, 1983, and 1984; in Gansu Province, there were three suppression campaigns in the 1950s followed by fresh ones in 1961 and 1987.[52] In Chapter 10, Xiaoxuan Wang shows that local officials were confused by the twists and turns of official policy toward folk religion, but it is hard to believe that this was case with respect to official policy on the sects. Indeed, if PSB reports can be trusted, it seems that some sect members deliberately used their official positions to protect their coreligionists. In Shanxi in 1958, among the 19 members of the CCP in Xiasai Village, which had a population of 384, 8 were officers and 4 were disciples of the Nine Palaces Way. Most had joined the Party as affiliates of the Way during the 1945–1949 civil war. In the 1951 suppression campaign, Zhang Shanjin, who was to become Party secretary and who held the rank of "red pen" (*hongbi*) in the Way, ordered that the "Buddha gate" be closed— i.e., that no new disciples be recruited: "each individual should uphold the faith and the pious should wait." In 1954, he declared that "The Old Buddha will soon return, so it is time to open the Buddha gate." By 1958, 41 percent of the population of Xiasai were members of the Way, including 16 officers, 56 old disciples, and 87 new recruits.[53] The higher authorities saw all such activity as a counterrevolutionary attempt to infiltrate state and Party organs from within, but it is likely that some officials and Party members saw no contradiction between their political and religious affiliations, especially in areas, such as Fanshi County, where the sects were fairly well integrated into community life. It is clear that despite repressive campaigns, Party members remained in or joined the redemptive societies throughout the Mao era. In Henan, the PSB uncovered ninety-seven cases of sectarian activity in six months between 1974 and 1975 in which 118 Party and Youth League members were involved.[54]

The Appeal of the Societies

The People's Republic had brought a degree of social stability and economic improvement for millions of people, compared with the ravages of the Republican era. Yet the Mao era witnessed turbulent socioeconomic transformation on a historically unprecedented scale: land reform and collectivization pulverized the centuries-old social landscape in the countryside; the Great Leap Forward led to famine and a staggering death toll; and barely had the country begun to recover than the Cultural Revolution loosed violence, factionalism, and chaos upon society. It is arguable that even in times of social stability, fear of imminent disaster is never irrational for people who live permanently close to the edge of subsistence. Yet during the Mao era, the uncertainties of nature were compounded by colossal state-induced economic and political transformation, and this led to pervasive psychological uncertainty that was receptive to eschatological sentiment. It is impossible to put a figure on the number who responded to the millenarian rhetoric of the redemptive societies, but it may have run into the low millions. For these, the message that the disturbing times they were living through were a sign of the imminent coming of the Maitreya offered hope. In 1957, the Nine Palaces Way proclaimed: "This year the eighth month is an intercalary month when the five oceans will overwhelm the Central Plain. During the Great Destruction, 70 percent of the population will die; the remaining 30 percent are those who have joined the Way. . . . When the Old Buddha comes down to earth, we will ascend to the throne."[55] In Shuangyang County, Jilin, the Mount Wutai sect predicted that 1967 would be the year when "heavenly soldiers and generals will come down and carry out killing and destruction, and after forty-nine days the third emperor will arrive." Hundreds flocked to join the sect, comforted by its message: "As we go into the city in the clouds, the Unborn Mother will write with a fountain pen that a Buddha is a Buddha, that an ancestor is an ancestor, that an immortal is an immortal." According to the PSB, the initiates claimed that it was pointless to work in the commune fields because heaven was about to arrive. "By autumn there will be good food to eat, good clothes to wear, and there will be no need for money."[56]

Salvation from disaster, however, was only ever one element in the appeal of the redemptive societies. David Ownby argues that the typical redemptive society was one that "offered healing and the promise of salvation through the practice of morality and bodily technologies."[57] Official ideology, however, obsessed as it was with the societies as vehicles of counterrevolution, occluded this religious raison d'être. Yet fundamental to understanding why the societies survived the Mao years is recognizing that they catered to a sense that life as experienced by the unenlightened is not true life—that there is another realm of being that transcends mundane existence.[58] The societies offered individuals the opportunity to live an ethical life liberated from sin and the prospect of eternal life. And this promise of salvation marked a difference between the redemptive societies and mainstream popular religion, which was rooted in relationships of family, lineage, and locality.[59] How important the beliefs and specific practices of a redemptive society were to its appeal is hard to gauge; but in many regions different societies competed for followers, so we may infer that the particular teachings on offer were of some significance in determining which society an individual elected to join. The basic appeal, however, lay less in doctrine or ritual than in the purer form of life the societies offered their followers—a life revolving variously around the reading of sutras; the practice of inner alchemy; meditation; or the renunciation of meat, alcohol, or sexual relations. During the reform era, when it became possible for people to talk about what attracted them to the societies, the most common—although by no means the only—reason they gave for joining a congregation was essentially spiritual: to "practice vegetarianism, do good deeds, and prepare for the next life"; to "avoid calamities and disasters and enjoy a peaceful existence"; to "become an immortal or Buddha and develop good karma."[60]

One should not underestimate the ethical appeal of the societies at a time when the regime vaunted its contempt for traditional norms and values. The Yiguandao, in particular, was closer to Confucian values than were many sects whose filiations were closer to the supposed "White Lotus" tradition.[61] Yiguandao leaders regularly preached respect for loyalty, filiality, and justice, and its literature used folk legends to promote upstanding behavior—such as the one about the good monk Zhigong who returned to earth to dwell among men in order to save them. More generally, the society celebrated values of hierarchy and harmony and deprecated selfishness and the pursuit of riches.[62] In 1988 in Weifang in Shandong, Li Yu, deputy head of a school and a Party member, was caught putting up ninety copies of an "appeal to people of good will" in support of the Great Sage Emperor Dynasty (*Dasheng wangchao*). The appeal explained that impending calamities would come about because "people no longer follow truth, bad men run amok, people covet wealth, they deceive one another, the authorities are stupid, they take bribes and flout the law and prey upon the common people."[63]

If spiritual and ethical appeals were primary, more worldly considerations also shaped the decision to join a redemptive society. In the Chengdu region in 1950, among 1,108 Yiguandao members, 31 percent joined to protect themselves and their families against natural disaster and other calamities, 29.3 percent in order to be healed, 14.9 percent to obtain material benefits, 12.3 percent to enjoy a blessed afterlife, 7.2 percent to become saints or immortals, and 5.5 percent to have children.[64] The stress on healing corresponds with findings in China today, in which one of the most common reasons for joining a religious group is to gain access to supernatural healing, especially in the case of chronic illness or infertility. Throughout the Mao era, a major element in the activity of the societies was the provision of healing, often through spirit mediums, exorcism, or therapies such as holy water or incense ashes. In April 1966, a report by a neighborhood socialist education committee in Tianjin said that the chief reason the sects had still not been eliminated was that they offered the sick "magic medicine" through qigong, prayer, and holy water. The report cited the example of a factory director and Party member whose wife was mentally ill: upon being told by a sect leader that his wife was possessed by the spirit of a yellow weasel, he spent three days trying to catch it.[65] In Lin County in Henan, Yang Maicun, one of two leaders of the Way of Flowers and Vegetarianism (*Huazhaidao*), declared that any sick person who joined the society would be cured. But when one initiate died, he reasoned that "evil spirits have congregated in this place and unless you join my society, more people will surely die."[66]

The Communists never tired of stating that the redemptive sects were organizations dominated by "landlord elements," rich peasants, and capitalists. Yet in reality they were largely plebeian in composition. In the Republican era, the societies had been cross-class organizations with members ranging from the political and economic elites down to the most marginal and impoverished strata. The destruction of the old ruling classes, however, meant that the societies lost the merchants, gentry, and officials who had once been their wealthy patrons. Moreover, whereas prior to 1949 the societies had had a substantial urban membership, the suppression campaign of the 1950s was more successful in incapacitating the societies in towns and cities than in the countryside. The early 1950s, for example, saw particular efforts to ensure that members of the working class withdrew from the sects. At the Number 1 Cigarette Factory in Shanghai, where 3,067 people were employed, the suppression campaign led to the withdrawal of 615 workers (one-fifth of the workforce) who were ordinary members of the societies and 11 who held positions in the sects. At the Number 1 Silk Weaving Mill, 23.5 percent of the workforce of 1,999 renounced their sect membership.[67] At the Huachang silk filature in Wuxi in 1951, 10 percent of the 377-strong workforce confessed to being members of the Yiguandao, including 2 Party members, 4 Youth League members, and several activists.[68] The consequence of the relatively greater success of the suppression campaign in urban areas was that the center of gravity of the societies shifted toward the countryside, and possibly to those layers of peasants who were least targeted in political campaigns. In Liaoning, a survey of 868 low-ranking altar masters showed that 41 percent were poor peasants or hired laborers, while 30 percent were middle peasants.[69]

Because the societies encouraged people to look beyond the confines of their families—and because many believed in a female deity—it is perhaps not surprising that women played a pivotal role as educators and organizers in these movements. In 1950 in Zhanhua County in Shandong, the Yiguandao had 112 male and 105 female altar masters, and women comprised 36 percent of the 686 disciples. The Way of Saints and the Virtuous had 42 male and 16 female officers, and women comprised 35 percent of the 2,339 members.[70] In 1982, 63 percent of the 133 members of the Buddha Sage sect (*Foshengmen*) in Xiayi County, in Henan, were female.[71] Although official propaganda construed the typical sectarian as an illiterate old woman—"the Yigundao targets mature women because their mentality is rather conservative and they are easily confused"—the figures do not suggest that women formed the majority in the redemptive societies.[72] That said, in 1982 in Liuhe County in Jiangsu, 6 out of 10 leaders of the Guanyin Society were illiterate women aged fifty or over, and another was a woman who had been educated only to primary school level.[73] Indeed, these statistics suggest that the likelihood of women rising to positions of leadership, even high-ranking ones, was greater than in the Communist Party. In 1976 in Daming County in Hebei, Yang Xuehua, empress of the Heavenly Palace sect (*Tiangongdao*), was accused of fomenting a rebellion scheduled for the fourteenth day of the seventh lunar month. This involved 1,530 disciples from six counties in Hebei, Henan, and Shanxi. For her alleged role as leader, she was put to death.[74] In 1988, thirty-nine-year-old Chao Yuhua, who had acquired a reputation for powers of miraculous healing that had been vested in her by the Jade Emperor, was crowned empress of the Great Sage Dynasty in a factory dormitory in Weifang in Shandong. Her photograph shows a severe-looking woman sitting in an ordinary chair, wearing slacks, a stylish jacket, and a pearl necklace. She is flanked by two "ministers," both wearing Mao jackets and neatly creased trousers.[75]

Historically, joining a sect had been a way for many ordinary people to achieve a small degree of upward social mobility. As Kenneth Dean has shown for the Three-in-One sect (*Sanyijiao*), the redemptive societies in the late imperial and Republican eras offered those without powerful bureaucratic or lineage connections some prospect of social advancement within a new, liturgical community.[76] This was no longer the case in the People's Republic. Certainly, a few charismatic individuals were able to acquire a degree of local prestige—and often a degree of wealth through donations from their followers—by forming redemptive societies and, in some cases, by declaring themselves emperors. No one in Maoist China, however, joined a redemptive sect for a comfortable or quiet life. Even the lowliest disciple could expect trouble: at best, a stain on his or her work or political record; at worst, a spell under surveillance or in a labor camp.

The Politics of the Societies

Notwithstanding the fact that a minority of redemptive societies engaged in active resistance to the regime, the security organs massively exaggerated the political threat they posed. Some, such as the Li sect or the Three-in-One Society, eschewed politics of any kind.[77] And we have seen that *fubi* was a label that might be pinned on something as innocuous as an attempt by the societies to revive their activities. Yet, making due allowance for paranoia in police reports, some of the largest redemptive societies were clearly hostile toward the Communist regime, which is hardly surprising given the persecution to which they were subjected.

The societies circulated their politico-religious messages in a variety of forms, some more or less explicit. In spring 1950, Sun Suzhen (1895–1975), the second, estranged wife of Zhang Guangbi, the founder of the modern Yiguandao, sent out an elliptical "altar order" (*tan xun*) that predicted that the Yiguandao would soon overthrow the Communists.

> When the lotus is green and the plum red, then you will have an inkling.
> When the chrysanthemum is yellow and the crab fat, the curtain will be raised.
> Hide your trail, but remember that the day of reckoning is at hand.
> Then vengeance for injustice will be achieved.[78]

Spirit writing furnished an endless stream of spiritual messages, warnings, exhortations, and reassurances to followers, much of the content of which was recondite, but some clearly anti-Communist. The year 1949— ubiquitously referred to as "liberation" in official discourse—was sometimes dubbed the *mo kao*, the demonic test; the five-star red flag was likened to the fifth watch of night (i.e., the period just before the sun rises to dispel the darkness, the sun in this case being the Yiguandao); and the Patriarch sect (*Laoyedao*) interpreted Lin Biao's defection to mean that the heavenly mandate had passed to it.[79] Much of the communications of the societies was in written form, circulated in the exchange of "precious volumes," sacred instructions (*shengpi*), or good tidings (*jiayin*). New movements emerged as individuals read and interpreted written texts in new, creative ways. In 1957 in Zitong in Mianyang Prefecture in Sichuan, Tu Nanting, a twenty-six-year-old soldier whose father had been suppressed as a despotic landlord, made a bid to become emperor after reading fifteen volumes of moral exhortation (*quanshan shu*), stelae inscriptions, and metaphorical books, including the *Tu bei tu,* a Tang dynasty book of prophecies in the form of arcane drawings and obscure poems.[80] At the same time, the authorities' relentless pursuit of forbidden written material meant that the societies also relied heavily on the circulation of their message through oral means—through apocalyptic rumors and tales of sinister omens. Again, some of these rumors were explicit in their antipathy to the regime. Some that circulated in Anhui during the Great Leap Forward variously announced: "The five demons will stir up trouble for China. Communist power will quickly come to an end." "Chiang Kai-shek will return to the mainland in time to celebrate his birthday." "Only when a True Dragon Emperor ascends the throne will it be possible to avoid the hardships of the kalpa."[81] Even when the rumors carried content more obviously spiritual, their dissemination disconcerted the authorities, since they put into circulation "news" and interpretations of events that ran counter to those pumped out by the news and propaganda media.[82]

Strictly speaking, *fubi* connoted an attempt to restore an imperial dynasty, and it continued to carry this connotation in the Mao era. Again, we must remind ourselves that by no means all redemptive societies were obsessed with emperors and with imperial rule: the emperor, for example, hardly figured in the writings of the Way of the Temple of the Heavenly Immortals (*Tianxianmiaodao*).[83] Moreover, it is entirely possible that the PSB construed as "emperors" sect leaders who claimed authority of an entirely supernatural kind. Even allowing for this, however, it is clear that there were hundreds—and possibly thousands—of attempts to establish new dynasties in all parts of China during the Mao years.[84] The Handan region of Hebei Province alone—admittedly a hotbed of sectarianism—saw no fewer than 104 self-styled emperors appear in the 1950s, followed by 69 between 1983 and 1987.[85] In 1965 in Jiangxi, there were 22 attempts at imperial restoration involving the True Emptiness Teaching, the Elegant Gate (*Yaomenjiao*), the Gold Immortality Pill sect (*Jindanjiao*), and others.[86] In Henan in six months between 1974 and 1975, 21 out of 97 police cases relating to the societies involved attempts to establish a new dynasty. In Anyang, for example, Yang

Zhaogong, who claimed to have "friends in the Central Committee," appointed several dozen ministers and drew up plans for three military districts and thirty-two armies.[87]

A typical claimant to the imperial throne was Li Zhu, who announced the inauguration of a new dynasty in 1954 on the border of Hebei and Inner Mongolia, predicting that "at the end of the year of the horse a new dynasty will appear, and eighteen sons will ascend the throne." Since 1954 was the year of the horse and the combination of the characters for "eighteen sons" formed his own surname, Li was clearly setting out his stall. He proceeded to appoint ministers (*dachen*), dukes (*zhuhou*), and governors (*zhouguan*), who met in underground caves and who apparently supported themselves through trade, transportation, magical healing, and fortune-telling.[88] In 1961, Song Jiufang, leader of Nine Palaces Way, and several colleagues set off from Changling County in Jilin to Beijing bearing a dragon banner; on October 3, they sneaked into the Taihedian in the Forbidden City and installed Song as emperor.[89] In Cangnan County in Zhejiang, Li Guangchang, an old team leader, became a monarch of impressive longevity. For almost five years from 1981 to 1986, he ruled as emperor of the land of Zishen, whose center was Changxiang Village, gaining a following among peasants in distant parts of Zhejiang and Fujian. It took the PSB four years to rumble the existence of this statelet, even though Li and his ministers were not afraid to publicize their cause. "Of the main military regions, four are already controlled by the Zishenguo." "The Zishenguo has nuclear weapons, and when the appointed time comes, we shall provoke a world war and bring about a change of dynasty." "The Troops of Heaven will come to our assistance, providing protection for the Emperor to take up the Throne." "If you join the Zishenguo, when the nuclear bombs explode, we will send vehicles to ferry you away." Li and his officials created a flag that featured a double-planet motif rendered in vermilion, blue, yellow, white, and black; a military banner; and an army uniform with epaulettes bearing a dragon-head design. The PSB claimed they also tried to manufacture a potion that would render people unconscious during the rebellion they were said to be planning.[90]

The loving detail with which claimants to the mandate of heaven set about recreating the structures, rituals, and paraphernalia of imperial rule attest to how deeply the imperial model was rooted in popular culture as the model of all political authority. Leaders of these sects often showed exhaustive knowledge of the functioning of the imperial bureaucracy and managed to conceal—or make?—lavish robes, banners, fans, seals, certificates of appointment, and ritual objects associated with dynastic rule. Some appear to have looked to the restoration of the Qing, but most believed that a new dynasty would be created as the Maitreya established his presence on earth. Yet the structures of Communist administration also influenced the way the political order was imagined. In Bin County in Heilongjiang, Liu Yi, prophesying that the three calamities and eight difficulties would arrive in 1974, announced that he would be taken to the underworld and would preside over a nine-dragon hall before returning to earth to found the Zhongchao kingdom. This would comprise China, Korea, Japan, and India, and it would divide the world into thirty-six states, each ruled by a "chairman" (*zhuxi*). Moral leadership would be provided by a loyal teaching organization, consisting of thirty children, twenty-one students, seventy-four commune members, three brigade officials, one commune official, four barefoot doctors, seven workers, four Party members, and four Youth League members.[91] In the same syncretic fashion, Yang Xuehua, empress of the Heavenly Palace sect in Hebei, formed a court comprising ministers with ranks modeled on those of the Qing bureaucracy; yet among them were also ministers of foreign affairs and of public security and army commanders whose ranks mirrored those of the People's Liberation Army.[92] This said, it bears repeating that insurgent sects were not bent on creating a secular regime, but rather saw the claim to the mandate of heaven as the modality through which the Maitreya would inaugurate a third age of peace. It is also likely that would-be emperors were perceived as messianic figures by their followers, figures around whom they should rally in order to survive the onset of the third kalpa. Any challenge to Communist authority was essentially secondary— the byproduct of a process whose destiny was determined by heaven.

Perpetuating the Tradition

Disciples were willing to face the risk of serious punishment in order to ensure the survival of their organizations. In Panshi County in Jilin, there were 459 sect members in 1949, including 100 ranking members; in September 1985, there were 320 members, including 31 leaders. Of these, 156 were long-standing members whereas 164 were "newly discovered" by the PSB; among the leaders, 11 were longstanding and 20 were "newly discovered."⁹³ In Handan in Hebei, 79 percent of 264 sectarian leaders and more than 1,000 followers who were arrested in 1961 were said to have undergone some form of punishment for sectarian activity in the past.⁹⁴ In Anyang County in Henan (where no fewer than 101 different sects operated in 1970), the number of members of redemptive societies fell from 22,838 in 1949 to 8,881 in 1970, while the number of ranking members fell from 1,318 to 678. Of the original 1,318 officers, 69 had been shot, 77 were imprisoned, 123 were put under surveillance, 379 died, 18 absconded, and 16 moved away.⁹⁵ By 1985 in Zhuozhou County in Hebei, 27 leaders had been executed, 60 imprisoned, 172 put under surveillance, and 163 released; 52 had run away.⁹⁶ As these numbers suggest, many displayed a reckless courage in the face of persecution. In 1981, the police in Yunnan uncovered a Yiguandao network headed by Yang Biao, who had served three terms of imprisonment since 1951. Of his 178 disciples, no fewer than 108 had been punished before: 1 had been given a suspended death sentence, 6 had been sentenced to life imprisonment, 87 had been sentenced to fixed terms of imprisonment, and 15 had undergone periods of criminal control (*juyi*).⁹⁷

For some, "passing on the incense" (*xu lao jie xiang*)—i.e., the transmission of the secret lore of the society to the next generation—was a divine commission that could not be gainsaid. Zhang Cheng was the eldest grandson of Zhang Guangbi, founder of the modern Yiguandao. His father was executed in Shanghai in 1953, when Zhang was seven, and the previous year his grandmother, Liu Shuaizhen, had been arrested in Qingdao and sentenced to death. In 1954, his mother died, leaving the eight-year-old an orphan. The following year, his unmarried aunt, Zhang Maojin, brought Zhang Cheng and his brother to Yuncheng County in Shandong, where she hid them in the home of Zhao Zhifeng, a transmitter of rites. She changed the boys' surname to Zhao, and in 1958 when Zhang Cheng became thirteen, she invested him as emperor. For this she was consigned to the Heze labor camp in Shandong, where she died in 1977. Zhang Cheng was sentenced to reeducation through labor, a sentence he completed eight years later in 1966, when he was twenty-one. About three years later, he established a sworn brotherhood with two transmitters of rites in Yuncheng County. The three quickly reestablished a Yiguandao network across seven counties in Shandong and two in Henan, and Zhang was active throughout the 1970s. He was only caught in 1983 (and executed).[98] Equally committed to passing on the lore of his sect was Wang Anting, whose father had been the leader of the Return to the Village sect (Huanxiangdao) in Hebei before his execution as a despotic landlord in 1947. During the 1950s, Wang knit together a network of disciples in Xian and in the mountainous region of Wuan County in Hebei, moving around under an assumed name and doing various jobs as a shirt-maker and seller of steamed buns. He was said to have established more than one hundred secure hiding places. Proclaiming himself a "representative of the spirit world who has received a special *dao* of government," he distributed "letters from the spirit world" and cured illness and, according to the police, fleeced disciples of money and seduced women. For a period of more than thirty years he managed to maintain a network of over 1,000 disciples in nine counties, until his arrest in 1984 by the Handan police.[99]

Secrecy, of course, was imperative in ensuring the survival of the societies. In the Republican era, the societies had proselytized more or less openly. After 1949 this was impossible. Societies were forced underground, sometimes quite literally, since there are examples where they created headquarters in caves. In Xingping County in Shaanxi, Liu Zhihui, grand master of the Middle Way, was said to have dug two *li* of caves in which his sect set up offices, a mimeograph machine, and pressure lamps. In one grim incident, five teenage youths allegedly died in caves in Shaanxi, where they had been studying the "immortal life," because they fell sick and did not have enough to eat.[100] Secrecy, in any case, was an element in the culture of the redemptive societies that was valued for its own sake, for most delighted in arcane rites of initiation and the transmission of esoteric knowledge. Yet the societies were never hermetically sealed from the wider community, and they sometimes benefitted from the protection of officials and from fellow villagers who were not disciples but who may have valued the services of healing, exorcism, festival rituals, or prayers for the dead that societies could provide.[101]

So far as recruitment was concerned, *guanxi* (social connections) were paramount. The Golden Line faction of the Yiguandao was said in 1955 to have a policy of "promoting guanxi and friendship," "visiting relatives, calling on friends, working as traveling merchants, and tending the sick."[102] And because society members recruited among those they knew, this could lead to entire sections of communities falling under their sway. In the

Number 5 Production Team of the Wangping Brigade in Huaxu Commune in Shaanxi, 45 out of 47 households joined the Yiguandao, as did 39 out of 48 households in the Number 6 Production Team. Of 111 families in Qianbao Brigade in Huli Commune in Pingyang County in Zhejiang, all but 5 joined the Way of Former Heaven, and these were Catholics.[103] This instance may also have been connected to the trend toward a "cellularization" of rural society as marketing networks were suppressed and controls over the movement of population tightened.[104] That said, the implementation of the commune and household registration (*hukou*) systems does not seem to have prevented determined individuals from developing sectarian networks that stretched well beyond village or commune. Traditionally, the societies had recruited peripatetically, with activists moving about on the back roads and waterways, expanding networks through the exchange of precious volumes and talismans, and recognizing one another through passwords and secret handshakes. This became more difficult in the Mao era, but it did not cease. In Lin County in Henan in 1981, the network of the Way of Flowers and Vegetarianism comprised only 1,300 members, but they were scattered across four counties in contiguous provinces.[105] In general, the societies were able to operate most easily in remote or mountainous areas and along the borders between counties and provinces. In such places communications were poor, Party organization was weak, and the level of economic development low.

Despite a formally hierarchical structure, most societies were highly localized and low-ranking officers enjoyed considerable autonomy, including in matters of doctrine and ritual. Although the tendency of the sects to split might be seen as a weakness, in the conditions that appertained it was probably a factor that aided survival, since local leaders were able to adapt easily to changing circumstances by setting up new organizations.[106] In 1972 in Beian County in Heilongjiang, if the statistics are to be believed, there were 78 Yiguandao members, 69 Li sect members, and a further 143 who belonged to no fewer than forty-five other societies, each with an average of 3 members! Since 1949, total society membership in the county had fallen by 80 percent (from 1,400), but the number of societies had increased from ten to forty-seven.[107] Running counter to this proliferation of small societies, however, may have been a strengthening of the trend toward the unification of different traditions that had been afoot since the late Qing—seen most strikingly in the Three-in-One teaching, which sought to merge China's three major religious traditions.[108] There is exiguous evidence that differences based on the exclusive use of certain scriptures or on particular lines of transmission lost significance during the Mao years. In Shaanxi, among thirty-eight leaders of the Way of Long Life (*Changshengdao*), one was originally from the Society for Common Good and eight were former leaders of the Yiguandao.[109] Slogans such as "fusion of three faiths" (*san jiao he yi*) and "ten thousand dao return to their common root" (*wan dao gui gen*) appear to have been quite common. A parallel trend was toward the simplification of initiation rites and avoidance of membership records. In Linxiang County in Hunan, the Yiguandao called on leaders to "simplify the initiation procedure and streamline the administration of Buddhist affairs." The Laorendao (Way of Old People) in Shou County, Anhui, for example, wrote down the name of an initiate on a slip of paper and burned it, and initiation was complete.[110]

For all the above reasons, despite the terrible drubbing they received at the hands of the state, the societies survived. Their recovery began in the late 1970s and took off in the 1980s. This had little to do with the publication of Document 19 in 1982, which liberalized China's religious policy. Indeed, it is doubtful that "liberalization" had any role to play in the revival of the sects— at least before the 1990s. For in 1983, the Ministry of Public Security reported with alarm that cases of "disruption and sabotage" by the societies had increased by 78.9 percent in 1981 (compared with 1980), by a further 31.4 percent in 1982, and by a further 29.7 percent in the first eight months of 1983. Henan, Shaanxi, Sichuan, and Yunnan, it reported, were most affected, but all provinces had suffered, with the exception of Tibet.[111] The government response was a "strike hard" (*yanda*) campaign against the redemptive societies that lasted from 1983 to 1986; in some areas it was still going on in the late 1980s. Nevertheless, the resurgence of the redemptive societies has been a key element in the general revival of religion that has taken place in China over the past quarter of a century. Significantly, many of the societies that are now flourishing are new, attesting to the capacity of the sectarian tradition to reinvent itself continually. One reasonably reliable report reckons that in the 1990s there were six big societies and about one hundred smaller societies operating, each of the big six having between 100,000 and 600,000 members.[112] The boundary between the redemptive societies and the new qigong sects—such as Falungong and the Zhonggong sect, which claimed 20 to 38 million followers until it fell under government proscription at the end of the 1990s—is very blurred. Clearly, political and socioeconomic conditions today are radically different from those of the Mao era when persecution and socioeconomic turmoil encouraged a responsiveness to the apocalyptic sentiment propagated by the sects. Yet some of the same characteristics that allowed the societies to survive then—determination in the face of adversity, absolute conviction in their righteousness, a qualified willingness to colonize the local structures of power, and, above all, ingenuity in adapting to new conditions—have powered their amazing growth in the reform era. Now, however, they react against—and adapt to—the market economy, consumerism, declining state provision of health care, a culture of increased individualism, rising nationalism, political corruption, and the desire of local officials to attract outside investment.[113] There is no sign that the redemptive societies will disappear anytime soon.

Epilogue

Mao's China—Putting Politics in Perspective

VIVIENNE SHUE

In the autumn of darkest 1973, the ever more ashen-faced Premier Zhou Enlai—then under an only thinly veiled and vicious political attack from the ultra-left—was somehow toughing it out in the struggles for political survival at the top, and everyone else in China was being set up to endure the excruciatingly long, drawn-out, theoretically debased, and utterly implausible Campaign to Criticize Lin Biao and Confucius. I was spending my days in the library at the old Universities Service Centre on Argyle Street in Kowloon, Hong Kong, collecting material for my dissertation on the agrarian reforms of the 1950s in central China, and, resolute in my imperviousness to the lively Cantonese chatter all around me, doing my level best to improve my proficiency in spoken Mandarin. In my search for a language tutor, I was introduced to a young man named Fu, who had very recently come, as a "refugee," from Beijing, under circumstances that were never discussed. In his early-to-mid twenties, intelligent and soft-spoken, a nonsmoker, very slight of build and wearing his straight hair more than halfway down to his shoulders, Fu possessed the glorious "standard" pronunciation I was seeking, and so I was gladdened when, for a fee I could afford, he agreed to meet with me for several hours every week.

Our working relationship was not to develop as I had hoped it might, however. Reserved, pensive, and seemingly rather melancholy, Fu showed little interest in me, my life, or my work. Searching for topics to kick off good sessions of "conversation" together, therefore, I asked him often about himself and about his former life in what I then imagined to be the all but utterly hollowed-out, bleak, and embattled capital to the north. I learned early on that Fu had not been "sent down" to the countryside—in fact, had never traveled much outside Beijing at all. And I was confused by this. He said his health had always been good, and he certainly was in the age cohort of those who should have been sent down, so I could not guess what had kept him in the city. He did not seem ever to have been assigned a job. And when I pressed him on precisely how he spent his days during the height of the Cultural Revolution, he told me simply that he stayed at home. He said he had lived serenely enough and had not actually faced any political problems. He wasn't interested in politics, he told me. He enjoyed reading, especially poetry, plays, and fiction. He spent much of his time practicing drawing. He thought he had some talent and wanted to be an artist. How, I wondered, had a clever youth such as Fu not been pressed by activist classmates into designing revolutionary propaganda posters and writing out big-character posters (*dazibao*)? How had it been possible to just opt out of politics, to simply "stay at home" during those days of revolutionary mass mobiliza- tion—of virtually universal criticism and self-criticism? Yes he had, he told me, sometimes heard the sounds—the beating drums, the clanging cym- bals, and all the other commotion—of mass demonstrations and rallies, quite near his parents' home. But no, no one ever came to disturb him, and no gangs ever stormed in to burn his family's books or "drag" him out for criticism. A personal indifference to politics, even in the hyperpoliticized city of Beijing, was not in itself a crime, at least not as this young man recounted to me his tranquil existence there. He had not decided to leave Beijing because he'd been attacked or felt persecuted. However, the rather cloistered life he led there was not offering him many opportunities to develop himself or his young talents, he believed. And so he had made the break to Hong Kong.

Although Fu always conveyed a certain air of diffident matter-of-factness as he gave me his colorless accounts of the Cultural Revolution as he had lived through it, I nevertheless began to wonder if there was something he was failing to disclose. His account did not tally with anything I thought I knew and understood about society and politics, educated youth, and mass political participation under Mao. Cultural Revolution politics, I believed then, had been so total and so toxic that it had penetrated and profoundly affected even the smallest and most innocent nooks and crannies of everyday urban social life. Perhaps, even if there had been no counterrevolutionary "crime" he had been thought to have committed, there was some misdemeanor or some oddity my language tutor (understandably enough) was now choosing to conceal from me—something that set him and his family apart, exempting them from involvement in the political maelstrom that had gone on around them. I could not put out of my mind the puzzle of his self-described quietism amid the ardor and the chaos of that era of maximum social mobilization. So I kept asking questions. But Fu had said he would try to help me learn to speak more fluent Mandarin; he had not agreed to be, in effect, clumsily interviewed two or three days a week about the Cultural Revolution and his past life in Beijing. Eventually, my questions about politics succeeded in annoying him, or else they just made him uneasy. He started making excuses and missing appointments, and before very long he told me he would be too busy to keep up the classes.

Fu did not fit the social imaginaries that were available to students then for thinking about urban youth during the Cultural Revolution, so I could never forget him. Many years later, it occurred to me to wonder if perhaps Fu was gay—as we might say now but would never have said then.[1] I speculated that he could have been known to be gay, and for that reason purposely isolated and ignored by those who were politically active. Or that he could have been known to be gay and given protection by someone, or some group, in a position to shield him. An explanation along those lines, however, had never even crossed my mind when Fu and I knew each other in Hong Kong—the life choices realistically available to persons known to be homosexual and surviving in the forbiddingly puritanical Chinese social context of the early 1970s being something seemingly so incongruous and remote, so very nearly impossible even to ponder, from my external vantage point on China at that time.

Politics in Command

While Mao Zedong still lived, experts in the West typically considered and wrote about the immensity of China's social revolution in the present tense as it were, and under the rubric of "current events." For academic researchers, maintaining such a present-day orientation to the subject dictated that making sense of Mao's China would belong not primarily to social historians, but to social scientists—and most prominently to political scientists. The whole of the Cold War was marked by such profound political-ideological division and perilously heightened international political tensions, after all, that most of us could hardly help but perceive it as entirely natural, at the time, that those whose scholarly speciality was "the political" would be the ones best equipped to weigh and interpret the course of the Chinese revolution, the succeeding permutations in Maoist socialism, and the genuine significance of these for people living on the other side of what then was still frequently referred to as the "bamboo curtain."

Early on in the United States, political and military authorities at the highest levels—having already secured funding for the Marshall Plan to help rebuild Western Europe and hold the line against Communism there, and then having steered the fight against Communism to a bloody standstill also on the Korean Peninsula—turned their attention more urgently to the question of reinforcing preparedness on the home front for waging what plainly was to become a bitter, and protracted, struggle ahead. Reacting apprehensively to the challenge unexpectedly posed by the Soviets' first Sputnik satellite launch in 1957, Congress, the following year, passed the National Defense Education Act. In its earliest form, this legislation allocated federal funding to advance higher education and research not only in strategic science and engineering subjects, but also to enhance the teaching and learning of certain foreign languages by students in America, and to seed some further study of the histories and cultures of certain world regions that were regarded as "critical" to national defense. The PRC, with which the United States would not even establish formal diplomatic relations for another twenty years to come, was judged to be one of those critical regions of the world about which there existed a discomfiting deficit of expertise. And so, along with a number of other geographically and linguistically demarcated "area studies" programs, a new set of China Studies centers began to take form, with the help of the federal funding being funneled into (what remained a select number of) U.S. universities. New language instructors, library acquisitions, course offerings, and scholarships provided novel opportunities for studying China to the just-then-ballooning numbers of American high school graduates aspiring to earn college degrees in the 1960s and '70s.

Many of those recruited to the study of Chinese and other "critical languages"[2] at that time were expected eventually to enter public service in defense-related roles. Some young people attracted to the field would ulti-mately opt for futures in academic research and teaching, however. And conspicuous among them in terms of the numbers—as was true also with those who would go on to work for government—were students of political science.[3] It was in this general context, then, that it was to fall largely to those who had received some training in the discipline of politics—and who were felt to have reasonable quantities of relevant official documents, speeches, and Chinese news reports to sift through in their research—to accomplish much of the foundational work of sketching the course of events and assem-bling and interpreting the key trends and turning points in what we then generally tended to approach as China's contemporary history and politics.

What we students of politics looked for, and found, in those early years was for the most part what we were trained to see: shifting and contending patterns of political discourse and practice inside China, needing to be explicated and accounted for. The succession of titanic "mass mobilization campaigns" presided over by the Chinese Communist Party was widely per-ceived to be among the most distinctive and prominent features of the Mao-era political system. And much effort was therefore devoted to tracing and dissecting those campaigns, as well as to piecing together a plausible, deeper political logic underlying them. Thus, with political campaigns featured as the most meaningful moments and markers in time, recitation of the course of social history inside China under Mao conventionally came to be ordered, in the West, very largely in accord with what Gail Hershatter has so aptly referred to as "campaign time."[4] With mass campaign after mass campaign to disentangle and record, it was but a short step for students of politics to envision and represent the China they knew as, in effect, a society in thrall to politics, a social field perpetually *politically saturated*—a complex society, to be sure, with numerous cross-cutting impulses, but one so thoroughly and repeatedly drenched in the obligatory enactment of "the political" that few, if any, other potently meaningful spaces remained for alternative dimensions of the human experience to be expressed. Politics, on our polit-ical scientists' account of it, was indeed "in command."

Nor was it only accidental, of course, that this particular vision of Chinese society, as saturated by "the political," reflected so well the ideals of "con-tinuous revolution" that Mao and other official voices were unceasingly advocating at the time. When Mao said that the historical mission of the Chinese Communist Party should be to "put politics in command," he meant that the greater goals of achieving a genuine social revolution should take priority over the interim calculus of economic benefit, even sometimes over the calculus of national economic "development"; revolutionary social goals should guide economic choices. For Mao, further, the core meaning of "putting politics in command" was to be found in what was perhaps his single most memorable injunction, uttered in 1962: "Never forget classes; never forget class struggle. Class struggle is the key link, everything else hinges on it." While Mao lived, the political struggle, and in particular class struggle, defined the essential contours of Chinese public life and public discourse. The politics of class struggle was to be deliberately magnified and kept ever at the center of view.

It was not until very shortly after Mao had left the scene, then—by which time it was becoming (ever-so-gradually) possible for foreign scholars to visit, talk with a greater and greater range of Chinese people, and even carry out modest field investigations inside China themselves—that we began to glimpse more clearly a variety of commonly accepted practices, habits, and patterns of speech still surviving: small scenes, private settings, and even whole unanticipated segments of the social field that did not fit comfortably into the austere archetype of continuous class-conscious struggle and endless political saturation we had been led to believe had prevailed for so long. Observed small spaces of accustomed ease and joy, beauty and indulgence, hope and faith, wit, menace, risk, or reserve—these did not chime well with our expectations of an all-pervasively political mentality having been in command, and seemed to point plainly instead to other domains of validation and attachment coexisting, if still somewhat covertly, with the values and the demands of "the political." Clearly there was to be room for different types of social scientists, not all primarily concerned with politics per se, but rather with culture, family and religion, or gender, or demography, or business and economics, or delinquency, or public health—all to shed light on Chinese affairs. Eager scholars from all these disciplines and more did, of course, rapidly join the field. But for obvious reasons, few then turned their research attentions backward in time or toward revising and deepening our understanding of what the Mao period had really been. Reliable testimony, not to mention hard "data" about the still-contested painful past, was nearly impossible to access then. And China in the early reform period was already changing in ways that seemed momentous to us all. Fascination with the present day and with predictions about the future remained as pressing as ever. Thus, when we did finally begin to glean our sharpened perceptions of those previously concealed recesses of social life that had survived, perhaps even flourished, despite all the attempts at political saturation under Mao, they came to us late, through fragments of first-hand experience, chance discoveries, and other nonreplicable, nonstandard sources. They came to us only as the experienced realities of the Maoist past themselves were being briskly swept away before our eyes, out of the present tense, and into the dustbin of history.

The Dustbin of History

Now, more than thirty-five years further on, the dustbin is being coaxed to give up some of its treasures. Sources of many kinds that earlier had been safeguarded or suppressed are now coming into the hands of (mostly) younger historians, who cannot help but read them as precious remains salvaged from an antique era: diaries and memoirs, letters and mimeographed newsletters, local-state archives including all manner of investigative and surveillance reports, political and criminal confessions, and other internal memoranda. Recovered sources of all these sorts make it possible for a colorful and absorbing collection of rich new research results such as those in this volume to be assembled. The findings presented in these essays are, for the most part, based on very partial—even fragmentary—bits of evidence, to be sure. Still, when read together, they do suggest that we may now, at long last, be in a position to start a serious and dispassionate reassessment of the nature and extent of the "political saturation" actually achieved and sustained under Mao.

The studies collected here take us some distance, in fact, toward reconceptualizing the contours of the basic social field in those days, as well as the options for individual and group actions within and across it. Here we see in detail how some Party-state policies and political requirements affected individuals and communities in ways that could be oppressive and liberating all at the same time. We see that young people especially, perhaps, may have experienced the Mao era in complex and convoluted ways, with the horizons of their futures shrunken in some respects but expanding in others. And we are reminded too that, demographically speaking, China—like

much of the rest of the world in the 1950s, '60s, and '70s—was overrun with
youthfulness.

In several of the essays gathered here, we are shown as well how, even
under the political absolutism of the high Mao era, some operational space
could still remain available for individual and small-group agency, if only in
electing how precisely to respond to certain Party-state expectations and
requirements. Confronting adverse circumstances and heavily constrained
by politics, people nonetheless actively went to work navigating the options
that were available to them in ways they hoped might enhance their own
preferred ends. The capacities of individuals and small groups of people to
establish links, remain in touch with one another, and even self-organize
ambitious events and activities under the Party-state's radar—even when
these groups and individuals were seemingly quite isolated and separated
from one another by great distances or other obstacles—emerges intrigu-
ingly in the accounts of several authors here. The Party's official norms of
public morality and its prescribed, highly politicized public culture evidently
encountered competition more or less unceasingly through the high socialist
era, from such scattered clusters and networks of individuals busying themselves in sustaining alternative philosophies, aesthetics, and norms of social
behavior. The research reported here strongly suggests the stubborn persistence of officially disapproved but popular cultural and social practices,
illicit associations, smuggling and gambling rings, black markets, and officially proscribed activities of all sorts throughout the entire period.

Even more often, perhaps, expressions and practices of individual and
group agency might fall well short of being illicit yet still fly in the face of the
official morality publicly promoted by the Party at the time. In reading Sha
Qingqing and Jeremy Brown's analysis of the writings of Tongshan (Chapter
7), a young Tianjin diarist who hoped to turn the disaster of the "Great
Tangshan Earthquake" into a beneficial opportunity for himself as he
maneuvered to avoid his imminently scheduled departure for the countryside, I was reminded of someone else who lived in Tianjin and would only
have been a few years older than Tongshan at that testing time. She told me,
years later—it must have been in 1992, as we were chatting about her teenage
son's upcoming birthday celebration—the story of how she had very deliberately tried to get pregnant in the immediate aftermath of the quake. She was
then just beginning a promising academic research career, but her unit was

shut down after the catastrophe, and all members were expected to suspend their research and help out instead with relief work and city reconstruction for months to come. (Although Tianjin was not at the epicenter, the damage done there still amounted to a major emergency.) Yet for her, she explained, the closing of her institute and the expectation that she would answer the call to assist in the recovery meant only months of doing nothing but dis-agreeable physical labor; and furthermore, she would be losing valuable time and would be set back on her own research agenda. If she were found to be carrying a child, however, she would be exempted from all that. She would be allowed instead just to gather up some of her books and papers and stay at home, continuing her research and writing—and so also gaining an edge on most of the other young academics assigned to her unit, who would be spending their time cleaning up the rubble. She and her husband agreed, talking it through together then, that it would be an opportune moment to conceive.

Tongshan, with typical teenage melodramatic self-absorption, declared in his diary that he felt as if his "life was over!" when he ultimately failed despite all to get a work assignment that would allow him to stay in the city. But my maternal academic friend, with a cunning gleam in her eye, could glance over at her (by then fifteen-year-old) son, glued to the television on the other side of the room that day as we talked, and congratulate herself again on just how clever she had been to arrange to fall pregnant when she did. Attempts at exercising agency in the Mao era sometimes succeeded—and sometimes they failed. They sometimes involved making proactive appeals or com-plaints to people in power, but they could take many other, more stealthy, preemptive, and even (pro)creative forms as well. And even those living in quite favored circumstances close to power then, including Party cadres themselves, as these studies show, could become adept at working the system to their own local community, or personal careerist, ends.

For those who could not or would not try to work the system to advantage, there were still other options available in pursuit of a more satisfying life. According to the records analyzed here by S. A. Smith, for example, hun-dreds of thousands, "possibly millions" of people over the years, remained so apparently untouched by (or became so confused and alienated from) the official ideology and public culture of the Mao era that, as a way of dealing with personal anxiety or moral uncertainty, they opted to respond instead to

the apocalyptic narratives put abroad by a resilient host of officially out-
lawed religious sects, underground charismatic leaders, and popular redemptive societies. Some went so far as to join in actual religiously inspired
rebellions against the Maoist state that, according to Smith, were "not
trivial." Many more—including large numbers of cadres again—may have
believed there to be no necessary contradictions entailed in working with
and for the Communist Party while participating just as faithfully in the
mystical activities of one or more of these doctrinally syncretic and univer-
salist societies. Drenched in the secular political categories of class and class
struggle these questing souls may have been—but not, apparently, to the
exclusion of older moral categories such as sin and the hope for redemption
in heaven.

Other themes running through these essays include the persistent ubiquity of whispered rumors about spies and clandestine plots, as well as the
troubles caused for the Party-state by rumor mongering and the anxiety and
psychological tension it could generate among ordinary people. A spirit of
suspicion and insecurity—when joined with the generalized material dearth,
the scarcity of services of all kinds, the common fears and traumatic memories of war and invasion, the disruptiveness of the mass campaigns, investigations and public shamings, the exhausting labor, the family separations,
and the frustration of natural personal desires that characterized life for so
many during the whole period—made the prevailing social atmosphere very
highly fraught for some, even psychologically punishing. And none of these
fascinating observations arising from the archival record in the essays collected here conforms very well to the vision of a society thoroughly transformed by its saturation in revolutionary class politics. Taken altogether,
these essays present a picture of very uneven penetration by "the political,"
at best.

Ruling Agonistically and over Rough Social Terrain

Like all modern states, the one that Mao and the Chinese Communist Party
built during the 1940s, '50s, and '60s projected its authority and ruled over
the geographical and social space under its sway *agonistically.* That is to say
that the actual tasks and routines of governing in Mao's China, as elsewhere

in the modern world, may best be characterized and understood as engagements in a more or less continuous process of striving and competing—competing against naysayers, challengers, and antagonists of all sorts arising potentially from every corner and crevice within the national society as well as from beyond state borders. Although state power-holders everywhere generally choose to depict what they do in entirely different and more socially palatable terms, to be sure, the essence of maintaining their authority and control lies in identifying the most potent challengers and competitors active or latent in the social terrain and devising means to neutralize or subdue them. Since the very acts of wielding and projecting power and authority over and into the social space so reliably serve only to provoke yet more new competitors and counterforces to arise, the agonistic quality of rule, when looked at over the longer term, is more or less continual and continually renewing. In this one sense at least perhaps, politics (the exercise and circulation of power) resembles the economy (the creation and circulation of value): it can never rest. And *the endeavoring restlessness* of "the political" in human societies—all the more static and smothering concepts and depictions of it that have been devised to the contrary notwithstanding—is *the most vital quality* that must be grasped. In modern states the hegemony of "the political," we might say, is forever condemned to remain aspirational—never quite realized.

Similarly, the social field over which the modern state must strive to rule tends to be characterized not only by significant variation and complexity, but also by its own capacity for restless shape-shifting, opacity, and ambiguity. Arguably also, the level of inaccessibility and the extent of flux exhibited across the national social field of China during the 1940s, '50s, and '60s made it nothing less than extraordinarily challenging for any aspiring rulers to read with much accuracy. The Maoist Party-state, although experienced in governing some portions of the country and some segments of society by the time it came to national power in 1949, nonetheless faced many daunting obstacles to effectively penetrating, comprehending, and establishing effective governance over others. All through the decades of the 1950s and '60s, the Party-state kept rediscovering, to its dismay, just how rough that social terrain remained; just how ragged, unreconciled, and unruly its subjects could still be. And in the course of all its episodic scuffles and skirmishes aimed at offsetting the capabilities of its adversaries and keeping a motley array of challenging social counterforces at bay, the Party-state's own capacities to think and act as a unified team forever remained, also, in some doubt.

Putting Politics in Perspective

Toward the end of their introductory essay here, the editors of this volume survey their contributors' main historical finds: an enormously varied and challenging social terrain to be governed; locally brokered, bargained, and consequently very uneven policy implementation; a Party-state made up of flawed individuals suffering from their own political ambivalences as well as other limitations; and a population often more consumed by coping with the struggles of everyday life than with the effort to achieve a revolutionary utopia. Who would have thought "Mao's China" could turn out to have been so "ordinary"?

Pretty "ordinary" life under Mao may have been much of the time, but for most historians of twentieth-century China, the substantive and method-ological lessons to be learned from the essays in this collection should, none-theless, be encouraging ones. For obviously there remains much more in the way of historical correction and genuine deepening of our understanding to be gained now from tapping further into China's newly opening archives and from targeting in particular other previously overlooked sorts of sources and materials. Although the rewards can be rich, the opportunities for piecing together extensive oral histories of China's high socialist era are rap-idly diminishing, as Hershatter's work reminds us. But then again, for what was still an underdeveloped economy at the time, the astonishingly high rates of basic literacy achieved in China under Mao—and the deep-rooted scribal passion for counting, record-keeping, and report-writing that both ordinary people and state officials, high and low, so consistently displayed all across the country—make the search for revelatory new written materials very likely now to return a rich harvest.

As it has been conceptualized in this collection, it may be mainly a matter of probing at the "grassroots" to find enlightening local or individual per-spectives. But invoking the familiar central/local organizing principle implied in the notion of seeking grassroots (as opposed to official) knowledge and experience may also be just one way for us to order future searches for the greater variety of perspectives we seek to illuminate. Looking for new sources originating from those segments of society regarded not merely as local, but as outcast or marginal, may be fruitful too. Even more so, perhaps, would be searching consciously for study materials arising out of the "liminal" regions—those betwixt and between the structures normally recognized as powerful in society. Records of the spiritual and self-sacrificing, the aesthetic and imaginative, the wily and cunning, and the reckless: traces remaining of spaces such as these, where that which is formal or official glimpses, but only fitfully and warily, that which is chaotic or creative—such spaces of experience and the traces they have left behind may be equally worth pursuing, into the past.

For social scientists in the China field, however, who remain mostly fixed on the present day and who have already had long and fruitful experience with reevaluating rhetoric and trends at the core of the polity with the benefit of insights gathered from the grassroots, the most important takeaway from reading the essays in this volume may be a little different. For today's social scientists it may boil down, in fact, to working out an adequate response in their own minds to the concluding rhetorical question posed by Brown and Johnson in their introductory essay about "whether Mao's China ever existed at all." Speaking only for myself—but perhaps other social scientists of China who lived through the period too would agree—the only satisfactory response to such a question must be an unambiguous "Yes and No!" In deep and important respects, to be sure, everyday life in China during those years was nothing so out of the "ordinary," and it is salutary now, finally, to be in a position to document and emphasize those quotidian dimensions of the historical reality. But in other respects, the Mao era has to stand as an emphatically extraordinary time, at least when compared with what we know of the China that came before it, and the one after. The comprehensive condition of life that conventionally tends to be conjured up with the phrase "Mao's China"—a truly massive social field over which a simply monumental effort was made, repeatedly, to put militant revolutionary politics in command—most certainly did exist. But as the studies collected here make apparent, that social field, in tangible action, often did not much resemble at all the ways in which it was imagined to exist, either by those writing hortatory *People's Daily* editorials in Beijing or by those looking on with fascination and alarm from the West.

The long, draining decades of the Cold War are, with good reason, remembered as an intensely "political" time by people living in almost all countries around the globe. And in China, this was especially so. The effort by Mao and the Communist Party to put politics in command, and to keep it there, had powerful effects, setting such lofty goals for positive societal transformation over the longer term, while sharply delimiting the parameters of the possible for so many in the shorter term. Almost everyone's life, public and private, was impacted by the purposefully heightened importance of "the political" in Mao's China. And yet, the totality of the human experience—including heart, mind, soul, wit, and will—was, even then, not by any means limited or confined to inhabit only the realm of the political. The life choices even of someone as politically disinterested as my onetime language tutor Fu, for example, were undoubtedly shaped and constrained by the magnification of "the political" in the early '70s. Yet he was still able to take his decision to quit the essentially tolerable life he lived in Beijing not because he was much bothered at all by politics; it was, rather, because somehow he could not keep from cherishing in himself other dimensions of value and other aspirations—artistic, professional, or, we might say, vocational.

Among the social scientists in our field, there are not a few who would give us to believe that, whatever degree of political saturation may or may not actually have been achieved in Chinese society under Mao, in the present day anyway, the ideals and values associated with putting politics in command are well and truly dead. In Chinese hearts and minds today it is economics, and only economics, in command, so they say. Social scientists of contemporary China reading this volume, with minds open to rethinking the intricately interlaced possibilities that lie embedded in the present day in light of a deepening comprehension of the multivalent past, may well be skeptical of such one-dimensional characterizations of contemporary Chinese social reality.

Should we social scientists now repeat the earlier pattern of thinking about the human experience from the perspective of whether it is, say, politics or economics, or yet some other system of values and beliefs, that is in command of people's lives? Or should we, rather, taking our cues from the findings of several of the twentieth-century historians here, be seeking to grasp in the kind of work we do—in our models, approaches, questions, and answers—more of that quality of restless striving that people in complex societies seem so steadfastly to be engaged in, striving to live what they would find it possible to accept and regard as a whole and decent, a satisfactory, human life? That ceaseless striving for validation and empowerment, amid always-competing systems of value and belief, within a densely packed and ever-shifting field of play is, arguably, what lies at the heart of the human experience of "the social." And so, perhaps it is only with a general orientation to our subject as multivalent and dynamic as this that we may succeed, one day, in putting "the political" in China—and even "the economic" for that matter—into proper perspective.

Notes

Introduction

1. Noteworthy scholarship about the underlying reality of the Mao years includes Victor C. Falkenheim, "Political Participation in China," *Problems in Communism* 27, no. 3 (May-June 1978): 18–32; Andrew G. Walder, *Communist Neo-Traditionalism: Work and Authority in Chinese Industry* (Berkeley: University of California Press, 1986); and Jean C. Oi, *State and Peasant in Contemporary China: The Political Economy of Village Government* (Berkeley: University of California Press, 1989).

2. Elizabeth J. Perry, "Trends in the Study of Chinese Politics: State-Society Relations," *China Quarterly* 139 (September 1994): 712–713.

3. Joseph W. Esherick, Paul G. Pickowicz, and Andrew G. Walder, eds., *The Chinese Cultural Revolution as History* (Stanford: Stanford University Press, 2006), 12–13.

4. At first glance, de Certeau's theory of everyday life, with its distinction between "producers" and "users," is a poor fit for China during the Mao years. It is meant to explain modern capitalist consumer society rather than a socialist planned economy. Nonetheless, his focus on how people transform, resist, and adapt to ideas, situations, and spaces that are imposed on them is applicable to a study of the grassroots during the Mao years, when people lived under severe constraints but behaved in ways contrary to what policy-makers, planners, and propagandists intended. Michel de Certeau, *The Practice of Everyday Life,* trans. Steven Rendall (Berkeley: University of California Press, 1984).

5. Perry, "Trends in the Study of Chinese Politics," 707.

6. Ibid., 708.

7. Joseph W. Esherick, "Deconstructing the Construction of the Party-State: Gulin County in the Shaan-Gan-Ning Border Region," *China Quarterly* 140 (December 1994): 1078.

8. Gail Hershatter, *The Gender of Memory: Rural Women and China's Collective Past* (Berkeley: University of California Press, 2011), 68.

9. Two important ethnographies in this regard are C. K. Yang, *Chinese Communist Society: The Family and the Village* (Cambridge, MA: MIT Press, 1965

[1959]); and Sulamith Heins Potter and Jack M. Potter, *China's Peasants: The Anthropology of a Revolution* (New York: Cambridge University Press, 1990). For other revealing studies of life in villages and cities, see Anita Chan, Richard Madsen, and Jonathan Unger, *Chen Village: Revolution to Globalization*, 3rd ed. (Berkeley: University of California Press, 2009); Edward Friedman, Paul G. Pickowicz, and Mark Selden, *Chinese Village, Socialist State* (New Haven, CT: Yale University Press, 1991); Friedman, Pickowicz, and Selden, *Revolution, Resistance, and Reform in Village China* (New Haven, CT: Yale University Press, 2005); and Martin King Whyte and William L. Parish, *Urban Life in Contemporary China* (Chicago: University of Chicago Press, 1984).

10. Scholarship about Mao by such political scientists as Roderick MacFarquhar and Frederick Teiwes sets a high standard that has stood the test of time. See especially MacFarquhar's trilogy *The Origins of the Cultural Revolution* (New York: Columbia University Press, 1974, 1983, 1997) and Frederick C. Teiwes, *Politics and Purges in China: Rectification and the Decline of Party Norms* (White Plains, NY: M. E. Sharpe, 1979). Recent cutting-edge scholarship centered on Mao can be found in Timothy Cheek, ed., *A Critical Introduction to Mao* (New York: Cambridge University Press, 2010).

11. Frederick C. Teiwes and Warren Sun, *The End of the Maoist Era: Chinese Politics during the Twilight of the Cultural Revolution, 1972–1976* (Armonk, NY: M. E. Sharpe), 446n150.

12. For notable examples of archival research, see Elizabeth J. Perry and Li Xun, *Proletarian Power: Shanghai in the Cultural Revolution* (Boulder, CO: Westview, 1997); Neil J. Diamant, *Revolutionizing the Family: Politics, Love, and Divorce in Urban and Rural China, 1949–1968* (Berkeley: University of California Press, 2000) and *Embattled Glory: Veterans, Military Families, and the Politics of Patriotism in China, 1949–2007* (Lanham, MD: Rowman & Littlefield, 2009); Kimberley Ens Manning and Felix Wemheuer, eds., *Eating Bitterness: New Perspectives on China's Great Leap Forward and Famine* (Vancouver: University of British Columbia Press, 2011); Thomas S. Mullaney, *Coming to Terms with the Nation: Ethnic Classification in Modern China* (Berkeley: University of California Press, 2011); Zhou Xun, *The Great Famine in China, 1958–1962* (New Haven, CT: Yale University Press, 2012); and Aminda M. Smith, *Thought Reform and China's Dangerous Classes* (Lanham, MD: Rowman & Littlefield, 2013). Other revelatory works that draw on a combination of never-before-unearthed sources and recently conducted oral history are Joel Andreas, *Rise of the Red Engineers: The Cultural Revolution and the Origins of China's New Class* (Stanford: Stanford University Press, 2009); Jacob Eyferth, *Eating Rice from Bamboo Roots: The Social History of a Community of Handicraft Papermakers in Rural Sichuan, 1920–2000* (Cambridge, MA: Harvard University Asia Center, 2009); Hershatter, *The Gender of Memory*; Sigrid Schmalzer, *The People's Peking Man: Popular Science and Human Identity in Twentieth-Century China* (Chicago: University of Chicago Press, 2008); and

Yiching Wu, *The Cultural Revolution at the Margins: Chinese Socialism in Crisis* (Cambridge, MA: Harvard University Press, 2014).

13. Jeremy Brown, "Finding and Using Grassroots Historical Sources from the Mao Era," *Dissertation Reviews,* December 15, 2010, http://dissertationreviews.org /archives/310. In addition to the chapters in this volume, recent works using substantial amounts of grassroots and unofficial sources include Roderick MacFarquhar and Michael Schoenhals, *Mao's Last Revolution* (Cambridge, MA: Belknap Press of Harvard University Press, 2006); Daniel Leese, *Mao Cult: Rhetoric and Ritual in China's Cultural Revolution* (New York: Cambridge University Press, 2011); Jeremy Brown, *City versus Countryside in Mao's China: Negotiating the Divide* (New York: Cambridge University Press, 2012); and Michael Schoenhals, *Spying for the People: Mao's Secret Agents, 1949–1967* (New York: Cambridge University Press, 2013).

14. Vivienne Shue, *The Reach of the State: Sketches of the Chinese Body Politic* (Stanford: Stanford University Press, 1988).

15. See also Elizabeth J. Perry and Merle Goldman, *Grassroots Political Reform in Contemporary China* (Cambridge, MA: Harvard University Press, 2007). In addition, our approach is informed by recent scholarly activity related to the production of a bottom-up and empirically informed post-1949 "contemporary history" (*dangdai shi*): Yang Kuisong et al., "'Zhongguo dangdai shi xueke jianshe' bitan" [An exchange of notes on the construction of the discipline of contemporary Chinese history], *Shehui kexue* 381 (May 2012): 147–169.

16. Rural women understood their own experiences during the Mao period in ways that differed from the state's "campaign time"; Hershatter, *The Gender of Memory*. Neil Diamant's research indicates that the implementation of such policies as land reform and the Marriage Law and the introduction of the 1954 constitution "telescoped" and "blended" at the local level in overlapping ways that confused citizens and confounded grassroots cadres. Diamant, *Revolutionizing the Family,* 139, and Neil J. Diamant, "Policy Blending, Fuzzy Chronology, and Local Understandings of National Initiatives," *Frontiers of History in China* 9, no. 1 (March 2014): 83–101.

17. Michael Schoenhals, "Is the Cultural Revolution Really Necessary?" in *China's Communist Revolutions: Fifty Years of the People's Republic of China,* ed. Werner Draguhn and David S. G. Goodman (New York: RoutledgeCurzon, 2002), 159–176.

18. Shue, *The Reach of the State.*

19. For two different accounts of rural conflict, see Vivienne Shue, *Peasant China in Transition: The Dynamics of Development toward Socialism, 1949–1956* (Cambridge, MA: Harvard University Press, 1980) and Friedman, Pickowicz, and Selden, *Chinese Village, Socialist State.*

20. A notable exception that focuses on neighbors killing neighbors is Yang Su, *Collective Killings in Rural China during the Cultural Revolution* (New York: Cambridge University Press, 2011).

21. Two violent eruptions are detailed in Melvyn C. Goldstein, Ben Jiao, and Lhundrup Tanzen, *On the Cultural Revolution in Tibet: The Nyemo Incident of 1969* (Berkeley: University of California Press, 2009); and Xian Wang, "Islamic Religiosity, Revolution, and State Violence in Southwest China: The 1975 Shadian Massacre" (master's thesis, University of British Columbia, 2013).

1. How a "Bad Element" Was Made

1. "Zhongyang shi ren xiaozu guanyu fangeming fenzi he qita huaifenzi de jieshi ji chuli de zhengzhi jiexian de zanxing guiding" [An interim provision by the central ten-member panel for the definition and treatment of the political demarcations of counterrevolutionaries and other bad elements], March 10, 1956, Shanghai Municipal Archive, J163/4/167/13–16.

2. Mao Zedong, "Guanyu zhengque chuli renmin neibu maodun de wenti" [On the correct handling of contradictions among the people], February 27, 1957, in *Mao Zedong xuanji* [Collected works of Mao Zedong] (Beijing: Renmin chubanshe, 1977), 5:366.

3. Undated personal résumé card in "Xuchang XX chang liumang anjuan—Zang Qiren" [Xuchang XX factory hooligan dossier—Zang Qiren], hereafter abbreviated as ZQR, 12.

4. "Tanbai dengji cailiao" [Registered confession materials], July 1958, ZQR, 14.

5. "Lüli dengji biao" [Personal résumé form], 1958?, ZQR, 89.

6. "Ganbu dengji biao" [Cadre registration form], January 5, 1953; "Gongsi heying XX chang zhigong dengji biao" [Joint State-Private Ownership XX factory staff registration form], January 24, 1957, ZQR, 18, 27.

7. "Ganbu dengji biao," January 5, 1953, 27.

8. "Baogao shu" [Report], May 3, 1953, ZQR, 27.

9. "Tanbai shu" [Written confession], September 23, 1956, ZQR, 28.

10. Ibid.

11. Ibid.

12. "Tanbai dengji cailiao," 14.

13. "Jianju Zang Qiren" [Reporting Zang Qiren], August 24, 1958, ZQR, 15.

14. "Diaocha zhengming cailiao jieshaoxin" [Introduction letter for evidence collected during investigation], with attachment "Diaocha xiansuo" [Investigation clues], December 20 and 22, 1960], in "Xuchang shi geming weiyuanhui shuangqing bangongshi qingli jieji duiwu anjuan—XX chang Zang Qiren" [Xuchang municipal revolutionary committee double cleanup office Cleansing the Class Ranks dossier—XX factory's Zang Qiren], hereafter abbreviated as XSG.

15. "Diaocha xiansuo biao" [Table of investigation clues], 1960, in "Xuchang XX Chang liumang anjuan—Zang Qiren," 58.

16. "Hong Zhenglong qingkuang jieshao" [An introduction of Hong Zhenglong's circumstances], December 17, 1960, ZQR, 58.

17. "Zhu Hongzhong diaocha baogao" [Zhu Hongzhong's investigation report], February 1, 1961, ZQR, 59–60.

18. "Luo Kezhen zhengming Zang Qiren de cailiao" [Luo Kezhen's testimony on Zang Qiren], April 6, 1961, ZQR, 70, 71.

19. "Chen Liang'en bishu" [Written account by Chen Liang'en], September 23, 1961, ZQR, 66.

20. "Zhonggong Xuchang shiwei gongye xitong shen'gan bangongshi zhi Xinjiang Chabucha'er Xibo zizhixian renmin jianchayuan han" [Letter from Xuchang Party Committee industrial system investigation office to People's Procuratorate of Qapqal Xibe Autonomous County, Xinjiang], August 5, 1961, February 16, 1962; "Xinjiang Chabucha'er Xibo zizhixian renmin jianchayuan zhi Zhonggong Xuchang shiwei gongye xitong shen'gan bangongshi han" [Letter from People's Procuratorate of Qapqal Xibe Autonomous County, Xinjiang to Xuchang Party Committee industrial system investigation office], October 19, 1961, April 25, 1962, ZQR, 73, 79, 80.

21. Zang Qiren, "Wo he Chen Wenlong de guanxi" [My relationship with Chen Wenlong], April 26, 1968, XSG.

22. Zang Qiren, "Wo de sixiang renshi" [My knowledge of ideology], April 26, 1968, XSG.

23. Zang Qiren, "Wo he Chen Wenlong de guanxi," "Wo de sixiang renshi," and "Jiefa pipan san fan fenzi Chen Wenlong" [Exposing and criticizing the three-antis element Chen Wenlong], April 26 and 28, 1968, XSG.

24. Zang Qiren, "Ziwo jiancha" [Self-criticism], May 1, 1968, XSG.

25. Zang Qiren, "Xiang quanchang geming zhigong jiancha" [Confession addressed to all the revolutionary staff of the factory], June 2, 1968, XSG.

26. Zang Qiren, "Guanyu wo taopao shi de sixiang qingkuang" [What I was thinking of when I was running away], June 3, 1968, XSG.

27. Zang Qiren, "Jiefa Chen Wenlong gao ziben zhuyi fubi" [Exposing Chen Wenlong's capitalist restoration], "Zai wenhua dageming zhong he Chen Wenlong de jiechu" [Interactions with Chen Wenlong during the Cultural Revolution], "Wo he Chen Wenlong de guanxi wenti" [Issues of my relationship with Chen Wenlong], June 9 and 10, 1968, XSG.

28. Zang Qiren, "Ziwo jiancha" [Self-criticism], June 12, 1968, XSG.

29. Zang Qiren, "Ziwo jiancha" [Self-criticism], June 17, 1968, XSG.

30. "Jiang Tao bilu" [Written records of Jiang Tao], September 16, 1968, XSG.

31. Zang Qiren, "Geren lishi jiaodai" [An account of personal history], December 25, 1968, XSG.

32. Jiang Tao, "Youguan Zang Qiren de qingkuang jiaodai" [Concerning Zang Qiren's account of circumstances], November 5, 1968, XSG.

33. Zang Qiren, "Guanyu wo lishi wenti de jiaodai" [Concerning the confessions of my historical problems], November 25, 1968, XSG.

34. Zang Qiren, "Buchong cailiao" [Additional materials], December 4, 1968, XSG.

35. Zang Qiren, "Geren lishi jiaodai" [An account of personal history], December 25, 1968, XSG.

36. "Zhang Ji'an guanyu wei Shaoxing xian Nanchi qu sanmin zhuyi qingnian tuan gaikuang" [An overview by Zhang Ji'an of the Three People's Principles Youth Corps in the collaborationist Nanchi District, Shaoxing County], January 18, 1969; "Lou Xing guanyu wei Nanchi qu qingnian zhandi fuwu dui qingkuang" [Concerning the situation of the Youth Battlefield Service Corps in the collaborationist Nanchi District by Lou Xing], January 19, 1969; Luo Kezhen, "Zhengming cailiao" [Evidence], January 17, 1969, in "Xuchang shi gongan jiguan junguanhui susong juanzong—Zang Qiren" [Xuchang municipal public security body military control's litigation file—Zang Qiren]; Xu Shuijing, "Guanyu Zang Qiren wenti de dafu" [Replies to the Zang Qiren question], February 3, 1969, XSG.

37. Zang Qiren, "Ziwo jiaodai" [Self-confession], June 17, 1970, in "Xuchang shi gongan jiguan junguanhui susong juanzong—Zang Qiren."

38. Zang Qiren, "Guanyu shouting ditai guangbo de jiaodai" [Confessions concerning listening to enemy radio], August 7, 1970, in "Xuchang shi gongan jiguan junguanhui susong juanzong—Zang Qiren."

39. Zang Qiren, "Qingkuang shuoming" [Explanation of circumstances], September 21, 1970, ZQR.

40. Zang Qiren, "Buchong shuoming" [Additional explanations], December 4, 1968, XSG.

41. "Zang Qiren zhi shi qinggongye zhuan'an zu" [From Zang Qiren to the Municipal Light Industries Bureau Special Investigations Group], January 22, 1972, ZQR.

42. Zang Qiren, "Tanbai shu" [Written confession], June 23, 1970, XSG.

43. Zang Qiren, "Wo zai shenghuo zuofeng shang de fanzui shishi xitong jiaodai" [My systematic confession of my lifestyle crimes], September 10, 1970, XSG.

44. Zang Qiren, "Wo fan yanzhong zuixing de genyuan" [The root of my serious crimes], September 16, 1970, ZQR, 29–39.

45. Zang Qiren, "Sixiang huibao" [Ideological report], October 3, 1971, ZQR, 61.

46. "Zang Qiren zhi shi qinggongye zhuan'anzu," January 22, 1972, ZQR, 46.

47. "Zhonggong Xuchang XX chang zongzhi weiyuanhui guanyu Zang Qiren wenti de shencha jielun he chuli yijian" [Xuchang XX factory Party Committee on the investigation conclusions and recommendations for dealing with the Zang Qiren question], April 14, 1972, ZQR, 54–55.

48. "Zuigao renmin fayuan guanyu chengnianren ziyuan jijian shifou fanzui wenti de pifu" [Supreme Court ruling on whether voluntary sodomy is a criminal matter], March 19, 1957, www.chinabaike.com/law/zhishi/yf/1421055.html.

49. See "Bugao" [Notice], January 21, 1977, ZQR, 3.

50. "Zhonggong Xuchang XX chang zongzhi wenyuanhui, Xuchang XX chang geming weiyuanhui guanyu Zang Qiren wenti chuli yijian de qingshi baogao"

[Report submitted by Xuchang XX factory Party Committee and the Xuchang XX factory revolutionary committee on recommendations of dealing with the Zang Qiren problem], August 1976, ZQR, 26.

51. Zang Qiren, "Sixiang huibao" [Ideological report], January 25, 1977, ZQR, 26.

52. Ibid.

53. "Bugao," January 21, 1977, ZQR, 3.

54. "Henan sheng Xuchang shi zhongji renmin fayuan xingshi panjue shu (77) faxingzi di 55 hao" [Criminal verdict (77) faxing number 55 of the Xuchang Municipal Intermediate People's Court, Henan Province], April 21, 1977, ZQR, 1.

2. Moving Targets

1. Lizhuang dadui diwu shengchan dui, *Guanyu Gao Qiwang you pinnong shangsheng wei er dizhu de cailiao* [Materials about Gao Qiwang rising from poor peasant to sub-landlord], May 30, 1966, Lankao County Office of Letters and Visits, Shanghai Jiaotong University History Department (hereafter abbreviated as LC), 22-3-3.

2. *Shencha cailiao zeren biao* [Investigation materials responsibility form], July 19, 1966, LC, 22-3-3. The Four Cleanups movement—which aimed to clean up politics, economy, ideology, and organization—is also known as the Socialist Education Movement. Following common usage in my sources, I use Four Cleanups in this chapter.

3. Henan sheng Lankao xian geming weiyuanhui, *Guanyu jiuzheng cuohua dizhu, funong chengfen de tongzhi* [Directive on correcting the class status of people mistakenly categorized as landlords and rich peasants], [1979] Lange jiuzi 3 hao, November 13, 1979, LC, 22-3-3.

4. Henan sheng Lankao xian difang shizhi bianzuan weiyuanhui, ed., *Lankao xianzhi* [Lankao County gazetteer] (Zhengzhou: Zhongzhou guji chubanshe, 1999), 59.

5. For an overview of land reform procedures and problems, see Richard Madsen, "The Countryside under Communism," in *The Cambridge History of China*, vol. 15, *The People's Republic, Part 2: Revolutions within the Chinese Revolution 1966–1982*, ed. Roderick MacFarquhar and John K. Fairbank (Cambridge: Cambridge University Press, 1991), 624–628.

6. "Zhonggong zhongyang guanyu tudi gaige zhong ge shehui jieji de huafen ji qi daiyu de guiding (cao'an)" [Party Center's draft regulation about the differentiation and treatment of each social class during land reform], April 27, 1948, in *Guanyu huafen nongcun jieji chengfen de jige wenjian* [Documents about differentiating rural class status], ed. Zhonggong Hebei shengwei siqing bangongshi (n.p., September 1964), 83–84. *Jiating chengfen* may have later morphed into the more commonly used "family background" (*jiating chushen*), but I have not seen

the latter term in class status differentiation documents from the late 1940s and 1950s.

7. For general and theoretical discussions, see Richard Curt Kraus, *Class Conflict in Chinese Socialism* (New York: Columbia University Press, 1981); and Jean-Francois Billeter, "The System of 'Class Status,'" in *The Scope of State Power in China,* ed. Stuart R. Schram (London: School of Oriental and African Studies, University of London, 1985), 127–169. For concrete examples of how class status labels affected everyday life in villages, see Anita Chan, Richard Madsen, and Jonathan Unger, *Chen Village: Revolution to Globalization,* 3rd ed. (Berkeley: University of California Press, 2009); and Jonathan Unger, "The Class System in Rural China: A Case Study," in *Class and Social Stratification in Post-Revolution China,* ed. James L. Watson (New York: Cambridge University Press, 1984), 121–141.

8. Geoffrey C. Bowker and Susan Leigh Star, *Sorting Things Out: Classification and Its Consequences* (Cambridge, MA: MIT Press, 1999), 53–54.

9. Ibid., 53.

10. China's population was at least 700,000,000 in 1966, and about 90 percent rural (630,000,000). Even if the Four Cleanups movement "had been completed in only about one-third of China's rural villages before the initiation of the Cultural Revolution," as Baum writes, the movement still affected at least 207,900,000 people. If between 1 and 5 percent of that number experienced a change in class status, the total comes to a low estimate of 2,079,000 and a high of 10,395,000. Richard Baum, *Prelude to Revolution: Mao, the Party, and the Peasant Question, 1962–66* (New York: Columbia University Press, 1975), 205n9.

11. Michael Schoenhals argues convincingly that relying on conventional assumptions about the "Cultural Revolution" can lead to misleading or inaccurate conclusions. I use the term in this chapter because people at the time used it to describe what was happening around them. See Schoenhals, "Is the Cultural Revolution Really Necessary?" in *China's Communist Revolutions: Fifty Years of the People's Republic of China,* ed. Werner Draguhn and David S. G. Goodman (New York: RoutledgeCurzon, 2002), 159–176.

12. Zhonggong zhongyang wenxian yanjiushi, ed., *Jianguo yilai Mao Zedong wengao* [Mao Zedong's manuscripts since the founding of the People's Republic of China], vol. 9 (Beijing: Zhongyang wenxian chubanshe, 1996), 349. Yang Jisheng attributes the first appearance of the phrase "the democratic revolution is incomplete" to a June 1960 report from the Handan Municipal Party Committee in Hebei Province and suggests that Liu Shaoqi may have used the wording before Mao. Yang Jisheng, *Mubei: Zhongguo liushi niandai dajihuang jishi* [Tombstone: A true history of the great famine in 1960s China], 6th ed. (Hong Kong: Cosmos Books, 2009), 2:1020, 1027n47.

13. Zhang Shufan, "Xinyang shijian: yige chentong de lishi jiaoxun" [The Xinyang incident: A painful historical lesson] *Bainianchao* 6 (1998): 43; Yang Jisheng, *Mubei,* 22–23.

14. Qiao Peihua, *Xinyang shijian* [The Xinyang incident] (Hong Kong: Kaifang chubanshe, 2009).

15. Zhonggong zhongyang wenxian yanjiushi, *Jianguo yilai Mao Zedong wengao*, vol. 9 (1996): 408–409.

16. *Jiuzheng cuohua dizhu, funong chengfen dengjibiao, 1–85 hao, 1979 de ren* [Registration form correcting the class status of mistakenly classified landlords and rich peasants, numbers 1–85, people from 1979], LC, 22–3–27. In this table of contents from Lankao County, thirty-nine out of eighty-five people listed had labels changed during the movement to reform the third type of brigade.

17. Henan sheng Lankao xian difang shizhi bianzuan weiyuanhui, *Lankao xianzhi*, 187.

18. Zhonggong zhongyang wenxian yanjiushi, ed., *Jianguo yilai zhongyao wenxian xuanbian* [Selected important documents since the founding of the People's Republic of China], vol. 1 (Beijing: Zhongyang wenxian chubanshe, 1992), 385.

19. Lankao xian Xiaosong renmin gongshe geming weiyuanhui, *Guanyu Guo Zhaotai zai 60 nian minzhu buke shi bei huading wei louwang dizhu de diaocha baogao* [Investigation report about Guo Zhaotai being categorized as a landlord who slipped through the net during the remedial course in democracy of 1960], October 13, 1979, LC, 22–3–17.

20. Yanlou renmin gongshe Xiaolizhuang dadui geming weiyuanhui, *Zuotan bilu* [Transcript of meeting], October 12, 1979, LC, 22–3–17. It is unclear whether Guo was sentenced to labor reform or to prison. He did not, however, serve a full sentence of fifteen years, because in 1972 he moved to a village six kilometers away from Xiaolizhuang.

21. Kong Lingfa, *Zhengming cailiao* [Testimony materials], April 2, 1979, LC, 22–3–17.

22. Guo Zhaotai, *Shensu shu* [Letter of appeal], April 1, 1979, LC, 22–3–17.

23. Felix Wemheuer has reported that local cadres in Henan were unhappy that they were treated as "scapegoats." Felix Wemheuer, "Dealing with Responsibility for the Great Leap Famine," *China Quarterly* 201 (March 2010): 187–188.

24. Literally "hat," I translate *maozi* as "label" because it referred to a punitive moniker that could be removed or reinstated.

25. On post-Leap rectification and the Socialist Education Movement, see Frederick C. Teiwes, *Politics and Purges in China: Rectification and the Decline of Party Norms* (White Plains, NY: M.E. Sharpe, 1979).

26. Baum, *Prelude to Revolution*; Roderick MacFarquhar, *The Origins of the Cultural Revolution, Vol. 3: The Coming of the Cataclysm, 1961–1966* (New York: Columbia University Press, 1997), 419–430.

27. Richard Baum and Frederick C. Teiwes, *Ssu-Ch'ing: The Socialist Education Movement of 1962–1966* (Berkeley: Center for Chinese Studies, University of California, 1968), 83.

28. Zhonggong zhongyang wenxian yanjiushi, *Jianguo yilai zhongyao wenxian xuanbian,* vol. 19 (1998), 231.

29. Ibid., 246. Emphasis mine.

30. Bo Yibo, *Ruogan zhongda juece yu shijian de huigu* [Reflections on certain major decisions and events] (Beijing: Zhonggong dangshi chubanshe, 2008 [1993]), 2:785.

31. Bo Yibo, *Ruogan zhongda juece yu shijian de huigu,* 2:790–791.

32. Jeremy Brown, *City versus Countryside in Mao's China: Negotiating the Divide* (New York: Cambridge University Press, 2012), 122.

33. MacFarquhar, *The Origins of the Cultural Revolution: Vol. 3,* 427.

34. Zhonggong zhongyang wenxian yanjiushi, *Jianguo yilai zhongyao wenxian xuanbian,* vol. 19 (1998), 18–30.

35. For example, Renmin chubanshe, ed., *Zenyang fenxi nongcun jieji* [How to do class analysis in villages] (Beijing: Renmin chubanshe, 1964 [1963]), was first printed in Beijing in December 1963 and reprinted in Tianjin in October 1964; Zhonggong Hebei shengwei siqing bangongshi, *Guanyu huafen nongcun jieji chengfen de jige wenjian;* Zhonggong Tianjin shiwei jiaoqu siqing gongzuo zong-tuan, *Shehuizhuyi jiaoyu xuexi wenjian* [Socialist education study documents] (n.p., January 1966).

36. The second list was posted in May 1965, and a villager mentioned a third list but did not provide a date. Houjiaying's class archives were filled out in August 1965. Letter of appeal from Liu Binqing to Mao Zedong Thought Propaganda Corps, Revolutionary Committee, and poor and lower-middle peasant comrades, January 13, 1969, Houjiaying Files, Chinese Social History Center, Nankai University (hereafter cited as HJY), A–10–13; *Hebei sheng Changli xian Nijing gongshe Houjiaying dadui di yi shengchan dui jieji chengfen dengjibiao* [Class reg-istration form for the number 1 production team, Houjiaying Brigade, Nijing Commune, Changli County, Hebei Province], August 25, 1965, HJY, F–37–1.

37. LC, 22–3–3.

38. Su Weimin, "Ting Yang Shangkun tan 'siqing'" [Listening to Yang Shangkun discuss the "Four Cleanups"], *Bainianchao* 10 (2007): 13.

39. Ibid., 13–14.

40. Edward Friedman, Paul G. Pickowicz, and Mark Selden, *Revolution, Resistance, and Reform in Village China* (New Haven, CT: Yale University Press, 2005), 54.

41. Zhonggong zhongyang wenxian yanjiushi, *Jianguo yilai zhongyao wenxian xuanbian,* vol. 18 (1998), 584.

42. Kaifeng xian Baliwan gongshe Liutie dadui Liutiecun di liu shengchandui, *Jieji chengfen dengji bo* [Class status registry], May 18, 1966, author's collection.

43. HJY, F–32–2.

44. Ibid. Neil Diamant shows that military service often did not translate into tangible benefits in the People's Republic. Neil J. Diamant, *Veterans, Military*

Families, and the Politics of Patriotism in China, 1949–2007 (Lanham, MD: Rowman & Littlefield, 2009).

45. Diwu shengchandui, *Guanyu Gao Qiwang*, May 30, 1966, LC, 22–3–3.

46. Ibid.

47. I assume that Gao dictated the self-criticism, because he described himself as "illiterate." His name chop appears at the end. *Gao Qiwang ziwo jiancha cailiao* [Gao Qiwang self-criticism materials], June 10, 1966, LC, 22–3–3.

48. Qin Xinde, *Kongsu shu* [Letter of appeal], April 9, 1966, LC, 22–3–10.

49. Zhuaying si dadui siqing gongzuo zu, *Guanyu Qin Xinde dizhu chengfen de er ci diaocha chuli yijian* [Opinion on handling the second investigation of Qin Xinde's landlord status], May 1, 1966, LC, 22–3–10.

50. Qin Xinde, *Qingshi cailiao* [Materials in support of my request], April 28, 1979, LC, 22–3–10.

51. Zhonggong Zhuaying gongshe weiyuanhui, *Guanyu Qin Xinde jiating chengfen wenti de qingshi baogao* [Report requesting instructions about Qin Xinde's family status problem], May 1, 1979, LC, 22–3–10.

52. *Zhonggong zhongyang guanyu duidai wuchan jieji wenhua da geming zhong gongzuo zu wenti de tongzhi* [Party Center directive addressing the question of work teams during the Great Proletarian Cultural Revolution], *Zhongfa* [67] 54 *hao*, February 17, 1967, in *Zhongguo wenhua da geming wenku* (Chinese Cultural Revolution database, hereafter cited as WDGW), ed. Song Yongyi (Hong Kong: Xianggang Zhongwen daxue Zhongguo yanjiu fuwu zhongxin, 2002), CD-ROM.

53. *Zhonggong zhongyang guanyu baowei siqing yundong chengguo de tongzhi* [Party Center directive about protecting the achievements of the Four Cleanups movement], *Zhongfa* [67] 30 *hao*, January 25, 1967, in WDGW.

54. *Hongqi zazhi* pinglun yuan, *Baowei siqing yundong de weida chengguo* [Protect the great achievements of the Four Cleanups movement], March 5, 1967, in WDGW.

55. There were four sons in the family, but one was not considered a member of the household during the class status registration.

56. HJY, F–37–1.

57. Letter from Liu Binqing to Nijing Four Cleanups work team Party Committee and Nijing Commune Party Committee, September 2, 1965, HJY, F–5.

58. Billeter, "The System of 'Class Status,'" 128.

59. Letter from Liu Binqing to Chairman Mao, October 31, 1965, HJY, F–2.

60. Letter from Liu Binqing to Nijing Commune, September 25, 1965, HJY, F–5.

61. Letter of appeal from Liu Binqing to Mao Zedong Thought Propaganda Corps, Revolutionary Committee, and poor and lower-middle peasant comrades, January 13, 1969, HJY, A–10–13.

62. Liu Binqing letter, April 20, 1966, HJY, A–14–2.

63. Letter from Liu Binqing to parents, February 23, 1966, sent from Four Cleanups work team in Xuanhua County, HJY, A–14–1.

64. Letter from Houjiaying Four Cleanups work team to Nijing Commune Four Cleanups work team, June 30, 1966, HJY, B–5–7. A mass meeting announcing the change was held on July 23, 1966.

65. HJY, A–13–10.

66. *Jiancha Liu Binxiang* [Liu Binxiang's self-criticism], August 2, 1966, HJY, C–1–4–3.

67. Letter from Liu Binqing to Shuili ting zhengzhi chu, Zhujun zhizuo bangongshi, January 1, 1968, HJY, A–15–12.

68. HJY, F–2.

69. HJY, B–9–14.

70. Letter from Liu Binqing to Liu Binxiang, April 20, 1967, HJY, A–10–18.

71. HJY, A–15–12.

72. Ibid.

73. HJY, A–10–13.

74. HJY, F–2.

75. *Renmin ribao* [People's Daily, hereafter cited as RMRB], January 19, 1979, 1.

76. The Cleansing the Class Ranks campaign was important in many villages and was as varied and confused as the Four Cleanups. As in remedial democracy and the Four Cleanups, family histories were twisted and reinterpreted during the Cleansing the Class Ranks campaign. See Roderick MacFarquhar and Michael Schoenhals, *Mao's Last Revolution* (Cambridge, MA: Belknap Press of Harvard University Press, 2006), 253–262; and Chan, Madsen, and Unger, *Chen Village*.

77. Hu Qiaomu, "Guanyu shehuizhuyi shiqi jieji douzheng de yixie tifa wenti" [On questions of formulation about class struggle during the socialist period], January 3, 1979, *Xinhuawang*, http://news.xinhuanet.com/ziliao/2005-02/05/content_2550214.htm.

78. *Zhonggong zhongyang guanyu dizhu funong fenzi zhaimao wenti he difu zinü chengfen wenti de jueding* [Party Center decision about the problem of removing labels from landlord and rich peasant elements and the status of children of landlords and rich peasants], *Zhongfa* (1979) 5 *hao*, January 11, 1979, in WDGW.

79. RMRB, January 30, 1979, 2.

80. Gao Laicheng, *Shangsu cailiao* [Petition materials], January 22, 1979, LC, 22–3–3.

81. Zhuaying gongshe geming weiyuanhui, *Guanyu Gao Qiwang jiating chengfen wenti de diaocha baogao* [Investigation report about Gao Qiwang's family status problem], October 23, 1979, LC, 22–3–3.

82. Zhonggong Zhuaying gongshe weiyuanhui, *Guanyu Ren Bowen jiating chengfen wenti de diaocha baogao* [Investigation report about Ren Bowen's family status problem], November 1, 1979, LC, 22–3–11.

3. An Overt Conspiracy

1. Notable scholarship on the Anti-Rightist Movement includes Roderick MacFarquhar, *The Hundred Flowers Campaign and the Chinese Intellectuals* (New York: Praeger, 1960); Roderick MacFarquhar, *The Origins of the Cultural Revolution, Vol. 1: Contradictions among the People, 1956–1957* (New York: Columbia University Press, 1974); Zhu Di, *1957 nian da zhuanwan zhi mi: zhengfeng fanyou shilu* [The mystery of China's great turning point in 1957: Annals of the rectification and anti-rightist movements] (Taiyuan: Shanxi renmin chubanshe, 1995); Ding Shu, *Yinmou: fanyoupai yundong shimo* [Covert conspiracy: The Anti-Rightist Movement from beginning to end] (Hong Kong: Kaifang zazhi she, 2006); Ding Shu, ed., *Wushi nian hou chongping "fanyou": Zhongguo dangdai zhishifenzi de mingyun* [Rethinking the Anti-Rightist Movement fifty years later: The fate of intellectuals in contemporary China] (Hong Kong: Tianyuan shuwu, 2007); Shen Zhihua, *Zhonghua renmin gongheguo shi, di san juan, Sikao yu xuanze—Cong zhishifenzi huiyi dao fanyoupai yundong (1956–1957)* [The History of the People's Republic of China, vol. 3, Reflections and Choices—from the Conference on Intellectuals to the Anti-Rightist Movement (1956–1957)] (Hong Kong: Xianggang Zhongwen daxue dangdai Zhongguo wenhua yanjiu zhongxin, 2008); Wu Xiaotao, "Guonei fanyoupai yundong yanjiu pingshu" [Assessment of mainland research on the Anti-Rightist Movement), *Jiangsu keji daxue xuebao* 8, no. 1 (March 2008): 26–31; and Zhonggong zhongyang dangshi yanjiushi, ed., *Zhongguo gongchandang lishi, di er juan, 1949–1978* [History of the Chinese Communist Party, vol. 2, 1949–1978), part 1 (Beijing: Zhonggong dangshi chubanshe, 2011), 453.

2. *Renmin ribao* [People's Daily], June 8, 1957, 1.

3. Song Yongyi, ed., *Zhongguo fanyou yundong shujuku, 1957–* [Chinese Anti-Rightist Campaign Database, 1957–), CD-ROM (Hong Kong: Universities Service Centre for China Studies, The Chinese University of Hong Kong, 2010).

4. "Nanyang jiaoyu: jiaoyu lingyu de fanyoupai douzheng" [Nanyang education: The anti-rightist struggle in the educational sector), originally posted at "Renwen Nanyang" [Nanyang people and culture], a website of the Nanyang Municipal Party Committee Propaganda Department no longer available online.

5. Zhonggong Tongbai xian weiyuanhui, "Guanyu dui youpai ji youqing cuowu renyuan de zhenbie jielun" [Conclusions upon reinvestigating rightists and people with rightist-tendency mistakes], May–July 1962, Tongbai County Archives [hereafter cited as TCA], 3–1–15–368.

6. Zhonggong Nanyang diwei dangshi weiyuanhui, ed., *Zhongguo Gongchandang Nanyang diqu lishi dashiji* [Chronology of the history of the Chinese Communist Party in Nanyang Prefecture] (Beijing: Zhonggong dangshi chubanshe, 1995), 199.

7. "Nanyang jiaoyu: jiaoyu lingyu de fanyoupai douzheng."

8. Zhonggong Tongbai xianwei, "Xianwei guanyu zuohao zhengfeng yundong de san dian zhishi" [The county committee's three-point instructions on the proper implementation of the rectification movement), May 20, 1957, TCA, 3–1–157.

9. Zhonggong Tongbai xianwei, "Xianwei guanyu zai quanxian fanweinei kaizhan zhengfeng yundong de chubu fang'an (cao'an)" [The county committee's preliminary program of the rectification movement launched within the entire county (draft)], September 17, 1957, TCA, 3–1–155.

10. See Cao Shuji and Liao Liying, "Guojia, nongmin yu 'yuliang': Tongbai xian de tonggou tongxiao (1953–1955)" [The state, the peasants, and 'excess grain': The state grain monopoly in Tongbai County, 1953–1955], *Xin shixue*, no. 3 (2011): 155–213.

11. Zhonggong Tongbai xianwei bangongshi, "Dui dangqian xuexi zhong jige wenti de baogao" [Report on several issues in the current study session], October 5, 1957, TCA, 3–1–157.

12. Ibid.

13. Ibid.

14. Zhonggong Tongbai xian weiyuanhui, "Guanyu sanji ganbu huiyi mingfang qingkuang baogao" [Report on the airing of views in the three-level cadres meeting], n.d., TCA, 3–1–145.

15. Ge Jinglu, "Zhonggong Tongbai xianwei gongzuo baogao" [Tongbai County committee work report], December 17, 1957, TCA, 3–1–142.

16. Zhonggong Tongbai xianwei bangongshi, ed., *Zhenggai jianbao* [Rectification bulletin], no. 2, December 19, 1957, TCA, 3–1–146.

17. Zhonggong Tongbai xian weiyuanhui, "Guanyu sanji ganbu huiyi zhengfeng he fanyoupai douzheng de zongjie (caogao)" [Regarding the conclusions of the rectification and anti-rightist struggle during the three-level cadres meeting (draft)], January 17, 1958, TCA, 3–1–145.

18. "Guanyu chexiao Pingshi qu lingdao xiaozu zuzhang Cao Qisheng de zhiwu de jueding" [Concerning the decision to strip Pingshi District leading group leader Cao Qisheng of his post], ed. Zhonggong Tongbai xianwei bangongshi, *Zhenggai jianbao* [Rectification bulletin], no. 3, December 20, 1957, TCA, 3–1–146.

19. Zhonggong Tongbai xian weiyuanhui, "Guanyu sanji ganbu huiyi zhengfeng he fanyoupai douzheng de zongjie (caogao)."

20. Zhonggong Tongbai xianwei, "Xianwei guanyu zai quanxian fanweinei kaizhan zhengfeng yundong de chubu fang'an (cao'an)."

21. Zhonggong Tongbai xianwei zhengfeng bangongshi, "Dui youpai fenzi zuzhi chuli gongzuo zongjie" [Conclusion of the organization and processing work of rightist elements], July 29, 1958, TCA, 3–1–159.

22. All material about the views aired at the December rectification meeting is from Zhonggong Tongbai xian weiyuanhui, "Xianwei sanji ganbu zhengfeng huiyi

zhongceng lingdao ganbu he weisheng xitong mingfang zuotan huiyi jilu" [Records of the airing-of-views meetings for middle-ranking leaders and cadres and the hygiene sector in the three-level rectification meetings of the county committee], n.d., TCA, 3-1-143.

23. Zhonggong Tongbai xianwei bangongshi, "Dui zichan jieji youpai fenzi Lu Jinfu kaizhan dahui douzheng de qingkuang baogao" [Report on the struggle meeting convened against the bourgeois rightist Lu Jinfu], January 14, 1958, TCA, 3-1-145.

24. Ye Fangying, "Wo jia chule liangge youpai" [My family produced two rightists], in *Huanghe* [Yellow River] 2, no. 78 (1999): 66–76; Li Shugang, "Yijiuwuqi nian Xinyang xian zhongxiaoxue jiaoshi fanyou suoyi" [Miscellaneous recollections of the anti-rightist movement of secondary and elementary schoolteachers in Xinyang County in 1957], in *Xinyang wenshi ziliao* [Historical materials on Xianyang], 10:165–167; and Feng Xianzhi, "Yi wo zai jiaoshi zhengfeng fanyou yundong zhong de jingli" [Recollections of my experiences in the rectification and anti-rightist movements among schoolteachers], in *Xinyang wenshi ziliao* [Historical materials on Xianyang], 10:170–175.

25. Ye Fangying, "Wo jia chule liangge youpai," 66.

26. Zhang Bojun (1895–1969) was chairman of the China Peasants' and Workers' Party and had served as transportation minister during the 1950s; Luo Longji (1896–1965) was an official in the China Democratic League and had served as minister of forestry; Chu Anping (1909–1966?) was editor of *Guangming Daily*.

27. Ye Fangying, "Wo jia chule liangge youpai," 68.

28. Feng Xianzhi, "Yi wo zai jiaoshi zhengfeng fanyou yundong zhong de jingli," 171.

29. Ye Fangying, "Wo jia chule liangge youpai," 68–69.

30. Ibid., 69.

31. Ibid., 69–70.

32. Li Shugang, "Yijiuwuqi nian Xinyang xian zhongxiaoxue jiaoshi fanyou suoyi," 167.

33. Ye Fangying, "Wo jia chule liangge youpai," 71–72.

34. Ibid., 73

35. Zhonggong Tongbai xian weiyuanhui, "Guanyu wenjiao, gongshangjie zhengfeng huiyi de jianbao" [A brief report on the rectification meeting for the educational and business sectors], January 14, 1958, TCA, 3-1-175.

36. Zhonggong Tongbai xian weiyuanhui, "Guanyu wenjiao, gongshangjie zhengfeng huiyi daming dafang de zongjie jianbao" [A brief concluding report on the rectification meeting for the educational and business sectors to air their views], January 14, 1958, TCA, 3-1-174.

37. Zhonggong Tongbai xianwei zhengfeng bangongshi, "Kaizhan ziyou bianlun, dianding xiabu duidi douzheng jichu" [Begin free debates to lay the foundation for the struggle against the enemy in the next step], January 17, 1958, TCA, 3-1-176.

38. Zhonggong Tongbai xian weiyuanhui zhengfeng bangongshi, "Tongbai xian zhongxiaoxue jiaoshi jiaoxin yundong de jianbao" [Bulletin of the "Opening your hearts to the Party" campaign among Tongbai County secondary and elementary schoolteachers], June 5, 1958, TCA, 3-1-177.

39. Zhonggong Tongbai xian weiyuanhui zhengfeng bangongshi, "Xuexiao jiaoxin yundong banyue lai qingkuang jianbao" [Bulletin on the situation after half a month of the "Opening your hearts to the Party" campaign in schools], July 4, 1958, TCA, 3-1-177.

40. Zhonggong Tongbai xianwei, "Guanyu dui youpai ji youqing cuowu renyuan de zhenbie jielun."

41. "Nanyang jiaoyu: jiaoyu lingyu de fanyoupai douzheng."

42. The prominent rightists from the central level who were not rehabilitated include Zhang Bojun, Luo Longji, Peng Wenying, Chu Anping, and Chen Renbing. See http://www.hudong.com/wiki/反右运动.

4. Revising Political Verdicts in Post-Mao China

The author gratefully acknowledges funding for this research by the Bavarian Academy of Sciences. He further thanks the editors and two anonymous reviewers for their very helpful comments. The epigraph is from Deng Xiaoping, "Emancipate the Mind: Seek Truth from Facts and Unite as One in Looking to the Future," in *Selected Works of Deng Xiaoping* (1975–1982) (Beijing: Foreign Languages Press, 1984), 157–158.

1. A recent overview is presented by Klaus Mühlhahn, *Criminal Justice in China: A History* (Cambridge, MA: Harvard University Press, 2009).

2. Dai Huang, *Hu Yaobang yu pingfan yuan jia cuo an* [Hu Yaobang and the reversal of unjust, false, and wrong cases] (Beijing: Zhongguo gongren chubanshe, 2004), and Xiao Donglian, *Lishi de zhuanzhe: cong boluan fanzheng dao gaige kaifang (1979–1981)* [Turning Point in History: From Bringing Order out of Chaos to Reform and Opening Up] (Hong Kong: Chinese University Press, 2008).

3. A notable exception, yet without court files, is Sue Trevaskes, "People's Justice and Injustice: Courts and the Redressing of Cultural Revolution Cases," *China Information* 16, no. 2 (2002): 1–26.

4. Beijing shi Fengtai qu renmin fayuan (BFRF), "Guanyu Wang XX wenti de fucha yijian" [Reexamination remarks regarding the problems of Wang XX], December 13, 1978. The court verdicts always contain the full names of the accused. To protect privacy rights, I have anonymized the accounts by replacing given names with "XX" throughout.

5. BFRF, "Guanyu Li XX wenti de fucha baogao" [Reexamination report regarding the problems of Li XX], December 13, 1978.

6. BFRF, "Guanyu dui fangeming fenzi Zhang XX yi an de fucha yijian" [Reexamination remarks regarding the case of the counterrevolutionary Zhang XX], February 21, 1979.

7. BFRF, "Dui Liu XX an de fucha yijian" [Reexamination remarks regarding the case of Liu XX], December 13, 1978.

8. Ibid.

9. Zhongyang pizhuan Zhonggong zui gao renmin fayuan dangzu, "Guanyu zhuajin fucha jiuzheng yuan, jia, cuo an renzhen luoshi dang de zhengce de qingshi baogao" [Report concerning the importance of revising and correcting unjust, false, and wrong cases and of earnestly implementing Party policies], *Zhongfa* [1978] 78, December 29, 1978, text available at http://www.reformdata .org/index.php?m=wap&c=index&a=show&catid=301&typeid=0&id=16516& remains=true.

10. Zhonggong zhongyang he guowuyuan, "Guanyu zai wenhua da geming zhong jiaqiang gongan gongzuo de ruogan guiding" [Several rules concerning the strengthening of public security work during the Great Proletarian Cultural Revolution], *Zhongfa* [67] 19, January 13, 1967, in *Zhongguo wenhua da geming wenku* (Chinese Cultural Revolution database, hereafter cited as WDGW), ed. Song Yongyi (Hong Kong: Xianggang Zhongwen daxue Zhongguo yanjiu fuwu zhongxin, 2002), CD-ROM.

11. Zui gao renmin fayuan, "Guanyu chuli jingshenbing huanzhe fanzui wenti de fuhan" [Reply on how to handle the question of criminal acts committed by mentally ill persons], June 2, 1956, author's collection.

12. On the history of China's political psychiatry see Robin Munro, *China's Psychiatric Inquisition: Dissent, Psychiatry, and the Law in Post-1949 China* (London: Wildy, Simmonds and Hill, 2006).

13. Zhonggong zhongyang pizhuan zui gao renmin fayuan dangzu, "Guanyu shanshi shanzhong de wancheng fucha jiuzheng yuan jia cuo an gongzuo ji ge wenti de qingshi baogao" [Report and request concerning certain questions about starting and ending well the work of completing the reexamination and correction of unjust, false, and wrong cases], *Zhongfa* [79] 96, December 31, 1979, in WDGW.

14. Courts handled 1.2 million cases, and public security organs another 795,000 cases; see Zhonggong zhongyang bangongting zhuan gong, jian, fa san dangzu, "Guanyu jin yi bu fucha pingfan zhengfa xitong jingshou banli de yuan, jia, cuo an de yijian de baogao" [Report concerning opinions about the further reversal and rehabilitation of unjust, false, and wrong cases handled by the political-legal system], *Zhongbanfa* [1983] 9, January 25, 1983, in WDGW.

15. He Lanjie and Lu Mingjian, eds., *Dangdai Zhongguo de shenpan gongzuo* [Trial work in contemporary China] (Beijing: Dangdai Zhongguo chubanshe, 1993), 1:148.

16. See Frederick C. Teiwes, *Politics and Purges in China: Rectification and the Decline of Party Norms, 1950–1965* (New York: M.E. Sharpe, 1979).

17. See Zhonggong zhongyang pizhuan gonganbu, "Guanyu gongan xitong luoshi ganbu zhengce qingkuang he yijian de baogao" (gaiyao) [Report concerning certain opinions and the situation of implementing cadre policies in the public security system (summary)], July 9, 1972, in WDGW.

18. Most prominently the article entitled "Wufa wutian zan" [In praise of lawlessness], *People's Daily*, January 31, 1967, 6.

19. Zhonggong zhongyang wenxian yanjiu shi, ed., *Jianguo yilai Mao Zedong wengao* [Mao Zedong's post-1949 manuscripts], vol. 13, 1969–1976 (Beijing: Zhongyang wenxian chubanshe, 1998), 334–335.

20. Ibid.

21. Beijing shi gonganju Chongwen fenju "Beijing Chongwen gongan shiliao" bianji, ed., *Beijing Chongwen gongan shiliao* [Historical materials on Beijing Chongwen public security] (Beijing: Neibu ziliao, 2001) 2:706.

22. Ibid.

23. See He Zai, *Yuan jia cuo an shi zheyang pingfan de* [This is how the unjust, false, and wrong cases were reversed] (Beijing: Zhonggong zhongyang dangxiao chubanshe, 1999), 208.

24. See Shao-Chuan Leng and Hungdah Chiu, *Criminal Justice in Post-Mao China: Analysis and Documents* (Albany: State University of New York Press, 1985), 299–303.

25. See *The Criminal Law and the Criminal Procedure Law of the People's Republic of China* (Beijing: Foreign Languages Press, 1984).

26. Beijing Fengtai qu difangzhi bianzuan weiyuanhui, ed., *Beijing shi Fengtai qu zhi* [Beijing Fengtai District gazetteer] (Beijing: Beijing chubanshe, 2001), 260.

27. Ji Tai, ed., *Beijing shi Fengtai qu jiexiang gaikuang* [Survey of Beijing Fengtai District's lanes and alleys] (Beijing: Zhishi chubanshe, 1994), 6.

28. Ibid., 3–4.

29. BFRF, "Guanyu Yang XX fan fangeming daoqie zui de fucha baogao" (Reexamination report concerning convict Yang XX's crime of counterrevolutionary theft), August 7, 1979, 1–2.

30. See Beijing Fengtai qu difangzhi bianzuan weiyuanhui, *Beijing shi Fengtai qu zhi*, 49.

31. The Military Control Committee was finally abolished in September 1973, ibid., 241.

32. See Carlos Wing-hung Lo, *China's Legal Awakening: Legal Theory and Criminal Justice in Deng's Era* (Hong Kong: Hong Kong University Press, 1995), 77.

33. Leng and Chiu, *Criminal Justice*, 22. See also Liao Junchang, "Duli shenpan yu shuji pi'an" [Independent trials and approving cases by secretary], *Xiandai faxue* 1 (1979): 6.

34. BFRF, "Guanyu Xi XX yi an de fucha qingshi baogao" [Report and request concerning the reexamination of the case of Xi XX], February 9, 1979.

35. Ibid., 2.

36. Ibid., 3.

37. Beijing Fengtai qu difangzhi bianzuan weiyuanhui, *Beijing shi Fengtai qu zhi,* 257.

38. See, for example, *Beijing Chongwen gongan shiliao* 2:737.

39. *Zhongfa* [1979] 96.

40. Ibid.

41. Beijing Fengtai qu difangzhi bianzuan weiyuanhui, *Beijing shi Fengtai qu zhi,* 260.

42. BFRF, "Guanyu dui fangeming Tan XX yi an de fucha baogao" [Reexamination report about the case of counterrevolutionary Tan XX], December 15, 1978.

43. Ibid., 2.

44. Ibid., 3.

45. The criterion of being "actively" caught in the act of spreading critical views or attacking Party policies fits both designations and cannot meaningfully be applied in these cases.

46. BFRF, "Guanyu Liu XX wenti de fucha baogao" [Reexamination report concerning the question of Liu XX], December 13, 1978.

47. BFRF, "Guanyu Song XX, Li XX yi an de fucha qingshi baogao" [Report and request concerning the reexamination of the case of Song XX and Li XX], February 9, 1979, 2.

48. Ibid., 1.

49. BFRF, "Guanyu Wang XX an fucha chuli yijian de qingshi baogao" [Report and request concerning opinions about reexamining and handling the case of Wang XX], December 13, 1978.

50. Ibid.

51. Among the present case materials is one example of a former landlord from Daxing County who unsuccessfully tried to form a gang to avenge the murder; see BFRF, "Guanyu Yang XX fangeming fucha yijian de baogao" [Report about opinions concerning the reexamination of counterrevolutionary Yang XX], February 6, 1979.

52. BFRF, "Guanyu Shen XX fan xianxing fangeming zui de fucha baogao" [Reexamination report concerning convict Shen XX's active counterrevolutionary crimes], July 1979.

53. Ibid.

54. BFRF, "Guanyu fucha Ren XX yi an de qingshi baogao" [Report and request concerning the reexamination of Ren XX's case], December 13, 1978.

55. BFRF, "Guanyu dui xianxing fangeming Zhao XX de chuxing yijian" [Preliminary opinions concerning active counterrevolutionary Zhao XX], December 6, 1977.

56. BFRF, "Guanyu dui Wei XX an fucha yijian de qingshi baogao" [Report and request concerning opinions about reexamining the case of Wei XX], December 15, 1978.

57. *Zhongfa* [1978] 78.

58. Ibid.

59. BFRF, "Guanyu Zhang XX fan xianxing fangeming zui de fucha baogao" [Reexamination report concerning convict Zhang XX's active counter-revolutionary crime], August 7, 1979.

60. BFRF, "Guanyu dui Fu XX fan jieji baofu daren zui de fucha baogao" [Reexamination report concerning convict Fu XX's crime of attacking others out of class vengeance], February 21, 1979.

61. BFRF, "Guanyu Gao XX fan fangeming jieji baofu zui de fucha baogao" [Reexamination report concerning convict Gao XX's counterrevolutionary class vengeance crime], August 1, 1979.

62. BFRF, "Guanyu dui Wu XX fan fangeming zui de fucha baogao" [Reexamination report concerning convict Wu XX's counterrevolutionary crime], March 1, 1979.

63. BFRF, "Guanyu dui Xie XX fan fangeming zui de fucha baogao" [Reexamination report concerning convict Xie XX's counterrevolutionary crime], February 14, 1979, 2.

64. Ibid.

65. BFRF, "Guanyu dui Zhou XX wenti de fucha baogao" [Reexamination report concerning the problem of Zhou XX], February 14, 1979.

66. BFRF, "Guanyu dui Wu XX fan fangeming," 2.

67. Ibid.

68. BFRF, "Guanyu dui Zhou XX wenti," 2.

69. BFRF, "Guanyu dui Wu XX fan fangeming zui de fucha baogao" [Reexamination report concerning convict Wu XX's counterrevolutionary crime], February 14, 1979, 2.

70. BFRF, "Guanyu dui Xie XX fan fangeming," 2.

71. *Zhongfa* [1979] 96.

72. BFRF, "Guanyu fangeming sharen fan Wang XX de fucha baogao" [Reexamination report concerning counterrevolutionary murderer Wang XX], December 13, 1978.

73. See the reprint of the document with accompanying commentary in the Supreme Court's internal journal *Renmin sifa* 1 (1978): 30.

74. BFRF, "Guanyu Yang XX fan fangeming daoqie zui," 1–2.

75. A pagoda in Hangzhou under which, according to the popular *Legend of the White Snake*, a captive spirit was held.

76. Mao Anlong (1927–1931) was the third son of Mao Zedong and Yang Kaihui. He died of dysentery in Shanghai in 1931 after being moved there with his two brothers in the wake of the execution of his mother by Guomindang troops.

Nevertheless, several legends have obscured his fate and given rise to rumors and impostors.

77. The legendary palace of moon goddess Chang'e.

78. BFRF, "Guanyu Yang XX fan fangeming daoqie zui de fucha baogao" [Reexamination report concerning convict Yang XX's crime of counter-revolutionary theft], 3.

79. For the publicized diary of Chen Lining and contemporary speeches by central leaders see the multiple editions of "Xin shidai de 'kuangren'" ['Mad man' of the new era] (Wuhan: printed pamphlet, May 1967).

80. *Zhongfa* [1979] 96.

81. For a general introduction see Ruti G. Teitel, *Transitional Justice* (Oxford: Oxford University Press, 2000). For the case of China see Thomas Richter, *China* (= *Strafrecht in Reaktion auf Systemunrecht. Vergleichende Einblicke in Transitionsprozesse,* vol. 9, hrsg. von Albin Eser, Ulrich Sieber und Jörg Arnold) (Berlin: Duncker & Humblot, 2006).

5. Liberation from the Loom?

1. Richard A. Kraus, "Cotton and Cotton Goods in China, 1918–1936: The Impact of Modernization on the Traditional Sector" (PhD diss., Harvard University, 1968), 143.

2. Anne E. McLaren, *Performing Grief: Bridal Laments in Rural China* (Honolulu: University of Hawaii Press, 2008).

3. Chao Kang, *The Development of Cotton Textile Production in China* (Cambridge, MA: Harvard University Press, 1977); Kraus, "Cotton and Cotton Goods in China;" Albert Feuerwerker, "Handicraft and Manufactured Cotton Textiles in China, 1871–1910," *Journal of Economic History* 30, no. 2 (1970): 338–378; Philip Huang, *The Peasant Family and Rural Development in the Yangzi Delta, 1350–1988* (Stanford: Stanford University Press, 1990).

4. Machine-spun yarn had greater tensile strength, making it ideal for warp threads that are stretched taught on the loom. Homespun was preferred for weft because it was thicker and warmer than factory yarn.

5. Sidney Gamble, *Ting Hsien: A North China Rural Community* (Stanford: Stanford University Press, 1954), 298–300; Zhang Shiwen, *Dingxian nongcun gongye diaocha* [Survey of Dingxian's rural industries] (Chengdu: Sichuan minzu chubanshe, 1991), 65–72.

6. Linda Grove, *A Chinese Economic Revolution: Rural Entrepreneurship in the Twentieth Century* (Lanham, MD: Rowman and Littlefield, 2006); Kathy Le Mons Walker, *Chinese Modernity and the Peasant Path: Semicolonialism in the Northern Yangzi Delta* (Stanford: Stanford University Press, 1999); H. D. Fong [Fang Xianting], *The Growth and Decline of Rural Industrial Enterprise in North China* (Tianjin: Nankai Institute of Economics, 1936).

7. Peng Zeyi, *Zhongguo jindai shougongye shi ziliao* [Historical materials on handicrafts in modern China] (Beijing: Sanlian chubanshe, 1957), 3:753.

8. It is true that the CCP encouraged manual spinning and weaving in the Yan'an era, mobilizing thousands of women to produce cloth for the revolution. However, this policy was reversed in 1949, when the government decided to phase out hand spinning and hand weaving in favor of modern industry in the next two to three years. See Zhang Zhong, "Fangzhi yu mianhua," [Textile industry and cotton], *Renmin ribao*, April 14, 1949, 1.

9. Internet reminiscences about everyday life under Mao contain much information about textile production. See, for example, Chen Zuo, "Tongzhou tubu" [Handmade cloth of Tongzhou], *Dongnan wenhua* 5 (1994): 31. In areas where little cotton was grown (e.g., Sichuan and the mountainous parts of Hebei and Shaanxi), *tubu* was replaced by factory cloth in the late 1960s and early 1970s. See Liu Changren, "Sichuan shougong mianfangzhiye shehuizhuyi gaizao" [The socialist transformation of handicraft cotton textile production in Sichuan], *Chengdu fangzhi gaodeng zhuanke xuexiao xuebao* 14, no. 2 (April 1997): 48; Zhongshan Yefu, "Wuliushi niandai Hebei nongcun de yishizhuxing" [Everyday needs in rural Hebei in the 1950–60s], http://sjzbsm.blog.163.com/blog/static/11992700420 0911243147514/.

10. These are my interview-based estimates. A 1954 *Renmin ribao* article estimates that it takes one person six months to provide clothes and shoes for a family of three. Kang Zenghui and Liu Shaoye, "Ma Tinghai nongyeshe shi zenyang fadong funü canjia nongye shengchan de" [How Ma Tinghai's agricultural cooperative promotes women's participation in agricultural production], *Renmin ribao*, February 2, 1954, 2.

11. From 2006 to 2013, I spent a total of eight weeks in the village of Gedatou, Zhouzhi County, and four weeks in the villages of Zhangli and Danbei, Xingping County.

12. Shaanxi sheng difangzhi bianzou weiyuanhui, ed., *Shaanxi sheng zhi: fangzhi gongyezhi* [Shaanxi provincial gazetteer: Textile industry] (Xi'an: Shaanxi renmin chubanshe, 1999), 36, 43–47; Eduard B. Vermeer, *Economic Development in Provincial China: The Central Shaanxi since 1930* (Cambridge: Cambridge University Press, 1988), 324–346.

13. Shaanxi sheng difangzhi bianzou weiyuanhui, *Shaanxi sheng zhi*, 46.

14. Interview Cao Yuqing and Zhao Xijie, November 17, 2006.

15. Kraus, "Cotton and Cotton Goods in China," 46.

16. Huang, *The Peasant Family,* chapter 5. For a more optimistic assessment of the earning capacity of spinners and weavers, see Kenneth Pomeranz, *The Great Divergence: China, Europe, and the Making of the Modern World Economy* (Princeton: Princeton University Press, 2000), 316–326.

17. Interview Cao Shiying and Tian Peijie, December 2, 2006.

18. Interview Yuan Aiying, August 13, 2010.

19. Interview Du Fengying, November 27, 2006.

20. Gail Hershatter, *The Gender of Memory: Rural Women and China's Collective Past* (Berkeley: University of California Press, 2011).

21. The fact that my interviewees remembered more indoor work than Hershatter's did may be because Hershatter's fieldwork area includes mountainous parts of Southern Shaanxi where no cotton was grown.

22. Interview Du Fengying and Guo Xiuzhen, November 27, 2006; interview Wang Xiuzhen and Feng Jinlian, September 4, 2008.

23. One memoir describes how a mother forced her daughters to redo their needlework over and over again until she was satisfied with the quality of the stitching. Zhang Zhanghuai, *Lao jingtai* [The old well] (Xi'an: Sanqin chubanshe, 2002), 104–105.

24. Ibid., 102–103; Wang Anquan, ed., *Zhouzhi geyao xuan* [A selection of songs from Zhouzhi] (Zhouzhi: Zhouzhi xian wenhuaguan, 1985), 67.

25. Zhang Zhanghuai, *Lao jingtai,* 105; Wang Anquan, *Zhouzhi geyao xuan,* 118–122.

26. Interview Chen Zi'an, August 2, 2010.

27. A bundle (*kun*) of cotton is equal to 10 jin (5 kg).

28. "One puts on graveclothes only once in a lifetime; the cloth therefore needs to be woven extra fine, and the cotton should be a bit thicker." Interview Peng Shu'e, September 15, 2008.

29. Kenneth Pomeranz, "Women's Work and the Economics of Respectability," in *Gender in Motion: Divisions of Labor and Cultural Change in Late Imperial and Modern China,* ed. Bryna Goodman and Wendy Larson (Lanham, MD: Rowman and Littlefield, 2005), 239–263.

30. See Mareile Flitsch, "Knowledge, Embodiment, Skill and Risk: Anthropological Perspectives on Women's Everyday Technologies in Rural North China," *East Asian Science, Technology, and Society* 2, no. 2 (2008): 265–288.

31. Wu Xiujie, *Ein Jahrhundert Licht: Eine technikethnologische Studie zur Beleuchtung im chinesischen ländlichen Alltag* [A century of light: An ethnological study of lighting technology in Chinese rural life] (Wiesbaden: Harrassowitz, 2009), 146–147.

32. Zhang Chong, "Fangzhi yu mianhua" [Textile production and cotton], *Renmin ribao,* April 14, 1949, 1.

33. Nicholas Lardy, *Agriculture in China's Modern Economic Development* (Cambridge, MA: Harvard University Press, 1983), 123–125.

34. Chao Kang, *The Development of Cotton Textile Production in China,* 279–283.

35. Women's mobilization for agricultural work is described in detail in Marina Thorborg, "Chinese Employment Policy in 1949–78 with Special Emphasis on Women in Rural Production," in *Chinese Economy Post-Mao,* Joint Economy

Committee, Congress of the United States, U.S. Government Printing Office, Washington DC, 1978.

36. Zhonghua quanguo gongxiao hezuo zongshe mianmaju, ed., *Zhongguo mianhua tongji ziliao huibian, 1949–2000* [Collected statistical materials on Chinese cotton from 1949 to 2000] (Beijing: Zhongguo tongji, 2005), 1:89. Area yields in the collective era grew from 13 kg/*mu* (1950) to 28 kg/*mu* (1978). See also Vermeer, *Economic Development*, 350–351.

37. Vermeer, *Economic Development*, 18–19, 346–354; Chao Kang, *The Development of Cotton Textile Production in China*, 252.

38. The mechanisms by which the state tried to increase its share of the cotton harvest resembled those described by Oi for the grain harvest—also in that in both cases, state procurement prices were below production costs. See Jean Oi, *State and Peasant: The Political Economy of Village Government* (Berkeley: University of California Press, 1989).

39. Shaanxisheng gouxu mian zhidao weiyuanhui, "Taolun xin hua shangshi qian nongcun mianhua cunliang" [A discussion of rural cotton stocks before the new cotton harvest hits the market], May 28, 1952, Shaanxi Provincial Archives (hereafter cited as SPA), Gongxiao hezuoshe folder, no. 230, file 44, 34.

40. Zhonghua quanguo gongxiao hezuo zongshe mianmaju, *Zhongguo mianhua tongji ziliao huibian, 1949–2000*, 1:270.

41. Xibeiqu hezuoshe, "Hansong yugou mianhua gongzuo jingyan zongjie" [Summary report on our experience in the advance purchase of cotton], May 12, 1952, SPA, Gongxiao hezuoshe folder, no. 230, file 44b, 8.

42. Ibid.; Shaanxi sheng renmin zhengfu, "Wei baogao woting zhaokai quansheng ge zhuyao mianchan xian . . ." [Report on meeting of all important cotton-growing counties of the province], March 30, 1954, SPA, Shaanxi sheng nongcun gongzuobu folder, no. 123.4, file 465, 38–40.

43. Vermeer, *Economic Development*, 348.

44. Xibei caiwei zong dangzu, "11 yue 27 ri He Jinshou Fujuzhang . . ." [November 27, Vice-Director He Jinshou . . .], December 7, 1953, SPA, Shaanxi sheng weiyuanhui bangongshe folder, no. 123.1, file 1261; Zhonggong Shaanxi shengwei, "Zi jiang sheng caijing dangzu guanyu mianhua baoguan gongzuo de jianbao . . ." [Summary report of the Party group of the provincial finance committee concerning cotton storage . . .], September 10, 1954, SPA, Shaanxi sheng weiyuanhui bangongshe folder, no. 123.1, file 1262; Zhongyang caijing weiyuanhui, "Guanyu 1953 nian shougou xinmian de zhishi" [Directive concerning the 1953 procurement of fresh cotton], August 28, 1953, SPA, Shaanxi sheng weiyuanhui bangongshe folder, no. 123.1, file 657.

45. Zhonggong Shaanxi shengwei, "Zi jiang sheng caijing dangzu guanyu mianhua baoguan gongzuo de jianbao . . ." [Provincial finance Party group report on the work of safely storing cotton . . .], September 10, 1954, SPA, Shaanxi sheng weiyuanhui bangongshe folder, no. 123.1, file 1262, 8.

46. Xibei caiwei, "Shaanxi sheng xinmian shangshi hou . . ." [Shaanxi Province: After new cotton hits the market . . .], September 10, 1954, SPA, Shaanxi sheng weiyuanhui bangongshe folder, no. 123.1, file 657.

47. Shaanxi sheng renmin weiyuanhui cai liang mao bangongshe, "Guanyu xinmian shougou zhong muqian cunzai de jige zhongyao wenti de yijian" [Advice concerning some important current problems in the procurement of fresh cotton], November 21, 1955, SPA, Gongxiao hezuoshe folder, no. 230, file 132.

48. See, for example, the immensely popular "Women's Freedom Song": "In the past, women were locked up in King Yama's Hall, now we have broken the iron chains / Women have become free persons who can take care of the great affairs of the nation / Liberation cannot be for one-half only; fully liberated, we participate in production / Let's weed out the Chiang Kai-shek reactionaries, vanguard and rearguard work together / Let's work hard in production and not be idle; let's all put in more effort / Let's build a new China for a million years." "Funü ziyou ge" [Women's Freedom Song], http://baike.baidu.com/view/2758318.htm.

49. Zhongguo shehui kexueyuan and Zhongyang dang'anguan, ed., *1953–1957 Zhonghua renmin gongheguo jingji dang'an ziliao xuanbian: shangye juan* [Selection of economic archival materials from 1953 to 1957: Commerce] (Beijing: Zhongguo wuzi chubanshe, 1995), 243–250; Shaanxi sheng renmin zhengfu, "Shaanxi sheng renmin zhengfu shixing mianbu jihua gongying zanxing banfa" [Temporary guidelines for the People's government's planned supply of cotton cloth], August 26, 1954, SPA, Shaanxi sheng weiyuanhui bangongshe folder, no. 123.1, file 1261, 9.

50. Gao Xiaoxian, " 'The Silver Flower Contest': Rural Women in the 1950s and the Gendered Division of Labour," in *Translating Feminisms in China,* ed. Dorothy Ko and Wang Zheng (Oxford: Blackwell, 2007), 166.

51. Men of the same age group contributed 150 labor days per year. Zhonggong Zhouzhi xian weiyuanhui, "Guanyu Beijingzhai nongye shengchan hezuoshe diaocha baogao" [Investigation report on the Beijingzhai agricultural cooperative], September 18, 1955, SPA, Shaanxi sheng nongcun gongzuobu folder, no. 123.4, file 547, 45.

52. Zhonggong Zhouzhi xian weiyuanhui, "Zhouzhi nongcun renmin gongshe zhengshe jieshushi jiben qingkuang diaocha" [Investigation of the basic situation of people's communes after commune rectification], August 25, 1959, SPA, Shaanxi sheng nongcun gongzuobu folder, no. 123.4, file 718, 23.

53. Zhonggong Baoji xianwei, "Zhonggong Baoji xianwei guanyu nongmin sixiang qingkuang de diaocha baogao" [Investigation report of the Baoji County Party Committee on farmers' ideological stance], August 17, 1957, SPA, Shaanxi sheng nongcun gongzuobu, folder 123.4, file 632, 2.

54. Kimberley E. Manning, "Making a Great Leap Forward? The Politics of Women's Liberation in Maoist China," *Gender and History* 18, no. 3 (November 2006): 586–587.

55. Xingping xian Fulian hehui, "Quan xian funü jinyibu dongyuan qilai zhuahao mianhua bozhong" [Women of the entire county are mobilized one step further to do a good job in sowing cotton], April 5, 1960, Xingping County Archives, Funü lianhehui folder, file 4.1.73, 74–79.

56. Gail Hershatter, "The Gender of Memory: Rural Chinese Women and the 1950s," *Signs: Journal of Women in Culture and Society* 28, no. 1 (Autumn 2002): 43–70; Hershatter, "Local Meanings of Gender and Work in Rural Shaanxi in the 1950s," in *Re-Drawing Boundaries: Work, Households, and Gender in China,* ed. Barbara Entwistle and Gail E. Henderson (Berkeley: University of California Press, 2000); Gao, "The Silver Flower Contest."

57. Xingping xian Fulian hehui, "Xingping xian fulian guanyu Huangzhong shengchandui zai xiashou zhong zuzhi youer shi mai deng wenti de baogao" [Report by the Xingping Women's Federation on Huangzhong Brigade organizing childcare during the summer harvest], March 6, 1961, Xingping County Archives, Funü lianhehui folder, file 4.1.92, 15–17. Guanzhong was spared the worst of the 1960–1961 famine, but suffered from poor harvests and high extraction longer than other provinces. Serious malnourishment was still widespread in late 1964.

58. Yu Zongxian and Zhao Gang, *Zhonggong fangzhiye zi fazhan jiqi dui woguo fangzhipin duiwai maoyi zhi yingxiang* [The development of textile production in Communist China and its impact on our country's foreign trade in textile products] (Taibei: Xingzhengyuan jingjihui, 1988), 105. See also Qian Zhiguang et al., *Dangdai Zhongguo de fangzhi gongye* [Textile industry in contemporary China] (Beijing, Zhongguo shehui kexue chubanshe, 1984), graph on p. 15 of statistical appendix.

59. Zhong Ling, *Mianbu wei shenme yao tonggou tongxiao?* [Why unified purchase and marketing for cotton cloth?] (Wuhan: Hubei renmin chubanshe, 1955), 18.

60. Zhonggong Shaanxi shengwei, "Guanyu mianbu shixing jihua gongying de zhishi" [Directive concerning the planned supply of cotton cloth], August 26, 1954, SPA, Zhonggong Shaanxi shengwei folder, no. 123.4, file 1261, 83; Shaanxi sheng difangzhi bianzou weiyuanhui, *Shaanxi sheng zhi,* 243.

61. Richard Kraus estimates a national average consumption of 360 g of cotton wool for padding, which I take as a minimum for northern China. Another 50 g out of each kg will be lost in spinning. See Kraus, "Cotton and Cotton Goods in China," 82.

62. Group interview, Yabei Township of Zhouzhi County, November 29, 2006.

63. Gao Xiaoxian, "Silver Flower Contest," 177.

64. Zhonggong Shaanxi shengwei nongcun gongzuobu, "Weinan diwei jiancha zuzhi duiyu Jingyang Sanqu xiang mianhua shengchan . . ." [Investigation group of Weinan District: Cotton production in Jingyang County, Sanqu Township . . .], September 23, 1953, SPA, Shaanxi nongcun gongzuobu folder, no. 123:4, file 11, 12–14.

65. Zhonggong Shaanxi shengwei nongcun gongzuobu, "Zi jiang Shaanxi sheng Fulian dui jianli nongye shengchan hezuoshe . . ." [Concerning the report on the provincial Women's Federation's establishment in agricultural production teams . . .], January 8, 1954, SPA, Shaanxi nongcun gongzuobu folder, no. 123:4, file 31.

66. Gao Xiaoxian, "Silver Flower Contest," 177–178.

67. Interview Jia Yumei, September 10, 2008. On Wang Baojing and Zhang Qiuxiang, see also Kojima Reiitsu, "The Bearers of Science and Technology Have Changed," *Modern China* 5, no. 2 (April 1979): 188–189, 203.

68. Interview Zhao Xijie, August 6, 2010; Wu Shu'e, August 7, 2010; Teng Jianyou, August 13, 2010.

69. Such textile cooperatives had been common in the Shaan-Gan-Ning border region, where women (as well as Eighth Route Army soldiers and Party leaders) were mobilized to spin and weave.

70. Hershatter, "The Gender of Memory: Rural Chinese Women and the 1950s," 63–64.

71. Lardy, *Agriculture,* 64, Chao Kang, *Development of Chinese Cotton Textile,* 238, 287–288.

72. Philip Huang, *The Peasant,* 323.

73. Vermeer, *Economic Development,* 276, 358–359.

74. Chao Kang, *Development of Chinese Cotton Textile,* 297–300; Qian Zhiguang et al., *Dangdai Zhongguo de fangzhi gongye,* graph on p. 11 of statistical appendix.

75. Yu Zongxian and Zhao Gang, *Zhonggong fangzhiye zhi fazhan,* 106.

6. Youth and the "Great Revolutionary Movement" of Scientific Experiment in 1960s–1970s Rural China

For their valuable help, I thank Jeremy Brown, Cao Xingsui, Lei Duan, Gail Hershatter, Matthew Johnson, Shuyu Kong, Ye Wa, Wang Zheng, members of the UMass History Department's history of science reading group, students in my UMass undergraduate history seminar on the Cultural Revolution, and two anonymous reviewers. I also thank the many people who generously granted me interviews, some of whom are credited below.

1. Song Haiting, "'Wenhua dageming' zhong zhishi qingnian shangshan xiaxiang yundong shu lun" [The up-to-the-mountains, down-to-the-villages educated youth movement during the Cultural Revolution], *Dangdai Zhongguo shi yanjiu* 1995.5: 73.

2. See, for example, Aileen Fyfe, "Reading Children's Books in Late Eighteenth-Century Dissenting Families," *Historical Journal* 43, no. 2 (June 2000): 453–473; Sally Gregory Kohlstedt, *Teaching Children Science: Hands-On Nature*

Study in North America, 1890–1930 (Chicago: University of Chicago Press, 2010); Melanie Keene, "'Every Boy and Girl a Scientist': Instruments for Children in Interwar Britain," *Isis* 98, no. 2 (June 2007): 266–289; Larry Owens, "Science 'Fiction' and the Mobilization of Youth in the Cold War," *Quest: The History of Spaceflight Quarterly* 14, no. 3 (2007): 52–57.

3. Mao Tse-tung, *Quotations from Chairman Mao,* 2nd ed. (Peking: Foreign Languages Press, 1966), 204.

4. Mao Tse-tung, "On Practice," in *Selected Works of Mao Tse-tung,* vol. 1 (Peking: Foreign Languages Press, 1967), 296.

5. Mao, *Quotations,* 40.

6. Mao Zedong, "Cast away Illusions, Prepare for Struggle," in *Selected Works,* vol. 4, 427.

7. Mao, *Quotations,* 290.

8. Michel Bonnin recognizes the existence of rural educated youth but none-theless reinforces the conflation of "educated youth" and "urban youth" in the title and content of his important book on educated youth, *The Lost Generation: The Rustication of China's Educated Youth (1968–1980),* Krystyna Horko trans. (Hong Kong: The Chinese University Press, 2013 [2004]). Bonnin also gives short shrift to youth participation in the scientific experiment movement. An exception to both patterns of omission is Miriam Gross's 2010 Ph.D. dissertation, which examines the role of rural educated youth in scientific activities to combat schis-tosomiasis and argues that the incorporation of rural youth into scientific and public health work helped consolidate state power. Gross, "Chasing Snails: Anti-Schistosomiasis Campaigns in the People's Republic of China" (PhD diss., University of California, San Diego, 2010), 626–664.

9. Mao Tse-tung, *Selected Works of Mao Tse-tung,* vol. 5 (Peking: Foreign Languages Press, 1977), 264.

10. Han Dongping, *The Unknown Cultural Revolution: Life and Change in a Chinese Village* (New York: Monthly Review Press, 2008), 29; Thomas Bernstein, *Up to the Mountains and Down to the Villages: The Transfer of Youth from Urban to Rural China* (New Haven, CT: Yale University Press, 1977), 61–62.

11. Bernstein comes to this conclusion (pp. 224–225), and the sources I have consulted support it. On the complexity of interpreting statistics on sent-down and returned educated youth, see Bernstein, *Up to the Mountains,* 22–32.

12. She Shiguang, ed., *Dangdai Zhongguo de qingnian he gongqingtuan* [Youth and the Communist Youth League in contemporary China] (Beijing: Dangdai Zhongguo chubanshe, 1998), 289–292.

13. Ibid., 291.

14. On environmental consequences of Mao-era agricultural policies, see, for example, Vaclav Smil, *The Bad Earth: Environmental Degradation in China* (Armonk, NY: M.E. Sharpe, 1984); Judith Shapiro, *Mao's War against Nature:*

Politics and Environment in Revolutionary China (Cambridge: Cambridge University Press, 2001).

15. Dongping Han, "Rural Agriculture: Scientific and Technological Development during the Cultural Revolution," in *Mr. Science and Chairman Mao's Cultural Revolution: Science and Technology in Modern China,* ed. Chunjuan Nancy Wei and Darryl E. Brock (Lanham, MD: Lexington Books, 2013), 281–303. My own current research also highlights some of the more successful aspects of Mao-era agricultural science, as do many of the Chinese agricultural officials and technicians I have been interviewing. The current Chinese political interest in revisiting Mao-era agricultural policies parallels the interest in revisiting the barefoot doctor program. See Xiaoping Fang, *Barefoot Doctors and Western Medicine in China* (Rochester, NY: University of Rochester Press, 2012).

16. *Renmin ribao* [People's Daily], December 20, 1972, 2.

17. Tuan shengwei Yangchun xianwei gongzuozu, "Guangdong Yangchun Sanjie dui qingnian kaizhan kexue shiyan huodong de jingyan" [The experience of youth in Sanjie Brigade, Yangchun, Guangdong carrying out scientific experiment activities], 1965, Guangdong Provincial Archives, 232–1–0084–106~108.

18. *Nongcun zhishi qingnian kexue shiyan jingyan xuanbian* [Selected experiences of rural educated youth in scientific experiment] (Beijing: Beijing renmin chubanshe, 1974), 21–22, 49, 64, 67. See also Gongqingtuan zhongyang qingnong bu, ed., *Wei geming gao nongye kexue shiyan* [Agricultural scientific experiment for the revolution] (Beijing: Zhongguo qingnian chubanshe, 1966), 40.

19. Lianjiangxian fulian, "Shengchan douzheng, kexue shiyan de jieguo, bian wo geng re'ai nongcun" [Results of the struggle for production and scientific experiment have deepened my love for the countryside], June 11, 1966, Guangdong Provincial Archives, 233–2–0332–23~29.

20. *Nongcun zhishi qingnian,* 19–20. Emphasis added.

21. See the sixth quotation in chapter 30, "Youth."

22. Gongqingtuan, *Wei geming,* 4.

23. *Renmin ribao,* October 30, 1965, 3.

24. *Renmin ribao,* October 16, 1972, 4.

25. *Renmin ribao,* October 16, 1972, 4.

26. Lu Youshang, "Guangkuo tiandi dayou zuowei" [In the vast land, great achievements are possible], *Kexue shiyan* 1976.7: 27.

27. *Kexue zhongtian de nianqing ren* [Youth in scientific experiment] (Beijing: Zhongguo qingnian chubanshe, 1966), 10.

28. *Nongcun zhishi qingnian,* 3.

29. Merle Goldman, *China's Intellectuals: Advise and Dissent* (Cambridge, MA: Harvard University Press, 1981), 135–138; James H. Williams, "Fang Lizhi's Big Bang: Science and Politics in Mao's China" (PhD diss., University of California, Berkeley, 1994), Book 2, 679; Sigrid Schmalzer, *The People's Peking Man: Popular*

Science and Human Identity in Twentieth-Century China (Chicago: University of Chicago Press, 2008), 124–125.

30. "Young Girl Fulfills Geological Prospecting Task by Several Times," *Survey of China Mainland Press* 2136 (November 7, 1959): 8–9.

31. *Nongcun zhishi qingnian*, 25.

32. E.g., *Nongcun zhishi qingnian*, 29, 50.

33. *Nongcun zhishi qingnian*, 36.

34. *Kexue zhongtian de nianqing ren*, 14–16.

35. Peter Seybolt, ed., *The Rustication of Urban Youth in China: A Social Experiment* (New York: M.E. Sharpe, 1975), 60–63. This is a translation of a Chinese collection entitled *Reqing guanhuai xiaxiang zhishi qingnian de chengzhang* [Have a warm concern for the maturation of sent-down educated youth] (Beijing: Renmin chubanshe, 1973). See also Heilongjiang sheng Binxian Xinlisi dui keyan xiaozu, "Bai ying dadou wang de xuanyu" [The selection of white-breast soybean king], *Nongye keji tongxun* 1973.12: 4; Zhang Renpeng, "Houlu duizhang Yang Liguo kexue zhongtian chuang gaochan" [Houlu Brigade leader Yang Liguo achieves high yields through scientific farming], *Xin nongye* 1974.14: 26.

36. Zhejiang sheng Huangyan xian Haimen qu baodao zu, "Pin xiazhongnong de 'guantianbing': zhishi qingnian Su Fuxing" [The poor and lower-middle peasants' "soldier who manages the heavens": The educated youth Su Fuxing], *Kexue shiyan* 1974.3: 8–9.

37. *Nongcun zhishi qingnian*, 5, 21.

38. *Kexue zhongtian de nianqing ren*, 3, 12, 19–20.

39. Yunnan shengchan jianshe bu dui mou bu sanjiehe keyan xiaozu, "Jinjina shumiao shi zenyang peizhi chenggong de?" [How are cinchona saplings successfully cultivated?], *Kexue shiyan* 1974.3: 6–7.

40. Carma Hinton, Geremie Barmé, and Richard Gordon, dir. *Morning Sun*, Long Bow Group (2003).

41. See also Anita Chan, Richard Madsen, and Jonathan Unger, *Chen Village under Mao and Deng* (Berkeley: University of California Press, 1992), 95.

42. Ibid., 239–240.

43. Gongqingtuan, *Wei geming*, 4.

44. See, e.g., Heilongjiang sheng, "Bai ying dadou wang," 4. On the other hand, a smaller number of cases warned against the opposite kind of error—that of assuming plants or methods from one area would fail in another—as in the story of the successful cultivation of the southern crop of white tree ears in a northern region. *Renmin ribao*, December 20, 1972, 2.

45. Gongqingtuan, *Wei geming*, 5.

46. Zhonggong Hunansheng Huarongxian weiyuanhui, "Women shi zenyang ban nongcun kexue shiyan wang de" [How we created a rural scientific experiment network], *Kexue shiyan* 1974.12: 1–3.

47. *Kexue zhongtian de nianqing ren,* 27–28, 31, 64; *Renmin ribao,* October 16, 1972, 4.

48. *Nongcun zhishi qingnian,* 37.

49. Bernstein, *Up to the Mountains,* 22.

50. Interview with Ye Wa, March 2012. See also the account in *Chen Village,* which finds a small silver lining in that "the amateur researchers enjoyed their adventures" because "however futile the results, they liked the opportunity to use their initiative." Chan, Madsen, and Unger, *Chen Village,* 238.

51. Shi Weimin, *Zhiqing riji,* 160–161.

52. Shen Dianzhong, *Sixiang,* 249, 255

53. Interview with Chen Yongning, June 2012.

54. Anita Chan, "The Culture of Survival: Lives of Migrant Workers through the Prism of Private Letters," in *Popular China: Unofficial Culture in a Globalizing Society,* ed. Perry Link, Richard Madsen, and Paul Pickowicz (Boulder, CO: Rowman & Littlefield, 2002), 181.

55. Interview with Cao Xingsui, June 2012.

56. Ibid.

57. Interview with Chen Yongning, June 2012.

58. Interview with Pan Yiwei, June 2012.

59. Interview with former returned educated youth, June 2012.

60. Bai Di, "Wandering Years in the Cultural Revolution," in *Some of Us: Chinese Women Growing Up in the Mao Era,* ed. Xueping Zhong, Wang Zheng, and Bai Di (New Brunswick, NJ: Rutgers University Press, 2001), 92.

61. Lihua Wang, "Gender Consciousness in My Teen Years," in Zhong, Wang, and Bai, *Some of Us,* 121.

62. Wang Zheng, "Call Me Qingnian but Not Funü," in Zhong, Wang, and Bai, *Some of Us,* 37.

63. Zhang Yang, *"Di'erci woshou" wenziyu* [The literary inquisition of *The Second Handshake*] (Beijing: Zhongguo shehui chubanshe, 1999), 91–99, 104, 105, 129, 405–407.

64. Ibid., 149.

65. Perry Link, "The Limits of Cultural Reform in Deng Xiaoping's China," *Modern China* 13, no. 2 (April 1987): 158.

66. Shen Dianzhong, *Sixiang chenfu lu* [Record of the ebb and flow of my thoughts] (Shenyang: Liaoning renmin chubanshe, 1998), 3–7; Paul Lafargue, "Reminiscences of Marx," in *Marx and Engels through the Eyes of Their Contemporaries* (Moscow: Progress Publishers, 1972), 23.

67. Shen Dianzhong, *Sixiang chenfu lu,* 249.

68. Ibid., 10, 360.

69. Interview with Ye Wa, March 2012.

70. Shen Dianzhong, *Sixiang,* 249–250.

71. Ibid., 297.

72. Bin Yang, "'We Want to Go Home!'—The Great Petition of the Zhiqing, Xishuangbanna, Yunnan, 1978–1979," *China Quarterly* 198 (2009): 401–421.

73. Guojia nongken zong ju kejiao ju, *Yong yu pandeng de nianqing ren* [Young people bravely scaling the heights] (Beijing: Nongye chubanshe, 1979), e.g., 46.

74. Ibid., 37–38.

75. Ibid., 5.

76. On protests by sent-down youth in Yunnan, see Bin Yang, "'We Want to Go Home!'"

77. Mao Zedong, "Mao Zhuxi gei Mao Anying, Mao Anqing tongzhi de xin" [A letter from Chairman Mao to Mao Anying and Mao Anqing], *Shaonian kexue* 1979.1: 3.

78. *Renmin ribao*, April 4, 1978, 4.

79. Gao Shiqi, "Chuntian" [Spring], *Shaonian kexue* 1979.1: 6–7. The slogan "Springtime for Science" emerged from the March 1978 national science conference.

80. Zhou Peiyuan, "Kexue de weilai jituo zai nimen de shenshang" [The future of science rests on your shoulders], *Shaonian kexue* 1979.10: 1.

7. Adrift in Tianjin, 1976

1. Tongshan's Diary (hereafter abbreviated TD), July 28, 1976. We thank Wee Kek Koon for his translation of an earlier draft of parts of this chapter.

2. Tianjin shi difangzhi bianxiu weiyuanhui, ed., *Tianjin tongzhi: dizhen zhi* [Tianjin gazetteer: Earthquake gazetteer] (Tianjin: Tianjin shehui kexueyuan chubanshe, 1995), 58–59, 63. See also Tianjin shi dizhen ju, *Tianjin ji fujin diqu dizhen dui Tianjin shi de yingxiang* [How earthquakes in Tianjin and nearby areas affected Tianjin Municipality] (Internal publication, 1982), 6.

3. In the thirty years following the Tangshan earthquake, major commemorative events organized by the people of Tianjin have been held at the Tianjin Earthquake Monument. The most symbolic ones were the 2006 commemoration of the thirtieth anniversary of the Tangshan earthquake and a memorial service for the victims of the 2008 Wenchuan earthquake.

4. The full names of the writer and his school are not mentioned in the diary. We only know from the entries that his given name was Tongshan.

5. TD, August 31, 1976. Tongshan never specifies what crime his brother committed.

6. In the oral recollections of sent-down youth, for example, apart from forgetting there are many cases of selective remembering. For the many oral interviewees who experienced the Cultural Revolution, the shadow of authoritarianism remains one of the key reasons for their reluctance to speak the truth. See Liu Xiaoming, "Guanyu zhiqing koushu shi" [On the oral history of sent-down youth],

Guangxi minzu xueyuan xuebao 5 (2003): 19–24; Liang Lifang, "Jiyi shangshan xiaxiang—zhiqing huiyilu de fenlei, gongxian ji qita" [Memories of going up to the mountains and down to the villages: Classification, contributions, and aspects of sent-down youth memoirs], *Ziyou pinglun, dangdai wentan* 1 (2008): 25–29; Wang Hansheng and Liu Yaqiu, "Shehui jiyi ji qi jiegou: yixiang guanyu zhiqing jiti jiyi de yanjiu" [Social memory and its structure: A study of the collective memory of sent-down youth], *Shehui* 3 (2006): 46–68.

7. Wu Yanhong and David J. Knottnerus, "Richang yishihua xingwei de xingcheng: cong *Lei Feng riji* dao zhiqing riji" [The formation of daily ritualized behavior: From *Lei Feng's Diary* to sent-down youth diaries], *Shehui* 1 (2007): 98–119.

8. For an example and an analysis of a Cultural Revolution diary written with the expectation that others would read it, see Richard King and Michael Schoenhals, "The Cultural Revolutionary 'Public Diary,'" *CCP Research Newsletter* 3 (Summer 1989): 18–22.

9. TD, September 9, 1976.

10. TD, July 28, 1976.

11. In the study of modern and contemporary history, researchers should take a special interest in historical sources that were not intended for publication—including diaries—and invest the effort, time, and money to collect them. See Jin Dalu, "Shanghai wenge yanjiu de shiliao zhunbei" [Preparing historical sources for the study of the Cultural Revolution in Shanghai], *Shehui kexue* 5 (2007): 164–170.

12. For detailed data, see Guojia dizhen ju dizhi yanjiusuo, "Tianjin diqu zhenhai dizhi tiaojian fenxi yu zhenhai yuce de tantao" [Analysis of earthquake geological conditions in the Tianjin region and an examination of earthquake prediction], in *Tangshan dizhen kaocha yu yanjiu,* ed. Guojia dizhen ju keyanchu (Beijing: Dizhen chubanshe, 1981), 45–55.

13. Ibid.

14. Tianjin shi geming weiyuanhui, "Tianjin shi kangzhen gongzuo qing-kuang" [Earthquake recovery work in Tianjin], in *Tangshan dizhen kangzhen diaocha zongjie ziliao xuanbian,* ed. Zhongguo jianzhu gongye chubanshe (Beijing: Zhongguo jianzhu gongye chubanshe, 1977), 10–17.

15. TD, July 28, 1976.

16. TD, July 31, 1976.

17. Tianjin shi difangzhi bianxiu weiyuanhui, *Tianjin tongzhi: dizhen zhi,* 78. The area in Tianjin with the highest casualty numbers was Hangu District in the northeast, with 4,380 people dead and 10,787 seriously injured. In the rural counties outside the city, the area with the highest casualty numbers was Ninghe County, with 16,097 people dead.

18. TD, July 28, 1976.

19. Ibid.

20. Tianjin shi dizhen ju, *Tianjin ji fujin diqu dizhen dui Tianjin shi de ying-xiang*, 8.

21. Tianjin shi difangzhi bianxiu weiyuanhui, *Tianjin tongzhi: dizhen zhi*, 285–286.

22. See Bian Jizhe, "Zai Tianjin dizhen de rizi" [My days in Tianjin during the earthquake], in *Suibi* [Random notes] (Guangzhou: Huacheng chubanshe, 1981), 14:29–31.

23. Tianjin shi difangzhi bianxiu weiyuanhui, *Tianjin tongzhi: dizhen zhi*, 208.

24. TD, July 29, 1976.

25. TD, July 30, 1976.

26. Ibid.

27. TD, August 1, 1976.

28. TD, July 30, 1976.

29. TD, August 3, 1976.

30. See Yang Wujin, "Languang shanguo zhihou: yi dizhen yu kangzhen" [After the flash of blue light: Recollections of the earthquake and relief work], *Tianjin Hebei wenshi* 4 (1990): 37–43.

31. Western scholars who have studied mass communication systems during disasters have described the different methods of information transmission during earthquakes. Chinese historians would benefit from exploring this topic further. See Gary J. Krug, "The Day the Earth Stood Still: Media Messages and Local Life in a Predicted Arkansas Earthquake," *Critical Studies in Mass Communication* 10, no. 3 (1993): 273–285.

32. TD, August 5, 1976.

33. TD, August 2, 1976.

34. TD, August 5, 1976.

35. In comparison, the selection of the so-called model disaster relief work began immediately. See Tianjin shi kangzhenban, "Tuixuan woshi chuxi zhong-yang zhan Tangshan Fengnan dizhen ji chuxi woshi kangzhen jiuzai xianjin jiti xianjin geren ming'e fenpei yijiangao" [Draft quota for the nomination of our city's advanced collectives and advanced individuals who were present in the center's battle against the Tangshan Fengnan earthquake and in our city's disaster relief work], Tianjin Municipal Archive, 401206800.

36. TD, July 28, 1976.

37. TD, August 3, 1976.

38. TD, August 5, 1976.

39. TD, August 6, 1976.

40. TD, August 20, 1976. Similar language about looters in Tangshan in the immediate aftermath of the earthquake was recorded by Li Lu, who saw "seven almost naked men tied together with a steel wire going through the flesh of their shoulders." The men had been accused of stealing wristwatches from corpses. Li

Lu, *Moving the Mountain: My Life in China from the Cultural Revolution to Tiananmen Square* (London: Macmillan, 1990), 53–54.

41. TD, July 25, 1976.

42. Ibid.

43. TD, July 27, 1976.

44. Ibid.

45. TD, August 3, 1976.

46. TD, August 10, 1976.

47. Anita Chan calls this phenomenon "political desocialization." She points out that the ebbing of the Red Guards' "revolutionary fervor" often began when they were working in the countryside. This was followed by the distrust of authority. See Anita Chan, *Children of Mao: Personality Development and Political Activism in the Red Guard Generation* (Seattle: University of Washington Press, 1985), 185–191. The starting point of Chan's thesis, however, is the concept of "authoritarian personality," which does not seem to apply to Tongshan's situation.

48. TD, August 3, 1976.

49. After the fall of Lin Biao, the CCP Center disseminated, over the period from December 1971 through July 1972, three batches of documents entitled "The struggle to crush the Lin and Chen anti-Party clique's counterrevolutionary coup" [Fensui Lin-Chen fandang jituan fangeming zhengbian de douzheng], allowing even ordinary citizens to read such important documents as the the "Summary of Project 571," supposedly the manifesto of the purported coup. At a time when curses against Lin Biao were resounding throughout the nation, various kinds of unorthodox thinking were quietly germinating. Critical words and phrases in "The Summary of Project 571" had inspired many people to rethink the Cultural Revolution.

50. TD, August 12, 1976.

51. TD, August 9, 1976.

52. TD, August 14, 1976.

53. TD, August 18, 1976.

54. TD, August 19, 1976.

55. TD, October 13, 1976.

56. TD, August 22, 1976.

57. TD, August 23, 1976.

58. Wang Yuqiao, "Zhenliu: feichang shiqi de mingzi" [Zhenliu: The name of extraordinary times], in *1976 nian dadizhen,* ed. Jia Changhua (Tianjin: Tianjin shehui kexueyuan chubanshe, 2006), 81–82.

59. TD, August 23, 1976.

60. TD, September 16, 1976.

61. TD, October 12, 1976.

62. TD, October 17, 1976.

63. TD, September 27, 1976.

64. TD, September 29, 1976.

65. TD, September 23, 1976.

66. TD, October 9, 1976.

67. TD, September 29, 1976.

68. TD, October 14, 1976.

69. TD, October 16, 1976.

70. TD, October 22, 1976.

71. TD, October 27, 1976.

72. TD, October 29, 1976.

73. TD, October 30, 1976.

74. TD, November 4, 1976.

75. TD, November 6, 1976.

76. TD, November 8, 1976.

77. TD, November 9, 1976.

78. TD, November 10, 1976.

79. TD, November 14, 1976.

80. TD, November 12, 1976.

81. TD, November 17, 1976.

82. Michel Bonnin, *The Lost Generation: The Rustication of China's Educated Youth,* trans. Krystyna Horko (Hong Kong: Chinese University Press, 2013), 275.

83. Ibid.

84. See Bonnin, *The Lost Generation,* 248–252.

85. *Zhongguo dizhen nianjian* bianji bu, ed., *Zhongguo dizhen nianjian: 1949–1981* [China earthquake yearbook: 1949–1981] (Beijing: Zhongguo dizhen chubanshe, 1990), 325–326.

86. TD, November 16, 1976.

87. TD, November 18, 1976.

88. TD, December 12, 1976.

89. TD, November 25, 1976.

8. Beneath the Propaganda State

Research and writing of this chapter was supported by: The Fulbright Program; Institute of International Education; Institute of International and Comparative Area Studies, University of California, San Diego; and Harris Faculty Fellowship, Grinnell College. I am also grateful for comments given by participants in the "China at the Grassroots" workshop held in May 2010 at Simon Fraser University— particularly those of Tim Cheek, Michael Schoenhals, Steve Smith, and Yang Kuisong. Subsequent drafts benefited immensely from additional readings by Vivienne Shue, the volume's two anonymous reviewers, and, once again, Tim

Cheek, whose insights opened new conceptual doors at just the right moment. All errors of fact and interpretation are mine alone.

1. On state-provided services as social wage in socialist societies, see Henry Veltmeyer and Mark Rushton, *The Cuban Revolution as Socialist Human Development* (Leiden: Brill, 2011), 87–92.

2. On state reach in the context of Chinese peasant society, see Vivienne Shue, *The Reach of the State: Sketches of the Chinese Body Politic* (Stanford: Stanford University Press, 1988).

3. On cultural geography and landscape in the context of China, see Yi-Fu Tuan, *A Historical Geography of China* (Piscataway, NJ: Transaction, 2008 [1969]); Kai-wing Chow, *Publishing, Culture, and Power in Early Modern China* (Stanford: Stanford University Press, 2004); Helen F. Siu, "The Cultural Landscape of Luxury Housing in South China: A Regional History," in *Locating China: Space, Place, and Popular Culture,* ed. Jing Wang (New York: Routledge, 2005), 72–93; Yu Luo Rioux, "Marketing the Revolution: Tourism, Landscape, and Ideology in China," (PhD diss., University of Colorado at Boulder, 2007).

4. On socialist construction as defined at the outset of the high socialist period, see Mao Zedong, "On the Ten Major Relationships" (April 25, 1956), *Selected Works of Mao Tse-tung,* vol. 5 (Beijing: Foreign Languages Press, 1977), transcribed by Maoist Documentation Project, accessed via https://www .marxists.org/reference/archive/mao/selected-works/volume-5/mswv5_51.htm, September 9, 2014.

5. The case for cultural unification and the successful creation of a "new socialist culture" in the context of Communist Party nation-building is made most forcefully in Chang-tai Hung, *Mao's New World: Political Culture in the Early People's Republic* (Ithaca: Cornell University Press, 2011). For a range of approaches to political culture in the People's Republic, see also Alan P. L. Liu, *Political Culture and Group Conflict in Communist China* (Santa Barbara, CA: Clio Books, 1971); Elizabeth J. Perry, "Introduction: Chinese Political Culture Revisited," in *Popular Protests and Political Culture in Modern China,* ed. Jeffrey N. Wasserstrom and Elizabeth J. Perry (Boulder, CO: Westview Press, 1994), 1–14; James Z. Gao, *The Communist Takeover of Hangzhou: The Transformation of City and Cadre, 1949–1954* (Honolulu: University of Hawaii Press, 2004).

6. For an example of post-Leap unofficial culture in the form of "superstitious" rumor, see S. A. Smith, "Talking Toads and Chinless Ghosts: The Politics of 'Superstitious' Rumors in the People's Republic of China, 1961–1965," *American Historical Review* 111, no. 2 (2006): 405–427.

7. The existence of particularist networks in local settings has been well documented for villages and factories of the People's Republic. On instrumental cliques and instrumental-personal ties in the industrial workplace, for example, see Andrew G. Walder, *Communist Neo-Traditionalism: Work and Authority in*

Chinese Industry (Berkeley: University of California Press, 1986), 162–189. However, particularist phenomena have yet to be fully documented within institutions of culture and propaganda; far better understood are factionalism and control at the level of production. For a detailed study of everyday control in China's socialist literary system, see Perry Link, *The Uses of Literature: Life in the Chinese Socialist Literary System* (Princeton: Princeton University Press, 2000), 56–103.

8. Mark W. Frazier, *The Making of the Chinese Industrial Workplace: State, Revolution, and Labor Management* (Cambridge: Cambridge University Press, 2002), 97–106.

9. Chunlan Zhao, "Socio-Spatial Transformation in Mao's China: Settlement Planning and Dwelling Architecture Revisited (1950s–1970s)," (PhD diss., University of Leuven), 182–188.

10. Zhongyang xuanchuan bu and Zhongyang bianzhi weiyuanhui, "Guanyu wen-jiao xitong tiaozheng jigou wenti de shuoming" [Explanation concerning the restructuring of institutions in the culture-education system] (January 1952); *Dang de xuanchuan gongzuo wenjian xuanbian* [Selected documents on the Party's propaganda work, hereafter cited as DXGWX] (Beijing: Zhonggong zhongyang dangxiao chubanshe, 1994): 99–100; Zhongyang xunchuan bu, "Yijiuwusannian gongzuo jihua yaodian" [Key points of 1953 work plan] (June 14, 1953), DXGWX, 158–159; Zhongyang xuanchuan bu, "Guanyu gaishan dang nei tongxin gongzuo de tongzhi" [Circular concerning improvement of communications within the Party] (September 1953), DXGWX, 160–164.

11. Zhonggong zhongyang, "Guanyu zhongyang zhengfu chengli hou dang de wenhua jiaoyu gongzuo wenti de zhishi" [Directive concerning issues in Party culture and education work following establishment of the central government] (December 5, 1949), DXGWX, 16–17. On the expansion of the propaganda system generally, see Huang Yan, "Xin Zhongguo lishi shang de xuanchuan wang zhidu" [The propaganda network system in the history of New China], *Zhonggong dangshi ziliao* [Materials on Chinese Communist Party history] 3 (2007): 117–128. Other pioneering works on post-1949 propaganda and propagandists include: Timothy Cheek, *Propaganda and Culture in Mao's China: Deng Tuo and the Intelligentsia* (Oxford: Oxford University Press, 1997); Julian Chang, "The Mechanics of State Propaganda: The People's Republic of China and the Soviet Union in the 1950s," in *New Perspectives on State Socialism in China*, ed. Timothy Cheek and Tony Saich (Armonk, NY: M.E. Sharpe, 1997): 76–124.

12. See Eddy U, "The Hiring of Rejects: Teacher Recruitment and the Crisis of Socialism in the Early PRC," *Modern China* 30, no. 1 (2004): 46–80; Brian DeMare, "Local Actors and National Politics: Rural Amateur Drama Troupes and Mass Campaigns in Hebei Province, 1949–1953," *Modern Chinese Literature and Culture* 24, no. 2 (2012): 129–178.

13. Zhonggong zhongyang, "Guanyu jiaqiang yu tiaozheng geji dangwei xuanchuan bu de gongzuo he jigou de zhishi" [Directive concerning strengthening

and restructuring the work of propaganda departments at all levels] (February 2, 1949), DXGWX, 69–72.

14. On the Communist Party as artistic patron and controller of the cultural marketplace during the Mao era, see Richard Kurt Kraus, *The Party and the Art in China: The New Politics of Culture* (Lanham, MD: Rowman & Littlefield, 2004).

15. Zhonggong zhongyang, "Guanyu xuanchuan wang wenti de tongzhi" [Circular concerning propaganda network issues] (1958.3.31), DXGWX, 356.

16. On the definition and phenomenon of corruption in socialist contexts, see Keith Jowitt, *New World Disorders: The Leninist Extinction* (Berkeley: University of California Press, 1992).

17. On the origin and evolution of the concept of the propaganda state in a comparative context, see Peter Kenez, *The Birth of the Propaganda State: Soviet Methods of Mass Mobilization, 1917–1929* (Cambridge: Cambridge University Press, 1985); David Brandenberger, *The Propaganda State in Crisis: Soviet Ideology, Indoctrination, and Terror under Stalin, 1927–1941* (New Haven, CT: Yale University Press, 2011).

18. Zhong Gong Shanghai shiwei zuzhi bu et al., *Zhongguo Gongchandang Shanghai shi zuzhi shiliao (1920.8–1987.10)* [Chinese Communist Party organizational materials, Shanghai, ...] (Shanghai: Shanghai renmin chubanshe, 1991), 350.

19. See also Zhonggong Shanghai shi wei dangshi ziliao zhengji weiyuanhui et al., *Shanghai geming wenhua shilüe* [Historical overview of Shanghai's revolutionary culture] (Shanghai: Shanghai renmin chubanshe, 1999), 477.

20. Zhonggong Shanghai dang zhi bianzuan weiyuanhui, *Zhonggong Shanghai dang zhi* [Chinese Communist Party Shanghai Party gazetteer] (Shanghai: Shanghai shehui kexueyuan chubanshe, 2001), 5.

21. Shanghai meishu zhi bianzuan weiyuanhui, *Shanghai meishu zhi* [Shanghai arts gazetteer] (Shanghai: Shanghai shuhua chubanshe, 2004), 752–754; Shanghai chuban zhi bianzuan weiyuanhui, *Shanghai chuban zhi* [Shanghai publishing gazetteer] (Shanghai: Shanghai shehui kexueyuan chubanshe, 2000), 904.

22. Shanghai guangbo dianshi zhi bianzuan weiyuanhui, *Shanghai guangbo dianshi zhi* [Shanghai radio broadcasting and television gazetteer] (Shanghai: Shanghai shehui kexueyuan chubanshe, 1999), 32–33.

23. Shanghai dianying zhi bianzuan weiyuanhui, *Shanghai dianying zhi* [Shanghai motion picture gazetteer] (Shanghai: Shanghai shehui kexueyuan chubanshe, 1999), 53.

24. Zhongguo xiqu zhi Shanghai juan bianji weiyuanhui, *Zhongguo xiqu zhi Shanghai juan* [China theater and opera gazetteer, Shanghai volume] (Beijing: Zhongguo ISBN zhongxin, 1996), 23, 67.

25. Tian Peize, "Jiefang sanshinian lai Shanghai qunzhong wenhua jianshe" [Construction of mass culture in Shanghai during the thirty years after Liberation], in *Fengyu licheng, 1949–1978* [A tempestuous course, 1949–1978, hereafter cited as

FYLC], ed. Zhonggong Shanghai shiwei dangshi yanjiu shi (Shanghai: Shanghai shudian chubanshe, 2005), 237.

26. *Shanghai meishu zhi*, 82–83.

27. *Shanghai chuban zhi*, 128.

28. *Shanghai guangbo dianshi zhi*, 32–33.

29. *Shanghai dianying zhi*, 569, 600.

30. Ibid., 572.

31. Ibid., 594; Tian, "Jiefang sanshinian lai," 245.

32. Liu Hongbing, " 'Gai xi, gai ren, gai zhi' zai Shanghai de guanche" [The implementation of "reform theater, reform people, reform the system" in Shanghai], FYLC, 253.

33. Yang Senyao, "Shanghai de wenhua yishu jiaoliu," [Cultural and artistic international exchange in Shanghai], FYLC, 283–284.

34. Yang Senyao and Wang Faji, "Quzhe fazhan de Shanghai chubanye" [The complicated development of Shanghai's publishing industry], FYLC, 216.

35. *Shanghai guangbo dianshi zhi*, 32–33.

36. *Shanghai dianying zhi*, 53; Shanghai Municipal Archive (hereafter SMA), B34-2-122; SMA, B177-1-324.

37. 'Shanghai zongjiao zhi bianzuan weiyuanhui, *Shanghai zongjiao zhi* [Shanghai religions gazetteer] (Shanghai: Shanghai shehui kexue yuan chubanshe, 2001), 39, 612; Zhongguo huidaomen shiliao jicheng bianzuan weiyuanhui, *Zhongguo huidaomen shiliao jicheng jin bainian lai huidaomen de zuzhi yu fenbu* [Integrated historical materials on the organization and distribution of China's religious sects during the past 100 years] (Beijing: Zhongguo shehui kexue chubanshe, 2004), 1:325–337.

38. Sun Xihong, "Shanghai dangyuan duiwu sici da fazhan" [Four moments of big development in the ranks of Shanghai Party members], FYLC, 1, 6; *Zhonggong Shanghai dang zhi*, 5.

39. *Zhonggong Shanghai dang zhi*, 293.

40. Tian, "Jiefang sanshinian lai," 237.

41. *Zhonggong Shanghai dang zhi*, 387.

42. Ibid., 399.

43. Ibid., 400.

44. *Zhongguo Gongchandang Shanghai shi zuzhi shiliao*, 353, 372–373.

45. See, for example, Wang Ruiyong, "Shanghai Jiao xian dianying faxing fangying sishinian" [Forty years of film distribution and projection in Shanghai's Jiao County], *Shanghai dianying shiliao* No. 2–3 (May 1993), 277–278.

46. SMA, B177-1-261.

47. Tian, "Jiefang sanshi nian lai," 245.

48. SMA, A22-2-184; SMA, A22-2-172.

49. SMA, B172-1-148.

50. SMA, A79-2-909.

51. SMA, B172–1–225; SMA, B172–1–149.
52. SMA, B172–1–592.
53. SMA, A22–2–958.
54. SMA, S319–4–12; SMA, B1–2–1632; SMA, C1–2–5679.
55. *Zhongguo Gongchandang Shanghai shi zuzhi shiliao*, 356.
56. On the general downsizing of China's urban population during this period, see Luo Pinghan, *Da qianxi: 1961–1963 nian de chengzhen renkou jingjian* [The great migration: Downsizing the urban population, 1961–1963] (Guangxi renmin chubanshe, 2003).
57. "Shanghai dangyuan duiwu," 6.
58. Shanghai shi wei dang shi bianxie zu, "Shanghai shi shangye xitong de jiceng dang zuzhi jianshe" [The construction of grassroots Party organizations in Shanghai's urban trade and commercial system], FYLC, 35.
59. SMA, A22–2–1093.
60. Ibid.
61. Ibid.
62. Ibid.
63. Ibid.
64. SMA, B3–2–147.
65. Ibid.
66. SMA, A22–1–615.
67. *Zhongguo xiqu zhi*, 23, 67.
68. SMA, A22–2–1093.
69. SMA, B3–2–147.
70. SMA, A22–2–1093.
71. Ibid.
72. SMA, B3–2–215.
73. SMA, B3–2–147.
74. Ibid.; SMA, A22–2–878.
75. SMA, A22–2–1093.
76. SMA, A22–1–878.
77. Ibid.
78. SMA, A22–2–1093.
79. Ibid.
80. SMA, A22–1–612.
81. Ibid.
82. Ibid.
83. SMA, A22–2–1093.
84. Ibid.
85. Ibid.
86. SMA, A22–1–615.
87. SMA, B3–2–222.

88. SMA, B3–2–180.

89. Ibid.

90. SMA, B3–2–192.

91. Ibid.

92. Ibid.

93. Ibid.

94. SMA, A22–1–615.

95. SMA, B3–2–101–53; SMA, A22–2–615.

96. SMA, B3–2–101–53.

97. See Qin Liyan, "The Sublime and the Profane: A Comparative Analysis of Two Fictional Narratives about Sent-Down Youth," in *The Chinese Cultural Revolution as History,* ed. Joseph W. Esherick, Paul G. Pickowicz, and Andrew G. Walder (Stanford: Stanford University Press, 2006): 240–265.

98. See Xiaobo Lü, *Cadres and Corruption: The Organizational Involution of the Chinese Communist Party* (Stanford: Stanford University Press, 2000).

9. China's "Great Proletarian Information Revolution" of 1966–1967

Initial research for this paper was made possible by a grant from the Swedish Research Council (VR) in support of "research on communist regimes." An earlier version of it was first presented at the University of Erfurt, Arbeitsstelle für Historische Anthropologie, in December 2005. This revised version draws on feedback received at a Lund University advanced seminar on media history, March 2010, and from my former student Fredrik Uddenfeldt.

1. Christopher Andrew and David Dilks, eds., *The Missing Dimension: Governments and Intelligence Communities in the Twentieth Century* (London: Macmillan, 1984), 1.

2. The emphasis here should be on *degrees* of *relative* autonomy. Something in the complex nature of the interplay between the Chinese state and Chinese society makes one hesitate to ascribe autonomous status to entities that may have been outwardly distinct from—and even vehemently opposed to—the local Communist Party apparat but whose membership at the same time insisted on referring to CCP Chairman Mao Zedong as their own "great helmsman."

3. See, for example, Andrew G. Walder, *Fractured Rebellion: The Beijing Red Guard Movement* (Cambridge, MA: Harvard University Press, 2009), and Elizabeth J. Perry and Xun Li, *Proletarian Power: Shanghai in the Cultural Revolution* (Boulder, CO: Westview Press, 1997).

4. *Wei Mao Zedong er zhan: sansi* Shoudu hongweibing *wenxuan* [Fighting for Mao Zedong: Selected articles from the 3rd HQ *Capital Red Guard*] (n.p., 1967), 204–205.

5. Beijing shi jixie gongyeju Dongfeng geming zaofan zongbu, ed., *Dongfeng zhanbao zengkan: Neibu cankao* [Supplement to the East Wind battlefield reports: Internal reference], no. 8, May 20, 1967.

6. *Baowei gongzuo shouce* [Protection work manual] ([Beijing], 1972), 48.

7. Mao Zedong, "Muster Our Forces to Repulse the Rightists' Wild Attacks," in *Selected Works of Mao Tse-tung,* vol. 5 (Beijing: Foreign Languages Press, 1977), 448–450.

8. *Jingji baowei gongzuo* [Economic protection work], vol. 9 (April 1958): 21.

9. Ibid.

10. *Luoshui ji* [They ended up in the water] (Beijing: Beijing shi gonganju, 1964), 28.

11. Hong Tingzhong, "Hengkong chushi: ji hongweibing de dansheng" [Over the earth: Recalling the birth of the Red Guards], in *Hongweibing wenyi,* no. 9 (June 1968): 7.

12. "Circular of the Central Committee of the Chinese Communist Party," in *Important Documents of the Great Proletarian Cultural Revolution* (Beijing: Foreign Languages Press, 1970), 123.

13. Zhonggong Beijing shiwei, "Guanyu chexiao ge dazhuan xuexiao gong-zuozu de jueding" [Decision to withdraw work teams from institutions of higher education], in *Wuchanjieji wenhua dageming ziliao,* ed. Beijing shi huaxue gongyeju jiguan hongse xuanchuanzhan (Beijing, 1966), 1:64.

14. "Zhang Chunqiao, Guan Feng, Yao Wenyuan tongzhi zai Zhonggong zhongyang, Guowuyuan wenge jiedai bangongshi de jianghua" [Speeches by Comrades Zhang Chunqiao, Guan Feng, and Yao Wenyuan at the Cultural Revolution Reception Offices of the CCP Center and State Council], in *Zhongyang fuze tongzhi guanyu wuchanjieji wenhua dageming de jianghua [bayue-shiyue],* ed. Shoudu dazhuan yuanxiao hongweibing daibiao dahui Zhengfa gongshe (Beijing, 1967), 303–307.

15. CCP Central Committee, "Decision Concerning the Great Proletarian Cultural Revolution," in Schoenhals, *China's Cultural Revolution,* 34.

16. The exhortation was Mao's. See his "Get Organized!" in *Selected Works of Mao Tsetung,* vol. 3 (Beijing: Foreign Languages Press, 1965), 153.

17. Tan Houlan, "Proletarian Dictatorship and Proletarian Extensive Democracy," in Schoenhals, *China's Cultural Revolution,* 152–154.

18. See reference to "Methods of Work of Party Committees" in Schoenhals, *China's Cultural Revolution,* 43.

19. Dong Chunhua et al., "Xianqi Beida yundong de xin gaochao!—zhi xiao wenge chouweihui de gongkaixin" [Launch a new high tide in the movement at Peking University: An open letter to the University Cultural Revolution Preparatory Committee], in *Shoudu guilai,* ed. Shanghai jiaoyu xueyuan "Tiejian" zhandoudui (Shanghai, 1966), 1:28.

20. "Lai zi shoudu Qinghua de yi feng xin" [A letter from Qinghua in the capital] in *Shu fengliu renwu hai kan jinzhao—Yunnan wenhua dageming yingxiong pu*, ed. Xiang Zhaobin and Wang Xianjin (Kunming: 8.23 gongren zongbu, 1968), 20–22.

21. See Roderick MacFarquhar and Michael Schoenhals, *Mao's Last Revolution* (Cambridge, MA: Harvard University Press, 2006), 90–91.

22. Lin Biao, "Zai jiejian zhongyang wenge xiaozu chengyuan shi de jianghua" [Speech at a reception for members of the Central Cultural Revolution Group], in *Lin Biao wenxuan* (Xi'an: Xi'an yejin jianzhu xueyuan geweihui xuanchuanbu, 1967), 2:274–275.

23. "Chen Boda, Kang Sheng, Li Xuefeng, Jiang Qing, Yao Wenyuan tongzhi deng zhongyao jianghua" [Important speeches by Comrades Chen Boda, Kang Sheng, Li Xuefeng, Jiang Qing, and Yao Wenyuan], in Shoudu dazhuan yuanxiao hongweibing daibiao dahui Zhengfa gongshe, *Zhongyang fuze tongzhi guanyu wuchanjieji wenhua dageming de jianghua*, 158–160.

24. Tao Zhu, "Jiejian Zhongguo renmin daxue wenge chouweihui Yu Jingqing deng ren he Wuhan diqu qi tongzhi de jianghua" [Speech at reception for Yu Jingqing et al. from the China People's University Cultural Revolution Preparatory Committee and seven comrades from the Wuhan region], in *Tao Zhu fangeming xiuzhengzhuyi yanlun huibian* (Beijing: Mao Zedong Sixiang zhexue shehui kexuebu hongweibing liandui, 1967), 210.

25. "Tao Zhu huida 'Fu Guangzhou zhuanjiu Wang Renzhong geming zaofantuan' wenti shi de shikuang" [Actual record of Tao Zhu responding to questions from the "Revolutionary rebel regiment headed for Guangzhou specifically to drag out Wang Renzhong"], in *Zhongyang fuze tongzhi guanyu wuchanjieji wenhua dageming de jianghua [shiyiyue–shieryue]*, ed. Shoudu dazhuan yuanxiao hongweibing daibiao dahui Zhengfa gongshe (Beijing, 1967), 282–283.

26. Xin Beida gongshe "Duli hanqiu" zhandoudui, ed., *Shoudu gaoxiao liangpai maodun de youlai, fazhan he Guan Feng, Wang Li youguan jianghua* [Guan Feng's and Wang Li's relevant speeches and the origins and development of the contradiction between the two factions in the universities of the capital] (Beijing, 1967), 13–14.

27. Tang Shaojie (historian of the Red Guard movement at Tsinghua University), interviewed by the author in Lund, Sweden, on September 7, 2010.

28. *Shoudu hongweibing* [Capital Red Guard], no. 19 (January 1, 1967): 4.

29. Wang Naiying, "Guanyu fanzui genyuan de chubu jiaodai cailiao" [Tentative account of the roots of my crimes], February 8, 1969. Handwritten document in the possession of the author, 3.

30. [Niu] Xiaohan and Mia Turner, *789 jizhongying: Zhongguo gaogan zinü zhong yige teshu qunti de gushi* [Camp 789: The story of a special group of Chinese senior cadres' children] (Brampton, ON: Mirror Books, 1998), 212.

31. Tang Xianzheng, telephone and address book formerly in the archive of the Hubei Geology Institute. Photographs of selected pages in the possession of the author.

32. "Zhai zi Wang Huiling jiaodai cailiao" [Excerpts from Wang Huiling's confessions] (November 12–22, 1970), copied by hand on April 5, 1971, in the Institute of Communication Engineering. Document in the possession of the author.

33. *Dongtai* [Current information], no. 144 (September 8, 1967).

34. *Lianhe fengbao* [Coalition tempest], no. 69 (December 19, 1967).

35. "Zhou zongli jiejian Xinjiang geming zaofanpai daibiaotuan tanhua jiyao" [Minutes of conversation at Premier Zhou's meeting with revolutionary rebel delegation from Xinjiang], in *Hongri zhao tianshan: Guanyu Xinjiang wenti Zhonggong zhongyang wenjian ji zhongyang shouzhang de jianghua*, ed. Xinjiang hong ersi *Xinjiang hongweibing bao* bianjibu (n.p., 1968), 24.

36. *414 zhanbao* [April 14 battle report], special issue (May 28, 1968): 4.

37. *Yaowen* [Important news], no. 94 (July 22, 1967): 3.

38. Ibid., no. 4.

39. *Dongtai jianbao* [Current information newsletter], no. 26 (February 3, 1967).

40. Ibid.

41. *Jiaogong dongtai* [Teachers and staff current information], no. 26 (May 6, 1967).

42. *Dongtai,* no. 73 (June 11, 1967).

43. Du Junfu, "Wo shi zemyang bei dacheng 'wuyaoliu' fenzi de" [How I was branded a "May 16" element], *Jiyi*, no. 30 (August 13, 2009): 31.

44. Walder, *Fractured Rebellion*, 215–219.

45. Wang Naiying, "Jiao xitong de jiefa cailiao" [A fairly systematic exposé], January 15, 1968. Handwritten document in the possession of the author, 73.

46. *Jiaogong dongtai*, no. 1 [March 25, 1967].

47. Quoted from original permit no. 000006, in the author's possession.

48. *Fandaodi tongxun* [Resist all the way bulletin], no. 7 (April 19, 1967).

49. Ibid., no. 23 (May 31, 1967).

50. Ibid., no. 16 (May 13, 1967).

51. *Wenge jianxun*, extra issue no. 60 (May 6, 1967).

52. *414 zhanbao*, special issue (May 28, 1968): 4.

53. Walder, *Fractured Rebellion*, 247.

54. *Quanwudi* [And are strong], no. 5 (August 21, 1967).

55. *Dongtai,* no. 115 (August 5, 1967).

56. Zhonggong zhongyang wenxian yanjiushi, ed., *Jianguo yilai Mao Zedong wengao* [Mao Zedong's manuscripts since the founding of the nation] (Beijing: Zhongyang wenxian chubanshe, 1998), vol. 12, 385.

57. *Ziliao* [Materials], no. 1 (September 11, 1967): 2.

58. *Zhou zongli, Chen Boda, Kang Sheng, Xie Fuzhi, Jiang Qing tongzhi zai Beijing dazhuan yuanxiao hongdaihui, gongdaihui, nongdaihui he zhu-Jing sanjun wuchanjieji gemingpai daibiao zuotanhui shang de jianghua* [Speeches by Premier Zhou and Comrades Chen Boda, Kang Sheng, Xie Fuzhi, and Jiang Qing at a meeting with delegates from the Capital Universities Red Guard Congress, Workers' Congress, Peasants' Congress, and Proletarian Revolutionary Faction Members of the three branches of the armed forces in Beijing] (Lijiang, 1967), 15.

59. *Zhongyang shouzhang zhongyao jianghua* [Important speeches by central leaders] (Beijing: Tsinghua daxue Jinggangshan bingtuan, 1967), 4.

60. *Ziliao,* 6.

61. *Dongfanghong bao* [East is red report], no. 75 (September 15, 1967).

62. *Zhongyang shouzhang fenbie jiejian dazhuan yuanxiao daibiao de jianghua* [Speeches by central leaders at receptions for delegates from institutions of higher education] (Beijing: Shoudu chubanjie geming zaofan zongbu, 1967), 15.

63. *Yaowen jianbao* [Important news report], no. 70 (September 20, 1967).

64. *Dongtai,* no. 155 (September 21, 1967).

65. *Dongtai bao* [Current information report], no. 134 (September 22, 1967).

66. *Xuexi ziliao* [Study material], no. 878 (December 18, 1967).

67. Ibid.

68. http://www.newschool.edu/cps/subpage.aspx?id=97320

10. The Dilemma of Implementation

1. In this study, "communal religion" or "communal religious activities" refers to locally based and oriented rituals, territorial cults, and temple organizations in rural China that the Communist government usually regarded as "superstition," in contrast to redemptive societies (*huidaomen*), newer religious movements with different organization, leadership, areas of operation, and scriptural traditions that the government viewed as counterrevolutionary.

2. Stephen Jones, "Chinese Ritual Music under Mao and Deng," *British Journal of Ethnomusicology* 8 (1999): 27–66; Steve A. Smith, "Talking Toads and Chinless Ghosts: The Politics of 'Superstitious' Rumors in the People's Republic of China, 1961–1965," *American Historical Review* 111, no. 2 (April 2006): 405–427; Steve A. Smith, "Local Cadres Confront the Supernatural: The Politics of Holy Water (*shengshui*) in the PRC, 1949–1966," *China Quarterly* 188 (December 2006): 999–1022; Joseph Tse-Hei Lee, "Politics of Faith: Christian Activism and the Maoist State in Chaozhou, Guangdong Province," *China Review* 9, no. 2 (September 2009): 17–39.

3. Richard J. Smith, "The Teachings of Ritual and the Rectification of Customs: Echoes of Tradition in the Political Culture of Modern China," in *Jinshi Zhongguo zhi chuantong yu tuibian: Liu Guangjing yuanshi qishiwu sui zhushou lunwenji*

[Tradition and metamorphosis in modern Chinese history: Essays in honor of Professor Kwang-Ching Liu's seventy-fifth birthday], ed. Hao Yanping and Wei Xiumei (Taipei: Institute of Modern History, Academia Sinica, 1998), 2:1173–1216; Daniel H. Bays, "A Tradition of State Dominance," in *God and Caesar in China*, ed. Jason Kindopp and Carol Lee Hamrin (Washington, DC: Brookings Institution Press, 2004), 25–39; Anthony C. Yu, *State and Religion in China: Historical and Textual Perspectives* (Chicago: Open Court, 2005).

4. For example, certain communal rituals such as dragon boat racing were sometimes defined as superstition and sometimes not, depending on the needs of the government. This was true even during the Maoist era.

5. Primary sources cited in this study come from local governmental archives (mainly Ruian Municipal Archives, but also other governmental archives in southern Zhejiang) and my fieldwork in Ruian's Tangxia, Xincheng, and Mayu Districts during the summers of 2004, 2011, and 2012. Other materials cited include local gazetteers, memoirs of local religious leaders, and the internal publications of local government organs.

6. As of the 2010 national census, the city had a population of about 1.19 million, covering 1,271 square kilometers of land.

7. See "Guanyu dangqian zongjiao huodong qingkuang de baogao" [Report on current religious activities], April 4, 1957, Ruian Municipal Archives (hereafter cited as RMA), 1–9–85.

8. These numbers were obtained from the Ruian Ethnic Minority and Religion Bureau, which I visited in August 2012. The number of registered religious sites includes 214 Christian churches (Protestant and Catholic), 228 Buddhist temples, and 153 Daoist temples. These numbers do not include temples and churches in Li'ao, Xianyan, and Meitou—three religiously important towns that were incorporated into Ouhai and Longwan Districts of the Wenzhou municipality in 2001.

9. Although dragon boat racing is mainly performed during the spring in the Wenzhou plains, a similar ritual of the Great Peace Dragon [Boat] (*taiping long*) is observed in mountainous areas in the winter, when people tour dragon boats made of paper throughout the community. See Jiang Zhun, *Qihai suotan* [Anecdotes of Wenzhou] (Shanghai: Shanghai shehui kexue yuan chubanshe, 2002), 243; Chen Ruizan, ed., *Dong'ou yishi huilu* [Collection of anecdotes from East Ou region], (Shanghai: Shanghai shehui kexue yuan chubanshe, 2006), 34; Lin Yixiu, "Longchuan: shequ gongtongti de lishi jiyi" [Dragon boat: Historical memories of the communities], *Minsu yanjiu* 4 (August 2007): 215–216.

10. Scholars often cite the opposing terms *zheng* (orthodox) and *xie* (heterodox) in the state classification of religious practices in late imperial China. My understanding is that *xie* primarily referred to millenarian sects. A subcategory of *su* practices should be distinguished from the category of *xie*, because *xie* connotes

"evil" and thus practices that cannot be tolerated. In contrast, the concept of *su* was often used to refer to religious practices that were tolerable in the eyes of the state. It should be noted, however, that a *su* practice could be categorized as *xie* once it was seen as a threat to imperial hegemony.

11. Vincent Goossaert, "1898: The Beginning of the End for Chinese Religion?" *Journal of Asian Studies* 65 (May 2006): 307–335.

12. Rebecca Nedostup, *Superstitious Regimes: Religion and the Politics of Chinese Modernity* (Cambridge, MA: Harvard Asia Center, 2009), 178.

13. See Lo Shih-Chieh, "The Order of Local Things: Popular Politics and Religion in Modern Wenzhou, 1840–1940" (PhD diss., Brown University, 2010), chapter 4.

14. Zhang Gang, *Zhang Gang riji* [Zhang Gang's diaries] (Shanghai: Shanghai shehui kexue yuan chubanshe, 2003), 306–307; see also Lo Shih-Chieh, "The Order of Local Things," chapter 5.

15. Among 609 temples (*miao*) listed in the "religion" section of the Republican Ruian gazetteer, only 10 communal temples were converted into schools or used for other purposes. See *Ruian xianzhi gao* [Draft gazetteer of Ruian County] (Ruian xian xiuzhiju, 1946–1948), 58–75.

16. Ibid., 7–45; 58–75.

17. Ibid., 1–6.

18. See Mo Fayou, *Wenzhou Jidujiao shi* [History of Christianity in Wenzhou] (Hong Kong: Alliance Bible Seminary Press, 1998), and Cao Nanlai, "Boss Christians: The Business of Religion in the 'Wenzhou Model' of Christian Revival," *China Journal* 59 (January 2008): 63–87. See also Lo Shih-Chieh, "The Order of Local Things," chapter 3.

19. David Holm, *Art and Ideology in Revolutionary China* (Oxford: Clarendon Press, 1991), 16.

20. Ibid., chapters 4–9; James A. Flath, *The Cult of Happiness: Nianhua, Art, and History in Rural North China* (Vancouver: University of British Columbia Press, 2004), chapter 6.

21. Holm, *Art and Ideology in Revolutionary China*, 49–74.

22. The land reform in Ruian took place between August 1950 and December 1951.

23. As in the Republican era, conversion of village temples was not complete in many cases. Local residents continued to use village temples for religious activities. See "Wei benxiang xiangxiao litang shang baiman fogui yuanbaozhuo fang'ai xuesheng jihui bufen mixin nongmin zhishi xuesheng kangyi yidong qing zhengfu xiezhu jiejue you" [On shrines and sacrifice tables occupying the auditorium of our town elementary school that obstructed school meetings, some superstitious peasants instigated students to protest against the plan to remove shrines and sacrifice tables, we ask for the assistance of the government in settling (the problem)], 1954, RMA, 4-6-69.

24. Interview with Zhang Junsun, on August 18, 2012.

25. Shi Shihu, *Ying Weixian zhuan* [Biography of Ying Weixian] (Xianggang chubanshe, 2009), 8–9; interview with Ying's grandson, Ying Weixian, on August 17, 2012. Ying Weixian has been the head of the Ruian Daoist Association since 1992.

26. In the "Decisions on Certain Issues in Land Struggle," issued by the Chinese Soviet Republic in 1933, it was suggested that priests, pastors, Daoist masters, Buddhist monks, temple workers, fengshui observers, fortune-tellers, and diviners should all be considered "religious professionals engaged in religious superstition [*zongjiao mixin*]." When the document was revised and reissued in 1948, this passage remained nearly unchanged. When the document was issued for the third time in 1950 after the founding of the People's Republic, the phrase "religious professionals" was changed to "religious professionals or superstition professionals," which paved the way for the possibility of differentiating "religion" from "superstition." However, a formal demarcation between "religious professionals" and "superstition professionals" was not established.

27. Mao Zedong, "Hunan nongmin yundong de kaocha baogao" [Report on the peasant movement in Hu'nan] in *Mao Zedong xuanji di yi juan* [Anthology of Mao Zedong, vol. 1] (Beijing: Renmin chubanshe, 1991), 33. This sentence was often quoted by officials dealing with the issue of "superstition" during the Maoist period.

28. "Guanyu ben xian gedi fasheng qunzhongxing zhaofo qiuyu ji saodong shijian de baogao" [Report on incidents of conjuring up deities to make rain and disturbances throughout the county], August 5, 1953, RMA, 1–5–3.

29. The county government in Yongkang, Zhejiang, allowed all county officials except for administrative heads (county head, district head, etc.) to participate in rainmaking ceremonies in order to better "educate" people. See Lü Shanxin, "Taiping xiang qiuyu mixin shijian huigu" [Memoir of the incident of rainmaking superstition at Taiping Town] in *Wushi niandai de Yongkang (Yongkang wenshi ziliao di shisan ji)* [Yongkang in the 1950s (Yongkang historical materials, vol. 13)], (Yongkang shi zhengxie wenshi weiyuanhui, 2001), 13:360.

30. The vice-head of Xincheng District, Xue Chongyin, was later forced to write a self-criticism for firing his guns into the air to dispel the masses and attacking a ritual organizer in Xinzhou Township. See "Guanyu Xincheng qu Xinzhou xiang saodong shijian geren jiantao" [Self-criticism on the riot in Xinzhou Township, Xincheng District], August 31, 1953, RMA, 1–5–90.

31. Ibid.

32. "Zhonggong Ruian xianwei pi zhuan Duanwujie wenyu huodong weiyuanhui guanyu Duanwujie wenyu huodong hualongzhou gongzuo yijian" [The Dragon Boat Festival Committee on Cultural Recreation's work opinion about dragon boat racing, circulated by the Ruian County Party Committee], May 30, 1955, RMA, 1–7–34.

33. "Guanyu zhengque chuli Duanwujie hualongzhou wenti de jidian yijian" [Some opinions on correctly handling the issue of dragon boat racing during the Dragon Boat Festival], May 27, 1957, RMA, 1–9–232.

34. "Guanyu zai Duanwujie jinzhi hualongzhou kaizhan aiguo huodong de tongzhi" [On prohibiting dragon boat racing and carrying out patriotic activities during the Dragon Boat Festival], June 16, 1958, RMA, 1–10–305.

35. "Guanyu Duanwujie hualongzhou huodong de tongzhi" [Notice on dragon boat racing during the Dragon Boat Festival], June 14, 1961, RMA, 1–13–108. The basket represents a group of divine spirits who possess the body of rowers during dragon boat race.

36. Gong Xuezeng, "Zhongguo Gongchandang de zongjiao—guojia guan" [The conception of religion and state of the Chinese Communist Party], *Xibei minzu daxue xuebao* 3 (March 2011): 13–24.

37. "Zhonggong zhongyang guanyu Hanminzu zhong Fojiao wenti de zhishi" [Party Center's instruction on the issue of Buddhism among Han people] and "Zhonggong zhongyang guanyu chuli Tianzhujiao wenti de zhishi" [Party Center's instruction on the issue of the Catholic Church]. See *Tongzhan zhengce wenjian huibian (di si juan)* [Collection of united front policies, vol. 4], ed. Zhonggong zhongyang tongyi zhanxian gongzuo zu (Zhonggong zhongyang tongyi zhanxian gongzuo zu, 1958), 140–149.

38. "Ruian xian gequ Fojiaojie Fojiaotu mingce" [Name list of Buddhists in the districts of Ruian County], October 1952, RMA, 4–4–74.

39. "Wei xi chaming Yueqing xian suo fasheng zongjiao wenti chuli bao shu you" [On clarifying the handling of the religious incidents in Yueqing County and reporting to the (Wenzhou regional) Commission], September 12, 1951, Yueqing Municipal Archives, 26–3–2.

40. "Zhixing zongjiao zhengce diaocha baogao" [Investigation report on the implementation of religious policies], April 9, 1953, RMA, 1–5–62.

41. "Jinhou bude shanzi zhanyong jiaotang" [Do not occupy churches without authorization from now on], March 17, 1956, RMA, 1–8–227.

42. "Jidujiao Tangxia qu Zilihui Xundao Neidi lianhe qingqiu zhunyu huifu juhui you ji pifu" [The joint petition for restoring gatherings by the Independent Church, Methodist Church, and the China Inland Mission at Tangxia District and the reply], January 20, 1952, RMA, 4–4–74.

43. "Wei qingshi benxian Fojiao choubeihui kefou zhunxu qi chengli you" [On asking whether the preparatory county Buddhist association should be established], October 10, 1952, RMA, 4–4–74.

44. "Wenzhou zhuanshu wei fu zhi jiaohui qingqiu huifu juhui wenti you" [Wenzhou special commission on the question of replying to the Christian congregations' petitions for restoring gatherings], May 11, 1952, RMA, 4–4–74; "Guanyu jiaohui zai tugai hou de huifu juhui wenti" [On the issue regarding the

restoration of church gatherings after land reform], July 29, 1952, RMA, 4–4–74. The situation was similar in Yueqing of Wenzhou and Wenling of Taizhou.

45. "Zhejiang shengwei xuanchuanbu guanyu diyici zongjiao gongzuo huiyi de zongjie baogao" [Zhejiang provincial Party propaganda department's summary report of the first meeting on religious affairs], December 15, 1952, Wenling Municipal Archives, J1–1–56.

46. "Ruian xianwei guanyu zongjiao gongzuo de pishi baogao" [Ruian County Party Committee's instruction and report on religious affairs], July 15, 1955, RMA, 1–7–35.

47. "Zongjiaotu bianhua qingkuang" [Changes in the number of religious believers], June 5, 1961, RMA, 4–13–42.

48. "Guanyu liji caiqu cuoshi jiaqiang fanghuo he zhizhi mixin huodong de yijian" [Opinions on immediately taking measures to reinforce the work of fire prevention and to stop superstitious activities], July 6, 1960, RMA, 4–13–12.

49. According to published data, the regional distribution of "superstition professionals" who resumed the profession in northern Zhejiang was 60 percent in Yuhang and 69 percent in Xinchang, in eastern Zhejiang, 84 percent in Cixi, 98 percent in Ninghai, and 92 percent in Tiantai; in southern Zhejiang, 74 percent in Yunhe and 98 percent in Pingyang. See *Yunhe xian gongan zhi* [Yunhe County public security gazetteer], ed. Chen Xubin (Yunhe xian gongan ju, 1994), 118; *Pingyang xian gongan zhi* [Pingyang County public security gazetteer], ed. Cheng Shicen (Tianjin: Nankai daxue chubanshe, 1997), 98; *Xinchang xian gongan zhi* [Xinchang County public security gazetteer], ed. Gao Shuibiao (Beijing: Dangdai Zhongguo chubanshe, 1994), 139; *Cixi shi gongan zhi* [Cixi Municipal County public security gazetteer], ed. Hu Yuntang (Beijing: Fangzhi chubanshe, 1998), 193; Xia Yuncheng, ed., *Tiantai xian gongan zhi* (Tiantai County public security gazetteer) (Beijing: Fangzhi chubanshe, 1998), 122–123; Xu Yaoxin et al., ed., *Yuhang gongan zhi* (Yuhang County public security gazetteer) (Hangzhou: Zhejiang daxue chubanshe, 1997), 294; and *Ninghai xian gongan zhi* [Ninghai County public security gazetteer], ed. Zhang Zhebin (Beijing: Zhonghua shuju, 2001), 256.

50. "Zhejiang sheng renmin weiyuanhui guanyu fandui fengjian mixin huodong de tongzhi" [The Zhejiang people's committee's notice on opposing feudal superstitious activities], December 26, 1964, RMA, 49–16–41.

51. "Guanyu Duanwujie hualongzhou huodong de tongzhi" [Notice on dragon boat race during the Dragon Boat Festival], June 14, 1961, RMA, 1–13–108; "Ruian xian Lingxia shengchan dadui nao longzhou" [Lingxia Production Brigade of Ruian County to hold dragon boat race], June 13, 1961, Wenling Municipal Archives, J79–1–48.

52. Zhang Chaoyin, ed., *Ruian shi longzhou huodong jianshi* [A concise history of dragon boat racing in Ruian] (Ruian shi shiwei dangshi yanjiushi and Difangzhi bangongshi, unpublished internal materials, 2004), 8.

53. In the same period, the distinction between religion and superstition became a central issue in theoretical debates between Party intellectuals, with Ya Hanzhang on one side and You Xiang and Liu Junwang on the other. The exchange between the two sides lasted for three years (September 1963–November 1965). Ya argued that religion should be separated from superstition, which must be suppressed. Religion would only gradually disappear through atheist education. You and Liu contended that religion and superstition were the same false illusions concerning supernatural power and that their separation would enhance religion. Conducting atheist education was not enough. Religion must be fought because it was not simply a thought issue (*sixiang wenti*) but also a sociopolitical one. Given the history in the following decade, the hardliners appear to have won the day. However, Ya's views on the separation of superstition from religion would have significant influence on religious policy after 1978. For the Ya vs. You and Liu debate, see Shinichi Hiroike, "Chuugoku no kyousan shugi niokeru 'shuukyou' gainen: 1960 nendai kiba ya kanshuu niyoru giron o chuushin ni" [The concept of "religion" in Chinese Communism: Ya Hanzhang's discussions in the 1960s], *Shuukyou kenkyuu* 336 (2003): 27–50.

54. "Pizhuan xianwei jianwei guanyu Tangxia Zhang Buwang tongzhi jinxing fengjian mixin huodong dasi huihuo langfei de diaocha baogao" [Issuing the investigation report by the county Party supervision committee on Comrade Zhang Buwang of Tangxia's engagement in feudal superstitious activities and extravagant expenditures], January 14, 1966, RMA, 1–18–8.

55. "Guanyu Tangxia Shao Yongsheng tongzhi canyu lingdao 'xiu jiapu' wenti de taolun" [Discussion on Comrade Shao Yongsheng of Tangxia District's involvement in organizing "genealogy compilation" activities], June 15, 1963, RMA, 1–15–143

56. Ibid.

57. "Guanyu dui Tangxia Zhang Buwang tongzhi jinxing fengjian fubi huodong de diaocha qingkuang he bianlun qingkuang" [Investigation and discussion on Comrade Zhang Buwang's engagement in the restoration of feudal order], January 17, 1966, RMA, 49–18–1.

58. "Guanyu zongjiaojie shehuizhuyi jiaoyu yundong zongjie baogao" [Summary report on the Socialist Education Movement in the religious sector], April 1958, RMA, 1–10–161.

59. Ibid.

60. Ibid.

61. "Guanyu Wenzhou diqu zongjiao zhengce zhixing qingkuang de baogao" [Report on the implementation of religious policies in the Wenzhou region], June 26, 1959, RMA, 1–11–248.

62. For instance, although the seventh national meeting on religious affairs in 1963 required striking firmly against counterrevolutionaries operating under the cloak of religion, it also emphasized "thoroughly enforcing religious freedom

policy and reinforcing the administration of religion" ("Diqici quanguo zongjiao gongzuo huiyi jiyao" [The minutes of the Seventh National Religious Affairs Conference], June 14, 1963, RMA, 1–5–164). Cadres were asked to make strictly clear "the boundary between political issues and the issues of thought and faith, the boundary between illegal activities and normal religious activities," in a command from Wenzhou prefectural government to attack counterrevolutionaries and bad elements within religious communities ("Guanyu daji zongjiao neibu fan huai fenzi de yijian baogao" [Opinions on attacking counterrevolutionaries and bad elements within the religious sector], June 1, 1964, RMA, 1–16–80).

63. Ibid.

64. "1961 nian zongjiao huodong qingkuang" [Situation of religious activities in 1961], November, 1961, RMA, 4–13–42.

65. "Guanyu muqian zongjiao huodong qingkuang" [On current religious activities], November 16, 1961, RMA, 4–13–42.

66. Ibid.

67. "Ruian xian Dayuejin qianhou jiaotang simiao bianhua qingkuang" [Changes to temples and churches before and after the Great Leap Forward in Ruian County], June 5, 1960, RMA, 4–13–42.

68. Tin was commonly used to make religious artifacts in traditional Chinese society.

69. Shu Chenqian, *Wushi nian jiaohui shenghuo huiyi* [Memoirs of fifty years of church life], unpublished manuscript, chapter 2.

70. Zhang Chaoyin, *Ruian shi longzhou huodong jianshi*, 78–91.

71. There was almost no rain for eighty-three days starting in mid-July. Even the Tang River, the longest river in the Wenrui plains, dried up.

72. Interview with Zhang Shisong at Lower Village, July 26, 2012; Tang Yijun, ed., *Xincheng zhen zhi* [Xincheng Town gazetteer] (Huangshan shushe, 1998), 280. In another case, representatives of Protestant churches in Wenzhou and Fuding of northern Fujian gathered in Nanchen Village, Xicheng, in spring 1971 to discuss merging all orders into one in order to act jointly—a critical historical moment for the development of the Protestant church in Wenzhou. It is said that more than 600 people joined the meeting. That year there was another, even larger meeting that took place in the same locale during the winter. Given the scale of the meetings, village cadres very likely played a role in shielding religious gatherings. See Miao Zhitong, *Wenzhou qu jiaohui shi* [Church history in Wenzhou] (unpublished internal materials, 2005–2006?), 138–139.

73. According to a provincial report, a few months after Nixon's August 1972 visit, a former student in a Catholic seminary, Cao Xiangde of Huangyan County, Taizhou, wrote letters to some overseas institutions accusing the government of religious persecution. Zhuo Peiliang, another former student of a Catholic seminary, assembled a group of people to draft a letter to Christians in the nation and plotted to send a delegation to Rome to seek help from the pope. In September,

Rev. Liao Zhongjie, a native of Wenzhou who was serving in the Methodist Church in Hong Kong, allegedly contacted his sister in Wenzhou, asking her to collect information and reconnect with old acquaintances. The provincial report is probably ideologically laden, given political conditions at the time. We should not, however, rule out the possibility that there were indeed attempts to contact the outside world after Nixon's visit. See the request of the Zhejiang provincial government to subordinate prefectural and county governments, "Guanyu daji liyong zongjiao jinxing pohuai huodong de fangeming fenzi de qingshi baogao" [Request for permission to attack counterrevolutionaries exploiting religion to conduct destructive activities], February 2, 1973, RMA, 1-21-60.

74. Chen Cunfu, "Zhejiang diqu Tianzhujiao he Xinjiao diaocha yanjiu" [Investigation of Catholicism and Protestantism in Zhejiang], *Ding* [Tripod], 131 (2004): 13; "Wenzhou diwei guanyu quanqu zongjiao gongzuo xianchanghui qingkuang baogao he Pingyang Huqian xiang dui zongjiao douzheng shidian zongjie baogao" [Wenzhou Party Committee's report of the regional on-the-spot religious affairs meeting and summary of the experiment on the struggle against religion at Huqian Township, Pingyang County], November 1, 1958, Longquan Municipal Archives, 1-5-172; "Guanyu daji liyong zongjiao jinxing pohuai huodong de fangeming fenzi de qingshi baogao."

75. Shu Chenqian, *Wushi nian jiaohui shenghuo huiyi,* chapter 16.

76. Interview with Liaozheng, head of the Buddhist association in Longshan Temple, Ruian, August 17, 2012.

77. There were two reports of attempts to restore "feudal superstition" and "feudal lineage" in the mountainous area of Huling District in the early 1970s. See "Guanyu dui Huling qu Chen Shicong Chen Wenzhu fengjian fubi an de chuli yijian baogao" [Opinions on the handling of the case of feudal restoration of Chen Shicong and Chen Wenzhu in Huling District], March 30, 1973, RMA, 1-21-9, and "Guanyu Huling qu Zheng Qingzan jinxing fengjian fubi de chuli jueding" [Decision on the handling of the case of feudal restoration of Zheng Qingzan in Huling District], July 8, 1977, RMA, 82-27-1. In addition, a small number of temples were rebuilt in the early 1970s. See Zhou Konghua and Ruan Zhensheng, eds., *Wenzhou Daojiao tonglan* [General survey of Daoism in Wenzhou] (Hong Kong: Tianma tushu youxian gongsi, 1999).

78. "Guanyu Ruian shi zongjiao wenti diaocha qingkuang de huibao" [Investigation report on the issue of religion in Ruian City], December 22, 1990, RMA, 1-38-6. There were 16,853 Christians (Catholics and Protestants) in Ruian in 1956. See "Guanyu dangqian zongjiao huodong qingkuang de baogao" [Report on current religious activities], April 4, 1957, RMA, 1-9-85.

79. Ruian's population increased from 456,900 in 1949 to 1,007,393 in 1982. *Zhejiang sheng renkou tongji ziliao huibian 1949–1985* [Census data collection in Zhejiang Province, 1949–1985] (Hangzhou: Zhejiang sheng renkou pucha bangongshi, 1986), 457–458.

80. This figure includes both baptized Christians and religious seekers (*mudaoyou*).

81. "Guanyu Ruian shi zongjiao wenti diaocha qingkuang de huibao" [Report on the investigation of religious issues in Ruian City], December 22, 1990, RMA, 1–38–6.

82. Li Yu, "Wenzhou (Ruian) diqu hualongzhou huodong anquan guanli wenti yu duice yanjiu" [Research on issues and strategies of public safety management in dragon boat activities in Wenzhou region (Ruian)] (master's thesis, Shanghai Tongji University, 2006), 7.

83. Some religious leaders told me that they had only vague knowledge of the new religious policy and accused the local government of intentionally delaying its implementation.

84. "1982 zongjiao gongzuo qingkuang he jinhou yijian" [Situation of religious affairs in 1982 and opinions on future activities], January 27, 1983, RMA, 1–31–45.

85. "Guanyu qingli miaoyu jianjue shazhu fengjian mixin he fengjian zongzu waifeng de tongzhi" [Notice on closing temples and resolutely stopping the evil trend of feudal superstition and feudal lineage], January 20, 1986, RMA, 1–7–20. For the situation of temple construction and reconstruction in Wenzhou, see also Mayfair Mei-Hui Yang, "Postcolonial Complex, State Disenchantment, and Popular Reappropriation of Space in Rural Southeast China," *Journal of Asian Studies* 63 (August 2004): 719–755.

86. "Zhang Guisheng tongzhi zai xianwei zongjiao gongzuo huiyi shang de jianghua tongzhi" [Notice on comrade Zhang Guisheng's speech at the meeting of county Party Committee on religious affairs], November 18, 1985, RMA, 1–33–7.

87. "Zhuanfa Mayu qugongsuo guanyu Yantougong chuli qingkuang de baogao tongzhi" [Issuing the report of Mayu district government on the handling of the problem of Yantou Palace], February 27, 1983, RMA, 1–34–3; "Qixinxieli bachu fengjian mixin de judian" [Pulling together to uproot the stronghold of feudal superstition], March 31, 1983, RMA, 1–31–46.

88. The most recent campaign occurred in 2000 and targeted unregistered temples. Private graveyards in the mountains were also targeted because the local government claimed that they damaged the environment. See also Mayfair Yang, "Postcolonial Complex."

89. "Zhuanfa shi gongan ju, shi tiwei 'Guanyu jinnian hualongzhou qingkuang ji jinhou yijian de baogao' de tongzhi" [Issuing municipal Public Security Bureau and municipal sports committee's notice on "Report about the situation of dragon boat racing this year and opinion on future activities"], July 12, 1984, RMA, 1–35–30.

90. See "Longzhou jingdu kaijin baixing jiaohao" [People cheer as the ban on dragon boat racing lifted], http://www.wzrb.com.cn/node2/node179/userobject 8ai142660.html. The removal of the ban on dragon boat racing and the introduction of new narratives was not only the result of local pressures, but was also

propelled by a national campaign to "defend the Dragon Boat Festival" (*baowei duanwu*) in 2003. During this campaign, local criticism against the ban on dragon boat racing intensified; the campaign also provided the incumbent Wenzhou government with a good excuse to reevaluate and publicly promote dragon boat racing. For details of the national campaign to defend the Dragon Boat Festival, see Shi Aidong, "Cong 'baowei Duanwu' dao 'baowei Chunjie': zhuizong yu xishuo" [From "defending the Dragon Boat Festival" to "defending Chinese New Year": Retracing and describing in detail], *Minzu yishu* 2 (April 2006): 6–19.

91. "Wenzhou shiqu minjian hualongzhou huodong guanli zanxing banfa" [Temporary regulation on civil dragon boat rowing in the Wenzhou municipality]. The regulation was issued in April 2004 but expired with the arrival of a new local regulation in 2008. Both regulations promoted dragon boat racing to the status of "traditional culture." See http://www.wenzhou.gov.cn/art/2008/5/23/art_4434_72223.html.

11. Radical Agricultural Collectivization and Ethnic Rebellion

1. *Dangdai Zhongguo* congshu bianjibu, ed., *Dangdai Zhongguo de nongye* [Contemporary Chinese agriculture] (Beijing: Dangdai Zhongguo chubanshe, 1992), 1992.

2. Hu Jun, "Guanyu shaoshu minzu diqu nongye shehuizhuyi gaizao zhong de ruogan wenti" [On several problems in the socialist reform of agriculture in minority areas], *Tongyi zhanxian gongzuo* 4 (1956): 28.

3. On holy water, see Steve A. Smith, "Local Cadres Confront the Supernatural: The Politics of Holy Water (Shenshui) in the PRC, 1949–1966," *China Quarterly*, no. 188 (December 2006): 999–1022.

4. Hu Jun, "Guanyu shaoshu minzue diqu," 29.

5. Zhonggong zhongyang wenxian yanjiushi, ed., *Jianguo yilai zhongyao wenxian xuanbian* [Selected important documents since the founding of the People's Republic], vol. 8 (Beijing: Zhongyang wenxian chubanshe, 1994), 254.

6. *Renmin ribao* [People's Daily], September 17, 1956, 4.

7. Li Ziyuan, *Zhongguo gongchandang minzu gongzuo shi* [History of the Chinese Communist Party's ethnicity work] (Nanning: Guangxi renmin chubanshe, 2000), 277.

8. Zhonggong zhongyang wenxian yanjiushi, ed., *Mao Zedong wenji* [Collected writings of Mao Zedong] (Beijing: Renmin chubanshe, 1999), 7:227.

9. The most detailed account can be found in Wei Guangxing, ed., *Zhongguo gongchandang Wangmo xian lishi, 1930–1978* [History of the Chinese Communist Party in Wangmo County, 1930–1978] (Guiyang: Guizhou renmin chubanshe, 2005). Useful gazetteers include Luodian xianzhi bianzuan weiyuanhui, *Luodian xianzhi* [Luodian County gazetteer] (Guiyang, Guizhou renmin chubanshe, 1994); and Guizhou sheng Wangmo xian difangzhi bianzuan weiyuanhui, *Wangmo*

xianzhi [Wangmo County gazetteer] (Guiyang: Guizhou renmin chubanshe, 2001). Two valuable articles include Lu Huilong and Chen Dean, "Mashan shijian qianhou" [The Mashan incident from beginning to end), *Qianxinanzhou wenshi ziliao xuanji*, no. 2 (October 1983): 349–374; and Jiang Shifei, "Wo suo zhidao de Mashan shijian" [All I know about the Mashan incident], *Qianxinanzhou tongxun* 2 (June 1990): 37–48. Jiang was a military officer in Wangmo County during the rebellion.

10. Wu Xiaotao, "Guizhou Mashan shijian shimo" [The whole story of the Guizhou Mashan incident], *Yanhuang chunqiu* 1 (2009): 40–43; Wu Xiaotao, "Wailai jingying yu bendi jingying de chongzhuang—1956 nian Qianxinan Mashan shijian" [A collision between local and outside elites—the Mashan incident in southwest Guizhou, 1956], *Gongshiwang*, January 20, 2010, http://21ccom .net/articles/lsjd/article_201001202836.html.

11. Wang Fengchang, *Mashan xiongying* [Eagle of Mashan] (Beijing: Renmin chubanshe, 2004); Wei Rang, *Mashan miwu* [Dense fog of Mashan] (Beijing: Zuojia chubanshe, 2003).

12. Guizhou sheng Wangmo xian difangzhi bianzuan weiyuanhui, *Wangmo xianzhi*, 1–2.

13. Liu Chaolun, "Mantan Wangmo" [A chat about Wangmo], *Guizhou ribao*, October 13, 1944, cited in *Kangzhan shiqi Qianjing yinxiang* [Impressions of scenes of Guizhou during the period of the War of Resistance], ed. Guiyang shi dang'anguan (Guiyang: Guizhou renmin chubanshe, 2008], 373.

14. Shi Chaojiang, *Shijie Miaozu qianxi shi* [A global history of Miao migration] (Guiyang: Guizhou renmin chubanshe, 2006), 167.

15. Zhonggong Xingren diwei gongzuozu, "Mashan xiang jingji qingkuang diaocha baogao" [Investigation report on the economic situation in Mashan Township], March 14, 1957, author's collection (hereafter abbreviated AC).

16. Guizhou sheng Wangmo xian difangzhi bianzuan weiyuanhui, *Wangmo xianzhi*, 124.

17. Zhonggong Xingren diwei gongzuozu, "Mashan xiang jingji qingkuang diaocha baogao."

18. See Wei Guangxing, *Zhongguo gongchandang Wangmo xian lishi*, chapters 1 and 2.

19. Xiong Liangchen interviewed in "Mashan fenghuo" [The flames of war in Mashan], *Guizhou wenzhi congkan* 4 (1984): 33; Qianxinan Buyi Miaozu zizhizhou zhi shizhi bianji weiyuanhui, *Qianxinan Buyi Miaozu zizhizhou zhi: junshi zhi* [Southwest Guizhou Buyi-Miao Autonomous Prefecture gazetteer: Military gazetteer] (Guiyang: Guizhou minzu chubanshe, 1988), 147.

20. Wu Tingshu, ed., *Zhongguo gongchandang Guizhou lishi, diyi juan: 1921– 1949* [History of the Chinese Communist Party in Guizhou, vol. 1: 1921–1949] (Guiyang: Guizhou renmin chubanshe, 2006), 317; Wei Guangxing, *Zhongguo gongchandang Wangmo xian lishi*, 31–40; Wang Zhenzhong, "Xiong Liangchen

lingdao de Mashan nongmin qiyi" [The Mashan peasant uprising led by Xiong Liangchen], *Qianxinan wenshi ziliao xuanji* 8 (1990): 194–211.

21. On the broad scope of anti-Communist resistance in Guizhou in the early 1950s, see Jeremy Brown, "From Resisting Communists to Resisting America: Civil War and Korean War in Southwest China, 1950–1951," in *Dilemmas of Victory: The Early Years of the People's Republic of China,* ed. Jeremy Brown and Paul G. Pickowicz (Cambridge, MA: Harvard University Press, 2007), 105–129.

22. Guizhou sheng junshizhi bianzuan weiyuanhui, ed., *Guizhou junshi dashiji* [Guizhou military chronology] (internal publication, 1990), 286.

23. Interview with Yang's niece and nephew, September 10, 2010.

24. Guizhou sheng Wangmo xian difangzhi bianzuan weiyuanhui, *Wangmo xianzhi,* 574.

25. Lu Huilong and Chen Dean, "Mashan shijian qianhou," 55.

26. See Zhonggong Wangmo xianwei zuzhibu, *Dui ge shaoshuminzu zhanyou renkou yu fengsu xiguan he tedian de diaocha ji zai jian dang zhong fazhan dang-yuan wenti zonghe baogao* [Comprehensive report on population ratios, customs, and special characteristics of ethnic minorities and the problem of developing Party members], July 15, 1952, AC.

27. Zhonggong Wangmo xianwei, *Zhonggong Wangmo xianwei dui saoluan shijian de jiancha baogao* [Self-criticism report on the riot incident by the Wangmo County Communist Party Committee], November 12, 1956, AC.

28. Wei Guangxing, *Zhongguo gongchandang Wangmo xian lishi,* 133.

29. According to a report delivered by Guizhou vice-governor Wu Shi at a cadre conference on October 25, 1956, 3,347 people took part in the uprising, including 127 Communist Party members, 144 Youth League members, 5 town-ship heads, 300 cadres in agriculture cooperatives, more than 300 members of local militia, 11 demobilized soldiers, 18 public security directors, and 56 public security committee members (AC).

30. Zhonggong Guizhou shengwei nongcun gongzuo bu, "Guanyu shao-shuminzu diqu huzhu hezuo yundong qingkuang he yijian de baogao" [Report on the situation and opinions about the mutual aid and cooperative movement in ethnic minority areas], March 25, 1955, in *Guizhou nongcun hezuo jingji shiliao* [Historical materials on the cooperative economy in Guizhou villages], ed. Guizhou nongye hezuohua shiliao bianxie weiyuanhui (Guiyang: Guizhou renmin chubanshe, 1987), 1:127–132.

31. "Zhou Lin tongzhi 1955 nian 9 yue 15 ri zai Zhongguo gongchandang Guizhou sheng di wu ci daibiao dahui shang de zongjie fayan" [Comrade Zhou Lin's speech at the Fifth Guizhou Chinese Communist Party Congress on September 15, 1955], in *Guizhou nongcun hezuo jingji shiliao,* 1:162.

32. "Zhonggong Guizhou shengwei guanyu yi nian lai nongye hezuohua yun-dong de chubu zongjie yu jindong mingchun gongzuo yijian [Guizhou Party Committee's initial summary of the cooperativization movement in the last year

and work plan for this winter and next spring], in *Guizhou nongcun hezuo jingji shiliao,* 1:283.

33. Guizhou sheng Wangmo xian difangzhi bianzuan weiyuanhui, *Wangmo xianzhi,* 15.

34. Wei Guangxing, *Zhongguo gongchandang Wangmo xian lishi,* 107–108.

35. Zhonggong Wangmo xianwei, *Zhonggong Wangmo xianwei dui saoluan shijian de jiancha baogao.*

36. Ibid.

37. Ibid.

38. Wei Guangxing, *Zhongguo gongchandang Wangmo xian lishi,* 125, 127, 129.

39. Zhonggong Wangmo xianwei, *Zhonggong Wangmo xianwei dui saoluan shijian de jiancha baogao.*

40. Guizhou sheng Xingyi zhuanyuan gongshu shuiwu ju *Anlong, Zhenfeng, Ceheng, Wangmo si xian 1950–1955 nian gongzuo qingkuang* [Report on work in Anlong, Zhenfeng, Ceheng, and Wangmo, 1950–1955), AC.

41. Wangmo xian shuiwuju, *1955 nian nianzhong zongjie* [Annual summary for 1955], January 16, 1956, AC.

42. Wangmo xianwei, *Guanyu junzheng ganbu huiyi qingkuang baogao* [Wangmo Party Committee report about the conference of military and government cadres], November 21, 1956, AC.

43. Guizhou sheng minzu fangwentuan erfentuan, *Wangmo xian minzu fangwen gongzuo qingkuang baogao* [Work report about visiting minorities in Wangmo County], November 19, 1956, AC.

44. Zhonggong Xingren diwei gongzuozu, "Mashan xiang jingji qingkuang diaocha baogao."

45. Zhonggong Wangmo xianwei, *Wangmo xian er, si qu hongnao chu huangdi shijian de diaocha baogao* [Investigation report on the stir about the emergence of an emperor], May 15, 1956, AC.

46. In his old age, Yang, who died in 2001, reportedly said that he himself did not actually believe Dog Granny Xiong's prophesy but that he used her to gain supporters. Interview with Yang's niece and nephew, September 10, 2010.

47. Zhonggong Wangmo xianwei, *Wangmo xian er, si qu hongnao chu huangdi shijian de diaocha baogao;* Zhonggong Wangmo xianwei, *Guanyu Mashan, Baiyi deng xiang hongnao chu huangdi shijian xiang diwei de baogao* [Report to the prefectural Party Committee on the stir about the emergence of an emperor in Mashan, Baiyi, and other townships], June 21, 1956, AC; Jiang Shifei, "Wo suo zhidao de Mashan shijian," 38.

48. Zhonggong Wangmo xianwei, *Wangmo xian er, si qu hongnao chu huangdi shijian de diaocha baogao;* Zhonggong Wangmo xianwei, *Zhonggong Wangmo xianwei dui saoluan shijian de jiancha baogao.*

49. Zhonggong Wangmo xianwei, *Guanyu Mashan, Baiyi deng xiang hongnao chu huangdi shijian xiang diwei de baogao,* June 21, 1956; Wei Guangxing, *Zhongguo*

gongchandang Wangmo xian lishi, 136. See also Wang Fengchang, *Mashan xiongying,* 467–470.

50. Zhonggong Wangmo xianwei, *Zhonggong Wangmo xianwei dui saoluan shijian de jiancha baogao;* Zhonggong Wangmo xianwei, *Guanyu Mashan, Baiyi deng xiang hongnao chu huangdi shijian xiang diwei de baogao.*

51. Zhonggong Xingyi diwei gongzuozu, *Guanyu dui Wangmo xian "chu huangdi" an kaizhan gongzuo qingkuang de jianbao,* June 28, 1956, AC.

52. Wang Gangzheng's report to the prefectural and provincial Party committees, July 3, 1956, AC.

53. Wang Fengchang, *Mashan xiongying,* 472–473.

54. Wangmo xianwei, *Guanyu junzheng ganbu huiyi qingkuang baogao.*

55. Luodian xianzhi bianzuan weiyuanhui, *Luodian xianzhi,* 170.

56. Zhonggong Wangmo xianwei, report of July 10, 1956, AC. According to another source, Meng Guanyi led the headquarters, other members of which included Vice-Directors Xiong Liangchen and Xin Peitian [Wangmo County magistrate], Political Commissar Wang Gangzheng, and Vice-Commissar Li Muzhen. See Wei Guangxing, *Zhongguo gongchandang Wangmo xian lishi,* 135–136.

57. Zhonggong Wangmo xianwei, *Wangmo xian er, si qu hongnao chu huangdi shijian de diaocha baogao.*

58. Zhonggong Wangmo xianwei, *Guanyu Mashan, Baiyi deng xiang hongnao chu huangdi shijian xiang diwei de baogao;* Zhonggong Xingyi diwei gongzuozu, *Guanyu dui Wangmo xian "chu huangdi" an kaizhan gongzuo qingkuang de jianbao.*

59. Report from Wang Gangzheng to the prefectural and provincial Party committees, July 3, 1956, AC; Battle plan sent from Meng Guanyi to the prefectural Party Committee and the military region, July 5, 1956, AC.

60. For a description of the meeting, see Wang Fengchang, *Mashan xiongying,* 490. Other sources indicate that Xiong Liangchen opposed using force to quell the rebellion. Xiong's younger brother Xiong Liangbin, a local vice–township head, was a supporter of the rebels and participated in the uprising; author interview with local villager, September 10, 2010.

61. Xingyi diwei, *Guanyu pingxi Wangmo baoluan shijian de zhishi* [Order on quelling the violent incident in Wangmo], July 19, 1956, AC.

62. Guizhou shengwei, *Guanyu pingxi panluan shijian wenti xiang zhongyang de baogao* [Report to Party Center about suppressing the riot incident problem], July 18, 1956, AC.

63. *Zhonggong zhongyang pifu Guizhou shengwei guanyu jiejue shaoshu minzu diqu saoluan shijian de jinji zhishi* [Party Center's comments on the Guizhou provincial Party Committee's urgent order about resolving the ethnic minority riot incident], August 9, 1957, AC.

64. Jiang Shifei, "Wo suo zhidao de Mashan shijian," 46.

65. Wangmo xianwei, *Guanyu jin 20 tian xin qingkuang gei diwei de jibao* [Urgent report to the prefectural Party Committee about the new situation in the past twenty days], August 31, 1956; Xingyi diwei, *Gei Wangmo xianwei de fuxin* [Reply to Wangmo Party Committee], September 3, 1956, AC.

66. Zhou Jinglin, "Miaozu nü fu xianzhang Xiong san mei," *Guizhou wenshi ziliao xuanji* 32 (December 1996): 22.

67. For more on Zhou Lin, see Gao Hua, "Zai Guizhou 'Siqing' de beihou" [Behind the "Four Cleanups" in Guizhou], *Ershiyi shiji*, no. 2 (2006), http://www .usc.cuhk.edu.hk/PaperCollection/Details.aspx?id=5172.

68. Wei Guangxing, *Zhongguo gongchandang Wangmo xian lishi, 1930–1978*, 137. According to Jiang Shifei, seventy rebels were killed and no fewer than fifty injured. Jiang Shifei, "Wo suo zhidao de Mashan shijian," 48.

69. Guizhou sheng Wangmo xian difangzhi bianzuan weiyuanhui, *Wangmo xianzhi*, 17.

70. Ibid., 17, 595; Wei Guangxing, *Zhongguo gongchandang Wangmo xian lishi, 1930–1978*, 137–138.

71. Wei Guangxing, *Zhongguo gongchandang Wangmo xian lishi, 1930–1978*, 137.

72. Ibid., 126.

73. Zhonggong Guizhou shengwei, *Guanyu pingxi Mashan shijian de baogao* [Report on suppressing the Mashan incident], February 23, 1957, AC.

74. On the 1958 uprising, see Wei Rang, *Mashan miwu*, 280–283. On the 1960 incident, in which five people died, see Wei Guangxing, *Zhongguo gongchandang Wangmo xian lishi*, and Guizhou sheng junshizhi bianzuan weiyuanhui, *Guizhou junshi dashiji*, 334.

75. Wei Rang, *Mashan miwu*, 284.

12. Caught between Opposing Han Chauvinism and Opposing Local Nationalism

1. The official phrase "local nationalism" (*difang minzuzhuyi*) was used to condemn political activity that was connected with advocacy of non-Han ethnic rights and interests or that circumvented Han-created institutions of authority.

2. *Renmin ribao* [People's Daily], October 1, 1950, 7.

3. Concerning Saifudin Azizi, see also Michael Dillon, *Xinjiang: China's Muslim Far Northwest* (New York: Routledge, 2004), 79. Azizi's first official title following the formation of the Xinjiang Uyghur Autonomous Region was Chairman of the Regional Government.

4. For an outstanding study of Xinjiang in the early 1960s from an international perspective, see Zhihua Shen and Danhui Li, "Antagonized Centers and Troubled Frontiers," *After Leaning to One Side: China and Its Allies in the Cold War* (Washington, DC: Woodrow Wilson Center Press, 2011), 167–195.

5. Xinjiang Uyghur Autonomous Region Archive (hereafter cited as XUARA), 0–4–1.

6. Zhonggong Xinjiang Weiwu'er zizhiqu weiyuanhui dangshi wenyuanhui, Zhonggong Xinjiang Weiwu'er zizhiqu weiyuanhui dangxiao, *Zhongguo gongchandang Xinjiang lishi dashiji (1949.10–1966.4)* [The Communist Party of China's annals of Xinjiang history (October 1949–April 1966), hereafter cited as XDSJ] (Urumqi: Xinjiang renmin chubanshe, 1994), 1:102.

7. Zhonghua renmin gongheguo minzu shiwu weiyuanhui zhengce yanjiushi, ed., *Zhongguo gongchandang zhuyao lingdaoren lun minzu wenti* [Key leaders of the Chinese Communist Party on ethnic minorities issues] (Beijing: Minzu chubanshe, 1994), 94–95, 113–114, 115–116.

8. XUARA, 0–7–115.

9. XUARA, 1–8–96.

10. XDSJ, 1:61.

11. XDSJ, 1:37; XUARA, 0–6–85.

12. Zhe Wu, "Cong 'guo zhong zhi guo' dao 'sheng zhong zhi sheng'—1945–1955 nian Yining yu Beijing zai Xinjiang minzu zizhi wenti shang jueli de beijing, guocheng yu jieguo" [From "a state within a state" to "a province within a province"—the background, process, and outcome of the tussle between Gulja and Beijing over the issue of autonomy for ethnic minorities in 1945–1955], *Liang'an fazhanshi yanjiu* 4 (December 2007): 217–275.

13. XUARA, 1–8–83.

14. Ibid.

15. Ibid.

16. See "Feishou Abudu Yimiti nantao renmin fawang" [Bandit chief Abdul Amet cannot escape justice], Hotan Mid-Level People's Court Archive, vol. 176; and Hetian diqu zhongji renmin fayuan, "Guanyu feishou Abudu Yimiti panchu sixing de bugao" [Bulletin on the death sentence of bandit chief Abdul Amet], Hotan Mid-Level People's Court Archive, vol. 59. For details, see 47 tuan dangshi ziliao zhengji bangongshi, "Hengchuan talimu, tunken hetian—yuan 2 jun 5 shi 15 tuan jinzhu hetian diqu zhuanti ziliao" [Across the Tarim Basin and settling in Hotan—topical data on the settlement of the Hotan region by the original 15th Regiment of the 2nd Army's 5th Division], in *Xinjiang shengchan jianshe bingtuan shiliao xuanji* [Selected historical material on the Production and Construction Military Corps in Xinjiang], ed. Xinjiang shengchan jianshe bingtuan shiliao bianji weiyuanhui and Xinjiang shengchan jianshe bingtuan shiliao xuanji bianjibu (Urumqi: Xinjiang renmin chubanshe, 1995), 5:185–198.

17. XDSJ, 1:137.

18. Zhongguo gongchandang Xinjiang Wei'wuer zizhiqu weiyuanhui dangshi yanjiushi, ed., *Zhonggong Xinjiang difangshi (1937 nian-1966 nian 4 yue)* [Local history of Xinjiang under the Chinese Communist Party (1937–April 1966)] (Urumqi: Xinjiang renmin chubanshe, 1999), 1:272–274.

19. XDSJ, 1:155.

20. XUARA, 1–8–97.

21. XUARA, 1–9–144.

22. Ibid.

23. XUARA, 1–9–153.

24. XDSJ, 1:153–155.

25. XUARA, 1–9–153.

26. Ibid.

27. Ibid.

28. On August 3, 1957 the 4th Meeting of the 1st Xinjiang People's Political Consultative Conference, centered on criticizing "rightist speech and actions," was convened. On the same day, *Xinjiang Daily* published the editorial "Bixu yansu renzhen di zhankai fanji youpai de douzheng" [The struggle against the rightists must be carried out seriously and in earnest], *Xinjiang ribao* [Xinjiang Daily], August 3, 1957, 1; August 4, 1957, 1.

29. Xinjiang shengchan jianshe bingtuan shizhi bianzuan weiyuahui, *Xinjiang shengchan jianshe bingtuan fazhanshi* [History of the development of the Production and Construction Military Corps in Xinjiang] (Urumqi: Xinjiang renmin chubanshe, 1998), 171–201.

30. Zhongguo gongchandang Xinjiang Wei'wuer zizhiqu weiyuanhui dangshi yanjiushi, *Zhonggong Xinjiang difangshi (1937 nian-1966 nian 4 yue)*, 1:304.

31. XDSJ, 1:158.

32. Li Danhui, "Dui 1962 nian Xinjiang Yi-Ta shijian qiyin the lishi kaocha" [A historical examination of the origin of the I-Ta Incident in Xinjiang in 1962], in *Beijing yu Mosike: Cong lianmeng zouxiang duikang* (Beijing and Moscow: From alliance toward antagonism), ed. Li Danhui (Guilin: Guangxi shifan daxue chubanshe, 2002), 480–509.

33. *Xinjiang ribao,* November 23, 2004, 4; XDSJ, 1:161–162.

34. XDSJ, 1:162.

35. Zhongguo gongchandang Yili Hasake zizhizhou weiyuanhui zuzhibu, Zhongguo gongchandang Yili Hasake zizhizhou weiyuanhui dangshi bangongshi, Yili Hasake zizhizhou dang'anju(guan), eds., *Zhongguo gongchandang Xinjiang Weiwu'er zizhiqu Yili Hasake zizhizhou zuzhishi ziliao (1940 nian 10 yue-1987 nian 10 yue)* [Materials on the organization history of Ili Kazak Autonomous Prefecture of the Xinjiang Uyghur Autonomous Region of the Chinese Communist Party (October 1940–October 1987)] (Urumqi: Xinjiang renmin chubanshe, 1993), 182–183.

36. Zhongguo gongchandang Xinjiang Wei'wuer zizhiqu weiyuanhui dangshi yanjiushi, *Zhonggong Xinjiang difangshi,* 1:308–309.

37. On October 1, 1958, Zhou Enlai said, "Henceforth, when any ethnic nationality creates or reforms its writing system, it should in principle be based on the Latin alphabet. [Where it is the same or very similar between Non-Han and Han

languages], the pronunciation and use of letters should be identical as far as possible to Hanyu Pinyin letters," Zhonghua renmin gongheguo minzu shiwu weiyuanhui zhengce yanjiushi, *Zhongguo gongchandang zhuyao lingdaoren lun minzu wenti*, 190–191.

38. XDSJ, 1:190.

39. Ma Dazheng, *Guojia liyi gaoyu yiqie* [National interests are paramount] (Urumqi: Xinjiang renmin chubanshe, 2003), 32–44.

40. XUARA, 1–11–88.

41. XUARA, 1–12–146.

42. XDSJ, 1:172–175.

43. Ibid., 1:178–179.

44. Yang Zhaoyuan (the first vice-director of the Cadres Department of the Xinjiang Production and Construction Military Corps), "Yang Zhaoyuan riji xuan" [Selections from Yang Zhaoyuan's diaries], February 17, 1960, in *Xinjiang shengchan jianshe bingtuan shiliao xuanji* (Selected historical material of the Xinjiang Production and Construction Military Corps), ed. Xinjiang shengchan jianshe bingtuan shizhi bianzuan weiyuanhui, Xinjiang shengchan jianshe bingtuan shiliao xuanji bianjibu (Urumqi: Xinjiang renmin chubanshe, 2001), 11:159–188.

45. XUARA, 1–13–129; XDSJ, 1:203, 227–228.

46. XDSJ, 1:195, 197–198.

47. XUARA, 1–12–59.

48. Ibid.

49. XUARA, 1–12–69.

50. Ibid.

51. Ibid.

52. Ibid.

53. Ibid.

54. XDSJ, 1:216.

55. XUARA, 181–30–6.

56. XUARA, 181–7–44.

57. XUARA, 181–7–44.

58. XDSJ, 1:227.

59. Zhonghua renmin gongheguo guojia minzu shiwu weiyuanhui wuzhong congshu bianji weiyuanhui Eluosizu jianshi bianxiezu, *Eluosizu jianshi* [Concise history of the ethnic Russian Chinese] (Urumqi: Xinjiang renmin chubanshe, 1986), 63–64.

60. Li Danhui, "Dui 1962 nian Xinjiang yita shijian qiyin the lishi kaocha," 480–509.

61. Zhongguo gongchandang zhongyang weiyuanhui tongyi zhanxian gongzuobu, "Di 11 ci quanguo tongzhan gongzuo huiyi" [The 11th National United Front Working Conference], in *Lici quanguo tongzhan gongzuo huiyi gaikuang he*

wenxian [Overview of and documents related to past National United Front Working Conferences], ed. Zhongguo gongchandang zhongyang weiyuanhui tongyi zhanxian gongzuobu (Beijing: Dang'an chubanshe, 1988), 198–204.

62. Zhonggong Xinjiang Weiwu'er zizhiqu dangwei tongyi zhanxian gongzuobu, "Guanyu jinyibu gonggu he fazhan shehui zhuyi minzu guanxi de jige wenti."

63. XDSJ, 1:204–205.

64. Ibid., 1:224–226.

65. XUARA, 1–13–141.

66. Zhonghua minguo zhu lianheguo jiaokewen zuzhi changren daibiao banshichu, "Baocheng Su'e zhichi 'ziyou Tu'erqisitan yundong qingxing'" [Report on Soviet Russia's support of "the Free Turkestan movement"], lianjiao (59) no. 130 (March 19, 1970), in *Waijiaobu dang'an congshu: jiewulei, di 3 ce, Xinjiang juan* [Ministry of Foreign Affairs files: Border issues, vol. 3, Xinjiang section], ed. Tang Yi, Zhao Zhucheng, and Lan Meihua (Taipei: Zhonghua minguo waijiaobu bianyin, 2001), 298.

67. Li Danhui, "Dui 1962 nian Xinjiang," 480–509; Li Danhui, "Dui Sulian qiaomin wenti de lishi kaocha" [A historical examination of the issue of Soviet citizens residing abroad], in *Lengzhan yu zhongguo de zhoubian guanxi* [The Cold War and China's relationships with its neighbors], ed. Niu Dayong and Shen Zhihua (Beijing: Shijie zhishi chubanshe, 2004), 16–66.

68. Li Danhui, "Dui 1962 nian Xinjiang," 480–509.

69. Ibid.

70. *Xinjiang ribao*, November 23, 2004, 4.

71. XUARA, 1–15–69.

72. XUARA, 1–15–126.

73. Someone in Xinjiang University shouted the slogan: "Destroy the Communist Party! Long live Turkestan!" XUARA, 1-15-66.

74. Zhang Shiqiu, "Guanyu Tacheng diqu jinxing shehuizhuyi he aiguo zhuyi jiaoyu jinxing qingkuang de baogao [Report on the progress of socialist and patriotic education in the Tarbagatay region], March 3, 1963, XUARA, 1-15-69."

75. XUARA, 1–15–66.

76. XUARA, 1–15–106.

77. XUARA, 1–15–90.

78. XUARA, 1–15–61.

79. Zhu Peimin, *20 shiji Xinjiang shi yanjiu* [Research on twentieth-century Xinjiang] (Urumqi: Xinjiang renmin chubanshe, 2001), 335; Donald H. McMillen, *Chinese Communist Power and Policy in Sinkiang* (Boulder, CO: Westview Press, 1979), 92–94.

80. Zhu Peimin, *20 shiji Xinjiang shi yanjiu*, 351–352.

13. Redemptive Religious Societies and the Communist State, 1949 to the 1980s

1. The "redemptive religious societies" were commonly referred to in imperial times as *xiejiao,* which is usually translated as "heterodox sects." Although I am not persuaded that the term "sect" is inappropriate, I have followed the important work of Goossaert and Palmer, who reject the term on the grounds that many of the societies were neither marginal nor exclusive communities. Vincent Goossaert and David A. Palmer, *The Religious Question in Modern China* (Chicago: University of Chicago Press, 2011), 26. Prasenjit Duara coined the term "redemptive societies," to underline their commitment to saving individuals and the world as a whole. Prasenjit Duara, *Sovereignty and Authenticity: Manchukuo and the East Asian Modern* (Lanham, MD: Rowman and Littlefield, 2003), 103–105.

2. The classic works in English on the Ming and Qing dynasties are Daniel Overmyer, *Folk Buddhist Religion: Dissenting Sects in Late Traditional China* (Cambridge, MA: Harvard University Press, 1976); Susan Naquin, *Millenarian Rebellion in China: The Eight Trigrams Uprising of 1813* (New Haven, CT: Yale University Press, 1976); Barend Ter Haar, *The White Lotus Teachings in Chinese Religious History* (Leiden: E. J. Brill, 1992); and Hubert Michael Seiwert (with Ma Xisha), *Popular Religious Movements and Heterodox Sects in Chinese History* (Leiden: E. J. Brill, 2003). Key works on the Republican era are Li Shiyu, *Xianzai Huabei mimi zongjiao* [Contemporary secret sects in North China] (Shanghai: Shanghai wenyi chubanshe, 1990 [1948]); Ma Xisha and Han Bingfang, *Zhongguo minjian zongjiao shi* [A history of Chinese popular religion] (Shanghai: Shanghai renmin chubanshe, 1992); Goossaert and Palmer, *The Religious Question,* ch.4; K. M. Tertitskii, *Kitaiskie sinkreticheskie religii v XX veke* (Moscow: Vostochnaia literatura, 2000); Thomas DuBois, *The Sacred Village: Social Change and Religious Life in North China* (Honolulu: University of Hawaii Press, 2005); Rebecca Nedostup, *Superstitious Regimes: Religion and the Politics of Chinese Modernity* (Cambridge, MA: Harvard University Press, 2010). Particularly valuable on the beliefs and rituals of the societies is Pu Wenqi, *Zhongguo minjian mimi zongjiao cidian* [Dictionary of Chinese secret popular religions] (Chengdu: Sichuan cishu chubanshe, 1996). Important works on the post-Mao era are David Palmer, *La fièvre du qigong. Guérison, religion et politique en Chine, 1949–1999* (Paris: Éditions de l'École des Hautes Études, 2005); Adam Yuet Chau, *Miraculous Response: Doing Popular Religion in Contemporary China* (Stanford: Stanford University Press, 2006); David Ownby, *Falun Gong and the Future of China* (New York: Oxford University Press, 2008).

3. I have drawn substantially on Zhongguo huidaomen shiliao jichang bianzuan weiyuanhui, ed., *Zhongguo huidaomen shiliao jicheng: jin bai nian lai huidaomen de zuzhi yi fenbu* [A collection of historical materials on the Chinese sects: Their organization and distribution across a century], 2 vols. (Beijing: Zhongguo shehui kexue chubanshe, 2004), hereafter cited as ZGHDMSL. This

includes a large amount of documentation drawn from county annals, much of which originated with the PSB; it contains little in the way of primary documentation and nothing in the way of texts produced by the societies themselves. Despite this limitation, used imaginatively and judiciously, it provides a huge amount of information about the strength, distribution, and leadership of the societies, and even a little about their beliefs and practices, although these are always ventriloquized through the voice of authority. On the problems of using official sources to reconstruct popular beliefs, see S. A. Smith, "Talking Toads and Chinless Ghosts: The Politics of Rumor in the People's Republic of China, 1961–65," *American Historical Review* 111, no. 2 (2006): 405–427.

4. Ter Haar, *White Lotus Teachings,* 200.

5. Qin Baoqi and Yan Lebin, *Dixia shenmi wangguo Yiguandao de xingshuai* [The rise and fall of the mysterious underground kingdom of the Yiguandao] (Fuzhou: Fujian renmin chubanshe, 2000), 241–247.

6. Kwang-Ching Liu and Richard Shek, "Afterword," *Heterodoxy in Late Imperial China* (Honolulu: University of Hawaii Press, 2004), 464.

7. Overmyer, *Folk Buddhist Religion,* 67–69.

8. Robert Weller, "Sectarian Religion and Political Action in China," *Modern China* 8, no. 4 (1982): 463–483.

9. Shao Yong, *Zhongguo huidaomen* [Chinese sects] (Shanghai: Shanghai renmin chubanshe, 1997), 452. A recent work puts the number of disciples at 30 million. Zheng Yonghua and Zhao Zhi, *Jindai yilai de huidaomen* (Beijing: Shehui kexue wenxian chubanshe, 2012), 230. A more detailed investigation counted 4,542 different societies over the course of the twentieth century, 908 with "society" (*hui*), 1,601 with "teaching" (*dao*), and 366 with "gate" (*men*) in their titles (the remainder being variously titled). ZGHDMSL, 2. The matter is complicated by the fact that it was not uncommon for them to change their names, especially in the PRC. In Sichuan it was said that the Yiguandao operated under some forty different names. *Xinan gongzuo* [Southwest work], no. 36 (January 16, 1951): 31.

10. DuBois, *Sacred Village,* 155.

11. Qin Baoqi and Yan Lebin, *Dixia shenmi wangguo,* 159, 155.

12. DuBois, *Sacred Village,* 134; Xu Zhengkang, "Yiguandao zai Ningbo diqu de zui'e neimu" [The inside story of the crimes of the Yiguandao in the Ningbo region], in *Wenshi ziliao cun gao xuanbian,* ed. Fan Jimin et al. (Beijing: Zhongguo wenshi chubanshe, 2002), 492.

13. Qin Baoqi and Yan Lebin, *Dixia shenmi wangguo,* 294–302.

14. Liu Ping and Wang Rui, "Shandong huidaomen de fenhua yanbian, 1945–1949" [The disintegration of the huidaomen in Shandong, 1945–1949], *Xuzhou shifan daxue xuebao* 38, no. 6 (2012): 70–75.

15. Jeremy Brown, "From Resisting Communists to Resisting America: Civil War and Korean War in Southwest China, 1950–51," in *Dilemmas of Victory: The Early Years of the People's Republic of China,* ed. Jeremy Brown and Paul G. Pickowicz (Cambridge MA: Harvard University Press, 2007), 105–129.

16. ZGHDMSL, 765; Hubei Provincial Archive, SZ–E–78.

17. In the Yiguandao, the hierarchy of officers was topped by a Grand Master (*shizun*), a position that was vacant under the Communists, followed by "leaders of the way" (*daozhang*) and "predecessors" (*qianren*), then by middle-ranking transmitters of rites (*dianchuanshi*), then by more-lowly altar masters (*tanzhu*) and "three talents" (*sancai*), who were responsible for spirit writing, and, finally, by the various officers (*banshi yuan*) who looked after local altars. *Xinan gongzuo,* no. 36 (January 16, 1951): 54.

18. Li Liangyu, "Guanyu zhenya fangeming yundong de jige wenti" [Several questions concerning the suppression of the counterrevolutionary movement], *Nanjing xiaozhuang xueyuan xuebao,* no. 5 (2013): 106.

19. Shao Yong, *Zhongguo huidaomen,* 454.

20. DuBois, *Sacred Village,* 143.

21. ZGHDMSL, 326.

22. *Xinan gongzuo,* no. 22 (October 18, 1950): 13.

23. *Survey of the China Mainland Press* (SCMP), no. 82 (March 11–12, 1951). For a good account of the methods used, see Chang-tai Hung, "The Anti-Unity Sect Campaign and Mass Mobilization in the Early People's Republic of China," *China Quarterly* 202 (June 2010): 400–420.

24. Kenneth Lieberthal, *Revolution and Tradition in Tientsin, 1949–1952* (Stanford: Stanford University Press, 1980), 112.

25. SCMP, no. 309 (April 3, 1952); Chi Po, ed., *Chanchu xiejiao: gongheguo chanchu fandong huidaomen shu shi* [Rooting out the heretical sects: A narrative history of how the Republic rooted out the reactionary sects] (Beijing: Zhongyang wenxian chubanshe, 1999), 1:307.

26. ZGHDMSL, 48.

27. Chi Po, *Chanchu xiejiao,* 293.

28. ZGHDMSL, 486.

29. ZGHDMSL, 426

30. ZGHDMSL, 632.

31. Shao Yong, *Zhongguo huidaomen,* 459.

32. ZGHDMSL, 766.

33. Jun Jing, *The Temple of Memories: History, Power and Morality in a Chinese Village* (Stanford: Stanford University Press, 1996), 51.

34. ZGHDMSL, 590.

35. Shao Yong, *Zhongguo huidaomen,* 459.

36. Qin Baoqi and Yan Lebin, *Dixia shenmi wangguo,* 311.

37. ZGHDMSL, 150.

38. ZGHDMSL, 197.

39. Daniel Leese, "Performative Politics and Petrified Image: The Mao Cult during China's Cultural Revolution" (PhD diss., International University of Bremen, 2006), 125.

40. ZGHDMSL, 343.

41. ZGHDMSL, 49.

42. ZGHDMSL, 31.

43. ZGHDMSL, 808.

44. ZGHDMSL, 689.

45. Proposal of the Ningxia Hui Autonomous Region Revolutionary Committee, January 1969. *Zhongguo wenhua dageming wenku* [Chinese Cultural Revolution Database], 2nd ed. (Hong Kong: Universities Service Centre for China Studies, Chinese University of Hong Kong, 2006).

46. ZGHDMSL, 1064–1065.

47. ZGHDMSL, 61.

48. Yang Kuisong, "The Sino-Soviet Border Clash of 1969: From Zhenbao Island to Sino-American Rapprochement," *Cold War History* 1, no. 1 (2000): 21–52.

49. ZGHDMSL, 275.

50. ZGHDMSL, 269.

51. Li Ruojian, "1950 niandai: yaoyan xijuan qianwan guoren" [The 1950s: Rumors swept across tens of millions of citizens], *Guojia lishi* 2 (2008): 85. DuBois, *Sacred Village*, 140.

52. ZGHDMSL, 1116; 653.

53. *Gongan jianshe*, no. 13 [224] (March 21, 1958): 17.

54. Tan Songlin and Peng Bangfu, ed., *Zhongguo mimi shehui* (Fuzhou: Fujian renmin chubanshe, 2002), 7:104.

55. *Gongan jianshe*, no. 13 [224] (March 21, 1958): 18.

56. ZGHDMSL, 275–276.

57. Ownby, *Falun Gong*, 43.

58. Seiwert, *Popular Religious Movements*, 469.

59. D. K. Jordan and D. L. Overmyer, *The Flying Phoenix: Aspects of Chinese Sectarianism in Taiwan* (Princeton: Princeton University Press, 1986), 274–276.

60. Robin Munro, ed. and trans., "Syncretic Sects and Secret Societies: Revival in the 1980s," *Chinese Sociology and Anthropology* 21, no. 4 (1989): 57. Hereafter cited as SSSS.

61. Seiwert, *Popular Religious Movements*, 428.

62. Lev Deliusin, "The I-kuan Tao Society," in *Popular Movements and Secret Societies in China, 1840–1950*, ed. Jean Chesneaux (Stanford: Stanford University Press, 1972), 227.

63. Mo Xin, *Di meng jing hua dangdai Zhongguo: "Cheng di" bi ju* [Imperial dreams that frighten China: The curtain falls on "declaring oneself emperor" in contemporary China] (Guangzhou: Guangzhou chubanshe, 1998), 161.

64. Deliusin, "The I-kuan Tao Society," 230.

65. Jilin Provincial Archive, 16–18–10.

66. SSSS, 57.

67. ZGHDMSL, 325.

68. Robert Kendall Cliver, "'Red Silk': Labor, Capital, and the State in the Yangzi Delta Silk Industry, 1945–1960" (PhD diss., Harvard University, 2007), 474.

69. Chi Po, *Chanchu xiejiao, 306.*

70. ZGHDMSL, 680–681.

71. SSSS, 53.

72. *Xinan gongzuo,* no. 36 (January 16, 1951): 58.

73. SSSS, 53.

74. ZGHDMSL, 50.

75. Mo Xin, *Di meng jing hua,* 163 and cover photograph.

76. Kenneth Dean, *Lord of the Three in One: The Spread of a Cult in Southeast China* (Princeton: Princeton University Press, 1998), 274.

77. On the Li sect, see DuBois, *Sacred Village,* chapter 5.

78. Tan Songlin and Peng Bangfu, *Zhongguo mimi shehui,* 36.

79. ZGHDMSL, 29, 186, 680.

80. *Gongan jianshe,* no. 10 [192] (June 20, 1957): 17–22.

81. ZGHDMSL, 479.

82. S. A. Smith, "Fear and Rumour in the People's Republic of China in the 1950s," *Cultural and Social History* 5, no. 3 (2008): 269–288.

83. David Ownby, "Imperial Fantasies: The Chinese Communists and Peasant Rebellion," *Comparative Studies in Society and History* 43, no. 1 (2001): 65–91.

84. For a rich discussion of one such case, see Chapter 11 in this volume by Wang Haiguang.

85. Qin Baoqi and Yan Lebin, *Dixia shenmi wangguo,* 312; SSSS, 25.

86. ZGHDMSL, 587.

87. Tan Songlin and Peng Bangfu, *Zhongguo mimi shehui,* 104.

88. Qin Baoqi and Yan Lebin, *Dixia shenmi wangguo,* 311.

89. ZGHDMSL, 268.

90. Chen Yu and Zhang Shenghua, "Zishen guo: fumie ji" [Account of the destruction of the Zishen kingdom], *Minzhu yu fazhi* 12 (1987): 25–27.

91. ZGHDMSL, 307.

92. Tan Songlin and Peng Bangfu, *Zhongguo mimi shehui,* 102.

93. ZGHDMSL, 284

94. ZGHDMSL, 49.

95. ZGHDMSL, 714–717.

96. ZGHDMSL, 107.

97. SSSS, 51.

98. Qin Baoqi and Yan Lebin, *Dixia shenmi wangguo,* 314.

99. ZGHDMSL, 54.

100. SCMP, no. 1092 (July 20, 1955).

101. DuBois, *Sacred Village,* 1.

102. SCMP, no. 1092 (July 20, 1955).

103. SSSS, 58–59.

104. Vivienne Shue, *The Reach of the State: Sketches of the Chinese Body Politic* (Stanford: Stanford University Press, 1988).

105. SSSS, 50.

106. DuBois, *Sacred Village*, 140.

107. ZGHDMSL, 310.

108. Seiwert, *Popular Religious Movements*, 433.

109. SSSS, 59.

110. SSSS, 59, 58.

111. Zhonghua renmin gongheguo gonganbu, ed., *Fandong huidaomen jianjie* [Short history of the reactionary sects] (Beijing: Qunzhong chubanshe, 1985), 25.

112. Thomas P. Bernstein and Xiaobo Lü, *Taxation without Representation in Contemporary Rural China* (New York: Cambridge University Press, 2003), 160.

113. Elizabeth J. Perry, *Challenging the Mandate of Heaven: Social Protest and State Power in China* (Armonk, NY: M.E. Sharpe, 2002), 309–331.

Epilogue

1. It was only in 1973, after all, that the American Psychiatric Association finally removed homosexuality from its official list of mental disorders.

2. Additional support for language study scholarships came also from the Ford Foundation, and the first languages designated as "critical" in the early 1960s included Chinese, Japanese, Russian, Arabic, Persian, and Turkish.

3. Again, this choice of topic and discipline made a kind of self-evident sense to most at the time. Only a very few brave souls interested in China's current affairs chose economics then; for China, following the Soviet model, had already instituted a thoroughly planned economy, while nearly all the stimulating economic theories and models being discussed and debated in the West then were designed to explain and predict the vicissitudes of market-based systems. Also, because mainland China remained resolutely closed to foreign field researchers, very few students fascinated by the study of anthropology then chose to study China either; and those who did most often did their first ethnographic apprenticeships in Taiwan. There was, however, a small handful of pioneering younger Western sociologists who were encouraged then and did turn their talents to understanding the new systems of social organization that revolution had brought to the mainland. In the absence of much reliable official documentation, social survey data, or statistics, several of those early scholars were nonetheless able to contribute important baseline sketches of China's emerging new social terrain, often by choosing to employ nonstandard sources for study, such as in-depth interviewing of mainland refugees living in Hong Kong.

4. Gail Hershatter, *The Gender of Memory: Rural Women and China's Collective Past* (Berkeley: University of California Press, 2011).

Contributors

Jeremy Brown is associate professor of history at Simon Fraser University. He is the author of *City versus Countryside in Mao's China: Negotiating the Divide* and editor of *Dilemmas of Victory: The Early Years of the People's Republic of China* (coedited with Paul G. Pickowicz).

Cao Shuji is professor of history at Shanghai Jiaotong University. He is the author of *Da jihuang: 1959–1961 nian de Zhongguo renkou* [The Great Famine: China's Population, 1959–1961].

Jacob Eyferth is a historian of twentieth-century China at the University of Chicago. He is the author of *Eating Rice from Bamboo Roots,* an ethnographic history of a community of rural papermakers in Sichuan.

Matthew D. Johnson is assistant professor of East Asian history at Grinnell College. He is the coeditor of two volumes, *China's iGeneration: Cinema and Moving Image Culture in the Twenty-First Century* and *Visualizing Modern China: Image, History, and Memory, 1750–Present.*

Daniel Leese is professor of modern Chinese history and politics at the University of Freiburg, Germany. He is the author of *Mao Cult: Rhetoric and Ritual in China's Cultural Revolution* and the editor in chief of *Brill's Encyclopedia of China.*

Sigrid Schmalzer is associate professor and a historian of modern China, science, and popular culture at the University of Massachusetts, Amherst. She is the author of *The People's Peking Man: Popular Science and Human Identity in Twentieth-Century China.*

Michael Schoenhals is professor of Chinese in the Centre for Languages and Literature, Lund University, Sweden. His most recent books are *Spying for the People: Mao's Secret Agents, 1949–1967* and, with Roderick MacFarquhar, *Mao's Last Revolution.*

Sha Qingqing is a researcher at the Shanghai Municipal Library. His article about the history of baseball during the early years of the People's Republic of China was published in *Zhonggong dangshi yanjiu* in 2014.

Vivienne Shue, FBA, is Professor Emeritus of Contemporary China Studies at the University of Oxford and a Fellow of St. Antony's College. Best known perhaps for one of her early works on China under Mao, *The Reach of the State,* other books include *Peasant China in Transition: The Dynamics of Development toward Socialism, State Power and Social Forces* (coedited with Joel Migdal and Atul Kohli), and *Tethered Deer: Government and Economy in a Chinese County* (coauthored with Marc Blecher).

Steve (S. A.) Smith is a Senior Research Fellow at All Souls College, Oxford. Among other books, he is author of *Revolution and the People in Russia and China: A Comparative History* and *Like Cattle and Horses: Nationalism and Labor in Shanghai, 1895–1927.*

Wang Haiguang is professor of history at the Central Party School in Beijing. His books and articles have focused on the Communist takeover of Guizhou, the Anti-Rightist Movement, the Lin Biao affair, and Hu Yaobang's efforts to deal with the aftermath of the Cultural Revolution at the Central Party School.

Xiaoxuan Wang is a PhD candidate in East Asian Languages and Civilizations at Harvard University. His dissertation examines the restructuring of associational life in rural China after 1949 by analyzing the reinvention of religious tradition.

Yang Kuisong is professor of history at East China Normal University. His most recent book is *Ren bu zhu de "guanhuai": 1949 nian qianhou de shusheng yu zhengzhi* [Unbearable "Concern": Intellectuals and Politics before and after 1949].

Zhe Wu is an assistant research Fellow at the Institute of Modern History, Academica Sinica. His articles have appeared in *Bulletin of the Institute of Modern History, Korean Studies of Modern Chinese History,* and *Asian Ethnicity,* among other venues.

Acknowledgments

Drafts of many of the chapters in this volume were presented at the "Between Revolution and Reform: China at the Grassroots, 1960–1980" workshop, held at Simon Fraser University in Vancouver, British Columbia, on May 28–30, 2010. We are grateful to Nara Dillon, Richard King, Shuyu Kong, and Huaiyin Li for sharing their research at the workshop and for their helpful comments on all of the papers. Timothy Cheek and Yuezhi Zhao were energetic and provocative discussants throughout the workshop, and the project has benefited enormously from their suggestions. Thanks also to Anna Belogurova, who served as rapporteur, and to Haruka Nakamura and Xian Wang, whose logistical assistance made the workshop a convivial and successful event.

Critical comments by Michael Schoenhals, Vivienne Shue, Andrew Walder, and Perry Link greatly improved our introduction and the volume as a whole. Special thanks go to Kathleen McDermott, Executive Editor for History at Harvard University Press, who provided crucial support at every stage, from the workshop itself to the decision to include new work by scholars from China and Taiwan. Our translator, Wee Kek Koon, was a pleasure to work with; Carolyn Brown's expert suggestions greatly improved the readability of five of the chapters. Katrina Ostler, John Shannon, and Lois Tardio were fantastic production and copy editors; and our indexer, Enid Zafran, has created a masterpiece.

We gratefully acknowledge the generous financial support for the conference, translation, and editorial phases of the project provided by the Social Sciences and Humanities Research Council of Canada; the Association for Asian Studies China and Inner Asia Council; Dean of the College, Grinnell College; and the following offices and organizations at Simon Fraser University: Vice-President, Academic; the David See Chai Lam Centre for International Communication; Dean, Faculty of Arts and Social Sciences; Vice-President, Research; and the Department of History. A Rapid Response Grant from the Simon Fraser University Publications Committee provided funding for the creation of the index.

Index